SOCIAL INDICATORS
OF WELL-BEING

Americans' Perceptions of
Life Quality

SOCIAL INDICATORS OF WELL-BEING

Americans' Perceptions of Life Quality

Frank M. Andrews
and
Stephen B. Withey
Institute for Social Research
University of Michigan
Ann Arbor, Michigan

PLENUM PRESS • NEW YORK AND LONDON

Library of Congress Cataloging in Publication Data

Andrews, Frank M
   Social indicators of well-being.

   Includes index.
   1. Social indicators—United States. 2. Social prediction. 3. United States—Social
conditions—1960-   —Public opinion. 4. Public opinion—United States. I.
Withey, Stephen Bassett, 1918-   joint author. II. Title.
HN60.A52   309'.07'2   76-26179
ISBN 0-306-30935-1

© 1976 Plenum Press, New York
A Division of Plenum Publishing Corporation
227 West 17th Street, New York, N.Y. 10011

Printed in the United States of America

Preface

This is a study about perceptions of well-being. Its purpose is to investigate how these perceptions are organized in the minds of different groups of American adults, to find valid and efficient ways of measuring these perceptions, to suggest ways these measurement methods could be implemented to yield a series of social indicators, and to provide some initial readings on these indicators; i.e., some information about the levels of well-being perceived by Americans. The findings are based on data from more than five thousand Americans and include results from four separate representative samplings of the American population.

One of the ways our research is unusual is that it includes a major methodological component. Typical surveys involve a modest effort at instrument development, the application of the instrument to a group of respondents, and an analysis of the resulting data that mainly describes the people studied. Our work, however, was implemented in a series of sequential cycles, each of which consisted of conceptual development, instrument design, data collection, analysis, and interpretation. Ideas and findings generated in prior cycles affected the design of subsequent cycles.

The book is organized into three major parts, which are preceded by a general introduction and followed by a series of appendices. Part 1 describes the methodological and conceptual explorations that provide the fundamental knowledge base on which one can begin to build a series of perceptual indicators. Part 2 examines a large number of perceptual indicators and what they tell about the well-being of the American population and of twenty-seven major subgroups defined on the basis of sex, age, race, socioeconomic status, and stage in the family life cycle. Part 3 is concerned with the application of our development efforts and is addressed to those who would use the indicators we have explored, or modifications of them, to assess perceived well-being in future investigations.

The introductory chapter (chap. 1) describes the nature of the concepts used in our research and presents the conceptual model that guided much of our work. The chapter concludes with details about the six separate bodies of data developed and analyzed for this investigation and the measurement methods that are common to them.

Chapters 2 and 3 constitute a pair in that they both describe the range of measures we have explored and report our analyses and conclusions about how well-being concerns are structured in the minds of Americans. The basic purpose of these chapters is to identify and "map" perceptions of well-being. Chapter 2 focuses on more than one hundred specific life concerns, while chapter 3 discusses sixty-eight global measures of well-being.

Chapters 4 and 5 constitute a second pair. These chapters address "accounting" questions: How, and to what extent, can more global evaluations of well-being be accounted for on the basis of evaluations of specific life concerns? Chapters 4 and 5 report the results of applying a variety of statistical models that simulate what may be the psychological processes people use in evaluating life quality.

Chapter 6 is concerned with the quality of measurement and brings together a wide range of results on validity and reliability to derive some recommendations about effective ways of assessing perceptions of well-being.

Chapter 7, on the dynamics of the evaluation process, describes a set of nine explorations intended to examine the underlying processes by which people come to hold the perceptions of well-being that they express. These explorations elaborate the basic statistical models developed in chapter. 4.

Chapters 8, 9, and 10 constitute part 2 of the book and present the major descriptive results on how Americans evaluated their lives. Chapter 8 focuses on a large number of life concerns and how they were evaluated by the American population as a whole. Chapter 9 takes the same concerns and reports results for various major demographic and social subgroups within the population. Chapter 10 examines various assessments of life-as-a-whole by both the general population and by major population subgroups. Taken together, these three chapters tell much about how the American people feel about their life quality—which components of life generated the most positive feelings and which the most negative, how various groups differed in their sense of well-being, and what changes people perceived from the past and expected in the future.

Chapter 11 is addressed to applications. It draws upon preceding material to suggest batteries of survey items that could be used in future surveys to yield coherent sets of indicators of well-being, and suggests various ways in which the resulting information might be analyzed and interpreted. It proposes numerous design alternatives, and describes some of the factors influencing the choice among these alternatives.

Data from carefully designed nationally representative samples of the American population constitute a source of information that may be useful for answering questions other than those posed by the original collectors of the data, and this is particularly likely in the present case where the surveys explored a new area—perceptions of well-being. With the expectation that these data will constitute an important historical record of Americans' perceived well-being in the early 1970s, and with the hope that other investigators may wish to use these data in new and innovative ways, we have placed the data in a publicly accessible archive. For a modest processing charge, the original sets of survey data (appropriately anonymized) and complete documentation can be obtained from the Social Science Archive, Institute for Social Research, University of Michigan, Box 1248, Ann Arbor, Michigan 48106, U.S.A.

Large-scale empirical research involves many people in addition to those who author the books. Ours is no exception. Marita DiLorenzi and Elizabeth Keogh have been our research associates from the beginning of the project and each has made important and varied contributions to all phases of the research. Three University of Michigan graduate students have been associated with us at various stages of the investigation: Jo Anne Coble helped us think through some aspects of the design for the first survey; and Rick Crandall and William Murphy participated in the design and analysis of the later surveys. Karen Keir, Carolynn Crandall, Heather O'Donnell, and Rhean Jones were particularly helpful with various clerical and typing tasks. Willard Rodgers and Philip Converse made numerous useful suggestions regarding a draft of this manuscript.

For the collection and processing of the data, we could not have proceeded without the service sections of the Survey Research Center, of the Center for Political Studies, and of the Institute for Social Research. The national probability samples were the work of the Sampling Section, headed by Irene Hess; the interviews were conducted by the national interviewing staff and supervisors of the Field Section, headed by John Scott; the data were coded by members of the Coding Section, headed by Joan Scheffler; computer analyses were performed with the assistance of the Computer Service Facility, headed by Duane Thomas, and the Survey Research Center's Computer Support Group, headed by Judith Rattenbury, using mainly the OSIRIS software system;[1] and the data were archived by the ISR Social Science Archive under the direction of Ann Robinson.

Our work has been financially supported from several sources. Grant GS-3322 from the National Science Foundation came first, was our principal source, and was what made the entire project feasible. The concluding phases of our work were made possible by Grant GS-42015, also from the National Science Foundation, a small internal grant from our Institute for Social Research (using certain funds provided to the institute from the National Science Foundation's program on Research Applied to National Needs), a portion of a grant for other work directed by Stephen Withey from the John and Mary R. Markle Foundation, sabbatical leave time provided to Frank Andrews by the Institute for Social Research, and the congenial and supportive environment at UNESCO's headquarters in Paris, where major portions of this volume were written. The crucial

[1]OSIRIS is a computer software system developed at the Institute for Social Research of the University of Michigan with funds from the National Science Foundation, the Inter-university Consortium for Political Research, and other sources.

support of the National Science Foundation is acknowledged with special thanks. Its program on Special Projects, headed by Murray Aborn, has provided much of the significant financial support for early research on social indicators and has played a major role in the development of the social indicator movement.

Finally, we would recognize the thousands of hours contributed to our work by those who have responded to our interviews and questionnaires. Ultimately, it is to their well-being, and the well-being of all the millions of Americans they represent, that our work is dedicated.

FRANK M. ANDREWS
STEPHEN B. WITHEY

Contents

List of Exhibits

xvii

CHAPTER 1

Introduction

Some nineteenth-century gardeners created living sundials. They arranged a circle of coincident indicators of the time of day by planting a clock-face of flowers, each bed blossoming at a different hour. On sunny days one could tell the time to within a half hour by glancing at the garden (Luce, 1970, p. 120).

The slower seasonal changes of spring or autumn do not catch us by surprise or mystify us. There are clear leading indicators of what is going to happen in such signs as lengthening days, rising temperatures, changing leaf colors, hoarding squirrels, or migrating birds. We understand the changing relations between the sun and the earth in the turnarounds of the seasonal solstice, but we also know something about the associated tides of mood, cycles of allergy, and the diurnal and seasonal fluctuations of our hormones that are also signaled.

Standardized, dispersed, and frequent observations enabled meteorologists to map the isobars of barometric pressure, the highs and lows of temperature, and the gusty fronts of weather change. In doing so they developed an understanding of how weather is made and moved. We now have daily indicators of the course of storms and the patterns of probabilities of precipitation.

SOCIAL INDICATORS

Like indicators of time, season, and weather, social indicators of the various conditions of human beings, and of the changes and trends that characterize their lives, offer much that is attractive. Some social indicators already exist and include population and housing statistics, unemployment rates, and various economic series. The U.S. Government publication titled *Social Indicators 1973* (Executive Office of the President, 1973) provides an example of a compilation of social indicators. However, in these days of growing interdependence and social complexity we need more adequate cues and indicators of the nature, meaning, pace, and course of social change.

1

We can do nothing about the earth's spin, and maybe we should do nothing about the weather except cope with it, but most social phenomena are of our own making and subject to our own direction. Bell comments, perhaps overconfidently, on guided social change:

> Perhaps the most important social change of our time is a process of direct and deliberate contrivance. Men now seek to anticipate change, measure the course of its direction and its impact, control it, and even shape it for predetermined ends. "The transformation of society" is no longer an abstract phrase but a process in which governments are actively engaged on a highly conscious basis. (Bell, 1973, p. 345)

The desirability of monitoring a broader range of social indicators has been accepted by growing numbers of people in recent years. The social indicator "movement" is gaining adherents all over the world: in both developed and developing countries; at international, national, subnational, and enterprise levels; and among persons with applied as well as theoretical interests. Numerous proposals for the further development of social indicators have been made. The following example from the Organization for Economic Cooperation and Development is representative:

> Increasingly sophisticated social indicators should be evolved to monitor [economic and social] trends and impacts, and to provide a system of "early warning" of growing imbalances, social disbenefits, dissatisfactions, and emerging social needs. *Major efforts should be stimulated to devise social indicators that will permit social components to be fully taken into account when evaluating cost and benefit in technological innovation.*

> Social indicators, however, if they are to be fully useful, must be formulated in such a way that public and private administrations can draw coherent and valid policy conclusions from them. Comparative studies between countries and the sharing of national insights and research results may have considerable advantages to offer in this regard. Parochial national biases and cultural traditions can often be better perceived through such a shared approach. (OECD, 1971, p. 104)

Interest in social indicators is, of course, not new. Lazarsfeld (1961) documents the fact that the idea that social topics could be subjected to quantitative analysis acquired prominence in the first part of the seventeenth century, and that the history of such efforts includes work by astronomers, chemists, naturalists, mathematicians, and others up to the pioneering surveys of poverty in nineteenth-century England.

> The "measurement of life" became an object of enduring interest to the Italian Alfredo Niceforo at the close of the nineteenth century. [In 1922 he published a work] in which he developed key indicators . . . for each dimension of the concept of civilization . . . and describes his effort . . . as the construction of a "social symptomology." (Lazarsfeld, 1961, p. 180)

And, as David reminds us, the long history of interest in social indicators, somewhat forgotten in the passion of current zeal, should lead one to surmise:

> The social indicators movement—a movement shaped by both a strong sense of social need and an underlying optimism concerning the roles of

purpose and rationality in the conduct of human affairs—may fail to realize how far into the future [it] will have to reach before the promises and hopes embedded in it, both scientific and political, begin to be realized. (David, 1972)

Nevertheless, these "promises and hopes" are generating considerable current enthusiasm for developing and monitoring social indicators.

Some enthusiasts believe social indicators will save mankind from predicted catastrophies of pollution and resource depletion. They suggest indicators will point to life purposes that are more sustainable than the consumption goals implicit in traditional economic indicators. Other adherents believe indicators will lead to better social systems based on new knowledge about the strengths and weaknesses of current social programs. Others think indicators will focus the attention of policymakers on current social problems and thus make societies more responsive to people's needs. Still others suggest indicators will help to predict the future, or to interpret the present in the light of the past.

That social indicators will produce all these results is most unlikely. However, monitoring a broadening range of social indicators does seem to have some potential for making contributions to these important goals and hence we believe social indicators deserve our serious attention and careful development efforts.

Characteristics of Social Indicators

Considerable debate has arisen as to what really constitutes a social indicator. The U.S. Department of Health, Education and Welfare, in their publication *Toward a Social Report*, defines the term as follows:

> A social indicator . . . may be defined to be a statistic of direct normative interest which facilitates concise, comprehensive and balanced judgments about the condition of major aspects of a society. (U.S. Department of Health, Education and Welfare, 1969, p. 97)

The key concepts here are "normative interest" and the implication of relevance to policymaking. Normative interest implies that an indicator measures something we care about directly and over which we want to maintain some control or guidance.

An article by Sheldon and Freeman says that "social indicators are time-series that allow comparisons over an extended period which permit one to grasp long-term trends as well as unusually sharp fluctuation rates . . ." (Sheldon and Freeman, 1970, p. 97). Here we have lost the emphasis on normative interest but have added the notion of time-series and processes. Hoffenberg writes about social indicators as being "measurements of social systems performance" (Hoffenberg, 1970, p. B779), and Elaine Carlisle says, "A social indicator is defined as the operational definition or part of the operational definition of any one of the concepts central to the generation of an information system descriptive of the social system" (Carlisle, 1972, p. 25). This differentiates a social indicator from just any social science variable by making it a characteristic of the social system. A paper by Sawhill (1969) describes social indicators as "quantitative measures of social conditions designed to guide choices at several levels of decision making."

Several facets of these definitions reflect the basic perspectives of the social indicator effort. The quest is for a *limited* yet *comprehensive* set of *coherent* and *significant* indicators, which can be *monitored* over time, and which can be *disaggregated* to the level of the relevant social unit. Discussion about the pros and cons of such a definition and the reasons for choosing such a set of terms occurs in articles by Land (1971) and by Andrews (1973).

The set of indicators should be "limited" so they can be understandable and not overly detailed, lengthy, or complex. The indicators should be "comprehensive" so that a substantial portion of the most salient or critical aspects of society is included. They should be "coherent" in that it would be helpful to our understanding if they hung together in some form that would eventually lead to a model or theory about how society operates. Any set of indicators would be "significant" if they fulfilled the foregoing demands but there is a further implication that they should be of "direct normative interest," which implies that they should relate to aspects of society that interest or concern us.

Quality of Life

A term that has arisen in social indicators work is "quality of life." The term sometimes refers to an "outsider's" judgments of quality covered in such measures as crowding, decibels of noise pollution, reported crimes, income levels, etc., but it may also refer to the privately known and privately evaluated aspects of life. Campbell and Converse (1972) point to the need for an understanding of how social conditions are perceived and evaluated. Commenting on the revolution of rising expectations, they write:

> Discontentment with objective conditions has appeared to be increasing over exactly the same period that those conditions have at most points and by almost all criteria been improving, a discrepancy with portentous social and political implications. (Campbell and Converse, 1972, p. 9)

A recent report from the Department of Health, Education and Welfare on *Work in America* remarks on the dull, repetitive, and mechanical tasks that

> . . . are causing discontent among workers at all occupational levels. This is not so much because work itself has greatly changed; indeed, one of the main problems is that work has not changed fast enough to keep up with the rapid and wide-scale changes in worker attitudes, aspirations and values. (*Work in America*, 1973)

The focus of these comments is not away from the physical and technological aspects of living but rather an urging to spotlight a larger stage of concern. Dalkey says:

> The notion of quality of life . . . is somewhat different from the one used by the news media and by most public officials. The more usual meaning is

related to the environment and to the external circumstances of an individual's life—pollution, quality of housing, aesthetic surroundings, traffic congestion, incidence of crime, and the like . . . And [these] have the additional feature that they appear to be more manageable by municipal, state, and national programs than attitudes or feelings. But they form only a limited aspect of the sum of satisfactions that make life worthwhile. An important question for policy is whether they constitute a major share of an individual's well-being, or whether they are dominated by factors such as sense of achievement, love and affection, perceived freedom and so on. To answer this question, a somewhat deeper look has to be taken at quality of life as the individual experiences it. (Dalkey, 1972, p. 9)

The proposition that quality of life is not adequately defined by physical variables is made in an extreme form by Bateson (1972), who proposes that what people care most about is not episodes or things as such but the pattern and setting of their personal relationships—how they stand in love, belonging, hate, respect, responsibility, dependency, trust, and other similar abstract but nonetheless real relations. He proposes that it is with respect to these relationships that we feel psychological pain, and that it is these pains that can reset the controls on our evaluations and behaviors.

Objective and Subjective Indicators

Many indicators of social conditions that are currently available would be classified as objective. Most of them are products of the accounting or record-keeping of institutions and agencies with specific interests and functions. Financial accounts, records of births and deaths, people-days of hospitalization, wages and prices, absenteeism, levels of chemical pollution, and building construction permits are all statistics that are maintained because there is need for them. However, since it is widely agreed that the notion of quality of life includes important perceptual and subjective elements, there is need for indicators that reflect these elements as well as for indicators that tap the more objective components.

It has become common to divide social indicators into two types—objective and subjective. We believe, however, that this classification is neither clear nor very useful. Even birth and death and what defines human life are currently matters of legal, medical, and doctrinaire dispute. Presumably objective indicators of these matters turn out to involve subjective judgments. Conversely, it can be argued that many subjective indicators (such as people's evaluations of their lives) provide rather direct and objective measurements of what they intend to measure.

Rather than focus on what we regard as a spurious division between objective and subjective indicators, we believe it is more helpful to consider the following three dimensions of the phenomena that are being indicated. The first is the extent to which people agree on how to characterize a given phenomenon. We may usually agree as to what constitutes a "house" but still have problems with whether to regard a hut, a shack, a pup tent, or a cave as a house. We may have even more difficulty in agreeing whether we are viewing a "good house" since our views about the characteristics of this concept may differ widely.

The second dimension is the degree to which the same sensory or neural input at some level of the nervous system is available to co-observers. The phenomenon of my pain is not the same to me and to my dentist; the evidence is totally different. A somewhat similar differentiation can be made for a teacher's and a parent's observations of the same child. If the observations are made in different settings, the child's role behavior is likely to be discrepant. If the adults are simultaneous observers, their different training, orientation, and experience may still result in their having divergent perceptions.

The third dimension is the extent to which different people can take similar action toward a phenomenon. Things that are seen as accessible and manipulable are commonly believed to be objective. Observers can behave toward an objective phenomenon similarly. They can do something to it: Move it, build it, tear it down, or block it from view. Hence, people who want to improve the human condition in a physical or technological way claim to be interested in objective entities. But it is equally possible, and probably equally important, to alter subjective things. The work of engineers, industrialists, construction workers, technological innovators, foresters, and farmers who alter the physical and biological environment is matched by educators, therapists, advertisers, lovers, friends, ministers, politicians, and issue advocates who are all interested and active in constructing, tearing down, and remodeling subjective appreciations and experiences.

Thus, it may be more helpful and meaningful to consider the individualistic or consensual aspects of phenomena, the private or public accessibility of evidence, and the different forms and patterns of behavior needed to change something rather than to cling to the more simplistic notions of objective and subjective.

THE RESEARCH PROBLEM

Once one grants the desirability of measuring, and monitoring over time, a wider range of social characteristics than are currently being observed, there arises an immediate question: What to measure?

The notion of measuring the quality of life could include the measurement of practically anything of interest to anybody. And, no doubt, everybody could find arguments supporting the selection of whichever set of indicators happened to be his choice. The vast range of potential research undertakings that might conceivably be relevant to life quality needs to be reduced, for the moment, to the point where a focused and manageable start can be made. The investigations reported here concentrate on *perceptions of well-being*.

Measurements of individual well-being seem to us, and to many others also,[1] a particularly promising place to begin. The promotion of individual well-being is a central goal of virtually all modern societies, and of many units within them. While there are real and important differences of opinion—both within societies and between them—about *how* individual well-being is to be maximized, there is nearly universal agreement that the goal itself is a worthy one and is to be actively pursued.

Citizen welfare, in the broad sense of the word, is the concern not only of national-level governments, but of state, county, city, and village governments as well. Universities, churches, hospitals, and many service organizations devote at least a portion of their effort toward the promotion of welfare and the reduction of "illfare." Many corporations take a strong interest in the welfare of their own employees, and the more enlightened corporations also show concerns for the welfare of "outside" people who are affected by their operations. Of course, individuals themselves take a healthy interest in their own well-being, and most also show concern about the well-being of certain other individuals.

Even when we focus on perceptions of well-being, however, there are a variety of possible research approaches. One possibility is to explore the *components* of perceived well-being. Alternatives are to identify and measure the factors that *influence* perceptions of well-being, or to investigate the social and psychological *effects* produced by differences in perceived well-being. Any one of these could (and probably should) motivate a series of major investigations. First, however, we need to learn about well-being itself: What its components are, how they relate to one another, combine, change over time, and vary across social, cultural, geographic groupings. After gaining knowledge about these matters, one would be ready to begin exploring the causes, and the effects, of differences in well-being.

We have no quarrel with those who choose to explore more externally based indicators of well-being. On the contrary, we feel each type of indicator can complement the other. Furthermore, we suggest that a fully developed set of social indicators might consist of two parallel series: one indicating how people themselves evaluate various aspects of their lives; and the other indicating the external or environmental conditions relevant to each of those aspects.

We would not expect the two series of indicators necessarily to move in the same direction from one measurement to another, or even to covary substantially across different individuals. It would be quite possible for the external conditions of life to "improve" while people's sense of well-being declined. (It has been suggested that this is just what occurred among blacks during the mid-1960s prior to the urban riots.) Similarly, we know of cases where people who live in areas with relatively low recorded crime rates feel less safe than

---

[1]The Organization for Economic Cooperation and Development, undertaking one of the most comprehensive attempts yet seen at the international level to initiate work on social indicators, placed primary emphasis on social concerns relevant to *individual well-being* (OECD, 1973, p. 9, italics ours).

those in areas with higher crime rates. Nor would we expect the two series of indicators to reflect the same set of criteria. Sound levels may be damaging to people's hearing even if they should happen to enjoy the din. On the other hand, people may be greatly bothered by annoying sounds even if their effect is not physically hazardous. The perceptual indicators complement the externally based ones because they provide different but no less important information about individual well-being.

Research Goals

Having determined to focus on indicators of perceived well-being, a host of theoretical and practical issues needs to be resolved. With appropriate "research and development" we hope to be able to obtain and to monitor a set of indicators that meet the following criteria:

1. Their coverage should be sufficiently broad to include all the most important concerns of the population whose well-being is to be monitored.

2. If the relevant population includes demographic or cultural subgroups that might be the targets of separate social policies, or that might be affected differentially by social policies, the indicators should have relevance for each of the subgroups as well as for the whole population.

3. Despite broad coverage, it should be possible to measure the indicators with a high degree of statistical and economic efficiency so that it is feasible to monitor them on a regular basis at reasonable cost.

4. The validity (i.e., accuracy) with which the indicators are measured should be high, and known.

5. The instrument used to measure the indicators should be flexible so that it can accommodate different trade-offs between resource input, accuracy of output, and degree of detail or specificity. In short, the indicators should be measured with breadth, relevance, efficiency, validity, and flexibility—a tall, but not impossible, order.

The order is not impossible because much of the basic technology is already in place. The methods of survey research, developed largely over the past thirty years, now make it possible to obtain perceptions from a few hundred to several thousand carefully selected people and derive accurate estimates of the perceptions of people in an entire nation, region, state, city, etc., and—at the same time—to derive good estimates of perceptions held by various overlapping sets of the bigger subgroups in those areas.

While the basic survey technology is now available, what has not been available is the detailed knowledge necessary to construct batteries of survey questions that would efficiently and validly cover a wide range of relevant life concerns. It is toward filling this gap in knowledge that our work is directed.

Specifically, we address the following issues:

—What are the more significant general concerns of the American people?

—Which of these concerns are relevant to Americans' sense of general well-being? What is the relative potency of each concern vis-à-vis well-being?

—How do the relevant concerns relate to one another? Which tend to covary; which are statistically distinct? What is the structure of American's perceptions about well-being? How can a broad range of concerns be measured with maximum efficiency?

—How do Americans arrive at their general sense of well-being? Can one understand their perception of general well-being in terms of their evaluations of particular concerns? How many different concerns need to be considered?

—To what extent can Americans easily identify and report their feelings about well-being? With what validity can one assess their evaluations of particular concerns and general well-being? To what extent will they bias their answers?

—How stable are Americans' evaluations of particular concerns? How stable are their feelings about general well-being?

—What are the costs and difficulties of collecting perceptual measures from Americans?

—How comparable are various subgroups within the American population with respect to each of the questions above?

Once answers to these questions are in hand—and we can now supply many of them—it becomes feasible to develop the desired broad-gauged, efficient, valid, and flexible instrument for monitoring perceptions of well-being.

Usefulness

What is the importance and usefulness of measuring people's perceptions of well-being? We propose six products of value to social scientists, to policy-makers and implementers of policy, and to people who want to influence the course of society.

First, there is value in getting some baseline measures against which we can compare subsequent measures and trends of change so that we will know whither we are tending. Are we getting more or less satisfied with our lives, whatever that may mean? Are we getting more satisfied in some areas and less satisfied in others? Is there stability in some areas and flux in others?

Second, there is value in knowing how satisfactions and dissatisfactions are distributed in society. How do different subgroups feel? Is decay of satisfactions with life rapid among the aged? How do young people feel? How about the rich and the poor, the married and unmarried, men and women? Is some subgroup of society changing while others are stable?

Third, there is value in getting to understand the structure and independence of various satisfactions. Does marital satisfaction contribute to or relate to job satisfaction? How is one's satisfaction with house and neighborhood influenced by local services and business practices? How do feelings about standard of living relate to satisfactions with local or national government?

Fourth, there is value in understanding how people evaluate and feel about their lives if the judgments are made about *domains* of life such as their families, their houses, their jobs, their neighborhoods, local governments, etc., and comparing such a picture with how they judge their lives if they consider the degree to which their *values* or criteria for evaluations are met, using standards such as freedom and independence, well-offness, respect by others, achieving success, and so forth. How does the picture of life evaluations differ when taking one approach or the other? Is our understanding of human feelings improved if the two approaches are combined?

Fifth, there is value in understanding how people combine their feelings into some overall evaluation of the value of life. What aspects of life are more important than others in determining one's global evaluations? How do different domains and value criteria relate to feelings about life as a whole? How do parts of life add together, or are they isolated and compartmentalized?

Sixth, there is value in understanding the whole process of human evaluating. Most would agree that anything that can be done to improve the human lot that is reflected as felt improvement is a condition to be coveted. The appreciation of life's conditions would often seem to be as important as what those conditions actually are.

Although the usefulness of research on human evaluations and processes of judgment may have to be displayed over a period of time, it would seem fair to say that the importance of human satisfaction does not need to be defended. Even the managers of human affairs who may lay claim to expertise on what is best or feasible for society tend to believe that their actions and policies will be vindicated in eventual human appreciation. Governments are often responsive to expressions of public dissatisfaction. Some who are interested in social action might well claim that people do little to improve their lot until they are aware of differences, deprivations, and opportunities that make them dissatisfied. People who make no case for contentment might regard dissatisfaction as evidence of striving, ambition, imagination, and goal setting. And even those who try to be satisfied with their lot, eking out satisfactions where they can be found, or those who put up a front of life satisfaction while masking the more desperate conditions of their daily lives, by so doing give importance to satisfaction as a needed component of human life.

One may justifiably claim, then, that people's evaluations are terribly important: to those who would like to raise satisfactions by trying to meet people's needs, to those who would like to raise dissatisfactions and stimulate new challenges, to those who would suppress or reduce feelings and public expressions of discontent, and above all, to the individuals themselves. It is their *perceptions* of their own well-being, or lack of well-being, that ultimately define the quality of their lives.

BASIC CONCEPTS AND A CONCEPTUAL MODEL

Implicit in the preceding discussion are most of the basic concepts that are central to our work.

We conceive of well-being indicators as occurring at several levels of specificity. The most global indicators are those that refer to life as a whole; they are not specific to any one particular aspect of life. We would regard questions such as How do you feel about your life as a whole? How happy are you these days? and Is your life better, worse, or about the same as other people's? as providing evaluations of well-being at the global level.

At a somewhat more specific level are general evaluations of what we call life "concerns."[2] Concerns are, simply, aspects of life about which people have feelings. Part of our work (reported in chap. 2) has been devoted to developing lists of life aspects that people say are of significant concern to them, and we have collected and analyzed data relevant to about one hundred concerns. Examples of questionnaire items that assess well-being at the concern level include How do you feel about your house or apartment? How do you feel about our political leaders? How do you feel about your marriage? How do you feel about what you are accomplishing in your life? and How do you feel about the amount of beauty and attractiveness in your world?

We suggest that concerns can usefully be divided into two types: "domains" and "criteria" (or "values"). The first three of the above examples (house, political leaders, marriage) represent domains. These are aspects of life that can be evaluated in the light of one's values. On the other hand, the last two examples (accomplishment and beauty) are themselves criteria that might be used in evaluating life domains.

Domains and Criteria

Based on our pilot work, we confirmed the idea that people could and did divide their lives up into domains that, although not isolated, were separate enough to be identified and evaluated as a distinguishable part of life. Considering levels of specificity, it is probably impossible to develop an exhaustive list of domains in life, but we did develop a long list with fairly broad coverage. Examples of such domains are your marriage, your own health and physical condition, your friends, your job, your religious faith, the operation of your local government, your neighborhood, and so forth.

We also developed a list of another set of concerns. These were the criteria, or values, by which one judged or evaluated how one felt about the various domains of life. One can ask people how they feel about their houses or their jobs without even raising the question of what criteria they use in making such judgments. Examples of such criteria are amount of challenge, privacy, comfort, fun, variety and diversity, independence and freedom, responsibility, and so forth. These, too, are important aspects of life and one can ask people how they feel about the independence and freedom in their lives without even raising the question of what domains of their lives are most satisfying or dissatisfying in this regard.

Domains of life are places, things, activities, people, and roles. There are domains that people do not all share. Some are married, some are not. Some people have jobs, others do not. Some people own cars, others travel by alternate means. For some people getting into or out of a domain would

---

[2]In choosing this term, we follow Cantril (1965).

improve their well-being. Many people feel that "getting married" or "getting a job" would enhance their quality of life, and there are others who feel that "getting a divorce" or "retiring from a job" would do the same thing.

Criteria are values, standards, aspirations, goals, and—in general—ways of judging what the domains of life afford. There are criteria that people do not share, but people seem to differ more in their particular standards and their ideas of relevance than in the presence or absence of criteria dimensions. Neatness or messiness, independence or dependence, may or may not be important to you and people may well differ in the desirableness of one or another point between those polarities but they are prevalent aspects of situations and relationships. For some people, changes in their standards or the relevance of criteria would improve their quality of life. For others, only the accomplishment of an aspiration will do because the importance or relevance of such a state to their quality of life seems unalterable.

A large subset of what we have termed "domains" turns out, although it was not our starting point or intent, to be a taxonomy of social institutions and agencies. The activities of social institutions are frequently regarded as the major focus of social indicators work. Families, schools, medical facilities, stores where you buy and businesses where you work, welfare offices and services, protective organizations and other units of local government, unions and union activities, recreational facilities, and so forth, constitute a listing of social institutions (people, facilities, functions, and services) created to meet people's needs and aspirations. All of them, within our schema, would be classified as domains.

A large subset of what we have termed "criteria" turns out to be a somewhat shared dream to be loved, liked and accepted, responsible, respected, somewhat independent, somewhat secure, interested in life, comfortable, competent, successful, and to have fun. While these are abstract concepts and probably vary somewhat in what they mean to different people, we suspect that people diverge more in how much of these attributes they want, and in what domains they want them, than in what the criteria mean to them.

The quality of life is not just a matter of the conditions of one's physical, interpersonal and social setting but also a matter of how these are judged and evaluated by oneself and others. The values that one brings to bear on life are in themselves determinants of one's assessed quality of life. Leave the situations of life stable and simply alter the standards of judgment and one's assessed quality of life could go up or down according to the value framework. It may well be that subjective quality of life is better understood by studying the nature and determinants of value structures than by assessing the more objective conditions of living. It is undoubtedly better to try and link them in a common understanding.

A Conceptual Model

The conceptual relationship between these two types of concerns—domains and criteria—is shown in Exhibit 1.1.

EXHIBIT 1.1. Two-Dimensional Conceptual Model with Examples of Possible Domains and Criteria and with Evaluations of Well-Being at Three Levels of Specificity

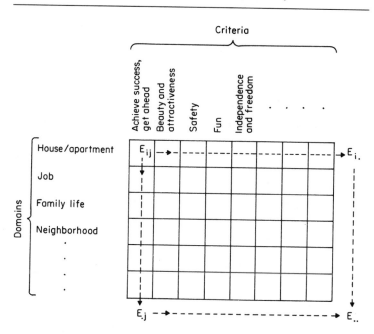

E_{ij} = Affective evaluative response to a particular domain with respect to a particular criterion

$E_{i.}$ = General affective evaluative response to a domain (across criteria)

$E_{.j}$ = General affective evaluative response to a criterion (across domains)

$E_{..}$ = General affective evaluative response to life-as-a-whole--i.e., perceived quality of life

We show in Exhibit 1.1 the two-dimensional matrix model that emerged in the course of our work and that guided its latter portions. Note that the domains define one of the dimensions (the rows in Exhibit 1.1) and that the criteria define the other dimension. Jointly they provide the framework in which a person's actual evaluations of well-being are hypothesized to occur.

Exhibit 1.1 also shows evaluations at three levels of specificity. The global and concern levels have already been mentioned. These are indicated in the Exhibit by $E_{..}$, for the global level, and by the $E_{i.}$s and $E_{.j}$s for the concern level. A still more specific level is represented by the E_{ij}s within the cells. These represent a person's evaluation of a specific domain with respect to a specific criterion. For example, the question, How do you feel about the beauty and attractiveness of your house?, involves such an evaluation.

Our basic hypothesis as to how evaluations may combine across levels is derived by treating the layout in Exhibit 1.1 as if it were a statistical table. It suggests that the evaluations located at the margins may be derived by some appropriate combination of the evaluations in their respective rows or columns. For example, how a person evaluates his house (an evaluation at the concern level, which would be represented by an E_i.) might be understood by considering how well the house is perceived to meet a range of relevant criteria; e.g., How do you feel about the beauty and attractiveness of your house? How well does your house meet your needs?, etc. Note, however, that we make no prior assumption that the combination is necessarily a simple addition of the various evaluations in the cells (though this is one possibility), and there is no requirement that every cell contain an evaluation; some may be irrelevant and hence "empty."

The example above is in terms of the rows of the diagram. We hypothesize that combinations can be made column-wise as well; i.e., for the criteria. Presumably, how a person feels about one of the particular values in his life is dependent upon its fulfillment in various domains. Thus, the evaluation, How do you feel about the beauty and attractiveness of your house?, may have relevance to the beauty criterion as well as to the house domain. However, one might go on to inquire about beauty and attractiveness at work, in the neighborhood, etc., if one were interested in the person's general evaluation of beauty and attractiveness.

The diagram is also intended to imply that global evaluations—i.e., how a person feels about life as a whole—may be the result of combining the domain evaluations *or* the criterion evaluations in a manner analogous to that outlined above. The corner entry can be obtained either by combining down the right margin or across the bottom margin. Again, there is no necessary requirement that the combination be a simple additive one, or even that all of the margin entires enter into the combination.

The model, of course, is no more than a representation of a set of hypotheses about the types of thoughts people may have when they evaluate their well-being and how these different thoughts may function with respect to one another. Nevertheless, as detailed in chapter 7, the model can be used to generate a large number of empirically correct predictions, which suggests that the model itself may be in reasonably close accord with reality.

Going Beyond the Model

The research results reported in this volume can all be tied in one way or another to the conceptual model that has just been described. The model itself, however, invites speculation beyond what has been empirically investigated, and we would briefly elaborate three such themes. The first involves a dimensional expansion of the model to incorporate evaluations at a still more specific level than any of those presently represented; the second involves the inclusion of "feedback loops" from general evaluations to specific evaluations in a multi-time (i.e., dynamic) version of the model; the third considers some of the processes by which the elementary affective evaluations of the model (the E_{ij}s) may be generated.

Dimensional Expansion of the Model. One may assume that people affectively evaluate their lives not only at the concern level, but also at the subconcern level. For example, people take an interest not only in the domain of "house," but also in subdomains such as kitchen, heating system, furnishings, and the like. Similarly, the criterion-type concern, "beauty and attractiveness," may include such subcriteria as balance, color schemes, and complementarity with surroundings. In principle, each of these subconcerns could themselves be subdivided, practically ad infinitum.

Subconcerns could easily be incorporated in the model by the inclusion of additional dimensions. If one wanted to represent both subdomains and subcriteria, two additional dimensions would be needed. Although it is hard to graphically portray a model in more than two dimensions, the basic structure of the model would remain similar to that in Exhibit 1.1. In addition to what is shown there, each of the domain-by-criterion entries (i.e., each of the E_{ij}s) would become analogous to a "corner" entry (such as E..) and be derived from its *own* matrix consisting of subdomains and subcriteria.

Feedback Loops. The common assumption about the development of feelings and evaluations is that individuals react to the details and elements of human experience. Feelings about one's house thus are based on how one feels about the kitchen, the bedroom, the storage areas, the patio, the view, and so forth. Feelings about the kitchen are in turn built up out of feelings about the stove, the sink, the refrigerator, work space, temperature control, etc. Thus, the direction of influence is assumed to be *from* the specific *to* the general.

However, once one has "arrived at" a set of feelings about a given concern (e.g., one's work, job, career, or profession) and organized a set of expectations, skills, and behaviors around it, it is likely that these feelings and behaviors will themselves influence future evaluations of some component such as job assignment or job pay. Thus, in a multitime model one may wish to incorporate feedback loops by which general evaluations can influence those at a more specific level.

Examples of such general-to-specific influences are numerous. Feelings about family are so organized that one can overlook occasional bursts of anger and cope with bouts of illness and handle limited interpersonal stresses without altering one's basic commitment to and evaluation of one's family. Similarly, one's orientations toward the national government may be so firm and entrenched that it is almost impossible to budge them.

Undoubtedly, influences both from specific-to-general and from general-to-specific occur and would need to be included in a dynamic model. These thoughts point to the limitations on the interpretations that are possible from single surveys. Data are needed over time and under the pressures and circumstances of social stress and change and from individuals in improving and retrogressing conditions in order for us to understand the dynamics of evaluative processes, the directions of influence, and the ways people can achieve improved states of well-being.

Processes That Generate Affective Evaluations. Our conceptual model describes how affective evaluations at more general levels are presumed to relate to, and be generated from, those at more specific levels. The model assumes that certain elementary (i.e., highly specific) affective evaluations already exist, but says nothing about the cognitive processes that produce them. Although investigation of these processes is not a major focus of our work (though chap. 7 devotes some attention to this matter), it may be useful to describe briefly some of the concepts that seem relevant. We draw on four streams of thought.

The first is a large literature on the behavior and evaluative interaction between perceived environmental conditions and internal reference signals, needs, abilities, and aspirations. Powers' (1973) work illustrates an approach that includes notions of continuous feedback to various levels of perception of the environment and the proposition that behavior is always in the service of prospective perception to enhance the fit between internal reference signals and input from the environment. French, Rodgers, and Cobb (1974) have proposed the person–environment fit model. It suggests that a person's sense of satisfaction (or, more generally, subjective "fit") stems from the degree of congruency between the environment, as the person perceives it, and the person's needs or aspirations, as these are also perceived by the person. Each of the two perceived entities (environment and needs/aspirations) is presumed to bear some relationship to objective reality, though it is granted that the relationship may be less than perfect owing to distortions introduced in the process of perception. Although the person–environment fit model is not a fully proven theory, we concur with its suggestion that satisfactions (and also evaluations of life aspects) are probably the result of some comparison between a perception of the environment and a set of needs or aspirations, or—as we have called them— criteria.

A second stream of thought stems from the literature on adaptation level (Helson, 1964, on perception; Lewin, 1942, on level of aspiration, etc.). Brickman and Campbell (1971) have particularly focused on hedonic level and adaptation as these processes apply to the quality of life. Their basic observation is that the human mind seems to include a built-in adaptation process by which people "adapt" to the peaks of delight, or depths of despair, and, after a while, cease to experience them as extremes, even when external conditions apparently remain unchanged. Although the precise nature and operation of the adaptation process remains unclear, it would seem that any full explanation of how people affectively evaluate life aspects would need to take adaptation into account. It may be that one's aspiration levels undergo slow change, moving downward when a person experiences unfavorable circumstances and upward when circumstances are good, so as to maintain some degree of discrepancy between what one actually experiences and what one hopes for (as suggested by Campbell, Converse, and Rodgers, 1976, chap. 6). This is highly speculative, however, for there may be exceptions where people continue to feel delighted, or terrible, about certain aspects of their lives for long periods.

A third stream of thought encompasses the wide variety of social judgment theories including work of Adams (1963) or Walster, Berscheid, and Walster (1973) on equity theory and the judgments people make based on values of fairness or justice and the perceived distribution of equities in a group.

Also, as another example, there is the work of Kelley (1971) on attribution theory and the evaluative imputation of motives, standards, and so forth to one's own actions and those of others. There is also the extensive work on framing and keying of social judgments encountered in reference group studies (Hyman and Singer, 1968).

A fourth stream of thought stems from the utility functions discussed by economists (e.g., Samuelson, 1955, p. 418). The basic notion (after adaptation to our terminology) is that there exists a function that relates the level of one's affective evaluation to some quantitative aspect of a particular life concern. Exhibit 1.2 includes several possible forms for the functional relationship and suggests life aspects to which each might apply.

One of the reasons we find such functional relationships interesting is that they may represent in quantitative terms the operation of a psychological "value." Furthermore, when one makes the casual observation that two people "have different values" the implication may be that they have differently shaped, or differently located, evaluation functions. One of the findings emerging from our work (reported in chap. 4) is that groups that might be assumed to have somewhat different values show remarkable similarity in the way they seem to combine evaluations of life concerns when evaluating life as a whole. This finding, however, is not incompatible with the groups having different values—in the sense described here—that generate the particular affective

EXHIBIT 1.2. Possible Functional Relationships Between Affective Evaluations and Life Concerns

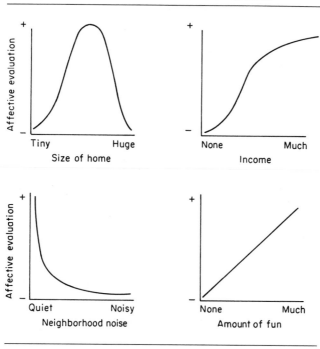

evaluations that we subsequently observe and analyze. In short, given the possibility of different evaluation functions, the observed *homogeneity* between groups in how affective evaluations seem to be manipulated is not incompatible with cultural *heterogeneity* in the generation of affective evaluations.

METHODS AND DATA

The Measurement of Affective Evaluations

The basic entries in the model, just described, are what we designate as "affective evaluations." The phrase suggests our hypothesis that a person's assessment of life quality involves both a cognitive evaluation and some degree of positive and/or negative feeling, i.e., "affect."

We have experimented with numerous different ways of measuring affective evaluations, and chapter 6 provides a detailed comparison of them. The approach that was used most extensively, and that we believe to have been most effective, used the Delighted–Terrible Scale (abbreviated to the D–T Scale). It will be convenient to describe this scale and the considerations that guided its development here at the very beginning.

The standard approach for measuring affective evaluations on the Delighted–Terrible Scale has been to present the respondent with a set of categories and to ask him to choose the one that came closest to representing his feelings. When used in an interview situation, the categories were printed on a card that was given to the respondent. One of these cards is reproduced in Exhibit 1.3.

The D–T Scale includes seven on-scale categories: "Delighted," "Pleased," "Mostly satisfied," "Mixed—about equally satisfied and dissatisfied," "Mostly dissatisfied," "Unhappy," and "Terrible." In addition, the scale includes three

EXHIBIT 1.3. Categories Used for Assessing Affective Evaluations

I feel:

7	6	5	4	3	2	1
Delighted	Pleased	Mostly satisfied	Mixed (about equally satisfied and dissatisfied)	Mostly dissatis- fied	Unhappy	Terrible

A   Neutral (neither satisfied nor dissatisfied)

B   I never thought about it

C   Does not apply to me

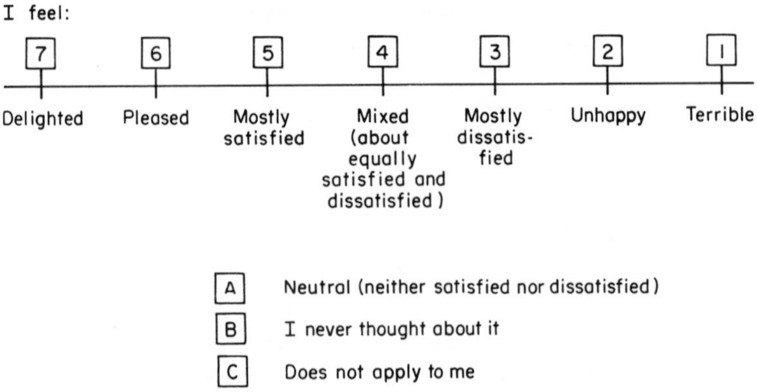

off-scale categories: "Neutral—neither satisfied nor dissatisfied," "Does not apply to me," and "I never thought about it." These off-scale categories are particularly useful for concerns that are irrelevant or difficult for some respondents.

Interview or questionnaire items that would be answered using the Delighted–Terrible Scale were preceded by a standard introduction that aimed to set the time frame as the "extended present." It read:

> In the next section of this interview/questionnaire we want to find out how you feel about various parts of your life, and life in this country as you see it. Please tell me the feelings you have now—taking into account what has happened in the last year and what you expect in the near future.

This portion of the introduction was followed by instructions to the respondent as to precisely how his answers were to be indicated.[3]

The Delighted–Terrible Scale represents an attempt to improve on previously available methods for measuring affective evaluations and its development was guided by several considerations.

In a survey of subjective well-being, Campbell, Converse, and Rodgers (1976) used a scale that ranged from "Completely satisfied" to "Completely dissatisfied," and obtained markedly skewed distributions for many of the domains they studied. Typically, half to two-thirds of their respondents selected one of the two most satisfied categories. While we do not question their finding (one might expect a substantial portion of the population to be at least "satisfied" with many basic aspects of their lives), we felt this concentration at the "Satisfied" end of the scale posed both conceptual and statistical problems. On the conceptual side, we suspected that the large group who said they were satisfied included some who were "merely" satisfied and others who experienced a more active and positive enjoyment. We wanted a scale that would separate these groups. On the statistical side, we knew that substantially skewed distributions pose certain problems in analysis, and that reducing the skew would enhance our ability to find meaningful relationships. Thus, we felt we could improve on the "Satisfaction" scale by adding more affect to it and, in the process, attempting to reduce the skew of the distributions generated.[4]

Another consideration affecting the development of the D–T Scale was that we wanted the main scale to have seven categories. There is considerable evidence that a seven-category division is about as fine a discrimination as the average person makes for many judgment tasks (Miller, 1956). Futhermore, from a purely statistical standpoint, seven categories are sufficient to capture essentially all of the potential variance (Cochran, 1968; Conner, 1972; Ramsay, 1973). Thus, psychological and statistical considerations converged, led us to a

---

[3]These instructions varied slightly, depending on whether the data were being collected by an interview or a questionnaire. The exact wordings can be seen in Appendix A.

[4]Although we here criticize some aspects of this satisfaction scale, we would note that it actually served its intended purpose reasonably well. Chapter 6 presents empirical data comparing the two scales (and others) when applied to the same respondents and notes the higher estimated validities and less skewed distributions associated with the D–T Scale.

preference for a seven category scale, and—as a consequence—led us to reject placing major dependence on the three-category happiness scales used in previous national surveys by Gurin, Veroff, and Feld (1960) and by Bradburn and Caplovitz (1965; Bradburn, 1969).

A third consideration concerned the explicit labeling of all categories of the scale. Some surveys present respondents with a set of categories that are laid out along a single dimension, label the end categories, and leave it to the respondent to infer appropriate meanings for the intermediate categories. While respondents can and do provide answers using such scales, we felt this left some ambiguity as to just what the respondent was expressing when he chose one of the intermediate, unlabeled categories. Thus, we wanted each of our categories explicitly labeled, and for this reason chose not to depend on the type of "ladder" scales used previously for assessing reactions to life quality by Kilpatrick and Cantril (1960; Cantril, 1965) or on the unlabeled satisfaction scales used by Abrams (1974) or Campbell, Converse, and Rodgers (1976).

Finally, we felt it important to make it easy for the respondent to "opt out" if none of the main categories represented his feelings. Many people are not married, do not have children, do not work at a paying job, do not own a car, etc., and are therefore unable to say how they feel when asked about them. As shown in Exhibit 1.3, the Delighted–Terrible Scale includes three off-scale categories for use when the respondent felt he or she had no feelings about a topic or had not thought enough about them to give a fair answer.[5]

Our goal, of course, was to design a measuring device that would yield more valid and discriminating information about people's evaluations of different aspects of life than had been produced by previously used scales. Part of our research was designed to test whether this had been achieved. As reported in chapter 6, there is evidence to suggest that the Delighted–Terrible Scale does indeed work somewhat better than others with which it has been compared.

Data Sources

Exhibit 1.4 lists the six major sources of data reported in this book. Included among them are four national sample surveys, each of which used a distinct battery of interview items, a local-level survey that used an unusually extensive questionnaire, and re-interviews of a sample of the respondents to one of the national surveys. In addition to the data from the 5,422 respondents indicated in Exhibit 1.4, we have made certain use of data from another national survey conducted by Campbell, Converse, and Rodgers (1976), and we conducted a series of exploratory interviews with a small set of heterogeneous individuals.

[5]The statistical results suggest that these off-scale categories functioned as we had intended. They were most likely to be used when reference was to one of the following aspects of life (figures are percentages of respondents choosing the off-scale categories in a national survey): Job, 43 percent; Organizations you belong to, 38 percent; Your spouse, 29 percent; Your marriage, 27 percent; Your children, 27 percent; Things you do to help people in this community, 18 percent; Your car, 16 percent; Sports and recreation facilities you use, 14 percent; Schools in this area, 12 percent; Services you can get for your home, 11 percent.

EXHIBIT 1.4. Major Data Sources

Name of data	Time of interviewing	Number of respondents	Population represented
May	May 1972	1,297	American adults
November Form 1	November 1972	1,072	American adults
November Form 2	November 1972	1,118	American adults
April	April 1973	1,433	American adults
July	July 1973	222	Local group
October[a]	October 1973	280	American adults

Notes: Appendix N describes two other data sources: national samples of respondents surveyed in 1974 and 1976.
[a]All October respondents are also present in the April data.

For convenience the several groups of respondents listed in Exhibit 1.4 will be named according to the month in which data were collected from them. For example, we shall talk about the "May respondents" (or the "May data"), "July respondents," etc.

National-Level Surveys. The four national surveys were independent from one another but nearly identical in original sample design. In each case the sample was intended to be representative of persons eighteen years of age or older (and married persons under eighteen) living in households within the coterminous United States exclusive of households on military reservations—in short (and approximately): American adults.

For each of the national surveys the sample design was that used by the Survey Research Center to select national probability samples of dwellings (Kish and Hess, 1965). Households were sampled at a constant rate and one respondent per household was chosen on a random basis for interview.[6]

Some people with only a casual acquaintance with survey methodology find it difficult to give much credibility to a survey finding. How can a few people represent such a large population? One or another respondent may well be unique and not like thousands of other people. The point is not whether each or any person interviewed is a template for tens of thousands of others. Rather, the questions is, Could you get a thousand or more people, randomly chosen, who presented a radically different composite picture? The answer is that it would be very unlikely indeed. Interviews with the first few hundred respondents show all the variety one expects from individual lives but as the number of respondents grows, the *distribution* of answers, life conditions, attitudes, feelings, etc., begins to be firmed up; around one thousand interviews the distribution of responses becomes quite stable. If interviews were carried on into the thousands, the distribution (proportions, percentages, averages, etc.) would not budge a significant amount. Probability sampling makes this result possible.

---

[6]To be mathematically precise, the data from each respondent could be weighted by the number of eligible persons in the household. A careful check, however, showed that the weighted results did not differ perceptibly from the unweighted results. For computational economy most of the results reported in this book are based on the unweighted data.

With a probability sampling design such as we have used, the magnitude of sampling errors due to taking a sample rather than a complete census can be estimated. The "sampling error" does not measure the actual error in a sample statistic; but it does allow one to estimate the range that will include the population value with a specified probability. As an example, suppose that the sample shows that 50 percent of the approximately fifteen hundred respondents to the April survey have a high life-satisfaction score. It turns out that there is a 95 percent chance—i.e., it is very likely—that the actual population value is within ±3.2 percentage points of this value. This result is typical: Most of the percentage figures reported in this book have a 95 percent chance of deviating from the true population values by no more than five percentage points, and for many the likely deviation is even less. (Appendix B includes a table of estimated sampling errors for percentages and samples of different sizes.) Other statistics, such as means, correlations, etc., have comparably small sampling errors.

It is impossible to interview everyone selected in a national probability sample. Some people are sick or on vacation during the interviewing period, others simply refuse to cooperate, and a very few present problems such as language barriers for the interviewer.

In these surveys we completed interviews in about three-quarters (75 percent) of the selected dwellings. (Appendix B presents the details.) It would be better if we had a higher completion rate, but persons not interviewed are not all alike or even similar to each other, so the final results are not seriously biased by their loss. These people, in other words, tend to be somewhat similar to the people that we did interview, and if they had been interviewed, the eventual results would in almost all cases not be different enough to fall outside the sampling error range that must always be tolerated.

Different samples show some variations but in our May 1972 sample, on comparing the proportions we obtained by sex, age, and race with national distributions reported by the Census Bureau, the largest difference between our results and that for the national population is a 4.6 percent underrepresentation of men. There was a slight underrepresentation of eighteen- and nineteen-year-olds (2.3 percent lower than census figures) and forty-five- to fifty-four-year-olds (2.5 percent lower). Other age group differences were less than 2 percent. By race, 8.9 percent of our respondents were black compared to a population figure of 10.0 percent, and 1.2 percent were other nonwhites compared to 1.4 percent in the census tabulations. One may conclude then that our samples compare quite satisfactorily with national figures.

In looking at survey results one is sometimes tempted, in trying to grasp the large picture, to ignore the small percents that represent minorities of feeling. But the population we are representing is big. It is estimated that this population, in the year 1972–73, totaled about 140 million adults. Thus, a single percent corresponds to the feelings of about 1½ million people; a percentage of 5 percent represents a group of people that might range in size from 5 to 9 million. (The same year our surveys were taken there were 3 million young people graduated from high school, 3 million were civilian employees of the federal government, about 2 million students enrolled for the first time in institutions of higher education, and about 2 million marriages occurred.) Even small percents can represent significant social groups, and in surveys of well-being one should pay attention to the quality of life of small segments of society as well as to the conditions of large sectors of the population.

The respondents in our national surveys spent one to two hours talking with an experienced interviewer about a variety of topics, one of which was their feelings about various life concerns. The size and coverage of the battery of items dealing with life quality varied from survey to survey, ranging in average interviewing time from about ten minutes to about twenty. (Appendix A includes the relevant portions of the interview schedules.)

Local-Level Survey. The local group consisted of 222 respondents who accepted payment to spend two to four hours answering a lengthy question-naire. These respondents all lived in or near Toledo, Ohio. Strictly speaking, these respondents do not constitute a sample of any group. However, because an informal quota system was used in their recruitment, they are a highly heterogeneous group of people whose distributions on major demographic variables, it turned out, were almost identical to those of a true random sample of the Toledo population. Furthermore, their distributions were rather similar to national distributions for sex, age, marital status, and employment status, but showed slightly higher education and income than the average American. (Appendix H compares these July respondents to Census Bureau profiles for United States adults and to a random sample of adults from Toledo. Selected portions of the questionnaire administered to these respondents appear in Appendix A.)

CHAPTER SUMMARY

Like indicators of time, season, and weather, social indicators of the various conditions of human beings offer much that is useful. Although certain social indicators already exist, the importance of monitoring a broader range of social indicators is acknowledged by growing numbers of people. The quest is for a limited yet comprehensive set of coherent and significant indicators of society that can be monitored over time and that can be disaggregated to the level of the relevant social unit.

An adequate monitoring of the quality of life requires attention not only to the physical and technological aspects of living but also to how conditions of life are perceived and evaluated by individuals. However, the current practice of dividing indicators into two types—objective and subjective—implies a difference between them that is not matched by reality.

Of the many possible aspects of life quality that might be measured, individual well-being, a central goal of all societies, merits special attention. Rather than looking at the causes or impacts of well-being, we chose first to examine its basic components. Furthermore, we chose to investigate direct perceptions of well-being, rather than more externally based inferences about it, though the potential contribution of both types of indicators is recognized.

An adequate monitoring of perceptual indicators of well-being requires that they be measured with breadth, with relevance to major subgroups in the population, with statistical and economic efficiency, with validity, and with flexibility. The technology of survey research now permits the achievement of some of these goals, but further research is needed before batteries of social indicator survey items that meet the above criteria can be designated. The present book aims to provide some of this knowledge. It also aims to provide baseline measures for assessing future changes, knowledge of how satisfactions and dissatisfactions are distributed in society, information about the structure of perceptions about well-being, and understanding about the process of evaluation, including how feelings are combined into an overall evaluation of life quality.

The basic concepts used in the present investigations include global evaluations, concern-level evaluations (subdivided into two types, domains and criteria), and domain-by-criteria evaluations. A conceptual model is presented that summarizes our hypotheses about how more general evaluations result from the combination of certain more specific evaluations. Several ways in which the model might be expanded are discussed: the inclusion of additional dimensions to handle still more specific evaluations, the incorporation of feedback loops in a multitime model, and the addition of certain psychological processes to generate the affective evaluations that are the present building blocks of the model.

The Delighted–Terrible Scale, used for measuring affective evaluations, is described, as are the considerations that led to its development and the reasons we chose not to use certain scales used previously by others. These considerations include the incorporation of both evaluative and affective components, the attempt to differentiate people who are actively pleased from those who are merely satisfied, the use of seven ordered categories plus additional off-scale categories, and the provision of labels for every category.

Six major data sources, plus two supplementary ones, provide the information that is analyzed in this study. The major sources include four nationally representative probability samples of the American adult population—some five thousand respondents in all—a 280-respondent re-interview sample from one of the national surveys, and a group of 222 heterogeneous individuals recruited in a midwest city who answered a lengthy questionnaire.

PART 1

DEVELOPING INDICATORS OF PERCEIVED WELL-BEING

CHAPTER 2

Identifying and Mapping Concerns

This chapter describes the assembly of a broad and extensive list of life concerns, and presents a series of analyses that explore the way Americans' feelings about these concerns are organized.

Identifying life concerns, and learning about their organization, generates basic knowledge that is necessary for the rational development of social indicators of perceived life quality. The basic assumption is that people's sense of well-being has a lot to do with their feelings about specific aspects of life that concern them. To test such an assumption, we need to identify a wide range of specific life concerns. Hence, for the moment, our goal is simply to cast the net widely, "catch" as many concerns as we can, and then cluster them into meaningful groups on the basis of their empirical and conceptual relationships to one another.

"Concerns" are what life—in the view of the people living it—is "all about." These are the aspects of each person's existence about which he or she has feelings. Surely, these deserve a central place in any assessment of life quality.

Each of us, through our own experience of life, as well as through our observation and participation in the lives of others, has some insight about life concerns. However, there seem to be few, if any, empirical studies devoted to identifying and mapping concerns. Yet, these matters are so fundamental—and at the same time so researchable—it seems unfortunate to leave the determination of the concerns to be investigated, measured, monitored, and eventually focused upon by the users of social indicators to less-than-perfect "insight."

The number of possible life concerns may be almost infinite, and one could argue that any attempt to identify them all is doomed to failure. While granting that this might be true, a more limited—and probably more useful—goal can be set: to identify those concerns that are commonly held, that are relatively broad in scope, and that have significant impacts on people's sense of well-being. Since people share much in the way of physical and psychological needs, and live within rather similar constraints imposed by the nature of the human body

27

and its physical and social environments, it is not unreasonable to expect substantial commonality in the concerns people have. This, at least, was the hypothesis that made it reasonable to undertake this investigation. We think the results presented in this and succeeding chapters show that our expectation was well-founded.

Examples of concerns are easy to find and can be identified in almost any conversation. The ones listed below were provided by our July respondents in response to the very general question, What are the best parts or characteristics of your life?

"I love my wife and family."
"Have a good job."
"Doing things I like to do."
"Able to do what I want."
"Have friends."
"Making a happy home for my husband and children."
"Have a good husband, happy marriage, nice children with whom I have good rapport, enough income, good home, car, clothes, friends, and good health."
"I really like going to church and taking part in it."
"I am getting a college education; I have good parents who provide for and love me; I have a boyfriend who loves me."

This next set came in response to a companion question, What are the worst parts or characteristics of your life?

"Life is too expensive."
"Tend to be depressive every once in a while."
"Pressure from others."
"The situation of the country today."
"My type of work I'm stuck with."
"Not enough intelligence."
"When the children are sick or there is a death of a close friend or relative."
"Sometimes living too far from family."
"I would like to have a great many more friends."
"I have a very difficult time coping with four children under seven years of age; I have a difficulty finding time for myself and my interests."
"My 'flesh' self—the drive in man which tries to have one yield to earthly or worldly desires; examples are rejection of the truth, hate, fear, restlessness, selfishness, etc."
"Being too sensitive and emotional; don't really know my father; have gained too much weight; am not a good money manager; can be very pessimistic; let people get me down."

For conceptual purposes, we find it helpful to think of concerns as varying in degree of specificity or "scope." As noted in chapter 1, "house" is a concern with rather broad scope (though it is not as broad as "life as a whole"). "Kitchen," "heating system," "color schemes," and "architectural balance" are somewhat more specific. "Scratch on refrigerator door" would be a highly specific concern. Our investigation will be confined to concerns of broader scope; partly because we suspect they hold the most promise as a basis for social indicators, and partly because investigation of the more specific concerns would seem to benefit from prior knowledge about the organization of broad-scope concerns.

As is also noted in chapter 1, concerns can be divided into two types: domains and criteria. We shall be interested in both types, so long as they are broad in scope.

Research Strategy

The basic strategy of our approach was first to assemble a very large number of possible life concerns and to write questionnaire items to tap people's feelings, if any, about them. Then, having administered these items to broad samples of Americans, we used the resulting data to empirically explore how people's feelings about these items are organized. The organization of these items, depicted in a series of maps, permits us to see the structure of perceptions of life concerns. We can do this both for the total American population and for major subgroups within it. The maps help us infer which questionnaire items tap which concerns, and how the concerns themselves fit together in people's thinking.

Knowing the general structure of perceptions about life concerns would permit, we expected, an informed selection of specific concerns for monitoring in a social indicator framework. If one's purpose were broad and general, one could ensure that the concerns selected were an adequate "sample" of the full range of life concerns, and at the same time avoid the inefficiencies of selecting concerns that were essentially redundant. Alternatively, if one's purpose were more focused, such as an interest in family indicators, or community indicators, one could select concerns from just the relevant portion of the structure.

Furthermore, knowing how the feelings tapped by specific questionnaire items are located within the structure allows one to tailor the measurement process to particular design goals. A study that needed higher validities and could afford the increased costs could select a large set of complementary questionnaire items to tap each of the selected concerns. A study that had to proceed with maximum economy could reduce the number of items tapping each concern to two, or even one, yet know that these few items would provide maximum coverage for the resources expended.

Finally, we suspected that knowledge of the structure with which aspects of well-being are perceived might have longer-range conceptual benefits as well. Such a structure might suggest how the findings from a research project investigating one concern might relate to (or be distinct from) the findings of projects focused on other concerns, and such a structure might suggest important aspects of life that deserve increased conceptual or empirical attention from scholars and/or policymakers.

IDENTIFYING CONCERNS

The task of identifying concerns involved examining four different types of sources.

One source was previous surveys that had included open questions about people's concerns. Two examples of such items are:

> All of us want certain things out of life. When you think about what really matters in your own life, what are your wishes and hopes for the future? In other words, if you imagine your future in the best possible light, what would your life look like then, if you are to be happy? (Cantril, 1965)

> In this study we are interested in people's views about many different things. What things going on in the United States these days worry or concern you? (Blumenthal *et al.*, 1972)

Such items are not uncommon in major surveys. They are often located very early in an interview, before the respondent has had a chance to learn the specific topics of the study; and are used to get the respondent thinking and talking about himself and his life. Answers to such items provide an unusually rich source of information about people's concerns since these questions have been included in various large surveys and answered by people from all walks of life.

In our search for expression of life concerns, we examined data from these very general unstructured questions in eight different surveys.[1] Most of the surveys were conducted on national samples of Americans (though data from twelve other countries were also represented). Most were conducted within the preceding five years. All focused on substantive issues of high social, political, and/or psychological interest. By scanning the coding categories developed for these studies, a list of some eight hundred concerns was developed.

A second type of source was structured interviews, typically lasting an hour or two with about a dozen people of heterogeneous background. These interviews focused on the respondents' daily activities and their reactions to those activities, were conducted by our project research staff (rather than the usual field-staff interviewers), and were recorded on tape. These interviews were useful in further expanding the list of concerns.

A third type of source, particularly useful for expanding our list of crite-

---

[1]These surveys included: (1) A series of studies carried out by Cantril (1965) and his colleagues in thirteen different nations that assessed human concerns; (2) a 1969 survey of the American population that focused on attitudes about the use of violence, subsequently reported in Blumenthal *et al.* (1972); (3) a 1969 national survey of American workers that assessed working conditions (Survey Research Center, 1971); (4) a recent national panel survey of American youth (Bachman *et al.*, 1967); (5) several hundred interviews taken in low-income urban neighborhoods during 1970 (Lansing *et al.*, 1971); (6) a 1971 national survey on issues relating to life quality conducted by our colleagues Campbell, Converse, and Rodgers, 1976; (7) a 1966 national survey conducted by our colleagues Miller, Converse, and Stokes dealing with political and election issues; and (8) a 1967 study of Detroit residents concerned with issues of race and civil disorder (Aberbach and Walker, 1973).

rion-type concerns, was previously published lists of values. The literature on values is old and extensive with its roots in aesthetics, ethics, religion, and philosophy. In its current treatment it cuts across all the humanities and the social sciences. Extensive empirical work on value measurement was partly initiated by the work of Thurstone (1959). It has been richly extended by many people using the armamentaria of statistical methods so that we now have a variety of assessment and analytic techniques and findings that provide factors, clusters, dimensions, etc., in value space. Allport and Vernon (1931) were one of the first to devise a test of values, and another early effort using the concept of styles of life was made by Morris (1942, 1956). Cantril's (1965) list of human concerns can be translated into a list of value concerns. Rokeach (1973) has developed two lists of value concerns that he regards as providing adequate coverage of value criteria, one list applied to "means" of accomplishing goals and the other list applied to the "ends" themselves. His research instrument requires a preference rank ordering of the listed values.

An attempt to discover value orientations common to all cultures and human groups within an anthropological perspective was made by the Kluckhohns (1951, 1953). The four value orientations they considered were adapted and elaborated by Spiegel (1971) as a framework for understanding the roles and interactions between the individual, the family, groups, institutions, and society. Parsons and Shils's work (1951) on value orientations is a sociological example of a similar effort focusing on the reciprocal influence of values on social structure. In philosophy, the axiology of Hartman (1959), building on the work of G. E. Moore, provides a logical, conceptual model for three levels of value considerations.

Finally, we checked to make sure that our list of concerns included those receiving attention from official national and international bodies doing work on social indicators, and from certain other researchers known to be working in this field. Lists proposed by the U.S. Department of Health, Education and Welfare (1969), by the U.S. Office of Management and the Budget (Executive Office of the President, 1973), by OECD (1973), and by a half-dozen other research groups in the United States were examined.

The number of concerns with which we were working grew rapidly at first, then more slowly. Starting with the list of about eight hundred concerns coded in previous surveys, supplemented where necessary by concerns drawn from the other sources, we performed a preliminary ad-hoc clustering to combine concerns that were near duplicates. After rewording these to reduce differences in level of specificity, and phrasing them in the form of questions appropriate for use in a survey interview, we arrived at an initial list of about sixty concern items. This was a number large enough to allow a moderately detailed initial exploration of life concerns, yet small enough to be a feasible set on which to collect data from survey respondents.

These items were all phrased in a standard format, How do you feel about——?, and could all be answered using the Delighted–Terrible Scale, which is described in chapter 1. These items, along with others developed later, appear in Exhibit 2.1.

EXHIBIT 2.1. Items Used to Assess Affective Evaluations of Specific Concerns

M = May national survey (N = 1297)
N′ = November national survey Form 1 (N = 1118)
N″ = November national survey Form 2 (N = 1072)
A = April national survey (N = 1433)
J = July respondents (N = 222)
O = October respondents (N = 280)

How do you feel about . . .

		M	N′	N″	A	J	O
1	Your children	M				J	
2	Your wife/husband	M				J	
3	Your marriage	M				J	
4	Your own family life—your wife/husband, your marriage, your children, if any			N″		J	
5	Close adult relatives—I mean people like parents, in-laws, brothers, and sisters	M				J	
6	The things you and your family do together	M		N″		J	
7	Your own health and physical condition	M		N″		J	
8	The extent to which your physical needs are met				A	J	
9	The responsibilities you have for members of your family	M				J	
10	How dependable and responsible you can be					J	
11	Your opportunity to change things around you that you don't like			N″		J	
12	Your chance of getting a good job if you went looking for one			N″		J	
13	The extent to which you are tough and can take it				A	J	
14	The way you handle the problems that come up in your life	M				J	
15	The extent to which you can accept life as it comes and adapt to it					J	
16	The extent to which you can adjust to changes in your life				A	J	
17	The extent to which you get what you are entitled to—what is rightfully yours					J	
18	The extent to which you are achieving success and getting ahead				A	J	
19	The extent to which you compete and win at things					J	
20	What you are accomplishing in your life	M	N′			J	
21	Yourself—what you are accomplishing and how you handle problems			N″		J	
22	Yourself	M			A	J	O
23	How interesting your day-to-day life is				A	J	
24	The amount of beauty and attractiveness in your world				A	J	
25	The chance you have to enjoy pleasant or beautiful things			N″		J	
26	Your sex life			N″		J	
27	How much fun you are having	M		N″			
28	The amount of fun and enjoyment you have				A	J	O
29	The amount of physical work and exercise in your life				A	J	
30	The way you spend your spare time, your nonworking activities	M		N″		J	
31	The amount of challenge in your life					J	
32	The usefulness, for you personally, of your education	M				J	
33	The extent to which you are developing yourself and broadening your life				A	J	
34	The variety and diversity in your life					J	
35	The amount of imagination and fantasy in your life					J	
36	How creative you can be			N″		J	
37	The extent to which you maintain links to the past and to traditions					J	
38	The amount of time you have for doing the things you want to do	M		N″		J	
39	The amount of pressure you are under				A	J	
40	The amount of relaxation in your life					J	
41	Your chances for relaxation—even for a short time			N″		J	

EXHIBIT 2.1. (*continued*)

42	The sleep you get		N"	J	
43	The freedom you have from being bothered and annoyed		A	J	
44	Your independence or freedom—the chance you have to do what you want		A	J	O
45	The privacy you have—being alone when you want to be		N"	J	
46	The amount of friendship and love in your life			J	
47	How much you are accepted and included by others			J	
48	How sincere and honest you are		A	J	
49	How sincere and honest other people are		A	J	
50	How generous and kind you are			J	
51	How generous and kind others are			J	
52	The way other people treat you	M		J	
53	The amount of respect you get from others		A	J	
54	How fairly you get treated		A	J	
55	How much you are admired or respected by other people		N"	J	
56	The respect other people have for your rights		N"	J	
57	The people who live in the houses/apartments near yours	M		J	
58	People who live in this community	M		J	
59	The people you see socially	M		J	
60	Your friends		N"	J	
61	The things you do and the times you have with your friends	M		J	
62	The chance you have to know people with whom you can really feel comfortable	M		J	
63	How you get on with other people	M		J	
64	How much you are accepted and included by others		A	J	
65	The reliability of the people you depend on		N"	J	
66	How dependable and responsible people around you are			J	
67	The extent to which your world seems consistent and understandable			J	
68	How much you are really contributing to other people's lives		A	J	
69	Your religious faith	M		J	
70	The religious fulfillment in your life		A	J	
71	Things you do to help people or groups in this community	M		J	
72	The organizations you belong to	M		J	
73	How neat, tidy, and clean things are around you		A	J	
74	Your housework—the work you need to do around your home	M	N"	J	
75	Your job	M	N"	J	
76	The people you work with—your co-workers	M		J	
77	The work you do on your job—the work itself	M		J	
78	The pay and fringe benefits you get, and security of your job	M		J	
79	What it is like where you work—the physical surroundings, the hours, and the amount of work you are asked to do	M		J	
80	What you have available for doing your job—I mean equipment, information, good supervision, and so on	M		J	
81	How secure you are financially		A	J	
82	How well your family agrees on how family income should be spent		N"	J	
83	The income you (and your family) have	M	N"	J	
84	How comfortable and well-off you are			J	
85	Your standard of living—the things you have like housing, car, furniture, recreation, and the like	M	N"	J	
86	Your car	M		J	
87	Your house/apartment	MN'N"		J	
88	The outdoor space there is for you to use outside your home	M		J	
89	This particular neighborhood as a place to live	M		J	

EXHIBIT 2.1. (*continued*)

90	This community as a place to live	M	N"	J	
91	The services you can get when you have to have someone come in to fix things around your home—like painting, repairs	M		J	
92	The services you get in this neighborhood—like garbage collection, street maintenance, fire and police protection	M		J	
93	The way the police and courts in this area are operating	M		J	
94	How safe you feel in this neighborhood	M		J	
95	Your safety		A	J	O
96	How secure you are from people who might steal or destroy your property		N"	J	
97	The way you can get around to work, schools, shopping, etc.	M		J	
98	The schools in this area	M		J	
99	The doctors, clinics, and hospitals you would use in this area	M		J	
100	What you have to pay for basic necessities such as food, housing, and clothing	M	N"	J	
101	The goods and services you can get when you buy in this area—things like food, applicances, clothes	M	N"	J	
102	The taxes you pay—I mean the local, state, and national taxes all together	M		J	
103	The way your local government is operating	M			
104	What your local government is doing		N"	J	
105	The way our national government is operating	M			
106	What our national government is doing		N'N"	J	
107	What our government is doing about the economy—jobs, prices, profits	M	N"	J	
108	Our national military activities	M		J	
109	The way our political leaders think and act	M	N"	J	
110	The condition of the natural environment—the air, land, and water in this area	M		J	
111	The weather in this part of the state	M		J	
112	Outdoor places you can go in your spare time	M		J	
113	Your closeness to nature			J	
114	Nearby places you can use for recreation or sports		N"	J	
115	The sports or recreation facilities you yourself use, or would like to use—I mean things like parks, bowling alleys, beaches	M		J	
116	The entertainment you get from TV, radio, movies, and local events and places	M		J	
117	The information you get from newspapers, magazines, TV, and radio	M		J	
118	The information and entertainment you get from TV, newspapers, radio, magazines		N"	J	
119	How the United States stands in the eyes of the rest of the world	M		J	
120	Life in the United States today	M		J	
121	The standards and values of today's society		N"	J	
122	The way people over 40 in this country are thinking and acting	M		J	
123	The way young people in this country are thinking and acting	M	N"	J	

In subsequent work, the list was modified and expanded. Some substitute items were written to provide a more clearly focused statement of the concern. In other cases we discovered that several items that we had thought might tap distinct concerns acted as though they represented just one, and we attempted to construct a single summary measure of that concern. Perhaps more significantly, as we encountered new concerns not well represented among the original list of about sixty, we constructed new items to tap them.

The expanding list of concern items was administered, in various overlapping subsets, to respondents in the four national surveys, and the complete list—which numbered 123 items—was administered to the July respondents. Exhibit 2.1 presents the full set of concern items and indicates the surveys in which each was used.

Exhibit 2.1 includes items that tap what we believe to be a reasonably comprehensive set of concerns for the chosen level of specificity. Of course, a nearly infinite number of alternative wordings could be imagined, and if one were to focus on concerns of greater specificity, many more concerns could be identified. While the range of concerns covered in this list is not guaranteed to be "complete," we have not (yet) noted omissions that seem of major importance. In short, we feel it represents an adequately broad basis from which to start exploring perceptions of well-being.

MAPPING THE CONCERNS

Given the list of 123 concern items, the next step was to explore how they fit together in people's thinking. Several mapping techniques were used to identify the organization of these items. On the basis of this organization, we were able to infer the general structure of perceptions about well-being.

Before describing the results of our mapping analyses, we briefly discuss the nature of maps in general and the processes by which our maps were constructed.

Maps and the Mapping Process

In many respects the maps of perceptual structures, which we shall shortly discuss, are similar to conventional geographic maps.

In geographic maps, the elements are places and their locations on the map are determined by their physical proximities. Geographic maps are usually portrayed in two dimensions, though sometimes—as in the case of the globe—three dimensions are needed to correctly locate all elements relative to one another. The map is a representation of a two- (or three-) dimensional physical space, and it summarizes in one compact presentation much knowledge about the distances between places.

Sometimes contiguous geographic locations are grouped together and considered a region. Much of our understanding of geography—including the identification of major geographic factors and types of climates—and our ability to correctly predict many types of differences between specific places, depends upon this simple conceptual abstraction, "region."

Maps of perceptual structures also have elements, which may be grouped into regions; they also occur in two or three dimensions; they also represent a space, a "perceptual" space; and they also compactly summarize a great deal of information about the interrelationships among the elements. In our perceptual maps, however, the elements are questionnaire items. Their location on the map is based upon the covariation of the answers they elicit. Two items are placed near one another on the map if they "behave similarly"—i.e., if a person's answers to them tend to be both high, or both low; and items are kept far apart if a person's answer to one tends to be unrelated to his answer to the other. Thus, covariation is the key to constructing, and interpreting, perceptual maps.

The main analytic procedure we have used for constructing maps has been Smallest Space Analysis (Guttman, 1968; Lingoes and Roskam, 1973).[2] This is a technique that locates points (representing the concern items) in a multidimensional space so that the rank order of the plotted distances between all pairs of points agrees as closely as possible with the rank order of the statistical relationships between the items.

With Smallest Space Analysis one can perform the mapping in any number of dimensions from one to ten and then choose the smallest number that allows reasonably good fit between the observed "distances" and the plotted distances. One measure of the degree of fit is the coefficient of alienation, which varies from 0.0 to 1.0. (Smaller values indicate less alienation and hence better fit.) Since nearly all real data contain some extraneous measurement errors,[3] one rarely tries to achieve a perfect fit. Rather, the choice of the number of dimensions is a compromise that permits reasonably good portrayal of the actual interrelationships in a number of dimensions small enough for easy visualization. Our maps, as will be seen, are portrayed in two, and occasionally three, dimensions.

Smallest Space Analysis is one of several recently developed multidimension mapping techniques, all of which give nearly identical results under normal circumstances (Spence, 1972).

Although Smallest Space Analysis was the most useful of the mapping techniques we applied, we would not have felt confident about its results unless we had also tried several complementary approaches. Factor analysis (Harman, 1967; Rummel, 1971) and a clustering technique known as ICLUST (Kulik, Revelle, and Kulik, 1970) were also used on the same data.[4]

---

[2] The computer program we used was MINISSA (Lingoes and Roskam, 1973).

[3] Chapter 6 describes a series of analyses that assess the extent of various types of error in the data.

[4] In nearly all of our analyses, input to Smallest Space Analysis, Factor Analysis, or ICLUST was a matrix of Pearson product–moment correlation coefficients (r's). Strictly speaking, the data do not fully meet all the statistical assumptions for r: Our scales are ordinal, many distributions are skewed, and some relationships are not perfectly linear. However, a careful check showed that the pattern of relationships in a matrix of gamma coefficients (for which the data *do* meet all the assumptions) was virtually identical to that in a matrix of r's. (The rank correlation—*rho*—between the r's and the gammas was .95 for the sixty-six pairs of variables we examined.) Whether our variables were collapsed to reduce skew prior to computing r's also proved to make virtually no difference. (*Rho* between r's based on collapsed scales and those based on uncollapsed scales was .98.)

These results are consistent with our own previous experience with similar kinds of variables, and with findings from a more general investigation of this issue by Labovitz (1970). They also suggest the interesting results that most relationships among affective evaluations of concern items, assessed using the Delighted–Terrible Scale, are reasonably linear.

Perceptual Structures—July Respondents

The actual course of our research involved a sequential series of mappings, each based on data from a different set of respondents and involving different (but overlapping) sets of concern items. However, it is most convenient to begin our description of the results with the complete and final set. These results come from the July respondents, who answered the full set of concern items. From their data we derived our most broad-ranging and detailed perceptual map, and it provides the best overview of the major features of what we believe to be a typical perceptual structure. Subsequently, we shall see that our inferences about this perceptual structure are in reasonably close accord with results derived from other sets of respondents selected to be representative of the whole adult American population.

Exhibit 2.2 is a map showing the location of 118 concern items in a three-dimensional space.[5]

In addition to the items, 34 subregions are indicated, most of which contain several items. Items were clustered together, and a subregion defined, only if the content of the items was similar and they were located close to one another in all three dimensions.[6] While the subregions help us to see the contents of people's perceptions, and how these contents relate to one another, there was no intent to define a subregion for every item.

Description of the Structure. In getting acquainted with the structure of perceptions that can be inferred from Exhibit 2.2, it is convenient to begin with the Self Adjustment subregion, near the right side of the map. It contains the

---

[5]Note that the item numbers are keyed to match Exhibit 2.1, which presents the exact wording of each item. Locations on the third dimension are approximately indicated by the shape of the enclosure around the item, and exactly indicated by the signed value that appears within the enclosure. (Locations on the first two dimensions are indicated by the position of the item in the exhibit.)

Exhibit 2.2 shows 118 items out of the 123 shown in Exhibit 2.1. Three items were reworded in the course of our work, and the earlier versions were not asked of the July respondents. Two concerns were each represented by a pair of items that were so similar there was no need to plot them separately. (In one case, items 47 and 64, the wording was identical and could be used to check the operation of our plotting techniques—which worked as expected—and to provide an estimate of reliability, discussed in chapter 6.)

Given the unusually large number of items plotted in Exhibit 2.2, it had to be produced by a combination of methods. The principal technique, used to plot eighty-nine of the items, was Smallest Space Analysis. Once these items were located, the remaining items were added by hand, using results obtained from ICLUST and inspection of their relationships to other items.

For the eighty-nine items plotted by Smallest Space Analysis, the coefficient of alienation was .24 in three dimensions. While still closer fits could undoubtedly have been achieved by adding dimensions, the modest gains expected were not judged worth the added difficulty of dealing with more than three dimensions.

[6]In clustering items that had been administered to national samples of respondents, an additional criterion was imposed: that the pattern of relationships among the items had to be *stable* across major subgroups of the population. Given the smaller number of July respondents, this could not be implemented in clustering the items shown in Exhibit 2.2, though insights gained from analysis of the national data (discussed subsequently) were allowed to affect clustering decisions represented in Exhibit 2.2.

EXHIBIT 2.2. Three-Dimensional Perceptual Map Showing Location of Thirty-Four Concern Clusters and 118 Items

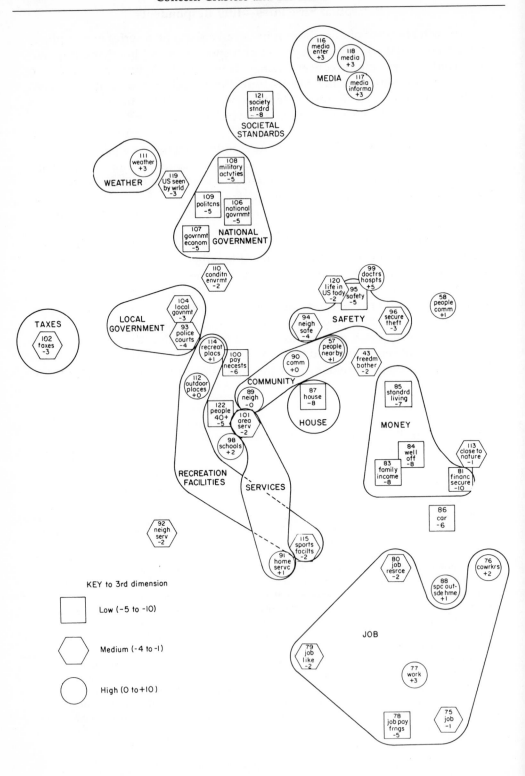

EXHIBIT 2.2. (*continued*)

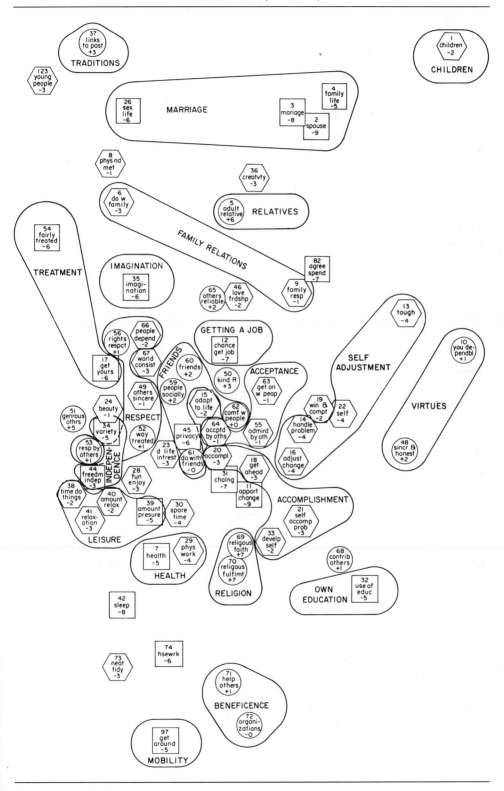

central item, How do you feel about yourself?, plus several others that ask essentially how the respondent adapts to his world.

To the left of Self Adjustment—and at roughly the same "altitude"—occur several other subregions, all of which suggest perspectives by which the respondent may evaluate his roles and positions in the world: Acceptance, Accomplishment, Independence, Respect, Leisure, Chances for getting a job, and the Quality of family relations. Also closely bunched here are several other subregions whose content is also relatively close to oneself: one's Own Education, Health, Religion, and Friends. (In contrast, the Virtues subregion—to the right of Self Adjustment—with its items about the respondent's own sincerity and dependability, suggests some of the ways the respondent relates to, and evaluates, himself.)

Children, Marriage, and Relatives are a set of subregions in the upper right of the map. Note that this Family region forms a kind of column in the third dimension: Spouse is at one end, Children in the middle, and Relatives at the other end.

Moving still farther left on the map, we encounter a set of subregions whose content is clearly distinct from the rather egocentric orientation of the regions discussed first. Here we find Job, Money, House, and Safety. The Job region, like the Family region mentioned previously, is another "column" of items ranging from the economic item (Pay and fringes) at the bottom, to Co-workers and the Nature of the work itself at the top. It is probably not accidental that the economic item in the Job region falls low on the third dimension—as do all items in the Money region—while the Co-workers item is at about the same (high) altitude as are other items having to do with friends.

Close to the House subregion, though clearly differentiated on the third dimension, are Community, Services, and Recreation Facilities.

Moving still farther left, and toward the upper part of the map, we find several subregions having to do with concerns beyond one's house and immediate community: Taxes, Local Government, National Government, Societal Standards, and Media.

Several other subregions, not mentioned here, as well as numerous single items not included in an identified subregion, can be seen in the exhibit.

Exhibit 2.3, which is derived directly from Exhibit 2.2, is an attempt to provide a more global picture of the basic structure. It takes the subregions we have just discussed and groups them into regions. Self and Family are major regions on the right, with Family located somewhat lower on the third dimension than Self. In the middle of the space come Other People (up high), and Economic Aspects (down low). Moving farther left, we find Job, Local Area, and the Larger Society—all at an intermediate level. House and Costs, both low down, like Economic Aspects, also appear on the left. Religion and Beneficence are set apart in the lower right.

One way to consider the organization of the domains and value-criteria is from the viewpoint of social roles. A social role is defined by Spiegel (1971) as a "goal-directed configuration of transactions patterned within a culture or subculture for the functions people carry out with respect to each other in a social

EXHIBIT 2.3. Three-Dimensional Perceptual Map Showing the General Structure of Concerns

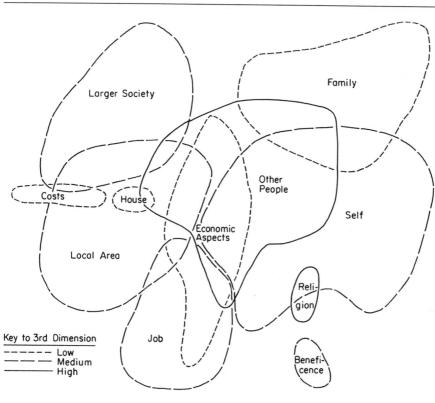

group or situation." The concept has the notion of a "program" within which one has set expectations of other people and considerable patterning for one's own behaviors and choices. These patternings of relationships among people establish a constellation of expectancies and demands on oneself and others, and they also organize a cluster of interdependent and related activities that have to be evaluated as a whole rather than singly.

One common role is that of family member. It seems clear that there is a general association of evaluations, in the average case, about one's spouse, one's children, and one's family life.

The role of being and having a friend is another set of behaviors and expectations that combine a number of domains and criteria. Being an employee and holding a job is another complex role with interdependent facets. The role of consumer establishes certain expectations of the way one should be treated by commercial enterprises and certain contexts for evaluation of those treatments, services, and products. The role of community resident may not be seen as very gratifying or very demanding, but there are clear expectations, not always reciprocated, of how one should be treated by neighbors or by local

government in its various functions. The role of national citizen is a further
extension of mutual interactions and expectancies that gets quite abstract but
sometimes very personally real and relevant.

The concept of roles as an organizer of sets of evaluations about aspects of
life serves to reduce the multiplicity and variety of facets of life that an
individual faces. It is of considerable theoretical interest that this concept of
social roles ties as closely as it does to the empirically derived structure of
perceptions shown in Exhibits 2.2 and 2.3.

Interpretation of Dimensions. Given the mapping shown in Exhibits 2.2 and
2.3, it is tempting to search for "meaning" in the dimensions derived. While
there may be an orderly progression of some concept along one or another of the
dimensions of a perceptual map, there is no necessity that this occur. The
situation is analagous to a geographic map: There is no intrinsic "meaning" to
the dimensions North-South or East-West, though it tends to be the case that
climates vary systematically with location on the North-South dimension.

The map in Exhibits 2.2 and 2.3 has one dimension for which it is easy to
infer a "meaning." The right-left dimension begins with concerns about
aspects of the self, which presumably seem psychologically "close" to oneself,
and then proceeds in an orderly fashion to concerns that are progressively more
remote: to one's relationships to other people, family members, and own
health; then to one's job, money, and house; then to one's community and its
various services and facilities; and finally to one's local and national governments, societal standards, media, weather, and taxes. Thus, psychological
closeness, or perhaps degree of control by the individual varies systematically
along the right-left dimension. This may be one of the underlying principles by
which individuals organize their feelings about life concerns.

Although we have sought similar orderly progressions along the second
and third dimensions, we have been unable to arrive at any interpretations that
seem as compelling as that for the first dimension.

Relationships Among Concerns. Quite aside from possible interpretations
one might give to the dimensions shown in Exhibits 2.2 and 2.3, these maps
contain a great deal of information about people's affective evaluations of life
concerns. Recalling that covariation is the basic metric that determines closeness or remoteness, and with the additional information that maximum distances on these maps correspond to approximate statistical independence, and
minimal distances to correlations generally in the range .6–.7,[7] we can see, for
example, that how one feels about one's family life tends to be unrelated to
one's evaluations of the local government or one's job (concerns that are rather
remote from the Family region), but bears a substantial relationship to how one
feels about one's spouse or children (items that are relatively close to the item
on family life).

Of course, these contrasts—and thousands of others that can be derived by

[7]Of the nearly seven thousand relationships that are summarized in Exhibit 2.2, most fell in the
range r = .0 to .4; the highest five ranged between .68 and .87; the lowest five ranged from −.08 to
−.19.

examining these exhibits—are eminently reasonable. It is this reasonableness that leads us to believe that there exists a rational structure to people's perceptions, and that our statistical mapping procedures have identified this structure.

Exhibits 2.2 and 2.3, while including the full set of concern items, are based on results from our July respondents, who do not constitute a nationally representative sample. It is our belief, however, that these exhibits provide a reasonably good representation of a perceptual structure that is typical for Americans generally. We turn next to the data that support this belief.

Perceptual Structures—May and November Respondents

The 1,297 May respondents, who constitute a representative national sample, were asked for their feelings regarding sixty-three concerns. Based on the interrelationships among their answers, the three-dimensional map shown in Exhibit 2.4 was derived.[8] While a comparison between the structure shown here and that in Exhibit 2.2 will show minor differences, the striking finding is the general similarity between them.

The principal dimension, shown vertically in Exhibit 2.4, closely matches the "psychological closeness" dimension that ran right-left in Exhibits 2.2 and 2.3. Note, in Exhibit 2.4, that this dimension begins with concerns having to do with family, self, and other people; proceeds through housing, income, and job; then taps services and other aspects of the local area; and ends with a variety of items assessing feelings about the nation and national government. As in Exhibit 2.2, items related to job and religion are displaced outward from the center on the second dimension; the House item is located rather close to the money items (Income and Standard of Living); and items assessing feelings about Weather, Media, and Young People are pushed out to the borders of the structure, reflecting their generally low relationships with other life concerns.

Another comparison can be made with results obtained from a different nationally representative sample, the 1,072 November respondents. These people were asked for their feelings about thirty-seven aspects of life, some of which overlapped with the prior set of sixty-three. A mapping of these thirty-seven concern items appears in Exhibit 2.5.[9] The by now familiar structure appears again.

While the match is not perfect, it is clear that the structure of the sixty-three items administered to the May respondents bears a substantial resemblance to the structure independently derived for the July respondents.

[8]For the data shown in Exhibit 2.4 (plus three global items that are not plotted), the coefficient of alienation was .26 in two dimensions, .19 in three dimensions, and .14 in four dimensions. Nearly all correlations among the sixty-three items of the May data were in the range .1 to .6. For results from a factor analysis of these data, see Appendix E.

[9]For these data, Smallest Space Analysis produced a coefficient of alienation in two dimensions of .24. In three dimensions this dropped to .17. Nearly all correlations among the thirty-seven items of the November data were in the range .1 to .5. For results from a factor analysis of these data, see Appendix E.

EXHIBIT 2.4. Three-Dimensional Perceptual Map Showing Location of Sixty-Three Concern Items

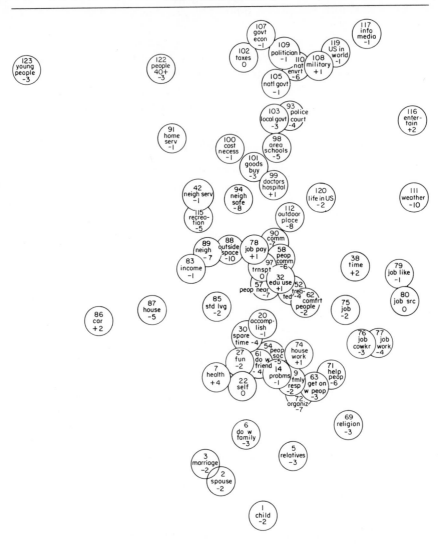

Data source: 1,297 respondents to May national survey. Item numbers match Exhibit 2.1.

To obtain a quantitative measure of the similarity between structures, we examined the relationships between pairs of concern items that had been included in both the May and November national surveys. Eighteen nearly identical items were included in both surveys.[10] These generated 153 relation-

[10]The sixteen identical items can be identified from information given in Exhibit 2.1. The nearly identical items were 103–104 and 105–106 respectively.

ships matchable from one survey to another, which varied in strength from .0 to .7 (Pearson *r*'s). When these relationships were correlated with one another, the result was an impressive correlation (*r*) of .89. This indicates that the relative magnitudes of the relationships in one survey were highly similar to those in the other, and hence shows a very high degree of replicability of the basic structure between two comparable but independent national surveys.

EXHIBIT 2.5. Two-Dimensional Perceptual Map Showing Location of Thirty-Seven Concern Items

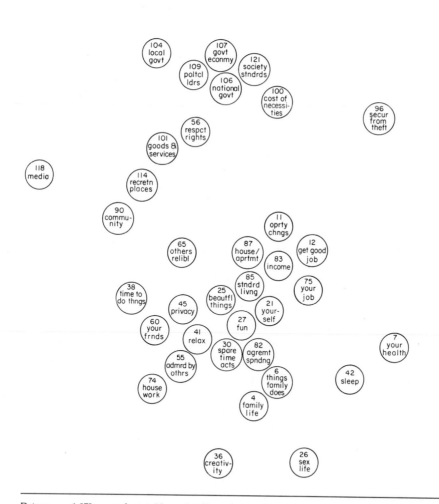

Perceptual Structures—April Respondents

The May and November national surveys, just discussed, included concerns that were mainly of the *domain* type, and it is for these that we observed replicable structures that arrayed concerns according to the degree of personal influence the respondent could exercise. When we turn to the organization of criterion-type concerns, we find distinctly different structures.

The April national survey included twenty-three concern items, nearly all of which were of the criterion type. A mapping based on a Smallest Space Analysis of these data is presented in Exhibit 2.6.[11]

These criteria items seem to be organized on a "sun-and-planets" principle: Substantial covariation is shown by a central core of items having to do with one's daily life and oneself (within the dotted line), and outside this are additional "satellite" concerns that show little covariation either with the central core or with each other. (The appropriateness of the sun-and-planets analogy is enhanced when one considers results for subgroups of the population, to be discussed shortly. For most subgroups, the central core continues to appear, but the "satellite" concerns "rotate" around it as their linkages to items in the central core vary from subgroup to subgroup.)

We interpret the observed structure to indicate that most of the criterion-type concerns having to do with oneself and one's daily life show relatively less differentiation than characterized the domain-type concerns. Essentially, respondents who felt positive about the fulfillment of one criterion having to do with themselves—e.g., the extent to which they were achieving success—tended also to feel positive about other criteria—e.g., the interestingness of their daily lives, their independence and freedom, or the extent to which they were developing themselves.

This relative homogeneity in feelings may reflect the way the world actually operates: Fulfillment of one set of values may tend to be accompanied by fulfillment of other sets. Or, alternatively, it may reflect a tendency for people to conceptualize and evaluate criteria less precisely than domains. A kind of halo may influence perceptions; people who feel some criteria are being fulfilled in their lives may tend to feel others are also.

While the criteria we measured showed more homogeneity of feeling than did the domains, the criteria certainly do not constitute a totally undifferentiated set. The correlation between most pairs was less than .4, indicating that feelings about the typical criterion explained less than 16 percent of the variance in feelings about most other criteria.

Further insight into the structure of perceptions about criterion-type concerns can be gained by examining where they are located relative to the domain-type concerns. The April data, which include few domains, do not permit this, but the July data, mapped in Exhibit 2.2, do. Two observations can be made.

---

[11]For these data, the coefficient of alienation in two dimensions was .20. In three dimensions it was .15. Nearly all correlations were in the range .2 to .5. For results from a factor analysis of these data, see Appendix E.

EXHIBIT 2.6. Two-Dimensional Perceptual Map of Twenty-Three Concern Items, Mostly of the Criterion Type

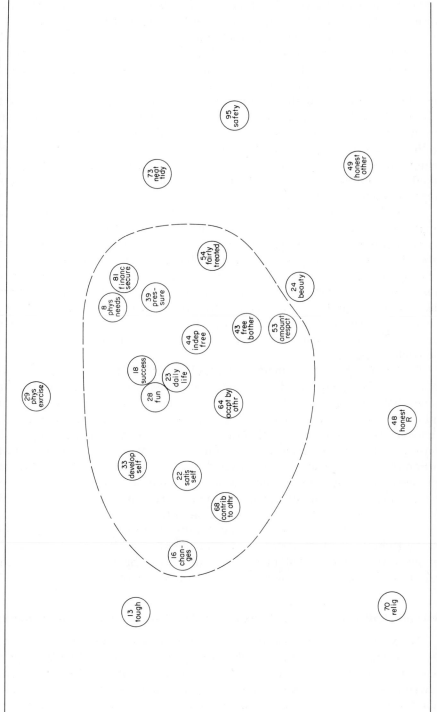

Data source: 1,433 respondents to April national survey. Item numbers match Exhibit 2.1.

First, most of the criterion-type items shown in Exhibit 2.2 are located within the densely packed region in the center-right of the map, and this is particularly true for concern items that make up the central core in Exhibit 2.6. While criteria that act like satellites in Exhibit 2.6 also tend to fall farther out from the center in Exhibit 2.2 (note, for example, the positions of Safety, Tough, Neat and tidy, and R's own sincerity and honesty), none of the criteria are as "remote" (i.e., close to the periphery of the structure) as are some of the domains. Despite our concerted attempt to assemble a heterogeneous list of criterion-type concerns, people's feelings about them showed less heterogeneity than their feelings about domain-type concerns. It would appear that feelings about the fulfillment of various possible life goals are more closely linked to evaluations of oneself than to evaluations of the social and physical world in which one lives.

Second, one can note that the criterion-type concerns are completely intermingled with the domain-type concerns in Exhibit 2.2. Although the two types can be distinguished conceptually, as was done in chapter 1, it appears that respondents do not make this distinction. The distinctions repondents make, as is clearly shown by the nature of the regions that emerge, are on the basis of substantive *topic* (e.g., money) rather than on the basis of domain versus criterion (e.g., Family income versus Financial security). The intermingling of domains and criteria in Exhibit 2.2 supports the feasibility of assessing perceptions of life quality using either a domains-oriented or a criteria-oriented approach, or both.

So far, we have examined perceptual structures of evaluations of well-being as these emerge in data from heterogeneous sets of people. We have shown that a reasonable and orderly structure can be identified, that it is highly replicable in independent nationally representative samples, and that its main extensiveness is defined by different domain-type concerns, with most criterion-type concerns being located near the domain of Self and within a limited portion of the total space. When mapped in three dimensions, the first dimension seems to array concerns according to degree of psychological closeness. The second and third dimensions, while necessary to permit correct positioning of the items, had no obvious and replicable interpretations.

Next, we turn to two checks on the stability of the structures just described. The first check involves a statistical adjustment to each person's answers to remove certain effects that may have influenced the structure. The second examines the relationships within certain subgroups of the population.

Perceptual Structures—After Equating for Level and Variability of Evaluations

To explore the extent to which the structures shown in Exhibits 2.4 and 2.5 might be truly representative of the way people organize their perceptions about life concerns, rather than a statistical artifact arising from differences between people, interrelationships among the items were recomputed using data that had been adjusted to remove two kinds of phenomena. Each of the May respondents' answers to the concern items were moved up or down, and spread out or contracted, so that after adjustment each person showed the *same* average level of satisfaction across the whole set of items, and the *same* degree of variability in satisfaction across the whole set.[12]

Part of our purpose in constructing these adjusted scores was to remove any differences that might have existed between people in how they used the Delighted–Terrible Scale. Thus, if some people had consistently interpreted the scale in a more optimistic way than others, this could have generated spurious relationships that would affect our mappings. Of course, in the process we removed the real differences in people's general level of satisfaction as well as the differences, if any, in their use of the scale, but for the present purpose of checking the structure this was not critical.[13]

The important and reassuring finding was that when interrelationships among the adjusted scores were examined (data not shown), a pattern emerged that was generally similar to that observed earlier. The size of the correlations was usually smaller, but the same clusterings tended to appear. This increased our confidence in the phenomenological reality of the basic structure we have identified.

Perceptual Structures—Subgroups of the Population

In what respects are the perceptual structures of major subgroups of the population similar to, or different from, the structures shown previously for the general population? (By "subgroup" we mean collectivities such as men, women, blacks, young people, old people, high status people, or low status people). This issue is important because social indicators of perceived well-being should be relevant to subgroup interests and perspectives if they are to be maximally useful, and hence should take account of how various subgroups structure their perceptions. Furthermore, it is conceivable that some of the relationships that emerged when we analyzed data for the total population, and that influenced the placement of items in our perceptual maps, could be the "spurious" result of having combined distinctively different groups. Our inferences about perceptual structures need to be checked using data from somewhat more homogeneous sets of people.

The structural results for subgroups derive from the two national surveys (the May and April respondents) whose general results appear in Exhibits 2.4 and 2.6.[14] Appendix D presents eighteen detailed plots, one for each of nine subgroups, as they answered each of the two sets of concern items.[15]

---

[12]Scores adjusted in this way are sometimes referred to as "ipsative scores."

[13]Chapter 6 describes an analysis in which the effect of response bias is estimated separately from the effect of true differences in satisfaction.

[14]Results from the November respondents were also examined. They generally agree with the results discussed below and were judged not worth separate presentation.

[15]To facilitate comparison among the subgroup structures, and between them and the structure for the general population, the plots in Appendix D maintain constant the position of the items, but include indications of the correlations observed in the particular subgroup. Substantial correlations between items that are shown as relatively far apart usually indicate a larger correlation in

Our purpose here is only to identify some of the more substantial and general differences that can be observed among perceptual structures of the various subgroups. This information will be used to supplement the results presented in Exhibits 2.2 through 2.6 and to guide us in constructing well-being measures that are relevant and meaningful to a wide range of people, and that— to the extent possible—will have *similar* meanings to members of different subgroups.

Men and Women. In both surveys, the results for men and women show perceptual structures rather similar to each other and to that derived from the general population (Exhibits D.1,2 and D.10,11). The major difference is one of degree of differentiation: In general, men differentiated their evaluations of life concerns more than did women; i.e., the general level of covariation was somewhat higher for women than for men. Most differences between these two groups, however, are small, and what is probably most important is the structural similarity each showed to the pattern derived for the general population.

Four Age Groups. Four age groups were examined: sixteen to twenty-nine, thirty to forty-four, forty-five to fifty-nine, and sixty or more years old. When we compare these four groups, using data from the May survey, in which the concern items were mainly of the domain type, several interesting shifts in perceptual structures appear (Exhibits D.3,4,5,6).

Respondents sixteen to twenty-nine years old showed relatively many linkages between evaluations of their job (and/or housework) and other aspects of their "private" life: their standard of living, how they are treated by other people, what they feel that are accomplishing, and their family responsibilities. In this formative period when young adults are just moving into formal work roles, success or failure on the job may play a central role in determining other aspects of well-being.

The thirty- to forty-four-year-old group shows a neatly structured pattern that is very similar to that for the total population. In this age group, job seems to be evaluated relatively independently of other life concerns.

In the forty-five- to fifty-nine-year-old group job items again tie more closely to several other aspects of one's life (to sense of accomplishment, to standard of living, and—a linkage not seen earlier—to feelings about helping other people). In addition to these job linkages, this forty-five- to fifty-nine-year-old group differs from the general population in the emergence of a distinct cluster of items having to do with feelings about relationships with other people: people in the community, people one sees socially, things one does with friends, things one does to help people, how other people treat one, how one gets on with other people, and community organizations. Feelings

the subgroup than was observed in the total population. Conversely, lack of correlation between items that are plotted close together usually indicates less covariation between these items in the subgroup than in the total population. (Four items that appear in Exhibit 2.4 are omitted from Exhibits D.1 to D.9. These tapped feelings about car, weather, young people, and people over forty.)

about relationships with other people, however, seem to be relatively independent of feelings about one's family and are tied more strongly to job or community concerns for this age group.

In our oldest age group, those sixty or more years of age, in contrast, feelings about other people tend to be linked to feelings about family responsibilities and relatives. Two other features of the structure for these older people are of interest: For the first time, we see a linkage between feelings about one's health and other aspects of life,[16] and feelings about jobs become irrelevant for many.[17]

Thus, across the four age groups we see several different patterns in the way feelings about jobs and other people relate to other aspects of one's life. Note, however, that despite these changing interrelationships among certain clusters, the *internal* structure of most clusters remains relatively constant: Family items continue to show linkages to other family items, community items to other community items, national government items to other national government items, and so on. This pattern of generally stable relationships *within* a set of substantively similar concern items, but sometimes varying relationships *between* different concerns, is one that we will also see in a number of other instances. It provides a key to constructing indicators of well-being that are appropriate for a wide range of subgroups.

When we compare the four age groups with respect to the structure of their feelings about criterion-type concerns (Exhibits D.12, 13, 14, 15), there is one clear and unmistakable trend: The older the group, the less differentiation there is among the several items. For people in their late teens and twenties, the linkages between criteria are relatively few and relatively weak; for those aged sixty or more, the linkages are numerous and strong. Whether this reflects a more integrated view of life on the part of our most senior respondents, or simply that they answered these items with a more global and less analytic perspective is impossible to tell. Whatever the cause, it is interesting that this trend of decreasing differentiation of the criterion-type items with increasing age does not appear for the domain-type items. Despite the differences in levels of interrelatedness, the basic sun-and-planets structure of the criterion items is maintained in all age groups. The "planets" tend to show their strongest linkages to different portions of the "sun" as one shifts from one age group to another, and the whole structure becomes more tightly tied together as age increases, but the basic composition of the structure is clearly seen at all age levels.

Blacks. The structure of domain-type items for blacks (Exhibit D.7) is somewhat different from that which emerges for the population as a whole. Among the many discrepancies one can see a general merging of feelings about different aspects of the larger society—the media, national government, local

---

[16]The results from the November data, not presented, show this increasing linkage of health to other aspects of life more strongly than do the May data in Exhibit D.6.

[17]Nearly all retired people (97 percent) chose the off-scale category "Does not apply to me" when asked to evaluate their jobs.

government, and the natural environment—into a much more tightly knit and less differentiated general evaluation.

One can also see interesting shifts in the relevant contexts for certain items: The question, How do you feel about the way other people treat you?, which in the total population showed most covariation with feelings about co-workers, relates most for blacks to feelings about one's spouse and one's organizations. Several other similar examples are evident.

Turning to the criterion-type items (Exhibit D.16), we again find interesting differences between blacks and the general population. The primary difference is that two of the items that are relatively distinct from the central core of items in the total population are more closely linked to this core for blacks. These are feelings about physical work and exercise, and feelings about neatness and tidiness. Perhaps achievement of these goals plays a more central role in the thinking of blacks than in the thinking of others.

Groups with High or Low Status. Finally, we turn to consider two groups extreme with respect to socioeconomic status.[18] The differences in perceptual structures between the general population and both the high and low socioeconomic status groups are substantial.

With respect to both domain- and criterion-type concerns, the low status group shows much less differentiation than the general population (Exhibits D.8, 17). What appear as relatively distinct concerns for the general population show up as one heavily interlinked set for this group (with the exception of job-relevant items, which were irrelevant for most people in this group, since they tended not to be employed for a variety of reasons).[19] For these people, apparently, life tends to be evaluated very generally, with much less differentiation among different aspects than is seen by most people.

The high status respondents, in contrast, show more than average differentiation among criterion-type items (Exhibit D.18). Their pattern among the domain-type items differs from that for the general population mainly by a closer integration of feelings about characteristics of oneself, one's job, one's family responsibilities, and one's income and standard of living (Exhibit D.9).

Selecting and Clustering Concern-Level Measures

The large array of concern items that have been assembled, and the perceptual structures that have been identified for the total population and for major subgroups, provide a rich source that can yield any of a wide variety of measures of perceived well-being at the concern level.

---

[18]Both of these groups were restricted to people thirty or more years of age, since our indicators of status—family income, and education of family head—were less applicable to young people, whose education, incomes, and family situations were, in many cases, still undergoing significant changes. The low socioeconomic status group was composed of people aged thirty or more who fell in SES category 1 (defined in Appendix L) while those in the high status group were aged thirty or more and fell in SES category 5 (also defined in Appendix L).

[19]In examining Exhibit D.17 note that, unlike other exhibits in the series, linkages are shown only for correlations of .60 or greater. Had all correlations of .40 or more been plotted, most items would have been linked to most others.

Our strategy for exploiting this source was a simple one: Sample the perceptual space to ensure breadth of coverage; do this by selecting one or more items from a dispersed set of subregions; where certain criteria can be met, enhance the validity of the measure by basing it on a cluster of items rather than just one; then check the relevancy and adequacy of the selected concern-level measures by examining their ability, when taken singly and jointly, to explain respondents' general sense of well-being.

This strategy represents an implementation of the basic model described in chapter 1, which suggests that one's overall sense of life quality is determined by feelings about the things in life that concern one. The strategy also explicitly checks for two types of possible "failures": (1) that some of the items did not tap anything about which respondents actually felt concerned—irrelevancy of the concern; and (2) that respondents' feelings about some aspects of life, while real, may not have any relation to their evaluation of life as a whole—irrelevancy of the feeling.

In this section we will not make specific recommendations about how to construct a social indicator battery for assessing perceived well-being. That is the topic of chapter 11. Here we simply describe certain clusterings of concern items used in the analyses reported in chapters 4 and 5, and the considerations that led us to construct these particular combinations. While our experience in using these measures leads us to suggest that some be preserved, and that others be modified or abandoned, we remain committed to the basic methodological approach that governed their construction.

Methodology. Three criteria had to be met before concern-level items were placed together within a cluster: (1) The items had to be substantively similar; (2) they had to exhibit substantial statistical covariation; and (3) the pattern of their covariation had to be reasonably stable across major subgroups of the American population.

The requirement for conceptual similarity helps assure that we can arrive at an appropriate understanding of the nature of the concern, and that we not place together items that may covary for some reason (such as cause and effect) other than that they are alternate ways of measuring what is essentially the same concern.

The requirement of substantial covariation assures that we place together only items that operate as though they had something in common and, therefore, that act as if they are tapping the same concern.

The requirement for similar patterns of relationships within different subgroups helps assure that the concern is relevant for a wide range of people and that its "internal" meaning is similar to different groups. Given the observed differences in perceptual structures, it seems that it will be impossible to construct a set of perceptual indicators that show the same relationship to each other in all groups of the population. However, by careful selection of concern items, it may be possible to construct a set of indicators that are internally stable across groups.

A specific example implementing our approach may be helpful. The four domain items having to do with national government were observed to relate to one another substantially and consistently in all of the subgroups examined.

Given their conceptual similarity, it was thus reasonable to treat them as alternate measures of a single general concern. Similarly, the two items, How do you feel about the way your local government is operating? and How do you feel about the way the police and courts in this area are operating?, were also observed to substantially and consistently covary. It was not hard to conceptualize these as tapping a concern about local government. For some groups (e.g., women, blacks), the linkages between the two sets were substantial, suggesting that these people evaluated these aspects of their lives in terms of a general perception of "government." However, certain other groups (e.g., men and people sixty or more years of age) showed rather weak linkage between the two sets of items. These people differentiated between local and national government. Thus, we decided to treat these items as if they were tapping two concerns and to measure each separately. This preserved a distinction that at least some people made, yet did little violence to the perspectives of those who perceived only "government" in general. For these latter people, we would simply observe that their evaluations of local government tended to be similar to their evaluations of national government. Essentially, the internal meaning of each concern was kept stable, though the relationships between concerns was allowed to vary from group to group.

Clusters. The results of our clustering decisions are shown in Exhibits 2.7 and 2.8, for the May and April national data sets, respectively. (The November data includes no clusters that do not also appear in the May data.) As can be seen in these exhibits, a substantial number of multi-item clusters could be formed that met the criteria just discussed.

Because the July data included fewer respondents than any of our national samples, the third clustering criterion—stability across subgroups—could not be used. The first two criteria, however, could be examined, and the series of clusters that emerged in the July data have been presented in Exhibit 2.2.[20]

In chapters 4 and 5 we explore the ability of various clusters, and of single concern items, to explain individuals' sense of well-being. Appendix C describes how each of the cluster scores was derived, and provides a convenient reference number for each of these measures. (Reference numbers for single item measures appear in Exhibit 2.1.)

AFFECTIVE EVALUATIONS VERSUS UNSPECIFIED FEELINGS

All of the explorations of perceptual structure discussed so far in this chapter have been based on data generated by using the Delighted–Terrible Scale. In mapping the locations of concern items, we have put them close together if people's affective evaluations of them showed substantial covaria-

---

[20] A second set of clusters of items in the July data, which grouped items into nine broad topical areas on the basis of their apparent content, was also scored. These appear as measures C40 to C48 in Appendix C.

EXHIBIT 2.7. Twelve Clusters Identified Among Sixty-Three Items of May National Survey

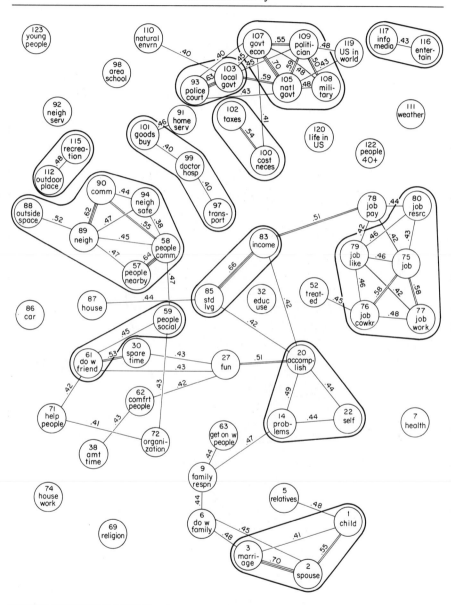

Item numbers match Exhibit 2.1. Location of items adapted from Exhibit 2.4.

EXHIBIT 2.8. Four Clusters Among Twenty-Three Criterion-Type Concerns

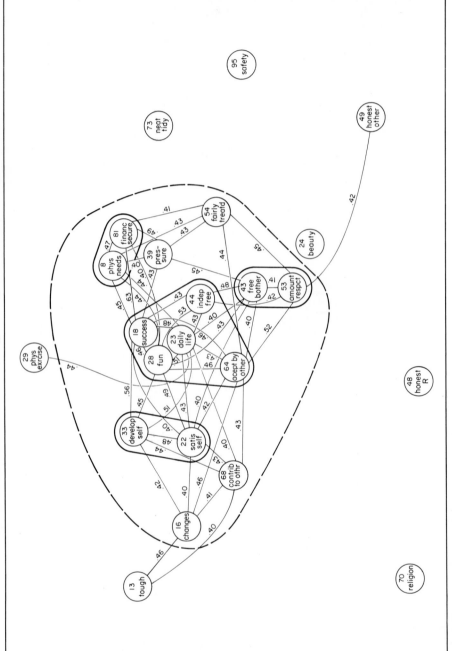

Data source: 1,433 respondents to April national survey. Item numbers match Exhibit 2.1; linkages show $r \geq .40$.

tion, and far from one another if affective evaluations were statistically independent. There remains, however, an important issue as to whether covariation
in *affective evaluations* provides the appropriate measure for assessing perceptual structures. It is conceivable, for example, that although people's affective
evaluations of "community" and "neighborhood" tended to covary, other
responses to these concerns might not show similar covariation. Perhaps if the
dimension were "comfort" to "distress," or "mine" versus "others," or "casual" versus "formal," or any of many other possible dimensions, the patterns of
covariation would appear quite different. Thus, an important question is
whether feelings of affective evaluation, assessed by the Delighted–Terrible
Scale, provide appropriate indications of the structure of feelings about life
concerns.

To help us answer this question, each of the July respondents, as his or her
very first task, was given a set of thirty-five cards. Each card named something
that might qualify as a life concern. For example, one card had "Your house or
apartment" printed on it. Others read "Taxes," "Your job (for pay)," "Your
independence or freedom," "Your last vacation," and so on.[21] Respondents
were asked to eliminate cards that did not apply to them (e.g., spouse, children,
car) and then to sort the remaining cards according to *similarity of feelings*. The
instruction read:

> Put in any one pile, those things or people for which you have roughly
> similar feelings. Cards that end up in any one pile should have some rough
> similarity in how you FEEL about them.

Respondents were told they could use as many or few piles as they wished, and
the nature of the feelings by which they were to classify the concerns was left
entirely to them.

Subsequently, the proportion of times respondents said they had the same
feelings about two concerns (relative to the number of times they might have
said this) was computed for each pair of concerns and treated as a measure of
similarity between the pairs. These similarity measures were then used to
explore the structure of people's feelings and the map shown in Exhibit 2.9
emerged.[22]

The striking aspect of this map is the general similarity of the structure to
the maps presented earlier in Exhibits 2.2, 2.4, and 2.5. Note that one dimension begins with concerns about family and self at one end (except for the three
time items and the vacation item, none of which was used previously), and

[21]Of the thirty-five cards, twenty-six contained concerns that appear in Exhibit 2.1 with the
following numbers: 1, 2, 4, 20, 22, 24, 26, 28, 30, 43, 44, 47, 57, 60, 74, 75, 83, 85, 86, 87, 89, 90, 95,
100, 102, and 106. The remaining concerns read as follows: "Your position in the community,"
"Popular music," "The last five years," "Your last vacation," "The circumstances and conditions
of your life," "Your clothes," "The food you eat," "The next five years," "The last year."

[22]This map was produced by the same statistical technique (Smallest Space Analysis) used in
producing the other maps in this chapter. In two dimensions, the coefficient of alienation was .24,
in three dimensions it was .18, in four dimensions, .11. Since only modest improvements in fit
were achieved by use of more than two dimensions, Exhibit 2.9 shows the simpler two-
dimensional solution.

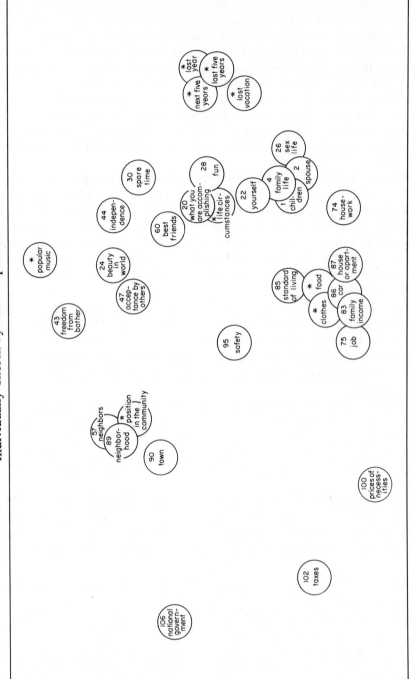

EXHIBIT 2.9. Two-Dimensional Perceptual Map Based on Similarity of Feelings Along Dimensions Individually Chosen by Each Respondent

Data source: July respondents. Item numbers match Exhibit 2.1; see footnote 21 in text for items with asterisks.

extends to concerns about the national government and taxes, at the other. Concerns about job, income, standard of living, house, relationships with other people, and community occur between the two. Clearly, this is the familiar main dimension that also appears in Exhibits 2.2 through 2.5. Note also the close proximity of several items having to do with family, of several other items dealing with neighborhood and community, and of the income/standard of living pair. These regions of the space closely replicate regions identified earlier.[23]

We interpret the similarities between this map, which is based on *whatever* feelings people had regarding life concerns, and the earlier maps, which were based on the specific feelings (affective evaluations) tapped by the Delighted–Terrible Scale, as demonstrating that affective evaluations play a major role in governing the organization of people's perceptions about life concerns. Although the previous structures were derived from just one prespecified type of possible feeling, rather similar structures emerge when respondents are left free to use whatever feelings seem most natural to them. We believe this supports the essential correctness of the perceptual structures shown in previous exhibits.

CHAPTER SUMMARY

Identifying aspects of life that concern people, and learning how people's feelings about these concerns are organized, generate basic knowledge needed for rational development of perceptual indicators. Knowing the structure of perceptions about life concerns permits an informed selection of specific concerns for assessment in a social indicators framework, and knowing the location of specific questionnaire items within this structure allows one to tailor the measurement process to achieve the desired balance among breadth of coverage, statistical efficiency, validity, and economy. Knowledge of this structure may have conceptual benefits as well, helping to interrelate information about different life concerns, and perhaps calling attention to concerns that have been neglected by scholars or policymakers.

An extensive list of possible life concerns was assembled, drawing from answers given to previous surveys, published lists of "values," important life aspects identified by various national and international organizations, and a series of wide-ranging interviews conducted by project staff. Exhibit 2.1 presents 123 questionnaire items written to tap these. The items were administered in various overlapping subsets to three nationally representative samples of

---

[23]To provide a quantitative measure of the degree of similarity between the structures shown in Exhibits 2.2 and 2.9, both of which are based on data from the July respondents, the magnitude of (a) the correlations between each pair of items was correlated with (b) the proportion of people saying they had similar feelings about that pair—for all pairs of items that appear in both exhibits. The resulting correlation was +.38.

respondents, and the full set was administered to a more restricted group, the July respondents. This list of 123 concern items provides a broad base from which to begin exploring perceptual structures, and major omissions from it have not yet been identified.

A series of maps locate these items in two- and three-dimensional spaces and permit inferences about how perceptions regarding life concerns are organized. These maps were derived on the basis of the amount of covariation observed among the concern items, through the application of Smallest Space Analysis.

The most all-inclusive map, based on data from the July respondents and presented in Exhibit 2.2, shows a reasonably clear grouping of items into content-oriented clusters, or subregions, and rational transitions from one subregion to another. Subregions could be aggregated into the following general regions: Self, Family, Other People, Economic Aspects, Job, House, Costs, Local Area, Larger Society, Religion, and Beneficence. One dimension of the map arrays concerns according to degree of psychological closeness, ranging from concerns about oneself, at one end, to concerns about the national government, at the other.

Maps of domain-type items, based on nationally representative samples of respondents, show structures generally similar to that for the July respondents, and structures that are highly replicable from one national sample to another.

Maps of criterion-type items suggest a sun-and-planets organization: a large central core of criteria dealing with aspects of one's daily life and oneself is surrounded by single concern items that are relatively independent from the central core and from each other. Criterion-type items, when mapped into the same space as domain-type items, intermingled with the domains (indicating respondents did not distinguish between them), were bunched somewhat more tightly (indicating evaluations of criteria were more homogeneous than evaluations of domains), and tended to be located in or near the Self region of the structure.

When the covariations among domain- and criterion-type items were examined for nine (overlapping) major subgroups of the American population (based on sex, age, race, and status) some variations in perceptual structure became evident. In most cases, however, the clusters of items that appear in maps based on the total population continued to appear for the subgroups, though the interrelationships between these clusters differed from group to group. (In constructing measures for use in later analysis, we imposed the requirement that patterns of relationship between a measure's component parts had to be similar in all subgroups. Two exhibits show the items that met this requirement and that also were conceptually similar and sufficiently interrelated to justify being combined.)

To check the appropriateness of using data from the Delighted–Terrible Scale for making inferences about perceptual structures, a special set of data were collected in which respondents indicated simply whether their feelings about certain pairs of concerns were similar or different. The nature of the feelings was left strictly up to the respondents. The structure of concerns that emerged from the analysis of these data is generally similar to the structures derived using data from the Delighted–Terrible Scale. This suggests that affective evaluations play a major role in governing the organization of people's perceptions, and supports our inferences regarding structures of perceptions about life concerns.

CHAPTER 3

Measuring Global Well-Being

The preceding chapter discussed life concerns, "domains" of life and "criteria" for evaluating life. Although the domains and criteria that we chose to investigate were all relatively broad in scope, each referred to an aspect of life that was substantially less inclusive than life-as-a-whole. In contrast, this chapter focuses on a wide range of "global" measures, measures intended to tap a variety of different qualities that characterize life-as-a-whole. It describes sixty-eight global measures and how they relate to one another, both conceptually and statistically.

In some respects this chapter is functionally parallel to the preceding one: It describes a large set of measures developed for assessing perceptions of well-being, it examines their interrelationships, and it leads toward the analyses (in chaps. 4 and 5) where we attempt to account for variation in the global measures on the basis of variation in the concern measures.

However, unlike our analysis of the concern measures, which we saw as relevant to a single psychologically coherent structure, we will not attempt to make inferences about a "structure" of global perceptions. We doubt that such a structure exists. Rather, when examining the interrelationships among the global measures, we shall focus on their statistical overlap or distinctiveness and on the evidence they give about the kinds of perspectives and dimensions respondents use when evaluating life-as-a-whole.

In developing a set of global measures, our purpose—as with the concern measures—was to be broad and inclusive. By asking people to assess their life-as-a-whole from a variety of perspectives and with respect to a variety of qualities, we expected to learn which of these were most meaningful to people, and how the more meaningful ones fit together. As with the concern measures, we wanted our global measures to include those used by certain other investigators in previous research on life quality, but also wanted to explore a broader and more extensive set of global measures than had previously been examined. In addition to developing the basic knowledge needed to guide our own subsequent analyses, we hoped our information about evaluations of life-as-a-

63

whole would be useful to others who might also wish to develop social indicators of perceived life quality.

Our basic conception of a global measure, as indicated in chapter 1, is of a *summary evaluation* about life-as-a-whole.

An analogy may be helpful. In choosing which of several cars to purchase, one may consider a wide range of different features—gas mileage, style, size, power, and many others. Some cars seem good with respect to some features, others with respect to other features. Yet, somehow the purchaser combines his evaluations of the more specific features and arrives at a decision about which car to buy; he makes a global assessment, a summary evaluation, of the overall desirability of ownership in such a way that one car (the one purchased) scores ahead of all others.

For the car purchaser only one global aspect is of immediate interest, the desirability of owning this car. In assessing well-being at the global level, however, the situation is not so clear. Do people actually evaluate their lives in global terms? If so, along what dimensions and from what perspectives do they make the evaluations? Before considering the nature of the evaluations that may be made, we consider the prior question as to whether such evaluations are made at all.

On the Existence of Global Assessments of Life Quality

Several considerations lead us to believe it is meaningful to attempt to measure global assessments of life quality.

One is the thought that each person, each day, is implicitly faced with a fundamental choice: whether to continue living. Unlike our car purchaser, the choice is not *which* life to "buy" (though over time one may be able to change major aspects of one's life), but whether to keep the present one "going." Of course, most people choose to continue their existence, but the occasional suicide reminds us that there is an alternative. The observation that most people continuously try to perform the functions required to keep them alive when they do not "have to," suggests that in some basic and perhaps unconscious way they have made a summary evaluation that comes out implying, "My life-as-a-whole scores high enough to be worth continuing."

A second consideration supporting the existence of global assessments of life quality is the way people behave when asked for global evaluations: They provide them, promptly and with apparent ease. In the course of our work we have put the question, How do you feel about your life as a whole?, to thousands of people and asked them to choose from a set of categories (the Delighted–Terrible Scale) that includes the answer, "Never thought about it." Virtually no one (less than 1 percent) chose the never-thought-about-it answer. Our experience is not unique. Other investigators have had similar success with questions about life-as-a-whole. Furthermore, such questions are often asked (and answered) in everyday conversations: "How's life going?" "How are things?" "How's life treating you today?"

A third line of evidence comes from investigations by Dalkey (1972). He posed this question to subjects participating in his research, What proportion of the adult population . . . maintain some form of running evaluation, explicit or implicit, of themselves or of their "life"? Based on his respondents' answers, Dalkey concludes, "The majority of respondents agreed that some evaluation is kept by most people" (Dalkey, 1972, p. 97).

Thus, we are persuaded that it is indeed meaningful to investigate assessments of life-as-a-whole. The next question, then, concerns the nature of these assessments. To investigate this we assembled a large number of measures that attempt to assess life-as-a-whole from a variety of perspectives and along a variety of dimensions. These perspectives and dimensions provide the basis for defining a typology of global measures.

The next section of this chapter describes the global measures we explored and the several "types" into which they fall. Next, the typology itself is laid out in more formal terms, and possibilities for constructing various other types of global measures are noted. The latter part of the chapter examines the statistical interrelationships among the global measures and shows that the typology, which is based on theoretical considerations, provides a classification scheme that ties in with the empirical similarities and dissimilarities among the measures.

THE GLOBAL MEASURES AND A TYPOLOGY FOR CLASSIFYING THEM

The global measures used in our research, and the concepts they were designed to tap, accumulated gradually during the course of our work. We did not undertake a systematic search for the terms people use when thinking about their life-as-a-whole, but as we encountered different ways of assessing life-as-a-whole—in our own thinking about the problem, in the ways respondents spoke about their lives, or in the work of other researchers—we incorporated these into our work.

Exhibit 3.1 presents the complete list of sixty-eight global measures we experimented with and an indication of the respondents to whom each measure was administered. The list is ordered according to what we believe are the conceptual differences between the measures. The major organizing principle is the *perspective* from which the evaluation is made: absolute, relative, long-range change, or short-range change. Within the absolute perspective, measures are subdivided into *general* evaluations versus evaluations of various *more specific qualities* of life-as-a-whole. Finally, the general evaluations are further subdivided into *full-range* and *part-range* measures. (At the very end of the list appear five supplementary global measures that refer to something other than the respondent's current life quality.)

EXHIBIT 3.1. Measures of Global Life Quality

M = May national survey (N = 1297)
N' = November national survey Form 1 (N = 1118)
N" = November national survey Form 2 (N = 1072)
A = April national survey (N = 1433)
J = July respondents (N = 222)
O = October respondents (N = 280)

A. *Absolute perspective, general evaluation, full-range measures*

G1 How do you feel about your life as a whole? (D–T Scale) Short name: M N'N" A J
Life 1

G2 Same measure as G1, asked later in interview. Short name: Life 2   M N" A J

G3 Derived measure: mean of coded answers to G1 and G2. Short name: M N" A J
Life 3

G4 Same as measure G2, but asked later in interview. Short name: Life 4   J

G5 Which face comes closest to expressing how you feel about your life as a   J
whole? (Scale: seven faces with varying smiles or frowns) Short name:
Faces: whole life

G6 Here is a picture of a ladder. At the bottom of the ladder is the worst life   A J
you might reasonably expect to have. At the top is the best life you might
expect to have. Of course, life from week to week falls somewhere in
between. Where was your life *most of the time during the past year?* (Scale:
ladder with nine rungs extending from "Best life I could expect to have"
to "Worse life I could expect to have") Short name: Ladder: most

G7 Here are some circles that we can imagine represent the lives of different   A J
people. Circle eight has all pluses in it, to represent a person who has all
good things in his life. Circle zero has all minuses in it, to represent a
person who has all bad things in his life. Other circles are in between.
Which circle do you think comes closest to matching your life? (Scale:
row of nine circles with contents ranging from eight +'s to eight −'s)
Short name: Circles: whole life

G8 Where would you put your life as a whole on the feeling thermometer?   N' N"
(Graphic scale from very cold, negative, to very warm, positive) Short
name: Thermometer

G9 Derived measure: weighted sum of number of weeks out of past ten with   J
given feelings. (Formula: 1(G18) + 2(G19) + 3(G20) + 4(G28) + 5(G26) +
6(G25) + 7(G24).) Short name: Weighted weeks

G10 Derived measure: regression weighted sum of number of weeks out of   J
past ten with given feelings. (Formula: 52.366 + 1.244(G18) + .869(G19)
− 1.507(G26) − 2.373(G25).) Short name: Regression weighted weeks

G11 Derived measure: regression weighted sum of number of good parts,   J
neutral parts, and bad parts of life—out of total of eight parts. (Formula:
50.321 + 1.492(G16) − 2.519(G22).) Short name: Weighted slices

G12 Derived measure: combination of Life 3 and five qualities. (Components   M
and relative weights: .647(G3) + .192(G40) + .163(G44) + .146(G43) +
.064(G39) + .034(G41). Scales were first standardized and, where
needed, reversed.) Short name: Rodgers' X

G13 Average of up to three ratings by persons nominated by the respondent   J
on how the respondent feels about life as a whole. (D–T Scale) Short
name: Rating by others

G14 Rating by interviewer of how respondent feels about life as a whole. (D–   A
T Scale) Short name: Interviewer rating

B. *Absolute perspective, general evaluation, part-range measures*

G15 Now, try and forget all the things in your life that annoy or worry you;   N'   J

EXHIBIT 3.1. (*continued*)

	how do you feel about the good and pleasant parts of your life? How do these nice aspects, by themselves, make you feel? (D–T Scale) Short name: Good parts		
G16	Here is a circle and we can imagine that it represents *your life*. The pie slices are parts of your life. There are eight slices, so let's imagine that you can divide your life up into eight parts. Now, put a plus sign (+) in those slices that are *good* parts of your life. Put a zero (0) in those slices that are *neutral* parts of your life, neither good nor bad. And, put a minus sign (−) in those slices that are *bad* parts of your life. Put some mark in every slice. Measure: number of +'s. Short name: Number of pluses.		J
G17	Where on the ladder would you say was your *best week in the past year*— on which rung would you put it? (See G6 for full wording and scale.) Short name: Ladder: best	A	J
G18	Think back over what your life has been like during the past ten weeks. It may help to try to remember some of the specific things that happened to you, or which you did during this period. YOUR ANSWERS SHOULD ADD UP TO TEN WEEKS. For what part of that time did you feel *delighted* about your life as a whole? . . . pleased . . . mostly satisfied . . . mixed—about equally satisfied and dissatisfied . . . mostly dissatisfied . . . unhappy . . . terrible. . . . Measure: number of weeks felt delighted. Short name: Weeks delighted		J
G19	Measure: number of weeks felt pleased out of ten. (See G18 for question wording.) Short name: Weeks pleased		J
G20	Measure: number of weeks felt mostly satisfied out of ten. (See G18 for question wording.) Short name: Weeks mostly satisfied		J
G21	Now try and forget all the good and pleasant parts of your life; how do you feel about the things that annoy or worry you? How do these poor aspects, by themselves, make you feel? (D–T Scale) Short name: Bad parts	N′	J
G22	Measure: number of −'s assigned to eight parts of life. (See G16 for full question wording.) Short name: Number of minuses		J
G23	Where on the ladder was your *worst week during the past year*—on which rung? (See G6 for full wording and scale.) Short name: Ladder: worst	A	J
G24	Measure: number of weeks felt terrible out of ten. (See G18 for question wording.) Short name: Weeks terrible		J
G25	Measure: number of weeks felt unhappy out of ten. (See G18 for question wording.) Short name: Weeks unhappy		J
G26	Measure: number of weeks felt mostly dissatisfied out of ten. (See G18 for question wording.) Short name: Weeks mostly dissatisfied		J
G27	Measure: number of 0's (neutrals) assigned to eight parts of life. (See G16 for question wording.) Short name: Number of neutrals		J
G28	Measure: number of weeks felt mixed—about equally satisfied and dissatisfied out of ten. (See G18 for question wording.) Short name: Weeks mixed		J

C. *Absolute perspective, measures of various more specific qualities*

G29	How satisfied are you with your life as a whole these days? (Seven-pt. scale: Completely satisfied . . . completely dissatisfied) Short name: Seven-pt. Satisfaction	N′ N″
G30	In general, how satisfying do you find the way you're spending your life these days? Would you call it completely satisfying, pretty satisfying, or not very satisfying? Short name: Three-pt. Satisfaction	N″

EXHIBIT 3.1. *(continued)*

		M	N"	J
G31	Taking all things together, how would you say things are these days— would you say you're very happy, pretty happy, or not too happy these days? Short name: Three-pt. Happiness	M	N"	J
G32	How do you feel about how happy you are? (D–T Scale) Short name: Seven-pt. Happiness		N"	J
G33	Most people worry more or less about somethings. Would you say you never worry, worry a little, worry sometimes, worry a lot, or worry all the time? Short name: Worries		N'N"	J
G34	Most people's moods change from day to day; sometimes you feel up, other times you feel down. How do you feel today? A lot worse than usual, somewhat worse than usual, about as usual, somewhat better than usual, a lot better than usual. Short name: Mood			J
G35	Bradburn's Positive Affect Scale: number of five positive events experienced. "During past few weeks did you ever feel . . . particularly excited or interested in something? . . . proud because someone complimented you on something you had done? . . . pleased about having accomplished something? . . . on top of the world? . . . that things were going your way?" Short name: Affect positive		N"	J
G36	Bradburn's Negative Affect Scale: number of five negative events experienced. "During the past few weeks did you ever feel . . . so restless that you couldn't sit long in a chair? . . . very lonely or remote from other people? . . . bored? . . . depressed or very unhappy? upset because someone criticized you?" Short name: Affect negative		N"	J
G37	Bradburn's Affect Balance Scale. (Formula: G35 − G36) Short name: Affect balance.		N"	J
G38	Total affect (Formula: G35 + G36) Short name: Affect total		N"	J
G39	Feelings about your life: Boring . . . Interesting (7-pt. scale)	M		J
G40	Feelings about your life: Enjoyable . . . Miserable (7-pt. scale)	M		J
G41	Feelings about your life: Useless . . . Worthwhile (7-pt. scale)	M		J
G42	Feelings about your life: Not lonely . . . Lonely (7-pt. scale)			J
G43	Feelings about your life: Full . . . Empty (7-pt. scale)	M		J
G44	Feelings about your life: Disappointing . . . Rewarding (7-pt. scale)	M		J
G45	Feelings about your life: Intolerable . . . Ideal (7-pt. scale)			J
G46	Feelings about your life: Angry . . . Contented (7-pt. scale)			J
G47	Feelings about your life: Disgusted . . . Enjoying (7-pt. scale)			J
G48	Feelings about your life: Helpless . . . Capable (7-pt. scale)			J

D. Measures using a relative perspective

				J
G49	Which of the following statements fits how you feel? My life is worse than nearly everyone else's . . . worse than most others' . . . about average—better than some and worse than some . . . better than most others' . . . better than nearly everyone else's. Short name: Better than everyone			J
G50	Which of the following statements fits how you feel? My life is much worse than most other people's . . . somewhat worse . . . about the same . . . somewhat better . . . much better. . . . Short name: Much better			J
G51	Measure: category selected as the one "in which you would put your own life" out of seven ranging from "People with the best kind of life" to "People with the worst kind of life." (See G52 for question wording.) Short name: Kind of life			J
G52	If all the adults in the United States were represented by cards—one person per card—and if you were sorting everyone into seven piles ordered from those who had the *best kind of life* to those who had the *worst kind of life,* some people would have to fall in the middle pile. We			J

EXHIBIT 3.1. (*continued*)

have drawn a line to represent the height of the pile of cards, representing people, in the middle group. Draw lines up from each of the other six points to show about how many people you *think* would be in the other piles. Just make your best guess. Draw a circle around the letter under the pile in which you would put your own life. Measure: respondent's decile position, as calculated from his perceived position within the distribution he gave. Short name: Decile position

G53 Derived measure: difference between respondent's estimate of the   A J
relative balance of good and bad parts in his own life and his estimate of
the balance that "would be chosen most often by people in this
country." (Formula: G7 − G67) Short name: Circles: R minus others

G54 Now let's compare your life . . . with the lives of six *people you know*   J
well. It does not matter to us who these people are, but for your
convenience write down the initials of each person in the boxes
provided below. (Think of real people you meet from time to time.)
Under each set of initials put a "B" if you think that on the whole your
life is better *for you* than that person's would be. Put an "S" if yours
seems about the same for you as that person's would be. Put a "W" if
yours seems worse for you than that person's would be. Measure:
average of up to six ratings, where B = 3, S = 2, and W = 1. Short name:
Social comparison

G55 Imagine that the lines below represent piles of cards. Each pile has   J
people whose lives are pretty similar. The person in Pile A below has a
life like nobody else. People in Pile G have lives like quite a lot of other
people. In which pile would you put *your life*? (Scale categories showed
1, 3, 5, 8, 12, 20, and 29 members, respectively.) Short name: Uniqueness

E. Measures using a long-term change perspective

G56 Derived measure: progress from past levels (Formula: G6 − G64) Short   A J
name: Past progress

G57 Derived measure: progress expected in the future (Formula: G65 − G6)   A J
Short name: Future progress

G58 Derived measure: progress from past to future (Formula: G65 − G64)   A J
Short name: Progress past and future

F. Measures using a short-term change perspective

G59 Derived measure: range of levels between best and worst weeks   A J
(Formula: G17 − G23) Short name: Ladder: best minus worst

G60 Derived measure: range of feelings about good parts and bad parts of   N" J
life. (Formula: G15 − G21) Short name: Range of feelings

G61 Feelings about your life: up and down and changing . . . even and   J
steady and stays the same (7-pt. scale) Short name: Up and down or
steady

G62 Please indicate how much your feelings about your life as a whole   J
change from month to month. (7-pt. scale ranging from "my feelings
about this never change" to "my feelings about this change a great
deal.") Short name: Variation in feelings

G63 Derived measure: stability in feeling across past ten weeks. (This   J
measure was based on measures G18, G19, G20, G24, G25, G26, and G28
and varied according to the number of weeks during which the modal
feeling was experienced.) Short name: Number of weeks stable

G. Supplementary measures

G64 Where was your life *five years ago*? (Same ladder scale as measure G6)   A J
Short name: Ladder: five years ago.

EXHIBIT 3.1. (continued)

G65	Where do you expect your life to be *five years from now?* (Same ladder scale as measure G6) Short name: Ladder: five years hence.	A	J
G66	Considering how your life is going, would you like to continue much the same way, change some parts of it, or change many parts of it? (3-pt. scale) Short name: Changes desired	N″	J
G67	Which circle do you think would be chosen most often by people in this country? (See G7 for full question wording and scale.) Short name: Circles: others	A	J
G68	Think of the neighbor who lives nearest to you, who is of the same sex as you, and who is at least eighteen years old. (If there are several such neighbors living equally close to your house or apartment, pick the one to the left as you walk into your place.) The following questions all concern how you *think* this person feels about aspects of his or her *own* life. Measure: how he/she feels about life as a whole. (D–T Scale). Short name: Neighbor whole life		J

General Assessments of Life-as-a-Whole from an "Absolute" Perspective

Full-Range Measures. The first set of measures in Exhibit 3.1 are all attempts to assess life-as-a-whole using very general response scales and from an "absolute" perspective. We shall call these Type A measures.

Measures G1 through G14 provide these kinds of assessments and attempt to cover life-as-a-whole in its entirety. Measures G1, G2, and G4 are based on essentially identical questions (How do you feel about your life as a whole?) that were answered using the Delighted–Terrible Scale; they differ only with respect to their serial position within the interview or questionnaire. Measure G3, the mean of answers given to G1 and G2, came to be known as Life 3 and is our most-used global measure. Various analyses to be reported in this chapter and in chapter 6 suggest it provides one of the best assessments of a person's general feeling about life-as-a-whole.

Measures G5 through G8 are attempts to assess general feelings about life-as-a-whole using nonverbal scales. Their purpose is identical to that of Measures G1 to G4, all of which were tied to the specific words of the Delighted–Terrible Scale, but G5 through G8 attempt to accomplish their purpose by use of various graphic devices. Measure G5 uses a series of seven stylized faces in which the shape of the mouth varies gradually from a big smile to a big frown. G6 uses a picture of a ladder with numbered rungs extending from "Best life I could expect to have" to "Worst life I could expect to have."[1] Measure G7, Circles: Whole life, consists of a row of nine circles, each divided into eight "pie slices" of equal size and labeled with plus and minus signs. The combinations of plus signs and minus signs vary across the nine circles to indicate different mixtures of positive and negative life aspects. Measure G8 uses a drawing of a thermometer to portray a scale ranging from positive to negative.[2]

---

[1] This ladder scale was adapted from Cantril (1965), as were the several questions applied to it.

[2] This thermometer format has been used on numerous previous occasions by the Survey Research Center and the Center for Political Studies at the University of Michigan to assess reactions toward political candidates.

Measures G9 through G12 are all derived by combining answers to two or more questions. G9 takes the durations that the various feelings that make up the Delighted–Terrible Scale were experienced over the past ten weeks and combines them into a single summary measure using a simple combination rule. G10 uses the same data but a slightly different combination statistically derived to provide a score maximally similar to the respondent's score on Life 3.[3] Measure G11 also attempts to match Life 3, using data from another series of questions in which the respondent was asked to consider his life as divided into eight parts of unspecified natures and to indicate for each whether his feelings about it were positive, neutral, or negative.[4] Measure G12 is an attempt to construct in our data a measure that would be conceptually parallel to one constructed by Campbell, Converse, and Rodgers (1976).[5]

The last two measures in this initial set, G13 and G14, are assessments of the respondent's general feelings about life-as-a-whole made by persons *other* than the respondent himself. G13 is an average of ratings made by up to three persons nominated by the respondent for this purpose; G14 is a rating made by the person who interviewed the respondent. Rarely would the interviewer have had any contact with the respondent other than during the approximately one-hour interview itself, but during this period the interviewer would have heard the respondent's opinion about a wide range of subjects, and would have been able to observe the respondent in his own home setting.

Part-Range Measures. In addition to the full-range measures just discussed, the global measures include some that apply a general scale and an absolute perspective, but that seek to assess only part of the range; i.e., are concerned only with those portions of life-as-a-whole that the respondent believes are especially good, especially bad, or neutral. Our purpose in constructing these measures was to enable us to follow up suggestions that, in their most extreme form, said it is only the "good things" or only the "bad things" in a person's life that really influence his overall evaluations.

Measures G15 through G20 all involve general responses to the "good" parts of life and ask essentially, *how* good are the good parts (G15), what *portion*

---

[3] After determining that a linear additive model was reasonably appropriate, a step-wise multiple regression was run using Life 3 as the dependent variable and the durations over which seven feelings were held (Measures G18, G19, G20, G24, G25, G26, and G28) as predictors. The maximum R^2 was a relatively low .34, and was reached after entering four of the seven predictors: Weeks unhappy, Weeks dissatisfied, Weeks delighted, and Weeks pleased (in that order).

[4] A multiple regression was run using Life 3 as the dependent variable and Number of pluses (G16) and Number of minuses (G22) as predictors. The R^2 was .17. Including Number of neutrals (G27) as an additional predictor did not increase the explained variance since, given the format of the original question, it contains no information not derivable from the other two predictors.

[5] The Campbell, Converse, and Rodgers measure combined the five qualities shown in Exhibit 3.1 as components of G12 with a seven-point satisfaction scale (our G28), and found the broader measure was somewhat more predictable from domain satisfaction scores than was the seven-point satisfaction scale alone. Since we did not have both the qualities and the satisfaction scale in the same data set, we constructed the measure using Life 3 as if it were the satisfaction scale, and used the weights derived by Campbell, Converse, and Rodgers. It turned out that in our data G12 was not more predictable than Life 3 alone, but this may be attributable to the fact that Life 3 is itself a more general measure than is seven-point satisfaction. (Evidence for this latter point appears later in this chapter and in chapter 6.)

of life consists of good parts (G16), how good was the *best week* (G17), and for how many weeks (out of the past ten) did the respondent feel "delighted," "pleased," and "mostly satisfied" (G18, G19, and G20, respectively).

A parallel set of measures (G21 through G26) assesses the other end of the range, the negative parts of life. Two additional measures (G27 and G28) tap the middle of the range.

We shall designate all these part-range measures as Type B.

More Specific Qualities of Life-as-a-Whole, "Absolute" Perspective

All of the preceding measures assess life-as-a-whole with respect to very general evaluative dimensions. They use either the categories of the Delighted–Terrible Scale, or nonverbal symbols that leave the definition of the categories entirely up to the respondent (faces, ladders, thermometers, or pluses and minuses and zeros). It is possible, however, to imagine that respondents evaluate life-as-a-whole on the basis of qualities that are somewhat more specific than the very general ones discussed so far. Whether these more specific assessments occur in addition to the general evaluations, instead of the general evaluations, or are simply conceptual abstractions without reality in the thoughts of respondents, are alternatives that will be examined in due course. Whatever the case, a number of these more specific assessments have been proposed and used by prior investigators, and thus seemed to merit attention in a developmental study such as ours. Although the measures to be discussed next assess various qualities of life, in each case it is life-as-a-whole that is being evaluated and the evaluation is made from an "absolute" perspective. We call these Type C measures.

Measure G29, the seven-point satisfaction scale applied to life-as-whole, was taken without modification from the work of Campbell, Converse, and Rodgers (1976).[6] The three-point happiness rating, measure G31, was developed by Gurin, Veroff, and Feld (1960) and has been used extensively in other surveys since. While an interesting measure, we felt its three categories were fewer than would be optimal, and so experimented with a seven-category modification involving the happiness concept and the Delighted–Terrible Scale, measure G32. From Gurin, Veroff, and Feld we also adopted a question on worries, shown as measure G33. The question on current mood, measure G34, was constructed by us, though it links conceptually to previous work on moods done by Wessman and Ricks (1966).

Measures G35 through G38 all derive from a set of items developed by Bradburn (1969) in his research on psychological well-being. Five items ask whether certain positive feelings (e.g., "feeling on top of the world") have been experienced during the past few weeks and were combined by Bradburn (and us) to provide a measure of Positive Affect (G35). A complementary set of five negative feelings (e.g., "depressed or unhappy") yielded a measure of Negative Affect (G36). The extent to which positive feelings predominated over negative

---

[6]Our description of the development of the Delighted–Terrible Scale in chapter 1 includes comments about possible weaknesses of the seven-point satisfaction scale.

feelings, or the reverse, is what Bradburn called Affect Balance (our measure G37). Finally, the sum of positive and negative affects provides an indication of the extent to which the respondent experiences any feelings at all (measure G38, Total Affect).

In an effort to tap a wide range of other qualities characteristic of a person's life-as-a-whole, we included a substantial number of bipolar scales portrayed in the format of the Semantic Differential developed by Osgood, Suci, and Tannenbaum (1957). These appear in Exhibit 3.1 as measures G39 through G48. Five of these were used previously by Campbell, Converse, and Rodgers (1976); others were developed by us.[7]

Assessments of Life-as-a-Whole from a Relative Perspective

In contrast to the "absolute" perspective that has characterized all of the global measures discussed so far, seven of the measures (G49–G55) depend on the respondent's comparison of himself with other people. These measures are "relative" in the sense that they involve a statement of the respondent's perceived level of well-being relative to his perception of the well-being of others. These were developed to let us check the possibility that what really matters to a person may not be his absolute evaluation of his well-being, but his evaluation of where he stands in comparison to other people in general and/or in comparison to his personal acquaintances.

Measures G49 and G50 constitute a pair with a rather subtle difference between them. G49 asks, essentially, how *many* people have lives better (or worse) than the respondent. G50 compares the respondent's life to that of "most other people" and asks how *much* better or worse it is.

Measures G51 and G52 constitute another pair. G51 is based on where the respondent places himself along a scale whose ends are labeled "People with the best kind of life" and "People with the worst kind of life." Measure G52 is the decile equivalent of that placement, given the respondent's own perception of how adults in the United States would be distributed along that scale.

Like the previous items in this set, G53 asks the respondent to compare himself to other Americans, but with respect to the relative balance of good parts and bad parts in his life. Measure G54 involves a comparison with up to six specific individuals the respondent "knows well" and was adapted from a technique used by Holmes and Tyler (1968; also, Holmes, 1971).

Measure G55, Uniqueness, is different from any of the preceding measures. Instead of asking for the relative position on a positive–negative scale, this measure assesses how *distinctive* the respondent thinks his life is. Is it like nobody else's, pretty similar to the lives of lots of other people, or at one of the various intermediate points?

All the relative measures will be called Type D.

---

[7]In addition to those shown in Exhibit 3.1, certain others appeared in the questionnaire developed for the July respondents. The questionnaire appears in Appendix A. A reversal in the way they were presented on the page apparently confused some respondents and led to our decision not to use the resulting data.

Assessment of Life-as-a-Whole from the Perspectives of Long- or Short-Term Change

In addition to the "absolute" and relative perspectives previously discussed, there exists the possibility that people base their evulations of life-as-a-whole on their sense of the rate and direction of change in their life. One could imagine that the present level of life quality is not as important as whether one thinks he is progressing or declining, and at what rate. To let us examine such possibilities, several measures incorporating a change perspective are included in our list.

Long-Term Change. Next in Exhibit 3.1 come three global measures (to be called Type E) based on the respondent's perception of long-term change: progress toward the "Best life I could expect to have" or retrogression toward the "Worst life I could expect to have." All three are similar to measures used previously by Cantril (1965). G56 assesses change perceived from five years ago to the present; G57, change expected in the coming five years; and G58, a combination of the two—i.e., the change when the level of well-being five years ago is compared to that expected five years in the future, a ten-year span.

Short-Term Change. In addition to the possible importance of a sense of progress or retrogression over a five- or ten-year period, one can imagine that perceptions of life quality might be related to the short-term variability of a person's feelings. What relationship to expect, however, is not immediately clear. Life quality in general may seem better to the person whose feelings are very stable than to the person whose feelings bounce around a great deal, even if both people have the same "average" feeling. Alternatively, one could argue that some variation in feelings about life—particularly the chance to occasionally experience high "peaks"—might be preferable to absolute steadiness. Although we did not choose among these alternatives, interest in the issue led us to include several measures assessing the frequency (or likelihood) of short-term change and the width of the range between the highest of the highs and the lowest of the lows. The range measures are G59 and G60; the frequency measures are G61 through G63; all are of Type F.

Neither of the range measures directly asks the respondent to *report* the range of his extreme feelings, since this seemed to be a rather difficult and abstract concept to ask questions about. Instead each measure is derived from answers to simpler questions. The first (G59) is the difference between the level reported for the "best" week (during the past year) and the level for the "worst" week. Both of these levels are assessed in terms of Cantril's ladder scale. The second range measure (G60) is the difference between how the respondent feels about the good parts of his life and how he feels about the bad parts of his life. Here, the feelings are measured along the Delighted–Terrible Scale.

Among the frequency of change measures, two ask for the respondent's own general assessment of how variable are his feelings about life (G61 and G62), and the third (G63) is an indirect measure computed from the respondent's answers to several items about the duration over which certain feelings were experienced.

Supplementary Global Measures

The final five items in Exhibit 3.1, measures G64 though G68, are not assessments of the respondent's own current life-as-a-whole, but are components of certain previous measures and/or figure in analyses to be reported later in the chapter.

Two of these measures ask for the respondent's assessment of his life-as-a-whole at some time other than the present: five years ago, or five years in the future (G64 and G65, respectively). One measure asks about changes the respondent would like to make in his life (G66).[8] And the final two ask for the respondent's assessment of other people's lives: other people in general (G67), and a specific other person, his nearest same-sexed adult neighbor (G68).

Formal Structure of the Typology

Having introduced the various types of global measures one by one, it will be helpful to note how these types interrelate to one another and form just part of a conceptual structure that involves still other possible types. As shown in the following diagram, the typology itself is based on three factors: (A) the *perspective* from which the evaluation is made (absolute, relative, long-range change, and short-range change); (B) the *generality* of the evaluation (general versus specific); and (C) the *range* of the evaluation (full-range versus part-range). Taken together the various categories on these three factors define sixteen possible types of global measures. Six of these types are represented in our data and are the focus of considerable comparative analysis in the remainder of this chapter and also in chapters 5 and 10.

A. Perspective of the evaluation				B. Generality of the evaluation	C. Range of the evaluation
Absolute	Relative	Long-range change	Short-range change		
Type A	Type D	Type E	Type F	General	Full-range
Type B	—	—	—	General	Part-range
Type C	—	—	—	Specific	Full-range
—	—	—	—	Specific	Part-range

While it would not be difficult to construct measures that would belong to still other types implicit in the above diagram, we feel that the six types we have examined provide a suitably broad base for an examination of the various possibilities. Furthermore, based on what we have learned from the six types we have examined, we suspect that the most useful indicators of perceived well-being will be among these types. (Among the remaining types, our results lead us to suspect that specific, full-range measures employing the relative, long-range change, or short-range change evaluative perspectives are likely to have more promise than any of the types involving part-range measures.)

[8]This item is adapted from one asked by Bradburn (1969; Bradburn and Caplovitz, 1965).

INTERRELATIONSHIPS AMONG GLOBAL MEASURES

As with the concern measures discussed in chapter 2, it is important to know how the global measures interrelate to one another. Here, however, we shall not use the interrelationships to make inferences about an underlying perceptual structure. There is little reason to believe that the heterogeneous set of global measures just described pertain to a single unified structure, or even that such a structure exists for assessments of life-as-a-whole. Our concern here is simply to explore the functional differences and similarities among the global measures. The resulting insights permit an informed selection of global measures for use in subsequent analyses and provide a foundation on which to base further development of global indicators.

To explore interrelationships among these measures, we applied the same multivariate analysis techniques as were used in chapter 2: Smallest Space Analysis, Factor Analysis, and ICLUST.[9] In many cases, however, a detailed examination of the actual matrix of relationships provided the most helpful insights about the measures. Three such matrices are presented in this chapter.

Overview of Results

It is convenient to present first a general overview of how we understand these many global measures fit together, and then describe the specific results on which our view is based.

The general picture is a simple one, and is closely tied to the basic organization of Exhibit 3.1. We find that the Type A measures, involving a *general* evaluation of the respondent's life-as-a-whole from an absolute perspective, tend to cluster together into what we shall call the core cluster. Measures that tap life-as-a-whole less generally, or from perspectives other than the absolute one, show positive relationships of varying strengths to the core cluster. Among these measures, those that utilize the same perspective sometimes form subsidiary clusters themselves. As the apparent content of noncore measures becomes increasingly different from a general evaluation of life-as-a-whole using an *absolute* perspective, their positive relationships to the core measures become progressively weaker, resulting in a scattering of these measures outward from the central cluster. Since these noncore measures also differ from one another, they scatter away from the core cluster in many directions. A few of the measures are so different from the core cluster as to be essentially independent from it.

If one seeks a visual analogy for what we conceive as the basic organization of these measures, one might consider a landscape: The landscape is dominated by one central "peak" (the core cluster). The level of the land gradually drops away from the peak in all directions (corresponding to the decreasing relationships of other measures to those in the core cluster). The outsloping land is broken by an occasional "hill" (corresponding to a subsidiary cluster).

---

[9]References that describe these techniques are cited in chapter 2.

While this analogy is admittedly fanciful, it has some correspondence in reality, both in where the global measures are located by a Smallest Space Analysis and in the way the global measures can be predicted by affective evaluations of life concerns. (As will be seen in chapter 5, the central core measures, our peak, are very predictable by appropriate combinations of concern items; as one moves farther and farther from the central core, the degree of predictability progressively declines.)

Results from April Respondents

Relationships Among Global Measures. Among our nationally representative samples of respondents, the largest number of global measures is available for the April group. Sixteen measures are available here. They constitute a heterogeneous set, including assessments from the absolute, relative and change perspectives, full-range and part-range measures, evaluations obtained directly from the respondent about both his own and others' lives, estimates made by an interviewer about the respondent's feelings, and use of both verbal and nonverbal scales. All of the measures, however, are *general* assessments of life-as-a-whole. None of the more specific assessments (Type C) appear in this set.

Exhibit 3.2 presents the list of measures and the intercorrelations among them.

In Exhibit 3.2, one can see that the first six measures (G1 through G14), all of which are full-range, general assessments of the respondent's life-as-a-whole from an absolute perspective (i.e., Type A measures), constitute a rather solid cluster. Each shows relationships to all of the others, and most of the correlations are above .5. This is an interesting and important finding. Here is a set of measures utilizing a variety of different scales—the Delighted–Terrible Scale, the Circles Scale, and the Ladder Scale—and two separate sources of information—the respondent and the interviewer—all of which seem to be tapping the same underlying phenomenon: general evaluations of life-as-a-whole. These items are among those that constitute the core cluster described in our earlier overview of results.

The correlation of .68 between Life 1 and Life 2—two administrations of essentially the same item separated by ten to twenty minutes of interviewing time—deserves special comment. This can be regarded as a reliability (stability) coefficient.[10] We have also been able to compute this same relationship in data from the May, November Form 2, and July respondents, where its values were .61, .71, and .64 respectively. So the .68 obtained here can be regarded as a typical value. To provide a further insight into the meaning of this particular relationship, Exhibit 3.3 presents the crosstabulation on which this correlation of .68 is based. It is instructive to note that 93 percent of the respondents chose a category in answering Life 2 that was either identical or immediately adjacent to the category they chose when answering Life 1 (54 percent chose identical

[10]Chapter 6 is devoted to an extensive investigation of reliability and validity.

EXHIBIT 3.2. Relationships (Pearson r's) Among Sixteen Global Measures

		G1	G2	G3	G6	G7	G14	G17	G23	G53	G56	G57	G58	G59	G64	G65
G1	Life 1															
G2	Life 2	.68														
G3	Life 3	.92	.94													
G6	Ladder: most	.51	.50	.54												
G7	Circles: whole life	.51	.46	.52	.59											
G14	Interviewer rating	.53	.52	.57	.45	.45										
G17	Ladder: best	.45	.44	.48	.68	.52	.36									
G23	Ladder: worst	.32	.30	.33	.52	.41	.31	.32								
G53	Circles: R-others	.39	.35	.40	.45	.74	.33	.41	.30							
G56	Past progress	.17	.18	.19	.37	.15	.16	.26	.18	.17						
G57	Future progress	-.04	-.01	-.03	-.41	-.10	-.06	-.10	-.25	-.07	-.07					
G58	Progress past and future	.11	.14	.13	.04	.05	.11	.14	-.03	.09	.78	.53				
G59	Ladder: best-worst	.03	.04	.04	.00	.00	-.05	.43	-.69	.01	.03	.18	.14			
G64	Ladder: five years ago	.18	.16	.18	.30	.26	.15	.21	.18	.14	-.74	-.19	-.76	-.02		
G65	Ladder: five years hence	.42	.42	.45	.48	.42	.34	.50	.23	.33	.25	.58	.53	.16	.10	
G67	Circles: others	.03	.04	.04	.04	.11	.05	.01	.06	-.54	-.05	-.01	-.06	-.03	.10	.04

Data source: 1,433 respondents to April national survey. Item numbers match Exhibit 3.1.

EXHIBIT 3.3. Life 1 by Life 2 for April Respondents

Life 1	Life 2							All	
	Delighted	Pleased	Mostly satisfied	Mixed	Mostly dissatisfied	Unhappy	Terrible	other	Total
Delighted	89	43	5	1	0	0	0	4	142
Pleased	80	293	79	11	0	2	0	6	471
Mostly satisfied	31	190	268	54	2	1	0	4	550
Mixed	3	25	57	73	6	1	0	5	170
Mostly dissatisfied	0	1	7	11	10	5	0	0	34
Unhappy	1	0	2	3	3	8	5	1	23
Terrible	0	0	1	0	1	1	3	1	7
All other	4	5	11	2	1	0	1	12	36
TOTAL	208	557	430	155	23	18	9	33	1,433

Notes: Pearson Correlation Coefficient = .68. Respondents with usable data on both measures: 1,376. Respondents with identical answers: 744 (= 54% of above group). Respondents with identical or immediately adjacent answers: 1,278 (= 93% of above group).

categories).[11] Thus, we find that a correlation of .68 in this case is indicative of a very substantial degree of agreement between answers to the Life 1 and Life 2 measures.

Two brief comments about the behavior of the Life 3 measure (G3) are also warranted. Life 3 is an index derived by combining answers to Life 1 and Life 2, and some of the gains of making such a combination can be seen in Exhibit 3.2. Note that for any measure with which the Life measures show any substantial correlation, Life 3 correlates with it more highly than do either Life 1 or 2. While the gains are often modest, they support, with perfect consistency, our expectation that the Life 3 index should provide a more reliable and valid indicator of respondents' true feelings about life-as-a-whole than either of its constituent parts. With a little computation, one can also discover that of the six measures in the core cluster, Life 3 has the highest average correlation with the others (when we omit the "incestuous" correlations among the three Life measures themselves). This indication of its centrality within the core cluster is the first of several that we shall encounter in this chapter, and is part of statistical evidence that suggests Life 3 is one of our most promising global measures.

Continuing with our examination of Exhibit 3.2, we find that the two part-range measures, G17 and G23 (Ladder: best and Ladder: worst) both show consistently positive relationships with all the Type A measures. These part-range measures apparently tap the same underlying phenomenon as do the Type A measures. However, they apparently tap it less efficiently, since their relationships to the Type A measures tend to be somewhat weaker than are the interrelationships among the Type A measures themselves. Of course, the simplest explanation for why they tap it less efficiently is that these part-range measures are sensitive to only a portion of the complete phenomenon, whereas the Type A measures are sensitive to the whole.

Although the Type A measures tend to relate slightly more strongly to the evaluation of the best week than to the evaluation of the worst week, there is support here for the view that *both* "good" experiences and "bad" experiences influence general evaluations of life-as-a-whole.[12]

Turning next to the relative measure (G53), we again find consistently positive relationships, of modest size,[13] between it and all of the preceding

[11]We computed a table parallel to that shown in Exhibit 3.3 using the May data and obtained essentially identical results with respect to the degree of agreement between answers to Life 1 and 2. In the May data, where the correlation between these two measures is .61, 92 percent of respondents gave an answer to Life 2 that was either identical to, or immediately adjacent to the answer they gave to Life 1 (52 percent answered both questions identically).

[12]The truth of this statement rests in part on the relatively modest relationship between the two part-range measures ($r = .32$), which lets us eliminate spurious association as an alternative explanation for the pattern of correlations between the part-range measures and those in the core cluster. The finding that both positive and negative experiences influence general evaluations of life-as-a-whole may seem "obvious," but the issue has been debated and it was this debate that led us to include the part-range measures among those to be investigated. A further, and somewhat more elegant, exploration of this issue appears later in the chapter in our description of results from the November respondents.

[13]The correlation of .74 between G53 and G7 is a trivial exception; this correlation involves one of the constituent parts of G53 (see Exhibit 3.1).

measures. The more positively the respondent evaluates his own life, the greater the advantage he perceived of his own position over that of the typical American.

Of the remaining measures in Exhibit 3.2, only Ladder: five years hence (G65) shows substantial and consistent relationships to measures in the core cluster. Apparently, the higher one's current evaluation of life-as-a-whole, the higher one's expectations for the future. The same trend, though at a weaker level, also obtains for one's perceptions of the past: Those who rate their current lives relatively high also tend to say their lives were above average five years ago. Both these results seem intuitively reasonable.

The three long-term change measures (G56, G57, and G58) are also interesting. The core measures show consistently positive, but rather mild, correlations with Past progress and zero or very slightly negative relationships to Future progress. The smallness of the correlations suggests that the core measures, which assess current level of perceived well-being, are not strongly affected by perceptions of previous levels, or future levels. However, the mild positive relationship that exists between sense of current level and Past progress is a reasonable one: there is a slight tendency for those who think they have progressed more than average in the past five years to say that they feel better than average about their current life. But neither past progress nor current level have much to do with expectations about future progress.

The independence of Past progress and Future progress from one another, and their slightly opposite relationships to the core measures, suggest that it was a mistake to combine them into measure G58: Progress past and future, and that this combination should probably be ignored.

The short-range change measure G59, which assesses the range between one's best week and worst week, shows no substantial correlation to any other measure in the entire matrix (other than to its own components). Either the measure is invalid, or the "range" notion is empirically distinct from the notions of level and change. We suspect the latter.

One final comment can be made on the basis of Exhibit 3.2. This concerns the Circles: others measure (G67). The fact that it is essentially unrelated to any of the core measures is reassuring. This indicates that respondents differentiated clearly between their own lives and the lives of other people and that the positive correlations in this matrix are not simply the result of massive response biases.

One interpretation of the set of results portrayed in Exhibit 3.2 is that the core measures (Type A) are relatively "pure" indicators of current well-being, uncontaminated by people's sense of the rate and direction of change in their lives, but showing reasonable relationships to both the positive and negative aspects of experience, and reasonable relationships—given the moderate social stability present in American society—to where people said they were in the past, and expect to be in the future.

Smallest Space Analysis. Exhibit 3.4 presents a two-dimensional plot of the measures appearing in Exhibit 3.2, based on a smallest Space Analysis.[14] The

[14] In two dimensions the coefficient of alienation was .19. In three dimensions this dropped to .13.

EXHIBIT 3.4. Two-Dimensional Plot Showing Location of Sixteen Global Measures

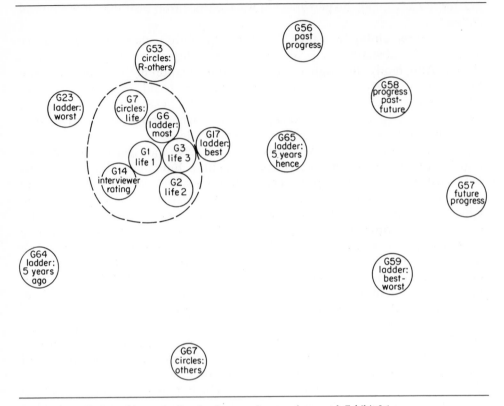

Data source: 1,433 respondents to April national survey. Item numbers match Exhibit 3.1.

plot is a straightforward representation of what has just been described. The Type A measures fall close together (within the dotted line); the two part-range measures and the relative measure fall close to this cluster; Ladder: five years hence comes next closest; and the other items tend to be scattered about, relatively far from the core cluster, and relatively far from each other.[15]

Results for Subgroups. As with the structure of people's perceptions of life concerns, discussed in chapter 2, we wanted to know whether the way global measures interrelated when analyzed in the total population would be maintained within subgroups of the population. Using the same nine demographically defined subgroups as were used in chapter 2 (men, women, four different

---

[15] Although we believe examination of the correlation matrix presented in Exhibit 3.2 and the plot in Exhibit 3.4 provides the most useful overview of how this heterogeneous set of global measures fit together, we did submit these sixteen measures to an orthogonal factor analysis to see whether any additional understanding would emerge when a set of independent factors were imposed on the data. Our conclusion is that it did not. The results appear in Appendix F.

age groups, blacks, and two groups extreme with respect to socioeconomic status), we recomputed some of the relationships shown in Exhibit 3.2.[16]

The results (not shown) indicated very substantial stabilities across the subgroups. In nearly all cases the correlations within the subgroups were within 0.1 of the correlations within the total population. For the group that appeared most different, we performed a Smallest Space Analysis (plot not shown) and found only minor variations from the plot in Exhibit 3.4.

We conclude that the general pattern of relationships just described is rather widely applicable throughout the American population.

Summary of Results from April Respondents. In this first set of empirical results, involving sixteen of the total set of sixty-eight global measures, one can see statistical support for some of the broad features described in our earlier section, Overview of Results.

Among the sixteen measures, all those that assess the current state of the respondent's life-as-a-whole from an absolute perspective and use the full range of a very general evaluative dimension (the Type A measures) cluster closely together, in what we designated as the core cluster. Within this cluster are measures using three different scales (the Delighted–Terrible Scale, the Circles Scale, and the Ladder Scale) and two separate sources of information (the respondent himself and the interviewer acting as an observer of the respondent). Life 3 proves to be the most central of the core measures.

Three other measures show substantial similarity to those in the core cluster. These are the two part-range measures (which are rather similar to the core measures in that they use a general dimension and an absolute perspective), and a measure of current well-being assessed from a relative perspective.

Showing mild relationships to the core measures are three others that assess not the current state of the respondent's life-as-a-whole but its state in the past, expectations about its state in the future, and its progress over the past five years.

The remaining measures include two long-range change measures, one short-term range of change measure, and one projective item on how other people would assess their own lives. None of these items show other than trivial relationships to other assessments of the respondent's own life.

The same set of relationships that occur among global measures for the total adult American population could also be seen in each of the nine demographically defined subgroups, suggesting the broad applicability of the observed pattern of relationships.

This pattern of relationships, once seen, has substantial rationality. It was results such as these that led to the development of the typology of global measures discussed in connection with Exhibit 3.1. In the April data we see the usefulness of distinguishing global measures on the basis of (1) what is assessed, (2) the perspective used in making the assessment, and (3) the range of the dimension on which the assessment is made. Since all of the measures in

---

[16]Twelve of the 120 relationships shown in Exhibit 3.2 were recomputed for each of the nine subgroups. These twelve were chosen to span the range from high relationships to low ones.

the April data use a *general* evaluative dimension, the appropriateness of the fourth aspect of the typology—the nature of the dimension used—does not appear. We turn next, however, to the November data, where this becomes relevant.

Results from November Respondents

The set of global measures available for the November respondents are, from a typological standpoint, more homogeneous than those just discussed. With only one exception, all the November measures assess the same thing (the respondent's own life-as-a-whole), use the same information souce (the respondent himself), and approach the assessment from an "absolute" perspective. The major difference among the November measures occurs in the qualities of life-as-a-whole that are evaluated. Included here are measures that assess well-being in general, as in the April data, and also measures tapping a variety of more specific qualities.

Although reference is made here to "November respondents," recall that there are two completely separate groups of November respondents, each of which constitutes a representative national sample. Each group answered a different questionnaire. Some of the global measures appeared in both questionnaires, and this let us examine the replicability of the relationships. As can be seen in Exhibit 3.5, the correspondence between the two sets of results, where these can be compared, is uniformly very high.

Relationships Among Global Measures. Exhibit 3.5 shows the global measures that are available for the November respondents, the particular sample(s) to which they were administered, and the correlations among the measures.

At the top of the exhibit are Life 1, Life 2, Life 3, and the Thermometer. These are all full-range general assessments of life-as-a-whole (i.e., Type A measures), and all show substantial relationships to one another (two of which are incestuous). The three Life measures were prominent members of the core cluster in the April data, and here again we find the emergence of a similar pattern.

Interestingly, the two part-range measures (G15 and G21—Good parts and Bad parts) are related to each other even more weakly ($r = -.06$) than the modest $+.32$ observed between the part-range measures in the April data. Of course, the measures being examined are not the same in April and November, so some discrepancy in findings might be expected. In both cases, however, we have evidence that the way people feel about the positive aspects of their lives has relatively little to do with how they feel about the negative aspects.

The two part-range measures each show positive relationships to the Type A measures, but—as in the April data—these relationships are weaker than those among the Type A measures themselves. Once again we have evidence that the part-range measures do not tap perceptions of well-being in the same way as the full-range measures, and that the full-range measures are sensitive to *both* the positive and negative aspects of life.

A small multivariate analysis explored this matter further by examining

EXHIBIT 3.5. Relationships (Pearson r's) Among Thirteen Global Measures

	Data	G1	G2	G3	G8	G15	G21	G29	G30	G31	G32	G33	G35	G36	G37	G38
G1 Life 1	a,b															
G2 Life 2	b	.71														
G3 Life 3	b	.92	.93													
G8 Thermometer	a,b	.49 .51	.49	.53												
G15 Good parts	a	.37	*	*	.25											
G21 Bad parts	a	.25	*	*	.23	-.06										
G29 7-pt. Satisfaction	a,b	.56 .64	.66	.70	.46 .47	.34	.27									
G30 3-pt. Satisfaction	b	.50	.49	.53	-.41	*	*	.51								
G31 3-pt. Happiness	b	.55	.54	.59	.39	*	*	.49	.55							
G32 7-pt. Happiness	b	.68	.74	.77	.50	*	*	.63	.49	.57						
G33 Worries	a,b	-.21 -.24	-.27	-.28	-.13 -.16	-.09	-.27	-.24 -.27	-.24	-.24	-.30					
G35 Affect positive	b	.33	.34	.36	.25	*	*	.30	.26	.39	.36	-.12				
G36 Affect negative	b	-.30	-.29	-.32	-.20	*	*	-.31	-.31	-.31	-.30	.32	.01			
G37 Affect balance	b	.44	.45	.48	.32	*	*	.43	.41	.50	.47	-.31	.71	-.70		
G38 Affect total	b	-.03	-.05	-.04	.02	*	*	-.01	-.05	-.04	-.04	.14	.71	.71	.01	
G66 Changes desired	b	-.44	-.39	-.45	-.36	*	*	-.44	-.40	-.37	-.37	.22	-.13	.36	-.35	.17

* These two measures were not assessed for the same respondents.

Data sources: a = 1,118 respondents to November (Form 1) national survey; b = 1,072 respondents to November (Form 2) national survey. Item numbers match Exhibit 3.1.

how Good parts and Bad parts, considered *jointly*, related to Life 1. A Multiple Classification Analysis showed that these two part-range measures used as predictors could explain 24 percent of the variance in Life 1 (multiple $r = .49$). Further checks showed that the relationships between each of the predictors and Life 1 were essentially linear, and that no interaction was present; i.e., that the relationship between Life 1 and one predictor was unaffected by the level of the other predictor. Although the two part-range measures, even considered together, were not very potent in explaining the variation in the full-range measure, the form and nature of the relationships were rather neat. There was no "overlap" in the part of the variance of Life 1 that each part-range measure explained, and regardless of how a person felt about his life experiences at one end of the evaluative extremes, the better he felt about those at the other extreme, the better he felt about life-as-a-whole.

Next in Exhibit 3.5 we encounter nine measures assessing various qualities of life-as-a-whole that are more specific than the general evaluations considered so far. G29 and G30 use a satisfaction dimension, G31 and G32 refer to happiness, G33 asks about worries, and G35 to G38 focus on affect. With the exception of Affect total, which does not relate to anything but its components, all of these assessments of more specific qualities show relationships in the expected directions to the Type A measures. For four of these measures—the two Satisfaction and the two Happiness items—relationships with the Type A measures, and with each other, are high enough to raise doubts as to whether distinct dimensions are being assessed. Although the wording of these items suggests that the evaluations being made are not completely general, it is clear that they act rather like general evaluations. Additional data bearing on this point is presented later in the chapter.

It can also be noted that for both Satisfaction and Happiness, the seven-point measures show the same pattern of relationships to other items as do the three-point measures but that the relationships tend to be somewhat higher for the seven-point versions. We suspect this is because the seven-point scales provide more sensitive indications of respondents' feelings than do the three-point scales.[17] (With respect to the Happiness measures, however, there remains some doubt as to whether the seven-point or three-point version provides the purer measure, as will be discussed shortly.)

The Worries measure shows rather weak relationships, in expected directions, with most other measures, the highest (.32) being with Affect negative. Apparently, the frequency of worrying is only modestly related to the general level of one's sense of well-being.

The four affect measures are of considerable interest. Bradburn (1969)

---

[17]This result was expected and was what motivated the development of the seven-point Happiness measure. Although three-pt Happiness has been used numerous times in the past fifteen years, relatively new evidence (Cochran, 1968; Conner, 1972; Ramsay, 1973) suggests that three-category scales capture only 80–90 percent of the total variation, whereas seven-category scales capture virtually 100 percent of it. One might have argued that the seven-point Happiness measure correlated better with the Life 1, 2, and 3 measures because they all used the same scale; however, this argument cannot be used to explain its higher correlations with Satisfaction and with Worries.

found—somewhat to his surprise—that positive and negative affect were independent of one another. Using his same items and constructing the measures similarly, we clearly replicate his result; note the correlation of .01 between G35 and G36.[18] Of course, this is consistent with the low correlation observed among the part-range measures (G15 and G21 in the November data, and G17 and G23 in the April data) and once again suggests that a person's response to the positive aspects of his life has little or nothing to do with his response to its negative aspects. Both of these (independent) responses, however, are moderately related to general evaluations of life-as-a-whole, to sense of satisfaction, and to happiness.

The Affect balance measure, the excess of positive feelings over negative feelings, relates more strongly than either the positive or negative feelings alone to all of the preceding measures. Although Affect balance is a "full-range measure," it nevertheless does not act like a core measure. It apparently does not tap general evaluations of life-as-a-whole as sensitively as do the core measures, presumably because Affect balance uses a more specific dimension for evaluation (i.e., affect) that constitutes only part of the entire phenomenon.

Affect total proves to be unrelated to any other global measure (except its components). While this eliminates Affect total as a useful measure for assessing well-being, the very low relationships are of some interest. They tell us that people who report relatively bland lives—few "highs" and few "lows"—tend to feel neither better nor worse off than people with lives that are rich in affective experiences. Apparently what counts in determining one's sense of well-being is *what* one feels, especially the relative balance of positives and negatives, rather than *how much* one feels.

The final measure in Exhibit 3.5 is based on the question, Considering how your life is going, would you like to continue much the same way, change some parts of it, or change many parts of it? This measure shows modest relationships with nearly all of the other global measures: The more negatively one evaluates one's life, the more likely one is to desire to change it.

If we compare how this item relates to Affect positive and Affect negative (G35 and G36) we find a somewhat stronger relationship with Affect negative (r's of $-.13$ and $.36$, respectively). This difference also seems understandable when one considers that it is the *bad* experiences in life that impel changes, not the good experiences.[19]

---

[18]Surprised by Bradburn's finding, we wondered whether it could be attributed to his having asked simply *whether* the feelings had been experienced rather than *how frequently* they were experienced. Consequently we designed our data collection to obtain not only a yes-no answer to each of the affect items (e.g., During the past few weeks did you ever feel bored?), but then followed up the "yesses" by an additional question that assessed frequency. Our hypothesis proved wrong. Essentially identical results were obtained regardless of whether the yes-no or the frequency scale was used.

[19]Unfortunately, the November data do not permit us to compare how the two part-range measures, Good parts and Bad parts, relate to Changes desired. Based on the consideration described here, one would predict that feelings about Bad parts would show a stronger relationship to Changes desired than feelings about Good parts. In the July data, which contains all three measures on the same respondents, the expectation is clearly supported with correlations of .11 (with Good parts) and $-.31$ (with Bad parts). See Exhibit 3.7.

The changes desired item was included to provide an indication of the respondent's desired behavior and contrasts with the purely evaluative focus of most other global measures. It is reassuring to find that reports of desired behaviors show at least moderate relationships, in reasonable directions, to the evaluative measures.

Before leaving Exhibit 3.5, we pause for one observation about the Life 3 measure, a measure that plays an especially significant role in later chapters. A careful examination of the exhibit will show that Life 3, with only trivial exceptions, has relationships to all other measures that are as high or higher than any other single measure, including the components of Life 3 (Life 1 and Life 2). Thus, we see in these November data, as we did in the April data, that Life 3 stands in a particularly central position among measures that tap evaluations of the respondent's current life-as-a-whole.

Given the rather straightforward nature of the results shown in Exhibit 3.5, we did not plot the variables by Smallest Space Analysis. The general pattern of results is clear, and the plot would have been structured rather like that shown in Exhibit 3.4; i.e., with one central cluster and with single items located at varying distances from it (and from each other). As usual, however, we submitted the matrix to exploratory factor analysis and, in this case, encountered some particularly interesting results.

Factor Analysis. The factor analysis to be reported here was an exploratory one, in the sense that it involved applying some conventional procedures to the matrix that has just been discussed to see what additional insights, if any, would result. The numerical output did help us consider our measures from a different perspective, however we approach the actual numbers produced by this factor analysis with considerable caution. The implicit causal model on which they are based is not the one that we feel is most appropriate and, as a consequence, we feel thay are misleading and/or uninterpretable in certain respects. What counts here is the basic pattern; chapters 6 and 7 explore the causal dynamics underlying assessments of well-being with greater care and sophistication.

As shown in Exhibit 3.6, three factors emerged when the matrix of Exhibit 3.5 was submitted to a conventional factor analysis.[20] The second and third factors were readily interpretable as representing negative and positive affect, respectively. Because of our belief that assessments of life-as-a-whole involve both cognitive and affective elements, we called the first factor Cognitive evaluation.

While the name, Cognitive evaluation, provides a needed label, it may imply a greater conceptual clarity than we believe actually exists. As this first factor was finally located by the exploratory factor analysis (after varimax rotation), it was not totally independent of the affect measures (Exhibit 3.6

---

[20]By "conventional factor analysis" we mean an orthogonal factor analysis that begins as a principal components analysis, in which the number of factors to be extracted is determined by the "Kaiser criterion" (truncation of components with eigenvalues less than 1.0), and in which the nontruncated factors are rotated to the varimax criterion.

EXHIBIT 3.6. Factor Analysis of Twelve Global Measures

| | Factor Loadings | | | |
	I Cognitive evaluation	II Negative affect	III Positive affect	Variance explained
Measures				
G1 Life 1	.85	.17	.14	78%
G2 Life 2	.86	.15	.18	79%
G3 Life 3	.92	.18	.17	91%
G8 Thermometer	.66	.09	.07	45%
G29 7-pt. Satisfaction	.75	.25	.13	64%
G31 3-pt. Happiness	.60	.22	.13	52%
G32 7-pt. Happiness	.80	.18	.21	72%
G33 Worries	.19	.60	.01	39%
G35 Affect positive	.27	−.12	.90	91%
G36 Affect negative	.11	.89	.18	84%
G37 Affect balance	.18	.51	.80	94%
G66 Changes desired	.47	.49	−.07	47%
Factor contributions				
To total variance	39%	16%	15%	70%
To explained variance	56%	23%	21%	100%

Notes: Communality estimates were entered at 1.0 and not iterated. Principal components with λ <1.0 were eliminated.
Data source: 1,072 respondents to November national survey (Form 2). Item numbers match Exhibit 3.1.

shows Affect positive relating .27 to this factor, and Affect negative relating .11); and furthermore, we suspect this first factor includes certain methods effects that are common to at least some of the measures, in addition to variance they share with respect to Cognitive evaluations. Nevertheless, cognitive evaluation is probably the major part of what this first factor represents and thus has claim to be represented in the name.

In Exhibit 3.6 one can see that the Type A measures—Life 1, Life 2, Life 3, and Thermometer—all show generally similar patterns of loadings on the three factors. Of the variance in each of these four measures that is explained by the factors, by far the largest part of it is first-factor variance. This is notably *not* the case for some measures assessing specific life qualities: Worries, Affect balance, Changes desired, and (of course) Affect positive and Affect negative. The seven-point Satisfaction measure and the two Happiness measures are like the Type A measures in having most of their explained variance attributed to the first factor, but they each differ from the Type A measures with respect to the other factors. Seven-point Satisfaction shows relatively more Negative affect variance, while the Happiness measures show relatively more Positive affect variance. Finally, the seven-point Happiness measure shows factor loadings that are more similar to those of the Type A measures than does three-point Happiness.

Of fundamental interest here is the suggestion that positive affect, negative affect, and cognitive evaluation are three "ingredients" that may be present (in differing proportions) in many global measures. This is not to say that these three ingredients account for all the variance of every global measure; many measures will include a unique component, and nearly all will include at least some random measurement error. Nevertheless, we shall have made a significant start toward understanding global assessments if we can begin to quantify their sometimes subtle differences in terms of a limited set of more basic components.

Some of the results in Exhibit 3.6 seem intuitively reasonable and/or could be clearly foreseen on the basis of our examination of the matrix in Exhibit 3.5. Other results, however, came as a surprise, or are seen here with an unanticipated clarity. Among the "expected" results is the assignment of separate factors to Affect positive and Affect negative (we had seen earlier that they did not relate to one another), the predominance of something other than positive and negative affect in the variance of the Type A measures (they show only modest relationships to the affect measures in Exhibit 3.5), and the sensitivity of the Worries measure and of Changes desired to negative affect. We were surprised, however, by the factor loadings of the Happiness measures. On an intuitive basis, we had expected Happiness to be heavily laden with positive affect. While Exhibit 3.6 does show these measures to contain more positive affect than any of the Type A measures, and more positive affect than negative, it also shows first-factor variance to be their main ingredient. Furthermore, we had not expected that the shift from the three-point scale to the seven-point scale would significantly alter the factor composition of the Happiness measures. (In the data from the July respondents, to be discussed shortly, we shall again encounter this shift in the sensitivity of the two Happiness measures to positive affect).

Summary of Results from November Respondents. The basic "tractability" of measures of perceived well-being emerges in our analysis of these November data. When the same measures were included in both of the independent November national surveys, similar results emerged in each survey, indicating the basic stability of the findings. Replications could also be observed between one or another of the November surveys and the April survey, discussed earlier: (1) in both data sets, full-range general measures of life-as-a-whole, evaluated from an absolute perspective, clustered together; (2) these measures showed modest relationships to part-range measures at either the positive or negative end of the evaluation spectrum, while the part-range measures showed little or no relationship to each other; (3) the Life 3 measure appeared unusually central among those that assess life-as-a-whole from an absolute perspective.

The November measures that assess the specific qualities of satisfaction, happiness, worries, and positive and negative affect (none of which were available in the April data) helped extend our understanding of the nature of global assessments of well-being. A factor analysis suggested that at least three independent sources of variation, or "ingredients," contribute to our measures: a Cognitive evaluation source, a Negative affect source, and a Positive affect source. Our measures assessing general evaluations of life-as-a-whole seemed to be mainly composed of Cognitive evaluation variance. The Satisfaction measure was also heavily laden with Cognitive evaluation variation, but was somewhat more sensitive to Negative affect than Positive affect. The two Happiness measures, also reflected (to our surprise) substantial Cognitive evaluation variance, but (as expected) were more sensitive to Positive than Negative affect. The Worries measure included large amounts of Negative affect variance.

A behaviorally oriented measure about desire to make changes in one's life related in reasonable directions and at moderate levels (r's of about .4) to the more evaluative measures and seemed more sensitive (as is reasonable) to the negative than the positive aspects of life.

Results from July Respondents

We turn next to the large number of global measures that were administered to the July respondents.[21] Sixty-three measures—all but five of the total set of sixty-eight global measures shown in Exhibit 3.1—are available for these people, and many are available for only this group.

In designing the questionnaire for the July respondents, one of our goals was to test global assessments from a wide range of perspectives and, within each perspective, to try out several different measurement approaches. The basic question we hoped to answer was, What are the most useful ways of assessing people's evaluations of life-as-a-whole?

Our approach to the analysis paralleled that used on other data sets. We computed and studied a large matrix of interrelationships, and we submitted that matrix to several "second level" multivariate analysis techniques, including factor analysis and ICLUST. As it turned out, the matrix itself contributed most to our understanding of these measures, and it is this we shall discuss in some detail here. One aspect of the factor analysis also proved interesting, and we shall devote some attention to it.[22]

Relationships Among Global Measures. Exhibit 3.7 presents the interrelationships and measures we shall discuss. Fifty very heterogeneous measures are represented here. However, in order to keep the analytic and descriptive tasks within reasonable bounds, nearly a quarter of the measures available for the July respondents do not appear in the exhibit. The omitted measures are ones that seemed (on the basis of ICLUST results available when we planned this analysis) redundant with measures that have been included.

---

[21]We do not devote a separate section of this chapter to the global measures in the May data. The measures available, as shown in Exhibit 3.1, include the three Life measures (G1–G3), one Happiness measure (G31), five self-descriptions using bipolar adjective scales (G39, G40, G41, G43, and G44), and one derived measure combining Life 3 and the bipolar adjective scales (G12). The principal results from our analyses of these measures have been mentioned earlier in the chapter (e.g., the relationship between Life 1 and Life 2, and the predictability of Life 3 compared with that of the more broadly based measure G12), or will be mentioned in conjunction with the July data (e.g., relationships among the bipolar adjective scales). We have not conducted extensive analyses of the bipolar self-descriptions, under the assumption—based on a preliminary check—that other global measures would prove more useful.

[22]The ICLUST results, which are not presented, confirmed the clustering of measures that was visible in the matrix, but did not add to our understanding.

EXHIBIT 3.7. Relationships (Pearson *r*'s) Among Fifty Global Measures[a]

			A								
			G 1	G 2	G 4	G 5	G 6	G 7	G 9	G10	G11
	G 1	Life 1									
	G 2	Life 2	6								
	G 4	Life 4	6	6							
	G 5	Faces: whole life	6	6	5						
A	G 6	Ladder: most	4	5	4	4					
	G 7	Circles: whole life	4	5	5	4	4				
	G 9	Weighted weeks†	5	5	5	5	5	4			
	G10	Reg. wtd. weeks	5	6	6	5	5	3	9		
	G11	Wtd. slices	4	4	4	4	3	5	4	4	
B₁	G15	Good parts	2	2	2	2	1	2	1	2	1
	G16	Number pluses	4	4	3	4	2	5	3	3	9
	G17	Ladder: best	3	2	3	3	5	3	4	4	2
	G18	Weeks delighted	3	4	3	3	3	2	3	3	2
B₂	G21	Bad parts	2	3	2	2	2	2	3	3	2
	G22	Number minuses	-4	-3	-3	-4	-3	-4	-3	-3	-9
	G23	Ladder: worst	3	3	3	2	4	2	3	3	2
	G25	Weeks unhappy	-4	-4	-4	-4	-4	-4	-7	-7	-3
B₃	G27	Number neutrals	-2	-2	-2	-2	-1	-3	-1	-1	-4
	G31	3-pt. Happiness†	5	5	4	6	3	4	5	5	4
	G32	7-pt. Happiness	7	7	6	6	5	5	5	5	4
	G33	Worries	-3	-3	-2	-3	-2	-3	-4	-3	-2
	G34	Mood today	1	2	1	1	1	1	1	1	-0
	G35	Affect positive	3	4	4	4	3	3	4	4	2
	G36	Affect negative	-3	-3	-2	-2	-2	-2	-4	-4	-2
	G37	Affect balance	4	4	4	4	4	4	6	6	3
C	G39	Interesting	5	5	5	5	3	4	5	5	3
	G41	Worthwhile	3	3	4	3	2	2	2	3	2
	G44	Rewarding	6	5	5	5	3	4	5	4	4
	G45	Ideal	6	4	4	4	3	3	5	3	3
	G46	Contented	4	4	4	4	3	5	3	3	3
	G47	Enjoying	5	5	4	4	3	4	4	4	3
	G48	Capable	5	5	4	4	3	3	4	4	2
D	G49	Better than everyone	4	3	4	4	3	4	3	3	3
	G50	Much better	5	4	4	5	3	4	4	4	3
	G51	Kind of life†	4	3	3	4	2	3	2	2	3
	G52	Decile position	3	2	3	3	2	2	2	2	2
	G53	Circles: R-others	2	2	2	2	2	5	2	2	4
	G54	Social comparison	2	1	2	1	1	2	2	2	1
	G55	Uniqueness	-0	-0	-1	0	-1	-1	-1	-0	0
E	G56	Past progress	2	2	2	2	4	1	3	3	1
	G57	Future progress	-0	-1	-1	-0	-5	-1	-1	-1	-0
	G58	Prog. past and future	1	1	0	1	0	-0	2	2	0
F	G59	Ladder: best-worst	-0	-0	-0	-0	-0	-0	-0	-0	-1
	G61	Up and down or steady	2	2	1	1	1	-0	1	1	1
	G62	Variation in feeling	-3	-2	-3	-2	-2	-2	-3	-3	-2
G	G64	Ladder: 5 yrs. ago	1	1	2	2	2	2	1	1	2
	G65	Ladder: 5 yrs. hence	4	4	3	4	4	3	4	4	3
	G66	Changes desired	-4	-3	-4	-4	-2	-2	-3	-4	-2
	G67	Circles: others	1	2	1	2	1	2	1	1	0
	G68	Neighbor whole life	2	2	2	2	-0	2	1	1	1

†The scale of the measure has been reversed so high scores imply greater well-being.
[a]Decimal points have been omitted.
Data source: 222 July respondents. Item numbers match Exhibit 3.1. Lettered sections group measures of the same type.

EXHIBIT 3.7. (continued)

	B₁				B₂			B₃		C				
G15	G16	G17	G18	G21	G22	G23	G25	G27	G31	G32	G33	G34	G35	G36
2														
3	2													
1	1	2												
-3	2	-0	1											
-1	-5	-1	-2	-2										
-1	2	0	1	4	-3									
-0	-2	-2	-2	-3	3	-3								
-2	-8	-2	1	-1	-0	-1	1							
2	4	2	3	2	-3	2	-3	-2						
2	4	3	3	3	-4	3	-4	-1	5					
0	-2	-1	-1	-3	2	-2	3	0	-3	4				
1	-0	0	1	1	0	0	-1	-0	1	1	-0			
2	2	3	2	1	-2	-0	-3	-1	4	3	-0	2		
1	-2	-1	-3	-3	3	-3	3	0	-3	-3	4	-1	0	
0	3	2	4	3	-3	2	-4	-1	5	4	-4	2	6	-8
2	2	2	3	2	-2	2	-4	-1	5	6	-3	1	4	-3
2	2	2	1	1	-1	2	-2	-2	2	3	-1	1	3	-1
3	3	2	3	2	-3	2	-3	-2	4	5	-3	1	2	-2
2	3	3	3	2	-2	3	-3	-2	4	5	-3	2	3	-2
2	2	3	3	2	-3	2	-3	-1	4	4	-3	1	2	-3
2	2	3	2	2	-2	2	-3	-1	4	5	-4	1	2	-3
1	2	2	3	1	-2	1	-4	-2	3	4	-3	2	3	-2
3	3	3	1	2	-2	2	-4	-2	4	4	-2	1	4	-0
2	3	3	-2	2	-2	2	-3	-2	4	4	-2	2	4	-0
1	3	2	0	2	-2	2	-2	-2	-4	4	-3	0	3	-1
2	3	1	-0	1	-1	3	-2	-2	3	3	-3	1	3	-1
1	4	2	1	1	-3	1	-2	-2	2	2	-1	0	3	-1
2	0	1	1	1	-0	1	-1	0	2	2	-1	1	2	-0
-1	-1	-2	0	-0	-1	-1	-0	2	1	0	0	-0	3	-2
-1	-0	1	2	1	-1	1	-2	1	2	2	-0	1	2	-2
-0	1	-2	-0	-2	1	-4	0	-1	0	2	1	0	1	0
-0	0	-1	1	-0	-1	-1	-1	0	2	1	1	1	2	-1
2	-0	5	1	-4	1	-8	1	-1	-1	-0	1	0	1	2
-2	1	1	1	2	-1	2	-0	0	1	1	-2	0	-1	-3
-1	-2	-2	-1	-2	1	-2	2	1	-2	-3	2	0	-2	2
2	2	3	-0	1	-1	2	-1	-2	0	1	-1	-1	1	0
1	3	2	2	1	-2	0	-3	-2	3	3	-0	1	2	-1
1	-1	-1	-2	-3	2	-3	3	-0	-3	-4	3	1	-2	3
1	0	0	1	1	0	0	-0	-0	0	2	-1	0	-0	-0
3	1	0	1	-0	-1	0	-0	-0	2	2	-1	1	1	-1

EXHIBIT 3.7. (*continued*)

			G37	G39	G41	G44	G45	G46	G47	G48	G49	G50
							C					
C	G39	Interesting	4									
	G41	Worthwhile	2	4								
	G44	Rewarding	4	5	4							
	G45	Ideal	3	5	3	7						
	G46	Contented	4	4	3	4	5					
	G47	Enjoying	4	4	3	7	6	6				
	G48	Capable	3	4	3	6	6	3	5			
D	G49	Better than everyone	2	3	2	3	3	3	3	3		
	G50	Much better	2	4	1	4	4	3	4	4	7	
	G51	Kind of life†	3	3	1	3	2	3	2	2	5	5
	G52	Decile position	2	2	1	3	2	2	2	2	6	5
	G53	Circles: R-others	2	2	1	2	1	2	2	2	3	3
	G54	Social comparison	1	2	0	1	2	1	2	1	1	2
	G55	Uniqueness	0	−1	−0	−2	−1	0	−2	−2	−2	−2
E	G56	Past progress	2	1	0	2	1	1	1	2	0	1
	G57	Future progress	0	1	−1	−0	−1	−2	−1	2	−1	0
	G58	Prog. past and future	2	1	−0	1	0	−0	0	2	−0	1
F	G59	Ladder: best-worst	−1	1	1	1	2	1	1	2	−0	−0
	G61	Up and down or steady	2	1	0	1	2	2	2	1	0	0
	G62	Variation in feeling	−3	−2	−1	−2	−2	−3	−2	−1	−2	−2
G	G64	Ladder: 5 yrs. ago	0	1	1	1	1	1	2	0	2	1
	G65	Ladder: 5 yrs. hence	2	3	1	3	3	1	2	5	2	3
	G66	Changes desired	−4	−3	−2	−2	−4	−3	−2	−3	−1	−2
	G67	Circles: others	0	1	1	1	1	1	0	1	−0	0
	G68	Neighbor whole life	1	1	2	2	2	2	1	1	1	2

EXHIBIT 3.7. (*continued*)

D					E			F			G				
G51	G52	G53	G54	G55	G56	G57	G58	G59	G61	G62	G64	G65	G66	G67	G68
8															
2	2														
1	3	1													
−2	−3	−1	−0												
0	0	1	1	0											
−0	0	0	0	−0	−0										
0	0	1	1	0	8	6									
−2	−1	−1	0	−0	−0	1	0								
1	1	−1	−0	2	−0	−1	−1	−0							
−2	−2	−0	−1	−0	−1	2	0	1	−2						
1	1	0	0	−1	−8	−2	−8	0	1	−0					
2	2	2	1	−1	3	6	6	0	0	0	−1				
−3	−2	−1	−1	−1	−1	2	1	2	−3	3	−1	−0			
−0	−1	−7	0	0	−0	−1	−1	0	1	−2	1	0	−1		
1	0	−0	−0	1	−1	1	−0	0	1	−1	2	1	−0	2	

The matrix in Exhibit 3.7 (like the previous matrices) is ordered as in Exhibit 3.1, which puts together items of the same "type." When the matrix is ordered this way, its basic patterns emerge with reasonable clarity. Lest the reader be surprised by the general neatness of our data, however, we would note that in the actual course of our research the matrix came before the typology, and our development of the typology was influenced by the statistical relationships in the matrix. This is not to say that the typology is inappropriate (on the contrary, we suspect it will prove quite useful), but simply that the typology has been designed in the light of the empirical as well as the conceptual information available. For ease of reference in the text that follows, the different types of measures are bracketed in Exhibit 3.7 and indicated by a unique letter.

At the top of the matrix in Exhibit 3.7 appear nine measures in Segment A, all full-range general evaluations of the respondent's own life-as-a-whole using an absolute perspective. Most of the relationships among these measures are in the range .4 to .6, and are among the highest in the entire matrix.[23] Included here are three Life measures, all single items using the Delighted–Terrible Scale; three other items using graphic scales (faces, ladder, and circles); and three derived measures, each of which combines data from several other questions. These are the core cluster items we have seen in the April and November data, with some new additions that were not available previously. One of the important things this cluster demonstrates is the eminent feasibility of measuring general evaluations of life-as-a-whole by a variety of very different methods.

Among this set of nine measures, Weighted slices (G11) seems noticeably less sensitive than others to whatever the core measures have in common, presumably the respondents' "true" evaluations of life-as-a-whole. Whether this is because Weighted slices is tapping something else, or simply contains a greater proportion of error variance, cannot be determined for sure. However, since its relationships with other variables in the matrix are generally below those of the other core measures, we suspect Weighted slices is simply a less valid measure.

For measures that are included here in the July data and also in one (or more) of the national data sets, one can compare their interrelationships to test both the stability of the relationship and the representativeness of the July respondents. Life 1, Life 2, and Ladder: most also appear in previous exhibits, and in no case is there a discrepancy greater than .1 between their correlation amongst the July respondents and their correlation in a national sample. This is the first of many indications that with respect to global measures, the July respondents provide results that are highly generalizable to the entire adult American population.

---

[23]The matrix includes a few correlations of .7, .8, and .9. Most of these will be disregarded in our discussion since most involve either alternate versions of the same measure or correlations of a derived measure with one of its components. Some of the other incestuous relationships have slightly lower correlations and these will also be disregarded.

The two versions of Weighted weeks also deserve comment. One version uses a very simple weighting scheme, the other uses weights derived from a special regression analysis. Given that these two measures correlate .9 with one another, and that they correlate almost identically with all other measures in the matrix, it seems that the refinement of using regression-derived weights did not produce a significantly different or improved measure.

Turning next to the part-range measures, we find four that attempt to assess positive experiences (Section B_1), four that are relevant to negative experiences (Section B_2), and one tapping neutral experiences (Section B_3).

In several respects correlations involving these measures show similar patterns to results seen in the April and November data. As previously, the positive part-range measures show little or no relationship to the negative part-range measures (most correlations are .2 or less; see Section B_1B_2 of the matrix). Once again we find an indication that how one feels about the good experiences in life has little to do with how one feels about the bad parts. Yet, as we have also seen previously, both the positive and negative part-range measures show consistent but moderate relationships to the full-range (Type A) measures (most r's are in the range .2 to .4; see Sections B_1A and B_2A).

The July data permit us to examine one matter concerning the part-range measures that we have not been able to consider previously, the extent to which measures that purport to measure the same part of the range correlate with one another. Exhibit 3.7 shows that these convergencies are rather modest: .1 to .3 for the positive-range measures (Section B_1B_1) and .2 to .4 for the negative-range measures (Section B_2B_2). While the correlations are all in the expected direction, their relatively low values raise certain doubts about the part-range measures. Are these measures markedly less valid than the Type A measures? Or, do they somehow tap different aspects of feelings about positive (or negative) experiences? Or, perhaps both?

Unfortunately, we cannot definitely answer these questions with the present data. We can note, however, that the meaningful relationships of the part-range measures to the Type A measures, relationships that are higher in many cases than those between similar part-range measures, suggests that the part-range measures do include at least some valid variance. (One can also note that two of the part-range measures, Good parts and Bad parts, tend to show lower correlations with the core measures than the other part-range measures, suggesting that these two may be less sensitive than the others.)

Our hunch is that the low convergencies can be attributed to *both* validity problems and to the measures tapping slightly different aspects of experience. It may be less natural for people to think about just the good aspects of their lives, or just the bad aspects, and hence the part-range questions may pose more difficult tasks for the respondents than the more natural full-range questions. This could cause lower validity. It is also true that the several part-range questions specifically ask about not only level of feelings, but also proportions, extremes, and durations, whereas most of the core measures focus on some *level* of well-being. Thus, the part-range measures may be more heterogeneous than the core measures.

Although we cannot be certain why these part-range measures show the relationships they do, one of the practical implications of these relationships is reasonably clear: These part-range measures look less promising as global social indicators than do the Type A measures.

The sections of the matrix involving the part-range measures and the Type A measures (B_1A and B_2A) can also be usefully examined from the perspective of the Type A measures. With one exception, all of the Type A measures tend to relate about equally to the part-range measures. The exception is Weighted slices, which generally shows weaker realtionships, and which, it will be recalled, was also less central among the Type A measures themselves. This reinforces our doubts about this measure.

Moving down the matrix to Section C, we find fourteen measures of various specific life qualities. Since the measures, in most cases, were not intended to assess the same thing, their interrelationships (Section CC) are of only modest interest, though one can note that some of the correlations here are rather high. The interrelationships among these specific evaluations and the more general evaluations (the Type A measures), however, are of fundamental interest, and appear in Section CA. Within this section we find two distinguishable patterns: The qualities vary in their relationship to the Type A measures, and—conceptually distinct from this—the Type A measures vary in their relationship to the qualities.

With respect to the *qualities,* we see that the Type A measures are most sensitive to: Happiness (G31, G32), Disappointing . . . Rewarding (G44), Intolerable . . . Ideal (G45), Boring . . . Interesting (G39), Disgusted . . . Enjoying (G47), and Helpless . . . Capable (G48). Thus, these data suggest that a high score on one of the Type A measures implies a life that is viewed as happy, rewarding, interesting, ideal, enjoyable, and capable. Here is an important indication of the "meaning" of a high score on a Type A measure.

While none of the specific qualities were totally unrelated to the Type A measures, it is clear from Section CA of the matrix that the Type A measures are less sensitive to the extent the respondent felt his life to be "worthwhile" (G41), to his frequency of worrying (G33), and to his experience of negative affects (G36) than to the qualities described earlier, and that the Type A measures are only very slightly related to the respondent's report of his mood on the day the data were collected (G34).

Although most of these qualities did not appear in data sets discussed previously, the Happiness measures, the Affect measures, and Worries were also asked of the November respondents. Once again, we find that the correlations from the July respondents are consistently within .1 of those from a national sample, which supports both the stability of the phenomena being examined and the generalizability of the July data.

Included among the July quality measures are both the three- and seven-point versions of Happiness. Which is better? It is clear that the seven-point version tends to show higher relationships with the Type A measures (Section CA) and with the part-range measures (Sections CB_1 and CB_2). It also tends to show higher correlations with the other qualities (Section CC), with two potentially significant exceptions. The exceptions are Affect positive and Affect balance, with which the *three-point* measure shows higher relationships. Since it could be argued that these two affect measures are especially relevant to the Happiness concept, the evidence supporting the superiority of the seven-point version of the Happiness measure is not unanimous. Furthermore, exactly the same pattern of relationships appeared in the November data (Exhibit 3.5): The seven-point version of Happiness related more strongly than the three-point version to all global measures except those tapping positive affect, and to these the three-point version related slightly higher.

Our conclusions about the Happiness measures run parallel to the results of the factor analysis (shown in Exhibit 3.6): that as an indicator of *general* well-being, the seven-point Happiness measure is the better of the two; but that it is not as sensitive as the three-point version to *affective* experiences of a positive kind. Thus, if one were committed to using just one of these two measures, the choice between them would depend on one's purposes. (Of course, if it is *general well-being* and/or *positive affect* that one wants to measure, neither version of Happiness offers as pure an indicator as would certain other measures; e.g., Life 3 and Affect positive, respectively.)

Section CA of the matrix can also be examined with respect to the *Type A measures,* and has some extremely interesting things to say about them. The highest relationships tend to be shown by Life 2, Life 1, Weighted weeks, Regression weighted weeks and Faces: whole life—in that order. The lowest relationships tend to be shown by Weighted slices, Ladder: most, and Circles: whole life—in order from bottom up. These findings suggest that among the Type A measures the Life measures, the Weeks measures, and the Faces measure are perhaps the most promising. Once again we have an indication that Weighted slices may be the least valid of these Type A measures, and that the Life measures are among the most promising.

In Section D of Exhibit 3.7 appear seven measures, all of which involve the respondent evaluating his life *relative* to the lives of other people. Within this set, the Uniqueness measure is conceptually distinct because it assesses degree of differentness rather than relative amount of well-being. Other than to note that how unique one believes himself to be bears virtually no relationship to any other measure in the matrix, an interesting finding in itself, we shall not pay further attention to this measure.

Of the remaining six relative measures, four show a very substantial convergence. Correlations range from .5 to .8 (Section DD) among Better than everyone, Much better, Kind of life, and Decile position.[24] Thus, we seem to have several different, but reasonably equivalent, ways of assessing respondents' perceptions of how their level of well-being compares with that of others.

The lower relationships of the remaining two relative measures (Circles: R-others, G53, and Social comparison, G54) with the other relative measures, combined with their lower relationships to other measures in the matrix,

---

[24]The .8 correlation between Kind of life (G51) and Decile position (G52) is likely to be spuriously high because these two measures were derived from the same sources.

particularly the Type A measures and the specific life qualities, lead us to suspect these measures to be less valid. Both of these measures, and especially the Social comparison measure, used rather indirect means of eliciting the respondent's sense of his relative well-being, and it seems that in this case the indirectness hurt rather than helped.

The relationships between the relative measures and the Type A measures, shown in Section DA of the matrix, are interesting for a number of reasons.

In terms of the general level of the correlations it is an important, though not unreasonable finding to see positive relationships of moderate strength (.2 to .5) between the more promising relative measures and the absolute (Type A) measures. The higher a person believes his relative position to be, the more likely he is to give a high rating to his own well-being.

When we compare the relative measures, it is clear that two show noticeably higher relationships to the Type A measures than the others, Better than everyone (G49) and Much better (G50). These measures are two variations on the same theme, and it is not surprising to see them showing the same pattern. The wording of the Much better measure seems slightly more sensitive to the kinds of variation tapped by the Type A measures (and also by the specific quality measures; see Section DC).

The next two measures in the exhibit, Kind of life (G51) and Decile position (G52), are another pair, derived from the same questions but scored in a different way. Their relationships to the Type A measures are a bit lower than the preceding pair, but here again the patterns are similar, and one member of the pair, Kind of life, seems slightly more sensitive than Decile position.

From the data appearing in Sections DA, DC, and DD, we suspect Much better (G50) may be the most useful of the relative measures.

The relationships between the relative measures and the Type A measures (Section DA) also provide some interesting comparisons among the Type A measures. Once again, the Life measures and the Faces: whole life measure tend to show stronger than average relationships, and Weighted Slices and Ladder: most show weaker than average relationships.

Section E of the matrix consists of three long-term change measures: Past progress, Future progress, and the combination of the two. Since sense of Past progress shows *no* relationship to expectations of future progress (Section EE), and since these two measures of change relate to the Type A measures and some of the life qualities in opposite directions (and since essentially identical results appeared in the April data), it now seems that it was a mistake to combine Past progress and Future progress. Hence measure G58, Progress past and future, is not one we would recommend for future use. The Type A measures show modest positive relationships to Past progress (r's of about .2 to .3)—the more respondents believed they had advanced over the past five years, the higher their sense of well-being—and very weak negative relationships (r's of about $-.1$) to expectations about future progress. Perhaps the most important result is that the Type A measures apparently tap sources of variation that are pretty much distinct from those tapped by the long-term change measures.

Section F consists of three short-term change measures. One was intended to assess the extreme range of feelings (G59), the other two were self-reports of the variability of feelings (G61 and G62). Since the range concept is to some extent distinct from the notion of variability (a person might experience many variations of small range), there is no necessity for the first measure to correlate with the other two, and in fact it does not (r's are .0 and .1; see Section FF). One would have hoped, however, that the two self-reports of variability of feelings would show more convergence than they do; although they correlate more with each other than with the range measure, the relationship between them ($r = .2$) is not substantial.

It is clear that the range measure shows virtually no association with most of the other measures in the matrix. This result replicates, using a more extensive set of measures, what was observed for the April respondents. The two variability measures, and particularly Variability in feelings (G62), show modest relationships with most other measures. However, even at their highest, which occurs with several of the Type A measures, the relationships are not very strong ($r = .3$). These correlations are reasonably consistent, however, in suggesting that greater sense of well-being shows a mild tendency to accompany greater steadiness (less variability) in feelings.[25]

Finally, in Section G, appear five supplementary measures, none of which is a direct assessment of the level of the respondent's current well-being. Two of the supplementary measures, the level of well-being the respondent expected five years in the future (G65) and the extent of change the respondent wanted to make in his life (G66), show moderate relationships to the global measures (r's in the range .2 to .4, Section GA). Both of these results are reasonable; the better off a person feels currently, the better off he expects to be in the future, and the less change he wants to bring about in his life. Both results replicate those seen previously in the April and November data, respectively.

The other three measures in this section show rather weak relationships to the Type A measures (r's of .2 or less). How one feels about one's current well-being has relatively little to do with perceptions of well-being five years ago or perceptions of others' well-being, either "the average American" or a specific neighbor.

This concludes our comments about Exhibit 3.7. Before summarizing these and previous findings, however, we wish to present one additional set of results, which themselves provide a partial summary.

[25] A supplementary analysis, which included all of the global measures using a short-term change perspective (G59 to G63), plus eighteen *domain* assessments that also used a short-term change perspective, provided a somewhat broader set of variables with which to explore the two notions, range-of-feelings and variability-of-feelings. The results (not shown) confirm those that appear in Exhibit 3.7: (1) two statistically independent clusters emerged, one consisting of range measures, the other of variability measures; and (2) even within these clusters the relationships tended to be weak except between pairs of items drawn from the same section of the questionnaire. Our conclusion is that the range notion should be conceptually distinguished from the variability notion. We remain somewhat unsatisfied, however, with the measures we have constructed for assessing those aspects of feelings about well-being.

Factor Analysis. When the matrix shown in Exhibit 3.7 was factor analyzed, one portion of the results proved quite interesting.[26] One of the early steps in the factor analysis process is to extract a "first principal component." This represents that one hypothetical source of variation that shows the highest overlap with each of the variables. Although well defined from a statistical point of view, the conceptual meaning of the first principal component is arbitrary and depends on the mix of variables being analyzed. In the present case, since nearly all the variables refer to the respondent's current well-being, the first principal component clearly has a lot to do with his feelings about it.[27]

We found it interesting to array the variables according to their sensitivity to the respondent's feelings about his life-as-a-whole (i.e., by their "loadings" on the first principal component). This ordered list appears as Exhibit 3.8.

Exhibit 3.8 shows that six measures have loadings of .70 or more on the first principal component. Five of these are Type A measures: two versions of the Weighted weeks measure, Life 1, Life 2, and Faces: whole life. The sixth is seven-point Happiness. These results are entirely consistent with our earlier comparisons of the Type A measures and again suggest that the Life measures and Faces: whole life are among our most promising global measures.

The high loadings of the Weighted weeks measures may in part be attributable to these measures each being indices composed of answers to several items and a reflection of the somewhat greater reliability one expects to obtain from such combinations. These two indices load almost identically on the first principal component, which is further evidence that the more simply constructed Weighted weeks is as adequate a measure as the more complicated Regression weighted weeks.

It would be interesting to see how Life 3, another composite measure,

[26]In general, however, the factor analysis was substantially affected by trivial methodological rather than conceptual aspects of the data and, as a consequence, proved not to be as enlightening as we had hoped. The pattern of factor loadings (not shown), before and after rotation, was very similar to that from the factor analysis of global measures administered to the April respondents (see Appendix F). Prior to rotation, the first factor explained about one-third of the common variance, and was followed by thirteen other factors, none of which explained as much as 10 percent of the common variance. The loadings on the first factor were roughly similar to the loadings on the first principal component, shown in Exhibit 3.8; the second factor was exclusively related to items and indices using the Ladder scale, which had not loaded strongly on the first factor; and the remaining twelve factors were conceptually unclear and showed virtually no loadings as big as .5. After a varimax rotation, some aspects of the former first factor were preserved, but many measures formerly here were split out. A few of the splits resulted in conceptually interesting factors—e.g., Positive affect, Negative affect, and Relative position—but most were the result of the high yet uninteresting correlations between indices and their components.

[27]Had we anticipated using the factor analysis in the way we do here, we would have omitted those few variables from the set shown in Exhibit 3.7 that do not refer to level of current well-being. Their presence slightly dilutes the purity of the first principal component as an indicator of the respondent's feelings about this level. However, the number of irrelevant variables is small, and in most cases they show only weak relationships to other variables, so their impact on the first principal component is small. The potential gains of revising the analysis and redoing the computations did not seem to justify the considerable cost.

In the present analysis, the first principal component by itself accounted for 25 percent of the total variance.

EXHIBIT 3.8. Fifty Global Measures Ordered by Loadings on First Principal Component

Measure		Loading	Measure		Loading
G10	Reg. wtd. weeks	.79	G65	Ladder: five yrs. hence	.49
G9	Wtd. weeks	.78	G66	Changes desired	.45
G1	Life 1	.76	G52	Decile position	.44
G32	Seven-pt. Happiness	.76	G36	Affect negative	.44
G2	Life 2	.74	G33	Worries	.44
G5	Faces: whole life	.72	G17	Ladder: best	.43
G4	Life 4	.69	G18	Weeks delighted	.42
G44	Rewarding	.68	G23	Ladder: worst	.40
G37	Affect balance	.67	G41	Worthwhile	.39
G31	Three-pt. Happiness	.66	G53	Circles: R-others	.38
G45	Ideal	.65	G21	Bad parts	.36
G39	Interesting	.65	G62	Variability of feelings	.33
G47	Enjoying	.64	G27	Number of neutrals	.30
G7	Circles: whole life	.63	G56	Past progress	.26
G11	Wtd. slices	.61	G15	Good parts	.26
G6	Ladder: most	.60	G54	Social comparison	.22
G50	Much better	.60	G55	Uniqueness	*
G25	Weeks unhappy	.59	G34	Mood today	*
G48	Capable	.59	G64	Ladder: five yrs. ago	*
G46	Contented	.58	G57	Future progress	*
G49	Better than everyone	.55	G58	Prog. past and future	*
G16	Number pluses	.53	G59	Ladder: best-worst	*
G22	Number minuses	.52	G67	Circles: others	*
G35	Affect positive	.51	G61	Up and down or steady	*
G51	Kind of life	.50	G68	Neighbor whole life	*

* Loading <.20.
Item numbers match Exhibit 3.1. July data.

would load on this first principal component and to compare its loading with those of the Weighted weeks measures. Unfortunately, this measure was not included in this analysis, but we can be sure its loadings would be at least in the mid-.70's since both its components, Life 1 and Life 2, load at this level. Given the expected gains in reliability of an index over single items, gains that we have seen for Life 3 in the April and November results, it would not be unreasonable to expect its loading to be about .8, making it another particularly promising measure.

In addition to the six measures that load .70 or more, eleven others load at least .60. These also show substantial sensitivity to the respondent's feelings about the level of his life-as-a-whole. Included here are all the rest of the Type A measures (Life 4, Circles: whole life, Ladder: most, and Weighted slices), certain of the more specific life qualities (Rewarding, Affect balance, Happiness, Ideal, Interesting, and Enjoying), and one of the relative–perspective measures (Much better). It is interesting to note that this set of measures includes exactly the same specific quality measures, and exactly the same relative–perspective measure, as were noted as being most sensitive on the basis of our earlier examination of the basic matrix of relationships (Exhibit 3.7).

The fact that a variable does not load at least .60 on the first principal component does not necessarily imply that it is a "poor" variable; i.e., one that does not validly measure anything. While we suspect that some of the low loadings are attributable to low validities, others undoubtedly occur because the variable assesses something different from the respondent's own current level of well-being. This is particularly clear when we examine the variables that show very low loadings in this analysis. To the extent that variables validly assess *something* they are "good" variables, but if this "something" is statistically distinct from the respondent's current level of well-being, these variables do not (and should not) show high loadings in Exhibit 3.8. Thus, the low loading variables include two types: "good" variables that measure other things, and "poor" variables that do not measure much of anything. Distinguishing the two, at least for certain selected variables, is one of the goals of the analyses on reliability and validity reported in chapter 6.

CHAPTER SUMMARY

This chapter describes sixty-eight global measures and the conceptual and statistical interrelationships among them. All are summary statements about life-as-a-whole, and most refer to the level of the respondent's own current well-being. Among the sixty-eight measures, some are taken from work by previous investigators, and many are new ones designed to let us investigate some of the different ways people may evaluate their life-as-a-whole.

In conjunction with the description of the complete list of measures, a conceptually oriented typology is presented. This typology distinguishes measures according to three characteristics: (1) the perspective from which the assessment is made (absolute, relative, long-term change or short-term change), (2) the nature of the evaluative dimension ("general" versus various more specific qualities), and (3) whether the assessment refers to the full range of life experiences or to only some part of the range.

Using this typology as a basic organizing principle, statistical results are discussed from the April, November, and July respondents. In each case, the relevant matrix of correlations is examined in detail and, where useful results emerged, additional findings from Smallest Space Analysis or Factor Analysis are presented. A clear and readily understandable pattern of relationships emerged, which was highly replicable from one data set to another.

All of the Type A measures, *general evaluations of the respondent's current life-as-a-whole from an absolute perspective and using the full range of experiences,* clustered together into what was called the core cluster. This clustering occurred despite the fact that the measures used a variety of different scales (some verbal, some graphic), a variety of different questions, and two different information sources (the respondent and the interviewer). Since the measures in this core cluster refer directly to one of the key matters of interest from a social indicators standpoint (the respondent's current level of well-being), since they show relatively high convergencies among themselves despite the methodological differences among them, and since they show substantial relationships to several more specific qualities that have obvious relevance to well-being (Happy, Satisfying, Rewarding, Ideal, Interesting, Enjoyable, Capable), these Type A measures have evident potential. Among them, the following appear most promising: Life 3, Weighted weeks, Faces: whole life.

A series of other measures that were typologically similar to the Type A measures except for reference to only a *part of the range* of experiences (positive experiences, negative experiences, or intermediate experiences) was also examined. These "Type B" measures showed relatively weak correlations between the positive-relevant and negative-relevant measures, but moderate relationships to the Type A measures. We suspected the low convergencies could be attributed both to the measures containing less valid variance than the Type A measures (perhaps because it was unnatural and/or difficult for a respondent to evaluate just his positive, or just his negative experiences), and to their being a more conceptually heterogeneous set than the Type A measures. The evidence that is available, however, suggests that how people feel about the positive aspects of their lives has relatively little to do with how they feel about the negative aspects, and yet that both of these contribute to how they feel about life-as-a-whole.

Among the global measures that tapped *specific qualities of life* (Type C measures), indices measuring positive and negative affect proved particularly interesting. When these were factor analyzed jointly with certain other global measures, including evaluations of several other specific qualities of life-as-a-whole and several general evaluations, three independent factors emerged: We named them Cognitive evaluation, Positive affect, and Negative affect. Results suggested that the Type A measures were nearly identical with respect to the proportions of these three sources of variance that each contained, mainly Cognitive evaluation variance, supplemented by Positive and Negative affect variance. In contrast, the measures tapping specific life qualities tended to contain relatively less Cognitive evaluation variance, relatively more (and unequal) affect variances, and more variance from other (unique) sources.

Of seven measures that asked the respondent to assess his well-being *relative* to that of other people (Type D measures), four showed satisfactory convergencies and moderate relationships to the core measures. Of these, the measure named Much better was most sensitive to the feelings that were also tapped by the core measures. Two other relative measures showed both weaker convergencies with the others, and weaker relationships to the core measures. We suspected these might be less valid. The final relative measure, the respondent's assessment of the uniqueness of his life, proved virtually unrelated to most other measures.

The *long-term change* (Type E) measures were each derived from direct estimates by the respondent of the level of his well-being five years ago, currently, and five years hence. Although the *level* of well-being expected five years hence showed moderate relationships to the core measures (all of which assess current level), none of the *change* measures showed other than weak relationships to current level. Apparently, people's feelings about current well-being are quite independent from their expectations about future progress, and only slightly more related to their sense of past progress. Furthermore, their sense of past progress was unrelated to their expectations about future progress. Given this latter point, plus the directions of some of the other relationships, we concluded that the measure named Progress past and future probably did not represent any thoughts that were real to most respondents and that it should be discarded.

The *short-term change* (Type F) measures included two distinct types of assessments: those tapping the *range* of feelings and those tapping the *likelihood* or *frequency* of any variation. Although our measures of these concepts seem less dependable than measures of some other concepts, perhaps because these concepts themselves were unnatural to the respondents, the available evidence suggests that the range of feelings was almost totally independent of the level of well-being (i.e., the Type A measures), while stability of feelings (lack of variation) showed a weak positive relationship to level.

To conclude this summary, it will be useful to bring together the types of measures that proved *un*related or only *weakly* related to the Type A measures. These are interesting for two reasons: (1) They suggest kinds of influences by which the core measures are not "contaminated"; and (2) they suggest (at least in some cases) aspects of well-being that are distinct from those tapped by the Type A measures and that would need to be tapped by other measures if these aspects are to be tapped at all. The Type A measures were largely independent of the respondent's self-reported "mood" on the day he participated in the study, his sense of uniqueness, his sense of progress or decline in either the past or the future, the range and variability of changes in his feelings, how he evaluated the well-being of other people in general, and how he evaluated the well-being of a specific neighbor. Although some of these aspects of well-being (particularly the change measures) may be of interest in a social indicators framework, we believe the Type A measures clearly deserve our primary attention. Thus, it is reassuring to find that the Type A measures provide a statistically defensible set of general evaluations of the level of current well-being, that these relate substantially to a variety of specific life qualities that support their meaningfulness, and that they are relatively uninfluenced by a variety of phenomena that might have made their interpretations less clear.

CHAPTER 4

Predicting Global Well-Being: I

This chapter and the next one focus on the prediction of global well-being. Here we undertake a relatively detailed exploration of the prediction of a single measure of global well-being, the Life 3 measure. Chapter 5 provides a broader, but less detailed, study of the prediction of a large number of other global measures.

The word "prediction" is used here in the statistical sense of attempting to account for the observed differences in peoples's feelings about their overall well-being. From the survey results we know how each respondent felt about a large number of life concerns, and we also know certain demographic facts about each respondent: age, education, sex, family income, and the like. Our goal is to see how well these bits of information, considered one at a time and in various combinations, enable us to accurately predict a respondent's feelings about life-as-a-whole.

An exploration such as this yields at least two kinds of returns. First, we can gain insights into some matters of real substantive interest: Which aspects of life have the most impact on people's sense of well-being? How do people go about integrating evaluations of the more specific aspects of their lives into a general evaluation? Such questions have obvious relevance both for the development of useful social policies and for the more basic-science goals of understanding how people respond to their environments.

The second kind of reward is more methodologically oriented. In developing batteries of social indicators, we need to decide how many, and which, of our measures would prove most useful under various conditions. By observing how they contribute to the prediction of global well-being, we can gain important information on how to construct broad-ranging yet statistically efficient batteries of indicators.

Life 3: A Measure of Global Well-Being

The Life 3 measure is just one of many global measures described in the preceding chapter. However, we regard it as one of our best measures of global well-being. It seems an appropriate measure to try to predict (i.e., as a dependent variable) in a series of detailed analyses for several reasons: (1) Its wording refers directly to a concept of immediate and obvious relevance from a social indicators standpoint: How do you feel about your life as a whole? (2) As shown in chapter 3, Life 3 is one of the most sensitive of a whole set of alternative measures (the Type A measures) that can be used to attain a global assessment of the respondent's own current life-as-a-whole, using the full range of a very general evaluative dimension, and making the evaluation from an absolute perspective. (3) As also shown in chapter 3, the Life 3 measure shows meaningful and reasonable relationships to a variety of more specific life qualities; it relates substantially to feelings of life being happy, satisfying, interesting, rewarding, ideal, enjoyable, and the respondent's sense of his or her own capability. (4) The measure is an index based on answers to two questionnaire items and thus is more stable than answers to just one question. (5) The scaling of the Life 3 index is transparently straightforward, a simple mean.

The Life 3 measure is available for most of our respondents, the requisite questions having been included in all interviews and questionnaires except the November Form 1 interview. Consequently, we shall be able to explore the predictability of this measure in the May, November (Form 2), and April national samples and for the July respondents as well.

Topics to Be Discussed and Overview of Results

Any attempt to account for the variation in one measure on the basis of other measures faces certain general analytic problems. Of course, we face these problems here and it is the sequential exploration of each that forms the basic organization of this chapter.

Although we shall discuss the issues in a logical order, we would note that the order of presentation is not necessarily the order in which we actually did the analyses. To some extent the problems interact and need to be addressed simultaneously, and to some extent the order in which they were addressed was dictated by the actual flow of our research, in which the full range of data was accumulated only after a series of distinct research cycles, each of which was designed in the light of preliminary results from prior cycles.

We begin with a brief look at how the respondents' feelings about various specific life concerns, each considered alone, relate to general sense of well-being. This is strictly preliminary to the main thrust of the chapter, which is multivariate prediction, but provides a useful initial scan of the concern measures and their relative potency when considered one at a time. As we shall see, the relationships (r's and eta's) range from .1 to .7 with some of the highest involving evaluations of oneself, one's immediate family and marriage, one's material and monetary resources, and how one is treated by other people.

Next we face questions about appropriate ways of combining information on feelings about two or more life concerns. Formally, this involves the selection of an appropriate statistical model for predicting Life 3.

Finding a statistical model that fits the data has real substantive interest, as well as methodological, because in these data the statistical model can also be considered as a psychological model. Not only is the model that method of combining feelings that provides the best predictions, it is also our best indication of what may go on in the minds of the respondents when they themselves combine feelings about specific life concerns to arrive at global evaluations. Thus, our statistical model can also be considered as a simulation of psychological processes.

We shall see that remarkably simple and orderly models, linear additive ones, fit the data well. They fit so well, in fact, that improvements in predicting people's feelings about life-as-a-whole seem likely to come about not by developing better models, but by developing better (i.e., more valid) indicators of people's true feelings.

Next, the chapter explores the accuracy with which Life 3 can be predicted using different combinations of predictors—the concern measures and the demographic characteristics of the respondents. We explore combinations of concerns that vary in number, in topical heterogeneity, and in type (domains and criteria), and conclude that reasonably good predictions of global well-being can be achieved using a relatively modest number of concerns (less than a dozen) so long as these concerns are topically heterogeneous. Using *optimal* sets of concern measures, multiple correlations of .7 to .8 can be achieved (i.e., 50–60 percent of the variance in Life 3 can be predicted). When adjusted for the estimated reliability of the measures themselves, these multiple correlations are close to the theoretical maximum of 1.0.

The prediction of global well-being from the demographic characteristics of the respondents produced straightforward results that have proved surprising to some observers: The demographic variables, either singly or jointly, account for very little of the variance in perceptions of global well-being (less than 10 percent), and they add nothing to what can be predicted (more accurately) from the concern measures.

The final major section of the chapter is devoted to questions of generalizability. Will means of predicting feelings about life-as-a-whole developed for the general population work well within demographically defined subgroups of the population? How well will means of predicting developed on one sample work for other samples? How much better would the predictions within a particular subgroup be if the means of making them were optimized for that particular group rather than for the general population? Answers to these kinds of questions show that the previously cited results are remarkably generalizable. Predictive equations developed for the total population prove to work reasonably well within each of a wide range of major subgroups, and excellent crossvalidations of the predictive equations can be demonstrated.

RELATIONSHIPS BETWEEN SINGLE CONCERN MEASURES AND LIFE 3

Before turning to the multivariate prediction of Life 3, we shall take a quick look at how the concern measures, considered one at a time, relate to global well-being. The discussion, however, merely lays the groundwork for the multivariate analyses that follow, for by its very nature we know that evaluation of life-as-a-whole must be a multiply determined phenomenon and hence should be understood within a multivariate context. It will be useful, however, to review the range of concern measures that are available, to note the form and range of the individual relationships, and to briefly describe the kinds of concerns that show high, medium, and low relationships to Life 3.

A preliminary, but fundamental, issue in any study of relationships is the form that they take—linear or curvilinear. Early in our work, we suspected there might be important curvilinearities between feelings about specific life concerns and feelings about life-as-a-whole. Would higher evaluations of specific life concerns be regularly associated with higher evaluations of general well-being? It was certainly possible to imagine that various ceiling effects, or "defense" effects, might result in people with higher evaluations of particular concerns showing no higher, or even lower, evaluations of life-as-a-whole. Such effects, if present, would result in nonlinear relationships that would have to be allowed for in subsequent analysis.

However, after examining many associations between feelings about specific life concerns and life-as-a-whole, we conclude that substantial curvilinearities do not occur when affective evaluations are assessed using the Delighted–Terrible Scale.[1]

At first we doubted the generality of this finding and so checked it for a very heterogeneous set of concerns and in several different sets of data, always finding that whatever association existed was essentially linear in nature. The finding is interesting for several reasons. It hints that evaluations of life-as-a-whole may be derived through a relatively simple process; it suggests that our means of assessing these evaluations by the Delighted–Terrible Scale may be appropriate;[2] and it simplifies our multivariate analyses (which are described later).

The relationships between people's feelings about specific concerns and the Life 3 measure (eta's and r's) were all positive and ranged from a low of about .1 to a high of about .7. Exhibit 4.1 shows these relationships for each of the four surveys in which the Life 3 measure was included. It groups the concerns according to the major "region" identified in Exhibit 2.3, and—within each group—it orders the concerns according to their relationship with Life 3 (with a few exceptions needed to keep substantively similar concerns together).[3]

[1]This conclusion is based on comparisons of the Pearson product–moment coefficient of correlation (which is sensitive only to the linear component of a relationship) with the eta statistic (which is sensitive to both linear and curvilinear components). When computed on the same data, the two statistics practically never deviated from each other by as much as .05, indicating that most relationships had no component other than a linear one.

[2]The finding is certainly not unique to the Delighted–Terrible Scale, though we have no good basis on which to estimate its generality. Campbell, Converse, and Rodgers (1976) also found generally linear relationships between measures based on a seven-point scale of satisfaction.

[3]The richness of our data complicates an exhibit such as 4.1, which brings together results from different surveys and from analyses performed at different times. The right-hand portion of the exhibit and the associated footnote provide full details on exactly what is presented. We would

The concerns that showed the highest individual relationships to Life 3 included feelings about the fun, enjoyment, and interestingness of one's life; one's own efficacy, accomplishments, and adjustment; one's marriage; how one is treated and accepted by other people; and such "economic" matters as one's income, standard of living, and the extent one's physical needs are met. These concerns generally showed relationships with Life 3 of .5 or more.

The above list is put into sharper focus when compared with a list of concerns with *low* relationships to feelings about life-as-a-whole. While none of the following were totally independent of Life 3, most showed relationships in the range .1 to .2. These concerns included feelings about local weather, the condition of the local environment, local government, the mass media, the way young people think and act, one's mobility (i.e., facilities for transportation), and one's links to the past. In contrast to the concerns that relate highly to Life 3, which tend to be matters in which a person was immediately and personally involved, and over which a person might have substantial personal influence, these low-relationship concerns tend to be matters much more remote from one's immediate personal life.

The organization of Exhibit 4.1, in which concerns are grouped according to their place in the perceptual structures identified in chapter 2, lets us perceive a rather nice orderliness in the way the concern measures relate to feelings about life-as-a-whole. There tends to be a substantial degree of consistency among the concerns of each major group. Note that the Oneself and own personal life group includes none of the concerns with very low relationships to Life 3, and that most of the relationships in the group are .35 or higher. The Family, Relations with other people, and Economics, housing, job, costs groups also contain concerns with relatively high relationships, but the ranges here are slightly lower than in the Self group. On the other hand, the Local area and Larger society groups contain concerns that show much lower relationships to life-as-a-whole. In the Local area group the relationships range from about .35 downward, and in the Larger society group the highest relationships barely exceed .25.

Exhibit 4.1 is also interesting for its demonstration of the essential replicative nature of relationships between individual concern measures and Life 3. Despite a number of factors that tend to make relationships somewhat higher for the November and July respondents than for the May and April ones, the relationships between most concerns and feelings about life-as-a-whole tend to be rather similar across the four surveys. (The similarity is further enhanced if one considers the *relative* sizes of the relationships rather than the absolute values shown in Exhibit 4.1. Note that the kinds of concerns that show the highest relationships to Life 3 in one survey tend to be the same as those showing the highest relationships in other surveys.)

---

caution, however, that the relationships between any particular concern and Life 3 vary from survey to survey for certain reasons beyond the usual ones of sampling fluctuations and real change over time. (These other reasons are listed in conjunction with our discussion of the replicability evident in Exhibit 4.1.)

EXHIBIT 4.1. Relationships of Concern Measures to Life 3

	Association with Life 3				Measure[a]			
	May	Nov.	Apr.	July	May	Nov.	Apr.	July
Oneself and own personal life								
Fun and enjoyment	.51	.61	.60	.61	27	27	28	28
Self-efficacy, adjustment, etc.	.55	.54	.54	.68	C3	21	22	C4
			.44	.63			16	C2
			.33				13	
			.51				18	29
			.47				33	
Interesting daily life	b	b	.54	.63	—	—	23	23
Independence and freedom	b	b	.43	.62	—	—	44	C15
Beauty, attractiveness	b	.55	.38	.50	—	25	24	24
Spare-time activities	.41	.47	b	.49	30	30	—	30
Amt. time, leisure, relaxation	.28	.31	.44	.52	38	38	39	C18
		.39				41		
Imagination, fantasy	b	b	b	.42	—	—	—	35
Contribution to others' lives	b	b	.43	.32	—	—	68	68
Chance of getting good job	b	.37	b	.44	—	12	—	12
Opportunities to change things	b	.37	b	.30	—	11	—	11
Freedom from bother	b	b	.38	.36	—	—	43	43
Privacy	b	.37	b	.36	—	45	—	45
Neat, tidy, clean	b	b	.38	.34	—	—	73	73
Own dependability, sincerity	b	b	.32	.37	—	—	48	C1
Health, physical exercise	.29	.38	.37	.49	7	7	29	C9
Sleep you get	b	.31	b	.24	—	42	—	42
Creativity	b	.32	b	.35	—	36	—	36
One's family								
Family, marriage	.38	.52	b	.60	C6	4	—	C7
				.14				1
Things do with family	.38	.51	b	.46	6	6	—	C8
Family agreement on spending	b	.42	b	.40	—	82	—	82
Sex life	b	.40	b	.42	—	26	—	26
Close adult relatives	.22	b	b	.27	5	—	—	5
Relations with other people								
Fair treatment by others	.30	b	.51	.58	52r	—	54	C14
Accepted, admired by others	.31	.34	.50	.53	63	55	64	C10
Your friends	.31	.36	b	.46	62	60	—	C12
	.34				C11	—	—	—
Others' sincerity, honesty	b	.28	.28	.48	—	56	49	C13
			.39				53	
Reliability of others	b	.38	b	.34	—	65	—	65
Economics, housing, job, costs								
Income, living standard, fin. security	.47	.57	.49	.49	C20	C20	81	C19
Physical needs met	b	b	.56	.44	—	—	8	8
House, apartment	.36	.44	b	.36	87	87	—	87
Job	.23	.37	b	.33	C23	75	—	C22
Costs, taxes	.26	.25	b	.15	C37	100r	—	102

EXHIBIT 4.1. (*continued*)

	Association with Life 3				Measure[a]			
	May	Nov.	Apr.	July	May	Nov.	Apr.	July
The local area								
Safety, security from theft	.24	.27	.38	.43	94r	96	95	C26
Community, neighborhood	.31	.32	b	.33	C24	90r	—	C25
Services, public and private	.20	.25	b	.27	92	101	—	C27
	.31				C28	—	—	—
Local schools	.17	b	b	.41	98	—	—	98
Recreation facilities, places	.22	.27	b	.27	C30	114	—	C29
Local government	.23	.19	b	.21	C32	104r	—	C31
Condition of local environment	.13	b	b	.21	110	—	—	110
Local weather	.12	b	b	.09	111	—	—	111
The larger society								
National government	.26	.25	b	.24	C34	C33	—	C33
Society's standards	b	.26	b	.25	—	121	—	121
Way people over 40 think, act	.22	b	b	.25	122	—	—	122
Way young people think, act	.15	.12	b	.31	123	123r	—	123
The mass media	.15	.17	b	.21	C36	118r	—	C35
Other concerns								
Housework, work around the home	.36	.32	b	.32	74	74r	—	74
Religious faith, fulfillment	.24	b	.33	.21	69	—	70	C38
Organizations, help of others	.21	b	b	.28	72	—	—	C39
Way you get around, mobility	.25	b	b	.20	97r	—	—	97
Use of own education	.33	b	b	.16	32	—	—	32
Your links to the past	b	b	b	.16	—	—	—	37

[a] Measure numbers refer to Exhibits 2.1 or C.1. Statistics for May, November, and April data are eta's except in the few cases where an *r* follows the measure number to indicate that the statistic shown is a Pearson correlation coefficient; statistics for the July data are all Pearson correlation coefficients.
[b] This concern was not evaluated by these respondents.
Data sources: 1,297 respondents to May national survey; 1,072 respondents to November (Form 2) national survey; 1,433 respondents to April national survey; and 222 respondents to July local survey.

Several factors in addition to the usual ones of sampling fluctuations and possible real changes over time (neither of which seems of major import) probably contribute to the modest variations among the relationships from survey to survey. These factors stem from differences in the characteristics of the respondents, in the methods of data collection, and in the composition of the concern measures. As mentioned in chapter 1, the July respondents tended to have somewhat more education than the respondents to the other (national) surveys and hence may have been able to give more precise answers to our questions. The July respondents also spent much more time (two to four hours) answering questions about quality of life, and this may have enabled them to more clearly focus their thoughts and feelings. In contrast, the November respondents encountered questions about life quality only in the latter part of a lengthy interview, and certain analyses (discussed in chap. 6) hint that their answers, while containing typical portions of valid variance, include a greater-than-usual portion of common methods variance (hence, relationships for them may be affected more than the relationships in other data by this spurious component). Finally, the best measure of a given concern in one survey was not always available in other surveys. (Note, in particular, that relationships to Life 3 tend to be slightly higher when a concern was measured by a *cluster* of items than when it was tapped by just a single item, and that the greater number of items put to the July respondents permits use of more clusters for them.)

Having noted the specific statistical results of Exhibit 4.1, let us consider them from several perspectives.

They might be seen as suggesting the aspects of life that are most potent for influencing general feelings of well-being. Interpreted in this light, our findings clearly corroborate Cantril's general observation, based on research in 13 countries (including the United States), that people were most concerned about matters which were rather close and personal. Cantril summarized his finding:

> The vast majority of people's hopes and fears revolve around the complex of personal well-being, and this is rather simply and genuinely defined: a decent standard of living; opportunities for children; technological advances; good health; a good job; decent housing; a happy home life; better educational facilities. (Cantril, 1967, p.145)

Although our data do not agree with all the specific components of Cantril's statement (our relationships for educational facilities are not uniformly strong, and we did not assess feelings about either opportunities for children or technological advances), the broad trend of our results is clearly in accord with those of Cantril: Concerns relevant to *personal* well-being relate most strongly to evaluations of life-as-a-whole.

Even though concerns that have a more immediate personal impact tend to show stronger relationships to Life 3, it is not the case that the more remote concerns are irrelevant. As our multivariate analyses will show, after one takes account of "close" concerns, some of the more remote ones still make their own distinct contribution to the prediction of feelings about life-as-a-whole.

The higher relationships shown by concerns that are close to the respondent carry implications for the design of social indicator systems. They suggest that these are particularly important matters and that a set of social indicators that aspires to be reasonably comprehensive should probably include measures of these more personal aspects of life. (One may note that indicators designed to tap these personal and immediate aspects of life are often neglected or only sparsely represented in many systems of indicators. Sometimes this is justified on the basis that such matters are not appropriate targets for policy action by those who monitor the indicators and/or because of fears of violating personal privacy. One might question the validity of both of these reasons.)

The final comment we wish to make regarding the findings of Exhibit 4.1 is that they suggest that some of our concern measures may be more "global" than others. In designing these surveys we made a sharp conceptual distinction between global measures and the more specific concern measures, and attempted to construct concern measures that were narrowly focused upon a single domain or criterion. Yet, as noted in chapter 1, measures can be conceived as varying in their degree of specificity, and the results in Exhibit 4.1 suggest that at least two of ours, those having to do with the criteria of Fun and Beauty, may be less specific than most of the others. Although one cannot be sure, we suspect that part of the reason for the relatively high relationships to Life 3 shown by these measures may be that the measures themselves come closer to being global statements about life-as-a-whole than do most of the other concern measures. However, one cannot really prove this, and despite an attempt to make each of these measures more specific, their relationships to Life 3 declined only slightly and remained relatively high.[4] An alternative explanation for the strength of these relationships is simply that Fun and Beauty are two very important criteria.

MULTIVARIATE PREDICTION OF LIFE 3

When we move from the bivariate relationships of the preceding section to a full multivariate "prediction" of Life 3, we approach the problem of accounting for feelings about life-as-a-whole with what we believe is a more appropriate degree of complexity. On a purely intuitive basis, one suspects that feelings about life-as-a-whole must be influenced by a host of more specific life experiences, and we have already described (in chap. 1) a formal matrix model that incorporates this basic intuition.[5] Our purpose here is not to "test" that particular model (though many of the results to be described are relevant to such a test), but rather to undertake a much broader exploration of the extent to which variation in the Life 3 measure can be accounted for.[6]

The explorations to be described can be divided into four topical areas. In formal terms these are: (1) identifying appropriate prediction models, (2) assessing the accuracy of prediction when using different sets of predictors, (3) testing the generalizability of the results, and (4) evaluating the levels of prediction achieved. We shall consider them in that order.

[4]Our original item to assess Beauty was worded, How do you feel about the chance you have to enjoy pleasant or beautiful things? Feeling that the word "pleasant" was too general, we altered the item in later surveys to, How do you feel about the amount of beauty and attractiveness in your world? Both items were asked of the July respondents and, as expected, the second version, which seemed somewhat more specific, showed a slightly lower relationship with Life 3. (The correlations with Life 3 were .56 and .50, for the first and second versions, respectively.) A similar, but smaller, shift occurred for two versions of the Fun measure (see items 27 and 28 in Exhibit 2.1). Both versions were also administered to the July respondents, with resulting correlations of .62 and .61.

[5]Our models and analysis designs incorporate the intuition that global feelings are "caused"—at least in part—by affective evaluations of more specific life concerns (rather than the reverse). Hence it will occasionally be convenient to describe our multivariate results using language that implicitly assumes this direction of causality; e.g., we shall speak of a concern's "influence," "impact," etc. Of course, none of our data or analyses permit a strict test of this assumption. In place of phrases such as "Concern X shows a modest impact on Y," cautious readers may wish to substitute a more clumsy but statistically precise phrase such as "Concern X shows a modest partial relationship to Y."

[6]Chapter 7 includes a section devoted to the testing of the matrix model.

Models for Predicting Life 3 from Concern Measures

The problem of finding an appropriate statistical model is the problem of finding an appropriate way to "combine" information on feelings about different life concerns to achieve an optimal prediction of feelings about life-as-a-whole. Of course, there are many ways in which information can be combined. The simplest would be just to add up the numerical scores assigned to the respondent's feelings about life concerns. More complex combinations would involve transformations of the original scores and/or differential weighting of them. Still more complex are various nonadditive combinations in which the *weight* of one variable is allowed to vary according to the *level* of one or more other variables.

Finding an appropriate means of combining variables is of considerably more than mere statistical interest. In the present data, all of the variables describe psychological states (affective evaluations), and hence the optimal statistical model can also be considered as our most adequate simulation of the actual mental process that a person may use to arrive at a "summary" evaluation of life-as-a-whole. Thus, the statistical model that proves most appropriate for predicting Life 3 can be regarded as a psychological model as well.

Our search for an appropriate prediction model involved three kinds of analyses: a search for curvilinearities, a search for statistical "interactions,"[7] and experimentation with several different approaches for weighting the predictor variables (i.e., the concern measures).

Linearities. In our discussion of results from the bivariate analyses, we noted the important finding that bivariate relationships between Life 3 and the various concern measures were almost exclusively linear. The same result emerged when we explored the matter in a multivariate context. We performed many of our most critical multivariate analyses twice, once using Multiple Classification Analysis[8] and once using Multiple Regression. Multiple Classification Analysis is the more flexible of the two techniques and indicates the maximum prediction of Life 3 that could be achieved using optimal transformations of each predictor (i.e., under any possible condition of curvilinearity). Multiple regression is a more restricted approach and assumes that all relationships are linear. With perfect consistency, the predictability achievable with the more flexible technique was virtually identical to that achievable using a strict assumption of linearity, indicating that there was little besides a linear aspect to the relationships being considered.

As one example of this result, we cite an analysis of the April data. Twenty-three concern measures were used to predict Life 3 via Multiple Classification Analysis and also via Multiple Regression. In each case the percentage of variance that could be accounted for after adjustment for the appropriate degrees of freedom, R^2_{adj}, was 61 percent. Results such as these were unexpected

---

[7]Alternative terms for "interactions" include nonadditivities, conditioning effects, moderating effects, and contingency effects.

[8]Andrews *et al.*, 1973.

by us, and, before we became convinced of their generality, we made extensive use of the more flexible of the two multivariate procedures. The consistency with which its results duplicated those from Multiple Regression—regardless of the data set, the number of concern measures used as predictors, or the type of concerns included (domains or criteria)—finally convinced us of the generality of the result.[9]

Lack of Interactions. Just as we were prepared to encounter curvilinearities in the data, so also were we ready for interactions. Although we ultimately became convinced that marked interactions were not present in our data, initially we had no trouble imagining many instances where they might plausibly occur. For example, we thought that people who were in poor health might care less about other aspects of their lives than healthy people. Such a situation, if it occurred, could show up as a lower relationship between Life 3 and feelings about various life concerns among those who were relatively dissatisfied with their health than among those who were satisfied. An opposite interaction can also be imagined: People who were highly satisfied with some psychologically central life concern (e.g., self, family, job) might show lower relationships between their evaluations of other concerns and feelings about life-as-a-whole than would people who were less "fulfilled" by some central concern.

Such interactions seemed very possible, and we checked more than two hundred pairs of concern measures searching for instances of their occurrence. Nowhere did we find an instance of marked interaction. In nearly all cases the interaction was virtually zero; the few remaining cases where mild interaction was observed were most plausibly attributed to sampling and measurement fluctuations.[10]

Since the scan for interactions just described involved examining combinations of *two* concern measures as they related to Life 3, it was sensitive only to "first order" interactions. Since higher order interactions, involving three or more concern measures simultaneously, were also theoretically possible, we submitted the May data to an analysis by the Automatic Interaction Detector (Sonquist, Baker, and Morgan, 1973). This computer program identifies the concern measures most useful for predicting Life 3 and determines their optimal sequential combination. The technique requires no assumptions whatsoever about the presence or absence of interactions and/or linearities. The AID-determined optimal combination can be compared with results from more restrictive techniques, and the effects of interactions at any of several levels of complexity among the most predictive vaiables can be determined. The results of applying the AID technique were in complete accord with the scan for

---

[9]Campbell, Converse, and Rodgers (1976) also obtained essentially identical results from Multiple Classification Analysis and Multiple Regression when performing multivariate analyses of measures based on their seven-category satisfaction scale.

[10]Because the technique we used to scan for interactions is not widely known, we describe it more fully in Appendix G, where we also present some of the specific results that we examined. Included there is one of the largest instances of interaction that we encountered and a demonstration that taking account of it would have produced minimal gains.

interactions described earlier: There was no evidence of any marked interaction.[11]

Weighting Schemes. The two preceding sections have reported that linear additive models involving no scale transformations, the simplest general form of a statistical model, seemed to provide optimal predictions of Life 3. There remains, however, a question as to how the variables that are to be combined to produce a prediction of Life 3—i.e., the concern measures—are to be weighted. Should they be weighted equally? Could a better prediction be achieved if they were weighted differentially? Is there any gain in predictability if we take account of how *important* the respondent tells us the concerns are to him; i.e., if we introduce information about his own reported weighting of the concerns in addition to the information about his affective evaluations of them?

Several explorations provide consistent and clear answers to these questions. A simple summing of answers to any of certain alternative sets of concern items (coded from 1 to 7 on the Delighted–Terrible Scale) provides a prediction of feelings about life-as-a-whole that correlates rather well with the respondent's actual scores on Life 3. Using twelve selected concerns[12] (mainly domains) and data from the May respondents, this correlation was .67 (based on 1,278 cases); using eight selected concerns[13] (all criteria) and data from the April respondents, the correlation was .77 (based on 1,070 cases). These relatively high values obtain in subgroups of the population as well as in the population as a whole: When the sum of answers to eight of the April concern items was correlated with Life 3 in twenty-one different subgroups of the national adult population, the correlation was never lower than .70 nor higher than .82.[14] Regardless of the type of concern measure, the demographic character of the respondents, or the particular data set, we consistently find high correlations between even a simple sum of appropriately selected concern measures and Life 3.

A slightly higher correlation between *predicted* feelings about life-as-a-whole and the Life 3 measure can be achieved in some cases (but not always) by appropriately weighting the concern measure scores as they enter the summation. Weights that will produce the most accurate prediction of Life 3 can be derived by either of two statistical techniques (Multiple Regression or Multiple Classification Analysis).[15] What is extremely interesting is that the optimally weighted combination of concern measures provides a prediction of Life 3 that

---

[11] As described near the end of this chapter, interaction also proved absent among predictors of Life 3 that combined: concern measures and social or demographic characteristics, concern measures and present mood, and concern measures and recent major events in the respondent's life; it was also absent among predictors of Life 3 consisting of two or more demographic characteristics.

[12] These concerns are the "Selected 12" shown in Exhibit 4.2.

[13] These concerns are the first eight listed in Exhibit 4.5.

[14] These subgroups, as more fully described later in this chapter, were defined on the basis of sex, race, education, age, income, marital status, or socioeconomic level.

[15] The weights produced by these two techniques are not the same. Multiple regression applies a uniform weight to each of the prescaled answers of each concern measure; Multiple Classification Analysis computes the optimum weight for each individual answer category. Nevertheless, as described previously, either set of weights generates an equally good prediction of Life 3.

is, at most, only modestly better than that provided by the simple sum. In the May data, the previous correlation of .67 could be increased to .71 by optimally weighting the twelve concern measures. In terms of the total variance of Life 3, this represents an accounting of about 5 percent more of it (from 45–50 percent). When all the April respondents were grouped together, use of an optimally weighted sum of the same eight concern measures produced *no* increase in explained variance, while in the twenty-one subgroups increases ranging from 0–6 percent (of the total variance of Life 3) were observed. Our conclusion is that the introduction of weights when summing answers to the concern measures is likely to produce a modest improvement, but that even a simple sum of the answers provides a prediction that is remarkably close to the best that can be statistically derived.

Still another form of weighted sum seemed, at an early stage in our explorations, to offer a promising way to predict feelings about life-as-a-whole. On an intuitive basis, we suspected that the various concern measures being used to make the prediction should perhaps be weighted by the "importance" that the respondent assigned to them. It seemed reasonable that a person's feelings about life-as-a-whole would be more influenced by his feelings about the life concerns that he said were important to him than by feelings about other concerns.

The idea was so deserving of a test, and the results would be so important for the design of subsequent surveys, that we undertook its investigation, jointly with some of our colleagues, before designing our first instrument, that administered to the May respondents. Data suitable for testing this idea were available from a survey of American adults conducted in 1971 by Campbell, Converse, and Rodgers (1976). About twenty-two-hundred adults, sampled representatively from the forty-eight coterminous states, had been asked to rate their satisfaction with life-as-a-whole[16] and the following ten concerns: house or apartment, city or place you live in, the national government, your work, your nonworking activities, your marriage, your family life, your friendships, your health and physical condition, and your financial situation. The respondents also rated each of the concerns for its importance, How important that thing really is to you.[17]

The significant finding that emerged is that there was no possible use of these importance data that produced the slightest increase in the accuracy with which feelings about life-as-a-whole could be predicted over what could be achieved using an optimally weighted combination of answers to the concern measures alone.[18] Although a number of questions remain with respect to the

[16]The life-as-a-whole measure was subsequently included in our work; see measure G29 in Exhibit 3.1. The same seven-point satisfaction scale that is described for measure G29 was also used to assess satisfaction with each of the concerns.

[17]The importance ratings were made on a five-point scale whose categories were labeled "extremely important," "very important," "quite important," "somewhat important," and "not at all important."

[18]The statement is based on a comparison of three Multiple Classification Analyses. The first used answers to the ten listed concerns to predict life-as-a-whole and achieved $R^2_{adj} = .44$; the second

nature and meaning of the importance measures (some are explored in chap. 7), we have an unambiguous answer to our original question: Data about the importance people assign to concerns did not increase the accuracy with which feelings about life-as-a-whole could be predicted.

Conclusions and Comments About the Prediction Model. On the basis of the three sets of analyses just described, we come to some clear conclusions about the form of statistical model that is most appropriate for predicting Life 3 from feelings about specific concerns: Our results point to a simple linear additive one, in which an optimal set of weights is only modestly better than no weights (i.e. equal weights).[19] We confess to both surprise and pleasure at these conclusions.

We are surprised because we were quite prepared to believe that the processes by which life-as-a-whole was evaluated might be quite complicated, and that these complications might need to be reflected in a rather complex statistical model. While the total process may indeed be complicated, it now appears that the final portion of it—the movement to global assessments once concern-level assessments are available—is simpler than we thought.

Our pleasure about the result stems from its implications for theoretical and analytical parsimony. One of the situations in which the need for complicated models arises is when the investigators have approached a phenomenon with an inappropriate set of concepts and/or measures. In such cases, the inappropriateness of the approach, even when applied to a basically "simple" phenomenon, produces a complex set of results. While the beautiful simplicity of the present results does not prove that our concepts involving global and concern-level assessments, and our measures based on the Delighted–Terrible

---

used ten "pattern variables" (each composed of a pair of variables relevant to a given concern—the rating on satisfaction and the rating on importance) to predict life-as-a-whole and achieved $R^2_{adj} = .40$; the third used the ten satisfaction ratings and the ten importance ratings in a twenty-predictor additive model and achieved $R^2_{adj} = .43$. The pattern variables were each twelve-category nominal scales in which each category referred to a particular combination of satisfaction and importance—e.g., low-low, low-medium, low-high, etc. If there had been *any* way in which the importance ratings could have increased the accuracy of the prediction via a weighting function, the analysis using pattern variables would have detected it, since this made no assumptions whatsoever about the nature of the optimal function. The third analysis showed that even when the importance ratings were not paired with the satisfaction measures domain by domain, they contained no information beyond that already in the satisfaction measures that could increase the accuracy of prediction.

The fact that the R^2_{adj}'s actually declined when the importance data were introduced is not surprising and simply reflects the fact that the adjustment for degrees of freedom had to be larger when more answer categories were represented in the analysis; the R^2's prior to adjustment were all very close to .45.

It would be desirable to attempt to replicate these results using an alternative set of data and different concern measures. While importance ratings of certain concerns are available in our July data, the number of respondents there is too small to permit a good replication. Assessments of importance were not included in any of our other instruments.

[19]It is not generally true that "no weights" is equivalent to "equal weights"; however, in our data, where the variances of the various concern measures are roughly equal, the statement is approximately correct.

Scale, are correct, they certainly do not suggest need for major modifications in these concepts and measures. The simplicity of the suggested model is pleasing for another, very practical, reason: It suggests that analyses involving a very large number of concern measures can appropriately and effectively be carried out on these data using well-established, widely available, and relatively economical statistical techniques; e.g., Multiple Regression, Multiple Classification Analysis, and (somewhat less desirably) calculations of simple sums.

Before too great acceptance and commitment are generated for the use of linear additive models on data assessing perceptions of well-being, we should note some of the limits of our finding. It is, of course, based on the use of *particular* concern measures as predictors of *Life 3*.

On the concern measure side, we have not, of course, tried all possible combinations of concerns. It is possible that some significant modification to our general findings would be required by some combination of concerns that we have not examined. We grant the possibility, but judge it unlikely. Our results have been remarkably consistent, despite our having investigated concerns of both types, data from several different surveys, and numerous divisions of the population. Although we have not looked at all possible sets of concerns, we have examined several hundred sets, and not once have we encountered a marked deviation from the suggestion that a linear additive model is the right one.

On the global measure side, one might argue that all our results pertain to the Life 3 measure only. Would significantly different models be required by other global measures? The possibility is there, but again we judge it remote for other global measures that are of the same type as Life 3 (i.e., for general evaluations of one's own current well-being using an absolute perspective). Chapter 3 shows that all the measures of this type act very similarly, and we have no reason to suspect they would not do so in relation to the concern measures. For measures that are not of the same typological category as Life 3, we make no statements about what constitutes an appropriate model. Chapter 5 shows that combining concern measures in linear additive ways produces predictions of these other global measures that are, in general, much less accurate than the predictions of Life 3. Whether this is because the concern measures are inappropriate or the model is inappropriate remains unclear, though our present hunch attributes the lower prediction to inappropriateness of the concern measures.

It should also be noted that our results are based on a cross section of Anerican adults outside of institutions, most of whom are in reasonable physical and mental health, and—by worldwide standards—reasonably assured of being able to meet their basic physical needs. Whether the linear additive model would apply equally well in populations that are markedly less well off is an important question worthy of scientific investigation.

If linear additive models are appropriate for statistical prediction of Life 3, what does this imply about the underlying psychological processes by which people integrate their affective evaluations of specific life concerns?

As noted earlier, all our measures are assessments of mental states; and we have no reason to suspect that the optimal statistical model is not also our best indication of the underlying psychological process. Interpreted in this light, the linear additive model suggests that somehow individuals themselves "add up" their joys and sorrows about specific concerns to arrive at a feeling about general well-being. It appears that joys in one area of life may be able to compensate for sorrows in other areas; that multiple joys accumulate to raise the level of felt well-being; and that multiple sorrows also accumulate to lower it.

If true, these have some important policy implications. A few examples will illustrate them. The sense of well-being of an involuntarily unemployed person might be increased by providing a more satisfying community for him to live in, even if the employment problem could not be solved. The sense of well-being of an ill patient might be increased by helping him to have more satisfying relationships with people around him, even if the illness could not be cured. The sense of well-being of a person who cannot escape some degree of discrimination and persecution might be increased by ensuring more satisfying public services. Obviously, these are but a few of many possible examples involving the compensatory principle. The cumulative principle suggests that those who will feel most distressed will be people who experience sorrows in many normally distinct areas of life, without compensating joys in others. Public policies might be designed to identify such multiple-sorrow people and to take effective action to alleviate at least some of the sources of distress.

In discussing these findings with various colleagues and commentators, the question has sometimes been raised as to whether the model implies a policy of "give them bread and circuses." The model does suggest that bread and circuses are likely to increase a population's sense of general well-being. However, the model does *not* suggest that bread and circuses alone will ensure a high level of well-being. On the contrary, it is quite specific in noting that concerns that are evaluated more negatively than average (e.g., poor housing, poor government, poor health facilities, etc.) would be expected to pull down the general sense of well-being, and that multiple negative feelings about life would be expected to have a cumulative impact on general well-being.

Predicting Life 3 Using Different Sets of Concern Measures

We turn next to some of the most fundamental questions explored by our research. How well can we predict feelings about life-as-a-whole? What set of life concerns, taken jointly, provide the best prediction? How many life concerns need to be considered to achieve a good prediction? Answers to such questions have major implications for the design and use of social indicators assessing perceptions of well-being.

The design of our research provides many varied opportunities for exploring these issues, and also includes some potential hazards to the correct interpretation of the answers. The potentialities stem from the fact that different groups of respondents were asked for their feelings about different, but overlapping, subsets of concerns. Thus, we have opportunities for exploring how numerous different combinations of concerns relate to feelings about life-as-a-whole, and in some cases we can replicate the same combination in more than one set of data.

The major hazard is that the level with which feelings about life-as-a-whole can be explained varies somewhat from survey to survey, even when substantively similar concerns are used as predictors. Hints of this phenomenon were evident in Exhibit 4.1, and it appears even more obviously in the multivariate analyses reported hereafter. Although the fluctuations are not large, there is a general tendency for the May respondents to show levels of predictability that are low relative to others, the July group to be at the high end, and those surveyed in November and April to fall in the middle. As detailed in our discussion of Exhibit 4.1, the potential causes of these variations include sampling fluctuations, real changes over time, differences in the characteristics of the respondents being surveyed, differences in the data collection procedures, and/or differences in the composition of the concern measures.

Results from May Respondents. In the May data we have a substantial national sample of respondents who answered a wide range of concern items that were mostly of the domain type. Based on the structural explorations described in chapter 2, we identified thirty semidistinct life concerns that promised to provide a rather complete coverage of the full range of concerns put to the May respondents. In many cases respondents' feelings about these concerns could be measured by an index composed of several items that clustered together (as described in chap. 2 and app. C); in other cases only a single item was available as a measure of a given concern.

Exhibit 4.2 shows how these thirty concern measures, both the total set and various subsets, related to Life 3. First, we shall consider results when all thirty measures were used as predictors.

In Column A of Exhibit 4.2 one sees that when Life 3 was predicted via Multiple Classification Analysis (MCA) from all thirty concern measures, 55 percent of the variance in the Life 3 measure could be accounted for. More importantly, when this figure was adjusted to allow for expected shrinkage upon cross-validation, an estimated 50 percent of the variance in Life 3 for the total U.S. adult population could be explained.[20] (This is equivalent to a multiple correlation—adjusted for shrinkage—of .71.) This 50 percent figure is of some interest in its own right, indicating a level of explanatory power that is high relative to levels achieved in many other areas of social science, and showing that a rather substantial portion of the variance in feelings about life-as-a-whole can be related to feelings about specific life concerns. Nevertheless, this 50 percent figure will assume its full meaning only after we have compared

---

[20]"Shrinkage" is a well-known phenomenon, and is discussed in many treatments of multivariate prediction (e.g., Ezekiel and Fox, 1966, Andrews *et al.* 1973). It results from essentially random perturbations of a particular sample that would probably not be present in any other sample. Since Multiple Classification Analysis, the technique used in columns A–D of Exhibit 4.2, requires fewer assumptions about the data than does Multiple Regression (the technique used in column E), MCA results are somewhat more subject to shrinkage.

EXHIBIT 4.2. Prediction of Life 3 by Four Combinations of Concern Measures

		Predictors used				
		A 30 concerns	B 16 with high β's	C 6 with high β's	D Selected 12	E Selected 12
Percent variance explained						
In present data		55%	54%	49%	52%	51%
Population estimate		50%	51%	48%	50%	51%
Concern measures		MCA β	MCA β	MCA β	MCA β	MR β
C3	Efficacy index	.26	.27	.28	.25	.23
C6	Family index	.19	.18	.17	.19	.22
C20	Money index	.15	.15	.20	.16	.12
27	Amount of fun	.15	.16	.21	.15	.17
87	House/apartment	.12	.12	.13	.11	.10
6	Things do with family	.11	.09	.10	.08	.05
38	Time to do things	.09	.09	a	.07	.02
123	Young people think	.09	.08	a	a	a
30	Spare-time activities	.09	.08	a	.08	.06
C30	Recreation index	.07	.06	a	a	a
C34	National govt. index	.07	.08	a	.09	.07
C28	Consumer index	.07	.06	a	.06	.03
C32	Local govt. index	.07	.06	a	a	a
74	Housework	.07	.07	a	a	a
C36	Media index	.06	.05	a	a	a
7	Your health	.06	.06	a	.06	.07
C37	Cost index	.06	a	a	a	a
98	Schools in area	.06	a	a	a	a
92	Services in nghbrhd.	.06	a	a	a	a
5	Close adult relatives	.06	a	a	a	a
110	Natural environment	.05	a	a	a	a
62	Comfortable people	.05	a	a	a	a
C24	Neighborhood index	.04	a	a	a	a
122	People over 40 think	.04	a	a	a	a
72	Organizations belong to	.04	a	a	a	a
111	Weather	.04	a	a	a	a
C11	Friends index	.03	a	a	a	a
C23	Job index	.03	a	a	.02	.05
69	Religious faith	.03	a	a	a	a
63	Getting on with people	.01	a	a	a	a

Notes: Measure numbers refer to Exhibits 2.1 or C.1.
[a] Predictor omitted.
MCA = Multiple Classification Analysis.
MR = Multiple Regression.
Data source: 1,297 respondents to May national survey.

it to various other attempts to explain Life 3, evaluated it relative to the maximum that one might expect with these data, and considered its several components.

The thirty concern measures used to predict Life 3 are presented in Exhibit 4.2 in order according to their relative potency in its prediction; i.e., by the

Multiple Classification Analysis (MCA) beta coefficients shown in Column A.[21] The order is interesting. At the top of the list are concerns about self-efficacy, family, money, fun, housing, and the time available for doing what one wants. After our examination of Exhibit 4.1, these items do not seem surprising, though again one can note that some of these concerns are outside the realm of what some would consider as relevant matters for social indicators. Here in the multivariate context, as in the previous bivariate analysis, our data point to the importance of concerns that are close to self and family in accounting for feelings about general well-being.

A surprise comes at the bottom of the list, where we find feelings about job seeming to play a relatively small role. Given the large amount of time most employed people spend at their jobs, and the widespread belief that work roles are important to the people who fulfill them, one might have expected job concerns to show more relationship to Life 3, even after holding constant the effects of other predictors.[22]

Although the order of the concern measures is intriguing, one must remember that when using predictors that are not absolutely independent of one another (ours show modest overlaps), the order among them will depend partially on the particular ones that are included in the analysis. We know from experience with these data that minor changes in an analysis (in the respondents and/or in the predictors being analyzed) can produce rather substantial changes in the order. Furthermore, as noted in our preceding discussions of prediction models, we know that quite good predictions of Life 3 can be achieved even when all predictors are given the same weight; i.e., "tied" for the same position in the rank order. Thus, it seems more useful to focus on the *set* of predictors used in a particular analysis and the magnitude of their joint explanatory power, rather than on the order of their individual impacts.

Columns B, C, and D of Exhibit 4.2 explore the effects of using different subsets of the thirty concern measures to predict Life 3. After having found that the thirty concerns could explain about 50 percent of the variance in Life 3, we wondered whether all thirty were required to achieve this level, or whether some smaller set would suffice. Column B shows the results of using only the sixteen concerns that showed the highest betas in Column A.[23] The percentage

---

[21]The reader is cautioned not to confuse MCA betas with those from Multiple Regression (MR). The beta of MCA is useful as an indicator of the relative strength of association between a given predictor and the dependent variable when holding constant all other predictors, but does not itself enter into the prediction equation. In contrast, the MR beta indicates both strength of association (holding other predictors constant) and is a component of the prediction equation.

[22]We were sufficiently puzzled by the low position of the Job measure that we conducted a series of subanalyses to explore the matter. These are described in conjunction with our discussion of Exhibit 4.3.

[23]Using the highest beta coefficients to select a smaller set of predictors provides only a very rough approximation to a stepwise procedure, which would have been the ideal way to choose a maximally efficient subset. At the time the analyses in columns A through D of Exhibit 4.2 were run, it was not clear that linear multiple regression should be applied to these data, and the Multiple Classificiation Analysis procedure did not include an option for running the analysis stepwise. Subsequently, we found we could apply stepwise multiple regression to these data, with results that are discussed below.

of variance explained by these sixteen predictors was virtually identical to that explained by the whole set of thirty.[24] Clearly, the thirty contained some redundancies with respect to predictive usefulness and could be substantially reduced with no loss in predictive accuracy.

Having found that sixteen predictors could do the work of thirty, we wondered whether some still smaller number could do the work of the sixteen. Column C of Exhibit 4.2 reports the result of an experiment with the six predictors that had the highest betas in column B. This time we observed a small drop in the estimate of the variance that could be explained for the population (from 51 to 48 percent), and concluded that these six predictors could not do quite what the earlier set of sixteen had.

As a third step in our exploration of the predictive power of different sets of concern measures, we undertook to explain the variation in Life 3 using a dozen predictors, chosen partly on the basis of their having performed effectively in preceding analyses, and partly on the basis of what we regarded as their potential relevance for public policy. As shown in column D of Exhibit 4.2, we decided to include—in addition to the highest-beta concerns having to do with Self, Family, Money, Fun, Housing, and Available time—other concerns dealing with Job, Health, Consumer services, the National government, and Spare-time activities. Some of these had quite low betas, but seemed potentially important from a social indicators perspective. As shown in Exhibit 4.2, the Selected 12 predictors proved able to account for variance in Life 3 (as estimated for the population) to the same degree, 50 percent, as the full set of thirty had. Although these Selected 12 are probably not the only set of twelve that could attain this level of predictive power, we believe the Selected 12 are a particularly interesting set because of the several considerations that governed their selection.

The Selected 12 predictors were submitted to several additional analyses, one of which appears in column E of Exhibit 4.2. Here we use the same predictors as in column D, but try making the prediction using Multiple Regression rather than Multiple Classification Analysis. Multiple Regression is more restrictive with respect to the assumptions it makes about the data, but if these assumptions can be met, it is the more efficient technique. A comparison of the explanatory powers achieved by the two techniques showed essentially no differences. Here is powerful evidence supporting the essential linearity of the relationships, the lack of need for transformation of the Delighted–Terrible Scale, and the appropriateness of using Multiple Regression on these data.[25]

---

[24] Although the percentage of variance that could be explained in the present data dropped slightly (from 55 percent to 54 percent), the estimate of the explanatory power for the population as a whole actually increased slightly (from 50 percent to 51 percent). The increase occurred because the small decrease in explanatory power was more than offset by a more efficient predictive system.

[25] When applying Multiple Regression, one must determine how to handle "missing data" respondents; e.g., those who have no feelings about a job because they have no job. Classic approaches are either to omit such respondents from the entire analysis or to arbitrarily assign them the mean of the other respondents' scores on any variable for which their own scores are lacking. However,

EXHIBIT 4.3. Prediction of Life 3 by Optimal Combinations of the Selected 12 Concerns

Concern measures[a]	Number of meassures[b]	% variance explained[c]	Gain[d]	Loss if deleted[e]
C3 Self-efficacy index	1	30	30.3	3.3
C6 Family index	2	39	9.1	3.6
C20 Money index	3	45	5.2	0.9
27 Amount of fun	4	48	3.3	1.7
87 House/apartment	5	49	1.1	0.7
C34 Natl. govt. index	6	50	0.7	0.4
C23 Job index	7	50	0.4	0.2
7 Your health	8	50	0.3	0.3
30 Spare-time activities	9	51	0.3	0.2
6 Things do with family	10	51	0.2	0.2
C28 Consumer index	11	51	0.1	0.1
38 Time to do things	12	51	0.0	0.0

[a] Measure numbers refer to Exhibit 2.1 or C.1.
[b] The particular measures that constitute an optimal set of any given size are those listed on the same line as the number and above that line. For example, the set of 3 concerns that provide the best possible prediction of Life 3 are measures C3, C6, and C20.
[c] The percent variance explained in the present data and the population estimates are identical for the results in this exhibit.
[d] The Gain column shows the increase in the predictive power achieved by adding the indicated predictor to those listed above it.
[e] The Loss if deleted column shows the decrease in predictive power if the indicated predictor were removed from the full set of 12 predictors.
Data source: 1,297 respondents to May national survey.

Having seen the appropriateness of applying Multiple Regression to these data, it is of considerable interest to examine the results of entering the Selected 12 predictors in a formal Stepwise Regression. This can tell us, for any given number of predictors, which concerns should be combined for maximal predictive power, and it can determine the decrease in predictive power that would result if any one predictor were omitted from an otherwise optimal set. The results appear in Exhibit 4.3.

Exhibit 4.3 shows that an explanatory power of 50 percent—almost the maximum possible—could be achieved with just six concern measures: Self-efficacy, Family, Money, Fun, Housing, and National government. (This optimal set of six differs in only one respect from the set of six shown in column C of the previous exhibit: Feelings about the National government came in and

in the present case it seemed undesirable to omit respondents who had "missing data" on any one predictor from the entire analysis because this would greatly reduce the size of the data base, and it seemed unrealistic to assume that their feelings about a concern that was irrelevant for them should be imputed at the mean. Consequently, the Multiple Regression was conducted using a previously computed matrix of correlations from which missing data respondents had been deleted on a variable-by-variable basis. This preserves the size of the data base, but makes slightly ambiguous the precise sample to which the regression results refer. Nevertheless, since the Multiple Regression results proved virtually identical to those from Multiple Classification Analysis (in which missing data cases present no problem since they are simply included as another category of each predictor and assigned their own coefficient), we believe this solution was a reasonable one.

feelings about Things done with one's family went out. However, feelings about one's family continue to be represented: by the Family index, which remains in.) By adding the concerns about Job, Health, and Spare-time activities to the previous set of six, one can raise the explanatory power one more percentage point, but the addition of more concerns has virtually no effect.

One must be struck by the topical heterogeneity of the concerns that go to make up the optimal six, or optimal nine. If one refers to the structural map presented in Exhibits 2.4 or 2.7 and identifies the locations of these most-efficient six (or nine) concerns, one finds that they tap different portions of the space (though with greater concentration in the Self region) and range over the full length of that space.[26] Such heterogeneity, of course, seems eminently reasonable. It supports our expectation that feelings about life-as-a-whole would be influenced by widely divergent aspects of life, and hence, our belief that a comprehensive battery of social indicators should tap the whole spectrum of concerns.

The right-most column in Exhibit 4.3 shows the number of percentage points by which the explanatory power would drop if the indicated concern measure were removed from the full set of twelve and the prediction of Life 3 were made using the remaining eleven. What is important here is the finding that none of the predictors, when part of this set of twelve concerns, plays a critical role by itself. The most critical is the Family index, and even the removal of this concern would reduce the explanatory power by less than four percentage points (from 51 percent to about 47 percent). The removal of other predictors would produce smaller decreases, most of them very trivial indeed.[27]

Our surprise at the low beta shown by the Job measure when it was included among all thirty predictors (column A, Exhibit 4.2), and its relatively late entry into the Stepwise Regression and small contribution here also (Exhibit 4.3), stimulated a series of subanalyses focusing on this measure. We checked to see whether the job-relevant items had been answered by the appropriate people (in general, employed people answered them, and the

[26] As a further test of the hypothesis that heterogeneous concerns would more effectively predict Life 3 than homogeneous ones, we compared the predictive power of pairs of items close in perceptual space with pairs of items that were remote from one another. Four items were selected—1, 6, 103, and 108 (see Exhibits 2.1 or 2.4)—and the six possible regressions involving all combinations of two predictors were run. The average multiple correlation from regressions involving *close* pairs was .35, while the average multiple correlation involving *remote* pairs was .41. Although the difference was not large, it was in the expected direction and thus tends to support the hypothesis.

[27] In our discussion of the relationships between single concern measures and Life 3, we noted that certain concerns (those having to do with Fun and with Beauty, particularly) may have shown high relationships because they may have operated more like another global measure rather than tapping just a specific aspect of life. This raises the possibility that the relatively high levels of explanatory power shown in Exhibits 4.2 and 4.3 might have resulted from our inadvertently including a global measure (the Fun measure) among the predictors. The right-most column of Exhibit 4.3, however, shows that the predictive power is not dependent upon the Fun measure, and that its removal would produce only a small decline in the percentage of Life 3 variance that could be accounted for.

unemployed marked them as not applicable, as should have been the case); and we checked to see that our Job index was appropriately representing the relationships that were shown by its various component items (it was). Having eliminated these reasons as causes of the weak relationships, we explored the behavior of the Job index in various subgroups of the population.

Among *employed men* this concern proved to make a modest, but clearly discernible contribution to the explanation of feelings about life-as-a-whole. In this subgroup of the population, the Selected 12 concerns (which included the Job concern) explained 51 percent of the variance in Life 3—essentially identical to the explanatory power of this set in the total population, and when the Job index was removed from this set the explanatory power dropped to 48 percent.[28]

Furthermore, among this group the Job concern showed an MCA-beta of .22 (sufficient to put it in fourth place, behind Money, Health, and Fun), whereas—as shown in Exhibit 4.2, column D—in the total population it showed a beta of .02, the lowest beta of all. Although there were not enough employed women in our sample to support a parallel analysis for them, various other analyses (not shown) suggest that feelings about Job would show even less impact on feelings about life-as-a-whole for employed women than they had for employed men. Thus, these multivariate results, as well as the bivariate results presented previously in Exhibit 4.1, suggest that in present-day America feelings about one's job tend to have a rather mild impact on people's general sense of well-being. Even among employed men, various other concerns seem to have more impact on feelings about life-as-a-whole, and job concerns show only modest relationships.[29] (Among the November respondents, as is described below, the Job concern showed a somewhat greater impact on feelings about life-as-a-whole, but even there its impact was not great).

Taken together, then, Exhibits 4.2 and 4.3 suggest that of the original set of thirty concerns assessed in the May data, only a certain heterogeneous nine are really needed for maximal prediction of feelings about life-as-a-whole, and close-to-maximal levels can be obtained with just six. Even using as few as four or five can be almost as effective. If one uses a dozen predictors, there is sufficient overlap among them that the removal of any one does not produce a marked decrement in explanatory power. Of course, we do not propose that assessment of only these few particular concerns would in any way constitute an adequate monitoring effort from a social indicators perspective. Ability to account for differences in feelings about life-as-a-whole is certainly not the only requirement of a set of indicators. Nevertheless, we believe these analyses that show that about half the variance of the Life 3 measure can be explained by

[28]Both these figures are estimates for the *population* of employed men; the explanatory powers in the *present data* were 58 percent and 54 percent, respectively.

[29]This inference about what influences the qualify of life in America is in marked contrast to what is claimed to be the case for certain socialist countries, where the work role is said to be an extremely central one for the individual. It would be interesting to undertake a crosscultural replication to see if job concerns really do have more impact in other settings.

concerns measured in the May data, and that indicate how many and which concerns are needed to achieve this level of explanation, have considerable import for the eventual design of a battery of perceptual indicators.

The results of using different subsets of concerns to account for variation in feelings about life-as-a-whole shown in Exhibits 4.2 and 4.3 have focused on the predictive power of sets that were specifically selected to provide *good* explanations. What if one selected other sets? Is it the case that *any* set of substantively heterogeneous concerns would provide good predictions of Life 3? What about sets that were not heterogeneous?

A series of five multiple regression analyses that used various sets of nine single concern items as predictors of Life 3 explored these issues. The items for these sets were selected according to their locations in perceptual space (mapped in Exhibits 2.4 and 2.7). Items that were well distributed throughout the space were presumed to represent substantively heterogeneous sets, while those that were located compactly in one portion of the space were presumed to represent homogeneous sets. The results[30] led us to three conclusions:

1. Any set of nine concern items that are well scattered throughout the space seems likely to provide a moderately good prediction of feelings about life-as-a-whole. Specifically, it appears that heterogeneous sets of nine concern items will show a predictive power of at least two-thirds that shown by a set of nine items selected for maximum predictive efficiency via a stepwise multiple regression procedure.

2. In general, heterogeneous sets of concern items provide better predictions of feelings about life-as-a-whole than do homogeneous sets. In these analyses, three heterogeneous sets showed an average predictive power that was about 40 percent higher than the average shown by two homogeneous sets.

3. The predictive power of a homogeneous set depends in part on what (one) portion of the perceptual space it taps. In our analyses, a set of nine items drawn from the Local area region showed a predictive power that was only about half that shown by a set drawn from the Self region.

While all three findings have significant import for the design of batteries of well-being indicators, we believe the first finding has a special importance from a scientific point of view. It shows that our ability to predict feelings about general well-being is not dependent on using a particular set of items, but rather depends on having taps into various regions of a much more generally

---

[30]The five sets of nine concern items, together with a brief indication of the purpose for which the set was assembled and the percentage of variance in Life 3 that it explained, are as follows (item numbers refer to Exhibit 2.1): Set A (nine domains selected for maximal predictive efficiency from sixteen domains common to May and November data, 44 percent): items 2, 3, 6, 30, 75, 83, 85, 87, 103; Set B (nine domains matched in space to Set A but including none of the "best" items, 32 percent): items 5, 9, 57, 61, 77, 78, 89, 93, 108; Set C (nine domains with same configuration in space as Set A, but with configuration rotated, and including none of the "best" items, 29 percent): items 1, 7, 38, 59, 61, 72, 94, 100, 112; Set D (nine domains or criteria compactly located in Self and Family regions of the space, 43 percent): items 1, 5, 7, 9, 14, 20, 22, 27, 63; Set E: (nine domains or criteria compactly located in Local area region of the space, 17 percent): items 57, 58, 89, 90, 91, 94, 97, 99, 101. Note that Set D included certain criteria-type items, which may have enhanced its predictive power relative to Sets A and B, which were restricted to domain-type items only.

conceived perceptual space. It demonstrates that it is not the items themselves that are critically important, but the regions of the space, and that any of numerous possible combinations of items that effectively tap a heterogeneous set of regions can provide the desired accounting for differences in feelings about life-as-a-whole.

Results from November Respondents. In determining the concern-level questions that would be administered to the November (Form 2) respondents, we sought to extend the range of topics beyond that which had been used for the May respondents, and to include enough overlap between the two sets of questions to permit some attempts at replicating the May results. We wondered, of course, whether expanding the range of concerns would enable us to predict still more of the variance of Life 3 than had been the case in the May data, and whether the May results would reappear in a separate but comparable national sample.

It turned out that the proportion of variance in Life 3 that could be explained in the November data was, in fact, higher than in the May data (the population estimates of the percentage of variance accounted for rose from 50 percent in the May data to 61 percent in the November data). This increase, however, could not be attributed to using a wider range of concern measures as predictors. This latter conclusion was clearly indicated when we replicated, using the November data, the analysis involving the Selected 12 concerns (presented in Exhibit 4.2, column D). In the May data the Selected 12 predictors had accounted for 50 percent of the variance in Life 3; in the November data these same twelve concerns accounted for 60 percent of the variance! Thus, relationships in *general* seemed somewhat higher in the November data.[31]

Despite this general upward shift in the strength of the relationships, the pattern of findings from the November respondents nicely replicated those obtained in the May data. Once again, the Selected 12 concerns proved to have virtually all the explanatory power possessed by a much larger set of concerns, and once again concerns having to do with Self, Family, Money, Housing, and Fun were the ones that showed large impacts on feelings about life-as-a-whole.

Exhibit 4.4 presents the statistical results on which these conclusions are based. Several details presented in the exhibit are worth separate comment.

The concerns that had the highest MCA-betas in the November data show remarkable overlap with those that had the highest MCA-betas among the May respondents (column C, Exhibit 4.2). Note that five of the top six are *identical.* The item, How do you feel about the things you and your family do together?, dropped slightly in relative position (and out of the top six) and was replaced by an item new in the November data, How do you feel about your chance to enjoy pleasant or beautiful things? This new item was intended to tap the criterion, Beauty, but upon seeing its first-place rank among these concerns, we wondered whether the inclusion of the word "pleasant" might have made the

---

[31] We suspect that the November measures may have about the same proportion of valid variance as the May measures, but may include somewhat larger portions of common methods variance. (Chapter 6 presents some of the explorations that suggest this.) This would account for the tendency for relationships to be a bit higher in the November data than for the May respondents.

EXHIBIT 4.4. Prediction of Life 3 by Two Combinations of
Concern Measures

		Predictors used	
		28 concerns	Selected 12
Percent variance explained			
In present data		67%	62%
Population estimate		61%	60%
Concern measures		MCAβ	MCA β
25	Pleasant/beautiful things	.16	[a]
27	Amount of fun	.15	.23
87	House/Apartment	.13	.11
4	Family life	.12	.19
C20	Money index	.12	.19
21	Yourself	.12	.17
65	Reliability of others	.10	[a]
75	Your job	.09	.10
7	Your health	.09	.09
38	Time to do things	.08	.10
6	Things do with family	.08	.09
42	Sleep	.08	[a]
26	Sex life	.07	[a]
45	Privacy	.07	[a]
12	Chance get good job	.07	[a]
55	Admired by others	.07	[a]
30	Spare-time activities	.06	.07
60	Your friends	.06	[a]
114	Recreational places	.06	[a]
41	Relaxation	.06	[a]
82	Agreement on spending	.06	[a]
C33	National govt. index	.05	.07
101	Goods and services	.05	.06
96	Secure from theft	.05	[a]
121	Society's standards	.05	[a]
56	Respect for rights	.04	[a]
11	Opportunity make changes	.04	[a]
36	Creativity	.02	[a]

Notes: Measure numbers refer to Exhibits 2.1 or C.1.
[a]Predictor omitted.
MCA = Multiple Classification Analysis.
Data Source: 1,072 respondents to November national survey (Form 2).

concern less specific (i.e., more like the global measure Life 3) than intended. (A subsequent alteration of the item to refer to Beauty and attractiveness reduced its relationship to Life 3; see Exhibit 4.1.) In Exhibit 4.4 it is also interesting to note that the Job concern, which had surprised us because of its low relationship to Life 3 in the May data, now showed a beta that ranked it in the upper-middle portion of the range.

Using the November data we also explored the effects of deleting certain predictors from the Selected 12. Our interest in this matter runs parallel to our interest in the results presented previously in the right-most column of Exhibit

4.3; i.e., how critical are various concerns for predicting Life 3 when included among the others of the Selected 12? Once again, a result emerged from the November data that was highly consistent with that discussed previously for the May respondents. None of the predictors among the Selected 12 played an especially critical role, and any one could be removed from the set without dropping the predictive power of the remaining eleven more than a few percentage points. (Data not shown.)

Finally, we undertook a formal crossvalidation of the earlier results from the May data. For each respondent in the November data, we attempted to predict his score on the Life 3 measure by entering his feelings about the Selected 12 concerns into the prediction equation derived from our previous analysis of data from the *May* respondents (shown in Exhibit 4.2, column D). Correlations between the actual and predicted scores were reasonably high. When all respondents were grouped together, the correlation was .75. Thus, we had predicted 56 percent of the variance in Life 3 scores of the November respondents by applying the model developed for the May respondents. This 56 percent is a predictive accuracy only slightly below the 60 percent which could be predicted using coefficients derived from the November data itself, and is actually slightly *higher* than that achieved in the May data. We also checked a few subgroups of the sample to see whether the predictive accuracy would show marked variations and found that it did not. Among 106 blacks the correlation was .76 (58 percent); among 759 women it was also .76 (58 percent); and among 752 men it was .73 (53 percent). Although these results did not surprise us, given what we knew about the relative nonimportance of the weights used in these prediction equations (discussed previously in our section on models), here was a formal demonstration that the results from one survey could be nicely crossvalidated in an independent national sample and, furthermore, that the ability to crossvalidate held for certain major segments of the sample as well as for the sample as a whole.[32]

All in all, then, the results from the November data showed many general similarities to those obtained previously. They strongly suggested that the patterns of the earlier results were not idiosyncratic to a single survey but could be satisfactorily replicated in an independent but comparable sample. At the same time, however, results from the November respondents alerted us to certain types of instabilities that seemed to occur in data about perceptions of well-being. We found that the general level of predictive power could vary somewhat from survey to survey, and that the impact—in both absolute and relative terms—of particular concerns could also show modest variations.

Perhaps the biggest disappointment to us, at the time the results reported in this section emerged in our work, was the conclusion that despite our inclusion of concerns that we felt considerably broadened the range of topics beyond those investigated in the May survey, we had failed to account for any more of the variance in Life 3 than could be predicted equally well by the Selected 12 concerns. The reasons for this apparent failure were suggested to us

---

[32]A later section of this chapter focuses directly on subgroups of the population.

only much later in our work, after we had analyzed data from the July respondents. We suspect there are two separate reasons.

1. Even though we had included among the November concerns a substantial number of criterion-type measures (in contrast to the almost exclusive focus
on domain-type concerns investigated in May), the actual heterogeneity of the
concerns may have been increased little if at all. Our mapping of domains and
criteria in the July data, the only data set in which extensive numbers of both
were present, suggests that the criteria fit in among the domains rather than
"pushing out" into new regions of the perceptual space. (See Exhibit 2.2.) Thus,
although the apparent content of the criteria items that were used for the first
time in the November survey seemed quite different from that of the domain
items, their actual meaning—in terms of how people reacted to them—was
sometimes not as different as one might have expected. An example will
illustrate the point: The May interview included the item, How do you feel
about the people you see socially?, which was intended to tap a suspected
domain of friends and social acquaintances; in November, there appeared a
criterion-type item, How do you feel about how much you are admired or
respected by other people?; when we constructed perceptual maps using the
July data, which included both these concerns, we observed that they fell rather
close together in the perceptual space (as can be seen in Exhibit 2.2).

2. Even if we had succeeded in finding concerns that lay on the perimeters
of the perceptual space, it is, however, extremely doubtful that they could have
further increased the percentage of variance in the Life 3 measure that could be
accounted for. As discussed in chapter 6, our estimates of the validity with
which we have measured feelings about specific concerns are such that it seems
that essentially all the variance that is potentially explainable has already been
accounted for. In short (although we had only a vague suspicion of it at the
time), it now appears that even the Selected 12 concerns have an explanatory
power that is, after adjustment for the effects of imperfect indication of people's
true feelings, close to the theoretical maximum of 100 percent. Thus, although
there may be other advantages from inquiring about additional specific life
concerns, it now seems unrealistic to expect that additional concerns will add to
our ability to predict feelings about life-as-a-whole.

Results from April Respondents. The concern items included in the April
interview were created to let us explore how feelings about a wide range of
criterion-type concerns would contribute to a person's general sense of well-
being. Twenty-three items were ultimately included, all being of the criterion
type (assuming one classifies the item, How do you feel about yourself?, as
tapping a criterion), and most in use for the first time. The major issue from the
standpoint of prediction was how well one's general sense of well-being could
be accounted for on the basis of feelings about criteria. Our Matrix Model
(described in chap. 1) clearly suggests that one should be able to understand
and predict feelings about life-as-a-whole on the basis of a person's feelings
about either domains or criteria, but at the time we designed the quality-of-life
section of the April interview instrument, we knew of no statistical evidence to
support this expectation.

EXHIBIT 4.5. Prediction of Life 3 by Optimal Combinations of Twenty-Three Criterion-Type Concerns

Concern measures[a]	Number of measures[b]	% variance explained[c]	Gain[d]	Loss if deleted[e]
28 Fun and enjoyment	1	37	36.5	2.0
8 Physical needs met	2	48	11.3	2.3
22 Yourself	3	53	5.5	1.4
54 How fairly treated	4	57	3.4	1.5
33 Develop, broaden self	5	58	1.7	0.3
23 Interesting daily life	6	59	1.0	0.7
16 Adjust to changes	7	60	0.8	0.4
81 Financial security	8	61	0.7	0.7
68 Contribute to others	9	61	0.3	0.2
70 Religious fulfillment	10	61	0.2	0.2
64 Acceptance by others	11	62	0.2	0.2
43 Freedom from bother	12	62	0.2	0.2
48 Own sincerity, honesty	13	62	0.1	f
73 Neat, tidy, clean	14	62	0.1	f
29 Physical work, exercise	15	62	0.1	f
49 Others' sincerity, honesty	16	62	0.0	f
18 Success, get ahead	17	62	0.1	f
39 Amount of pressure	18	62	0.1	f
24 Beauty, attractiveness	19	62	0.0	f
44 Independence, freedom	20	62	0.0	f
13 Be tough, can take it	21	62	0.0	f
95 Your safety	22	62	0.0	f
53 Respect from others	23	62	0.0	f

[a] Measure numbers refer to Exhibit 2.1.
[b] The particular measures that constitute an optimal set of any given size are those listed on the same line as the number and above that line. For example, the set of 3 concerns that provide the best possible prediction of Life 3 are measures 28, 8, and 22.
[c] The percent variance explained in the present data and the population estimates are identical for the results in this exhibit except for the last three lines where the population estimates would, in each case, be 61%.
[d] The Gain column shows the increase in the predictive power achieved by adding the indicated predictor to those listed above it.
[e] The Loss if deleted column shows the decrease in predictive power if the indicated predictor were removed from a set consisting of the first 12 predictors.
[f] This predictor not among the first 12; see note e.
Data source: 1,433 respondents to April national survey.

Exhibit 4.5 shows that, indeed, a rather substantial portion of the variance in Life 3 could be predicted on the basis of people's feelings about criteria. The twenty-three criterion-type concerns taken together accounted for 62 percent of the variance in Life 3 among the April respondents.[33] Interestingly, this level of explanatory power is very similar to that achieved in the November data, and as

[33]Exhibit 4.5 shows results from an analysis of the April data using stepwise multiple regression, and is thus parallel to Exhibit 4.3 for the May data. As noted previously, the April data were also subjected to a series of analyses using Multiple Classification Analysis (similar to those applied to the May data and reported in Exhibit 4.2). The percentage of variance explained by the Multiple Classification Analysis was essentially identical to that explained using Multiple Regression when the same number of concern measures were entered, thereby once again demonstrating the basic linearity of these relationships.

will be discussed later, seems close to the theoretical maximum of 100 percent after allowing for the estimated reliability of the measures. Clearly, the expectations generated by the Matrix Model were supported.

Exhibit 4.5 also shows that the 62 percent level of predictive power can be achieved by using substantially fewer than twenty-three concerns. Only eleven are needed to achieve the 62 percent level, and a mere half-dozen can do almost as well.

According to these results the criterion measures that, taken jointly, produce the best accounting of one's general sense of well-being are those that tap four types of feelings: (1) the character of one's daily life—how much fun, enjoyment, and interest it has; (2) the extent to which one's physical needs are met, and the related matter of financial security; (3) the nature of oneself, including the extent to which one is developing and broadening oneself, and how one adapts to changes; and (4) how one is treated by other people. The first four concerns listed in Exhibit 4.5 each tap one of these areas, and the second four essentially add a second tap on each of the four areas. With even one measure of each of the four areas, one can explain most of what can ultimately be explained (57 percent of the variance, out of a maximum of 62 percent), and after the second tap is added to each, the explanatory power is essentially at the maximum.

It is interesting to note that these four types of criteria show a neat spatial relationship to one another, and a clear distinction from other criteria, as these were located on the perceptual map discussed in chapter 2 and shown in Exhibit 2.6. The criteria that make up the most efficient sets of predictors of Life 3 all come from the central "sun" portion of the structure. Together, they span the full extent of the "sun." Only when one gets to the tenth-listed criterion, Religious fulfillment, does one encounter the first "satellite" predictor, and by the time one encounters even this first satellite, essentially all the variance in Life 3 that can be explained has already been accounted for. Clearly, the satellite criteria, which won their locations, and hence their name, because of their generally low relationships to other criteria, contribute virtually nothing to our ability to predict Life 3.[34]

The final aspect of interest in Exhibit 4.5 is the information provided in the right-most column. Here we examine the uniqueness of predictive contribution made by each of the first twelve predictors when included with the other eleven. The small numbers in the column show that, given these twelve predictors, no single one is critically important. There is sufficient overlap within the set that any one could be deleted and our ability to predict Life 3 would be hardly affected.

As in our analysis of the May data, discussed previously, we wished to see

[34]Several attempts to predict Life 3 using sets of predictors that included cluster scores (clusters C5, C16, C17, and C21, as shown in appendix C and Exhibit 2.8) resulted in predictive powers somewhat below the 62 percent maximum level shown in Exhibit 4.5. The reason seems to lie not in any deficiency of the cluster scores themselves, but in our not having appreciated the importance of a full tapping of the various areas of the "sun" region, and our (incorrect) initial expectation that the peripheral (i.e., "satellite") criteria would prove useful as predictors.

how much our ability to predict Life 3 was dependent on our using a particular set of "good" predictors, and to what extent Life 3 could be predicted using a less-than-best set of criterion-type concerns. Starting from the results presented in Exhibit 4.5, which show those predictors that constitute an optimal set of six, and that the optimal set has an explanatory power close to the maximum, we chose an *alternative* set of six predictors. This alternative set included none of the optimal predictors, but six others that were "space-matched" to the optimal ones. Thus, for each optimal predictor, we picked another concern item that was close to it in the perceptual space (as mapped in Exhibit 2.6).[35]

The prediction of Life 3 using this alternative set of predictors nicely replicated results from the similar analysis applied to the May data. The alternative set showed a predictive power that, while not as high as the optimal set, was still substantial. The alternative set explained 46 percent of the variance in Life 3 (multiple correlation = .68). The 46 percent figure is about three-quarters of the 59 percent explained by the optimal set of six predictors, a result comfortably within the "at least two-thirds" range suggested by the May results. Thus, once again we find that the ability to predict feelings about general well-being is not critically dependent upon a particular set of concern items, but can be achieved with somewhat similar levels of predictive power using other items selected from the same regions of the perceptual structure.

Results from July Respondents. In the July data the number of cases is much smaller (222) than in the national-level surveys, and the number of different concerns that were measured is much larger. Hence, it was not feasible to search among all concerns for sets that would provide optimal predictions of Life 3. Nevertheless, it was possible to take sets of predictors selected on some prior basis and to see how well they could predict Life 3.

In one series of analyses, four sets of concern measures, selected because of their optimal performance in a national survey, or because they were space-matched to an optimal set, were applied again, using the July data.[36] Because we knew the explanatory power shown by each set when applied to national data, we could see whether the set worked better, the same, or worse, in the July data. The results were consistent in showing that the level of predictive power achieved in the July data was *higher* than what had been observed when the same predictors were applied in the national data (the differences were not

---

[35]The alternative six consisted of the following items (item numbers match Exhibit 2.1): 18, 39, 44, 53, 64, and 68.

[36]These four sets of concern items have all been discussed previously in this chapter. They are: (1) nine optimal domains from the May data, Set A as described in a previous footnote; (2) nine space-matched domains in the May data, Set B; (3) six optimal criteria from the April data, shown in Exhibit 4.5; and (4) six space-matched criteria from the April data, the alternative set detailed in our discussion of the April results. When applied in the *July* data to predict Life 3, these sets explained, respectively, the following percentages of variance: 57 percent, 33 percent, 63 percent, and 57 percent. Note that although the same predictors were used to achieve the prediction, new regression equations were calculated. Thus, each comparison is made between the predictive powers of two regresion equations, each derived from the data to which they are applied. Thus, it is the effectiveness of the *predictors* that is being crossvalidated, not the effectiveness of a particular prediction *equation.*

large; they averaged seven percentage points). Of course, these gains in predictive power reflect, in part, the somewhat higher general level of relationships
that we know characterizes the July data and that are discussed earlier in this
chapter. More importantly, however, they provide one more indication of the
substantial extent to which results relevant to the prediction of general well-
being obtained in one survey can be obtained again in an independent set of
data.

One other predictive analysis was undertaken using the July data, this time
applying a set of nine cluster scores that had been derived to tap certain broad
areas of conceptual interest.[37] These nine broadly based clusters accounted for
62 percent of the variance in Life 3 (population estimate: 61 percent), a level that
is, again, wholly consistent with the levels of explanatory power reached in
other data sets when a wide range of concerns were included among the
predictors.

Using Classification Variables to Predict Life 3

The preceding section has shown that feelings about general well-being, as
assessed by the Life 3 measure, can be predicted moderately well from people's
feelings about various combinations of specific life concerns. Another obvious
set of predictors consists of people's demographic or social characteristics: their
age, sex, race, and the like. In considering the need for, or the impacts of, public
policies that affect well-being, decision-makers frequently think of the population in such demographic terms. Furthermore, these classification variables are
frequently the main focus of much sociological analysis. An important question, then, is: How well can demographic variables account for differences in
perceived well-being?

The answer is clear, and perhaps surprising: Poorly.

Results from May Respondents. Results from analyses of the May national
data are shown in Exhibit 4.6. Six classification variables were used to predict
Life 3. These included Sex, Race, Age, Education, Family income, and Family
life-cycle stage.[38] As can be seen in column A, these six variables could account
for only 8 percent of the variance in feelings about general well-being in the
present data, and an estimated 5 percent for the population as a whole.[39]

---

[37]These were clusters C40 through C48 as listed in appendix C and described in chapter 2.

[38]Respondents were grouped into eight age categories: 15–19 years, 20–24, 25–29, 30–34, 35–44, 45–
54, 55–64, 65+. The education groups were: 0–5 grades, 6–8, 9–11, 9–11 plus formal noncollege
training, 12, 12 plus formal noncollege training, some college, BA, more than BA. The family
income groups were: under $4,000 per year, $4,000–5,999, $6,000–7,499, $7,500–9,999, $10,000–
12,499, $12,500–14,999, $15,000–24,999, $25,000+. Family life-cycle stage was determined on the
basis of the respondent's own age and marital status, and the age of the youngest child living in
the family (see chap. 9 for a description of the categories used).

[39]The use of Multiple Classification Analysis, rather than Multiple Regression, was important in
these analyses since some of the classification variables are of a categorical nature (e.g., Family
life-cycle stage, Race) and an assumption of linear relations existing between Life 3 and the other
predictors seemed unwarranted. Of course, Multiple Classification Analysis assumes that the
effects of each predictor simply add on to effects of other predictors, and various tests of this
assumption suggest it to be reasonable (as is described later in the chapter).

EXHIBIT 4.6. Prediction of Life 3 by Six Classification Variables and the Selected 12 Concerns

	Predictors used			
	A	B	C	D
	6 clas. vars.	Sel. 12 concerns	6 clas. + 12 concerns	
Percent variance explained				
In present data	8%	52%	53%	
Population estimate	5%	50%	50%	
Predictors				Bivariate
Classification variables	MCA β	MCA β	MCA β	η
Family life-cycle stage	.19	a	.13	.20
Age	.12	a	.08	.20
Family income	.16	a	.05	.18
Education	.06	a	.03	.07
Race	.03	a	.03	.03
Sex	.01	a	.02	.04
Concern measures				
C3 Efficacy index	a	.25	.25	.55
C6 Family index	a	.19	.15	.38
C20 Money index	a	.15	.15	.47
27 Amount of fun	a	.16	.15	.51
87 House/apartment	a	.11	.12	.36
30 Spare-time activities	a	.08	.09	.41
C34 National govt. index	a	.09	.09	.26
6 Things do with family	a	.08	.08	.38
C28 Consumer index	a	.06	.07	.31
38 Time to do things	a	.07	.07	.28
7 Your health	a	.06	.05	.29
C23 Job index	a	.02	.03	.23

Notes: Measure numbers refer to Exhibits 2.1 or C.1.
  MCA = Multiple Classification Analysis.
a Predictor omitted.
Data source: 1,297 respondents to May national survey.

Compared to the 50 percent explanatory power of the Selected 12 concerns (discussed previously in connection with Exhibit 4.2, and repeated in Column B of Exhibit 4.6), the 5 percent figure seems meager indeed.

The Exhibit indicates that Family life-cycle stage, Age, and Family income showed somewhat stronger relationships to Life 3 than Education, Race, or Sex. As is discussed in greater detail in chapter 10, respondents in the "married" categories of the life-cycle variable, younger people, those with more income and education, and whites tended to give above-average evaluations to life-as-a-whole (see Exhibit 10.12).

Special comment needs to be made about the Race variable, whose weak relationship to Life 3 in both the multivariate and bivariate analyses (columns A and D, respectively) may be surprising to some. The weakness of the relationship is attributable to two things: (1) the difference between blacks and whites in their feelings about life-as-a-whole was only modest; and (2) because only a relatively small proportion of the total population is other than white, Race, as a variable, does not pull the sample apart very much and hence has limited chance to explain variation that is distributed across the whole sample.

Although there are some modest (and very interesting) differences between the various "demographically" defined subgroups in the American population, the important finding at the moment is that the six classification variables examined in Exhibit 4.6 showed only *weak* relationships to feelings about life-as-a-whole. Furthermore, by comparing columns B and C of Exhibit 4.6, one can see that these classification variables accounted for *none* of the variance in Life 3 that could not be alternatively, and more effectively, accounted for by the concern measures. Note that the Selected 12 concern measures explained 50 percent of the Life 3 variance, and that adding the six classification variables to the set of predictors resulted in no increase whatsoever in the population estimate for the variance explained.

This result was so surprising it needed to be replicated with an independent set of data. We undertook such a replication using our April respondents, and will describe that next.

Results from April Respondents. A series of analyses parallel to those just described, but using the data from the April respondents and a different set of concern measures, is shown is Exhibit 4.7.

In columns A and D we find that the same six classification variables that were used previously can again explain only a very modest portion of the variation in Life 3. No one variable by itself explains as much as 6 percent, and jointly they account for only about 9 percent. Although the relative impacts of these variables are not precisely the same as in the May data, Family life-cycle stage and Family income again rank near the top, while Sex and Race rank near the bottom.[40]

Column B repeats a portion of the results from Exhibit 4.5, which showed that an optimal set of eight criterion-type concerns can explain virtually all the variation in Life 3 (61 percent) that is potentially explainable by the full set of twenty-three concerns. By comparing the figures for percentage-of-variance-explained shown in column C, which uses both the optimal eight concerns and the six classification variables, with those in column B, one sees that, again, the classification variables made no marginal contribution to the prediction of Life 3. (The population estimate actually declined fractionally, because the prediction equation employed more coefficients and thus became less efficient.)

It is clear then that the following findings are replicable: (1) classification variables predict variation in the Life 3 measure only poorly; and (2) classification variables make no net contribution to what can be predicted much better by the concern measures.

Lack of Statistical Interactions. The weak explanatory power shown by the classification variables led us to wonder whether we had inadvertently missed part of their impact because we had used an analysis technique that assumed that the effect of one classification variable would simply add on to the effects of

[40]Exhibit 10.12 presents a related analysis.

EXHIBIT 4.7. Prediction of Life 3 by Six Classification Variables and Eight Criterion-
Type Concerns

	Predictors used			
	A 6 clas. vars.	B 8 criteria	C 6 clas. + 8 criteria	D
Percent variance explained				
In present data	11%	61%	62%	
Population estimate	9%	61%	60%	
Predictors	MCA	MR	MCA	Bivariate
Classification variables	β	β	β	η
Family life-cycle stage	.23	a	.12	.24
Age	.14	a	.05	.09
Family income	.15	a	.06	.21
Education	.06	a	.06	.14
Race	.08	a	.02	.13
Sex	.07	a	.03	.03
Concern measures				
28 Fun and enjoyment	a	.19	.19	.60
8 Physical needs met	a	.19	.19	.56
22 Yourself	a	.17	.18	.54
54 How fairly treated	a	.16	.17	.51
33 Develop, broaden self	a	.08	.10	.47
23 Interesting daily life	a	.12	.13	.54
16 Adjust to changes	a	.10	.10	.44
81 Financial security	a	.10	.11	.49

Notes: Measure numbers refer to Exhibit 2.1.
MCA = Multiple Classification Analysis.
MR = Multiple Regression.
a Predictor omitted.
Data source: 1,433 respondents to April national survey.

others. To explore this matter, we undertook another analysis using the same
six classification variables and a technique that did not make this additive
assumption, the AID technique (Sonquist, Baker, and Morgan, 1973). Results
from this more flexible technique showed the classification variables to have a
predictive power that was essentially identical to that shown in Exhibit 4.6, and
hence indicated that the low level of explanation could not be attributed to our
having applied an inappropriate statistical model. In a further search for reasons why the relationships were so low, we tried using a wider range of
classification variables as predictors. To the six already mentioned, ten more
were added: degree of urbanization, employment status, relationship to the
head of the household, occupation, marital status, time married, political party
preference, religious preference, socioeconomic status of household head, and
type of structure in which the respondent lived. The previous analysis using the
nonrestrictive AID procedure was repeated, now using sixteen classification
variables, and the same result emerged: Weak explanatory power (9 percent of
the variance in Life 3 could be predicted using sixteen classification variables).

The conclusion seems inescapable that there is no strong and direct relationship between membership in these social subgroups and feelings about life-as-a-whole. (Nor, as four other analyses showed, was there a strong relationship between them and feelings about any of the following very distinct life concerns: House, National government, Self-efficacy, Money.[41])

Evaluation of Predictive Levels Achieved

We have described how people's feelings about various life concerns can be used to predict their general sense of well-being and shown that 50–62 percent of the variation in people's scores on the Life 3 measure can be explained in this way. The question to be addressed here is, How good is that 50–62 percent explanatory level?

Since the logical maximum of a percentage figure is 100 percent, one might at first be tempted to believe that our 50–62 percent explanatory powers are just slightly more than half of what might be achieved. However, while 100 percent may stand as an ideal, this is an unrealistic and impractical ideal. When using measures with any component of random error, one cannot hope to explain 100 percent of the variance, and virtually all social science measures, including ours, do have a random component. Thus, it is important to know not what the logical maximum explanatory level is, but rather what the theoretical maximum is, when using measures of a certain quality. While we do not contest the desirability of developing better measures, and hence increasing the potential for accurate predictions, this is essentially a *measurement* problem, and needs to be carefully distinguished from the *prediction* problem, which tries to achieve the best possible prediction with a given set of measures.[42]

For the present discussion it will be useful to distinguish three factors that may influence people's scores on the measures we have analyzed. The first is people's true feelings. Ideally, we would like this to be the *only* factor that would influence the scores, but we know it is not. The degree to which the scores actually reflect people's true feelings is the validity of the measure. The variation among people's scores that reflects actual differences in their true feelings is the *valid component* of the total variation.

The second factor affecting people's scores is a methods factor. Some people will use a particular scale (in the present case, our Delighted–Terrible Scale) in ways that are systematically different from other people, and hence

---

[41]All four analyses used the same core of seven predicting variables, supplemented in two analyses by an additional (eighth) predictor. The core predictors were Marital status, Sex, Race, Age, Family income, Family life-cycle stage, and Degree of urbanization. In predicting feelings about House, Type of structure was added as an additional predictor; in predicting feelings about the National government, Political party preference was added. All analyses were made using the AID technique. Explanatory powers were as follows: House, 9 percent, National government, 6 percent, Self-efficacy, 2 percent, Money, 14 percent.

[42]These issues have long been recognized by social science methodologists. Bohrnstedt and Carter (1971) have recently stressed the need for researchers to be sensitive to the influence measurement errors have on the results obtained, and procedures for adjusting results for "attenuation" due to random measurement error have been developed by statisticians (e.g., McNemar, 1969).

people may appear to be more (or less) different from one another than is really the case. One would hope to use methods that have minimal impact of their own (the Delighted–Terrible Scale is reasonably good compared to other methods we have tried, as is described in chapter 6), but it is rare that the *method component* is absolutely zero.

The third factor is a mixture of all the "random" influences that affect answers to different questions in different ways. Momentary shifts in mood, lapses of memory, misunderstandings, and numerous other possible errors produce the *random error component* of a score, which—like the methods component—one tries to keep as low as possible.

The methods and random error components both represent "errors," but they have very different effects. When the variables used to make a prediction are based on the same methods as is the dependent variable, the methods components are shared, and hence appear to contribute to the prediction. In contrast, the random error components, because they are (by definition) not shared, must detract from the prediction.

Chapter 6 describes various explorations that provide estimates of the proportion of variance attributable to these valid, methods, and error components for some of the variables used in this chapter. Because the methods for deriving such estimates for the kinds of data used here are only presently being developed, the estimates are probably not precisely correct. They probably are, however, approximately right, and evaluating our predictive level in the light of these estimates produces some very interesting results.

May Data. Chapter 6 (Exhibit 6.4) suggests that answers to a typical item from the May survey may have a validity coefficient of about .70, and a methods coefficient of about .34 (i.e., variables based on single items would contain 49 percent valid variance, 12 percent methods variance, and 39 percent random error variance). Much of the analysis of May data reported in the present chapter, however, used not answers to single items but scales based on multiple items. Life 3, for example, is a scale based on two items. Such scales have lower proportions of random error variance, and higher proportions of other variance, than the single items on which they are based. Thus, the measures we actually used to make predictions can be estimated to have validity coefficients of roughly .77 and methods coefficients of about .35 (i.e., to contain about 60 percent valid variance, 13 percent methods variance, and 27 percent random error variance).[43] Since the valid and methods components both appear as "reliable" variance, the reliability of such multi-item measures can be estimated at .73.

With this reliability figure in hand, one can compute the maximum percentage of variance in feelings about life-as-a-whole that could theoretically be predicted using measures from the May data. The result of applying a formula presented by Cochran (1970) is 53 percent. The explanatory levels for the May

---

[43]These estimates for multi-item scales, and similar estimates discussed later in this section of the chapter, were derived using Formula 14.37 in Guilford, 1954. The formula requires an estimate of the reliability of the item, which can be deduced to be .61 for a single item in the May data, given our estimates for validity and methods variance.

data (presented in Exhibit 4.2) are all remarkably close to this theoretical maximum and suggest that essentially 100 percent of what is theoretically predictable using these measures has been predicted.

July Data. Chapter 6 also describes an analysis of the July data that estimates validity and methods coefficients for answers to single items (shown in Exhibit 6.3). For items employing the Delighted–Terrible Scale (on which analyses of the present chapter are based), validity coefficients were estimated at about .82, and methods coefficients at about .27 (i.e., variables based on single items would contain 67 percent valid variance, 7 percent methods variance, and 26 percent random error variance, and would have a reliability of .74). Again, we must allow for the fact that Life 3 is a two-item measure, for which a reliability of .85 can be derived (based on estimates of its containing 77 percent valid variance, 8 percent methods variance, and 15 percent error variance). If we again apply the Cochran formula, we find that the maximum percent of variance in Life 3 that could be explained by a set of predictors based on single items is 63 percent. This figure is again remarkably consistent with the maximum explanatory powers actually observed in the July data. Once again, it suggests that some of our analyses have come very close to explaining virtually all of the variance in Life 3 that is potentially explainable with these measures.

November and April Data. We have not conducted the same detailed analyses designed to estimate measurement parameters on the data from the November and April respondents. Hence, we cannot duplicate the computations of theoretically maximal explanatory power just described. It is notable, however, that the explanatory levels achieved in the November and April data (about 60 percent) fall within the rather narrow range of what has been found to be maximal levels for May and July data (53 percent and 63 percent, respectively). Since we have repeatedly seen excellent replications of results from one data set to another, the inference is rather strong that for these respondents, also, close to maximal levels of explanatory power have been achieved.

Prediction of Life 3 in Subgroups of the Population

Previous sections of this chapter show that with knowledge of people's feelings about certain specific life concerns, one can account for rather substantial portions of how people feel about life-as-a-whole. The analyses that show this, however, are based on the total population considered as a single group. There remain several important questions concerning *subgroups* of the population; i.e., groups of people who are similar with respect to sex, age, education, race, and the like. Can the explanatory levels of 50–62 percent described previously for the total population be achieved within the subgroups by using the same concern measures as predictors and combining them in the same way? How much could the predictive power be raised by combining the same concern measures in a *new* way that is optimal for a given subgroup? These are questions that speak to the generality of our previous findings and the extent to

which they are appropriately applicable throughout the entire population.[44]
The answers have obvious importance for the design of social indicators that
might be applied to widely different subgroups.

Exhibit 4.8 brings together a rather substantial number of analyses that
address this issue of generality. In all, twenty-three subgroups, some of which
overlap with others, are examined. These are defined on the basis of sex, age,
socioeconomic status, income, education, employment status, marital status,
race, and certain combinations of these. Results are presented from three
independent national surveys. For the May and November surveys, the same
Selected 12 concerns are used as predictors of general well-being, and thus the
results constitute replications of one another; for the April survey, eight criterion-type concerns are used as predictors. In each survey, the predictor sets are
ones that, as described previously, showed optimal—or close to optimal—
explanatory powers within their respective data. Exhibit 4.8 shows results from
more than forty separate regression-type analyses.

In column B of the exhibit we find an answer to the question as to how well
the same predictors that worked well for the total population, if combined in
the same way, would work for each subgroup. These results, based on the May
data, show that the Selected 12 concerns could explain 52 percent of the variance
in Life 3 for the population as a whole (as also shown in Exhibit 4.2), and that
using the same way of making the prediction—i.e., the "All-Respondent
model"—the percentages of variance explained in the subgroups varied from 60
percent, for people thirty to forty-four years old, to 45 percent, for people aged
sixty and above. Clearly, this one prediction model works reasonably well in
each of the subgroups. A similar result, using the April respondents and a
different set of concern measures, can be seen in column I of Exhibit 4.8. Here,
an optimal set of eight criterion-type concerns explained 61 percent of the
variance in Life 3 for the total population (as we saw previously in Exhibit 4.5),
and these same concerns, combined in the same way, explained between 50
percent and 66 percent in each of the subgroups. Thus, based on results from

---

[44]In formal terms, our analysis here can be regarded as a search for possible statistical interactions
involving concern measures and classification variables when predicting Life 3. Earlier sections of
the chapter have indicated that the concern measures among themselves do not involve interactions, nor do the classification variables among themselves. Here we combine the two types of
measures, and show that these combinations do not involve major interactions either.

Several other searches for interaction involving combinations of concern measures and other
types of variables as predictors of Life 3 were also made, and in no case were marked interactions
found. One search involved five "personality" scales derived using an oblique factor analysis of
the July data. The following characteristics were assessed (numbers refer to items administered to
the July respondents in question 9): pessimistic about own future $(4 + 7 + 8 + 14 - 19)$; positive self-
image $(1+3+12+29+31)$; fatalistic $(-6+22+24+30+32)$; tendency to endorse socially undesirable
self-attributes $(17+23 + 34 + 35 +36 +38)$; and tendency to endorse socially desirable self-attributes
$(-10+16+27+39)$. Another search examined the effect of self-reported "mood" on the day the data
were being collected (item 4.1 of the July questionnaire). Still another checked the influence of
of any especially positive or negative events in the respondent's life (item 5.0 of the July questionnaire).

EXHIBIT 4.8. Prediction of Life 3 for Subgroups of the Population by Combinations of Concern Measures

Concern set:	Selected 12 concerns							8 criteria	
National survey: Data shown:	N	May Variation explained			N	November Var. exp.		N	April Var. exp.
Model used: Results for:		All-R model sample	Group- specific sample pop.			Group- specific sample pop.			All-R model sample
	A	B	C	D	E	F	G	H	I
Respondent set									
All respondents	1297	52%	52%	(50%)	1072	62%	(60%)	1433	61%
Men	547	50%	54%	(49%)	465	66%	(60%)	440	58%
Women	750	53%	55%	(51%)	607	65%	(61%)	630	61%
16–29 years old	358	52%	59%	(51%)	297	66%	(58%)	328	50%
16–29 hshld. head/spouse	276	—	63%	(53%)	233	71%	(62%)	—	—
30–44 years old	356	60%	69%	(63%)	284	75%	(69%)	348	58%
45–59 years old	275	50%	61%	(51%)	236	75%	(67%)	—	—
45–64 years old	363	49%	56%	(48%)	308	69%	(62%)	363	66%
60–97 years old	305	45%	53%	(42%)	251	63%	(51%)	259	64%
Low socioeconomic status	337	48%	57%	(48%)	303	68%	(60%)	277	62%
Mid socioeconomic status	268	52%	65%	(55%)	227	71%	(60%)	241	56%
High socioeconomic status	408	53%	60%	(54%)	321	73%	(66%)	447	59%
Employed men	413	—	58%	(51%)	349	71%	(65%)	—	—
Low income	480	52%	57%	(51%)	457	60%	(53%)	432	61%
Medium income	346	50%	60%	(52%)	272	74%	(68%)	308	52%
High income	403	49%	56%	(49%)	317	76%	(70%)	342	56%
Married	890	48%	49%	(46%)	718	65%	(62%)	822	53%
Nonmarried	406	56%	61%	(54%)	350	64%	(56%)	386	64%
0–11 grades of school	423	54%	63%	(58%)	398	68%	(62%)	392	58%
High school graduate	307	54%	64%	(55%)	347	67%	(60%)	420	61%
Some college education	330	—	58%	(49%)	186	79%	(69%)	237	58%
College degree	223	47%	60%	(46%)	141	74%	(56%)	156	62%
Married & employed	512	—	55%	(50%)	—	—	—	—	—
Blacks	115	50%	—	—	—	—	—	92	55%

Notes: Results are based on Multiple Classification Analyses of May and November data, and Multiple Regression analyses of April data. Predictors were as follows: for May data, the Selected 12 concerns as shown in Exhibit 4.2; for November data, the Selected 12 concerns as shown in Exhibit 4.4; for April data, the first eight concerns listed in Exhibit 4.5.

Data sources: May, November, and April national surveys.

two separate national surveys, and using two differert sets of predictors, it is clear that predictive models developed for the whole population are rather generally applicable.

In column C of Exhibit 4.8 one sees the explanatory power achievable in subgroups of the May data when the Selected 12 concerns are combined in a way that is *optimal* for each subgroup. Column D presents the estimated explanatory power when applying the group-specific prediction model to the entire set of American adults who are members of the group.[45] By comparing the figures in column B (which pertain to the sample, but which would show only small declines when shrunk back to estimate population-wide results) with the figures in columns C and D, one sees that the potential gains of deriving a special prediction model for each subgroup are uniformly small. Thus, it appears that the general prediction model works just about as well as the group-specific models. Finally, columns F and G of Exhibit 4.8 present the results of predicting Life 3 from the Selected 12 concerns in the November data. Once again, one can see that reasonably high levels of predictive power—population estimates ranging from 51 percent to 70 percent—can be achieved in each of the subgroups, as well as for the population as a whole.

It would be tempting, if one saw just part of the data in Exhibit 4.8, to make inferences to the effect that better predictions about people's sense of well-being were possible in some groups than others. For example, on the basis of figures in column D, it would appear that well-being is less predictable for people with a college degree than for those with less education. Note the consistent trend across the different education groups. Figures in columns G and I, however, do not show this trend, and one is led to conclude that the apparent trend in the May data is not a replicable phenomenon. Exhibit 4.8 contains other examples of apparent trends across subgroups, some of which seem replicable (e.g., the sex split, where women consistently show slightly higher predictive levels) and others where apparently substantial differences appear only once.

All in all, the figures show that there are *no* large and stable differences between subgroups in the extent to which their feelings about general well-being can be predicted on the basis of these concern measures; and that, on the contrary, the predictive power achievable in each of the subgroups is remarkably similar to that achieved for the population as a whole. In short, results presented earlier in this chapter seem widely applicable throughout the American population.

CHAPTER SUMMARY

This chapter focuses on the prediction of a person's general sense of well-being, as this is assessed by our global measure, Life 3. (The following chapter describes predictions of other global measures.) "Prediction" is used in the statistical sense of trying to account for variation among people on the basis of other differences that are known about them. The purpose of these analyses is to identify the life concerns that have most impact on feelings about life as a

---

[45]Column D values derive from those in column C and include an adjustment for estimated shrinkage upon crossvalidation. This adjustment becomes rather substantial for some of the smaller groups, and would have become excessive had this analysis been run for blacks, of whom there were only 115.

whole, to explore how people seem to integrate their feelings about these concerns, and to suggest ways in which broad yet statistically efficient batteries of social indicators may be constructed.

The Life 3 measure of general well-being seems a particularly appropriate one to analyze in detail because it is based on questions that address the matter of interest directly (How do you feel about your life as a whole?); it has proved to be one of the most sensitive of the full-range general global measures; and it relates meaningfully to other life qualities, suggesting it taps what it should. Furthermore, the Life 3 measure, an index based on two items that have been combined in a straightforward way, is available for respondents to four different surveys, three national and one local.

A preliminary examination of how the concern measures related individually to Life 3 shows that the highest relationships to general well-being are those involving concerns that are close and immediate to people's personal lives and over which they may have direct influence. Included here were characteristics of one's own life: how much fun, enjoyment, and interest it has; aspects of oneself—self-efficacy, adjustment, accomplishment; one's marriage; how one is treated and accepted by other people; and such economic matters as one's income, standard of living, and the extent one's physical needs are met. The relationship between individual concerns and Life 3 varied systematically according to the "region" of the perceptual space (as this was mapped in chap. 2) in which the concern was located. For example, all concerns in the Self region tended to show substantial relationships to general well-being, while—at the other extreme—all concerns in the Larger society region tended to show rather weak relationships. Furthermore, the relative sizes of relationships between the concerns and Life 3 were highly stable from one survey to another.

Given the apparent complexity of an evaluation of life-as-a-whole, it seems most appropriate to attempt to understand it as a multiply determined phenomenon. This requires finding an effective statistical model to indicate how information from the variables used to make the prediction should be combined.

A series of analyses show that surprisingly simple combination schemes fit the data as well as more complex ones. When feelings about life concerns are measured using the Delighted–Terrible Scale, one feeling just seems to "add on" to another, and although slightly better predictions of Life 3 can be achieved by appropriately "weighting" the concerns, the gain is only slight over predictions made by a simple unweighted addition of the D–T Scale scores. The simplicity of this additive linear model suggests that the D–T Scale may indeed be an appropriate way to assess people's feelings about their lives, and makes reasonable the use of certain powerful multivariate analysis techniques. This indication that people simply add up their joys and sorrows has implications for public decision-makers, who, it is suggested, might succeed in raising people's sense of well-being through policies designed to provide compensatory benefits where normal ones are unobtainable.

Having determined that additive linear models are appropriate for making predictions of Life 3, these are then applied in an extended exploration designed to determine how well different sets of concern measures can predict people's affective evaluations of life-as-a-whole. It is found that information about people's feelings regarding a modest number (six to twelve) of heterogeneous life concerns is sufficient to predict 50–62 percent of the variance in the Life 3 measure, essentially all that can be predicted even with additional concerns, and essentially 100 percent of the variance that is potentially predictable with measures having the reliability estimated for these.

The precise set of concern measures used to make the prediction is shown not to be critical (though some sets are better than others). Predictions at close to maximum possible levels were achieved using modest numbers of domain-type items, *or* of criterion-type items (or both). Even less-than-optimal sets of concern measures achieved reasonably good predictive levels if the measures tapped a heterogeneous combination of regions of the perceptual structure.

Various attempts were made to replicate the predictive power of a set of concern measures in more than one survey, and one formal attempt was made to crossvalidate a prediction equation derived in one survey by applying it to data of another. With perfect consistency, it was found that results were replicable and the crossvalidation produced an actual *increase* in predictive power.

The usefulness of various classification variables (Sex, Race, Age, Income, Education, Family life-cycle stage, etc.) for accounting for differences in people's sense of general well-being was also explored. None of these variables individually was able to account for more than 6 percent of the variance of Life 3, and jointly they accounted for less than 10 percent of its variance. Furthermore, these classification variables were found to contribute nothing to the prediction of Life 3 beyond what could be predicted (much better) by appropriate combinations of concern measures. This same pattern of findings was obtained in two independent national surveys, and several checks showed that the low predictive power of these variables was not the result of having applied an overly restrictive model, was not increased when ten other classification variables were added to the list, and applied to feelings about certain specific life concerns as well as to feelings about life-as-a-whole.

To assess the generality of the predictive power of the concern measures, an extensive series of subgroup analyses was undertaken. Using data from more than twenty (sometimes overlapping) subgroups, defined on the basis of sex, age, race, education, income, employment status, marital status, and/or combinations of these, from three different national surveys, and involving two distinct sets of concern measures, it was found that the same predictive equations that worked well for the total population worked well in all of the subgroups, and that only small gains could be achieved by recomputing the prediction equation to optimize it for the subgroup. On the basis of these subgroup results it seems that the results of the chapter are widely applicable throughout the American adult population.

CHAPTER 5

Predicting Global Well-Being: II

In this chapter we continue the examination begun in chapter 4 of the relationships between feelings about specific life concerns and more global aspects of well-being. Whereas the previous chapter focused exclusively and in considerable detail on the prediction of one global measure, Life 3, we here explore the full set of global measures much more broadly but in less detail.

Two general issues guide the analyses and discussion presented in this chapter. One issue concerns the global measures, the other the concern measures.

With respect to the global measures, we shall examine the extent to which assessments of life-as-a-whole incorporating widely different evaluative perspectives are predictable from the concern measures. Chapter 3 described a typology of global measures, and we here compare the predictabilities of the different types. Of course, we shall also compare the predictabilities of measures within a given type.

With respect to the concern measures, we shall be interested to see whether the pattern of their relationships to Life 3 so clearly evident in chapter 4 also obtains for other global measures. Will feelings about self, family, other people, and personal "economics" continue to show the stronger relationships to general well-being; and will feelings about the local area, the larger society, and other concerns show weaker relationships—even when general well-being is evaluated from perspectives that are different from that embodied in the Life 3 measure? In other words, does using different perspectives for evaluating life-as-a-whole change the relative importance of specific life concerns, or does the basic pattern stay the same?

In one sense, the present chapter stands as a further exploration of the extent to which the results of chapter 4 are generalizable. In this case, the generalizations involve, first, extensions to global measures that are of the same type as the Life 3 measure but that use different devices for obtaining the evaluations, and second, extensions to global measures that are of different types from Life 3. However, the chapter provides much more than a simple "test" of the earlier results. Its basic organization, and the rationale of its analyses, derive from the structure of perceptions about life concerns, and the typology of global measures, as these were described in chapters 2 and 3, respectively. In showing much about the statistical "behavior" of both the global measures and the concern measures, as they relate to one another, the chapter addresses in an integrated way many of the topics that have previously been raised as separate issues. Of course, the concern measures and global measures are simply means to particular goals; and in this case the goals include an improved understanding of how people perceive and evaluate their well-being, and an improved ability to measure those perceptions.

Plan of the Chapter and Overview of Results

As in the preceding chapter, results presented here are divided into two main sections, one reporting bivariate relationships and the other focusing on multivariate relationships.

Because we have many global measures to consider here, instead of the single one on which chapter 4 concentrated, our emphasis on the basic bivariate relationships will be more extensive than in the preceding chapter. The results from the bivariate analysis proved sufficiently clear that we could develop rather specific expectations about what the multivariate analyses would show, and a number of tests of these expectations showed them to be well founded. Accordingly, our multivariate analyses are relatively few.

The section on bivariate relationships is divided into several subsections, each of which focuses on global measures of a particular type and relates them to a standard set of twenty-two concerns. With respect to the level of relationships between global measures and concerns, we find that they vary systematically with the type of global measure and to a lesser extent among the measures of a given type. Our Type A measures, assessments that use an *absolute* perspective and the *full* range of a *general* evaluative dimension, tend to show the highest relationships, though certain of the specific (Type C) global measures also show high relationships. Part-range global measures (Type B) and relative measures (Type D) tend to show medium relationships. Global measures based on a change perspective, either long-range (Type E) or short-range (Type F), show only very weak relationships to the concerns.

The pattern of relationships across the different concern measures also proves interesting. There seems to be just one basic pattern, that which has been identified and described in chapter 4 (and summarized at the beginning of this chapter), that appears over and over again. Except for minor perturbations that seem not to be replicable, it is this pattern or nothing. The uniformity with which it appears, despite numerous variations in how feelings about life-as-a-whole are measured, and in precisely what feelings are measured, is one of the major consistencies of the bivariate results.

Another consistency has to do with replication of results. The nature of our data permits parallel analyses employing similar measures collected in different surveys. For the bivariate results presented in this chapter, just as has been the case in preceding chapters, good replications are consistently found.

The second major section of the chapter takes a few global measures selected from among the various types and examines the extent to which they can be predicted by combinations of concerns that were known to work well in predicting Life 3. It is shown that certain of the Type A and Type C global measures are moderately well predicted by combinations of concerns, that a Type B measure is only modestly predicted, and that Type E and F measures are hardly predicted at all. It is reasoned that these differences in predictive levels can be understood according to the varying sensitivities of different types of global measures to the one global-level phenomenon with which the concern measures seem jointly associated, a person's perception of his general well-being.

RELATIONSHIPS BETWEEN SINGLE CONCERN MEASURES AND THE GLOBAL MEASURES

In this section we take a rather broad look at how feelings about specific life concerns, each considered one at a time, relate to many different indicators of global well-being. To keep the analysis within reasonable bounds, we have grouped the global measures into the seven "types" described in chapter 3. In successive sets, we relate the measures of each type to a standard subset of twenty-two concern measures.

The twenty-two concern measures were intended as a broadly representative set that could be used for diverse exploratory purposes, and were not selected primarily for their optimal power to predict a particular global measure (though they include this as one of their characteristics). The concern measures were selected on the basis of results shown in Exhibit 4.1, which groups concerns as they seem to be organized in people's minds (closely linked to the topical content of the concern, as shown in chap. 2), and which shows how the concern measures in each group relate to Life 3. In selecting the twenty-two concerns from this larger set, we picked a few from each group, some because they showed relatively *high* relationships to Life 3, and some because they showed relatively *low* relationships to Life 3. (The low-relationship concerns were included so as not to bias the set toward the prediction of Life 3 to the exclusion of other global measures, and to ensure that the subset of twenty-two concerns would mirror the same basic patterns of relationship visible among the full set of concerns.) Where there was some choice among the concerns to be included, we favored those that had been assessed in at least two of the three surveys that were richest with respect to global measures (November Form 2, April, and July). The final subset, which will be referred to as the Selected 22 Concerns, is extremely heterogeneous, yet very powerful for predicting Life 3. It includes a mixture of both domains and criteria; it spans the full extent of the perceptual space, as this was mapped in chapter 2; it includes representatives from all the major "regions" of that space; it includes ten of the Selected 12 concerns discussed in chapter 4; and it includes *all* of the eight concerns that constitute an optimal set for predicting the Life 3 measure in the May data, and most of optimal eight for predicting Life 3 in the April data. These Selected 22 concerns are listed in Exhibits 5.1 through 5.4.

The majority of analyses reported in this section will be of data from the July respondents, because they are the people whose general well-being was assessed from the widest range of perspectives. We have, however, examined the behavior of the global measures in each of the other data sets, and a few of these analyses are included in the relevant exhibits. It may be noted at the outset that in these analyses, as has been the case in previous chapters, results from the July respondents consistently showed patterns very much like those from the national-level samples.[1]

Before turning to the tables of relationships, we would note that the coefficients shown are all Pearson r's. This is a coefficient that measures the *linear* component of a relationship. In chapter 4 we noted that relationships between our concern measures and Life 3 consisted almost exclusively of linear components; and to enhance the comparability between the various analyses, we focus exclusively on the strength of this component here.

Type A Global Measures

As detailed in chapter 2, the Type A global measures are assessments of life-as-a-whole using the full range of a very general evaluative dimension and an absolute perspective. A total of fourteen such measures were explored during our work, and nine of these are included in Exhibit 5.1.

In the left-most column of Exhibit 5.1 are results for the Life 3 measure. These have already been examined in considerable detail in the discussion of Exhibit 4.1, but are included here also for comparative purposes. Note that the coefficients shown here were derived by averaging the coefficients shown in Exhibit 4.1 for the November, April, and July respondents, the data sets from which most other results in this chapter come.

Because of the way the concerns were selected and organized for Exhibit 5.1, the basic pattern of their relationships to Life 3 is clearly evident. The groups of concerns vary from high-relationship groups (at the top of Exhibit 5.1) to low-relationship groups (at the bottom), and within each group one or two concerns were included that show high correlations to Life 3 relative to what is typical for the group, and there are also one or two that show relatively low correlations. Note that each of the four groups of concerns that show the highest relationships to Life 3—feelings about oneself, and one's own life, about one's family, about relations with other people, and about family economics, housing, job and costs—starts with a concern that relates to Life 3 in the .50's, and includes other concerns whose correlations range downward but nevertheless remain substantial. In contrast, the other groups of concerns—

---

[1]Chapter 4 includes a discussion of factors other than sheer sampling fluctuations that may have affected the replicability of results from one survey to another.

feelings about one's local area, the larger society, and other matters—start with concerns that relate to Life 3 only in the .20's and .30's, and range downward from there.

Of course, the pattern of relationships shown by the Life 3 measure does not represent a new finding, but simply demonstrates that the Selected 22 concerns clearly reflect the patterns observed previously when many more concerns were examined. Nevertheless, we have noted them in detail because the pattern and level of these relationships provide a "standard" against which results from other global measures can be compared.

In scanning the correlations shown by the other eight Type A measures included in Exhibit 5.1, three things stand out: (1) All measures show at least moderate relationships to the concerns listed in the upper part of Exhibit 5.1; (2) most of the relationships are somewhat lower than the comparable relationship shown by Life 3; and (3) all global measures show the same basic pattern.

The fact that Life 3 is the global measure that tends to be the most closely associated with the concern measures is perhaps not surprising when one considers that Life 3 shares a common measurement method (the Delighted–Terrible Scale) with the concern measures, and when it is recalled that Life 3 has the "advantage" of being based on more than a single answer. (But note that Regression weighted weeks, Weighted slices, and Others' ratings are also scales based on multiple answers.) What seems more important about Exhibit 5.1 is its demonstration that a wide range of different measurement methods, all of which are designed to assess the same underlying phenomenon from the same general perspective, in fact produce reasonably comparable results.

In chapter 3 we noted various indications, based on relationships among global measures, of the relative "goodness" of the Type A measures and concluded that the Life measures, the Weighted weeks measures, and Faces: whole life seemed most promising. Now we are able to compare how different Type A measures relate to life concerns, and in general our earlier judgements are upheld. The same global measures that looked promising when related to other global measures also tend to show the highest relationships to feelings about specific concerns.

In Exhibit 5.1 one measure stands out as notably least sensitive of all. This is Others' rating, which consists of estimates made by the respondent's friends and neighbors of how the respondent feels about his life-as-a-whole. Given that other people would not be expected to have as good knowledge about the respondent's true feelings as the respondent himself, it is not surprising that the relationships are lower here. The facts that they are nearly all positive, and that some attain moderate size, are the important ones to note.

Exhibit 5.1 includes two pairs of columns that let us see the extent to which results from the April national survey and the July local survey replicate one another. These occur for the Ladder: most and Circles: whole life measures. Although differences occur for certain pairs of correlations, both the general level of relationships in the different concern groups and the general pattern of these relationships across the groups show substantial similarities.

Before leaving Exhibit 5.1, brief mention might be made of the five Type A

EXHIBIT 5.1. Relationships of Concern Measures to Global Measures of Type A

| | Global measures | | | | | | | | | | | Concern measures | | |
	Life 3 Mean[b]	Faces: life G5, J	Ladder: most G6, A	G6, J	Circles: whole life G7, A	G7, J	Thermtr. G8, N	R.wtd. weeks G10, J	Wtd. slices G11, J	Othrs. rating G13, J	Intvr. rating G14, A	N	A	J
Concern measures														
Oneself and own personal life														
Self-efficacy, adjstmnt., etc.	.59	.57	.30	.42	.28	.51	.33	.59	.42	.41	.37	21	22	C4
Amt. time, leisure, relax.	.42	.41	.39	.30	.36	.39	.21	.38	.41	.18	.43	38	39	C18
Health, physical exercise	.41	.48	.28	.39	.29	.31	.20	.38	.35	.25	.27	7	29	C9
One's family														
Marriage	.56	.49	a	.35	a	.35	.32	.39	.39	.11	a	4	—	C7
Things do with family	.48	.39	a	.27	a	.37	.31	.41	.32	.20	a	6	—	C8
Close adult relatives	.27	.31	a	.13	a	.33	a	.22	.23	.09	a	—	—	5
Relations with other people														
Fair treatment by others	.55	.38	.39	.29	.38	.28	a	.45	.33	.23	.37	—	54	C14
Accepted, admired	.46	.38	.35	.15	.36	.35	.25	.38	.42	.26	.38	55	64	C10
Others' sincerity, honesty	.35	.33	.25	.35	.26	.43	.17	.41	.34	.09	.22	56	49	C13

												C20	81	C19
Economics, housing, job, costs														
Income, living stndrd., sec.	.52	.33	.45	.36	.43	.22	.35	.32	.21	.30	.41	87		87
House, apartment	.40	.29	a	.26	a	.15	.22	.27	.14	.07	a	75		C22
Your job	.35	.22	a	.24	a	.12	.30	.29	.20	.07	a	100		102
Costs, taxes	.20	.10	a	.12	a	.09	.10	.14	.27	.05	a			
The local area														
Safety, security from theft	.36	.36	.29	.26	.23	.36	.15	.31	.22	.21	.23	96	95	C26
Community, neighborhood	.32	.27	a	.18	a	.32	.20	.22	.15	.11	a	90		C25
Local government	.20	.18	a	.16	a	.14	.13	.27	.23	.04	a	104		C31
Local weather	.09	.10	a	.03	a	.08	a	.07	.07	.13	a			111
The larger society														
Society's standards	.25	.16	a	.22	a	.16	.17	.17	.09	.04	a	121		121
National government	.24	.17	a	.20	a	.10	.18	.34	.26	.01	a	C33		C33
Mass media	.19	.11	a	.14	a	.10	.11	.20	.14	-.11	a	118		C35
Other														
Religious faith, fulfillment	.27	.20	.20	.02	.16	.09	a	.07	.18	.12	.20		70	C38
Way you get around	.20	.24	a	.15	a	.15	a	.31	.16	.23	a			97

Notes: Global measure numbers match Exhibit 3.1; concern measure numbers match Exhibits 2.1 or C.1. Coefficients are Pearson r's.

a This concern not evaluated by these respondents.

b Shown here is the mean relationship for November, April, and July respondents.

Data sources: N: 1,072 November R's; A: 1,433 April R's; J: 222 July R's.

global measures that are not included. Two of these, Life 1 and Life 2, are the single-item components of Life 3; another, Life 4, is another parallel item. As expected, these three measures all show the same pattern as Life 3, and tend to relate to the concern measures at levels just slightly lower than Life 3. (The lower relationships presumably stem from the single-item versions of the Life measure containing proportionately more random measurement error than the multi-item index, Life 3. Of course, the original reason for constructing the index was to increase the validity and reliability of the measure through a reduction in the proportion of random variance.)

Another Type A measure omitted from Exhibit 5.1 is Weighted weeks (G9), which is so similar to Regression weighted weeks (data for which are shown) that there was no need to include them both. The final omitted measure is the experimental Rodgers's X (G12), which, as described in chapter 2, was only an approximate replication of a measure constructed by Campbell, Converse, and Rodgers (1976) and which did not seem especially promising in our data.

Type B Global Measures

We turn next to the Type B global measures, of which seven (out of fourteen) are included in Exhibit 5.2.[2]

The Type B measures differ in just one important respect from those of Type A. Type B measures assess a particular part of the feeling range—positive, negative, or intermediate—whereas each of the Type A measures covers the full range.

The markedly lower general level of the relationships in Exhibit 5.2, as compared to what appears in Exhibit 5.1, suggests that the part-range measures as a group are much less sensitive to feelings about general well-being than are the Type A measures. As noted in chapter 3, the convergencies among the part-range measures that were intended to measure the same thing were rather modest, and we suspect that the measures might have substantially less validity than those of Type A. (It was noted that the lower validity might stem from an inherent difficulty or unnaturalness in trying to assess just the positive, or just the negative, aspects of life.) The generally low level of relationships in Exhibit 5.2 is consistent with this notion that the measures themselves may be of relatively low validity.

The original reason for experimenting with part-range measures lay in the proposal that measures tapping the positive part of the range would behave rather differently from those tapping the negative part. This is a question of the similarity between patterns of relationships to other variables, and Exhibit 5.2 provides extensive opportunities for exploring this issue. Two interrelated questions can be addressed: (1) Do any of the part-range measures show a

[2]The seven Type B measures omitted from Exhibit 5.2 all inquired about the proportion of time over the past ten weeks that specific feelings were experienced. These measures were combined to form the Weighted weeks measures (G9 and G10), a representative of which is included in Exhibit 5.1.

EXHIBIT 5.2. Relationships of Concern Measures to Global Measures of Type B

| | | | Global measures | | | | | |
Concern measures	Good parts G15, J	Number pluses G16, J	Ladder: best G17, A	Ladder: best G17, J	Bad parts G21, J	Number minus G22, J	Ladder: worst G23, A	Ladder: worst G23, J
Oneself and own personal life								
Self-efficacy, adjstmnt., etc.	.23	.37	.26	.24	.28	−.37	.18	.33
Amt. time, leisure, relaxation	.16	.32	.32	.18	.30	−.40	.34	.22
Health, physical exercise	.18	.32	.22	.27	.21	−.30	.19	.28
One's family								
Marriage	.18	.30	a	.23	.28	−.37	a	.24
Things do with family	.21	.29	a	.24	.12	−.27	a	.13
Close adult relatives	.16	.25	a	.12	.01	−.15	a	.11
Relations with other people								
Fair treatment by others	.28	.29	.32	.34	.19	−.29	.25	.23
Accepted, admired by others	.30	.37	.33	.11	.15	−.36	.19	.12
Others' sincerity, honesty	.20	.33	.17	.25	.21	−.28	.22	.12
Economics, housing, job, costs								
Income, living stndrd., fin. sec.	.12	.15	.39	.25	.24	−.22	.35	.25
House, apartment	.28	.12	a	.23	.12	−.12	a	.15
Your job	.06	.24	a	.06	.15	−.11	a	.13
Costs, taxes	−.02	.28	a	.11	.07	−.18	a	.15
The local area								
Safety, security from theft	.19	.28	.26	.29	.15	−.09	.16	.04
Community, neighborhood	.15	.21	a	.20	.15	−.04	a	.05
Local government	.14	.26	a	.22	.09	−.14	a	.12
Local weather	.02	.13	a	.16	.05	.01	a	.04
The larger society								
Society's standards	.08	.06	a	.25	.13	−.10	a	.15
National government	.00	.25	a	.16	.24	−.21	a	.10
Mass media	.10	.10	a	−.01	.08	−.14	a	.10
Other								
Religious faith, fulfillment	.07	.08	.15	−.06	.12	−.23	.13	.09
Way you get around, mobility	.22	.20	a	.16	.05	−.09	a	.12

Notes: Global measure numbers match Exhibit 3.1; for concern measure numbers, see Exhibit 5.1. Coefficients are Pearson r's.
[a] This concern not evaluated by these respondents.
Data Sources: A: 1,433 April Rs; J: 222 July Rs.

pattern of relationships that is different from the full-range measures? (2) Do measures tapping one part of the range show a pattern that is different from those tapping other parts?

Although certain colums of Exhibit 5.2 show minor departures from the basic pattern shown by the Type A measures, the departures are rather small and are generally not replicated by other measures designed to tap the same portion of the range. Here, as with the Type A measures, the higher relationships tend to involve concerns that are listed early rather than late within their respective groups, and with groups that are listed in the upper part of the exhibit.

Some of the apparent trends, if observed in isolation, would be tempting to report as "findings." For example, one may note that the Good parts measure shows its highest relationships with concerns having to do with other people, whereas the Bad parts measure has its highest relationships with concerns having to do with oneself. Does this hint that other people are the source of life's joys, while its sorrows stem from feelings about oneself? One can check such a notion against other data in Exhibit 5.2. The intriguing difference either fails to appear or does so only very weakly when we look at other pairs of variables: e.g., Number of pluses and Number of minuses, or Ladder: best and Ladder: worst.

On the whole, our inability to find replicably different patterns of relationship between global measures tapping different parts of the evaluative range, and the generally low level of relationships throughout Exhibit 5.2, reinforce the doubts we expressed in chapter 3 about the potential usefulness of part-range global measures. We suspect these, and also previous results involving the part-range measures, may be best interpreted as reflecting the behavior of a set of measures that tap just part of what is essentially a unitary whole, and that may suffer in their validity from an unnatural restriction on the range of the phenomenon being assessed.

In addition to these observations about the level and pattern of relationships in Exhibit 5.2, it can be examined for what it has to show about the replicability of the relationships in different surveys. Two replications are shown, one involving two administrations of the Ladder: best measure, the other involving two administrations of Ladder: worst. In both cases, it can be seen that reasonable replications were obtained.

Type C Global Measures

The Type C measures involve an evaluation of life-as-a-whole with respect to some specific quality, and in the course of our work a substantial number of different qualities were explored. As shown in Exhibit 3.1, twenty global measures are included in Type C, though of these, only the nine that seem to offer the most interest will receive attention in this chapter. Most of the ones we shall examine here have figured prominently in the work of other investigators. We shall examine the seven-point satisfaction measure developed by Campbell, Converse, and Rodgers (1976); two different assessments of the Happiness concept, one of which—three-point Happiness—has been used in numerous previous surveys; the Worries measure developed by Gurin, Feld, and Veroff (1960), and several affect scales developed by Bradburn (1969). Relationships of these Type C measures to the Selected 22 concerns appear in Exhibit 5.3. To facilitate comparisons, correlations between the concerns and Life 3 (a Type A measure) also appear in this exhibit, repeated from Exhibit 5.1.

One specific-quality global measure in Exhibit 5.3 stands out from all the rest for being strongly associated with feelings about certain life concerns: seven-point Happiness. Note that its correlations tend to be in the same range as those for Life 3, and that they show the same pattern. Of course, part of the reason seven-point Happiness shows the high relationships it does is probably because it is based on the same Delighted–Terrible Scale as the concern measures themselves. (As described in chapter 6, we estimate that roughly 10 percent of the total variance in measures based on the Delighted–Terrible Scale is attributable to the method of measurement.) However, the .5 and .6 correlations between people's evaluations of "how happy they are" and their reported feelings about themselves, their families, and their relations with other people stand out as unusual in our findings. Seven-point Happiness is a measure we shall examine further in the latter part of this chapter.

It is interesting to note that the three-point Happiness measure shows substantially lower associations than does seven-point Happiness, but still shows the same pattern. We suspect the reduction in the level of the associations has two causes: (1) Three-point Happiness does not use the same assessment method as the concern measures; and (2) in offering the respondent only three possible reply options, this measure may fail to reflect the full variation in happiness that exists among people. Nevertheless, the associations shown by three-point Happiness are still moderately high when compared with those shown by most other global measures.

The seven-point Satisfaction measure, included here to see how a measure that plays a prominent role in the investigations of Campbell, Converse, and Rodgers (1976) would relate to our concern measures, produces moderate-level relationships, rather similar to those shown by the three-point Happiness measure just described. The relationships tend to be lower than those shown by Life 3, but nearly identical in pattern. It is unclear how much of the reduction in the level of the relationships is attributable to the fact that seven-point Satisfaction does not include the same shared methods variance as do Life 3 and the concern measures, how much of the reduction results from a fundamental difference in the underlying phenomena that each measure taps, and how much results from differences in the sensitivities of the measures to these phenomena (i.e., to differences in validities).[3] For reasons stated in chapter 1, our preference is for the Life 3 measure, and the present results seem consistent with that preference.

[3]We did check, however, to see whether the lower relationships might have resulted from our having missed part of the relationship through use of a statistic that is sensitive only to the linear component of an association. We found that associations between the concern measures and seven-point Satisfaction are essentially linear.

In chapter 6 we explore the issue of validity and conclude that Life 3 is somewhat more sensitive than other global measures to feelings of general well-being.

EXHIBIT 5.3. Relationships of Concern Measures to Global Measures of Type C

Concern measures	Life 3 Mean[b]	Sat. 7-pt. G29, N	Happy 3-pt. G31, J	Happy 7-pt. G32, J	Worries G33, N	Worries G33, J	Affect pos. G35, J	Affect neg. G36, J	Affect bal. G37, J
Oneself and own personal life									
Self-efficacy, adjstmnt., etc.	.59	.46	.41	.63	−.26	−.38	.31	−.27	.39
Amt. time, leisure, relaxation	.42	.25	.33	.55	−.17	−.33	.09	−.29	.29
Health, physical exercise	.41	.32	.33	.55	−.17	−.30	.20	−.18	.26
One's family									
Marriage	.56	.50	.49	.60	−.17	−.14	.26	−.34	.43
Things do with family	.48	.40	.29	.51	−.20	−.21	.15	−.28	.32
Close adult relatives	.27	a	.13	.24	a	−.01	.24	−.24	.13
Relations with other people									
Fair treatment by others	.55	a	.39	.56	a	−.28	.22	−.17	.27
Accepted, admired by others	.46	.27	.30	.53	−.15	−.19	.22	−.15	.24
Others' sincerity, honesty	.35	.24	.30	.50	−.14	−.20	.26	−.27	.37
Economics, housing, job, costs									
Income, living stndrd., fin. sec.	.52	.49	.32	.52	−.21	−.32	.11	−.15	.19
House, apartment	.40	.32	.24	.41	−.13	−.07	.16	−.15	.22
Your job	.35	.32	.21	.29	−.15	−.06	.10	−.23	.26
Costs, taxes	.20	.20	.22	.06	−.17	−.13	.05	−.06	.07
The local area									
Safety, security from theft	.36	.23	.33	.36	−.14	−.23	.22	−.13	.23
Community, neighborhood	.32	.24	.18	.29	−.07	−.05	.16	−.12	.19
Local government	.20	.17	.16	.27	−.01	−.14	.07	−.21	.22
Local weather	.09	a	−.02	.07	a	−.20	.07	−.05	.09
The larger society									
Society's standards	.25	.20	.25	.28	−.08	−.16	.14	−.05	.12
National government	.24	.25	.18	.27	−.12	−.23	.04	−.30	.28
Mass media	.19	.15	.07	.22	−.03	−.04	.00	−.16	.14
Other									
Religious faith, fulfillment	.27	a	.12	.17	a	−.05	.02	−.19	.17
Way you get around, mobility	.20	a	.13	.26	a	−.18	.06	−.08	.10

Notes: Global measure numbers match Exhibit 3.1; for concern measure numbers, see Exhibit 5.1. Coefficients are Pearson r's.
a This concern not evaluated by these respondents.
b Shown here is the mean relationship for November, April, and July respondents. Life 3, a Type A measure, is shown here for comparative purposes.
Data sources: N: 1.072 November Rs; J: 222 July Rs.

All of the remaining global measures in Exhibit 5.3, Worries and the several affect measures, showed lower associations with the concern measures, though in each case there were some relationships of moderate size. Interestingly, the general pattern that has characterized the relationships between the concern measures and all preceding global measures continues to appear here. Once again, the concern groups listed in the upper portion of Exhibit 5.3 tend to show higher relationships than those listed in the lower portion, and within each group, concerns listed early tend to have higher correlations than those listed late.

If we examine just the July results for the Worries measure, we might sense a modest variation on the basic pattern, for it seems that feelings about oneself (and about income and standard of living) have more to do with worries than family and relations with other people. Although this variation appears in the July data, it is not well replicated in the November data and does not appear for the Negative affect measure, even in the July data, where one might expect to see it again if the variation were a stable phenomenon. On the whole, it seems that all of these Type C measures of diverse life qualities show approximately the *same* pattern of relationships to the concern measures.

It is interesting to compare the level of relationships among the three affect-based measures. On the whole, there are not major differences between Affect positive and Affect negative, which suggests that the concern measures are equally sensitive to positive and negative emotional responses. On the other hand, correlations involving the Affect balance measure tend to be a little higher than those involving the other two affect measures. Thus the concerns seem more sensitive to the relative *balance* of positive and negative affects than to either one separately.

None of the affect measures shows correlations that are as high as those involving Life 3, Satisfaction, or Happiness. Why? We suspect (from Exhibit 3.6) that each of these latter three measures includes a major cognitive component and minor affective components, and that the relative sizes of the components are reversed in the affect measures. Given the observed difference in the levels of relationship, it would seem that the concern measures themselves may be richer with respect to cognitive than affective components.

Although the space available in Exhibit 5.3 prevented our including many additional columns, we can note that here (with the minor exception of the Worries measure, already mentioned), as in Exhibits 5.1 and 5.2, good replications were obtained when parallel analyses were performed on different sets of data. For the affect-based measures, nearly all of the relationships in the November data were within .1 of those that appear in Exhibit 5.3 for the July data.

In addition to the seven Type C global measures shown in Exhibit 5.3, two others were examined with some care. These were Mood (G34) and another of the affect-based measures, Affect total (G38). Results for them are easy to describe: They show only very weak relationships to the Selected 22 concerns. Affect total has no relationship greater than .1. Mood has only two that exceed .1; in the July data it relates .20 to health and .18 to mobility.

The results for Affect total are consistent with what we saw in chapter 3. There it did not relate to other global measures (other than its components, Affect positive and Affect negative); here we find it does not relate to any of the concern measures. Although just what Affect total does relate to remains a mystery, it is perhaps reassuring to know that none of the concern measures is systematically higher or lower according to a person's overall emotionality.

The generally low relationships between Mood and the concern measures are also reassuring. It would be unfortunate, from the perspective of monitoring social indicators, if people's evaluations of major aspects of their lives were heavily influenced by what they themselves recognized as transitory changes in "mood." The low relationships between our Mood measure and the Selected 22 concerns, which are consistent with the low relationships noted in chapter 3 between Mood and other global measures, suggests this does not happen.

Type D Global Measures

The seven Type D global measures each involves an assessment of how the respondent's life-as-a-whole compares to the lives of other people. For one of the measures (Uniqueness, G55) the comparison involves merely the degree of similarity or difference; for the other six, the comparison is specifically with respect to the level of well-being. The Type D measures are all *relative* measures, and are thus distinct from preceding types that involve "absolute" assessments.

Two of the Type D measures can be quickly dispensed with. Uniqueness showed only weak relationships to the Selected 22 concerns. The highest correlations, none of which exceeded .2, showed mild tendencies for those who thought themselves to be unusual to also feel more positive than average about their job, their religious fulfillment, the national government, and below average with respect to their safety. Although this pattern of relationships is distinctively different from what we have encountered before, the pattern is just barely discernible and cannot be checked for replication elsewhere in our data. The other Type D measure that seems of little interest is Social comparison (G54). Results presented in chapter 6 suggest this measure suffers from a rather severe lack of validity, which is consistent with the low relationships it shows with all other global measures, as noted in chapter 3, and we have not explored this measure further.

The remaining relative measures all show moderate-level relationships to feelings about certain life concerns, and the patterns of these relationships tend to be similar to one another, and similar to our "basic" pattern; i.e., that shown by the Type A measures. Results for the three Type D measures that were identified in chapter 3 as most promising—Much better, Better than everyone, and Decile position—appear in Exhibit 5.4. The level of relationships shown by other measures in this group tends to be slightly lower than those that are included in Exhibit 5.4, but not markedly different otherwise.

Given the generally good convergencies among the Type D measures shown in chapter 3, and the fact that some of the measures are methodologically

EXHIBIT 5.4. Relationships of Concern Measures to Global Measures of Types D, F, and G

Concern measures	Global measures						
	Better than G49, J	Much better G50, J	Decile pos. G52, J	Var. feel. G62, J	Weeks stable G63, J	Lad: 5 hence G65, A	Changes desired G66, J
Oneself and own personal life							
Self-efficacy, adjstmnt., etc.	.31	.36	.32	−.22	.14	.27	−.39
Amt. time, leisure, relaxation	.15	.24	.20	−.21	.12	.22	−.35
Health, physical exercise	.31	.37	.24	−.23	.11	.22	−.28
One's family							
Marriage	.25	.23	.12	−.24	.21	a	−.28
Things do with family	.24	.28	.22	−.20	.13	a	−.19
Close adult relatives	.13	.14	.04	−.18	.02	a	−.18
Relations with other people							
Fair treatment by others	.28	.31	.23	−.22	.20	.24	−.24
Accepted, admired by others	.21	.24	.06	−.22	.04	.29	−.18
Others' sincerity, honesty	.20	.20	.05	−.19	.18	.12	−.22
Economics, housing, job, costs							
Income, living stndrd., fin. sec.	.32	.29	.28	−.11	.10	.29	−.38
House, apartment	.19	.21	.12	−.16	.19	a	−.19
Your job	.04	.09	.10	−.03	.00	a	−.21
Costs, taxes	.19	.20	.16	−.09	.18	a	−.13
The local area							
Safety, security from theft	.30	.36	.15	−.14	.36	.26	−.14
Community, neighborhood	.12	.19	−.03	−.08	.10	a	−.21
Local government	.11	.15	.12	−.20	.31	a	−.21
Local weather	.01	.12	.07	−.09	.15	a	−.24
The larger society							
Society's standards	.19	.25	−.02	−.04	.09	a	−.10
National government	.04	.13	−.06	−.11	.20	a	−.18
Mass media	−.05	−.06	−.07	−.12	.06	a	−.25
Other							
Religious faith, fulfillment	.08	.07	.10	−.11	.04	.13	−.21
Way you get around, mobility	.18	.24	.19	−.10	.08	a	−.12

Notes: Global measure numbers match Exhibit 3.1; for concern measure numbers, see Exhibit 5.1. Coefficients are Pearson r's.
[a] This concern not evaluated by these respondents.
Data sources: A: 1,433 April Rs; J: 222 July Rs.

distinct from one another, we suspect that the Type D measures included in Exhibit 5.4 provide reasonably valid indications of people's sense of relative well-being. Assuming this to be the case, the moderate levels of the relationships between these relative measures and the concern measures, which depend on *absolute* assessments, would suggest that there is substantial overlap between how one feels about life concerns, and one's sense of relative "well-offness." Of course, this is not at all surprising—perceptions of relative position may well affect one's absolute evaluations, and vice versa—and is perfectly consistent with the moderate correlations we noted in chapter 3 between the Type D global measures and the Type A global measures. Nevertheless, the relative perspective is clearly not identical with the absolute one, for the level of the relationships for Type D measures shown in Exhibit 5.4 is clearly a bit below the general level for the Type A measures seen in Exhibit 5.1.

Type E Global Measures

The Type E global measures indicate perceptions of long-term change. Three measures were originally tried: Progress over the past five years, Progress expected over the next five years, and a combined ten-year progress measure. Based on the analysis reported in chapter 3, we concluded that the ten-year measure, while mathematically derivable, did not correspond to any unitary concept in most respondent's minds, and hence should be dropped.

Results for the remaining two long-term change measures could be examined in both the April and July data sets, which provided good replications of one another. Neither Past progress nor Future progress showed much relationship to any of the concern measurs (most correlations were .1 or less; data not shown). The only exception was a slight tendency for people who felt especially positive about themselves and their own personal life to report that their well-being had increased more than average over the past years, and to expect less than average increases in the next five years. But even here the relationships were weak (never more than .2). The general finding is that current evaluations of a wide range of life concerns have very little to do with changes in perceived well-being in either the past or the future.

Of course, this finding could be the result of low validities in our measures of long-term change, but we have other evidence that suggests this is not the cause of the low relationships. The Future progress measure, for example, is derived by taking the difference between Ladder: five years hence and Ladder: most. We have already seen in Exhibit 5.1 that Ladder: most relates well to feelings about various life concerns, and a parallel finding will be described later for Ladder: five years hence. Thus, each of the components of the Future progress measure shows something other than random error.

On the contrary, we suspect the consistent lack of relationships between all of our heterogeneous concerns and both of the Type E global measures, in both of the surveys in which the data could be examined, actually reflects how people evaluate their lives. It would appear that people are quite able to keep notions about *change* in well-being distinct from notions about its current *level*, and that their answers to questions about current levels are relatively uninfluenced by whatever may be their personal histories of past change, or expectations about futures changes. Just as we noted in chapter 3 that the Type A global measures proved to be relatively pure measures of current general well-being, unrelated to perceptions of change, we here note that the same relative purity seems to characterize the concern measures.

Type F Global Measures

Like the preceding set of global measures, Type F measures also assess changes in general well-being, but in this type the focus is on short-term change. In chapter 3 we noted that the Type F measures could be divided into two subtypes, those that assessed the *range* of variation in feelings, and those that assessed the *frequency* or *likelihood* of variation.

We find no evidence that the *range* measures relate to feelings about any of our Selected 22 concerns. In the July data, for example, the Ladder: best–worst measure (G59) shows no correlations with any of the concern measures higher than .12, and the highest correlation in a parallel analysis of the April data was an even lower .07 (data not shown).

Among the other Type F measures (G61–G63) there was a mild but consistent tendency for lower frequencies of variation (or higher likelihoods of stability) to be associated with more positive evaluations of numerous concerns. Results from two of the three relevant measures, Variation in feelings and Number of weeks stable, appear in Exhibit 5.4. (The third measure, Up and down or steady (G61), showed the same tendencies but generally weaker relationships.) Although the tendencies here are consistent, the level of the relationships is quite low, and the major conclusion is that the Type F measures of short-term change, like the Type E measures of long-term change, show no marked association with any of the concern measures.

Type G Global Measures

Finally, we come to five supplementary global measures that do not fit within any of the preceding types. Two refer to the respondents' perceptions of *other* peoples' lives and were excluded from the present analysis; the other three are of potential interest.

Exhibit 5.4 shows results for two of them, Ladder: five years hence and Changes desired. It is clear that how well off one expects to be five years in the future bears moderate positive relationships to how positive one feels currently about a wide range of life concerns. Since radical shifts in well-being are not common in American society, the finding is not surprising. A similarly reasonable result appears for the Changes desired measure. The more positive were people's feelings about numerous life concerns, the less likely were they to desire major changes in their lives. Interestingly, the pattern of relationships for both these global measures is basically similar to that observed for the Type A measures: Both one's expected well-being in the future and present desires for change have more to do with aspects of life that are close—self, marriage, family economics—than with the more remote concerns.[4]

Comment

The results described so far in this chapter show that affective evaluations of life concerns relate to nearly all global measures we have examined with approximately the same patterns, though with strengths that differ from one global measure to another. What could account for the remarkable consistency in the patterns, and the varying levels of the relationships?

---

[4]The final Type G global measure, Ladder: five years ago (G64), showed only weak relationships to the concern measures (most were .1 or less).

We suspect that the explanation is that the components of each global measure that bear some association to the concern measures are one and the same. Put in other words, we suspect that how one affectively evaluates various life concerns relates to essentially *one* phenomenon at the global level. Furthermore, we suspect differences in the *levels* of the relationships can be attributed to differences in the degree to which the global measures are sensitive to this one phenomenon.

What is this "one phenomenon"? It would seem to be perceptions of general well-being. This is the most reasonable thing for the heterogeneous concern measures to bear a common relationship to, and this would make sense of our findings that Type A measures, which are *direct* assessments of general well-being, tend to show the highest levels of relationship; that the part-range (Type B), specific-quality (Type C), and relative (Type D) measures—all of which *indirectly* tap general well-being—tend to show intermediate level relationships; and that the long- and short-range change measures (Types E and F)—which tap *change*, not present level—show the lowest relationships.

We would not go on to suggest that the global measures are insensitive to all other phenomena. On the contrary, the results described in chapter 3 show that there are systematic differences among the global measures in the extent to which they reflect absolute well-being, relative well-being, long-term change, and short-term change. Our point is that despite the heterogeneity among the global measures, they seem to have just one common intersection with the concern measures.

This insight has important implications for the multivariate prediction of global measures on the basis of feelings about life concerns. We turn to this matter next.

MULTIVARIATE PREDICTION OF GLOBAL MEASURES

Given the configuration of results obtained when we related individual concern measures to the global measures, just described, an extensive exploration of the extent to which each global measure could be predicted by combinations of concern measures, parallel to that undertaken for Life 3 in chapter 4, did not seem warranted. There seems to be just a single (common) component of the global measures, perceived general well-being, that is associated with feelings about life concerns; and we have already identified combinations of concern measures, and simple prediction models, which have proved effective in predicting one global measure, Life 3, which we believe to be among the most sensitive to this component. Accordingly, the multivariate questions that seem most interesting focus on the predictive power of these previously identified combinations and models when the global measure is other than Life 3.

Our expectations about predictive power are clear. We would expect selected concern measures, when combined additively, to yield relatively good predictions of those global measures that substantially reflect perceptions of general well-being, and poorer predictions of global measures that are less sensitive to this phenomenon. As noted among our comments about the results of the preceding section, the typological classification of a global measure, which depends on its manifest content and method of assessment, and the level of its bivariate relationships with the Selected 22 concerns provide indications of the extent to which each global measure reflects perceptions of general well-being.

To explore these ideas, a few global measures were selected for attention and we looked to see how well they could be predicted on the basis of feelings about life concerns. The analyses were performed on the November (Form 2) and April respondents, the two national-level data sets that included the largest number of global measures.

For the November respondents, the Selected 12 concerns were used to predict two Type C measures: Satisfaction and Happiness (seven-point). The Selected 12 concerns had proved to have a substantial predictive power for Life 3 (as great as all the concerns together), and we expected them also to show considerable predictive power for these Type C measures. This was because these Type C measures have a factorial composition rather similar to that of Life 3 (as shown in Exhibit 3.6), because Exhibit 5.3 shows that both of these Type C measures produce substantial correlations with at least some of the Selected 22 concerns, and because the Happiness measure, like Life 3, is based on the same Delighted–Terrible Scale as are the concern measures being used to predict it.

Exhibit 5.5 presents the results of predicting these global measures from the Selected 12 concerns, and includes—for comparison purposes—a parallel

EXHIBIT 5.5 Prediction of Three Global Measures by the Selected 12 Concerns

	Global measure predicted		
	Type A Life 3 G3	Type C Sat. G29	Type C Happy G32
Percent variance explained			
In present data	62%	43%	57%
Population estimate	60%	40%	54%
	MCA	MCA	MCA
Concern measures	β	β	β
27 Amount of fun	.23	.22	.25
4 Family life	.19	.20	.25
C20 Money index	.19	.18	.12
21 Yourself	.17	.11	.15
87 House/apartment	.11	.07	.06
38 Time to do things	.10	.08	.11
75 Your job	.10	.07	.08
6 Things do with family	.09	.04	.11
7 Your health	.09	.12	.07
30 Spare-time activities	.07	.07	.08
C33 Nat. govt. index	.07	.06	.04
101 Goods and services	.06	.08	.04

Notes: Measure numbers refer to Exhibits 2.1, 3.1, or C.1.
MCA= Multiple Classification Analysis.
Data Source:1,072 respondents to November national survey (Form 2).

EXHIBIT 5.6. Predictions of Five Global Measures from the Sum of Eight Criterion-Type Concerns in the Total Population and in Three Subgroups

		Global measures				
	Number of cases[a]	Type A Life 3 G3	Type B Ladder: best G17	Type E Past progress G56	Type E Future progress G57	Type F Ladder best-worst G59
All respondents	1070	59%	26%	3%	0%	0%
Men	440	55%	22%	1%	0%	0%
Women	630	61%	29%	5%	0%	0%
Blacks	92	52%	18%	6%	4%	0%

Notes: Shown here is the percentage of variance explained in designated global measures by the sum of answers to eight criterion-type concerns. The eight concerns are the first eight listed in Exhibit 4.5. Global measure numbers match Exhibit 3.1.
[a] The respondents analyzed here are those who answered *all* of the first twelve items listed in Exhibit 4.5.
Data source: Respondents to April national survey.

analysis in the same data for Life 3, which also appears in Exhibit 4.4. It is interesting to see that although the predictive levels are relatively high, 54 percent for Happiness and 40 percent for Satisfaction, neither is as high as the 60 percent achieved for Life 3. A check of the MCA beta coefficients shows that their relative sizes tend to be roughly the same, regardless of which of these three global measures is being predicted.[5]

The two type C measures included in Exhibit 5.5 were selected because of their high potential predictability. For contrast, we chose four additional global measures of other types from the April data. They were predicted from an unweighted additive combination of the eight criterion-type concerns that had proved most effective in predicting Life 3 in these same data.[6] These results appear in Exhibit 5.6, for the sample as a whole and also separately for men, women, and blacks.

Results in Exhibit 5.6 are much as expected. A rather substantial 59 percent of the variance in the Type A measure Life 3 is predictable from a simple sum of the selected eight concerns (as we knew from chap. 4); the same sum predicts a much more modest 26 percent of the variance of the part-range (Type B) measure, Ladder: best, and this sum predicts little or none (3 percent or less) of

[5] A somewhat similar pair of multivariate analyses in the July data replicate two of the results shown in Exhibit 5.5. Nine broad concern clusters (measures C40 to C48, as shown in Exhibit C.1) were used to predict both Life 3 and seven-point Happiness via multiple regression. The population estimates for the percentages of variance accounted for were 61 percent and 55 percent respectively, figures that are nearly identical with those just shown for the November respondents.

[6] Chapter 4 notes that for the April respondents an unweighted sum of these eight concerns produced as accurate a prediction of Life 3 as a more complicated, statistically derived weighted sum.

the variance in the long-range (Type E) or short-range (Type F) change measures. The same pattern of results also appears in each of the three subgroups.[7]

On the basis of results shown in Exhibits 5.5 and 5.6, which corroborate our expectations developed from the bivariate analyses, it appears that feelings about life concerns have quite a lot to do with evaluations of general well-being as these are assessed by the Life 3 measure, a moderate amount to do with the specific qualities of happiness and satisfaction in life-as-a-whole, and relatively little to do with perceptions of change.

Although our analysis has not examined all global measures, or even all ways of predicting the few global measures included in Exhibits 5.5 and 5.6, the close adherence of the results of this chapter to a broad general pattern leads us to suspect that further and more sophisticated multivariate analysis using concern measures as predictors of global measures would not yield fundamentally new insights.

CHAPTER SUMMARY

This chapter continues the explorations begun in chapter 4 of relationships between feelings about specific aspects of life and perceptions of general well-being. Here we examine how a standard subset of the concern measures relates to a wide range of global measures. The analysis and discussion focus on two broad issues: (1) the predictabilities of global measures of different types and within the same type; and (2) the patterns of relationships shown between the concern measures and the global measures. In drawing on the structure of perceptions about life concerns elucidated in chapter 2, the typological classification and interrelationships among global measures described in chapter 3, and the results of predicting Life 3 detailed in chapter 4, this chapter depends heavily on the results of previous chapters and elaborates in an integrated fashion some of the issues that have previously been considered in relative isolation.

The first major section of the chapter examines bivariate relationships: associations between the Selected 22 concerns, considered one at a time, and a wide range of global measures. The Selected 22 concerns are a set intended for exploratory purposes. The set includes representatives from each of the major groups of concerns, and within each group, one or two concerns that show relatively high relationships to Life 3, and one or two that show relatively low relationships. As such, it well demonstrates the basic pattern of relationships among the concerns and Life 3, has substantial power to predict Life 3, and yet is not restricted to the prediction of this measure to the exclusion of others.

The section on bivariate relationships is divided into several subsections, each of which focuses on global measures of a particular type. Among the Type

---

[7]Results for the Type A and E measures were examined in an additional eighteen population subgroups (those shown in Exhibit 4.8), and the same consistent pattern evident in Exhibit 5.6 continued to appear.

A global measures, assessments of life-as-a-whole that use the full range of a very general evaluative dimension and an absolute perspective, we find that the Life 3 measure tends to show the highest relationships to individual concern measures. All of the other Type A global measures show relationships that are highly similar in pattern to Life 3, and only modestly weaker in strength. The broad similarities in the way these measures relate to the individual concerns suggests that full-range, general, absolute evaluations of life-as-a-whole can be obtained using a wide variety of different measurement approaches. The graphical Faces, Ladder, and Circles scales, as well as the frequency-based Weighted weeks measures, all seem to be effective alternatives to the Delighted–Terrible Scale on which the Life 3 measure is based. Where parallel analyses from two separate surveys are performed, good replications are evident.

The next subsection of the chapter focuses on the part-range measures (Type B). In general, their relationships to the concerns are substantially lower than those shown by the Type A global measures. These results, combined with the observation that the positive-range, midrange, and negative-range measures all tend to show the same pattern of relationships to specific concern measures, reinforce our skepticism, first expressed in chapter 3, about the ultimate usefulness of these measures. Again, parallel analyses on different sets of data show the results to be replicable.

The following subsection examines how feelings about life concerns relate to certain Type C measures. (The Type C measures assess various specific qualities of life-as-a-whole: Satisfaction, Happiness, Worries, Positive and Negative affect, etc.) It is found that the level of relationships shown by the Type C measures varies greatly. The highest, at levels close to those shown by Life 3, involve the seven-point Happiness measure. Another measure of Happiness, and measures of Satisfaction, Affect balance, and certain other qualities show intermediate levels. Measures of current Mood and Total affect show virtually no relationships. Despite the differences in levels, the same pattern that characterized the relationships of the Type A and B global measures appears again for the Type C measures, with only minor variations that seem not to be replicable. The relationships shown by the Selected 22 concerns suggest that concern measures are about equally sensitive to positive and negative emotional reactions, but that they are not much influenced by either the respondent's current mood or his general propensity to respond emotionally.

Among the Type D measures, which involve explicit comparisons with other people, those that focus on one's relative well-being tend to show relationships to concern measures of moderate levels and with the same pattern as seen for other types of global measures. Measures of long- and short-term change (Types E and F) show very weak relationships, leading to the potentially important observation that our concern measures, which are current evaluations of specific aspects of life, seem essentially unaffected by notions of past progress (or decline), or by changes expected in the future. Results from two supplementary global measures (Type G) produced the not unexpected findings that more positive feelings about specific aspects of life tend to be associated with expecting to be well-off in the future and desiring to make relatively few major changes in one's life.

The remarkable consistency of the *patterns* of relationships between global measures and the Selected 22 concerns, and the differences in the *levels* of the relationships, suggested that (1) there is just one single phenomenon, perceived general well-being, to which the concern measures are related in the global measures, and (2) that the global measures reflect this phenomenon with differing degrees of sensitivity. This led to a few multivariate analyses where combinations of concerns known to be effective for predicting this phenomenon, as it was reflected in the Life 3 measure, were applied in parallel fashion to other global measures. As expected, the multivariate predictive power of certain combinations of concerns varied systematically from a high of about 60 percent for Life 3, a Type A measure, through intermediate levels for global measures of Types B and C, to essentially zero for global measures of Types E and F. Identical analyses within a wide range of population subgroups showed consistent results in all groups.

CHAPTER 6

Evaluating the Measures of Well-Being

How good are the measures of perceived well-being reported in previous chapters of this book? More specifically, to what extent do the data produced by the various measurement methods indicate a person's true feelings about his life? To what extent do the methods permit discrimination among people according to their feelings? How clear are the meanings of the categories used to describe people's feelings? How easy are the methods to use? And to what extent do our measures of perceived well-being have anything to do with respondents' other feelings, behaviors, and life situations? These are the primary questions addressed in this chapter.

These issues have obvious importance. One of our major goals is to develop a set of measures of perceived well-being that could be used as social indicators, and to that end we have experimented with many different measurement methods. These various methods are almost certainly not all equally good. To permit rational choices among them for subsequent application, it is necessary to determine which are the better ones. In addition, continued development efforts by ourselves or others need to be guided by a realistic assessment of how well different approaches have worked in the past and what has been achieved so far.

Furthermore, we have no illusions that our measures are perfectly valid, and we know that the bivariate and multivariate results reported in previous chapters are to some extent affected by the invalidities in the data. Random errors act to decrease the size of relationships while correlated errors spuriously increase them. Hence, an informed interpretation of any observed relationship requires information about the composition of the variables that are being related. (Chapter 4 notes that when predictions of feelings about life-as-a-whole are adjusted for the estimated validity of the scales, multiple correlations close to 1.00 can be obtained. One of the purposes of the present chapter is to develop the validity estimates cited there.)

While the validity of a measure—i.e., the degree to which it reflects what it is supposed to—is an important criterion for evaluating the goodness of a measure, it is not the only one. Measures without validity are worthless, but measures with high validities are not necessarily useful. One must also be concerned about the conceptual and practical relevance of a measure and the related matter of the degree to which it permits discrimination among the objects being measured.

Unfortunately, evaluating measures of perceived well-being presents formidable problems. Feelings about one's life are internal, subjective matters. While very real and important to the person concerned, these feelings are not necessarily manifested in any direct way. If people are asked about these feelings, most can and will speak about them, but a few may lie outright, others may shade their answers to some degree, and probably most are influenced to some extent by the framework in which the questions are put and the format in which the answers are expected. Thus, there is no assurance that the answers people give fully represent their true feelings.

Some of the things that can be directly observed about people include their behavior and characteristics of the world in which they live. Does their observability offer a solution to the problem of evaluating our measures? Only partially, we feel. Clearly, measures of perceived well-being that had nothing to do with behaviors, with objective conditions, or with people's other feelings would be irrelevant and would seem of very limited practical usefulness. Nevertheless, we have no expectation that there exists a one-to-one relationship between feelings and behavior or feelings and the environment. Furthermore, it is not behavior or external conditions that we are seeking to measure and understand at this point. It is the *feelings* about life that are of direct interest to us.

The reason we expect only modest relationships between a person's feelings and behavior and between feelings and his environment is that what a person actually does at any one time, and where and how he lives, almost certainly depend on many things in addition to his current feelings. For example, whether a person moves out of an apartment, while probably related to some extent to his feeling about the apartment, will also depend on factors such as the availability of alternative housing, the costs of other housing and his ability to pay them, the terms and period of his lease, the location of jobs, schools, shopping and other activities of the family, and on many other things. Some people remain in apartments they do not care much for, and some people vacate apartments that they like very much. This is but one example of the multidetermination of behavior. Its dependence on a host of factors in addition to feelings implies that there are no strong and necessary links between feelings (even if truly reported) and behavior at any one time, or between feelings and objective life conditions.

We believe that a person's feelings about his or her life have an importance—and hence a claim to be considered as social indicators—in their own right. A person's feeling of "delight" or "satisfaction" or "unhappiness," or whatever else may be the feeling, engendered by some aspect of life is itself a significant fact. For the person himself, the mixture of different feelings he has about life is an important part of what life *is*. If enhancement, maintenance, and/or redistribution of well-being are significant concerns of society, as we believe they are, then the lives people are actually experiencing are worth knowing about. From this perspective, perceptions of well-being have an interest in their own right, and measures of them need to be validated against the true perceptions, not against other phenomena such as behavior or environmental conditions, which are not the same and which are only indirectly relevant.

Plan of the Chapter and Overview of Results

The organization of the chapter follows from the above considerations. The first major section is devoted to deriving estimates of the validity of our measures of perceived well-being. The second section examines how people are distributed on the measures produced by various methods. There follows a section that adds two other evaluative criteria and that then provides an integrated evaluation of the several measurement methods. This third section concludes with a short speculation as to how the highest ranking methods might be still further inproved. The final section examines how measures of respondents' feelings about selected aspects of life relate to their reports of behaviors, environmental conditions, and other feelings.

The first section begins with a short discussion of our assumptions about the validity and error composition of measures and shows how these assumptions can be incorporated in causal measurement models. Using data from the July respondents, validity and error component estimates are then derived for six different measurement methods as used to assess perceptions of five different life concerns and life-as-a-whole (thirty-seven measures in all). It is shown that the validity of these measures depends mainly on the measurement method used and does not vary much with what is being assessed. The Delighted–Terrible, Faces, and Circles Scales are shown to produce measures (based on single questionnaire items) with validities of about .8; for the Ladder Scale, the estimated validity is .7; and for the Social comparison and Rating-by-others approaches, the validities are about .4. The two error components of the measures, random error and correlated error, are also separately estimated for each of these six measurement methods. The section then proceeds to compare the magnitudes of the validity and error components estimated from the July data with estimates for the same methods (and certain additional methods as well) when used in various national level surveys. In all, validity estimates for ten different measurement methods are derived and reasonably good replication is demonstrated from survey to survey.

The findings from the first major section of the chapter suggest that the better methods, even in their present form, yield rather effective measures of perceived well-being. For measures based on multiple items, such as many of those used in chapters 4 and 5, estimates of about 75 percent valid variance, about 10 percent correlated error variance, and about 15 percent residual variance can be derived. While not perfect, such a composition is quite good relative to what is believed to be the case in many surveys and clearly good enough to give the measures significant potential as social indicators.

The second and third sections of the chapter evaluate the five measurement methods having the highest estimated validity on several other criteria: distribution forms, ease of use, and precision of category meanings. None of the five methods appears ideal with respect to all criteria, but we conclude that the Delighted–Terrible Scale looks best, closely followed by the Circles and Faces Scales. The Ladder and seven-point Satisfaction Scales, while not as attractive as the first three, nevertheless represent useful alternative methods for assessing perceptions of life quality.

The final section, relating perceptions of well-being to reported behaviors, environmental conditions, and other feelings, shows that while relationships are uniformly in the expected direction, they tend to be rather modest in strength. Most correlations are in the range .2 to .4. Given that strong relationships were not expected and that the observed relationships are in the expected direction, these findings seem congruent with the earlier conclusions that presently available methods for measuring perceived well-being offer potentially useful indicators.

ESTIMATION OF THE VALIDITY AND ERROR COMPONENTS OF THE MEASURES

Measurement Theory and Models

The analyses to be reported in this major section of the chapter begin from the fact that the variance of any measure can be partitioned into three parts: a valid component, a correlated (i.e., systematic) error component, and a random error (or "residual") component. Our general analysis goal is to estimate, for measures of different types, from different surveys, and derived from different methods, how the total variance can be divided among these three components. Our procedures involve the application of a recently developed technology for specifying and estimating causal models, and before describing the analysis results it is essential that the conceptual underpinnings of the approach itself be clearly understood. Accordingly, we devote a few paragraphs to the nature of the variance components to be investigated and the relevance of each for validity and reliability, a few paragraphs to measurement models, and a few to the basis on which estimates of construct validity can be inferred from such models.

Variance Components. The *valid component* of a measure is that portion of the total variance which reflects what the measure is intended to measure. For our measures of perceived well-being, it is that portion of the variance which reflects people's true feelings about the particular aspect of life referenced by the measure. In other words, it is the variance that results from the "true effect" of people's actual feelings. We assume that measures which refer to different aspects of life, and/or which derive from different measurement approaches, may differ in the proportion of their variance that is valid; i.e., in their "validity."

A "validity coefficient," as this term is commonly used by social scientists, is the correlation (Pearson's product–moment r) between the true conditions and the obtained measure of those conditions. The square of the validity coefficient gives the proportion of observed variance that is true variance; e.g., a measure that has a validity coefficient of .8 contains 64 percent valid variance; similarly, a measure that contains 49 percent valid variance has a validity of .7.

As noted previously, validity is not the only criterion of a measure's quality but is an important one.

The *correlated error component* of a measure is that portion of the variance which reflects influences other than those that the measure was primarily designed to tap and which influence other measures as well. Several types of influences may result in correlated errors.

A person's answers reflect, in addition to his true feelings, the effect of his biases and the particular meanings or interpretations he gives to the words in which he expresses his answers. Different people have different biases and may give slightly different interpretations to the words used in the questions and answers of a survey. Among possible biases are a tendency to view the world positively, to be negative about the future, to answer "yes," to give socially desirable or socially acceptable answers, and many others. The effects of individuals biases and differences in interpretation are essentially "errors". and if they show up in more than one measure—as is especially likely to happen when the measures are based on the same method—they result in a spurious degree of correlation between the measures.

A special form of bias is what is sometimes known as "halo." One would hope that a respondent, when answering a series of questions about different aspects of something—e.g., his own life, or someone else's life—would distinguish clearly among those aspects. Sometimes, however, the answers are substantially affected by the respondent's *general* impression and are not as distinct from one another as an external observer might think they should be. This is particularly likely to happen when the respondent is not well acquainted with the details of what is being investigated or when the questions and/or answer categories are themselves unclear. Of course, "halo," which produces an *undesired* source of correlation among the measures, must be distinguished from the sources of *true* correlation among the measures.[1]

As will be seen later, our data suggest that different measurement methods activate different biases and/or different degrees of halo, which then act to produce different patterns of correlation among the measures. By examining

[1]Occasionally one encounters in the social science literature references to a "general factor." In the terminology of our present discussion, a general factor is one that combines both the true and halo effects (and sometimes other bias effects as well).

these patterns, we can obtain estimates of the effects of correlated errors associated with a particular method, and it will sometimes be appropriate to call these effects a method effect. One of our goals will be to estimate the impact of the method effect of each of the different measurement methods we have used.

The *residual* component of a measure is that portion of the variance that can be attributed neither to true effects nor to correlated errors. Since it is not true variance, it must be error variance, and since correlated errors account for all of the common (i.e., shared) error variance, the remaining variance must be "random" errors; i.e., invalid variance that does not appear in any other measure. Included here are the effects of all the quirks of fate that may influence a particular data-point: The respondent may not have correctly heard the question and/or may have lied about this item, the interviewer may have misunderstood the answer given and/or recorded the wrong answer, or possibly some error may have been introduced as the answer was being prepared for computer processing.

We have already noted that the *validity* of a measure is its correlation with the true state of whatever was intended to be measured, and that this is reflected by the proportion of the total variance that is valid variance. The *reliability* of a measure, on the other hand, is the correlation between two parallel versions of the measure. The parallel versions may be measures of the same thing (1) taken at two different times, or (2) stemming from alternate sources (as, for example, when judgments about the same thing are obtained from two different people), or (3) consisting of different, but equivalent, component items.

The reliability of a measure depends on *both* its true variance and its correlated error variance. As either or both of these increase, the reliability increases. While it is usually true that more reliable measures are better measures (because this usually indicates that their validity is also higher), it is possible to have a measure that has perfect reliability but zero validity. This would be the result if all of its variance were correlated error variance. This extreme case shows the importance of separately estimating the three variance components we have been discussing: the valid component, the correlated error component, and the residual.

Measurement Models. The diagram in Exhibit 6.1 portrays in graphic form the ideas we have been discussing and, at the same time, introduces the basic measurement model which guides the analyses in this section of the chapter. In the two rectangles are different but parallel measures of *x*, perhaps respondents' feelings about life-as-a-whole. Three separate effects influence each measure: true effects, correlated error effects, and everything else (what we have called residual effects, or random errors). These effects are shown by the various arrows indicating the flow of influence. Since the measures measure the same thing, they are both influenced, presumably, by the same true condition (represented by the oval on the left). Also, since both measures might be influenced by some of the same nonvalid effects, e.g., biases, we include correlated errors as a component of the model (represented by the oval on the

EXHIBIT 6.1. A Rudimentary Measurement Model

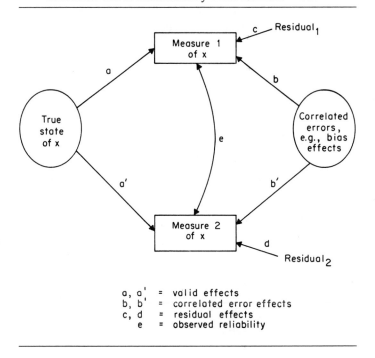

a, a' = valid effects
b, b' = correlated error effects
c, d = residual effects
e = observed reliability

right). The residual errors, however, are by definition different for each measure, and hence the residual arrows come from different points in the diagram.[2]

In Exhibit 6.1 the linkages labeled a and a' would be validity coefficients (assuming all variables, measured and unmeasured, had been standardized so variances were 1.0). The linkages labeled b and b' are the correlated error effects. The linkages labeled c and d are the residual effects. And the linkage e is the reliability.[3]

Given just the two measures in Exhibit 6.1, the only thing one could observe is their correlation (i.e., their reliability). While this puts a value on linkage e, the values of the other linkages remain undetermined. With two measures and no assumptions, this model is "underidentified"; i.e., there is insufficient information to provide unique estimates for all the parameters. Note, however, that by introducing certain assumptions even this rudimentary

[2]In accordance with usual conventions for displaying structural models, of which this is a simple one, we do not show the residual arrows as coming from ovals, though such ovals could have been included. According to the convention, ovals are reserved for unmeasured but specific concepts, whereas the residual effects are from a nonspecific "everything else."

[3]The absence of a linkage between the two ovals in Exhibit 6.1 represents an important and fundamental assumption of the model; i.e., that the magnitude of the correlated error is independent of the true state of whatever is being measured.

model could be estimated. If, for example, one were prepared to assume that there were no methods effects (i.e., that b and b' each equaled zero) and that the validities of the two measures were identical (i.e., that $a = a'$), then one could derive the validities (and the residuals) for any observed reliability using the standard procedures of structural equation modeling.[4] If, for example, the reliability were observed to be .70, and if one accepted the above assumptions, the validities of the measures would each be .84 ($.84 \times .84 + .00 \times .00 = .70$) and the magnitudes of the residual effects would each be .55 ($.84^2 + .00^2 + .55^2 = 1.00$). Precisely these assumptions as applied to this model lead to the sometimes-quoted and overly simple observation that "validity equals the square root of the reliability." We would stress that this statement applies only in the absence of correlated errors, and that the presence of correlated errors in our data requires that validity and reliability be treated as distinct concepts, not immediately derivable from one another.[5]

Although the model in Exhibit 6.1 is too rudimentary to permit useful estimation except under special assumptions, given more information (i.e., observed relationships among more measures) and a somewhat more complex version of this model, interesting estimates can be derived.

Construct Validity and Measurement Models. The social science literature traditionally distinguishes three types of validity: construct validity, concurrent validity, and predictive validity. The first refers to the relationship of an observed measure to a theoretical construct (or "concept"); concurrent and predictive validities both involve relating an observed measure to some observable criterion variable. As noted previously, we believe that appropriate criterion variables do not exist for validating affective evaluations of life conditions, and hence our discussion of validity will focus on construct validity.

Since theoretical constructs are unmeasured variables, a study of construct validity requires the estimation of relationships between observed measures and hypothetical (unobserved) variables. Such an investigation depends on both (1) a network of interrelationships among observed measures and (2) a set of theoretical assumptions about the relationships of the unobserved variables to one another and to the observed measures. At the time the term "construct validity" entered the social science vocabulary,[6] techniques had not been developed for specifying or estimating the types of theoretical models that were required. In the last several years, however, the means of doing this has been developed, and it is now possible to portray one's theoretical assumptions in the form of a structural model, and if the model and data are appropriate, to

---

[4]See, for example, Duncan, 1966; Land, 1969.

[5]Definitions of reliability that neglect the possible presence of correlated errors can be found in Wiley and Wiley (1970), and Cochran (1970). The discussions of validity and reliability presented by Heise and Bohrnstedt (1970) and by Guilford (1954) are examples of what we regard as a more useful approach that distinguishes validity and reliability according to whether the effects of correlated errors are excluded or included, respectively. This is the perspective used in this chapter.

[6]Cronbach and Meehl, 1955.

compute estimates of construct validity by fitting the parameters of the model to the data.[7]

It should be stressed, however, that the development of sophisticated procedures for estimating the parameters of a model does not reduce the importance of the theoretical assumptions that are made. Through suitable computing one can generate parameters; whether one chooses to interpret those parameters as estimates of validity—i.e., of the relationship between an observed measure and what that measure was *intended* to measure—will depend on how appropriate one believes the model (i.e., the theoretical assumptions) to be. The mere fact that a variable of the model is labeled in a certain way, (e.g., "true feelings about life-as-a-whole") does not make it so; rather, its meaning derives from its linkages and nonlinkages to other variables (both measured and unmeasured) and from the equality constraints imposed on the parameter estimates.

In describing our various modeling results, we indicate which parameters seem interpretable as validity coefficients. We also describe the model itself in sufficient detail that the cautious reader can himself assess the assumptions that are being made.

Estimates Derived from the July Data

Our most extensive analyses estimating validity and methods effects occur for the July respondents, who answered a questionnaire designed specifically to permit such analyses. Accordingly, we begin our discussion on the evaluation of well-being measures by describing the results from these data, and subsequently examine the extent to which the July results can be replicated and extended in the nationally representative data sets.

Nature of the July Data. Scattered throughout the July questionnaire was a set of thirty-seven items that, when brought together for the purposes of the present analysis, forms a nearly complete six-by-six multimethod–multitrait matrix; i.e., a matrix in which six different "traits" (aspects of well-being) are assessed by each of six different methods.[8] The aspects of well-being are at both the global and the concern levels.

[7]Work by Blalock (1964) and Duncan (1966) signaled the start of broad interest by sociologists in causal analysis. In a subsequent series of proposals it was shown that unmeasured constructs were incorporable within path models (e.g., Blalock, 1970; Costner, 1969; Heise, 1969; Land, 1970). After it became evident that methods involving path models and factor analytic techniques were both special cases of structural equation models (Goldberger, 1972; Goldberger and Duncan, 1973), only one development remained. Joreskog (1969, 1970, 1973) developed a powerful maximum-likelihood technique for simultaneously estimating parameters for observed and unobserved variables in a structural model that allowed error components to be correlated.

[8]Use of a multimethod–multitrait design for assessing validity was first formally suggested by Campbell and Fiske (1959). The approach represented an important advance at the time but was unable to provide precise estimates of construct validity. Several later suggestions and counter-suggestions for methods of quantifying this approach were made in the psychological literature (Conger, 1971; Jackson, 1969, 1971), but the most precise use of this technique seems to be

The concerns were chosen to be well spread in the perceptual structure (as shown in Exhibit 2.2) and to include both domains and criteria. The following six aspects of well-being are represented: Life-as-a-whole, House or apartment, Spare-time activities, National government, Standard of living, and Independence or Freedom. The six measurement methods involve: self-ratings on the Delighted–Terrible, Faces, Circles, and Ladder Scales, the Social Comparison technique, and Ratings by others. (The exact wording of each of the concern-level items appears in Exhibit 2.1; see items 30, 44, 85, 87, and 105. For descriptions of the six methods used to assess life-as-a-whole, see Exhibit 3.1, measures G1, G5, G6, G7, G13, and G54, these same methods were also used to assess the concern-level aspects.[9])

It is important to note that the measures used in the analysis to be described are all based on single items. In this respect they are different from many of the measures discussed in previous chapters, which were based on clusters of items. Single-item measures are generally somewhat less valid and reliable than well-constructed multiple-item measures. After deriving estimates for these single-item measures, we will use those estimates to develop a second set of estimates for measures based on multiple items.

The Measurement Model. The general form of the structural model whose parameters provide estimates of the validity and error components of our measures appears in Exhibit 6.2, together with the results of applying the model to one subset of the measures.[10] (Had a model of this form been applied to all thirty-seven measures simultaneously, it would have required estimating a very large number of parameters: well over one hundred, which is beyond the capacity of even the largest computer program known to be relevant for this purpose.[11] Instead, as will be discussed in greater detail later, three smaller analyses were performed using overlapping subsets of the measures.)

The analytic task is to estimate a set of parameters for this model that will come as close as possible to accounting for the observed covariations among the measures, given what is assumed to be their linkages to the unmeasured causal

---

possible only when it is wedded to methods of structural analysis. Boruch and Wolins (1970), Althauser and Heberlein (1970), and Alwin (1974) all discuss such applications of structural analysis. Although our analyses were designed prior to encountering the works of Boruch and Wolins and of Alwin, we subsequently found that their proposals closely coincided with what we had done.

[9]Although the design of our analysis is based on a six-by-six multimethod–multitrait matrix, there are actually thirty-seven measures relevant to a total of thirty-five cells. The Social comparison technique was not applicable for assessing affective evaluations of the National government (since all respondents had the *same* national government), hence this cell was empty; and two cells each contained a pair of parallel measures, assessment of Life-as-a-whole and Housing, using the Delighted–Terrible Scale.

[10]Models of this form have sometimes been called "confirmatory" or "restricted" factor analysis models (e.g., Joreskog, 1969; Boruch and Wolins, 1970).

[11]Estimates were obtained using LISREL (Joreskog and Van Thillo, 1972). This computer program provides maximum-likelihood estimates for the parameters of a linear structural equation system that may involve multiple indicators of unmeasured variables.

EXHIBIT 6.2. General Form of the Measurement Model Used for the
July Data and Parameter Estimates for One Subset of the Measures
(Analysis 1)

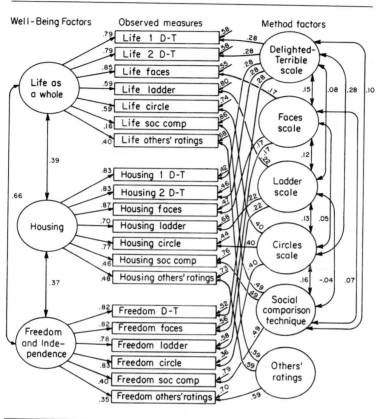

variables (the hypothetical constructs) and the presumed linkages among these unmeasured variables.

The theoretical assumptions that make it seem reasonable to interpret some of the obtained parameters as estimates of the validity and method effects are portrayed in the model or incorporated in the constraints imposed on the parameter values. Note that the variance of each observed measure (represented by the rectangles) is assumed to derive from three distinct sources: the respondents' "true feelings" about the relevant aspect of well-being (shown in the ovals on the left), the sensitivity of the particular method of measurement to effects of biases and/or halo, i.e., correlated errors or "method effects" (shown in the ovals on the right), and a residual. The true component represents valid variance; both of the other components represent error variance.

For each of the ovals on the left, direct linkages are provided to all of the measures intended to tap an identical aspect of well-being, but *not* to measures intended to tap other aspects. This helps to determine the "meaning" of the ovals on the left; i.e., they come to mean what the observed measures to which they are linked have in common, which in this case is feelings about a particular (identically defined) aspect of well-being. Although there are no direct linkages between true feelings about one aspect of well-being and measures of other aspects, the model does provide direct linkages between the ovals on the left. This incorporates our theoretical expectation that feelings about one aspect of life may well be related to feelings about other aspects (which is in accord with results described in preceding chapters).

A similar set of theoretical assumptions governs the specification of linkages involving the ovals on the right, which are intended to represent the method effects. We assume that a method can have a direct effect only on measures that use that method, but that there may be relationships among certain of the method factors themselves. (Because measures derived from Others' ratings were obtained from a source totally separate from that used for the remaining methods, this effect was constrained to be independent of the others; i.e., no linkages were provided between this oval and any of the others.)

In addition to the pattern of linkages, certain constraints imposed on the parameter values help to ensure that the ovals on the left and right take on the meanings intended for them. The most significant constraint involved linkages from the right-hand ovals to the measures. The magnitude (whatever it might be) of the linkages from any one oval had to be the *same* for all of the measures using the same method.[12] This forces the oval to mean something that has equal applicability to all of the measures using the same method, and is in accord with our expectations about the nature of a method effect. One main constraint was imposed on the parameter estimates associated with linkages from the ovals on the left and the observed measures: Estimates for the same aspect of well-being measured by the same method should be equal. (Two such cases occur in Exhibit 6.2: There are two measures of feelings about life-as-a-whole based on the Delighted–Terrible Scale and two measures of feelings about Housing using this scale.) For the analysis shown in Exhibit 6.2, there were no constraints on the parameter estimates for linkages *between* any pair of linked ovals.[13]

A couple of other assumptions are embedded in the analysis and deserve brief mention. These are that relationships among the variables of the model

[12] In the analysis of one subset of measures (later identified as "Analysis 3"), this constraint could be relaxed for measures employing the Delighted–Terrible Scale without making the model itself underidentified (i.e. unable to yield a unique set of parameter estimates). The result of permitting this relaxation, as shown in Exhibit 6.3, suggests that the constraint of requiring effects of the same method to be equal is not unrealistic.

[13] As described previously, models of the general form described here were applied to three overlapping subsets of the measures. Exhibit 6.2 shows results from one of these analyses; in the other two, one additional constraint was introduced: The linkages between the ovals on the right were fixed at zero. Since estimates for these linkages are close to zero in any case (as shown in Exhibit 6.2), imposition of this additional restriction, when it occurred, made little actual difference in the estimates of the other parameters (as shown by the similarity of the doubly estimated parameters presented in Exhibit 6.3).

(both observed and unobserved) are assumed linear, and their effects, where more than one is involved, are assumed additive. Although the truth of these assumptions could not be examined for all of the situations to which they might apply, we remind the reader that our measures of perceived well-being have shown reasonably linear relationships and reasonably additive effects whenever these matters have been examined (as described in preceding chapters). A linear additive model then seems appropriate to the data. It is also in accord with our theoretical expectations.

Because the model shown in Exhibit 6.2 incorporates our theoretical expectations about how various phenomena influenced the validity and error components of the observed measures, because serious alternative theories have not come to our attention, and because the model in fact fits the data rather well (as will be described shortly), it seems reasonable to use it to estimate the validity and error components of the measures. We shall interpret the parameter estimates associated with linkages between the measures and the ovals intended to represent true feelings as *construct validity coefficients,* and the estimates associated with the linkages between the measures and the ovals intended to represent the method factors as *method effect coefficients.*

The Results. Exhibit 6.2 shows results from the analysis of one subset of the measures.[14] Exhibit 6.3 brings together the complete set of validity and method effect coefficients.[15]

Before examining these results in detail we would note that the parameter estimates in fact fit the data well. For the analysis shown in Exhibit 6.2, the estimated relationships among the measures (there are 190 such relationships) showed a mean deviation from the observed correlations of 0.055. In no case was the discrepancy more than 0.19.[16] The other two analyses showed similarly good fits.

As shown in Exhibit 6.3, three of the methods—the D–T,[17] the Faces, and the Circles Scales—produced data with median validity coefficients approxi-

---

[14] All parameter estimates reported in this chapter pertain to standardized variables, i.e., the variance of unobserved variables has been set at 1.0, and all observed variables have been implicitly transformed to have variance of 1.0 (however, the model-generated *estimates* of variance in the observed variables may differ slightly from 1.0).

[15] Analysis 1, shown in Exhibit 6.2, included assessments of Life-as-a-whole, of Housing, and of Freedom and independence by all of the measurement methods. Analysis 2 included assessments of Freedom and independence, Standard of living, Spare-time activities, and the National government by all of the measurement methods. Analysis 3 included assessments of Life-as-a-whole and Housing by all of the methods.

[16] Using a significance test considered in Joreskog and Van Thillo (1972), these deviations could be statistically significant. However, the significance level is inflated by large sample sizes while the estimated parameters do not vary (Joreskog, 1969), and for our present purposes the absolute size of the deviations is of greater interest than their statistical probability.

[17] For convenience this chapter will use the short phrase, Delighted–Terrible Scale (or D–T Scale), to refer to the measurement method that involves self-ratings by the respondent using the Delighted–Terrible Scale in face-to-face interview or in group-administered questionnaire settings. Note that certain *other* measurement methods discussed in this chapter also use the answer categories of the D–T Scale: These include the methods called Others' ratings, Interviewer's ratings, and Telephone interview.

EXHIBIT 6.3. Estimated Validity and Method Effects Coefficients for the July Data

Measurement method:	D–T scale	Faces scale	Circles scale	Ladder scale	Social comparison	Others' rating
Validity coefficients:						
Housing	.83 (.85)	.87 (.85)	.77 (.83)	.70 (.70)	.46 (.45)	.48 (.51)
Spare time	.69	.77	.73	.82	.44	.37
National government	.87	.81	.85	.85	a	.38
Standard of living	.79	.77	.80	.70	.38	.37
Freedom or independence	.82 (.84)	.82 (.83)	.83 (.82)	.78 (.79)	.40 (.46)	.35 (.31)
Life-as-a-whole	.79 (.78)	.85 (.80)	.59 (.58)	.59 (.59)	.16 (.15)	.40 (.42)
Median validity	.82	.82	.80	.70	.42	.38
Method effects:[b]						
Analysis 1 (Exh. 6.2)	.28	.17	.40	.22	.49	.59
Analysis 2	.23	.27	.30	.29	.48	.55
Analysis 3	.29 (.25)	.27	.28	.00	.50	.52
Median method effect	.27	.27	.30	.22	.49	.55

[a] Data not obtained.
[b] Method effects parameters were constrained to be equal across aspects of well-being in each analysis (with one exception, as indicated in Analysis 3).
Values in parentheses are replications from independent solutions involving overlapping subsets of the well-being measures.

mating .8. Data obtained using the Ladder Scale had slightly lower median validity .7. And the two other methods, the Social Comparison Technique and the Rating by others, showed validities of about .4. It was no surprise to find that the respondents' feelings were assessed less accurately by other people than by the respondents themselves,[18] but the low validity of the social comparison technique had not been expected.[19]

Although there was nothing in the analysis to require that the validity estimates be consistent for different aspects of life quality when assessed by the same method, it is reassuring to observe that they turn out to be. Nearly all are within ±.10 of the median validity·value for the method. Thus, the analysis includes within itself a series of internal replications that provide further

[18]From other data available for the July respondents we are led to believe that the low validities shown in Exhibit 6.3 for measures derived from Others' ratings are quite general. The average correlation between measures based on the D–T Scale and measures based on Others' ratings for the six aspects of well-being included in the modeling analysis was .33. Exactly the same average correlation between D–T Scale ratings and Others' ratings was also obtained for eight *other* aspects of well-being.

[19]It might be argued that the validity of the Social comparison technique is wrongly estimated by this analysis on the grounds that the technique produces measures of *relative* well-being (a Type D perspective as these are described in chap. 3) whereas all the other methods yield measures of *absolute* well-being (a Type A perspective). While treating measures based upon the Social comparison technique as conceptually parallel to the others may represent a possible flaw in the design of the analysis, we would remind the reader that even when measures from the Social comparison method were put together with other Type D measures (in Exhibit 3.7). the Social comparison method performed very poorly. Thus, we feel that the validity estimates shown for this method in Exhibit 6.3 are reasonably correct.

support. Note, also, the generally close agreement of independent estimates of the parameters that were included in more than one analysis.

On the basis of these results we infer that single item measures using the D–T, Faces, or Circles Scales to assess any of a wide range of different aspects of perceived well-being contain approximately 65 percent valid variance. Assessing the same aspects of well-being by either the Social comparison technique or through Others' ratings results in only about 15 percent valid variance. The Ladder method falls in between and produced about 50 percent valid variance. Clearly, these differences are substantial.

Exhibit 6.3 also shows the magnitudes of the method effects. Here also there are sharp differences between the different methods. For the D–T, Faces, and Circles Scales, roughly 8 percent of the total variance can be attributed to method effects, whereas about 25 percent of the total variance is due to method effects when using the Social comparison technique, and 30 percent when using Ratings by others. For the Ladder Scale, about 5 percent of the total variance is due to the method.

The relatively high method effects in measures obtained from Others' ratings is notable, but not terribly surprising. Since other people have less direct access to the respondents' feelings than do the respondents themselves, one would expect substantially more "halo" in the Others' ratings than in the respondents' own ratings. This would be a reasonable explanation for the large amount of correlated error in these scores.

It is important to note the substantial similarity across the three analyses in the independent estimates of the method effect for any given method, despite the fact that these were derived in the context of different combinations of life aspects. This suggests that the equality constraint on the method effect parameters did not impose an unreasonable assumption. This conclusion is reinforced by the finding of similar method effects for the Delighted–Terrible Scale in Analysis 3 (.29 and .25), where separate method effects were estimated for Life-as-a-whole and for Housing.

Two other types of parameters appear in Exhibit 6.2. Concerned that the several method effects might themselves be correlated, we introduced linkages between all of the methods involving data obtained directly from the respondent. As can be seen in Exhibit 6.2, these parameters turn out to be very close to zero. The second type of parameter involves correlations among the "true" (unmeasured) perceptions of well-being. Here, of course, we expected substantial relationships, and they do in fact appear. (Although these latter relationships are interesting in their own right, they are essentially irrelevant to the main focus of the present chapter, other than as linkages necessary to complete the measurement model.[20])

---

[20]The estimates for these parameters in Analysis 1 appear in Exhibit 6.2. In Analysis 3 there is only one such parameter (between Life-as-a-whole and Housing) and its value is .40, a figure essentially identical to that obtained in Analysis 1. In Analysis 2 there are six such parameters whose values are as follows: Standard of living and Freedom, .49; Standard of living and Spare time, .40; Standard of living and National government, .20; Freedom and Spare time, .64; Freedom and National government, .33; Spare time and National government, .25.

Summary and Comments Regarding July Results. It appears that of the six measurement methods investigated here the three yielding the highest validity are those using the Delighted–Terrible, Faces, and Circles Scales. These three all yield measures with about the same composition: 65 percent valid variance, 8 percent correlated error (method) variance, and 27 percent residual variance. Although it is difficult to find many similar evaluations of social science measures, the information available to us suggests that measures with this composition are rather good compared to many single-item survey scales. (As will be seen later in this chapter, they compare well with various other methods with which we have experimented.) The Ladder Scale does not look as good with respect to validity, though is not bad: It contains about 50 percent valid variance. The Social comparison technique and Others' ratings seem rather poor indeed: only about 15 percent of their variance is valid.

By appropriate combination of several items that tap the same underlying perception, a composite measure can be formed that will have somewhat higher validity than any of the single items. For example, given measures with the composition of those from our more effective methods (i.e., containing 65 percent valid variance and 8 percent correlated error variance), a measure based on two items would be expected to contain not 65 percent valid variance but 76 percent; for a measure based on three items the figure is 79 percent; and for five items the figure is 83 percent. (The theoretical maximum is 89 percent.[21]) Since the conventional "validity" coefficient is the square root of the proportion of variance that is valid, these estimates imply that a three-item measure could have a validity of just under .9, and that the validity of a five-item measure could be just over .9. Thus, while one would not want to claim that social indicators of perceived well-being are perfectly valid, it would appear that fairly substantial validities can be achieved through use of appropriate measurement and scale construction techniques. This conclusion seems important because the usefulness of perceptual or "subjective" social indicators has sometimes been disputed on the grounds that all such indicators must have low validity. Obviously, our figures dispute this.

The notably low validity shown by the Others' ratings is interesting and may prove to be a significant empirical result in its own right. We think it is not the result of poor data collection procedures. Recall that the July respondents were people who had volunteered to participate in the study (for a modest fee), and who had taken the trouble to show up at an appointed time and place to fill out the questionnaires. They themselves provided us the names of the people used as other raters, in response to the following:

> We would like to contact two or three people who know you pretty well and ask them about a dozen short questions. We would like their guesses as to how you feel about certain things—your house or apartment, your neighborhood, your freedom from annoyance, and the like—the same items we asked you to estimate how your nearest neighbor felt about.

---

[21]These results are derived by application of Guilford's (1954) formula 14.37.

We'll contact these people by mail or phone, and send them a short questionnaire, telling them that you gave us their names.

What we need from you are the names of three people who know you pretty well and as good a mailing address for each as you can remember. (This may be any person—including your husband or wife.)

We are not going to tell these people how you answered any questions, nor will we tell you how they answer.

The response rate when we contacted the people who had been nominated was good, and we ended with an average of 2.3 other raters per respondent.

What is of interest is that even people who the respondents felt knew them pretty well were in fact relatively poor judges of the respondents' perceptions. This suggests that perceptions of well-being may be rather private matters. While people can—and did—give reasonably reliable answers (and, we estimate reasonably *valid* answers) regarding their affective evaluations of a wide range of life concerns, it would seem that they do not communicate their perceptions even to their friends and neighbors with much precision. Of course, they may see little reason to do so, and perhaps they see some reasons for not doing so. But the fact remains that these raters were not well informed about the feelings of our respondents. Since, as has been noted, the July respondents are reasonably representative of adult Americans generally, the inference is strong that we as a people do not really know how each other feels about many rather central life concerns. Of course, the lack of such knowledge is precisely why it has seemed important to survey perceptions of well-being. What is new here, however, is that the lack is not only at the society level, but also at the individual level. When critics question the validity or usefulness of perceptual indicators, some of their doubts may arise from the impression that they have a good understanding of other people's views. These results would suggest they probably do not.

We turn next to a series of analyses of national-level data to check the extent to which these validity and method effect estimates from the July data can be more widely generalized, and to develop validity estimates for additional measurement methods.

The Reliability of the Life Measures in National Data

One of the simplest comparisons to make between the estimates just derived from July data and national-level data involves the reliability of the Life measures. Three of the four national surveys included both Life 1 and Life 2, two measures that focus on the identical global aspect of well-being and assess it using the same method (the Delighted–Terrible Scale). Since these two measures were separated from one another by only ten to twenty minutes of interviewing time, it is reasonable to view the correlation between them as a classical short-term test-retest reliability coefficient. How well do these reliability figures agree with what we would expect from the preceding analysis?

The reliabilities of the Life measures in the national surveys are as follows: May data, .61, November Form 2 data, .71, and April data, .68.[22] If we use the estimates of the validity and method effects for Life-as-a-whole measured by the Delighted–Terrible Scale that appear in Exhibit 6.3, we obtain an estimated reliability of .70 ($.79^2 + .27^2 = .70$). Clearly, the estimate falls within the range of the observed reliabilities.

Although this comparison of observed reliability coefficients with estimates given by the measurement model is too simple to provide a very detailed check, its results are encouraging. It suggests that the joint impact that we have estimated for validity and method effects (which is what determines reliability) is reasonably generalizable to measures collected from national samples.

Estimates Derived from the May Data

Although the May survey was not designed with the same measurement evaluation goals as applied to the July questionnaire, the application of a structural model with some of the same features as the models of Exhibits 6.1 and 6.2 yields some interesting and relevant results.

Exhibit 6.4 shows the model, the measures, and the parameter estimates obtained.

With respect to the sources of variation in the observed measures, this model is identical to those described previously: It assumes the variance in each observed measure can be apportioned into a "true" component, a "method" component, and a "residual" component. The model differs, however, in three respects: (1) There is only a single method effect, since all measures are based on self-ratings using the Delighted–Terrible Scale; (2) it is explicitly assumed that "true" feelings about Life-as-a-whole are the result of "true" feelings about Self-efficacy, Family life, Material well-being, and an unspecified residual component; and (3) the constructs shown at the left of the figure are not defined by a series of items with identical content (as was the case in Exhibit 6.3, and as is the case on the right side of Exhibit 6.4), but by items with somewhat differing content. For the right side of Exhibit 6.4, these differences do not affect our interpretation of the validity- and method-effect linkages. However, for the left side of the figure, the linkages between the measures and the "true" feelings about aspects of well-being are more appropriately interpreted as factor loadings than as true validity coefficients. As previously, the method effect parameters were constrained to be equal, as were validity parameters that pertained to parallel measures, the two Life measures shown on the right side of Exhibit 6.4.

The measures entered in the analysis were each based on a single interview

---

[22]The reliability of these measures can also be considered from the perspective of the percent of respondents who gave similar answers to the two questions. As noted in chapter 3, the May data show 92 percent of respondents providing an answer to Life 2 that was either identical, or immediately adjacent, to the answer they gave to Life 1 (52 percent answered both questions identically). In the April data the figures are 93 percent and 54 percent, respectively.

The observed reliability of Life 1 and Life 2 in the July data is .64.

EXHIBIT 6.4. Structural Model Applied to Data from May Respondents

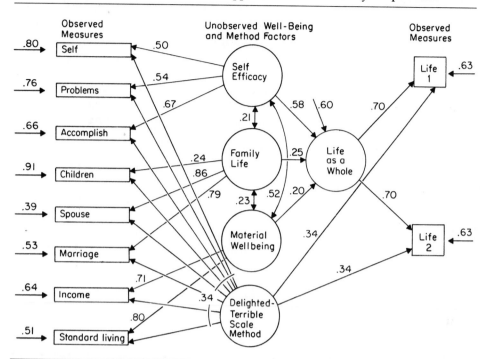

item that had been answered using the Delighted–Terrible Scale. The global measures are Life 1 and Life 2 (Measures G1 and G2, as shown in Exhibit 3.1), and the concern-level measures are those numbered 1, 2, 3, 14, 20, 22, 83, and 85 in Exhibit 2.1. Note that the concern-level measures are linked to their respective ovals in a way that is consistent with the way they were found to cluster in the perceptual structure (shown in Exhibit 2.7).

As previously, the LISREL computer program was used to generate estimates of the parameters of the specified model that would provide the best reproduction of the correlations observed among the measures. Once again, the fit was good: The average discrepancy between the observed and estimated correlations was 0.032, with a maximum discrepancy of 0.09.

As shown in Exhibit 6.4, the validity estimates for the measures of Life-as-a-whole are .70 and the method effects are .34. While not identical to results obtained for the July data, both these figures are reasonably close. (The July data provided two estimates of the validity of Life-as-a-whole measured by self-ratings on the D–T Scale—.79 and .78—and four estimates of the method effect—median = .27; see Exhibit 6.3)

While the differences are small, it is of interest to conjecture why the answers of the May respondents might show somewhat lower validities and somewhat higher method effects than those of the July respondents. This could result from the above-average education of the July respondents, the greater time they spent considering the quality of their lives, and/or the use of a questionnaire rather than interview survey procedure.[23]

The linkages on the left side of Exhibit 6.4 between the observed measures and the several aspects of well-being, while not interpretable as validity coefficients, are also interesting. The Standard of living item reflects the Material well-being construct with just about the same accuracy for these respondents (.80) as its estimated validity in the July data (.79). With the exception of the item about Children, most of the other parameters are estimated at similar or only slightly lower levels than typical validities estimated in Exhibit 6.3 for self-report measures using the D–T Scale format. (The low coefficient for feelings about Children is probably not attributable to low item validity but a reflection of the fact that the Children, Spouse, and Marriage items refer to different sets of feelings.)

In general, the results of the analysis of the May data suggest that the estimates of validity and method effects derived for the July measures based on self-reports using the Delighted–Terrible Scale can be generalized to typical national-level survey applications with only slight modification. The validity estimates from the July data may be slightly high, and the method effects slightly low, but the appropriate adjustments in the coefficients are probably less than .1.

Estimates Derived from the April Data

Our treatment of the April data from the measurement evaluation standpoint consists of an analysis using a very simple measurement model. More complex models could undoubtedly be applied to these data, but for developing a few validity estimates that can be compared with those from other data sets even the simple model seems reasonably adequate.

Four different methods were used to assess how the April respondents felt about their Life-as-a-whole. The respondent himself provided answers on the Delighted–Terrible, the Circles, and the Ladder Scales, and in addition the interviewer provided a rating of how the respondent seemed to feel. The resulting data yielded four "Type A" global measures. They are listed in Exhibit 3.1 as G3, G6, G7, and G14. Their interrelationships appear in Exhibit 3.2. It is these interrelationships that our present modeling analysis seeks to "explain" on the basis of more fundamental structural parameters.

The model applied to the data, and the estimated parameters, appear in Exhibit 6.5. The model assumes that each global measure is influenced in part by the respondents' true feelings about Life-as-a-whole and in part by other phenomena ("error") unique to that measure. The model also assumes that the four measures show the intercorrelations they do because they all reflect feelings about Life-as-a-whole, but that they are differentially sensitive to these

---

[23]Chapter 4 includes a more extended discussion of factors that may distinguish data provided by the July respondents from these obtained in the national surveys. Appendix H shows how the July respondents compare with national averages on various sociodemographic characteristics.

EXHIBIT 6.5. Measurement Model Applied to Data
from April Respondents

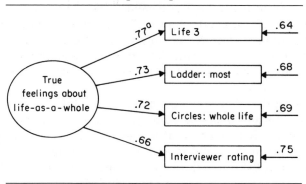

[a] Equivalent to validity of .71 for a single-item measure; see text.

feelings. Of course, given our assumption about what the oval shown in the exhibit represents, the parameter estimates for the linkages between the oval and each of the measures are interpretable as construct validity estimates.

One might question the absence of a correlated error factor from the model in Exhibit 6.5. In previous models this factor has been explicitly a *method* factor, necessitated by the presence in the model of two or more measures based on the same method and by our (well-supported) assumption that the method of measurement is likely to have some influence of its own on the scores obtained. While we believe our assumption applies equally well to these April data, there seems no need to introduce a common method factor because no two measures derive from the same method. (Since each method effect is assumed to be separate and essentially uncorrelated with the others, its effect is combined with other unique "residual" inputs to its respective measure.)

Of course, it is conceivable that there are certain biases that might have similar impacts even when measures are derived from different methods. What about these? We suspect that in the present analysis (though *not* in general) such effects will be quite small. One of the measures (the Interviewer rating) is based on a completely different source from the others, and an argument of common biases is hard to sustain here. Among the other three measures, all of which derive directly from the respondent, the formats of the assessment methods are distinctly different. One (the D–T Scale) involves the choice of a verbally defined category, another involves use of a nonverbal "ladder," the third requires picking from a set of circles that differ with respect to the *proportion* of "good things" and "bad things." The substantial heterogeneity among these three scale formats would be expected to reduce the effects of common (crossmethod) biases, and in fact our analysis of the July data showed that relationships among the effects of these methods tended to be very weak (as shown in Exhibit 6.2). In short, given the substantial heterogeneity among these methods, we are prepared to assume that the impact of correlated errors, if any, would be small enough to be ignored. (The result of an error in this assumption will be an overestimate of the validity coefficients.)

As can be seen in Exhibit 6.5, the validity estimates turn out to be .77 for the Life 3 measure, .73 for Ladder: most, .72 for Circles: whole life, and .66 for the Interviewer rating.[24] Despite the simplicity of the model, these parameters fit the data rather well. The average deviation between correlations estimated from these parameters and those actually observed is .037, and in no case is the discrepancy larger than .06.

In considering the .77 validity estimate for the Life 3 measure, it must be recalled that Life 3 is a measure based on two items, Life 1 and Life 2, and that its validity is undoubtedly somewhat higher than that of either of its components. However, given this validity and the observed reliability of its components (.68, shown in Exhibit 3.2), one can estimate that the validity of each of the components must have been about .71.[25] This figure is what should be compared with the .79 estimated for Life 1 or Life 2 in the July data, and the estimate of .70 for these measures in the May data. We find that a totally independent analysis again yields an estimate that is consistent with previous ones. In fact, the estimated validity of Life 1 and Life 2 is almost identical in the two data sets that come from national-level surveys.

The validity estimates shown in Exhibit 6.5 for the Ladder and Circle measures (.73 and .72 respectively) can also be compared with similar estimates from the July data. When used to assess *Life-as-a-whole*, these methods each yielded validity coefficients of .59 in the July data (see Exhibit 6.3); hence, the present estimates are moderately higher. On the other hand, when these methods were evaluated against a broader set of six measures, the Ladder method showed a median validity of .70 and the Circles method showed a median validity of .80 (also shown in Exhibit 6.3). Against these more broadly based figures, the present estimate for the Ladder Scale is very close to the July figure, and the Circles estimate is modestly lower. All in all, we conclude that the present estimates are reasonably consistent with the July results.

The validity coefficient of .66 for the Interviewer's rating is not directly comparable with any previous estimate. The figure, however, meshes well with estimates we have for other assessment methods. Given that the interviewers probably assessed the respondents' feelings less accurately than did the respondents themselves, it is not surprising to find a lower validity for the interviewer ratings than for any of the measures provided by the April respondents themselves. And given that the interviewers actually heard the respondents answer questions about their feelings of well-being (including feelings about Life-as-a-whole), it is not surprising that the interviewer ratings show higher validity than the method of Others' ratings (shown in Exhibit 6.3), which obtained assessments from people who were well acquainted with the respondent but who had probably not recently discussed perceptions of well-being with this person.

---

[24]These estimates were derived by applying the algebra of path analysis (Duncan, 1966) to all possible three-variable combinations and averaging the results. In no case did any individual parameter estimate deviate from the average shown in Exhibit 6.5 by more than .08.

[25]This figure was derived by applying formula 14.37 from Guilford, 1954.

Estimates Derived from the November Data

The November Form 2 data, based on another independent national sample, include measures derived by several assessment methods not previously examined in this chapter. In addition to the Life measures, which appear in other data sets as well, the November data include a measure of Life-as-a-whole utilizing the seven-point Satisfaction Scale, and another global assessment using the Thermometer Scale.

Our present analysis focuses on three global assessments: measures G3, G8, and G29 in Exhibit 3.1. Their interrelationships appear in Exhibit 3.5. Two versions of a simple measurement model have been applied to them. Both versions appear in Exhibit 6.6.

The rationale for Version 1 of the model is identical to what has already been described regarding the model applied to the April data. Essentially, this version assumes that all three global measures reflect, to possibly varying degrees, the respondents' true feelings about Life-as-a-whole, and that this is the only phenomenon the measures have in common. The absence of a correlated error factor might be justified on the same grounds as were used for the

EXHIBIT 6.6. Two Versions of Measurement Model Applied to Data from November Form 2 Respondents

Version 1

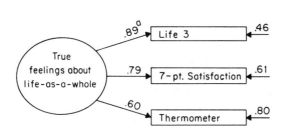

Version 2

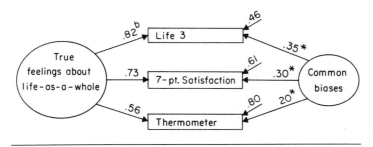

* In Version 2 of the model the parameter estimates for the common bias effects are assumed values.
[a] Equivalent to a validity of .82 for a single-item measure; see text.
[b] Equivalent to a validity of .76 for a single-item measure; see text.

April model: that no two of these measures use the same method, and that the effects of biases that would have similar effects across two or more methods are either nonexistent or small enough to be ignored.

Given the heterogeneity of the measures in the April data, the assumption of there being only small crossmethod bias effects seemed reasonable, and thus it seemed appropriate not to include a common bias factor in the model. In the November data, however, the correctness of such an assumption is more questionable. Although the measures being analysed derive from methods that are formally different, the differences between these methods are less substantial than between the April measures. Consequently, we have also experimented with another version of the model to see what impact the inclusion of a common error factor would have on the estimated validities. Unfortunately, in order to derive any estimates at all from Version 2 of the model it is necessary to base certain of the parameter estimates on assumed values. (Given just three measures, there is not enough information to estimate six independent parameters.) We have made some guesses about the extent to which each of the three measures might reflect common biases, and these are the values that appear in Exhibit 6.6 as the bias effects in Version 2.

The assumed values for the bias effects were based on considerations regarding the nature of the measures, the similarity between them, and the magnitudes of correlated error effects empirically derived in other data. We reasoned that (1) the Delighted–Terrible Scale (on which the Life measures are based) and the seven-point Satisfaction Scale were more similar to one another than either was to the Thermometer Scale, and hence would be more affected by common biases; (2) the Life 3 measure, which is itself based on a combination of Life 1 and Life 2, would reflect these biases somewhat more than the single-item Satisfaction measure; and (3) the crossmethod bias effects would probably not exceed the method effects estimated in the July or May data sets. Considerations 1 and 2 suggest an order for the assumed values, and consideration 3 suggests a level. While the values we chose—.35, .30, and .20, for Life 3, seven-point Satisfaction, and Thermometer, respectively—are admittedly somewhat arbitrary, they are not unreasonable in the light of previous analyses, and they permit us to see the impact on the validity estimates of allowing for correlated errors.

As shown in Exhibit 6.6, the estimated validities for Life 3 in the November data are .89 and .82 in Versions 1 and 2 of the model, respectively.[26] Since Life 3 is a two-item measure, it is necessary to adjust these estimates downward to arrive at estimates applicable for a single-item measure employing the Delighted–Terrible Scale. The appropriate values turn out to be .82 and .76 for Versions 1 and 2 of the model.[27] It is worth noting that these November

---

[26]All estimates for the November data were derived by the algebra of path analysis (Duncan, 1966). The estimated parameters fit the observed correlations perfectly, but this is trivial since the number of parameters being estimated in each version of the model is equal to the number of observed relationships among the measures.

[27]These adjustments are based on Formula 14.37 of Guilford (1954) and the reliability of Life 1 and 2 observed in these November data (.71, as shown in Exhibit 3.5).

estimates are just slightly below the estimates derived from the July data for Life 1 and Life 2 (.79), and somewhat above the estimates for these same measures in the May and April national surveys (.70 and .71, respectively). All in all, the November estimates seem consistent with those derived previously.

The seven-point Satisfaction measure has estimated validities of .79 and .73 in the two versions of the model, slightly lower, in each case, than the estimated validities of single item measures utilizing the Delighted–Terrible Scale (.82 and .76, as just noted). Regardless of whether one uses the estimates from Version 1 or Version 2, the figures suggest that the Delighted–Terrible Scale produces measures that contain about 8 percent more valid variance than that produced by the seven-point Satisfaction Scale ($(.76^2 - .73^2)/.73^2 = 8$ percent).

In both versions of the model, the Thermometer Scale appears distinctly inferior to either of the other two measures. Its validities are estimated at .60 and .56, among the lowest we have seen for measures derived directly from the respondent.

Before closing this section we would note that the seven-point Satisfaction scale, which we replicated from the work of Campbell, Converse, and Rodgers (1976), is not the only measure of feelings about Life-as-a-whole used by them. While they sometimes used this measure to assess evaluations of "general well-being" (e.g., in their chaps. 12 and 13), and while their "primary investment was made in a portfolio of measures involving 'satisfaction' as a key word" (quoted from their chap. 2), they also developed and used a more broadly based Index of Well-being. Their Index of Well-being combined evaluations of Life-as-a-whole made on the seven-point Satisfaction Scale with evaluations of eight other life qualities ("enjoyable," "full," "rewarding," etc.). Because of its broader coverage, we would classify this Index of Well-being as a Type A global measure and would have included it (rather than seven-point Satisfaction, which is classified in our chap. 3 as a Type C measure) in the analyses of Exhibit 6.6 had it been feasible to do so. The fact that the Index of Well-being requires nine items, most of which were not present in our November data, precluded our doing so.

Estimates Derived from the October Data

As described in chapter 1, a random sample of 280 respondents who had participated in the April survey were recontacted by telephone the following October and asked for their current evaluations of several aspects of their lives. Six questions relating to life quality were read to them over the phone, five of which were identical to questions asked six months earlier and were to be answered using the categories of the Delighted–Terrible Scale.[28] The sixth question asked: "Compared to six months ago, do you think your life as a whole now is better, worse, or about the same?" These six questions were just

[28]The items included evaluations of Life-as-a-whole, Yourself, Fun and enjoyment, Independence and freedom, and Safety. (See items G1, 22, 28, 44, and 95 in Exhibits 2.1 and 3.1 for the exact wording.)

part of the total telephone interview. The consistency of their answers over the six-month interval is one indication of the reliability of the measures, and by making certain assumptions, can also be used to estimate their validity. Because the April and October data were collected by different methods, a face-to-face interview in April and a telephone interview in October, it would be inappropriate to regard the correlation between them as a strict reliability coefficient; instead we shall use the term "consistency coefficient."

For all October respondents, the consistency coefficients (i.e., the Pearson r's between their answers in April and their answers in October) range from .32 to .52, with a mean of .40. Among the 68 percent of the respondents who said their lives were "about the same" in October as they had been in April, the range of the consistency coefficients is slightly wider—from .29 to .57—and the mean has the same value of .40. To the Life-as-a-whole item, 88 percent of the people who said their lives were "about the same" gave an answer in October that was the same or within one scale category of the answer they gave in April (51 percent gave identical answers) and the consistency coefficient for this item among those people was exactly at the mean, .40. The percentage-agreement figures for answers to other items are rather similar.[29]

The shifts in mean levels of satisfaction between April and October tend to be small, but in expected directions. To the item inquiring about Life-as-a-whole, the people who reported that their lives were "about the same" gave answers that average just about the same as in April; people who said things were "better now" gave answers that have a higher mean; those who said things were "worse now" show a lower mean.[30]

The model we have used to estimate the validity of measures obtained by the telephone interview appears in Exhibit 6.7. As in previous exhibits, the ovals on the left represent true feelings about a particular aspect of well-being, the oval on the right represents correlated errors arising from common biases, methods, and the like, and the rectangles in the middle represent the actual measures of particular feelings. As indicated in the exhibit, it is assumed that true feelings about x (any of the five life aspects being discussed) at the time of the April survey influenced the measurement of those feelings in April, and that these true feelings in April also influenced the true feelings the following October, which then in turn influenced the October measurement of those feelings. Since both measurements derive from the same source (the respondents) and depend on a similar, but not identical, assessment method (the April

[29]A small side analysis shows, as we expected, that respondents who had been perfectly consistent in the two answers they gave regarding Life-as-a-whole in the April interview (i.e., who gave the *same* answers to Life 1 and Life 2) show higher reliability over the six-month period than do respondents who had been less consistent within the April interview (mean reliabilities are .47 for respondents who had been consistent in April and .35 for the others). To our surprise, however, respondents with lower education show higher average reliabilities than those with more education. Further analysis suggests this is an artifact of the less educated respondents expressing a wider *range* of feelings. The more educated respondents, as we expected, show a modestly higher percentage of consistent answers.

[30]These differences, in terms of categories of the D–T Scale are −.08, +.29, and −.85, respectively; the number of cases in three groups are 191, 74, and 14, respectively.

**EXHIBIT 6.7. Measurement Model to Account for Reliability Assessed
over a Six-Month Period**

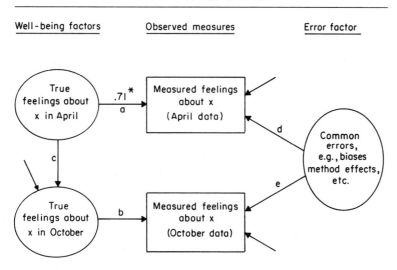

Estimated validity for October measures, given average reliability of .40 and assumed values for parameters c and d as follows:

	c = .9	c = .8	c = .7
d x e = .01 (e.g., d=e=.1)	.61	.69	.78
d x e = .04 (e.g., d=e=.2)	.55	.63	.72
d x e = .09 (e.g., d=e=.3)	.49	.55	.62

*.71 is the validity estimate for single-item measures based on the D–T Scale in the April data; see Exhibit 6.5.

survey was a face-to-face interview using the D–T Scale; the October survey was a telephone interview using the D–T Scale), it seems desirable to allow for the possibility that various biases may have had similar effects on both measurements, thereby creating correlated errors.

The model as depicted in Exhibit 6.7 involves five independent parameters (plus three "residual" parameters). The parameter labeled *b* is the validity estimate we desire for single-item measures using the Delighted–Terrible Scale in a telephone interview format. The only datum we have is the observed consistency between our measures of respondents' feelings in April and October; i.e., the correlation between the two rectangles in Exhibit 6.7. With five independent parameters and only one datum, the model would be hopelessly underidentified except for the fact that the results of previous analyses and some assumptions about the October measurement situation permit us to make informed guesses about some of the parameters. By experimenting with a range of guesses (a rather narrow range, it turns out) we can derive a range for the validity estimates we seek.

Let us review the bases on which we can make *a priori* estimates for some of the parameters. For parameter a we have a previous result (from the model shown in Exhibit 6.5) that can be used. We have already estimated that single item measures employing the Delighted–Terrible Scale in the April data had a validity of .71. This is precisely what parameter a is, and we accordingly assign it this value.

Parameter c is the stability of true feelings over a six-month interval. It is virtually certain that they are not perfectly stable (i.e. a value of 1.0 would be unrealistic), and it is also very likely that they are reasonably stable. Most people's lives do not change radically in a six-month period. We experimented with values of .9, .8, .7, and .6 for this parameter and found that when it became as low as .6 it implied certain other outcomes that were quite unreasonable (such as validity coefficients close to 1.00). Hence, we believe an estimate in the range of .7 to .9 is most reasonable for parameter c.

Parameters d and e refer to the effects of correlated errors. What matters for the estimation of the validity coefficient we desire is not the individual values of d and e but their product. What is a reasonable range for this product? The two empirically based estimates of the impact of method factors associated with the Delighted–Terrible Scale yielded parameter estimates of .27 and .34 (Exhibits 6.3 and 6.4). If d and e were set equal to each other and at the higher of these two levels, their product would be .12; at the lower of the two levels it would be .08. However, the nature of the present measurement situation suggests that the impact of common errors would be lower here than in the situations where these estimates were made. The assessment methods differ somewhat between the April and October measures, and the six-month interval between the data collections should reduce the impact of common biases. Furthermore, in the present situation there seems no reason to expect that parameters d and e should be constrained to be equal, and even if one were at the .34 level the product of the two would be substantially below .12 if the other were even modestly lower. Since there is almost certainly *some* correlated error effect, we have experimented with products ranging from .01 to .09.

Exhibit 6.7 includes a small table showing the validity with which single item measures in the October data would be estimated to tap true feelings about well-being (i.e., the value of parameter b) given that the mean reliability was .40, given that the April validity was estimated at .71, and given nine different combinations of assumptions about the values of parameters c, d, and e. The validity estimates range from approximately .5 to approximately .8, with the median being .62. If we set parameters c, d, and e each at the middle of the ranges we have been discussing, the resulting validity estimate would be .63. Hence .60 seems a realistic, perhaps slightly conservative, estimate for the validity of the measures in the October data. While we would grant that this estimate is heavily dependent on its accompanying assumptions, most alternative assumptions that seem reasonable would not alter the value by more than .1.

A validity estimate of .60 for the October data seems quite reasonable when compared with the .71 independently estimated for the April data. One might expect that an interview conducted over the telephone might yield somewhat less valid information than one in a face-to-face setting. Opportunities for "training" the respondent in the use of the answer scales are more limited, the establishment of good rapport between the interviewer and the respondent is more difficult, and some of the visual and physical cues that trained interviewers use to know whether a respondent has fully understood a question and given a reasonable answer are absent.

Comparison of Validity Estimates for Different Methods

This major section of the chapter has reported validity estimates for single-item measures derived from ten different assessment methods. Since one of our purposes is to identify the more effective methods for measuring perceptions of well-being, and since the ability of a measure to validly reflect those perceptions is an important criterion of effectiveness, it will be useful to compare the methods with respect to their estimated validity.

The comparison is complicated somewhat by the fact that not all measures were included in all data sets, and by the fact that the general level of validity seemed to run a bit higher in some data sets than others. This may result from some special characteristics of the respondents (as in the July data), or from differences between the measurement models used to make the estimates. Although the differences between parallel validity estimates are not large (the maximum discrepancy from different data sets for the same measure is about .10), the differences are sufficient to make a simple averaging of the obtained estimates inappropriate.

Nevertheless within any one data set the rank order of the validity estimates is clear, and with just a few minor exceptions the relative sizes remain constant across the different sets of respondents. Since measures based on the Delighted–Terrible Scale are present in each of the data sets, and since these measures consistently show validity coefficients that are either the highest in the group or very close to the highest, these can be used to provide a common point of reference.

Exhibit 6.8 summarizes the relative validities produced by the methods we have examined. The proportion of valid variance produced by single-item measures based on the Delighted–Terrible Scale (as shown in Exhibits 6.3 through 6.6) is taken as the base (= 100 percent) for each data set, and the proportion of valid variance in single-item measures derived from other methods, relative to this base, is shown for all other methods. For example, the last entry in the first column of Exhibit 6.8 shows that measures based on Others'

EXHIBIT 6.8. Comparison of Amounts of Valid Variance in Single-Item Measures Derived by Designated Assessment Methods

Measurement method	Survey			November[a]		Average
	July	May	Apr./Oct.	Version 1	Version 2	
D–T scale	100%	100%	100%	100%	100%	100%
Faces scale	100%	—	—	—	—	100%
Circles scale	95%	—	103%	—	—	99%
Seven-pt. Sat. scale	—	—	—	92%	93%	93%
Ladder scale	73%	—	106%	—	—	90%
Interviewer's rating	—	—	87%	—	—	87%
Telephone interview	—	—	71%	—	—	71%
Thermometer scale	—	—	—	54%	52%	53%
Social comp. tech.	27%	—	—	—	—	27%
Others' ratings	21%	—	—	—	—	21%

[a] Results are shown separately for Version 1 and Version 2 of the measurement model applied to the November data.

Figures show the valid variance produced by designated methods as a percentage of the valid variance in measures based on the Delighted–Terrible Scale used in the same survey and estimated by the same model.

ratings were estimated to contain only 21 percent as much valid variance as those based on the Delighted–Terrible Scale.[31]

From the Average column in Exhibit 6.8 one gets a clear idea of the relative validity ranking of the various methods. Three methods stand out at the top: the D–T, The Faces, and the Circles Scales. The data that we have suggest these are nearly equivalent with respect to their sensitivity to respondents' true feelings. From Exhibits 6.3 to 6.6, one can see that estimates of their validity coefficients ranged from .82 to .70, suggesting that half to two-thirds of their variance is valid variance. (Exhibit 6.3 shows that all three appear about equally sensitive to method effects, and that these account for approximately another 8 percent of their variance.)

A second set of three methods, less effective than the first three but nevertheless relatively good, also appears in Exhibit 6.7. These include the seven-point Satisfaction Scale, the Ladder Scale, and the Interviewer's ratings. These were estimated to produce about 90 percent as much valid variance as the top-ranked methods, with the seven-point Satisfaction Scale looking slightly better than this and the Interviewer s ratings looking slightly worse. Somewhat below this second set comes the Telephone interview technique, yielding roughly three-quarters as much valid variance as the top-ranked methods, and somewhat lower still comes the Thermometer Scale, which produced only about half as much valid variance as the top-ranked methods. At the very bottom

---

[31]The derivation is as follows: The validity estimate for the D–T Scale (from Exhibit 6.3) = .82, i.e., 67 percent of the total variance of these measures is estimated to be valid ($.82^2 = .67$); the validity estimate for Others' ratings (also from Exhibit 6.3) = .38, for 14 percent valid variance ($.38^2 = .14$); this latter figure (.14) is 21 percent of the former (.67).

come the Social comparison technique and Others' ratings. They produced only about a quarter as much valid variance as the top-ranked ones and look very poor indeed.

In considering the results shown in Exhibit 6.8, one needs constantly to remember the dependence of our validity estimates on the assumptions we have made about the measurement process and, in the case of the November and October data sets, the fact that some parameters had to be estimated from theoretical considerations rather than empirically. For several reasons, however, we feel reasonably confident about the ranking implied by the right-most column of Exhibit 6.8.

First, despite the use of five different sets of data, and measurement models whose details differed in significant ways, in the cases where independent but parallel validity estimates could be compared they proved to be reasonably close.[32]

Second, even when we tried modestly different models on the same data, the results, particularly when transformed to relative validities, were not very different. Exhibit 6.8 shows the similarity of the results derived from the two versions of the model applied to the November data. Likewise, most of the nine versions of the model applied to the October data would not have markedly changed the rank assigned to the Telephone interview technique.

Third, the rank order of the various methods with respect to estimated validity is generally consistent with the relative levels of relationships described in chapter 5. There we saw that virtually all measures of global well-being showed the same *pattern* of relationships to a standard set of twenty-two concerns, but that the *level* of the relationships depended upon the method used to assess the global feelings. We now encounter a result that is consistent with the latter one, and that in fact could well explain it: In general, the level of the relationships shown by the various methods in Exhibits 5.1 and 5.3 is closely related to the relative validities estimated for the various methods in Exhibit 6.8. The higher relationships are exactly what one would expect as a result of more valid measurements, and the consistency of the two sets of findings, despite the fact that they were derived by quite different approaches and from largely independent sets of relationships, gives added credence to the validity rankings.

In addition to these statistically oriented considerations, it should be noted that the results of Exhibit 6.8 are entirely reasonable in the light of our more generally based expectations. Methods that involve direct questioning of the respondent and that use a set of precisely labeled categories all have high validities (the D–T, Faces, and Circles Scales). Those that involve direct questioning but involve mostly unlabeled categories (the seven-point Satisfaction, the Ladder, and the Thermometer Scales) tend to show somewhat lower validi-

---

[32]In looking at Exhibit 6.8, one might note the apparently substantial discrepancy in the two relative estimates for the Ladder Scale. While we do not have a satisfying explanation for this discrepancy, we would note that the absolute validity estimates were almost identical: .70 in July and .73 in April.

ties. Measures based on data from other people (Interviewer's rating, Others' ratings), or on a very indirect assessment of perceived well-being (the Social comparison technique), tend to rank low.

We suspect that some of the validity estimates we have derived are particularly dependent upon the specific way in which the measurement method was applied. The validity of the Telephone interview, for example, was probably reduced relative to others because the respondent was asked only a very few questions about well-being, and hence probably had limited opportunity to focus his thoughts on this matter and to refamiliarize himself with the Delighted–Terrible Scale, from which he was to choose his answers. Had more time been available in the total telephone interview for questions about life quality, we suspect the validity of this technique would have been somewhat higher. Similarly, the Interviewer's rating was made after the interviewer had heard the respondent answer a whole series of questions about both specific and general aspects of well-being. One would expect the validity of this technique to change considerably if the interviewer's opportunity to become familiar with the respondent's views was different.

Despite these limitations, we believe Exhibit 6.8 can be helpful in choosing methods for assessing perceptions of well-being. The methods listed near the top of Exhibit 6.8 seem to be much more sensitive to these perceptions than those listed near the bottom. In fact, the methods near the bottom seem so poor that we feel a rather special defense would be required to justify any major subsequent effort devoted to them.

Exhibit 6.8 summarizes much of what we have to present regarding the differential validities of the measurement methods we have investigated. While we regard validity as one of the primary criteria for evaluating measurement methods, it is not the only one. We turn next to a brief examination of another criterion: the ability of a measurement method to discriminate among the respondents. We shall consider the five measurement methods that rank highest in estimated validity.

DISTRIBUTIONS PRODUCED BY THE MORE VALID METHODS

In evaluating the appropriateness of various methods for assessing feelings about well-being, one of the considerations is the form of the distribution that method provides. Methods that result in the population being well and reasonably symmetrically spread on the resulting scale are generally to be preferred over methods that fail to achieve this.

If a large proportion of a population is lumped together into the same category of a scale, the scale is unable to discriminate among these people, which may represent a liability when the data are analyzed. If heavy clustering occurs at one end of a scale, the situation is particularly undesirable because the scale is, in a sense, inappropriately "centered" with respect to the population being investigated. The scale not only fails to discriminate among the people in the cluster, but would be relatively insensitive to future changes that moved the population still further toward the end at which people are already heavily clustered. Furthermore, a reasonably symmetric distribution is assumed by many statistical techniques, and the presence of heavy clustering at one end of a scale may make the results of applying such techniques either incorrect or subject to misinterpretation.

Our interest in distribution forms is not independent of our earlier concerns about validity. We make no assumption that the real world contains only phenomena that show statistically normal (i.e., "bell-shaped") distributions. On the contrary, there are undoubtedly many phenomena that are not normally, or even symmetrically distributed. Scales that are intended to tap such phenomena must reproduce the actual distribution, however skewed it may be, if they are to be perfectly valid.

Having recognized this, however, we would go on to note that expectations about how phenomena are "really" distributed is one of the criteria that influences the choice of what is to be investigated and how one's interests are to be defined. To cite an extreme example, phenomena on which the population shows great clustering (e.g., the number of legs possessed by respondents) are simply not very useful as potential variables, however validly they might be measured. While the distribution form is just one of many factors that influence the choice of phenomena, other things equal, one would usually choose phenomena on which the population is believed to be well spread.

These considerations were partly what motivated our development of the Delighted–Terrible Scale. We had observed that when Campbell, Converse, and Rodgers (1976) used the seven-point Satisfaction Scale to assess people's feelings about life quality, rather heavy clustering occurred at the "satisfied" end of the scale. For the ten concern-level aspects most central to their study the average distribution showed two-thirds of adult Americans falling in the first two scale categories. While this may be an accurate reflection of the proportion of people who were *satisfied* with their lives, we felt that a different measurement method might prove able to discriminate a somewhat wider range of feelings. The Delighted–Terrible Scale was designed, in part, to provide differentiation among the large group of people who seemed to be "satisfied," but who, we suspected, did not all feel equally positive about their lives.

Statistical Results

Our data clearly show that the Delighted–Terrible Scale produces greater differentiation at the positive end of the scale than the seven-point Satisfaction Scale. For the nine life concerns that can be closely matched between our May data and the Campbell-Converse-Rodgers data, we found an average of 54 percent of the population locating themselves in the top two categories of the Delighted–Terrible Scale, whereas the comparable figure for the seven-point Satisfaction Scale is 65 percent.

The difference between the distributions given by these two measurement methods is shown somewhat more precisely in the results from our two groups of November respondents. The *same* respondents were asked to assess the same phenomenon (Life-as-a-whole), using the Delighted–Terrible Scale and—at a different point in the interview—using the seven-point Satisfaction Scale. The results appear in Exhibit 6.9 and again demonstrate that, as intended, the Delighted–Terrible Scale permits more discrimination at the positive end. Both of the independent but simultaneous November national surveys showed this result. Exhibit N. 2 in appendix N provides a similar comparison.

The Delighted–Terrible and seven-point Satisfaction Scales are not the only measurement methods whose estimated validity ranks fairly high. It is of interest also to examine the distributions that result from the Faces, the Circles, and the Ladder Scale. These were all used in the questionnaire administered to the July respondents, and two of the three (Circles and Ladder) also appeared in the April national survey. The distributions produced by these scales when used to evaluate Life-as-a-whole appear in Exhibit 6.10. The exhibit also includes the distributions produced by the Delighted–Terrible Scale in these surveys.

As can be seen in Exhibit 6.10, in the April survey the Ladder and Circles Scales produced well-spread distributions with somewhat less clustering at the positive end than the Delighted–Terrible Scale. In the July data all scales show higher means than in the April data with a consequent upward shift of the distributions. Here again, however, the clustering at the positive end is less for the Ladder and Circles Scales than for the Delighted–Terrible Scale. The July data show a modest difference between the Ladder and Circles Scales, with the lesser clustering being for the Ladder distribution. The April data show this

EXHIBIT 6.9. Comparison of Distributions Produced by the Delighted–Terrible and Seven-Point Satisfaction Scales for Feelings About Life-as-a-Whole

Survey:		Nov. Form 1		Nov. Form 2		
Scale:		D–T	Sat.	D–T	D–T	Sat.
Measure:[a]		G1	G29	G1	G2	G29
Scale categories[b]						
Positive feelings	7	10.6%	12.5%	8.5%	11.3%	14.1%
	6	34.6%	40.9%	35.3%	36.7%	43.8%
	5	39.5%	26.7%	39.8%	36.9%	23.5%
	4	11.8%	13.6%	12.6%	10.6%	11.2%
	3	2.2%	4.3%	2.3%	2.9%	4.9%
	2	0.8%	1.5%	1.1%	0.7%	1.5%
Negative feelings	1	0.5%	0.5%	0.4%	0.9%	1.0%
Total		100.0%	100.0%	100.0%	100.0%	100.0%
Mean:		5.34	5.37	5.30	5.38	5.42
s.d.:		1.00	1.14	0.99	1.05	1.20
skew:		0.72	0.89	0.77	0.95	1.11

[a] All items assess feelings about Life-as-a-whole. Measure G1 is what we have called Life 1, G2 is Life 2, and G29 is Seven-point Satisfaction. See Exhibit 3.1 for question wording.
[b] See Exhibit 3.1 for labeling of scale categories.
Data Sources: 1,118 respondents to November Form 1 national survey; 1,072 respondents to November Form 2 national survey.

EXHIBIT 6.10. Comparison of Distributions Produced by the Delighted–Terrible, Faces, Ladder, and Circles Scales for Feelings About Life-as-a-Whole

Survey:		April			July			
Scale: Measure:[a]		D–T G1	Ladder G6	Circles G7	D–T G1	Faces G5	Ladder G6	Circles G7
Scale categories:[b]								
Positive feelings	9	[c]	7%	11%	[c]	[c]	4%	3%
	8	[c]	11%	15%	[c]	[c]	10%	24%
	7	10%	23%	27%	8%	20%	29%	35%
	6	34%	23%	20%	40%	46%	29%	25%
	5	39%	23%	22%	36%	27%	18%	10%
	4	12%	7%	3%	10%	4%	4%	2%
	3	2%	3%	1%	3%	1%	3%	0%
	2	2%	2%	0%	3%	2%	2%	1%
Negative feelings	1	1%	1%	1%	0%	0%	1%	0%
Total:		100%	100%	100%	100%	100%	100%	100%
Mean:		5.30	6.06	6.53	5.32	5.72	6.11	6.76
s.d.:		1.05	1.58	1.51	1.04	1.02	1.46	1.15
skew:		1.05	0.29	0.41	0.97	1.40	0.68	0.64

[a] All items assess feelings about life-as-a-whole. Measure G1 is what we have called Life 1, G5 is Faces: whole life, G6 is Ladder: whole life, G7 is Circles: whole life. See Exhibit 3.1 for question wordings.
[b] See Exhibit 3.1 for labeling of scale categories.
[c] Nonexistent category for this scale.
Data sources: 1,433 respondents to April national survey; 222 respondents to July local survey.

same difference, though there it is less pronounced. The distribution for the Faces Scale proves to be more clustered at the positive end than any of the others in this set.

The same pattern of results emerges when one compares the distributions produced by the Circles, D–T, and Faces Scales for concern-level aspects of life in the July data: the Faces Scale produces more clustering at the positive end than the D–T Scale, which in turn produces more clustering than the Circles Scale. Comparable data are available for five concerns: Housing, National government, Spare-time activities, Independence and freedom, and Standard of living, and appear in Appendix I. Across these five, the average percentage of respondents locating themselves in the top two categories of the Circles, D–T, and Faces Scales are, respectively, 23 percent, 33 percent, and 43 percent.

Conclusions and Comments About Distribution Forms

The results of examining distribution forms produced by the five measurement methods with the highest estimated validities are clear. From the standpoint of providing well-spread and reasonably symmetric distributions on assessments of Life-as-a-whole, the Ladder and Circles Scales come closest, the Delighted–Terrible Scale comes next, and the seven-point Satisfaction and Faces Scales do least well. Although not all surveys included all measurement methods, this rank order is perfectly maintained within each of the surveys examined. Furthermore, it holds well for various concern-level aspects of life as well as for Life-as-a-whole.

It is of interest to speculate why the Circles and Ladder formats produce distributions that are closer to the abstract ideal. Two possible explanations come to mind. One concerns the extremity of the most positive category. In both the Ladder and Circles Scales the most positive category is defined as essentially perfect. In the Ladder Scale, this category is explicitly "the best life you might expect to have"; in the Circles Scale it is represented by a circle with eight plus signs and *no* minuses. It may be that despite feelings of very substantial satisfaction or even delight, relatively few people are prepared to pick a category that suggests their life could not be improved.

The other explanation is suggested by the fact that the Ladder and Circles Scales both have nine categories while all others have seven. We know that most people rate their own lives somewhat more positively than they think is typical for the average American, and it is possible that when presented with just seven categories, the need to place themselves above average, perhaps coupled with an assumption that the middle category represents the average, results in a substantial clustering at the positive end. In its pure form, this argument would suggest that any verbal or graphic labels attached to the scale categories would have no effect, and we know that this is not true for we have just observed that changes in the labels are accompanied by consistent differences in the distributions. Nevertheless, the number of categories in a scale may have some independent impact on where people place themselves.

OVERALL EVALUATIONS, ADDITIONAL CRITERIA, FURTHER IMPROVEMENTS

Preceding sections of this chapter have considered how various methods for assessing perceptions of well-being rank with respect to two criteria, validity and form of distribution. It happens that the methods do not rank the same on these criteria. This makes the process of arriving at an overall integrated evaluation less than straightforward. The task will be facilitated by first considering two additional criteria that will help us discriminate still further among the measurement methods.

Category Labeling and Ease of Use

For a variety of reasons we believe it desirable that the categories of a scale, each and every one, be accompanied by an explicit verbal or graphic label. All the categories of the Delighted–Terrible, the Faces, and Circles Scales have such labels, but this is not true for the Ladder and seven-point Satisfaction scales. The meanings of the categories in these latter scales are largely determined by the definitions of the ends of the scale and the distances of the categories from each end.

While both labeled-category and nonlabeled-category scales have long histories in survey research, we believe the labeled-category scales have an inherent advantage at several stages in the research process. At the time data are being collected, the greater precision in meaning given by category labels should ensure greater comparability in the way respondents use the scales and result in somewhat higher validity of measurement. (Note that the three methods that rank highest for estimated validity in Exhibit 6.8 are all labeled-category scales.) At the time data are being analyzed and interpreted, the presence of category labels makes it possible to know exactly what the respondent was endorsing. And at the time when research results are reported to potential users, the presence of category labels makes it possible to explain a particular summary statistic, such as a mean, it the same terms that were originally given to the respondents.[33]

A fourth criterion that deserves brief mention is ease of use. Clearly, methods that are readily accepted and understood by respondents, interviewers, and any others who may be involved in their use are to be preferred over others. While each of the five most valid methods proved quite acceptable to those who were asked to use it—the percentages of nonresponse, for example, did not differ substantially between the methods—we have the impression that the Faces, Ladder, Delighted–Terrible, and seven-point Satisfaction Scales have a transparent obviousness about them that is lacking in the case of Circles Scale. With its nine circles, each containing various numbers of plus and minus signs, the Circles Scale appears more complicated than the other formats and requires more initial explanation.[34]

Overall Evaluations

Given these four criteria—validity, distribution form, category labeling, and ease of use—how would we evaluate our various measurement methods? Of the four, we believe validity deserves first attention, partly because scales that have low validity hold little other interest. As shown in Exhibit 6.8, the Delighted–Terrible, Faces, Circles, seven-point Satisfaction, and Ladder Scales were ranked highest with respect to estimated validity. All of these methods seem highly serviceable, yet some seem more desirable than others.

The Delighted–Terrible Scale looks very good with respect to validity, has

---

[33] If a scale is to be used in languages other than that for which it was originally developed, and if the scale uses verbal category labels, finding suitable translations requires some effort. (This is much less of a problem if the categories are defined by graphic labels, as in our Faces and Circles Scales.) While it has been proposed to us that scales in which most categories are unlabeled may be more easily duplicated in another language, we know of no empirical evidence that would support this assertion. In fact, just the opposite position can also be proposed; i.e., that crosslinguistic comparability may be enhanced if the scale includes multiple opportunities for doing so through full category labeling rather than depending exclusively on an adequate translation of just the end points.

[34] This statement assumes data are being collected in a face-to-face interview where the respondent can be shown a card on which the scale appears.

labeled categories, and is easy to use. With respect to distribution form, it ranks in the middle among these five methods, better than the Faces and seven-point Satisfaction Scales, not as good as the Circles or Ladder Scales. While not perfect with respect to our four criteria, we believe the Delighted–Terrible Scale ranks ahead of all other methods.

Next in our overall ranking we put the Circles and Faces Scales. Each does well on three of the four criteria, and each scores last on one of the criteria. The Circles Scale shows relatively high validity, has explicitly labeled categories, and yields good distributions, but seems somewhat complicated when first presented. The Faces Scale also does well with respect to validity and has labeled categories; it is easy to use, but it produces rather heavily skewed distributions. One of these scales might be the one to choose if it was particularly desirable to use a graphic rather than purely verbal method.

The Ladder and seven-point Satisfaction Scales come fourth and fifth in our overall ranking. Both are easy to use; the Ladder Scale seems significantly better than the seven-point Satisfaction Scale with respect to the distributions it provides; the seven-point Satisfaction Scale is a shade better than the Ladder Scale with respect to estimated validity; both lack labeled categories. While we feel that neither of these methods is as desirable as those listed earlier, we would repeat our earlier comment that these are not bad methods: We feel they are reasonably good, certainly better than any of the five approaches that scored in the bottom half of our estimated validity rankings, but not the best that is available.

Toward Further Improvements

Having specified a variety of criteria and evaluated the methods we have investigated with respect to them, it is notable that none of the methods seems ideal. There is obvious room for improvement. This raises the question as to how improvements might be achieved. Some of the results described in this chapter suggest directions for further investigation.

With respect to the Delighted–Terrible Scale, it would be desirable to alter the distribution to provide more discrimination among people at the positive end. An examination of Exhibits 6.9 and 6.10 shows that the problem is not with the extreme positive category but with the two immediately adjacent to it, those labeled "pleased" and "mostly satisfied." It is in these categories that relatively large percentages of people tend to cluster. While it is likely that this simply reflects the fact that a large proportion of people feel reasonably positive about many aspects of their lives, it might be possible to distinguish more degrees of positive feeling by altering the scale to have three categories at this point instead of the present two. Of course, appropriate category descriptions would have to be found, and to retain the present balance of the scale, one might want to add an additional category in the negative portions of the scale as well.

The Faces Scale also produces a less-than-optimal distribution with substantial clustering at the positive end. Adding additional categories might improve this scale also. Unlike the D–T Scale, however, where the label on the extreme category seems to capture an appropriate portion of the population, it might be desirable to assign a still more extreme label to the most positive category of the Faces Scale. Of course, this requires drawing a face that is even more positive than the one that presently anchors the positive end of the scale, and there may be some limit as to how extreme an expression can become and still retain the essential characteristics of a human face.

The Circles Scale could be improved by making the essential meaning of the circles and their relationship to one another more immediately obvious. It is possible that this could be achieved by substituting shades of light and dark, or colors if that were feasible, for the present pie slices with their plus and minus signs.

RELATIONSHIPS BETWEEN MEASURES OF PERCEIVED WELL-BEING AND OTHER TYPES OF VARIABLES

A chapter devoted to evaluating measures of perceived well-being would be incomplete without some discussion of how the obtained measures related to other variables describing relevant characteristics of respondents' lives, behavior, and attitudes. Our work includes a number of investigations of these matters.

It is about the lives of the July respondents that we have the most extensive information. One part of the questionnaire administered to these people con- sisted of a systematic attempt to explore life conditions relevant to each of fourteen specific concerns. For the Standard of living concern, for example, respondents were asked to indicate the extent to which each of the following statements applied to them: "I can have a night on the town when I feel like it without worrying about the cost"; "I spend all I want and still have money left over at the end of the month"; "I have all the material things I want"; "My home is not very well equipped"; and "I would have trouble borrowing $1000 if I needed it." The fourteen concerns investigated in this way were chosen to span the range from life aspects that were very close to self and home, such as feelings about one's own accomplishments, freedom and independence, and family, to much more remote aspects such as feelings about the national government. All together seventy questionnaire items yielded information about life conditions relevant to these fourteen concerns.[35] An additional fifty items elicited information about traditional "demographic" matters such as family status, amount of education, level of family income, religious prefer- ence and attendance at religious services, characteristics of the living quarters and of the neighborhood, and many more. Thanks to these 120 items we know a moderate amount about the attitudes, reported behaviors, and life conditions of our July respondents.

When we related affective evaluations of specific life concerns, as measured

[35]The full set of items are in Question 26 of the July questionnaire (see app. A).

on the Delighted–Terrible Scale, to these other types of variables, a reasonably consistent and not very surprising pattern emerged. Nearly always, relationships were in the "expected" direction, and most were rather weak. In a few cases moderate relationships emerged: Evaluations of House or apartment on the Delighted–Terrible Scale correlated .56 with the applicability of the item "I find my house fits my needs," and .51 with "My home is comfortable all year around." Evaluations of Job on the D–T Scale correlated .48 with the item "I look forward to going to work." Evaluations of the National government correlated .54 with "I support the President's policies," and .48 with "I trust the government to find the best solutions to problems." Evaluations of Safety correlated .47 with "It would be safe to take an evening stroll in my neighborhood." And evaluations of Self-accomplishment correlated .58 with the item, "I am getting what I want out of life." But relationships exceeding .45 were not typical.

In our most systematic attempt to explore relationships between affective evaluations of life concerns and these other variables, three members of our project staff independently rated the relevance of selected life concerns assessed on the D–T Scale to seventy of these other variables. For example, concerns about Neighborhood, Community, and People nearby were judged relevant to the item, "I could count on my neighbors to help out if something were to happen to my family," and the National government concern was judged irrelevant. After ascertaining that the three staff members agreed well in their judgments about relevance, the average correlations between the evaluations of the concerns and the other items were computed. Where concerns had been judged relevant to the other items, the average correlation was .31; where staff members had been uncertain as to the concerns' relevance, the average correlation was .25; and where concerns had been judged irrelevant the average correlation was .15.

Two things can be said about these results. First, they show that evaluations of well-being on our concern measures related more to conditions of life that seem relevant to the concern than to conditions that pertain to other concerns. This, of course, is just as expected, and is a crucial demonstration that the concern-level well-being measures perform as they should. Second, even where life conditions are relevant to the concerns being assessed, they show, in general, only rather modest relationships to perceptions of well-being.

The average correlation of about .3 between our perceived well-being measures and somewhat more "objective" conditions of life relevant to the same concern is typical of what we find in analyses of other data as well. In each case we encounter a few relationships of .4 or .5, where it would be easy to say, "Yes, of course, that is reasonable"; but in other cases that one might well judge just as reasonable, the relationship turns out to be much lower. Our general conclusion is that one will not usually find strong and direct relationships between *measures* of perceived well-being and reports of most life conditions or behaviors.

Part of the explanation for the usually modest relationships, of course, lies in the estimated validities and reliabilities both of our well-being measures and of the other variables to which we relate them. As noted earlier in this chapter, the well-being measures based on the Delighted–Terrible Scale have validities estimated in the range of .7 to .8. Although the other variables have not received the same extended development effort, we suspect their validities are probably no higher than this, and quite likely somewhat lower. It follows that even if the true relationship were 1.00, the observed relationships would have a maximum of perhaps .6, even after allowing for modest contributions from common but nonvalid sources of variance.

Another part of the explanation, and one that is more important from the theoretical standpoint, is that it seems unrealistic to expect that the true underlying correlations would even begin to approach 1.00 in most cases. It would be naive, we believe, to think that a person's behavior at any one time could be closely predicted from his feelings without taking into account the social and physical constraints that impinge on that person. Similarly, it would be naive to think that a person's feelings about various aspects of life could be perfectly predicted by knowing only the characteristics of the person's present environment. Developing adequate explanations for why people feel as they do about various life concerns would be a challenging undertaking in its own right. While we believe this could prove scientifically fruitful, such an investigation is not part of the work we are presently reporting. Our present analysis just barely opens up this area by showing that (1) our well-being measures relate more to aspects of life for which they are relevant than to other aspects (i.e., that the well-being measures discriminate as they should among aspects of life); and (2) that feelings about well-being are phenomena that do not tend to be related highly to the behaviors and life conditions reported by the holders of those feelings.

CHAPTER SUMMARY

This chapter evaluates the measures of perceived well-being reported in previous chapters of this book. The evaluation suggests which assessment methods are most appropriate for subsequent use, suggests how the best of the methods might be further improved, and yields information permitting a more informed interpretation of other statistical analyses.

Evaluating measures of people's feelings about their lives presents major problems because there seem to be no clear and directly observable phenomena that can serve as criteria. People's behavior and the conditions under which they live, while related to their perceptions of well-being, are influenced by many factors in addition to their feelings and hence are not appropriate criterion variables. It is the *feelings* themselves that we seek to measure. Although very real and important to the people who hold them, they are internal and inherently unobservable phenomena.

The investigation of how an observed measure relates to an unobserved theoretical concept (e.g., people's true feelings about some aspect of life) is a study of construct validity. Construct validity can be estimated by using appropriate measurement models. The procedure requires a network of relationships among observed measures and a set of theoretical assumptions about how the measures link to concepts and how the concepts link to one another. These relationships and sets of assumptions can be conveniently portrayed and analyzed through use of structural measurement models. Most of our models assume that people's answers reflect three types of influences: their true feelings, which yield valid variance; their individual biases and interpretations, which yield correlated error variance if such biases influence more than one variable among those being analyzed; and unique residual effects. By fitting appropriate models to the data, we can estimate what proportion of a measure's variance is of each kind. From these the construct validity (and also the reliability) of the measure can be derived.

The July questionnaire was designed to yield measures that fit into a multimethod-multitrait matrix: six aspects of life each assessed by six different measurement methods. By applying a complex measurement model to overlapping subsets of these data, it was discovered that the method of assessment had far more to do with the validity and error components of the resulting measures than did the particular aspect of life that was being assessed. The measures with the highest validities resulted from the Delighted–Terrible, Faces, and Circles Scales. These methods produced single-item measures with validities estimated at about .8 (variance composition: 65 percent valid variance, 8 percent correlated error variance, 27 percent residual variance). The Ladder Scale yielded measures with estimated validities of about .7 (50 percent valid variance, 5 percent correlated error, 45 percent residual). The Social comparison technique and Others' ratings each produced estimated validities of about .4 (15 percent valid variance, 30 percent correlated error, 55 percent residual).

From these figures one can estimate that a three- to five-item index combining several measures obtained by the more valid methods could achieve a validity of about .9; i.e., include about 80 percent valid variance. While not perfect, such figures suggest that the more valid methods are capable of producing measures with more than enough validity to be useful as social indicators. On the other hand, the very low validities estimated for the Social comparison technique and the Others' ratings indicate that these methods are not appropriate for future use. Furthermore, the low validity of Others' ratings shows that perceptions of well-being are rather private matters that tend to be poorly judged, even by people ralatively well acquainted with the person who holds them.

The chapter then proceeds to a series of analyses that estimate the validities produced by various measurement methods when used in national-level surveys. A complex model is applied to certain data from the May respondents, and simpler models are fitted to data from the April, November Form 2, and October respondents. These analyses show that the validity estimates obtained from the July data are reasonably replicative at the national level. They also yield validity estimates for four additional assessment methods that were not used with the July respondents. When results from all the modeling analyses are brought together, it is found that the ten methods being evaluated rank as follows with respect to estimated validity: first, the Delighted–Terrible, Faces, and Circles Scales (at the top, and about equal); then the seven-point Satisfac tion and Ladder Scales and the Interviewer's ratings (each yielding about 90 percent as much valid variance as the top-ranked methods); then the Telephone interview (71 percent as much valid variance); then the Thermometer Scale (53 percent); and finally the Social comparison technique and Others' ratings (about 25 percent).

A second criterion for evaluating assessment methods is the form of the distributions they produce. Well spread and reasonably symmetrical distributions are, in general, preferable to those that lump large portions of the population into just one or two categories. Large clumps imply an inability to discriminate possibly different feelings. If such clumps occur at one end of a distribution, they indicate that the scale may be inappropriately centered with respect to the population's feelings and may be relatively insensitive to future changes that move the population still further toward the end where it is already clumped.

The development of the Delighted–Terrible Scale was motivated in part by the suspected weakness of the seven-point Satisfaction Scale in discriminating different degrees of positive feelings. A comparison of the distributions produced by these two scales in several national surveys shows that the distributions produced by the D–T Scale tend, as expected, to be better spread than those from the seven-point Satisfaction Scale. Other data show that the distributions from the Ladder and Circles Scales tend to be still better spread than those from the D–T Scale, while distributions from the Faces Scale tend to show substantial clumping at the positive end.

Before making an overall evaluation among the five methods that had the highest estimated validities, two other criteria are described: ease of use, and the incorporation of explicit labels for each category of the scale. It is noted that the Circles Scale seems more complicated than others in the group of five, and that the seven-point Satisfaction and Ladder Scales lack category labels. Considering all criteria together, the Delighted–Terrible Scale is judged to rank highest, followed by the Circles and Faces Scales, followed by the Ladder and seven-point Satisfaction Scales. The findings suggest that the D–T and Faces Scales might be still further improved by adding one category at or near the positive end (and perhaps a balancing category in the negative range), and that a minor change in the presentation format of the Circles Scale might further improve it.

The final section of the chapter examines how measures of perceived well-being (based on the D–T Scale) relate to various characteristics of the respondents' lives and their reported behaviors. After scanning a wide-ranging set of data, it is concluded that the well-being measures discriminate as they should among aspects of life (i.e., they show higher relationships to conditions of life that seem relevant to the concern than to conditions pertaining to other concerns), that relationships tend to be in the expected directions, but that relationships are not very strong. It is noted that it would be naive to expect strong relationships, and that it is precisely because strong relationships are not expected that it seems worthwhile to develop good ways of independently measuring people's perceived well-being.

CHAPTER 7

Exploring the Dynamics of Evaluation

The major topic of our research is perceptions of well-being, what we have called affective evaluations of various aspects of one's life. Preceding chapters have described how affective evaluations relate to one another, how how they seem to be organized in people's thinking, how global evaluations can be "accounted for" on the basis of concern-level evaluations, and how different assessment methods influence the validity of the resulting measures. There remain important questions concerning the psychological dynamics that generate these affective evaluations, and the related matter of the "meaning" of any particular answer a respondent may give.

There are at least the following "models" for evaluation:

One may be satisfied, or say so, because one's life has just improved. The reference is between now and an hour ago, or between today and yesterday. On comparing two states, one is better than the other, so one says one is happy, delighted, satisfied, gratified, etc. The model for such satisfaction is usually a dichotomous comparison: I'm not tired now (but I was), I'm having fun now (I was bored), and the like.

Another model of evaluation invokes the notion of an ideal: an ideal house, car, marital mate, income level, etc. A person may compare his present house, car, etc. against this ideal, and conceptualize not just a direction of difference (which is better) but also how far away he is from his ideal.

Another model of comparison would be that which involved a minimum set of characteristics rather than an ideal or dream. One may hold an image of one's dream house but keep it as part of one's fantasy life. In day-to-day evaluations one might be prone to use some picture of a "good enough" house and be very satisfied with housing that met such a minimum requirement. The same comparison is suggested when wives talk of their husbands as just being good providers, or when people speak of their cars as "still running."

Another point for comparison that may be used is the idea of a neutral or "swing" point. Above such a point things get better and below that things get worse. Feelings of satisfaction or dissatisfaction might then be engendered by how far one is from such a neutral point. One such point could be the middle of a range; for example, the range of pay rates in an organization, or the median of the distribution of wages. Alternatively, one might prefer to regard the average (i.e., the mean), which is heavily influenced by high salaries, as a better neutral point for comparison. Parducci (1965) has shown that the psychologically neutral point used by many people is still a different point that lies half way between the midpoint of the range and the mean of the distribution.

Still another model for evaluation may depend on the pace of change. It may be that people have ideal points or neutral points or both but that it is the slope of progress or rate of improvement that is crucial for their evaluations. People may feel satisfied even though they are a long way from their ideal because they feel they are making satisfactory progress and they are at a good point for their present age, time on the job, etc.

Another point of reference may be perception of a norm about how people ought to feel. People ought to be satisfied (and loyal, etc.) with their president. People ought to be satisfied (and loving, etc.) with their wives or husbands. People ought to be satisfied with what they have just spent money for. Such a framework may be applicable particularly for verbal statements to other people.

But there are also people who establish their own self-pictures and self-images and they include notions of being contented, easygoing, accommodating, etc. By working at such orientations it is quite possible to inhibit and repress or simply not to have responses that would arise readily without such a perspective toward oneself and one's life circumstances. Another self-picture might be one in which bad circumstances are not whitewashed or disguised but readily admitted, yet the individual might feel constrained to be long-suffering, enduring, patient, etc., and actually feel some small degree of satisfaction in doing so.

Another orientation that is not as self-oriented is a complementary or symbiotic one. It is not focused on comparisons of external conditions or internal states. The two or the several or the many belong together, conditions are shared, and the accounting of exchanges is a foreign concept. The relationship is lived and enjoyed for itself. Some conditions of love are like that and questions of the ideal mate or the average spouse or what one or another owes the relationship do not arise. The uncritical commitment is satisfying.

Thus, there are different attitudes and orientations toward evaluation itself. Any one framework or context does not have to hold for a person in all his or her judgments. They do not have to be personality characteristics. One may well hold one approach toward satisfaction with one's children or marriage and another toward one's car or local businesses and services.

Questions about the dynamics and meaning of evaluations are large and basic topics in their own right and will probably require extended investigation before a reasonably comprehensive understanding can be achieved. Although these have not been the major topics of our present research, some initial explorations have been made, and it is these that form the substance of this chapter. Unlike previous chapters, which have reported series of integrated analyses, each focused on a single theme, the present chapter consists of nine separate and largely independent explorations.

Organization of the Chapter and Summary of Results

This chapter consists of nine distinct reports, each intended to explore a different facet of the dynamics of evaluation. The first three explorations are essentially statistical translations of the categories of the Delighted–Terrible Scale into the categories of other scales; the results contribute to our understanding of what a respondent is really feeling when he or she chooses a particular answer category on the D–T Scale. Explorations 4 to 6 all focus on the perceptual processes that do (or do not) appear to contribute to the affective evaluations a respondent finally expresses. The final three reports focus, respectively, on self-other comparisons, on the nature of importance ratings, and on whether there exist separate and distinct patterns of perceptions about well-being.

In the first of the "statistical translations," the categories of the Delighted–Terrible Scale, the scale on which we have depended most heavily and the scale we regard as the most promising, are linked to corresponding categories on several other promising scales, those using the Faces, Circles, and Ladder formats. The results provide a basis for making comparisons when data have been collected on different scales. There is also evidence that all four scales tend to be used in approximately the same way, that the meanings of the D–T Scale categories seem not to be much influenced by what is being evaluated, that most of the categories of the D–T Scale seem to be separated by roughly one-step intervals on the comparison scales, and that there is a reasonably close correspondence between the categories of the D–T Scale and those of the Faces Scale.

In the second exploration the categories of the Delighted–Terrible Scale are linked to three more general levels of evaluation. These three levels represent, respectively, high satisfaction, a more modified fulfillment in which existing constraints and limitations are recognized, and a level that is no better than "tolerable" and possibly very unsatisfactory. The results, which are based on the July data, show that even when people described an aspect of their lives as "ideal" or as the kind they "most want to have" only a relatively small proportion describe their feelings as those of "delight" (the typical answer on the D–T Scale was "pleased). Based on these results it would appear that the D–T Scale extends in a positive direction beyond the range of feelings most people experience even when in a state of complete fulfillment. It follows that the "Delighted" category implies a very positive set of feelings indeed.

The third report examines the meaning of the categories of the Delighted–Terrible Scale in terms of amounts of family income. This analysis explores the relationship between various evaluative feelings and the amount of income that would lead to each. The analysis shows the expected but reassuring results that the more positive the category on the D–T Scale, the higher the income associated with it. More interesting, this analysis, in conjunction with those reported previously, suggests that the categories of the D–T Scale seem to be approximately evenly distributed along the dimension of affective evalutions.

The fourth report also focuses on economic matters and changes in them. It examines how perceptions of past changes and anticipations of future changes relate to one's present evaluation of economic well-being. The results show that perceptions of what has happened in the past bear a moderate but not very strong relationship to present evaluations, and that anticiaptions for the future show practically no relationship. Changes over the past five years and past one year seem to exert separate additive impacts on present evaluations.

The fifth report explores the importance of six frames of reference in people's evaluations of various life concerns. The frames of reference are satisfaction of one's own needs, fairness, resource input, the ease or difficulty of effecting changes, one's perception of how other people will react, and one's present social position. The results suggest that concern-level evaluations mainly reflect a needs-satisfaction perspective, with fairness and social position playing secondary roles, and the remaining perspectives having little or no independent impact.

A more elaborate analysis oriented toward some of the same issues is presented in the sixth report. Implementing the theoretical model that is described in chapter 1, we take forty-eight evaluations specific with respect to both domain and criterion, and use them to account for fourteen more general concern-level evaluations and, ultimately, for Life-as-a-whole. The model generates a variety of expectations involving the size and direction of relationships, the relative magnitudes of relationships, situations in which combinations of variables should be able to predict a dependent variable, and situations in which variables should be unable to predict. In all cases the empirical results prove to be in accord with what the model would lead one to expect. It is concluded that the theoretical model provides a useful way of conceptualizing the evaluation process.

The seventh report compares evaluations of various aspects of one's own life with estimates of how other people evaluate *their* lives. For Life-as-a-whole and for specific concerns that are rather "close" to oneself (in the sense of the perceptual structures mapped in chap. 2), people tend to rate their own well-being higher than that of others, while for life concerns that are relatively remote, they rate their own well-being below that of others. Since the methods by which our data were collected let us infer that such differences do not actually exist, we attribute them to an unexplained but potentially significant selective misperception of others' feelings. Although respondents—on average—estimate that others would rank order the different life concerns in roughly the same order they themselves do, for any particular concern there tends to be only a weak correlation between one's own feelings and one's estimate of a neighbor's feelings. This suggests that estimates of others' feelings are not simply projections of one's own feelings.

The eighth report concerns judgments by respondents of the "importance" of various life concerns. As noted in chapter 4, the importance data proved not to be useful in enhancing the accuracy with which evaluations of Life-as-a-whole could be predicted. Here, we encounter a parallel finding that the importance of a concern bears little relationship to the strength of the association between that concern and Life-as-a-whole. What importance ratings *do* relate to, however, is the position of the concern in the perceptual structure.

The closer the concern to the Self and Family regions, the higher its importance tends to be rated.

The ninth report describes an attempt to find groups of people who could be distinguished on the basis of a unique pattern of feelings about their well-being. The attempt proved unsuccessful, despite a concerted effort and use of powerful methods, and we conclude that while Americans differ in their views about well-being, these differences seem to shade gradually from one to another. We could find no sharp breaks that made people with one pattern of feelings stand separate from all other people.

EXPLORATION 1: A STATISTICAL TRANSLATION BETWEEN THE DELIGHTED–TERRIBLE SCALE AND THE FACES, CIRCLES, AND LADDER SCALES

One way of gaining insight about the meaning of the words of one language is to translate them into those of another language. The same applies to the categories of answer scales. We can gain added insight as to what the categories of the Delighted–Terrible Scale may mean by seeing what categories respondents choose on other scales to express the same feelings.

The July respondents were asked to record their feelings about Life-as-a-whole and five specific concerns on four different scales: the Delighted–Terrible, Faces, Circles, and Ladder Scales.[1] The last three are nonverbal graphic scales, and in two of them (Circles and Ladder) the categories progress in an unambiguously regular way. On the Circles Scale increasing positivity is represented by the progressive substitution of minus signs by plus signs, and on the Ladder Scale this is indicated by evenly spaced rungs up the ladder.

Exhibit 7.1 shows the mean of the respondents' answers on each of the three comparison scales according to the answer chosen on the Delighted–Terrible Scale. Parallel data are shown for two global- and five concern-level assessments. Perhaps most useful are the means that summarize results across the seven more detailed analyses. (These are the figures shown in the final row for each scale.)

Several interesting results appear in Exhibit 7.1. First is the obvious monotonic progression in the means of all three comparison scales as the D–T Scale categories change. In only two instances is there the slightest deviation from the expected progression, and in each case the deviating mean is based on only a very small number of respondents (six).[2] The comparison scales are clearly showing the same trends as does the Delighted–Terrible Scale.

Second, it is important to note that, for any given answer on the Delighted–Terrible Scale, the answers on the comparison scales are pretty much the same regardless of the particular aspect of life that is being assessed. Note that there

[1]These scales are briefly described in Exhibit 3.1 (see measures G1, G5, G6, and G7) and are portrayed in questions 11, 13, 15, and 18 of the questionnaire administered to the July respondents (see app. A).

[2]Appendix J presents the number of cases on which each mean in Exhibit 7.1 is based.

EXHIBIT 7.1. Mean Answers on Faces, Circles, and Ladder Scales Associated with Each Category of the D-T Scale for Designated Aspects of Well-Being

		Categories of the D-T Scale					
	Delighted	Pleased	Mostly sat.	Mixed	Mostly dissat.	Unhappy	Terrible
Results for Faces Scale (range: 1–7)							
Measures[b]							
G1 Life 1	6.6	6.2	5.5	4.9	4.7	3.3	[a]
G2 Life 2	6.4	6.1	5.6	4.0	4.3	[a]	[a]
87 House	6.8	6.1	5.2	4.4	3.6	[a]	[a]
30 Spare time	6.6	5.9	5.3	4.3	4.2	[a]	[a]
106 Nat. govt.	[a]	5.6	4.1	3.1	2.2	1.8	1.1
85 Stand. lvg.	6.9	6.0	5.2	4.7	4.1	[a]	[a]
44 Ind., free.	6.5	6.0	5.4	4.9	3.8	2.1	[a]
Mean[c]	6.6	6.1	5.3	4.2	3.2	2.0	1.1
Interval	(0.5)	(0.8)	(1.1)	(1.0)	(1.2)	(0.9)	
Results for Circles Scale (range: 0–8)							
Measures[b]							
G1 Life 1	6.3	6.1	5.7	4.9	5.5	4.0	[a]
G2 Life 2	6.2	6.1	5.6	4.9	3.8	[a]	[a]
87 House	7.1	6.4	5.0	3.9	3.3	[a]	[a]

30	Spare time	6.3	a	6.2	5.4	4.6	3.2	a
								1.8
106	Nat. govt.	a	6.0	4.4	3.7	2.5	1.8	0.8
85	Stand. lvg.	7.0	6.1	5.3	4.5	3.1	a	a
44	Ind., free.	7.3	6.4	5.6	4.5	3.1	1.8	a
	Mean[c]	6.7	6.2	5.4	4.3	3.0	2.1	1.0
	Interval	(0.5)	(0.8)	(1.1)	(1.3)	(0.9)	(0.9)	

Results for Ladder Scale (range: 1–9)

Measures[b]

G1	Life 1	6.8	6.7	5.8	5.0	5.8	4.0	a
G2	Life 2	6.9	6.6	5.7	5.1	4.8	a	a
87	House	8.5	7.3	6.3	5.6	5.3	a	a
30	Spare time	7.1	7.0	6.2	5.2	4.7	a	a
106	Nat. govt.	a	7.0	4.9	4.0	2.7	2.2	1.5
85	Stand. lvg.	7.5	7.2	6.3	5.6	4.8	a	a
44	Ind., free.	8.1	7.5	6.7	5.9	4.5	3.3	a
	Mean[c]	7.5	7.0	6.1	5.0	3.9	2.5	1.4
	Interval	(0.5)	(0.9)	(0.9)	(1.1)	(1.4)	(1.1)	

Notes: Appendix J presents the number of cases on which each of these means is based.
[a] Fewer than three cases available.
[b] Measure numbers refer to Exhibits 2.1 or 3.1.
[c] Figures are means of the means immediately above, are weighted for the number of cases on which each of the above means is based, and represent all available data (including data for which an a has been substituted in this exhibit).
Data source: 222 July respondents.

is relatively little variation within any one column of Exhibit 7.1 (and most of the variation that does appear can be attributed to the small numbers of respondents on which a few of the means are based). It would appear that the "meaning" of the scale categories remains reasonably stable from one concern to another.[3]

Third, it is interesting to see that the seven categories of the D–T Scale and the respective seven categories of the Faces Scale seem to have been assigned highly similar meanings by these respondents. As shown by the composite means, respondents who chose the Terrible answer also tended to choose the first face (the most "distressed" one); note the mean of 1.1. Similarly, those who chose the second (Unhappy) category on the D–T Scale tended to choose the second category on the Faces Scale. The match remains closely parallel throughout the scale except for the last category, and even here the discrepancy is not great.[4]

The final observation we would make about Exhibit 7.1 is based on an examination of the intervals between the composite means. Since the Circles and Ladder Scales each involve categories that are evenly spaced (at least in abstract geometric terms), it is of interest to compare the categories of the D–T Scale to them. We find that relative to the Circles and Ladder Scales the intervals between the five least positive categories of the D–T Scale are all approximately equal (and equivalent to about one rung on the Ladder, or one plus-for-minus substitution on the Circles Scale). However, the interval between Mostly satisfied and Pleased is somewhat less than that between the more negative categories, and the interval between Pleased and Delighted is only about half the size of the others. The results derived from the Circles and Ladder scales are remarkably similar in suggesting that the difference in meaning between Delighted and Pleased may be somewhat less than between most other categories of the scale.[5]

[3] A possible exception may have occurred for evaluations of the National government. This seems to have been evaluated relatively more positively on the D–T Scale than on the comparison scales. (For example, Exhibit 7.1 shows that people who said they were Mostly satisfied with the National government tended to rank it lower on the comparison scales than they ranked any of the other aspects of life.) Whether this should be attributed to a shift in the "meaning" of the D–T Scale categories when applied to the National government, or to an unexpected context effect in which the content of preceding items acted to raise people's evaluations of the National government, cannot be determined from the present data.

[4] Before one concludes that the word "Delighted" in the context of the D–T Scale has a less positive meaning than the most positive face (a conclusion that might be suggested by the mean of 6.6 on the Faces Scale for people who chose the Delighted category on the D–T Scale), we would raise two cautions. First, Exhibit 6.10 shows that respondents were *more* clustered at the positive end of the Faces Scale than at the positive end of the D–T Scale, a result contrary to the above conclusion. Second, given that the Faces and D–T Scales have approximately equal means and variances (see Exhibit 6.10) and are less than perfectly correlated, the well-known effect of "regression toward the mean" (Bohrnstedt, 1969) could well account for the observed result even if the Delighted category implied the *same* feeling as the most positive face. Since the seventh face is at the end of the scale, deviations from it can occur in only one direction and the mean can shift only downward.

[5] The intervals computed among the mean responses to the Faces Scale show exactly the same pattern as for the Circles and Ladder Scales, but since the argument of geometrically even spacing cannot be applied to this scale, we would urge caution in interpreting these results.

The above findings suggest that respondents tend to use all of the most promising scales in approximately the same way, that the meaning they attach to scale categories seems not to be much influenced by what is being evaluated, that most of the categories of the D–T Scale seem to be separated by roughly one-step intervals on the other comparison scales, except for the most positive categories where the separation may be less, and that there is a reasonably close correspondence between the seven categories of the D–T Scale and those of the Faces Scale.

EXPLORATION 2: THE D–T SCALE CATEGORIES AND THREE MORE GENERAL LEVELS OF EVALUATION

In another exploration of the meaning of the categories of the Delighted–Terrible Scale, answers on this scale were related to three more general levels of evaluation.

The first of these levels was intended to represent high satisfaction. Either of two answers (out of a total of six possible answers) resulted in a respondent being assigned to this level. When applied to evaluations of housing, the relevant answers were, An ideal house or apartment for you, or The kind you most want to have. The second evaluative level represents a more modified fulfillment and includes the notion that the thing being evaluated, while not perfect or ideal, is quite acceptable considering the constraints and limitations that the evaluator faces. The relevant answers (again with respect to Housing) were, The best house or apartment you are able to get now, or A good-enough house or apartment for now. The third evaluative level captures the whole range below the first two. The operational phrases were "tolerable" and "very unsatisfactory."[6]

These categories were applied by the July respondents to evaluate four aspects of their lives: Life-as-a-whole, Housing, Work (for pay or at home), and Oneself. When their general evaluations of these four aspects were compared to the way they had described their feelings about the same four aspects using the Delighted–Terrible Scale, a clear and consistent pattern of results emerged. Among those who evaluted an aspect of life as highly satisfying, the median response on the D–T Scale was Pleased. Some claimed feelings more positive than this, but there were also others who expressed feelings less positive than pleased. People who scored at the level of modified fulfillment tended to describe their feelings as Mostly satisifed on the D–T Scale. Finally, the group who evaluated things as no better than Tolerable tended to choose the Mixed category of the D–T Scale to represent their feelings.

Although these results are not surprising, they provide further evidence regarding the meaning of the D–T Scale categories and how these categories map into another evaluative perspective. One of the most interesting findings concerns the meaning of the Delighted category. Even among the group of

[6]Question 16 of the questionnaire administered to the July respondents is the source of the data reported here (see app. A).

people who expressed high satisfaction, less than one-fifth described their feelings as those of delight. This suggests that the Delighted category of the D–T Scale may represent a very positive affective evaluation indeed. In this respect Exploration 2 provides a useful complement to Exploration 1. Although Exploration 1 suggested that the interval between the Delighted and Pleased categories of the D–T Scale may be smaller than the interval between other categories, the present analysis suggests that the interval is sufficient to extend the scale beyond the range of feelings most people have even when in a state of high satisfaction.

EXPLORATION 3: HYPOTHETICAL FAMILY INCOMES AND AFFECTIVE EVALUATIONS ON THE D–T SCALE

A third exploration of the meaning of the categories of the Delighted–Terrible Scale and of the width of the intervals between them involved relating different amounts of family income to evaluations of those amounts.

The July respondents were asked a series of questions from which it was possible to map out their "evaluation function" with regard to income. One of these items read, What is the smallest amount that would make you feel *delighted* with your income? Parallel questions inquired about amounts of income that would lead the respondent to feel Pleased, Mostly satisfied, and each of the other feelings of the D–T Scale. The last item read, What is the largest amount that would leave you feeling *terrible* about your income? The answers were expressed relative to present family income—e.g., Double my present family income—and since the respondents also provided information on the amount of their family income, the relative amounts can be converted to actual dollar amounts.[7]

One of the interesting aspects of this approach is that the effects of the actual differences in family income can be held constant. If one simply relates evaluations of actual family income to the present amount of that income, those who feel Pleased (for example) with their incomes are different people from those who express other feelings, they are likely to have different incomes, and they may well be applying different standards of evaluation. However, by using the present approach, *all* respondents say how much money they would need to experience each of the feelings; the distribution of their actual incomes remains constant; and the same mixture of frames of reference that applied in answering one item is also present for all the others.

Exhibit 7.2 shows the median amounts of family income that the July respondents said would be needed to place them in each category of the Delighted–Terrible Scale.[8] One may note that as feelings about family income

---

[7]See question 17 of the questionnaire administered to the July respondents (reproduced in app. A) for the exact wording of these items.

[8]Although it is not our purpose here to focus on absolute dollar amounts, Exhibit 7.2 takes on added meaning when one notes that the median family income for these respondents is just over $12,500 (see app. H), an amount very close to that which the average respondent said would leave

EXHIBIT 7.2. Family Income and Affective Evaluations

Item	Median amount	Interval
Smallest amount for *delighted*	$18,500	
Smallest amount for *pleased*	15,370	3,130
Smallest amount for *mostly satisfied*	13,970	1,400
Amount for *equally satisfied and dissatisfied*	12,900	1,070
Largest amount for *mostly dissatisfied*	9,220	3,680
Largest amount for *unhappy*	7,780	1,440
Largest amount for *terrible*	6,490	1,290

Note: Each item was administered to all respondents. Dollar amounts shown are not actual incomes but the median amount that respondents said was necessary for (or would leave them with) the indicated feeling.
Data source: 222 July respondents.

become more positive, the amounts of that income become progressively higher, an expected, but nevertheless reassuring result. Of greater interest, however, is the difference in median dollar amount required to move from one D–T Scale category to another. Four of the six intervals are approximately equal in size and correspond to differences just over one thousand dollars. The remaining two intervals, between Delighted and Pleased, and between Equally satisfied and dissatisfied and Mostly dissatisfied, are somewhat over three thousand dollars.

Although the sizes of the intervals are not all equal, our general conclusion is that in absolute dollar terms there are no gross differences among them. The fact that this analysis suggests a somewhat larger-than-average interval between Delighted and Pleased stands in direct contrast to the suggestion in Exploration 1 of a smaller-than-average interval between this pair. We have no real explanation for the difference, and suspect it simply reflects the instabilities inherent in this kind of fine-grained analysis when conducted on rather limited numbers of respondents. Taken together, the two results seem to cancel one another, and we conclude that the difference in the meanings of Delighted and Pleased, when used in the context of the D–T Scale, is probably roughly equivalent to the difference in meanings between other adjacent scale categories.

EXPLORATION 4: THE ROLE OF PERCEPTIONS ABOUT THE PAST AND FUTURE IN PREDICTING PRESENT EVALUATIONS

In trying to understand how people arrive at their evaluations of life quality, one might guess that changes from the past and changes expected in the future would play an important role. One might imagine that perceptions of

---

him feeling "equally satisfied and dissatisfied." The median amount of income on which respondents felt they could "just get by" was $10,580, an amount that, in Exhibit 7.2, falls between the feelings of Mostly dissatisfied and Equally satisfied and dissatisfied.

progress over past conditions might lead to greater acceptance and satisfaction with present conditions, and that perceptions of decline might be associated with reduced satisfaction about the present. How expections about future changes would influence present evaluations is less clear, but there seems a real possibility that such influences might occur.

One exploration of these matters was reported in chapter 3 in connection with our discussion of global measures. It was noted there that none of the long-term (five-year) change measures showed any very substantial relationships to current assessments of Life-as-a-whole. Assessments of past progress tended to relate to present evaluations in the range .1 to .3, while expectations about future progress never showed relationships greater than .1. These results suggested that neither perceptions of the past nor perceptions of the future have much to do with current evaluations, but that of the two, perceptions of the past may exercise the greater influence.

A parallel but more detailed exploration of this same issue has been carried out at the concern level. People's evaluations of their current economic well-being were related to their perceptions of progress (or decline) in personal economic matters over four time periods: the past five years, the past one year, the coming year, and the coming five years.[9] The information derives from the national sample of May respondents.

The results of this analysis of the economic concern are consistent with those just described for more global evaluations of Life-as-a-whole. Evaluations of past progress explained small but noticeable amounts of variance in current perceptions of well-being, but expectations about the future showed hardly any relationships. Perceptions about progress over the past five years explained 8 percent of the variance in current evaluations of economic well-being (equivalent to a relationship of about .3); exactly the same predictive power was shown by perceptions of progress over the past one year; and the two together could account for 11 percent of the variance.[10] In contrast, perceptions about future economic well-being accounted for less than 2 percent of the variance in present evaluations.

This analysis, which is based on a totally different set of respondents from those used for the analysis of the global measures, again suggests that current evaluations have virtually nothing to do with expectations about the future, and bear only rather modest relationships to perceptions of progress or decline from conditions obtaining in the past. While information about perceptions of

---

[9] A typical item used to assess perceived change in economic well-being reads as follows: We are interested in how people are getting along financially these days. Would you say that you (and your family) are *better off* or *worse off* financially than you were *a year ago?* The answers included "Better now," "Same," "Worse now," "Uncertain." The complete set of economic change items consists of questions B1, B4, B4a, B5, B6, and B6a of the questionnaire administered to the May respondents (see appendix A). The measure of current economic well-being is our Money index (cluster C20) and is described in appendix C.

[10] A check showed that the effect of progress over the past five years simply added on to the effect of progress over the past one year; there was no evidence of statistical interaction involving these two predictors and evaluations of current well-being.

progress and decline may well be interesting and important in its own right, this is apparently not the major factor that explains how people come to feel as they do about conditions in the present.

EXPLORATION 5: SIX FRAMES OF REFERENCE AND EVALUATIONS OF WELL-BEING

When people make affective evaluations of life concerns, what are the frames of reference they use? In what contexts, or against which values, or with what perspectives, do people make their judgments of well-being? Exploration 4 suggested that perceptions of past changes play, at most, a rather modest role, and that expectations about future changes have very little impact. The present analysis explores six other contexts.

The basic design of this exploration involves a matrix of twenty-one measures: six context-specific evaluations for each of three life concerns, plus one general evaluation for each concern. The three concerns are heterogeneous and were selected from different portions of the perceptual structure (as this is mapped in chap. 2). The concerns are: Self-accomplishment, Housing, and the National government.

The six frames of reference are also heterogeneous. They include the following: the context of Need satisfaction (operationalized by the phrase, Thinking only of yourself and your own needs, how do you feel about . . .); the context of Fairness (your values as to what is appropriate or fair); the context of Resource inputs (the resources of money, time, and energy being put in); the context of Ease or difficulty of effecting change (what it would take to [bring about a] change); the context of Other people's evaluations (how you think most people would feel); and the context of One's own position in society (thinking of your age and position in life).

Typical context-specific questions read as follows: Thinking only of your own needs, how do you feel about your house/apartment? How do you think most people would feel about what you are accomplishing in life? With your values about what is appropriate and fair, how do you feel about what the national government is doing? All answers were expressed in terms of the categories of the Delighted–Terrible Scale, both for the context-specific items and for the more general items (e.g., How do you feel about what you are accomplishing in life?).[11] The data to be reported come from the 1,118 respondents to the November Form 1 questionnaire.

As expected, the answers pertaining to any one concern, but involving the use of different frames of reference, showed substantial overlaps with one another (correlations ranged from .4 to .7). Interestingly, the pattern of overlaps was almost identical for each of the three concerns. Four contexts showed relatively high interrelationships with one another (Need satisfaction, Fairness,

[11]For the exact wording of all items, see questions S5, S6, and S7 in the November Form 1 questionnaire in appendix A.

Costs, and Social position) while the other two (Ease of effecting a change and Others' evaluations) were somewhat more distinct from the first set and also from each other.

Not only did these last two contexts tend to show greater differentiation from the others, they also were the contexts that were apparently least "natural" for people. Roughly 10 percent of our respondents chose the "I can't answer" option when asked to evaluate the concerns with respect to the Ease of effecting a change and Others' feelings, while the percentage of people choosing this option with respect to the other contexts was generally less then 5 percent. The context for which fewest people chose the "I can't answer" option was that of Need satisfaction, suggesting that this was the frame of reference that people were most accustomed to using.

Exhibit 7.3 shows the results of three parallel multivariate analyses in which the respondents' context-specific answers were used to account for their more general evaluations of each concern. One of the first things that stands out is the relatively high explanatory powers achieved. For each of the three concerns, just over two-thirds of the variance could be explained by the six context measures included in the analysis. How "good" is this level of explanation? Although we have no empirical estimates of the validity and reliability of the context-specific measures, if we can assume that the results derived in chapter 6 for the validity and reliability of concern-level and global measures based on the Delighted–Terrible Scale are even roughly applicable to these measures (which are also based on the D–T Scale), we can estimate that the limit of explanatory power has essentially been reached. In short, the six frames of reference tapped by the predictors in this analysis seem sufficient to account for virtually all of the potentially explainable variance.

A second aspect of the results worth noting is the striking consistency across the three different concerns. The levels of explanatory power are virtually

EXHIBIT 7.3. Prediction of Three General Concern-Level Evaluations by Six Context-Specific Evaluations

	Concern					
	Self-accomplishments		House or apartment		National government	
Percent variance explained						
In present data	69%		69%		68%	
Population estimate	68%		68%		67%	
Contexts	η^2	β^2	η^2	β^2	η^2	β^2
Need satisfaction	.58	.13	.59	.18	.52	.08
Social position	.52	.07	.49	.06	.53	.07
Fairness	.53	.04	.51	.02	.55	.06
Resource input	.43	.02	.32	.00	.46	.03
Others' feelings	.28	.01	.32	.01	.22	.00
Ease of change	.31	.00	.21	.00	.39	.01

Note: Results based on Multiple Classification Analysis.
Data source: 1,118 respondents to November Form 1 national survey.

identical, and the relative importance of the different contexts is also highly similar.

This rank order of importance deserves particular attention. Of the six contexts, three show noticeably higher relationships to the general evaluations than the others. These are the contexts of Need satisfaction, Social position, and Fairness. Any one of these alone can explain about half of the variance in any concern measure (as shown by the eta^{2}'s). None of the other three contexts— Resource input, Others' feelings, or Ease of effecting changes—can explain this much, and the latter two clearly rank below Resource input. When we examine the predictive power of each context while statistically controlling all of the others (results that are shown by the beta^{2}'s), it appears that the Need satisfaction frame of reference clearly outranks all others. Social position and Fairness rank second and third, respectively. Resource input, Others' feelings, and the Ease of effecting changes show hardly any independent relationships.

These analyses suggest that concern-level evaluations are substantially related to people's perceptions of how well their needs are being met, but that the Needs satisfaction perspective by itself is not sufficient to fully explain the evaluations. Other frames of reference are apparently also being considered. While we cannot be certain what they are, this analysis suggests that particularly promising candidates include considerations of one's position in the social structure and consideration of one's values of what is appropriate and fair.

EXPLORATION 6: AN IMPLEMENTATION OF THE DOMAINS-BY-CRITERIA MODEL

The Problem

Chapter 1 describes a conceptual model of how people may arrive at concern-level and global-level evaluations of well-being. These are the evaluations that have been the primary subject of this book. The model, expanded to show presumed causal linkages and made relevant to the particular analysis to be described here, appears in Exhibit 7.4.

The essential ideas are that *domains* of life (such as Housing, Job, Family life, etc.) may be evaluated with respect to how well they meet various value *criteria*; and, conversely, that the *criteria* themselves (e.g., Achieving one's desired standard of living, Having fun, experiencing Independence and freedom, etc.) may be evaluated with respect to the degree of their implementation or achievement in various *domains*. As shown in Exhibits 1.1 and 7.4, the model is two-dimensional and assumes that the same set of elementary domain-by-criterion evaluations, when combined in different ways, can account for *both* concern-level evaluations of the domain type and concern-level evaluations of the criterion type. (The two sets of linkages at the left of Exhibit 7.4 represent these assumptions.) The model also assumes that either type of concern-level evaluations could be used to account for global evaluations (as suggested by the two linkages at the right of Exhibit 7.4).

EXHIBIT 7.4. A Causal Model to Explain Evaluations of Well-Being

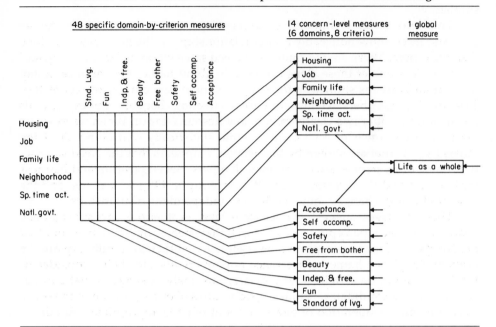

Chapters 4 and 5 explore the relationships between concern-level measures and global measures, and the results reported there provide substantial support for the assumptions of the model regarding the linkages between concern-level measures and global measures. We have not, however, previously examined data relevant to the linkages between domain-by-criterion measures and concern-level measures. This is one of the purposes of the present analysis.

A comprehensive "test" of this model is probably not feasible because of the difficulty of identifying all relevant criteria and all relevant domains, the practical problems of collecting the very large amount of detailed information that would be required, and the impossibility of measuring people's affective evaluations with perfect validity. Nevertheless we have assembled a set of sixty-three measures that permit an initial and partial implementation of the model. The data we have available will not be able to "prove" that our model is right, but they could show that the model is wrong. The model implies certain basic patterns in the bivariate and multivariate relationships, and to the extent that they appear, our willingness to accept the model will be enhanced.

Design of the Analysis and Measures Employed

As shown in Exhibit 7.4, the basic design of this analysis employs a matrix of measures relevant to six domains and eight criteria. The six domains are Housing, Job, Family life, Neighborhood, Spare-time activities, and the National government. The eight criteria are Standard of living, Fun, Independence and freedom, Beauty, Freedom from bother, Safety, Self-accomplish-ment, and Acceptance by other people. Both the domains and criteria were chosen to be well spread in the perceptual structure (as mapped in chap. 2), and hence the concerns in each set are relatively heterogeneous and show relatively little redundancy.

Within the matrix are forty-eight (six × eight) measures, each of which taps an evaluation of just one domain with respect to just one criterion. (These domain-by-criterion measures correspond to the E_{ij}'s of Exhibit 1.1. Sometimes we shall call them cell measures.) In addition, outside the matrix are fourteen more general concern-level measures, six that tap evaluations of domains, and eight that tap evaluations of criteria. (These correspond to the $E_{i.}$'s and $E_{.j}$'s, respectively, of Exhibit 1.1.) Finally, there is one global measure of feelings about Life-as-a whole (corresponding to the $E_{..}$ of Exhibit 1.1).

All data come from the 222 July respondents, and all evaluations have been made on the Delighted–Terrible Scale. The fourteen concern-level measures and the global measure have been used in analyses reported in preceding chapters, and are based on items with a relatively simple and straightforward wording.[12] The forty-eight domain-by-criterion measures come from questions 19.2 to 19.7 of the July questionnaire (reproduced in Appendix A). For example, the respondents' evaluation of the Housing domain with respect to the Stan-dard of living criterion was assessed by the following item, How would you feel about your house or apartment if you considered only the standard of living it enables you to have? Similarly, the evaluation of Housing with respect to the criterion of Fun is based on the item, How would you fee about your house or apartment if you considered only the fun it enables you to have? The same pattern, with only minor grammatical variations, was used for each of the other domain-by-criterion items.

Results

To explore the extent to which the assumptions of the model seem to match reality a series of bivariate and multivariate analyses have been performed. If the model is correct, certain patterns of relationships should appear.

Bivariate Relationships. One of the most elementary patterns concerns sim-ply the sign and magnitude of individual relationships. First, if the model is correct, the concern measures should relate positively to the global measure, and the relationships should be strong enough to suggest some "real" relation-ship; i.e., a relationship stronger than that which could be attributed to the measures being derived from the same method and hence probably sharing some common method effects. Since the fourteen correlations between the concern measures and the global measure range from .23 to .63 (mean $r = .43$), and since the common method effect, as estimated in chapter 6, would yield a correlation of only about .1, this first condition is clearly met.

[12]The fourteen concern-level measures appear in Exhibit 2.1 with numbers 4, 20, 24, 27, 30, 43, 44, 64, 75, 85, 87, 89, 95, and 106. The global measure is Life 3, measure G3 in Exhibit 3.1.

Second, positive relationships strong enough to suggest a real effect should also exist between each concern-level measure and at least some of the cell measures relevant to that particular concern. This condition also seems to be met. The forty-eight correlations involving domain measures (six domains, each correlated with eight cell measures) range from .12 to .63 and average .48; the forty-eight correlations involving criterion measures (eight criteria each correlated with six cell measures) range from .06 to .56 and average .37. Although we have no firm estimates of the impact of the shared method effect on the cell measures, it seems unlikely that it could even approximate 1.00, the figure that would be needed if the average .37 correlation were to be attributed mainly to shared method effects.

Third, if evaluations of Life-as-a-whole are traceable to evaluations at the cell level, one would expect positive relationships between the cell measures and the global measure. Again, the data support the expectation: The forty-eight correlations involved range from .13 to .41 with a mean of .20. Here also the typical relationship is stronger than could be reasonably attributed to shared method effects. (A method effect of .6 would be required for the cell variables, a value that seems unreasonably high, given that other measures based on the D–T Scale have shown method effects of about .3.)

In terms of the simple bivariate relationships, then, the model seems in accord with reality. We can also check the model with respect to certain patterns involving *comparisons* among bivariate relationships.

If the model is right, each concern-level variable should tend to have higher relationships with the cell variables that are assumed to influence it than with other cell variables. This expectation also proves to be supported by the data. For the domains, the average of the forty-eight correlations with "relevant" cell variables is .48 (as noted previously) while the average of the 240 correlations with "irrelevant" cell variables is .20. For the criteria, a similar but somewhat smaller difference exists: The forty-eight correlations with "relevant" cell variables average .37, while the 320 correlations with "irrelevant" cell variables average .27. Furthermore, these differences are not reversed for any of the fourteen concern measures considered individually.

A second important comparison involves the strength of the relationships between the global measure and the concern measures relative to the strength of the relationships between the global measure and the cell measures. Since the model suggests that the concern measures intervene between the global measure and the cell measures, and since the concern measures include evaluative inputs in addition to those represented among these particular cell measures (and hence can be presumed to more comprehensively represent the respondent's feelings), one would expect that the first set of relationships should tend to be higher than the second set. Once again, the results are clearly in accord with the expectation. Relationships between the concern measures and the global measure average .43 while those involving the cell measures and the global measure average .20. The difference holds not only when we average across all fourteen concerns, but also for each of the concerns individually.

Multivariate Relationships. Another way in which data relevant to this model can be examined is from the multivariate perspective. A series of sixteen Multiple Regression analyses, summarized in Exhibit 7.5, let us examine the relative impact of each cell variable in predicting both its relevant domain and also its relevant criterion, and also let us examine how the domains and criteria predict the global measure.

In the upper part of Exhibit 7.5 are the results of using the cell measures to predict concern measures of the domain type (in the first six rows) and of using criterion measures to predict Life 3 (in the bottom row). In all cases the prediction is made by combining *criteria.* Results of performing the complementary operation—combining *domains*—appear in the lower portion of Exhibit 7.5.

For each of the sixteen analyses included here, Exhibit 7.5 shows the beta values (which provide an indication of the importance of the predictors) and an estimate of the percentage of variance that could be explained in the population (i.e., the value of R^2 after adjusting for degrees of freedom and converting from a proportion to a percentage). For example, the top row in the upper portion of Exhibit 7.5 refers to the prediction of the domain-type measure, feelings about Housing, on the basis of eight cell measures. One can see that 41 percent of the variance in feelings about Housing could be explained by the eight predictors. Of the eight criteria used as predictors, the most important were Standard of living and Beauty, with betas of .37 and .25, respectively. (The slightly negative

EXHIBIT 7.5. Implementation of the Matrix Model

	St.Lv.	Fun	Indep.	Beauty	Bother	Safety	Accom.	Accpt.	
Combining criteria to predict domains or Life 3 (prediction: across)									
Housing	.37	.16	−.05	.25	.06	−.14	.00	.10	41%
Job	.10	−.14	.02	.17	.04	.03	.57	.01	43%
Family	−.08	.28	.00	−.06	.08	−.18	.51	−.04	24%
Neigh.	.23	.33	.03	.26	.31	.18	−.47	−.13	52%
Sp.-time	−.03	.27	.17	.01	.21	−.25	.24	−.13	27%
Nat. govt.	.38	.06	.01	.02	.31	.22	−.05	−.26	38%
Life 3	.07	.30	.14	.05	.02	.01	.34	.11	58%

	St.Lv.	Fun	Indep.	Beauty	Bother	Safety	Accom.	Accpt.	Life 3
Combining domains to predict criteria or Life 3 (prediction: downward)									
Housing	.16	−.06	.11	.11	.07	.22	.07	.04	.24
Job	.18	.25	.29	.31	.23	.40	.31	.29	.18
Family	.23	.28	.28	.16	.05	−.13	.10	.04	.35
Neigh.	.20	.07	−.09	.03	.05	.31	−.31	−.20	−.03
Sp.-time	−.07	.24	.18	.08	.00	−.08	.26	.45	.29
Nat. govt.	.04	.08	−.02	.00	.21	.09	.00	−.10	−.06
	29%	41%	31%	22%	19%	44%	16%	23%	43%

Notes: Decimal figures are Multiple Regression betas. Percentage figures show % variance explained (pop. estimates).
Data source: 222 July respondents.

beta of $-.14$ for the Housing-Safety cell measure shows that after holding constant all other predictors, more positive evaluations of the Safety of one's Housing tended to be related to less positive overall evaluations of one's Housing.)

The results in Exhibit 7.5 are interesting for a number of reasons. First, note that fairly substantial predictive powers have been achieved throughout. The eight criteria included in this implementation of the model proved able to explain from 24 percent to 52 percent of the variance in the domain measures, the value depending on the particular domain being predicted. The six domains yielded predictions of criterion measures ranging in power from 16 percent to 44 percent.

Second, note that as we shift from domain to domain different criteria have relevance. For example, in the upper portion of Exhibit 7.5 we see that Freedom from bother has more relevance for evaluating one's Neighborhood and the National government than for any of the other domains included in the analysis. Self-accomplishment, on the other hand, seems most relevant for evaluting one's Job and one's Family life. The criterion of Freedom and independence does not seem particularly important for evaluating any of the six domains included here. The criterion of Fun has more relevance for evaluating one's Family life, one's Neighborhood, and one's Spare-time activities than for evaluating one's Housing, Job, or National government. Additional descriptive statements can be derived by further examination of the upper portion of Exhibit 7.5, and many complementary statements can be derived from the lower portion of Exhibit 7.5. Since we have performed a rather intensive analysis on data from a relatively small number of respondents, we would not want to give undue importance to the particular descriptive results that emerge. What seems significant for our present purpose is that even this relatively simple conceptual model proves capable of "handling" such complex but nevertheless quite reasonable relationships.

The final statistical exploration of this conceptual model involved computing a large number of relationships (160), all of which we expected should be close to zero if the model were correct. Our reasoning, based on the model, was as follows: (1) For any one domain measure, there are only a few cell measures (eight) that are presumed to have a direct causal influence; (2) any relationship between other cell measures and this domain must, therefore, be the result of an indirect effect that occurs because the cell measures themselves happen to be correlated; (3) by removing from a domain measure all variance that can be attributed to its presumed direct causes (the eight "relevant" cell measures), we should effectively break the two-step linkage by which nonrelevant cell measures exert their indirect effects; (4) therefore, the nonrelevant cell measures should be unable to explain any of the remaining variance in the domain measure. A complementary argument could be presented for the criterion measures.

To see how well the model met this "test," we performed four parallel analyses. Each involved removing the variance explained by the presumed causes from one domain measure and then relating each of the presumably nonrelevant cell measures to the variance that remained.[13] The four domains for which the analyses were done were Housing, Neighborhood, Spare-time activities, and National government. The results were much as expected and provide substantial support for the model. Across the four analyses the average explanatory power of the cell variables was less than one percent (0.74 percent), and in none of the analyses did the average exceed 1.5 percent. Among the 160 individual relationships (forty nonrelevant cell variables for each of four domains), there were only three in which a cell variable proved able to explain more than 5 percent of the variance in a domain measure that could not be explained by its presumed causes, and in no case did the explanatory power exceed 10 percent.

In short, cell variables that the model suggested should have no direct causal impact on a concern measure showed virtually no relationships to such measures once the possibilities for indirect linkages had been removed. This result was independently replicated for four different domains.

Conclusions

As was stated at the beginning of this section, no amount of empirical analysis can "prove" that a conceptual model is correct. Our several analyses have, however, provided a variety of opportunities in which the model could be shown wrong, and this has not happened. On the contrary, a variety of expectations involving the size and direction of relationships, the relative magnitudes of relationships, situations in which combinations of variables should be able to predict a dependent variable, and situations in which variables should be unable to predict, have all been borne out. To the extent that the model has been testable against empirical data, it seems to accord well with reality. Whatever its ultimate "correctness," the model has already had unquestionable heuristic value in helping us to think about the evaluation process.

EXPLORATION 7: COMPARISONS BETWEEN ONE'S OWN WELL-BEING AND THAT OF OTHERS

How do people think their own well-being compares with that of others? Since it is probable that one's sense of being well-off or deprived depends in part on how well-off one believes other people are, it is of interest to examine how respondents' own feelings relate to what they believe to be the feelings of other people. We have explored this for several types of "others" and with respect to both feelings about Life-as-a-whole and a variety of more specific life concerns.

[13]For each domain measure this was accomplished by using the results of the relevant regression shown in Exhibit 7.5 to compute a predicted score for each respondent, and then constructing a new, residualized domain measure by subtracting the predicted score from the actual score. Correlations were then computed between the residualized domain measure and each of the nonrelevant cell measures.

When Life-as-a-whole is being assessed, the consistent finding is that most people think they are better off than either other people in general ("all the adults in the U.S.") or their nearest same-sexed neighbor. The average scores that respondents assign themselves on measures such as Life 3 or Circles: whole life tend to be roughly one half standard deviation higher than their average estimate of how others would evaluate their lives. This pattern appears in data from both the nationally representative April respondents and the more restricted group of July respondents.

People's tendency to be more satisfied with their lives than they believe others to be with *theirs* suggests what we might call a negative bias in perceptions of other people's feelings about Life-as-a-Whole. While this negative bias is of some interest in its own right and could be attributed to any of several psychological coping mechanisms, it gains added significance when we discover that, at the concern level, it is not a uniform phenomenon. Certain concerns also show this negative bias, but others show no bias or even a positive bias!

The data to be reported in some detail here come from the July respondents. Their questionnaire included a series of items introduced by the following instructions:

> Think who is the neighbor who lives nearest to you, who is of the same sex as you, and who is at least 18 years old. (If there are several such neighbors living equally close to your house or apartment, pick the one to the left as you walk into your place.) The following questions all concern how you *think* this person feels about aspects of his or her *own* life.

The respondents were then asked for their estimates of the neighbor's feelings about Life-as-a-whole and fourteen life concerns. Their answers were on the Delighted–Terrible Scale. These estimates of neighbors' feelings were then compared with the respondents' evaluations (also made on the Delighted–Terrible Scale) of the same aspects in their own lives. The results appear in Exhibit 7.6.

One particularly interesting result shown in Exhibit 7.6 involves the magnitude and direction of the difference between the mean scores for the various concerns, the amount of negative or positive bias. There is a remarkable correspondence between this bias and the position of the concerns in the perceptual structure (as mapped in Exhibit 2.2). Concerns that are closely associated with Self and Family show the strongest negative biases; those most remote from Self and Family show *positive* bias. In other words, these respondents tend to think that other people are less satisfied than they themselves are with closely personal aspects of life, but that other people are *more* satisfied with aspects of the local and national society.

For the Family life concern, where the negative bias is most pronounced, the respondents' average estimates of their neighbors' feelings were three-quarters of a scale category lower than what they reported as their own feelings (5.02 for the neighbors, which corresponds to the Mostly satisfied category on the D–T Scale, compared with 5.77 for the respondents, which approaches the "Pleased" category). A difference almost as great, but in the opposite direction

EXHIBIT 7.6. Evaluations of Life-as-a-Whole and of Fourteen Life Concerns: Own Feelings and Estimates of Nearest Neighbor's Feelings

	Aspect of life	Estimate for neighbor	Own rating	Difference
G3	Life-as-a-whole	5.12	5.42	−.30
4	Family life	5.02	5.77	−.75
27	Fun	4.90	5.20	−.30
64	Acceptance by others	5.09	5.31	−.22
20	Self-accomplishment	4.94	5.13	−.19
43	Freedom from bother	4.65	4.77	−.12
87	Housing	5.10	5.20	−.10
30	Spare-time activities	5.07	5.11	−.04
44	Independence & freedom	4.97	4.99	−.02
85	Standard of living	5.18	5.19	−.01
24	Beauty	5.01	5.02	−.01
95	Safety	4.91	4.88	+.03
75	Job	5.09	5.05	+.04
89	Neighborhood	5.22	5.10	+.12
106	National government	3.81	3.15	+.66

Notes: Measure numbers refer to Exhibits 2.1 or 3.1. The standard deviations of both the estimates for neighbors' and own ratings are approximately 1.0 for all aspects of life (range: .84 to 1.27). Data source: 222 July respondents. Figures show mean scores on D–T Scale.

can be seen for the National government concern. Here respondents thought their neighbors were substantially *more* satisfied than were they themselves (means are 3.81 for the neighbors and 3.15 for the respondents).

Although we do not have information directly from the neighbors as to how they really felt about their lives, it seems most unlikely that they could—on average—have felt much different from the respondents.[14] Thus, these results suggest that there are selective misperceptions of how others evaluate their lives.

Such misperceptions are potentially significant from two perspectives. From a scientific standpoint, identifying the factors that produce positive or negative biases may help us better understand how people come to feel as they do about their lives. These biases may also have relevance from a decision-making standpoint: Ours is a society that tries to increase well-being by allocating resources according to judgments by one set of people about how other people will feel and react.

A second interesting result in Exhibit 7.6 is the finding that, on the whole, respondents think that their neighbors would rank order their evaluations of the concerns in approximately the same way as do the respondents themselves. Within the group of concerns examined here, respondents are least positive regarding National government, Freedom from being bothered and annoyed,

[14]The basis for this statement is that the respondents form a reasonably representative sample of all the people (neighbors included) in the area from which they were selected, and hence the best estimate of the neighbors' actual feelings is the mean feelings shown by the respondents.

Safety, and Independence and freedom. These are the concerns that also get some of the lowest evaluations in terms of how respondents estimated their neighbors felt. (The rank correlation of the two sets of means across the fourteen concern-level evaluations is rho = .52.)

It does not follow, however, that respondents are simply imputing to their neighbors the same feelings that they themselves have. Within any one concern, the typical correlation between the respondents' own feelings and their estimates of their neighbors' feelings is a rather modest .24. As expected, this correlation tends to be highest for those concerns where the same phenomena impinge on both respondent and neighbor (e.g., for National government and Safety, where correlations are .43 and .48, respectively), and lowest for concerns where the evaluators could be expected to experience different situations (e.g., Acceptance by other people, Housing, and Spare-time activities, where the correlations range from .11 to .13). While the mild positive relationship within any one concern may be partly attributable to measurement artifacts and biases common to both sets of evaluations, part is almost certainly a reflection of reality. People within a single neighborhood tend to have certain social and demographic similarities, and one would expect they might also tend to make similar evaluations about their lives, particularly about those aspects that they experience in common.

This analysis has identified several interesting aspects about perceptions of other people's well-being. With respect to any one concern, there seems not to be great "projection"; on the whole people do not believe that others feel the same as they do about any one concern. There seems, nevertheless, to be an assumption that if neighbors were asked to rank-order a set of concerns from positive to negative, they would order them in roughly the same way as the respondents themselves. This seems a realistic assumption. Furthermore, there is a tendency to believe other people are less satisfied than the respondents themselves about matters that are close and personal (including one's Life-as-a-whole), but *more* satisfied regarding more remote concerns. We see no basis for believing that other people would in fact show such differences and suspect that these differences represent an unexplained but possibly significant bias in perceptions of others' well-being.

EXPLORATION 8: JUDGMENTS OF THE "IMPORTANCE" OF CONCERNS

One of the hypotheses with which we started was that the relative importance a person assigned to various life concerns should be taken into account when combining concern-level evaluations to predict feelings about Life-as-a-whole. The hypothesis is based on the expectation that when forming evaluations of overall well-being people would give greater "weight" to those concerns they felt were important, and less weight to those they regarded as less significant.

As described in chapter 4, a careful examination of this hypothesis showed it to be untrue. There was no way in which importance data could be combined with satisfaction data to increase the accuracy of predictions of feelings about Life-as-a-whole over what could be achieved using satisfaction data alone. This result puzzled us when it first emerged and led to a number of further explorations.

Two sets of data that included importance judgments have been available to us. One source is our own July respondents; the other is a separate national survey run by some of our colleagues.[15]

In one analysis we looked to see whether the mean importance assigned to a given concern bore any relationship to its association with feelings about Life-as-a-whole. If our original hypothesis had been correct, one would have expected a high relationship here; feelings about Life-as-a-whole would have had more to do with feelings about the important concerns than with feelings about the others. Using the data from our colleagues' survey the answer was essentially "no." Over ten concerns, the rank correlation between mean importance and the size of the simple bivariate relationship (measured by the eta statistic) was $-.39$: There was a modest tendency for the concerns that had higher relationships to Life-as-a-whole to be judged *less* important: When we performed the same analysis using a more complex multivariate relationship derived by holding constant the effects of all other nine concerns (measured by the beta statistic from Multiple Classification Analysis), the rank correlation was $+.15$. A similar analysis in the July data produced a rank correlation of $+.30$ between the importance of concerns and the size of their (bivariate) relationships to the Life 3 measure. It seems clear that the mean importance assigned to a concern has little to do with the relationship between that concern and feelings about Life-as-a-whole.

Further insight about the meaning of importance judgments emerged when we checked to see whether the importance assigned to a concern has anything to do with the position of the concern in the psychological structure. We compared the importance data for the ten concerns as assessed in our colleagues' survey with the position of those concerns in the structural maps derived from our own national sample of May respondents (see Exhibit 2.4).[16] There was a distinct tendency for concerns that were closer to Self and Family to receive higher importance ratings than those that were more remote (rho = .52). When the analysis was repeated using the importance of the concerns as judged by our July respondents, a parallel result emerged (rho = .43). Still a third version of the analysis took the importance of the concerns as judged by the July respondents and checked the location of the concerns in the plot derived from these same respondents (Exhibit 2.2). Here the relationship was somewhat higher (rho = .59).

We conclude that importance ratings are substantially linked to the posi-

---

[15]Question 20 of the July questionnaire, reproduced in appendix A, elicited the importance judgments from the July respondents. The questions used in the study designed by our colleagues Campbell, Converse, and Rodgers are detailed in chapter 4.

[16]We turned to our own May data for a mapping of the perceptual structure because we believed our own more extensive list of concerns produced a better defined map than that available from the smaller number of concerns investigated by our colleagues.

tion of the concern in the perceptual structure, and that concerns that are seen as being closely associated with oneself and one's family tend to be ranked as more important than others. However, the importance assigned to a concern does not have much to do with the strength of its relationships to feelings about Life-as-a-whole.

EXPLORATION 9: SEARCHING FOR PEOPLE WITH DISTINCTIVE PATTERNS OF FEELINGS ABOUT WELL-BEING

The final analysis to be reported in this chapter looked for groups of people who would show distinctive patterns of feelings about their well-being and who would be distinctively different from people with other patterns. Although we had no theoretical reason for believing such groups existed, we knew of no reason why they might not, and it seemed desirable to examine our data to see if they were present. It turned out that groups that were distinctive and separate, and that could be replicated in independent samples of respondents, could not be found despite an extensive and sophisticated search. The failure to find such groups, and our inference that distinctive groups of substantial size do not exist, represent important outcomes in their own right.

The meaning of the phrase "distinct separate group" needs to be clearly understood for this analysis to be properly interpreted. The search was for "types" or "clusters" of people. These are sets of individuals who show the same pattern of characteristics, and whose pattern is sharply different from that shown by other people. In the technical sense of the word, biological species qualify as "types," for there are clear distinctions between them; on the other hand, rocks graded by size and shape would not usually constitute distinct types, even though they were not all the same, because there are (usually) continuous gradations of size and shape. What we wanted to know was whether there were particular patterns of feelings about one's own well-being (e.g., a combination of being especially satisfied about one's Family, especially displeased with one's Job, and about average on other concerns) that would be characteristic of a substantial proportion of people but that would be distinctly different from even the most similar other patterns.

Two separate searches were undertaken. The first involved selecting two random subsamples from our May respondents and examining each individual's pattern of feelings with respect to the Selected 12 concerns.[17] We were unable in this search to find distinctive groups that could be matched in the two subsamples. The second involved a random sample of five hundred people selected from our May respondents and another sample of five hundred people selected from respondents to another national survey (that of Campbell, Converse, and Rodgers). These two samples were examined for feelings about

---

[17]The two subsamples consisted of 300 and 212 cases, respectively. See chapter 4 for a list of the particular measures included among the Selected 12 concerns.

seven concerns that had been assessed in both surveys.[18] Again, we were unable to find distinctive groups that could be matched in both subsamples. All searches were made using a sophisticated computer program called MIKCA: A Fortran IV Program for Multivariate Iterative K-means Cluster Analysis (McRae, 1971).

Our consistent failure to find groups of people who were distinct and separate with respect to their feelings about well-being suggests that patterns in feelings about well-being show reasonably continous variation throughout the population. Of course, this is not to say that all people have the same pattern of feelings, or even that different patterns are uniformly distributed throughout the population. From previous analyses we know that neither of these is true. Rather, the findings suggest that there seem to be continuous gradations from one pattern to another, with no sharp concentrations on certain patterns that are set apart by total absences of others.

The result is not surprising, but it helps to define the nature of perceptions about well-being. It probably simplifies, rather than complicates, the task of explaining the dynamics of perceptions about well-being. If it had appeared that people clustered into distinctive "types" with respect to feelings about life concerns, there would immediately arise questions as to why certain feelings went together and why other combinations of feelings did not appear. As it is, we are spared those questions. The results suggest that the issue of how people come to feel as they do can be approached by examining the various concerns individually.

CHAPTER SUMMARY

Since this chapter consists of nine separate reports of exploratory analyses, we shall break from our previous practice of presenting a general chapter summary. Individual summaries for each exploration appear near the beginning of the chapter under the subtitle "Organization of the chapter and summary of results."

---

[18]The concerns were Community, Own education, Job, Spare-time activities, Health, Standard of living, and Family life.

PART 2

WELL-BEING IN THE UNITED STATES: AMERICANS' PERCEPTIONS

CHAPTER 8

Americans' Well-Being: Specific Life Concerns

We have traced the structure of peoples' evaluations of well-being and established a framework for understanding the integration of these judgments. We will now look at these data from a simple, descriptive point of view to see what they tell us about well-being in the United States. This chapter presents the distributions (and arithmetic means) of responses from our complete national samples of American adults.[1] The results tell us much about how Americans evaluate many different aspects of their lives. (Chapter 9 focuses on differences in well-being among subgroups of the American population and Chapter 10 considers evaluations of life-as-a-whole.)

THE NATION

"How do you feel about: Life in the United States today?" (May 1972)

Delighted	7%	(coded 7)
Pleased	22%	(coded 6)
Mostly satisfied	39%	(coded 5)
Mixed	23%	(coded 4)
Mostly dissatisfied	5%	(coded 3)
Unhappy	3%	(coded 2)
Terrible	1%	(coded 1)
Total	100%	Mean = 4.9

The most common evaluation about "life in the United States today" is "mostly satisfied." Other feelings are distributed about equally on either side of that position. You can pick your own position and see what proportion of the population feels better than you do or what fraction feels worse. You can look at

[1]Appendix N presents additional data from national surveys conducted in 1974 and 1976.

the almost one in ten who feel "mostly dissatisfied," "unhappy," or "terrible" and wonder who they are and why they feel that way and whether they represent a distressed minority of about 14 million that deserves attention. You can surmise who the more than one in four are who are "pleased" or "delighted" with life in the United States and try and guess what it is that makes their picture of the nation so attractive. If you do these things you are beginning to confront the problems of subjective social indicators, and obviously one thing to do is to look at more feelings of the American public and try to piece them together into a more meaningful pattern. We will go on. (To conserve space we will present the percentage distributions horizontally instead of vertically, drop the 100 percent total, and abbreviate the scale, which is repetitive. In the text of this chapter we present the distributions and means from single items; appendix K contains similar information for selected combinations of items; i.e., for some of the clusters identified in chapter 2.)

"How do you feel about: How the United States stands in the eyes of the rest of the world?"

Delig.	Pleas.	Mos. sat.	Mixed	Mos. diss.	Unhap.	Terr.		(Mean)
1%	7%	18%	33%	20%	13%	8%	(May)[2]	3.7

The modal response on our international image moved down one whole scale step from that given to "life in the United States" and responses piled up somewhat more on the critical side. These data were collected a few months after United States détente with China, in the same month as the president held summit talks with Soviet leaders, and long before a cease-fire in Vietnam. It was also the month in which Governor Wallace was shot at a political rally.

"How do you feel about: The standards and values of today's society?"

Delig.	Pleas.	Mos. sat.	Mixed	Mos. diss.	Unhap.	Terr.		(Mean)
1%	6%	22%	42%	19%	7%	3%	(Nov.)	4.0

This pattern of responses is somewhat similar to the pattern on the last question, but there is no reason to assume that people were thinking internationally. Although 1972 was notable for slayings, bombings, and hijackings, the year also saw the ITT affair, the bugging of Democratic headquarters, and Irving's fake autobiography, but people were more likely thinking of the splits in values in our society that were evidenced in protests, life-styles, and generational conflicts.

"How do you feel about: The way young people in this country are thinking and acting?

[2]"May," "Nov.," and "April" indicate the particular national survey from which the data are taken. The surveys were conducted in May 1972, November 1972, and April 1973 (see chap. 1 and app. B for details on number of respondents, sampling procedures, etc.) Unless specified otherwise, "Nov." refers to data from respondents who answered the November Form 2 interview.

Delig.	Pleas.	Mos. sat.	Mixed	Mos. diss.	Unhap.	Terr.		(Mean)
2%	7%	21%	34%	15%	10%	11%	(May)	3.7

"How do you feel about: The way people over forty in this country are thinking and acting?"

Delig.	Pleas.	Mos. sat.	Mixed	Mos. diss.	Unhap.	Terr.		(Mean)
1%	8%	32%	39%	12%	5%	3%	(May)	4.2

There was no wave of pleasure or delight over the young or the middle-aged, though more unhappiness was expressed regarding young people than the over-forties. It is clear, however, that there were mixed feelings and probably some sensible reticence to generalize feelings about such a broad social category. There was greater dispersion of feelings expressed about young people, and this could reflect a greater variety of images as to what young people were thinking and doing as much as it may reflect varying standards of judgment about those activities.

Most of what we know about the nation and life in America is arrayed and displayed for us on the pages and screens of the mass media. The managers and craftsmen of the media also have a large hand in programming our entertainment, staging and waging our competitions, and molding our fantasies and fun. There are also local sources of information and entertainment that can be clearly separated from the national scene, but we lumped them together in our questions and it is often difficult in these days to separate the two.

"How do you feel about: The entertainment you get from TV, radio, movies, and local events and places?"

Delig.	Pleas.	Mos. sat.	Mixed	Mos. diss.	Unhap.	Terr.		(Mean)
4%	16%	36%	27%	10%	4%	3%	(May)	4.5

"How do you feel about: the information you get from newspapers, magazines, TV, and radio?"

Delig.	Pleas.	Mos. sat.	Mixed	Mos. diss.	Unhap.	Terr.		(Mean)
2%	12%	34%	29%	12%	7%	4%	(May)	4.3

Entertainment raised only a little more approval than information in the national media, the difference is trival, and the general impression is rather that the two were regarded about equally well or equally poorly. It is difficult to establish a standard of judgment for these results. The information and entertainment programs of the media obviously have to cater to various audiences and interests, and although inclusion of the phrase "you get" in the question wording may have excluded some programs that were never turned on or publications that were not read, it would seem that respondents were probably thinking of the variety and spread of offerings that one might reasonably expect to lead to mixed feelings and evaluations.

THE NATIONAL GOVERNMENT

The year 1972 was a year of war and a year of political campaigning, a year of both international and domestic concerns and problems. The activities of the federal government are indeed broad, and any evaluator would have to hold clear priorities regarding governmental policies to express extreme approval or disapproval. The schisms of feeling in the country are partly expressed by the high proportion who reported mixed feelings of satisfaction and dissatisfaction. Neither side of the midpoint on our scale mustered a majority of support or opposition in either May or November of 1972.

"How do you feel about: The way our national government is operating?" (May 1972)

What our national government is doing?" (November 1972)

Delig.	Pleas.	Mos. sat.	Mixed	Mos. diss.	Unhap.	Terr.		(Means)
1%	8%	25%	38%	15%	7%	6%	(May)	4.0
1%	5%	28%	45%	14%	5%	2%	(Nov.1)	4.1
1%	4%	21%	42%	18%	10%	4%	(Nov.2)	3.8

(The fact that the two national samples in November yielded slightly different proportions in the various scale categories is an indication of sampling variability.)

We also asked people their feelings about the military activities of the United States, a major political issue of that period and of that year's presidential campaign. It was clear (in May 1972) that across the nation there was more dissatisfaction than satisfaction with our national military posture and practice. One can see that the distribution of responses was skewed toward the "feel bad" end of the scale, but we have seen that this was true for several topics of national phenomena at this time.

"How do you feel about: Our national military activities?"

Delig.	Pleas.	Mos. sat.	Mixed	Mos. diss.	Unhap.	Terr.		(Mean)
1%	7%	20%	28%	19%	12%	13%	(May)	3.5

Much of what is governmental action is personalized and seen as the thinking or action of political leaders, so when the topic turns to them instead of government there is very little difference in the public's feelings or evaluations.

There was also very little shift in the overall distributions from May to November 1972 even though the November measure was taken at the time of a national election and heavy political campaigning.

"How do you feel about: The way our political leaders think and act?"

Delig.	Pleas.	Mos. sat.	Mixed	Mos. diss.	Unhap.	Terr.		(Means)
1%	3%	16%	44%	17%	11%	8%	(May)	3.6
1%	3%	20%	48%	18%	6%	4%	(Nov.)	3.9

LOCAL GOVERNMENT

Turning our attention away from the national scene, we raised the topic of local government, which is, of course, even more varied than national government since the term refers to the hundreds of separate governmental units where our respondents lived. These local units do not share the "sameness" of the federal government even though regions are differentially affected by various federal policies. What is shared, perhaps, is the replicative nature of problems and attempted solutions from one local governmental unit to another within the context of national economic and political conditions. We asked about local government in the same way that we queried feelings for the federal establishment. We also asked about a few governmental services such as schools, etc., but they are grouped under community and neighborhood in later presentation. However, we do include "police and courts" here since they usually have somewhat more of the character of a governmental unit than a neighborhood.

"How do you feel about: The way your local government is operating?" (May 1972)
What your local government is doing?" (Nov. 1972)

Delig.	Pleas.	Mos. sat.	Mixed	Mos. diss.	Unhap.	Terr.		(Means)
1%	13%	32%	30%	13%	6%	5%	(May)	4.2
<1%	5%	34%	37%	15%	5%	4%	(Nov.)	4.1

Local government in its various forms and policies was more favorably evaluated than the federal government but certainly not much better, and differential feelings even within the single respondent are reflected in the concentration of choices in the middle-scale units. The distributions are not symmetric and there was more satisfaction than dissatisfaction but certainly little enthusiasm, and one person in four felt mostly dissatisfied or worse. The police and courts received about the same degree of criticism and support as the larger activities of local government:

"How do you feel about: The way the police and courts in this area are operating?"

Delig.	Pleas.	Mos. sat.	Mixed	Mos. diss.	Unhap.	Terr.		(Mean)
2%	16%	33%	26%	13%	5%	5%	(May)	4.3

Since these are a mix of evaluations on a national sample, we do not know whether this picture reflects a mixture of communities or a replicated mixture of reactions in the areas, cities, and communities that make up a national sample. Probably some local communities receive more support and satisfaction than others but a national sample cannot well evaluate such a hypothesis. It is likely that although some local government units may do better than others, there will be a dispersion of evaluations in every civic unit.

ECONOMIC SITUATION

Economic problems are tremendously worse for some people than others, but there are also shared economic problems such as inflation that affect everyone, some worse than others. Our questions in this area, therefore, ran the gamut from activities and policies of the federal government to family standards of living and family agreement on expenditures. The items are perhaps best surveyed as a group.

	Delig.	Pleas.	Mos. sat.	Mixed	Mos. diss.	Unhap.	Terr.		(Means)
"How do you feel about:									
What the government is doing about the economy—jobs, prices, profits?"	1%	6%	19%	38%	20%	10%	6%	(May)	3.7
	1%	3%	15%	38%	24%	13%	6%	(Nov.)	3.4
The taxes you pay—I mean the local, state, and national taxes all together?"	1%	5%	16%	22%	23%	17%	16%	(May)	3.2
What you have to pay for basic necessities such as food, housing, and clothing?"	1%	9%	26%	29%	21%	9%	5%	(May)	3.9
	1%	4%	17%	24%	33%	13%	8%	(Nov.)	3.5
The income you (and your family) have?"	5%	29%	36%	15%	8%	5%	2%	(May)	4.8
	3%	23%	36%	14%	14%	5%	5%	(Nov.)	4.5
The pay and fringe benefits you get, and the security of your job?"	10%	30%	32%	13%	7%	4%	4%	(May)	5.0
How secure you are financially?"	6%	20%	32%	21%	11%	6%	4%	(April)	4.5

	Delig.	Pleas.	Mos. sat.	Mixed	Mos. diss.	Unhap.	Terr.		(Means)
Your standard of living—the things you have like housing, car, furniture, recreation, and the like?"	8%	34%	39%	12%	4%	2%	1%	(May)	5.2
	8%	33%	37%	12%	7%	2%	1%	(Nov.)	5.1
How well your family agrees on how family income should be spent?"	8%	32%	41%	13%	4%	1%	1%	(Nov.)	5.2

It is clear that feelings differed about various aspects of the economic problems that were apparent in 1972. Taxes came in for the most widespread criticism and unhappiness, though about one in four were mostly satisfied (or more enthusiastic) with them. What the government is doing about the economy received more disapproval than approval, and this distribution is close to that of feelings about the prices of necessities at a time of inflation. It is also apparent that the situation worsened between May and November 1972, with significant shifts away from satisfaction with then-current price levels.

Nevertheless, the picture of feelings about family income was somewhat rosier though it too dropped just a little between May and November. Although the impact of rising prices was being felt, it was not being equally shared across income levels. Job pay and security was even more satisfactory and was probably evaluated in a somewhat different context than overall family income, especially if there was more than one income earner in the family unit. Evaluations of financial security were distributed about the same as feelings about family income but with just enough difference to make one think that there were millions of families who were satisfied with their current incomes but not as many who were confident about their income security as they looked ahead.

However, when it came to judging one's standard of living, even though prices of necessities were rising, and—even closer to home—when it came to family decisions on how the available income was to be spent, then a large majority felt satisfied, and many were pleased, with what they had and how available resources were being apportioned. One senses strong feelings of dissatisfaction with the inflation in the economy and dissatisfaction with government action, but the financial strains, at least in 1972, had not as yet hit hard at family economics although there were portents of concern and some apprehension about the future.

COMMUNITY

A community is partly local government but there are other aspects of community life and setting that make up peoples' appreciation or dissatisfaction with the larger-than-neighborhood area where they live. We asked a number of questions that dealt with conditions, people, services, facilities, and so forth, but first we will deal with the most general aspects under this particular heading.

"How do you feel about: The weather in this part of the state?"

Delig.	Pleas.	Mos. sat.	Mixed	Mos. diss.	Unhap.	Terr.		(Mean)
10%	28%	34%	16%	6%	2%	4%	(May)	5.0

"How do you feel about: The conditions of the natural environment—the air, land, and water in this area?"

Delig.	Pleas.	Mos. sat.	Mixed	Mos. diss.	Unhap.	Terr.		(Mean)
5%	18%	27%	21%	12%	10%	7%	(May)	4.3

There may be no better time of the year to ask about the weather than in spring and perhaps the natural environment is at its best then, though it is also possible that pollution is more noticeable where it occurs. Whether the evaluation of weather varies seasonally or not and whether peoples' memories are long or short, at least one in three was pleased or delighted with the weather where they lived. Only one in eight felt mostly dissatisfied or worse. But, in this period of increased sensitivity to ecological problems, feelings about the state of the natural environment reflected more criticism and dissatisfaction than the God-given weather. People were more satisfied with their financial resources than they were with the present state of nature and its conservation.

"How do you feel about: This community as a place to live?"

Delig.	Pleas.	Mos. sat.	Mixed	Mos. diss.	Unhap.	Terr.		(Means)
18%	39%	27%	9%	3%	2%	2%	(May)	5.5
10%	35%	35%	12%	5%	1%	2%	(Nov.)	5.2

"How do you feel about: People who live in this community?"

Delig.	Pleas.	Mos. sat.	Mixed	Mos. diss.	Unhap.	Terr.		(Mean)
7%	41%	36%	12%	2%	1%	1%	(May)	5.4

A community may not seem quite as delightful a place in November as in May but satisfaction seems to run high at any time of the year. In mobile America one's community is to a large extent a personal decision, and one can grow to appreciate a community more as one pushes one's roots deeper into community life. Whatever the reason, satisfaction with community ran high and "delight" with one's town was a little more frequent than similar enthusiasm over the people who live there, but the difference is small and, in general, community reflects people as much as it reflects other appreciated and familiar characteristics.

SERVICES AND FACILITIES

Part of what makes up a community is the network and variety of facilities, personnel and services, some provided by government and others provided by individuals and business enterprises, that meet the needs of people who live together in settlements. We asked about broad categories of such services, assuming they might well vary in quality and the satisfaction they provided. (Evaluations of the police and courts have already been reported and feelings about some other community facilities such as those dealing with education and leisure are discussed under their own headings.)

Although one in eight reported "mostly dissatisfaction" or worse feelings with medical services, a proportion that implies a population total of about 17 million, this is the type of service that received the strongest endorsement. Forty-five percent said they were "pleased" or "delighted" with the doctors, clinics, and hospitals they would use. We did not ask about actual use or personal experience and some of the responses may have been based on hearsay, nor do we know whether there is any relationship between evaluation and exposure. (A good social indicator of community services would need to tie such loose ends together, but at this stage of our investigation we are exploring the broad pattern of human evaluations rather than delving deeply into the meaning and interpretation to be given each probe into a respondent's world.)

The set of services provided by local government in most communities received more favorable ratings as a group than did police and courts taken alone. The distribution of satisfaction and dissatisfaction that they elicited is very close to that given to medical services and both groups of services share characteristics of routine need and emergency crises.

"How do you feel about: The doctors, clinics, and hospitals you would use in this area?"

Delig.	Pleas.	Mos. sat.	Mixed	Mos. diss.	Unhap.	Terr.		(Mean)
11%	34%	32%	11%	5%	4%	3%	(May)	5.1

"How do you feel about: The services you get in this neighborhood—like garbage collection, street maintenance, fire and police protection?"

Delig.	Pleas.	Mos. sat.	Mixed	Mos. diss.	Unhap.	Terr.		(Mean)
7%	32%	35%	13%	6%	3%	4%	(May)	5.0

"How do you feel about: The goods and services you can get when you buy in this area—things like food, appliances, clothes?"

Delig.	Pleas.	Mos. sat.	Mixed	Mos. diss.	Unhap.	Terr.		(Mean)
4%	26%	40%	18%	8%	2%	2%	(May)	4.9

"How do you feel about: The services you can get when you have to have someone come in to fix things around your home—like painting, repairs?"

Delig.	Pleas.	Mos. sat.	Mixed	Mos. diss.	Unhap.	Terr.		(Mean)
4%	19%	33%	21%	13%	5%	5%	(May)	4.4

The business enterprises did not elicit the same proportions of delight and pleasure from their customers that was reported for the medical and on-the-street governmental services but the heavily dissatisfied proportion of the population stayed about one in eight. But even this group grew to about one in four when home services and repairs were the community service being evaluated. Yet, even though sizable numbers of people were unhappy with the cost, caliber, or promptness of the service they are able to get, there were still more satisfied than dissatisfied customers.

EDUCATION

The largest bite out of local civic budgets is usually made for schools and education services. Only 12 percent of our respondents felt they could *not* make an evaluation of local schools so many answers must have been based on evidence other than having one's own child presently in the local school system. Schools got a pretty fair report card, not an "A," because one in eight felt "mostly dissatisfied" or worse, but over 40 percent said that they felt pleased or delighted. This distribution of supportive and critical feelings is about the same as that obtained by the medical and on-the-street services to the community.

As a longer-term evaluation of educational services and an evaluation that could be made by everyone, we also asked our respondents about the usefulness of their own education. There is not much difference in the distribution of replies to that question and the one on local schools, but the two sets of evaluations are not correlated at any level worth our attention! "Usefulness," here, seems mostly to refer to what the respondent is accomplishing and what he or she is achieving financially. The evaluation of local schools does not seem to relate to one's feelings about anything else that we raised.

"How do you feel about: The schools in this area?"

Delig.	Pleas.	Mos. sat.	Mixed	Mos. diss.	Unhap.	Terr.		(Mean)
8%	35%	31%	14%	6%	3%	3%	(May)	5.0

"How do you feel about: The usefulness, for you personally, of your education?"

Delig.	Pleas.	Mos. sat.	Mixed	Mos. diss.	Unhap.	Terr.		(Mean)
8%	34%	36%	12%	7%	2%	1%	(May)	5.1

JOBS

We have already referred to our question about "job pay" but we asked a number of other questions about the work situation developed out of the study of factors in job evaluation by Quinn *et al.* (1971). Not everyone in a national sample of the adult population has paid employment, of course, and the following percentages refer to the population of employed workers rather than all adults. (In May the proportion who could not evaluate a "job" was 42 percent and in November it was 35 percent, which should largely be attributed to sampling variations and not a significant change in employment rolls. The number of unemployed who want jobs is sufficiently small that a much larger sample is required to measure that proportion with accuracy.)

Two aspects of the job receive as much reported satisfaction as the job in general and they may well be the two aspects of the work situation that engender the high levels of gratification. One was a question that limited evaluation to the work itself, what the worker did on the job; and the other was a query about how the respondent felt about co-workers on the job. No other aspects of the job situation receive stronger ratings of pleasure and satisfaction.

	Delig.	Pleas.	Mos. sat.	Mixed	Mos. diss.	Unhap.	Terr.		(Means)
"How do you feel about:									
Your job?' (Answered by 58% in May and 65% in November.)	17%	41%	24%	11%	3%	3%	1%	(May)	5.5
	13%	35%	33%	12%	4%	2%	1%	(Nov.)	5.3
The people you work with—your co-workers?"	16%	43%	29%	8%	2%	1%	1%	(May)	5.6
The work you do on the job—the work itself?"	20%	41%	25%	9%	3%	1%	1%	(May)	5.6
What you have available for doing your job—I mean equipment, information, good supervision and so on?"	11%	37%	34%	9%	5%	2%	2%	(May)	5.3
What it is like where you work—the physical surroundings, the hours, and the amount of work you are asked to do?"	9%	34%	36%	13%	5%	2%	1%	(May)	5.2
The pay and fringe benefits you get, and the security of your job?"	10%	30%	32%	13%	7%	4%	4%	(May)	5.0

When we asked about job resources, communication, and supervision—admittedly a mixed bag but all related to management for the employed worker—the ratings of enthusiasm were lowered somewhat though satisfaction was still high. The physical conditions of work and work load constrained the degree of enthusiasm for the job a ratchet click or two and asking about job pay squeezed a few more people out of the "pleased" and "delighted" categories. Nevertheless, about 70 percent of employed workers still said they are at least "mostly satisfied" with their job pay.

The percentages on the right side of the above distributions appear small and we have not emphasized them since they do not reflect the modal picture for United States workers, but when one is considering the quality of life of Americans workers those small percents still refer to the work experiences and conditions of millions of employed people. Over 8 million American workers in 1972 felt "mostly dissatisfied" or worse with their job pay.

NEIGHBORHOOD

The image of neighborhood suggests aspects of quality of life that are very pervasive in a person's daily life and personal situation. Respondents turned out to be as enthusiastic about their neighborhood as their community and about equally as pleased with their neighbors as with the presumably less well known "people in this community."

"How do you feel about: This particular neighborhood as a place to live?"

Delig.	Pleas.	Mos. sat.	Mixed	Mos. diss.	Unhap.	Terr.		(Mean)
18%	39%	24%	10%	4%	2%	3%	(May)	5.4

"How do you feel about: The people who live in the houses/apartments near yours?"

Delig.	Pleas.	Mos. sat.	Mixed	Mos. diss.	Unhap.	Terr.		(Mean)
11%	42%	30%	11%	3%	2%	1%	(May)	5.4

A neighborhood lies in a community setting of services, facilities, etc., and often one's job, whose evaluations we have already reported. One problem is to get to these places, and neighborhoods differ in the availability of mass transit and convenient highways. We did not separate transportation needs into their various forms but lumped them together in a general question on "the way you get around." Half the population turned out to be "pleased" or "delighted" with their personal transportation situation and over 80 percent were at least mostly satisfied, which is about the way people felt about their neighborhoods in general. We also asked how neat, tidy, and clean things are around you, and although this may refer to conditions inside one's home or on the job for some, it probably also refers to conditions in the immediate neighborhood of dwellings. Things were not quite as pleasant from this point of view but real dissatisfaction was limited to one in ten.

"How do you feel about: The way you can get around to work, schools, shopping, etc.?"

Delig.	Pleas.	Mos. sat.	Mixed	Mos. diss.	Unhap.	Terr.		(Mean)
10%	43%	31%	7%	5%	2%	2%	(May)	5.3

"How do you feel about: How neat, tidy, and clean things are around you?"

Delig.	Pleas.	Mos. sat.	Mixed	Mos. diss.	Unhap.	Terr.		(Mean)
12%	27%	35%	16%	6%	2%	2%	(April)	5.1

A problem of neighborhoods that has pushed some into moving away is the question of personal safety and property security. Three different questions were asked on three national surveys and lead to some indications of anxiety over theft but less concern regarding personal injury. When we asked people how safe they feel in their neighborhoods, over 80 percent said they are mostly satisfied with what they see as their local situation. If we asked about just "your safety," this group dropped to about 70 percent, and if the query explicitly and only mentioned stealing or property destruction, the size of the "mostly satisfied" or better aggregation dropped to about 60 percent. But it is certainly disturbing and very serious to find that one in ten said they are "mostly dissatisfied" or "unhappy" about their safety in their own neighborhoods, and that roughly twice that number indicated the same feelings about the security of their property.

"How do you feel about: How safe you feel in this neighborhood?"

Delig.	Pleas.	Mos. sat.	Mixed	Mos. diss.	Unhap.	Terr.		(Mean)
11%	38%	34%	8%	4%	2%	3%	(May)	5.2

"How do you feel about: Your safety?"

Delig.	Pleas.	Mos. sat.	Mixed	Mos. diss.	Unhap.	Terr.		(Mean)
8%	29%	35%	15%	7%	4%	2%	(April)	4.9

"How do you feel about: How secure you are from people who might steal or destroy your property?"

Delig.	Pleas.	Mos. sat.	Mixed	Mos. diss.	Unhap.	Terr.		(Mean)
3%	22%	37%	20%	9%	6%	3%	(Nov.)	4.6

FRIENDS AND ASSOCIATES

Friends are somewhat of a reciprocal choice adding meaning and pleasure to life, and one would expect them to be evaluated with pleasure. But there are also people one sees socially, casually, and in organizational settings, and individuals may vary in their feelings about such associations. We know that good interpersonal activities have a lot to do with making a neighborhood pleasant and making one's personal life meaningful and rewarding, so we asked several questions in this broad area of interest.

	Delig.	Pleas.	Mos. sat.	Mixed	Mos. diss.	Unhap.	Terr.		(Means)
"How do you feel about:									
Your friends?"	12%	45%	37%	5%	1%	<1%	<1%	(Nov.)	5.6
The things you do and the times you have with your friends?"	15%	43%	31%	8%	2%	1%	<1%	(Nov.)	5.6
The people you see socially?"	16%	55%	24%	4%	1%	<1%	<1%	(May)	5.8
The organizations you belong to?" (38% did not answer, belonging to no organizations.)	15%	46%	28%	9%	1%	<1%	1%	(May)	5.6
The chance you have to know people with whom you can really feel comfortable?"	7%	33%	37%	13%	7%	3%	<1%	(May)	5.1

It apparently is a little easier to feel pleased with the people one sees socially than with one's friends with whom there is more interaction, but it is clear that friendships and social activities are very satisfying and there is very little difference between one's friends and one's neighbors who, in many cases, are probably the same people. There is a slightly poignant note introduced, however, in answers to the question on people's chances to know people with whom they feel comfortable. It is true that 40 percent were "pleased" or "delighted" with their chances, a situation that sounds very agreeable, but almost one in four rather sadly said that they felt "mixed," "mostly dissatisfied," or "unhappy" with their chances of knowing people with whom they could feel really comfortable.

HOME

"How do you feel about: Your house/apartment?"

Delig.	Pleas.	Mos. sat.	Mixed	Mos. diss.	Unhap.	Terr.		(Means)
14%	35%	29%	11%	6%	3%	2%	(May)	5.3
10%	34%	36%	11%	5%	3%	1%	(Nov.1)	5.2
15%	33%	32%	11%	5%	2%	2%	(Nov.2)	5.3

"How do you feel about: The outdoor space there is for you to use outside your home?"

Delig.	Pleas.	Mos. sat.	Mixed	Mos. diss.	Unhap.	Terr.		(Mean)
18%	37%	24%	8%	5%	4%	4%	(May)	5.3

"How do you feel about: The privacy you have—being alone when you want to be?"

Delig.	Pleas.	Mos. sat.	Mixed	Mos. diss.	Unhap.	Terr.		(Mean)
10%	36%	37%	10%	5%	1%	1%	(Nov.)	5.3

"How do you feel about: Your housework—the work you need to do around your home?"

Delig.	Pleas.	Mos. sat.	Mixed	Mos. diss.	Unhap.	Terr.		(Means)
9%	29%	32%	17%	7%	3%	3%	(May)	4.9
5%	23%	39%	17%	10%	3%	3%	(Nov.)	4.8

Housing was not regarded as favorably as neighborhood, nor as favorably as neighbors or friends, but it was very close and most people, as far as the population as a whole is concerned, live in housing with which they were at least "mostly satisfied" (but about 13 million felt "mostly dissatisfied" or worse). They felt the same way about the available space around their homes, however varied their standards may have been, and about 80 percent were "mostly satisfied" with the amount of privacy they have. (This question may well refer also to areas other than the home in which privacy may be desirable.) Work that needs to be done around the home was not evaluated quite so positively, though the men and women who answered this question were more varied in their feelings on housework than on other aspects of their homes.

LEISURE AND LEISURE-TIME FACILITIES

Leisure activities are largely of one's own choosing and unless people feel deprived or limited in resources they should, one would expect, feel quite pleased with their leisure hours. They did, a little more so in spring than late fall.

	Delig.	Pleas.	Mos. sat.	Mixed	Mos. diss.	Unhap.	Terr.		(Means)
"How do you feel about:									
The way you spend your spare time, your nonworking activities?"	14%	36%	33%	9%	5%	2%	1%	(May)	5.4
	8%	29%	40%	14%	7%	1%	1%	(Nov.)	5.1
The amount of time you have for doing the things you want to do?"	7%	24%	32%	17%	13%	5%	2%	(May)	4.7
	5%	24%	35%	16%	13%	5%	2%	(Nov.)	4.7
Outdoor places you can go in your spare time?"	17%	34%	29%	9%	7%	3%	1%	(May)	5.3
The sports or recreation facilities you yourself use, or would like to use—I mean things like parks, bowling alleys, beaches?" (14% chose not to answer this question.)	9%	32%	33%	12%	7%	4%	3%	(May)	5.0
Nearby places you can use for recreation or sports?"	5%	25%	34%	15%	12%	5%	4%	(Nov.)	4.6
Your chances for relaxation—even for a short time?"	6%	33%	42%	10%	6%	2%	1%	(Nov.)	5.1

Respondents were equally pleased with the outdoor places they could go to in their spare time, although as many as one in five were clearly dissatisfied with what they found available to them. Sports and recreation facilities did not seem quite as satisfactory, though majorities were still satisfied. About one in five was less than "mostly satisfied" with the chances he or she had for grabbing periods of relaxation, and about one in three was less than "mostly satisfied" with the time available for doing the things they wanted to. (Some of these things might not be leisure activities but certainly many, if not most, of them must be.)

FAMILY

The family is a social institution that is changing in size and style and meaning. It is under stress, if not attack, but in some form it is the most meaningful group for continued and intimate relations among human individuals. How do people feel about their families?

	Delig.	Pleas.	Mos. sat.	Mixed	Mos. diss.	Unhap.	Terr.		(Means)
"How do you feel about:									
Your children?"	60%	28%	9%	1%	1%	1%	<1%	(May)	6.5
Your wife/husband?"	58%	31%	8%	1%	<1%	1%	1%	(May)	6.3
Your marriage?" (27–29% did not respond to above questions.)	50%	34%	11%	2%	<1%	1%	2%	(May)	6.2
Your own family life—your wife/husband, your marriage, your children, if any?"	22%	41%	28%	7%	1%	1%	<1%	(Nov.)	5.7
The things you and your family do together?"	28%	41%	22%	6%	2%	1%	<1%	(May)	5.8
	12%	40%	32%	11%	4%	1%	<1%	(Nov.)	5.4
The responsibilities you have for members of your family?"	17%	47%	29%	6%	1%	<1%	0%	(May)	5.7
Close adult relatives—I mean people like parents, in-laws, brothers, and sisters?"	30%	43%	18%	7%	1%	1%	<1%	(May)	5.9

Here we have the strongest expressions of delight and pleasure of any of the domains of life. People were so favorable that it is easy to be misbelieving even though they have been critical and dissatisfied on other issues and topics. Marriage and spouse were rated with only a trickle of unhappiness, and even though this is typical of responses to this question, a note of skepticism might be sounded. But these evaluations are, after all, admissions in an interview with some stranger, and in such a situation who would choose to denigrate one's family? In such a conversation even saying "*mostly* satisfied" may imply considerable reservation and lack of ease. It is interesting that when the family is lumped together—children, spouse, marriage—there was a considerable drop in the expressions of sheer delight and a large jump in the number who simply choose "mostly satisfied." Perhaps it is just that—the mixture—that creates stresses and strains or more easily allows their expression. A drop from between 50 and 61 percent to 22 percent in the proportion who said they are "delighted" surely cannot be due to asking the question in November! However, late fall did bring a drop in the number who said they are "delighted" with the things the family does together.

Even relatives are a pleasure and there were only isolated expressions of dissatisfaction and unhappiness. Family responsibilities were also well accepted and usually enjoyed. This is one of only two questions in which not a single person in the national sample said he or she felt "terrible." The family seems to be a rather robust source of pleasure when talked about in these terms.

SELF

So far, although we have been reporting feelings and evaluations, we have focused on expressions about people, activities, situations, things, and their characteristics that an observer might also view and react to, perhaps with difficulty and probably with different appreciations. The referent is sometimes ambiguous since people differ in their perceptions, their experience, and their information. What people react to when they state their feelings about local schools, what the government is doing about the economy, or the safety of their neighborhoods may be difficult to assess, but conceptually, at least, crime rates, government policies and practices, or school conditions and offerings could be separately measured. But we propose that part of the quality of life is how you feel about yourself and your chances, opportunities, and progress. A close observer of "you" might be able to gauge these in some objective fashion but it would be much harder than checking out your income, your home, or the conditions of your neighborhood.

We asked a number of questions about the personal world of the respondent, not just about her home or his family, which other people share, but about own health, feelings of time pressure, religious faith, etc., where both the feelings and the referent are internal, though not always unobservable and certainly not independent of conditions external to the individual respondent. At any rate, though the transition may be subtle, we move to a number of questions in which a respondent could not possibly avoid talking about himself or herself.

"How do you feel about: Yourself?"

Delig.	Pleas.	Mos. sat.	Mixed	Mos. diss.	Unhap.	Terr.		(Means)
8%	30%	41%	17%	2%	2%	<1%	(May)	5.2
10%	31%	38%	16%	2%	2%	1%	(April)	5.2

The delight with members of the family is gone when the self is mirrored. Perhaps as pleasure over family members is superficially mandated and deeply desired, equal delight with oneself should be played down in public though around 8 or 10 percent are uninhibited, but other considerations are probably working. One knows oneself in all situations and they are all yours: failures, problems, successes, delights. As a result, it is possible to get somewhat varied self-evaluations and the summary one may suffer by focusing on one or another aspect of self-experience.

> "How do you feel about: What you are accomplishing in your life?" (May, Nov.1)
>
> Yourself—what you are accomplishing and how you handle problems?" (Nov. 2)

Delig.	Pleas.	Mos. sat.	Mixed	Mos. diss.	Unhap.	Terr.		(Means)
6%	32%	38%	17%	5%	1%	1%	(May)	5.1
6%	25%	39%	20%	7%	2%	1%	(Nov.1)	5.0
4%	30%	41%	17%	5%	2%	1%	(Nov.2)	5.1

Asking about personal accomplishments did not alter the distribution picture noticeably and that facet is clearly not a more encouraging perspective than the mixture of considerations used in the general evaluation. If the criteria for self-judgment are made a little tougher in terms of "achieving success," self criticism or self-questioning was even more apparent.

> "How do you feel about: The extent to which you are achieving success and getting ahead?"

Delig.	Pleas.	Mos. sat.	Mixed	Mos. diss.	Unhap.	Terr.		(Mean)
7%	22%	35%	21%	9%	4%	2%	(April)	4.8

When the criteria were made still more challenging, about half the adult population was at least "mostly satisfied" with their opportunities to change situations they do not like or get a good job if they went looking for new employment.

> "How do you feel about: Your opportunity to change things around you that you don't like?"

Delig.	Pleas.	Mos. sat.	Mixed	Mos. diss.	Unhap.	Terr.		(Mean)
3%	13%	36%	29%	14%	4%	1%	(Nov.)	4.5

"How do you feel about: Your chance of getting a good job if you went looking for one?" (Questions not answered by 25 percent of the sample.)

Delig.	Pleas.	Mos. sat.	Mixed	Mos. diss.	Unhap.	Terr.		(Mean)
5%	21%	28%	20%	13%	6%	7%	(Nov.)	4.4

A number of questions dealt with physical aspects of life and answers were as varied as one might expect. Feelings about one's health and one's sex life were reported with pleasure and delight more often than they were about one's sleep or the amount of exercise one had.

	Delig.	Pleas.	Mos. sat.	Mixed	Mos. diss.	Unhap.	Terr.		(Means)
"How do you feel about:									
Your own health and	17%	36%	28%	8%	5%	4%	2%	(May)	5.3
physical condition?"	11%	34%	34%	8%	7%	4%	2%	(Nov.)	5.1
The extent to which your physical needs are met?"	11%	32%	38%	12%	4%	2%	1%	(April)	5.2
The sleep you get?"	7%	31%	38%	12%	7%	3%	2%	(Nov.)	5.0
The amount of physical work and exercise in your life?"	9%	26%	34%	18%	8%	3%	2%	(April)	4.9
Your sex life?"	15%	37%	31%	9%	2%	2%	4%	(Nov.)	5.4

If life turns out to be pleasant, interesting, and fun much of the time, one might assume that people would feel good about themselves. At least such experiences reflect back on the experiencing self. About three adults in four were satisfied, pleased, or delighted with the fun they are having. Add the words "fun and enjoyment" and people felt as good or a little better. Ask in November and there is a slight drop in the number who were "delighted." This image of three in four being satisfied or better appeared also with the degree to which day-to-day life is interesting, how the respondent's life is developing and broadening, and respondents' chances for independence and freedom to do what they want. Two different questions about their chances to enjoy beauty resulted in people saying in about the same proportions that they were "mostly satisfied" or felt even better about their chances and experiences. About 80 percent felt the same way about how happy they were and very few felt so bad that they were "unhappy" or "mostly dissatisfied" with however happy they were.

	Delig.	Pleas.	Mos. sat.	Mixed	Mos. diss.	Unhap.	Terr.		(Means)
"How do you feel about:									
How much fun you are	12%	33%	33%	14%	6%	1%	1%	(May)	5.2
having?"	5%	24%	44%	17%	5%	3%	2%	(Nov.)	4.9
The amount of fun and enjoyment you have?"	17%	34%	29%	12%	4%	2%	2%	(April)	5.3
How interesting your day-to-day life is?"	10%	27%	37%	19%	4%	2%	1%	(April)	5.1
The extent to which you are developing yourself and broadening your life?"	10%	26%	35%	19%	7%	2%	1%	(April)	5.0

How happy you are?"	13%	40%	33%	9%	3%	1%	1%	(Nov.)	5.5
The chance you have to enjoy pleasant or beautiful things?"	7%	27%	42%	13%	7%	3%	1%	(Nov.)	5.0
The amount of beauty and attractiveness in your world?"	15%	30%	29%	18%	5%	2%	1%	(April)	5.2
Your independence or freedom—the chance you have to do what you want?"	20%	34%	26%	11%	5%	3%	1%	(April)	5.4

But some people did not share in this rather rosy picture. On almost all of these queries about one in four reported mixed feelings or dissatisfaction, and there is a tinge of sadness in so many saying that they have mixed feelings about the amount of fun they are having, or the interest in their day-to-day life, or the amount of beauty in their world. One in four is not really an infrequent incidence, and although very few felt as badly as "unhappy" or "terrible" in replying to these questions, there is certainly a feeling of compromise lying back of some of the answers. Even to say one is "mostly satisfied" with how happy one is implies that one has given up a little on how happy one would perhaps like to be and tempered one's aspirations with the reality of what one can get.

In trying further to sample a large variety of ways people might look at themselves and evaluate their personal lives, we asked about their religious and ethical appraisals of themselves. This is like asking how "good" he or she is and people responded as one might expect. They thought they were pretty good from their own point of view. Almost 60 percent were "pleased" or "delighted" with how sincere and honest they are and only occasional individuals, not even 1 percent of the population, felt unhappy about themselves on that count. People felt equally good about their religious faith, though many more felt dissatisfied about that than about their own sincerity and honesty. When asked about "religious fulfillment" instead of "faith," there is a slight drop in the number who reported that they are gratified but not much change in the number who were dissatisfied.

	Delig.	Pleas.	Mos. sat.	Mixed	Mos. diss.	Unhap.	Terr.		(Means)
"How do you feel about:									
How sincere and honest you are?"	18%	41%	32%	8%	1%	<1%	<1%	(April)	5.6
Your religious faith?"	24%	36%	23%	10%	4%	2%	1%	(May)	5.6
The religious fulfillment in your life?"	20%	31%	28%	15%	4%	1%	1%	(April)	5.4

Part of the picture of the self must also be formed taking into account stresses and problems, and we included some items on these concerns to round out our effort to cover various aspects of self-appraisal. If problems are handled too easily, the status and difficulty of the problem might be questioned, yet if problems are handled at all there might be some gratification at mastery and most people encounter genuine problems at most stages of life. The majority of people were satisfied or pleased with the way they have handled their problems and only a minority seem to have been overcome by them, but we do not know the caliber of the problems they have encountered or people's aspirations about their solutions.

	Delig.	Pleas.	Mos. sat.	Mixed	Mos. diss.	Unhap.	Terr.		(Means)
"How do you feel about:									
The way you handle the problems that come up in your life?"	6%	31%	46%	14%	2%	1%	<1%	(May)	5.2
The extent to which you can adjust to changes in your life?"	10%	31%	40%	14%	4%	1%	<1%	(April)	5.2
The extent to which you are tough and can take it?"	12%	30%	34%	16%	5%	2%	1%	(April)	5.1
The amount of pressure you are under?"	6%	17%	30%	28%	10%	6%	3%	(April)	4.5

People felt better about the way they handle problems, about their ability to adjust to changes in life, and about their own ability to "take it" than about the amount of pressure they are under. Perhaps many saw pressure as an unsolved or unsolvable problem and a continuing characteristic of their lives, even though some probably enjoyed it.

INTERPERSONAL RELATIONS

We have claimed that how you see yourself is part of the quality of life; how you see other people treating you and how you relate to other people is certainly also a major part of that picture. We asked one question that was the counterpart of the one just reported on how people felt about their own sincerity and honesty. When this query is turned around and asked about the sincerity and honesty of "other people," there is a large discrepancy. People evaluated their own sincerity and honesty much more positively than that of others.

	Delig.	Pleas.	Mos. sat.	Mixed	Mos. diss.	Unhap.	Terr.		(Means)
"How do you feel about:									
How sincere and honest other people are?"	3%	16%	32%	30%	10%	5%	4%	(April)	4.4
How sincere and honest you are?"	17%	41%	32%	8%	1%	<1%	<1%	(April)	5.6

We asked another pair of questions that are also somewhat complementary: "How you get on with other people" and "the way other people treat you." Here also people felt better about their actions toward others than about others' actions toward oneself.

	Delig.	Pleas.	Mos. sat.	Mixed	Mos. diss.	Unhap.	Terr.		(Means)
"How do you feel about:									
How you get on with other people?"	14%	49%	31%	4%	1%	1%	0%	(May)	5.7
The way other people treat you?"	7%	44%	39%	8%	1%	1%	<1%	(May)	5.4

It is interesting that the two sets of responses correlate (Pearson's r) a little less than 0.4 and that the items correlate more with other items than with each other. Answers to "how you get on with other people" is better correlated with "how you feel about your family responsibilities," while "the way other people treat you" is better correlated with feelings about co-workers and friends. This suggests that respondents are thinking of two different sets of people when they answer these questions. So the two questions are not really very complementary but the two may well merge in some fashion in an individual's self-picture.

We did not ask people how they felt about the love and affection they got from other people, though it is certainly included in considerations of how one feels about one's marriage, one's friends, one's children, etc. But we did ask about more broadly distributed relations with large groups of people; however, in no case did we indicate who should be implied by the term "others" or "other people." The individual respondent could decide how inclusive or restricted he or she would like to make those terms. We asked about being accepted and included by others, being respected, and being admired. We asked our respondents how they felt about how fairly they were treated, and with perhaps the broadest referent for "others," how they felt about the respect other people had for their rights. People did not feel so good about this last item. Seventy percent said they are "mostly satisfied" or feel "mixed" about the respect for their rights. Being treated *fairly* is another matter and people felt quite a bit better about this, so perhaps they were thinking of a different group of "others" in the two questions. About one in five felt less than "mostly satisfied" with the degree of fair treatment they receive and one in eight said they are "delighted," which in this question setting sounds almost like surprise.

About half the population was "pleased" or "delighted" with the degree to which they are accepted and included, which makes their lives sound very hospitable. About the same proportions felt they are respected, but putting "admired or respected" together seems to demand more of others and oneself and people were more likely to say that they are just "mostly satisfied" on these joint criteria.

"How do you feel about:	Delig.	Pleas.	Mos. sat.	Mixed	Mos. diss.	Unhap.	Terr.		(Means)
How much you are accepted and included by others?"	11%	39%	37%	9%	2%	1%	1%	(April)	5.4
The amount of respect you get from others?"	10%	35%	38%	12%	3%	1%	1%	(April)	5.3
How much you are admired or respected by other people?"	6%	33%	46%	13%	1%	<1%	<1%	(Nov.)	5.3
How fairly you get treated?"	12%	33%	36%	13%	3%	2%	1%	(April)	5.3
The respect other people have for your rights?"	2%	15%	44%	26%	8%	4%	1%	(Nov.)	4.6

One aspect of relating well with other people is the chance to extend oneself in helping others and making contributions to their lives. Sometimes this is done in simple, informal, and paired interactions and sometimes it is more formalized and organized into group activity. We included both kinds of contribution to others in our questions. The responses we got showed it did not make much difference how the question was asked, though it might have been different if we had emphasized highly formal, group activity. Over one-third of the respondents were "pleased" or "delighted" with what they are contributing to the lives of others.

	Delig.	Pleas.	Mos. sat.	Mixed	Mos. diss.	Unhap.	Terr.		(Means)
"How do you feel about:									
Things you do to help people or groups in this community?"	9%	28%	34%	19%	7%	2%	1%	(May)	5.0
How much you are contributing to other people's lives?"	7%	28%	38%	19%	5%	2%	1%	(April)	5.0

Whatever one's interpersonal relations with close intimate family or business associates, friends, or governmental leaders, one needs to depend on some of them to be certain kinds of people and to do certain kinds of things. We asked people in our sample how they felt about the reliability of people on whom they depended and the distribution of responses shows some shaky positions. About one-third were pleased or delighted, but about one in five were less than satisfied and a little uncertain about some of the people on whom they feel they depend.

"How do you feel about: The reliability of the people you depend on?"

Delig.	Pleas.	Mos. sat.	Mixed	Mos. diss.	Unhap.	Terr.		(Mean)
5%	30%	46%	12%	4%	2%	1%	(Nov.)	5.1

SEASONAL CHANGES

Dissatisfaction with the costs of necessities increased significantly between May and November 1972, and this shift may reflect the increasing inroads of inflation. However, it is interesting that none of the other questions that were asked in both May and November showed any significant improvement, though some showed stability. There is certainly a suggestion that respondents surveyed in the spring (April or May) may express slightly stronger feelings of delight and pleasure than those queried in the grayer days of November. Notice the very slight drop in the proportions choosing the most pleasant categories of response for "things you do with your family," "your job," "your community," "the way you spend your spare time," "your health," and "how much fun you are having" in the results presented previously.

COMPARISONS AMONG MEANS

A quick scanning of the previous list of human concerns, looking at the averages or means of evaluative feelings, begins to give one a feel for some of the structural properties of domains and values. It is quite clear that family and friends were sources of high satisfaction. It is equally clear that the various queries about government did not, on the average, arouse more than feelings of mixed satisfaction and dissatisfaction. In between these two extremes there is a rough ordering of satisfactions from one's family to one's neighborhood, to community characteristics and services, to characteristics of the economy and media information and entertainment, and finally to the national government. This ordering is not only from near to far but also from private to public and from things one might personally influence to circumstances of our common situation.

Interspersed through this ordering are the value–criteria that start with high satisfaction values such as your own sincerity and honesty and how you get on with other people. The values about which people were least satisfied are such criteria as respect for your rights, others' sincerity, and your safety and security. In between these extremes are a group of values about interests and gratifications, how others treat you, your ability to handle problems and changes and some broader conditions having to do with achieving success and the amount of pressure in your life. A meaningful ordering is not as apparent as in the domains but there is, in the extremes, a sense of similar ordering from intimate values in one's private world to the scene of interaction with others, then to problems and competencies, and finally to rather widespread conditions with which people have to cope.

There are also some rather wild ties or near ties, as far as statistical averages are concerned, in people's feelings about quite disparate areas of life that are *not* correlated with each other but end up similarly evaluated. Schools and weather ended up with the same arithmetic average. One's job and one's sex life were about the same, as were health and housing. Feelings of safety in the neighborhood averaged out at the same level as feelings about medical services. Individuals did not necessarily make the same evaluations of these pairs, but the averages came out equal for the total sample.

By bringing together the results presented previously in this chapter we obtained the distribution of means shown in Exhibit 8.1.

One can see a substantial concentration of means in the range 5.1 to 5.3 (which implies a feeling just slightly more positive than "mostly satisfied" on our Delighted = 7–Terrible = 1 Scale). The items with means at or above 5.7 almost all involve family. They are your children, your spouse; your marriage; your own family life; close adult relatives; the things you and your family do together; responsibilities you have for members of your family; people you see socially; and how you get on with other people—and they all involve people. At the other end of the distribution the items with means of 4.0 or less all involve national conditions and largely the national government. They are the standards and values of today's society; the way young people in this country are thinking and acting; what you have to pay for basic necessities such as food, housing, and clothing; the taxes you pay; the way our national government is operating; what our national government is doing; what our government is doing about the economy; our national military activities; the way our political

EXHIBIT 8.1. Distribution of Mean Evaluations of Life Concerns
(Summary of Means Presented in This Chapter)

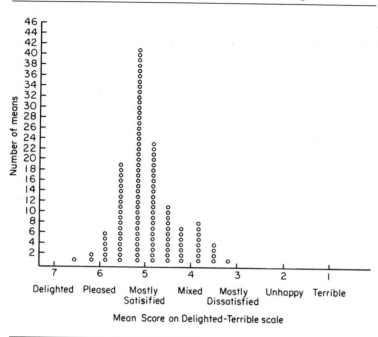

leaders think and act; and how the United States stands in the eyes of the rest of the world.

Although there is some overlap, one can almost divide the distribution of means into three groups referring to personal, local community, and national conditions. An individual's evaluations of the national government or conditions in the United States today are reactions to situations that, by and large, are common to all citizens and known to most of the population either through direct experience of prices and taxes or through mass media accounts of national news. Local conditions are also shared but with a much smaller group, namely, the residents of a particular neighborhood or community who share the same schools, commercial services, and neighborhood conditions. An individual's personal world is shared with only one's most intimate associates and is experienced directly with very limited information about the family and social life of other people.

It is clear from our data that the level of peoples' evaluations of conditions in these three areas—personal, local, and national—did indeed differ although there was also some overlap. One must conclude that people's subjective well-being was different for their personal, local neighborhood, and national interests and concerns. An index or set of indexes on quality of life that omitted personal life would, on the average, barely register as "mostly satisfied." If an index focused only on national conditions, one would arrive, at least in 1972, at the most pessimistic picture. On the other hand, an index based only on one's personal life of family and friends would give the impression that people were more satisfied than they really were.

It is interesting to note in this comparison of sample means that people's average evaluations of life-as-a-whole fell at about 5.4, slightly above the modal category of means. However, peoples' average feelings about themselves, in answers to how do you feel about "yourself," fell in the modal category at 5.2. Average feelings about "yourself" are relatively low within the distribution of feelings about one's personal world, but this average fell higher than that of any item referring to the national scene.

It might also be noted that concerns expressed as broad generalizations and abstractions usually seem to receive higher ratings of satisfaction than topics that are less general, more narrowly specified, and more specific. For instance, among national topics, "life in the United States today" receives the most positive rating, and the "national government" is rated better than any of its activities or components. Also, "community" is rated slightly higher than "neighborhood" and both a trifle better than "house or apartment" though all three are close together.

SKEWNESS, BIAS, AND SPREAD

As some of the distributions seemed improbably crowded toward the "pleased" portion of the scale, so the national averages on those same items appear incredibly high. Is it really true that at least one partner in half of the marriages in the United States was "delighted" with his or her marriage? Is it true that 60 percent of parents were "delighted" with their children? We tend to believe what people say in interviews, but we regard it as our task to find out what they mean, while still realizing that some people do distort or bias their answers in an interview situation.

At this point we must accept the fact that people's responses may not always mean *what we think they mean*. People's contexts for evaluative decisions vary. People's statements may have a bias toward expressing satisfaction. People don't like to appear miserable or unhappy, and they do not like to *be* unhappy. However, even if some bias exists, there is no reason to assume that the bias will change very rapidly from survey to survey.

Our results on marriage evaluations parallel those of previous researchers (Gurin, Veroff, and Feld, 1960; Bradburn, 1969). Bradburn, in comparing his results on the marriage question with those on other questions, notes the marked shewness of the distribution toward the "very happy" end of his scale:

> Although sometimes difficult, it is possible for most people to terminate a marriage relationship if it is an unhappy one. Thus, a high degree of self-selection is probable, and many who were generally miserable in their marriages have most likely ended them. Therefore those in our sample who do in fact report current unhappiness in their marriages probably represent

those who are either having transitory difficulties or whose marriages are in
the process of breaking up. (Bradburn, 1969, p. 157)

We find that about 4 percent of respondents who are presently married felt
"mostly dissatisfied," "unhappy," or "terrible" about their marriages. Some
viewers of our present culture who are aware of the frequency of broken
marriages and divorce might regard this figure as too low. However, this 4
percent amounts to a total of about 4 million couples in which at least one
partner feels "mostly dissatisfied" or worse. Although the cumulative rate of
broken marriages is regarded as high in our society, the number of divorces in
any one year is only about 1 percent, which is about one-quarter of our
dissatisfied figure. Looked at this way, the distribution of evaluations of
marriage seems more acceptable. It is undoubtedly true that many couples will
shift their feelings about their marriages as years go by and that those who felt
very unhappy may have already broken up.

Presumably there might be three good reasons for only a thin tail to many
of the distributions at the unhappy and dissatisfied end of the scale. First, the
biggest skewness occurs on those domains that are very satisfying in primary
interpersonal relations and the self-definition that follows from being included
and belonging, being liked and liking, and having meaningful social ties. Not
only are these relations often satisfying but most people would struggle to try
and make them pleasant and self-fulfilling because these relations are the major
investment of one's feelings, emotions, time, and effort.

Second, there are a number of domains that permit one, in most cases, to
do something about the situation. It is not too difficult to move to another house
or apartment unless one's resources are severely limited. Many people can get
their car fixed or buy another; they can change where they shop and even
switch jobs. Thus, at any one time there should be a minority of the population
unhappy about aspects of their lives that many of them can remedy or
ameliorate.

Third, there are some domains in which one is relatively quite powerless to
improve conditions, and although one does not have to be delighted or even
pleased with what one can do little about, one may be able to be somewhat
accepting and perhaps even satisfied. Only one in ten is delighted with the
weather but fewer than that proportion feel unhappy or terrible about it. The
case is similar for housework, television, local home services, and schools.

One could summarize these perspectives by classfying domains into those
that "should be good," those that "can be good," those that "you've got to live
with" and "those you don't care about." But there are some domains where
dissatisfaction seems to be most common where people are unwilling to be
tolerant and accepting, even though they may also be largely incapable of
altering conditions. These areas seem to be those showing deviations from
what is expected and rapid changes from what is desired. The most conspicu-
ous domains showing dissatisfaction are costs and taxes that were rising, and
national governmental activities that seemed to be wrong or inadequate.

But perceptions and expectations were really quite varied in the population. There are people who fell in every category of our response scales, and

whereas there is a skewness of the distribution on family items, the distributions on national government are closer to normal. Standard deviations of the distributions of evaluations ranged from 0.782 to 1.584. Among the items with the lowest standard deviations were items such as your children (0.84), family responsibilities (0.87), and adult relatives (0.99). The items with the highest standard deviations are domains such as taxes and the national government, topics that evidence more variety of evaluations and less agreement, even though they present the lowest arithmetic means as far as the total population is concerned.

DISCUSSION

It is almost impossible to ask a question about peoples' evaluation of one or another aspect of life and not find some people who will say they are delighted and others who will claim that they feel terrible about that same topic. This partly reflects the wide variety and spread of conditions in which people find themselves across this nation, but it also is a reflection of the diverse evaluations made of shared phenomena that may be seen in different lights and from varying perspectives.

With an array of over one hundred topics spread from marriage to how the United States stands in the eyes of the world, people's average evaluations on a scale of feeling coded "delighted," "pleased," "mostly satisfied," "mixed," "mostly dissatisfied," "unhappy" and "terrible," ranged from halfway between "delighted" and "pleased" with "your children" to about the point of "mostly dissatisfied" with "the taxes you pay." Peoples' evaluations ranged from heavily skewed distributions with a tapering tail at the unhappy end of the scale to more symmetric distributions for the less well-evaluated topics. Nevertheless, someone was "delighted" with every topic raised and someone was at least "unhappy" on every item. If these topics refer to aspects of the quality of life in the United States today, these answers reflect a great dispersion of "quality" across the population.

Average satisfactions ranged from "pleased" with one's immediate family, to "mostly satisfied" with friends, oneself, home, neighborhood, and job, to some increasing expressions of dissatisfaction with local services, prices, financial security, and government operations. With "delighted" scored as "7" and "terrible" scored as "1," the average for feelings about community was 5.5, for neighborhood 5.4 and for home 5.3; local government dropped to 4.2 and the United States government to 4.0. People tend, on the average, to rate "themselves" at about 5.2, a sort of middling rating among the variety of items they were asked to consider. It is interesting to notice the public's position on one or another topic and to compare relative strengths of feeling for this or that concern. It is possible that changes in national administrations and the passage of time will result in an improvement in the average evaluation of the federal government, but that will probably hinge on what happens on other issues such as the economy. One is almost forced to wonder and speculate whether absolute levels of satisfaction are important or only relative levels. Only repeated and replicated studies can answer that query well.

If evaluations of the people, things, and activities in an individual's private worlds of family, home, and friends were averaged, they would be less than "pleased" but more than "mostly satisfied." The local world of neighborhood and community would average to 5.0, "mostly satisfied," while the national scene would, on the average, be evaluated at 3.8, more dissatisfied than satisfied. These three areas of life could be regarded as yielding three different indicators of human assessment and social well-being. Leaving any one of them out of a social accounting would certainly alter the picture quite radically from the image that appears when they are included.

It is easy to wonder, as one scans these distributions, how many people it takes to make a social problem. On almost every aspect and part of life that was raised in our surveys, there are millions of citizens who feel "mostly dissatisfied," "unhappy," or "terrible." What is the portent and import of that many people expressing that kind of feeling? What is the stability of that discontent? We know that there was considerable pressure in 1972 against the then-current military activities of the United States. Our data show that about 40 million people felt "mostly satisfied" or better about that matter and about 60 million felt "mostly dissatisfied" or worse. Should one read something into the size of those less-than-majorities or is their ratio significant?

It is clear that when asked about certain aspects of life, people crowd into the categories of "pleased" and "delighted." This seems to be most true for questions about one's children and one's marriage. We asked no question about a facet of life in response to which people crowded with similar density into the categories reflecting that they felt "unhappy" or "terrible." A large number of people did not feel good about their taxes but these people amounted to nothing like the proportion who felt good about their children. Apparently discontent does not get so pervasive; people carry out their own adjustments or they may become tolerant or, as in the case of the Vietnam War, the government eventually does something about that aspect of life. It is probably not impossible to ask a question that would solicit large majorities at the discontented end of our scale. All of our questions asked about conditions over a period of time. If we restricted the time to, for instance, the weather last Tuesday evening when there was a storm, we might have crammed majorities into the "terrible" category. Also, if we had asked about crime in your city or the pollution you can find in sections of your town instead of "your safety" and "the condition of the natural environment," we would have undoubtedly pushed respondents into positions of greater criticism and discontent.

The long list of topics that we covered tapped many facets of life's experience, but there is a tendency to interpret the findings variously according to the topic. Feeling dissatisfied with life in the United States may indicate a certain malaise that has little of the concrete focus of being dissatisfied with one's house, but there may be more legitimate concern about dissatisfaction with what the government is doing about the economy than with reported dissatisfaction on "how creative you can be." The topics also vary considerably in the degree to which they deal with content areas of some public responsibility or domains in which it is reasonable to think of social improvement as opposed to individual improvement. The policymaker might well be much more selective than we were in choosing restricted topics for inquiry but our task was a different one, at this stage, since we chose to explore the whole field of perceived well-being and then place areas of social policy concern into the larger structure of concerns that the public might have. The distribution of evaluative feelings is about the same for local weather and the on-the-street services of local government. There is no correlation between those two sets of responses and there are certainly two totally different contexts for interpreting the significance of the shape of the distributions of evaluations of those two concerns.

The nature of each topic is not so neutral, however, that one can reasonably expect all respondents to see the midpoint of our scale as the neutral point of evaluation on every subject of inquiry. The center point of our scale is expressed as mixed satisfaction and dissatisfaction, which sounds middling enough for the topics of weather, family income, entertainment in the mass media, and so forth, but such a position sounds almost enthusiastic if the topic is "the taxes you pay" and quite despairing if the topic is "your religious faith." As psychologists have pointed out, the assumed or perceived shape of the distribution of peoples' feelings or behaviors has an influence on how people evaluate their own feelings. If you expect most people to express delight with their children, the choice of "mostly satisfied," however rationally sensible or calculatingly accurate, has tinges and overtones of some criticism.

One context for interpreting findings is the relative one of how one group compares with another and how conditions during this year compare with conditions at another period of measurement. These relative judgments cannot be suggested until we compare the standings of various subgroups on these measures, and also not until there is an accrued body of data with similar or identical measures collected over a period of years that permit the study of trends.

CHAPTER SUMMARY

There is tremendous variability in people's quality of life. Except for two of the 123 domain and criteria questions that we posed, there were some respondents in every one of the scale categories from "delighted" to "terrible." Some distributions were skewed, particularly those dealing with family and marriage, but many approached a more symmetric curve and means varied from "pleased" to "mostly dissatisfied."

Although there is some overlap one can discern three separate sets of domains and criteria wherein the distributions and their means tend to fill separate regions of the Delighted–Terrible Scale. Up at the "pleased" end of the scale are such items as one's children, spouse and marriage, one's friends and relatives, and other items that one can categorize as components of one's personal and somewhat private world. At the opposite end of the scale are the publicly shared concerns that refer to costs of goods and services, taxes, local and national government activities, and phenomena that characterize the national scene. In between fall those concerns that can be best described as domains that one shares with one's neighbors, co-workers, and fellow community residents.

This grouping and the ordering of mean satisfactions from private to local to national conditions are reflected in several other analyses. This ordering characterized the main dimension in the maps of concerns described in chapter 2. In addition, this ordering is similar to what results when concerns are ordered according to the strength of their relationship to feelings about life-as-a-whole (Life 3, as described in chap. 4 and 5). It is also apparent that this ordering goes from one's personal world that one knows constantly by direct experience to national conditions that one occasionally encounters under the name of inflation or taxes but usually knows only through the mass media and other secondhand channels of communication.

CHAPTER 9

Americans' Well-Being: Differences Among Population Groups

Any study of the distributions of perspectives on well-being in American society should find out whether particular perspectives occur more often in one social group or social category than in another. This chapter reports such an analysis. When we think of social conditions we tend to think of the rich and the poor, the educated and uneducated, men and women, the old and the young, and so forth. Such images often involve stereotypes of the life of the relatively well-off, the roles of the housewife and mother, or the restricted lives of senior citizens. Though differences among these groups may sometimes be overdramatized and almost caricatured, they frequently do serve as indicators of social conditions that are shared by large proportions of the people so categorized.

However, to characterize individuals only by wealth, sex, age or race, for instance, is not to say very much about them or their life situations. In a national comparison of men versus women, a host of other characteristics are left uncontrolled and uncompared. The life situations of those in their twenties, or those over sixty-five years of age, may show great variation despite their shared positions in the cycle of generations. A more sophisticated approach to the characterization of somewhat homogeneous social groups would identify complex combinations of the characteristics by which people or sectors of society are superficially described. Being young and poor and male and black and urban may begin to identify a social group with less varied attributes than the larger group referred to by any one of these characteristics taken alone. The trouble is, however, that on a national sample study of about twelve hundred people, which is quite adequate for describing national conditions, there are not enough cases for a reasonable analysis of a group such as that which is female, over forty-five, college educated and employed, or of people who are young, poor, male, and high school dropouts.

Nevertheless, we will examine various large groups in our society to see what differences in perceived well-being may be associated with these broad divisions of the population. It may well be that social-group differences will appear on specific domains such as job or neighborhood or standard of living that are more relevant than others to the life conditions of people characterized as young or parents of young children or wealthy. Such differences among broad groups would cast light on the quality of life of a large number of the members of an objectively definable social group even if such conditions were not characteristic of the whole social category. Significant differences, if they are found, are invitations to further thought on what accounts for the observed dissimilarities. If differences tend to hold across several question areas, one's inferences may have more substance.

Labels used for identifying large social groups such as "male," "female," "white," "middle-aged," "poor," and the like are really rough indicators of social situations, roles, resources, problems, etc., that are supposedly widely shared. If we find significant differences by the sex of the respondents, it is very unlikely that many of these differences are due to the biology of sex; they are more likely to be due to the social roles adopted by members of one sex or the other. With the exception of health, differences by age, if they occur, are more likely to be due to events and roles that go with generational position than just the passage of time. Thus, one is left with questions as to just what the associated social conditions are that make for different feelings among social groups. Since we asked about many domains of life, we may be able to get some insights into what conditions lie back of the overly terse labels that identify large social groups.

GROUPS IDENTIFIED

We were able to identify a variety of demographic groups among our respondents and have selected five classifications (yielding twenty-seven groups) for examination in this chapter. The classifications are sex, age, race, stage in the family life-cycle (FLC) and socioeconomic status (SES).

The groups defined on the basis of sex, age, or race are self-explanatory, but those for family life-cycle and socioeconomic status need some explication. To arrive at a family life-cycle scale, respondents were divided into those who had a child (usually considered to be age seventeen or less) living at home and those who did not, those who were married and those unmarried, and those under forty-five years of age and those older. The following analytic categories were then developed:

1. Unmarried, under forty-five years of age, no children at home.
2. Married, under forty-five years of age, no children at home.
3. Married, any age, youngest child under five years of age.
4. Married, any age, youngest child five–fourteen years old.
5. Married, any age, youngest child fifteen–seventeen years old.
6. Married, forty-five years of age or older, no children at home.

7. Unmarried, forty-five years of age or older, no children at home.

8. Unmarried, any age, children of any age.

Obviously those in category 6, for instance, may never have had children while some others may have gone through the years of child rearing. There are no subcategories for divorced, widowed, etc.

The concept of socioeconomic status was measured by combining family income and the educational attainment of the family head. People in categories 1 through 5 of the Socioeconomic Status Scale were in families characterized by "consistent" levels of income and education: both low (category 1), both high (category 5), or both at some intermediate level. For example, people in category 1 lived in families with less than four thousand dollars annual income and the family head had not completed high school. People assigned to category 6 had relatively low family income and were in families where the head had relatively high education; for those in category 7 the income outranked the education. (Appendix L shows the exact combinations of education and income associated with each category of the Socioeconomic Status Scale.)

Most of the groups to be examined in this chapter are represented by at least a hundred respondents in each national survey and some groups by many more than this. The smallest of the groups is the teen-agers, of whom there were about forty in each national survey. The number of respondents in each group is shown in appendix M.

COMPARISON OF GENERAL WELL-BEING IN DIFFERENT GROUPS

Did the general level of perceived well-being differ from one population group to another? To explore this matter we performed two parallel analyses. The first took all the concern-level items included in each of our national surveys and obtained a composite mean evaluation of them all. Since all groups evaluated the same concerns, we can compare the mean evaluations given by various groups for a rough indication of whether some groups experienced a higher level of general well-being than others. (However, since the concerns included in one survey were different from those included in other surveys, it would not be appropriate to compare composite means from one survey with those from another.) The second analysis looked not at a composite of concern-level evaluations but at how respondents themselves directly evaluated their "Life as a whole." (In Life-as-a-whole it *is* possible to compare means from different surveys since the same measure was used in each.) Results from both analyses, replicated in three national surveys, appear in Exhibit 9.1.[1]

The major finding emerging from Exhibit 9.1 is that there were only small variations in *general* well-being from group to group. Sex differences were clearly nonexistent using these summary statistics, and only some small sam-

---

[1] In Exhibit 9.1 and throughout this chapter the measure of feelings about Life-as-a-whole is Life 3 (which is described in chap. 3). References to "November" data are to the November Form 2 national survey. Means were computed from evaluations expressed on the Delighted–Terrible Scale.

EXHIBIT 9.1. Mean Evaluations by Social Groups in Three National Surveys[a]

	All concerns			Life-as-a-whole[b]		
Category	May	Nov.	April	May	Nov.	April
Men	5.0	4.8	5.1	5.5	5.4	5.4
Women	5.0	4.8	5.1	5.4	5.3	5.4
Age: 15–19	4.9	4.4	5.1	5.6	5.4	5.6
20–24	5.3	4.6	5.0	5.5	5.2	5.5
25–29	5.0	4.8	5.0	5.6	5.5	5.4
30–34	4.9	4.7	5.1	5.4	5.4	5.5
35–44	5.0	4.8	5.1	5.5	5.3	5.3
45–54	5.0	4.8	5.1	5.3	5.3	5.4
55–64	5.2	4.9	5.1	5.5	5.4	5.3
65+	5.1	4.9	5.2	5.4	5.3	5.3
FLC:[c] 1	4.8	4.7	4.9	5.2	5.1	5.2
2	5.0	4.7	5.1	5.7	5.5	5.6
3	5.1	4.7	5.1	5.7	5.4	5.6
4	5.0	4.8	5.2	5.5	5.5	5.6
5	5.0	4.8	5.1	5.5	5.6	5.4
6	5.1	4.9	5.3	5.5	5.5	5.5
7	5.1	4.8	5.0	5.3	5.1	5.0
8	4.8	4.6	4.8	5.1	5.0	4.9
SES:[c] 1 (low)	5.0	4.7	4.8	5.3	5.1	5.0
2	5.0	4.5	5.0	5.4	5.2	5.3
3	5.0	4.8	5.1	5.5	5.4	5.4
4	5.0	4.8	5.1	5.6	5.4	5.5
5 (high)	5.1	4.9	5.3	5.7	5.6	5.7
6	4.8	4.6	4.9	5.2	5.1	5.2
7	5.0	4.9	5.2	5.5	5.5	5.4
Blacks	4.9	4.3	4.7	5.4	4.8	5.0
Whites	5.0	4.8	5.2	5.5	5.4	5.4

[a] Given the sizes of these samples (shown in app. M), most differences of at least 0.4 between means are statistically significant at the .05 level.
[b] Evaluations of Life-as-a-whole are represented by the Life 3 measure, described in chapter 3.
[c] See text (section titled "Groups Identified") for description of categories of the Family Life-Cycle and Socioeconomic Status Scales.
Figures show mean scores on the Delighted–Terrible Scale.

pling variation is shown from survey to survey. Age seems to have made no clear difference either. Family life-cycle, looking just at categories 2 through 6 (all married with children of increasing age), shows no more variance or change than is apparent in the progressive age categories. Although the differences are not large, it is noticeable that people in categories 1, 7, and 8 (all unmarried) reported slightly lower figures consistently. In particular, one notes that in category 8 (unmarried with children), a category that includes a fair proportion of divorced people, the levels of average satisfaction with specific concerns or Life-as-a-whole reach the nadir of any category in the columns.

The groupings of socioeconomic status show very meager differences on means for concerns and not significant single steps for Life-as-a-whole means, though these do indicate a steady progression and the discrepancies between the top and bottom socioeconomic categories are statistically significant. However, one tends to note the smallness of differences because many observers of the American scene would have expected larger ones.

When blacks are compared with whites the May survey would suggest that there were no differences, but the following two surveys show a barely significant picture of less satisfaction among the black population.

Before leaving Exhibit 9.1 one might note that most composite means for the concerns were close to 5.0. While this implies an average evaluation of Mostly satisfied on the Delighted–Terrible Scale, one must remember that the average is only one position and most people did not fall there but somewhere else, either above or below. To obtain a mean of 5.0, sizable proportions of people must have given evaluations of Mixed, Mostly dissatisfied, or worse. It is also interesting to note that people's evaluations of their Life-as-a-whole tended to be somewhat more positive than the average of their responses to all the separate concern items.

Having seen that only rather modest differences between these groups appear when very general indicators of perceived well-being are examined, we can turn to the question of differences that may exist on concerns taken individually or as clusters, differences that could well get masked or discounted in an overall averaging, whether that "averaging" is done by the individual respondent or the analyst. An examination of differences between all groups for all concerns could get lengthy and confusing, so we will scan for those differences that merit some attention and skip those that are meaningless. We will present only differences in group means that are at least 0.4 or that generate eta's (a measure of bivariate association) of at least 0.15. Most differences that large are statistically significant (p = .05 level), but differences may have to be substantially larger before they are substantively important. The exhibits that follow in this chapter show results based on individual interview items; appendix K presents parallel results for selected indices.

MEN AND WOMEN

There were no differences of statistically significant magnitude on any of our concern-level measures using sex comparisons.

AGE GROUPS

As shown in Exhibit 9.2, evaluations of most concerns increased very slightly with age or stayed more or less steady over the age span. The few concerns that showed a drop do not have much conceptual interest. Health showed a drop in reported satisfaction, but not until the mid-forties, and satisfaction with one's children shaded down a little with advancing years but generally stayed so high (average above Pleased) that such a meager difference

EXHIBIT 9.2. Evaluations of Life Concerns by Age in Three National Surveys

Concern	Survey	Age of respondent[a]								η
		15–19	20–24	25–29	30–34	35–44	45–54	55–64	65+	
Concerns for which satisfaction decreases with age										
Health	(M)	5.4	5.7	5.8	5.5	5.6	5.1	5.0	4.8	.25
Health	(N)	5.7	5.5	5.5	5.3	5.3	5.0	4.9	4.6	.25
Children	(M)	—	6.8	6.7	6.6	6.4	6.4	6.3	6.3	.19
Concerns for which satisfaction increases with age										
Economic										
Cost of Necessities	(M)	3.8	3.8	3.6	3.8	3.8	4.0	4.2	4.1	.15
Neighborhood										
Community	(N)	4.9	4.7	5.0	5.3	5.3	5.3	5.5	5.5	.20
Community	(M)	4.8	5.0	5.3	5.5	5.5	5.7	5.7	5.6	.19
Neighborhood	(M)	5.1	5.2	5.1	5.1	5.5	5.5	5.8	5.5	.16
People nearby	(M)	5.0	5.1	5.1	5.2	5.4	5.5	5.7	5.6	.20
People in community	(M)	5.0	5.2	5.2	5.2	5.4	5.4	5.5	5.5	.15
Recreation facilities	(M)	4.7	4.8	4.9	4.6	5.0	5.1	5.4	5.1	.15
Recreational places	(N)	4.1	4.2	4.4	4.7	4.8	4.7	4.9	5.0	.19
Privacy	(N)	4.7	4.9	5.3	5.2	5.1	5.3	5.6	5.5	.21
Space outside home	(M)	4.9	4.8	4.7	4.9	5.4	5.5	5.8	5.5	.23

Interpersonal									
Respect	(A)	5.3	5.1	5.1	5.2	5.3	5.3	5.5	5.6	.17
Respect for rights	(N)	4.5	4.2	4.4	4.3	4.6	4.6	4.8	4.9	.21
Others' sincerity	(A)	4.3	3.9	4.0	4.3	4.4	4.6	4.7	4.8	.24
Own sincerity	(A)	5.4	5.2	5.4	5.8	5.7	5.7	5.7	5.9	.22
Government									
Police and courts	(M)	4.1	3.9	4.2	4.2	4.3	4.4	4.6	4.7	.18
Local government	(M)	3.9	3.9	4.2	4.1	4.1	4.2	4.5	4.6	.18
Taxes	(M)	3.2	3.1	3.1	3.1	3.0	3.1	3.6	3.6	.16
Government economy	(N)	3.5	3.2	3.4	3.5	3.5	3.5	3.7	3.8	.15
National government	(N)	4.1	3.5	3.7	3.7	3.7	3.8	4.0	4.1	.15
Miscellaneous									
Job	(N)	5.2	5.0	5.0	5.2	5.6	5.3	5.6	5.6	.20
Sleep	(N)	4.8	4.5	5.0	4.8	5.0	5.2	5.1	5.3	.19
Relaxation	(N)	5.3	4.7	5.0	5.1	4.9	5.1	5.4	5.5	.23
Free from bother	(A)	4.8	4.9	4.8	5.0	5.0	5.0	5.2	5.5	.18
Amount of pressure	(A)	4.4	4.2	4.4	4.3	4.4	4.4	4.6	5.0	.18
Time to do things	(M)	4.8	4.5	4.5	4.4	4.3	4.6	5.0	5.4	.18
Spare-time activities	(M)	5.5	5.0	5.1	5.1	5.5	5.4	5.6	5.5	.27
Natural environment	(M)	3.9	3.9	4.0	3.9	4.3	4.4	4.6	4.7	.17
Religious faith	(M)	5.3	5.3	5.3	5.3	5.6	5.7	5.8	5.9	.19
Religious fulfillment	(A)	5.5	5.1	5.0	5.5	5.3	5.3	5.5	5.8	.18

[a] Appendix M shows number of cases in each age group.
Figures show mean scores on the Delighted–Terrible Scale.

as is found cannot have much importance. The only other concern that showed a drop over the years of as much as 0.4 in group means was the question on how one felt about one's chances of getting a good job if one were to change, and this showed no decline until middle age.

Most of the distributions do not show any general tendency with aging as a gradient of change; wherever there are small differences that might be noted they tend to be associated with differences in the very young or the very old, or there seems to be a kind of step shift at some point in the middle-age categories. The group of teen-agers is relatively small so statistics for that category are somewhat unstable.

Most of the not very significant increase-with-age relationships fit two kinds of pictures: that of changing conditions with age, or a condition for an age cohort that is not true for younger or older generations. As people get older they tend to establish themselves in a neighborhood and community of their liking or they put down roots that make the area attractive to them. Similarly, the job becomes a little more satisfying. Aging also brings certain conditions of life that allow one to be less harried, hurried, and pressured. The greater satisfaction with governmental activities may also be due to a settling into local conditions or a longer time perspective, but it may also represent an age cohort that was always less critical of governmental policies and was always somewhat more religious than the present generation of younger adults. Aging may also represent a lowering of standards and aspirations that is an acceptance of conditions without struggle or resentment. The fact that income, standard of living, job pay, etc., do not show up among the items that drop significantly for those aged sixty-five and older is probably a reflection of expected and accepted conditions.

FAMILY LIFE-CYCLE

The normative picture of adulthood is more than just getting older and gaining maturity and seniority. The prevalent image is one of getting married, raising a family, the younger generation leaving home, and parents living alone again as they approach retirement. It is difficult to code life-cycle in a meaningful way because people get married at various ages, then have or do not or delay having children; some get unmarried for various reasons; the age span of children in the family varies, and children vary in the age at which they leave home. Our code roughly separates, in categories 2 through 6, married people under forty-five years of age who do not have children, have a preschool child, have a child in school but prehigh school, have a child of high school age, or are over forty-five with children gone. Families with several children could obviously have posthigh schoolers and preschoolers at the same time or other patterns of age mixes. Nevertheless, the Family Life-Cycle Scale focuses on the age of the youngest child since we suspect this exerts particular influence over family life.

There are essentially two components of our life-cycle code that are very different from simple age continuities. One is *being married:* married without children (code 2), married with children of certain age levels (codes 3, 4, and 5), and married with children gone (code 6). Categories 2 and 6 are by no means "clean" since the people in category 6 may never have had children, and in category 2 we have combined young people who have not yet had children with married people who may have lost their children through divorce, death, etc., and with married people in their early forties who have never had children— obviously a somewhat mixed group.

The second component is *not being married.* People in categories 1, 7, and 8 were all unmarried at the time of interview, though they might have been married at some previous time. Category 8 includes those who were not married but had children under eighteen years of age. They are mostly women and the bulk of them are divorcees, though some widows and never-marrieds are included. One should not therefore expect continuous differences to be apparent in the data since the family life-cycle categories represent various kinds of component characteristics that are not thoroughly separated.

The data first of all show that there are *no* differences in respondents' feelings that can be uniquely attributed to the presence or absence of children or the age of the youngest child.

A comparison of columns two through six in Exhibit 9.3 shows no significant differences that are not paralleled in the differences by the age data just discussed. Some of the age-related factors do not reoccur in Exhibit 9.3, but that is not surprising, considering the gross age categories used in the life-cycle code. Satisfaction with the neighborhood, for instance, rises a little, but we have already noted that happens with age without taking children or their ages into account.

What is clear from these data, however, is that being married or not did make a difference on a number of measures, and being *"un*married" with children (category 8) made a big difference, particularly economically and in the abysmal evaluations these people made of their marriages and some associated aspects of interpersonal relationships. On only one measure, Freedom from bother, do we find more satisfaction expressed by this group, though they were less satisfied on Amount of pressure. A comparison of the figures for categories 7 and 8 with those in the middle of the table shows the various effects of being over forty-five or under (most of those in category 8 are under forty-five), with children or without, and being married or not married.

Those parents who were unmarried or de-married felt much worse about their past marriages and they were left in more severe economic straits. But on feelings about the neighborhood the unmarried, over-forty-five respondents were much more like their married neighbors. In the self-evaluative items of one's Success in getting ahead and one's Accomplishments as well as in the situational evaluations of amount of Fun and enjoyment and Interesting daily life, the married group and the young, unmarried respondents reported higher satisfactions than did the older unmarried group or the single parents with children.

EXHIBIT 9.3. Evaluations of Life Concerns by Family Life-Cycle Stage in Three National Surveys

			Stage in the family life-cycle[a]								
		Category:	1	2	3	4	5	6	7	8	
		Married:	No	Yes	Yes	Yes	Yes	Yes	No	No	
		R's age:	<45	<45	any	any	any	45+	45+	any	
Concern	Survey	Children:	no	no	5	5–14	15–17	no	no	yes	η
Economic											
Income	(M)		4.7	5.0	4.9	5.0	5.0	4.9	4.8	4.1	.15
Income	(N)		4.2	4.3	4.5	4.9	4.7	4.8	4.4	3.8	.22
Financial security	(A)		4.2	4.9	4.5	4.7	4.4	4.9	4.3	3.6	.23
Standard of living	(M)		5.1	5.3	5.1	5.3	5.3	5.3	5.2	4.6	.15
Standard of living	(N)		5.1	5.0	5.0	5.3	5.3	5.4	5.1	4.6	.17
Cost of necessities	(M)		3.9	3.8	3.7	3.8	3.7	4.0	4.3	3.5	.15
Cost of necessities	(N)		3.6	3.3	3.0	3.4	3.4	3.6	3.7	3.4	.19
Marital relationships											
Marriage	(M)		—	6.3	6.5	6.3	6.4	6.3	—	—	.09[b]
Your wife/husband	(M)		—	6.6	6.6	6.4	6.4	6.4	—	—	.12[b]
Your sex life	(N)		4.7	5.9	5.7	5.6	5.4	5.3	4.6	4.3	.34
Your own family life	(N)		5.2	6.0	5.9	5.8	5.5	5.8	5.4	5.0	.26
Things family does	(N)		5.2	5.7	5.5	5.4	5.4	5.5	5.2	5.2	.15
Agreement on spending	(N)		4.9	5.2	5.2	5.2	5.1	5.5	5.2	4.6	.20
Interpersonal relationships											
Treated fairly	(A)		5.0	5.1	5.4	5.4	5.4	5.5	5.3	4.8	.18
Others' sincerity	(A)		4.0	4.4	4.1	4.5	4.6	4.7	4.7	3.9	.22
Respect for rights	(N)		4.4	4.1	4.4	4.6	4.7	4.8	4.8	4.7	.20
Respect you get	(A)		4.9	5.2	5.3	5.3	5.4	5.5	5.5	5.0	.19
Privacy you have	(N)		5.0	5.3	5.0	5.1	5.5	5.6	5.5	5.3	.20
Neighborhood											
Community	(M)		5.0	5.4	5.5	5.5	5.7	5.7	5.6	5.0	.17
Community	(N)		4.9	5.0	5.0	5.5	5.3	5.5	5.3	5.1	.20
Neighborhood	(M)		5.1	5.3	5.4	5.4	5.8	5.6	5.5	4.8	.15
Neighborhood safety	(M)		5.2	5.2	5.3	5.3	5.7	5.3	5.2	4.8	.12

									Eta[b]
People nearby (M)	5.1	5.2	5.2	5.4	5.6	5.6	5.6	4.9	.20
House/apartment (N)	5.2	5.2	5.1	5.5	5.5	5.5	5.3	4.7	.18
Space outside home (M)	4.7	4.9	5.1	5.3	5.5	5.6	5.5	5.0	.20
Recreation facilities (M)	5.1	4.6	4.9	5.0	4.9	5.4	5.0	4.5	.18
Recreation places (N)	4.5	4.5	4.3	4.8	4.8	5.0	4.9	4.2	.19
Government									
Police and courts (M)	3.8	4.2	4.3	4.4	4.4	4.5	4.6	4.0	.17
Local government (M)	3.7	4.0	4.3	4.2	4.3	4.4	4.6	4.1	.18
Taxes (M)	3.1	2.8	3.2	3.1	3.1	3.2	3.2	2.7	.18
Miscellaneous									
Physical needs (A)	5.1	5.5	5.3	5.4	5.4	5.4	4.8	4.6	.24
Your health (N)	5.5	5.7	5.3	5.3	5.3	4.9	4.6	5.1	.25
Sleep (N)	4.9	5.3	4.7	5.0	4.8	5.2	5.2	4.7	.17
Housework (N)	4.6	4.2	4.7	4.8	4.9	5.0	4.8	4.4	.15
Spare-time activities (M)	5.3	5.3	5.2	5.3	5.2	5.5	5.5	4.8	.14
Time to do things (M)	4.7	4.4	4.5	4.4	4.7	4.9	5.2	4.5	.21
Time to do things (N)	4.4	4.5	4.3	4.5	4.7	5.2	5.4	4.6	.30
Media (N)	4.6	4.3	4.5	4.7	4.4	4.7	5.1	4.8	.18
Fun and enjoyment (A)	5.4	5.6	5.5	5.4	5.5	5.4	4.8	5.0	.19
Your accomplishments (M)	4.9	5.3	5.3	5.2	5.1	5.2	5.0	4.6	.16
Success, get ahead (A)	4.7	5.0	4.8	5.0	4.8	4.9	4.3	4.2	.21
Chances of good job (N)	4.3	4.5	4.5	4.6	4.6	4.2	3.9	4.1	.15
Your job (N)	5.1	4.8	5.2	5.6	5.2	5.4	5.7	4.9	.20
Interesting daily life (A)	4.9	5.2	5.1	5.2	5.1	5.4	4.8	4.7	.18
Young people (N)	4.3	4.2	3.7	3.8	4.1	3.5	3.8	4.0	.20
Amount of pressure (A)	4.2	4.5	4.4	4.5	4.4	4.8	4.6	3.6	.19
Free from bother (A)	4.9	5.1	4.7	5.0	5.0	5.3	5.3	5.7	.17
Chance to relax (N)	5.1	5.1	4.8	5.0	5.1	5.4	5.4	4.8	.20
Own sincerity (A)	5.3	5.4	5.5	5.7	5.9	5.8	5.8	5.5	.20
Natural environment (M)	3.9	4.0	4.0	4.3	4.3	4.5	4.7	4.0	.18

[a] See text (section titled "Groups Identified") for description of categories of the Family Life-Cycle Scale. Appendix M shows the number of cases in each group.
[b] A few unmarried respondents (in family life-cycle categories 1, 7, or 8) answered these items, presumably referring to a former spouse or marriage. These people are excluded from the computation of the eta.

Figures show mean scores on the Delighted–Terrible Scale.

SOCIOECONOMIC STATUS

There are many who would regard socioeconomic status and quality of life as almost stand-ins for each other. Education increases sensitivity and skills and entrée to better jobs while higher levels of income provide the resources for some of the components of what many would regard as a "better life."

Measuring socioeconomic status (SES) presents certain conceptual difficulties. We have tried to handle some of these problems, but some remain. Since education and income are not perfectly correlated, we find situations of status inconsistency: There are people who have high education and relatively low income (e.g., nurses, teachers, social workers, etc.), and there are some entrepreneurs and others who have "made it" financially without much of an educational background. These groups are excluded from our presentation, even though they are interesting, in order to see the workings of SES by itself and to simplify the display of results. Another problem arises for people who reported a low income. Many of them fit the picture of payroll poverty but others are just young and not yet established, or now old and with a lifetime of different experiences, or just temporary occupants of a low income classification.

Exhibit 9.4 shows that SES clearly made a large difference, as one would expect, in evaluations of financial matters. All of the questions on economic matters show large differences between low- and high-SES persons, three of them larger than one step on the Delighted–Terrible scale (1.0). Low-SES people also reported less than average satisfaction with most marital concerns. Actually, there is only a low correlation (less than 0.4) between economic and marital concerns though there is somewhat more of an association among higher-SES persons. Nevertheless, there is a tendency for the dissatisfactions with these two areas to be characteristic of the lowest-SES group.[2]

A feeling of deprivation is also apparent in the responses of low SES people to questions on their physical needs, their health, their jobs, and to some extent, in the amount of fun and enjoyment they experience. A picture of sharp discouragement also appears in their evaluations of their chances of getting a good job, if they tried, and the degree to which they were achieving success and getting ahead (differences of about 1.5).

The rather bleak picture is only broken by the absence of differences in the evaluations of interpersonal relationships outside of the family and in almost all of the evaluations of community, neighborhood, house, etc. The low-SES group also reported better than average satisfaction with their time to do things and

[2]According to the U.S. Bureau of the Census (1971, Table 4, pp. 22–24), the average annual number of divorces in the years 1960–1966 was higher for low-income men than it was for men earning over eight thousand dollars a year (eight per one thousand married men versus four per one thousand married men). Men earning less than three thousand dollars per year were three times as likely as those earning over eight thousand dollars per year to have been divorced during the first through twentieth year of their first marriage. The divorce rate did not differ by income bracket for men who had been married for over twenty years. There are no comparable statistics for women.

they reported less dissatisfaction than higher-SES groups with housework and work around the house. In addition, the low-SES category members reported more satisfaction than average- or higher-SES people with the condition of the natural environment, the informational media, and political leaders. One can make a clear case that low-SES people were not more critical than others of government, government services, and public institutions of information and entertainment. It is their personal situation that aroused their expressed dissatisfactions. They appear preoccupied and overwhelmed with the clear problems of being poor.

BLACKS AND WHITES

As in other groups we have studied, distinguished by sex, by age, by family pattern, and by income and education, there is a large variety of situations and circumstances in which blacks find themselves. As we cannot characterize the sexes by any distinctions in reported satisfactions, we also cannot characterize all low-SES people with the description that identifies the average for their group. One cannot say that low-SES people have poor marriages. On an average they did report less satisfaction than higher-SES individuals but even "on the average" they reported feelings more positive than Mostly satisfied! Thus, our characterizations of groups are relative to other groups and one should still keep in mind the absolute evaluations expressed and the range and variety of feelings that are not communicated by the single "average figure."

The question we are raising is not what characterizes the members of some social grouping but rather whether there is a sizable proportion of that social group that has some common feelings; and if there is, whether that proportion is larger in one group than in another with which we are comparing it.

When we look at the differences between means for the two racial groups, shown in Exhibit 9.5, we find a large number of differences and one cannot help asking the question, To what can we attribute these differences? First of all, we find large differences in evaluations of economic or financial items and in evaluations of items on marital relationships. We found these differences characteristic, in a higher likelihood of occurrence sense, for low-SES families and we are led to interpret these figures as due to the larger *proportion* of blacks than whites who are poor (although there are more poor whites than poor blacks). In 1970, 10 percent of the white population of the country and 32 percent of the black population were below the low-income level established by the federal government (U.S. Bureau of the Census, 1972, Table 539, p. 329).

The significance of income in marital satisfaction is shown in Exhibit 9.6 and is sharply exemplified by the status inconsistent groups (categories 6 and 7). Both concerns included in Exhibit 9.6 show a higher level of marital satisfaction associated with the higher levels of income. The similar discrepancies between blacks and whites may be attributable to the differential income levels of the two racial groups that are evident from the census data just reported.

EXHIBIT 9.4. Evaluations of Life Concerns by Socioeconomic Status in Three National Surveys

Concern	Survey	National mean	Difference from national mean		Socioeconomic status group[a]					η
			Low SES	High SES	1 (low)	2	3	4	5 (high)	
Economic										
Family income	(M)	4.8	−.6	+.7	4.2	4.7	4.9	5.1	5.5	.33
Income	(N)	4.5	−.5	+.6	4.0	4.4	4.5	4.7	5.1	.24
Job—pay	(M)	5.0	−.5	+.3	4.5	4.6	5.0	5.0	5.3	.20
Standard of living	(M)	5.2	−.3	+.4	4.9	5.0	5.2	5.3	5.6	.24
Standard of living	(N)	5.2	−.5	+.4	4.7	5.1	5.1	5.2	5.6	.22
Financial security	(A)	4.5	−.8	+.7	3.7	4.3	4.5	5.9	5.2	.34
Cost of necessities	(M)	3.9	0	+.4	3.9	3.7	3.8	4.0	4.3	.15
Marriage and family										
Marriage	(M)	6.2	−.5	+.2	5.7	6.0	6.3	6.4	6.4	.21
Your wife/husband	(M)	6.3	−.4	+.3	5.9	6.3	6.3	6.5	6.6	.19
Your children	(M)	6.5	−.3	−.1	6.2	6.5	6.6	6.5	6.4	.15
Sex life	(N)	5.4	−.6	+.3	4.8	5.1	5.5	5.6	5.7	.21
Interpersonal relationships										
(No concerns showed significant differences.)										
Neighborhood										
Secure from theft	(N)	4.6	−.3	+.3	4.3	4.3	4.6	4.7	4.9	.15

Government
(No concerns showed significant differences.)

Miscellaneous

Physical needs	(A)	5.2	−.6	+.5	4.6	5.1	5.3	5.4	5.7	.28
Health	(M)	5.3	−.5	+.3	4.8	5.2	5.5	5.6	5.6	.19
Health	(N)	5.1	−.7	+.3	4.4	5.0	5.4	5.2	5.4	.23
Chances of good job	(N)	4.4	−.8	+.5	3.6	4.2	4.3	4.5	4.9	.21
Use of education	(M)	5.1	−.1	+.4	5.0	4.8	5.1	5.3	5.5	.20
Beautiful things	(N)	5.0	−.2	+.3	4.8	4.9	5.0	5.1	5.3	.15
Natural environment	(M)	4.3	+.6	−.2	4.9	4.4	4.0	4.2	4.1	.16
Time to do things	(M)	4.7	+.6	−.1	5.3	4.9	4.5	4.6	4.6	.19
Time to do things	(N)	4.7	+.6	−.3	5.3	5.0	4.5	4.5	4.4	.22
Achieving success	(A)	4.8	−1.0	+.4	3.8	4.5	4.8	5.1	5.2	.31
Fun and enjoyment	(A)	5.3	−.6	+.4	4.7	5.2	5.3	5.5	5.7	.22
Information—media	(M)	4.3	+.4	−.2	4.7	4.6	4.2	4.1	4.1	.16
What young people think	(M)	3.7	−.2	+.5	3.5	3.4	3.6	3.9	4.2	.20
What young people think	(N)	3.8	−.3	+.4	3.5	3.7	3.8	3.8	4.2	.20

[a] Appendix L describes the Socioeconomic Status Scale and appendix M shows the number of cases in each group. Figures based on mean scores on the Delighted–Terrible Scale.

EXHIBIT 9.5. Evaluations of Life Concerns by Race in Three National Surveys

Concern	Survey	Mean for whites	Difference for blacks
Economic			
Standard of living	(M)	5.3	−.6
Standard of living	(N)	5.2	−.8
Family income	(M)	4.9	−.6
Family income	(N)	4.5	−.8
Financial security	(A)	4.7	−1.2
Marital relationships			
Agreement on spending	(N)	5.2	−.8
Family life	(N)	5.8	−.7
Marriage	(M)	6.3	−.9
Your wife/husband	(M)	6.4	−.6
Things you do with family	(M)	5.8	0[a]
Things you do with family	(N)	5.5	−.6
Interpersonal relationships			
How others treat you	(M)	5.5	−.5
Treated fairly	(A)	5.4	−.8
Others' sincerity	(A)	4.5	−.7
Respect you get	(A)	5.4	−.5
Acceptance and inclusion	(A)	5.5	−.6
Neighborhood			
Community	(M)	5.5	−.4[a]
Community	(N)	5.3	−.9
Neighborhood	(M)	5.5	−.5
On-the-street public services	(M)	5.0	−.7
Goods and services	(M)	4.9	−.4[a]
Goods and services	(N)	4.8	−.6
Neighborhood safety	(M)	5.3	−.7
Your safety	(A)	4.9	−.7
Secure from theft	(N)	4.7	−1.0
Outdoor places	(M)	5.4	−.5
Recreation facilities	(M)	5.0	−.6
Recreation facilities	(N)	4.7	−1.0
House/apartment	(M)	5.3	−.4[a]
House/apartment	(N)	5.4	−.9
Neat and clean	(A)	5.1	−.6
Government			
Local government	(N)	4.1	−.5
National government	(M)	4.0	−.2[a]
National government	(N)	3.8	−.5
Miscellaneous			
Health	(M)	5.3	+.1[a]
Health	(N)	5.4	−.7
Chances of getting a good job	(N)	4.4	−.7
Amount of pressure	(A)	4.6	−.8

EXHIBIT 9.5 (*continued*)

Concern	Survey	Mean for whites	Difference for blacks
Physical needs	(A)	5.3	−.6
Fun and enjoyment	(A)	5.4	−.5
Fun and enjoyment	(N)	5.0	−.6
Independence and freedom	(A)	5.4	−.5
Beautiful things	(N)	5.1	−.9
What people over 40 think	(M)	4.2	−.5
Opportunity to change things	(N)	4.5	−.6
Achieving success	(A)	4.8	−.7
Entertainment	(M)	4.5	+.5

[a] Because of the size of the sample of blacks, differences of 0.5 rather than 0.4 are statistically significant in this two-group comparison. Appendix M shows the number of cases in each racial group.

Figures based on mean scores on the Delighted–Terrible Scale.

Our finding of less marital satisfactions among blacks is matched by census figures that indicate that blacks have had a higher divorce rate than whites: In 1967, of all men under seventy who had ever married, 14 percent of the whites and 28 percent of the blacks were known to have been divorced. For women, 15 percent of the whites and 31 percent of the blacks had been divorced (U.S. Bureau of the Census, 1971, Table A, p. 1). In 1971, of those black women born between 1900 and 1954 who had ever been married, 21 percent had been divorced compared to 14 percent of the comparable group of white women (U.S. Bureau of the Census, 1972, Table F, p. 7).

Two sets of concerns show a pattern of responses among blacks that is sharply divergent from the pattern apparent among low-SES respondents. On many of the questions on interpersonal relationships ("how others treat you," etc.), blacks reported less satisfaction than did whites (but the average was still around the Mostly satisfied category). The lowest rating is found for "how sincere and honest other people are." It would seem that these evaluations are a reflection of the prejudice that many blacks often encountered.

The other set of concerns on which blacks and whites differed significantly is the group of items that refer to various aspects of the neighborhood and dwelling of respondents. Almost every (though not all) aspect of the living environment was, on average, evaluated more poorly by blacks than by whites. This pattern cannot be explained away as one associated with low SES; it is rather one that seems to be characteristic of some significant proportion of the black population. The restricted housing opportunities faced by many blacks and conditions frequently associated with ghetto conditions would seem to be an apparent cause of this pattern of lower evaluations of neighborhood, housing, and related concerns. To pull down a group average for the nation to about

EXHIBIT 9.6. Evaluations of Marriage and Spouse by Race and
by Socioeconomic Status in the May National Survey

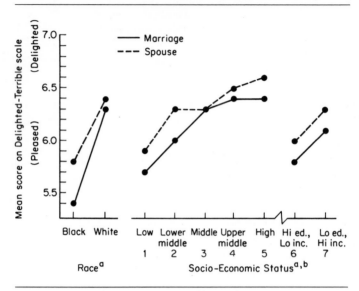

[a] Appendix M shows number of cases in each group.
[b] See Appendix L for description of categories of the Socioeconomic Status Scale.

the midpoint of the scale on some of these measures, many blacks must have
felt relatively disagreeable about their neighborhoods. Schuman and Gruenberg analyzed data collected by Campbell and Schuman (1968) on neighborhood and local services and concluded:

> The primary source of racial difference in dissatisfaction with city services
> lies in variations by neighborhood within cities. These variations are essen-
> tially along a status dimension defined in our study by race and social class.
> It is not one's own race or class that is more relevant, however, but that of
> one's neighborhood. Persons living in largely black and lower-income areas
> are most dissatisfied with the services they receive—regardless of their race
> or income; persons living in largely white and upper-income areas are most
> satisfied with their services, again regardless of their own race or income.
> (Schuman and Gruenberg, 1972, pp. 386–387).

Some of the other items such as Health, Physical needs, Fun and enjoyment, and Achieving success display a pattern similar to that found among low
SES, but other items such as Independence and freedom, Opportunity to
change things, and disaffections with Government are not characteristics of low
SES.

NONDIFFERENCES

It is of interest to notice which concerns showed no statistically significant
differences across various social groups. These are topics that seem impervious

to influences that one would associate with social group factors, at least those social groups that we examined. The concerns fall in the following categories:

Family:
Close adult relatives—I mean people like parents, in-laws, brothers, and sisters.
The responsibilities you have for members of your family.

Friends and Acquaintances:
The people you see socially.
The things you do and the times you have with your friends.
The organizations you belong to.
The chance you have to know people with whom you can really feel comfortable.
Your friends.

Interpersonal Relations (how you treat other people):
How much you are really contributing to other peoples' lives.
Things you do to help people or groups in this community.
How you get on with other people.

Self-Worth:
The way you handle the problems that come up in your life.
How creative you can be.
The extent to which you can adjust to changes in your life.
Yourself.
The extent to which you are developing yourself and broadening your life.
The extent to which you are tough and can take it.

Neighborhood and Community:
The doctors, clinics, and hospitals you would use in this area.
The schools in this area.
The way you can get around to work, schools, shopping, etc.
Privacy.

Job:
The people you work with—your co-workers.
The work you do on your job—the work itself.
What you have available for doing your job—I mean equipment, information, good supervision, and so on.
What it is like where you work—the physical surroundings, the hours, and the amount of work you are asked to do.

Miscellaneous:
Your car.
The amount of beauty and attractiveness in your world.
The weather in this part of the state.
The amount of physical work and exercise in your life.
Life in the United States today.
The standards and values of today's society.
How the United States stands in the eyes of the rest of the world.

Mallmann (1973) proposes plotting curves for the quality or quantity of (or time of working at) consumption of products in the satisfaction of an aspiration and then says:

> We shall term a distribution curve for a healthy population of a given age genuine, if the same curve is obtained when we replace the percentage of the population being considered, by the percentage of that population that is of a certain race, origin, sex, activity, residence or ideology. In such a case, the distribution is not the result of imposition, but of genuine value differences in the population.

Distributions of degrees of satisfaction, as we have in our data, are not the same as the curves of differential interest and consumption Mallmann proposes, but the idea of similar "plots" for groups as an indication that differences are not imposed by aspects of sex, race, income, etc., is relevant.

Four observations are suggested by these stable concerns. One is that evaluations of self, as a person, apart from conditions of circumstance, show equal distribution and variation across the various settings that are characterized by our social group categories. The self is apparently somewhat insulated from many of the problems and conditions of living. The items on how you treat other people share much of this self-worth flavor.

Secondly, although some group differences were found in evaluations of Neighbors and Neighborhood, friends and activities with friends seem not to be related to age, class, sex, etc. Even the two items under Family, Close adult relatives and Family responsibilities, seem to fit into this picture of people one sees socially or the picture of self-worth. If anyone can bolster one's feelings of self-worth, friends should have a share in providing such support.

It is interesting that although blacks showed no *statistically significant* difference on these items when compared with whites, they consistently showed slightly higher scores on both Family items, the same or higher on four of the five items under Friends, higher on two of the three items on "How you treat other people," and twice (two surveys) higher on evaluations of "yourself." This pattern merits some attention even if no one of the differences is statistically significant, given the sizes of our samples. Blacks' satisfactions on the self-worth items—handling problems, adjusting to changes, developing oneself and being tough—were equal to (first item) or slightly below (never significantly) the averages among whites. Whatever the context for these evaluations, they suggest a pattern that might be further explored.

Thirdly, it is noticeable that medical and school facilities did not come under more or less criticism or support from any of our social groups. Evaluations of these services ranged across all alternatives of our scale from Delighted to Terrible and there is some shift in the shape (skewness) of the distributions when groups are compared, but the group means stay fairly stable. The question on transportation also leads to stable means across groups but it is so broad, frequently alluding to car travel, that it cannot be regarded as any clear reflection or evaluation of public transportation systems.

Fourthly, it may be surprising to some that so many of the job items show no differences in mean satisfaction across groups. "Co-workers" and "the work itself" were almost significant for teen-age workers but not quite, and this age subsample is very small indeed. The general question on "job" and a more specific query on "job pay" did show statistically significant differences by socioeconomic status and the "job" item showed rising satisfaction with age. (Among blacks the job items showed lower satisfaction twice but the difference between blacks and whites was not statistically significant on either occasion.) One will recall the frequent differences in evaluations of family income but apparently job pay is sometimes evaluated in a different context. The range of means from low to high SES is less for job pay (5.3 to 4.5) than for family income (5.5 to 4.2); thus, people in the extremes of the SES scale tended to feel worse (for low SES) and better (for high SES) about family income than they did for job pay. It may be that pay is evaluated more in the setting of what the work is worth or what is fair, especially when one is evaluating other aspects of the job at the same time, while income is evaluated much more in the context of expenses, costs, and financial needs. Income and standard of living evaluations correlate about .6 for all groups.

This last point illustrates well some of the complexities of social indicator measures and the shifting contexts for subjective assessments. There are many family units with multiple income earners but there also is a sizable proportion of respondents who were referring to the same dollar amount when they evaluated "pay" and when they reported their feelings about "income." There is a correlation of .51 between feelings about income and feelings about job pay, which indicates considerable similarity or interdependence of feelings. For respondents over the age of forty-five, the correlation rises to 0.68, but for income earners younger than that, the correlation drops down into the thirties and it does so also for the low socioeconomic and black groups.

As Mallman (1973) suggests, individual differences pervade society, and where access to satisfaction is not inhibited or facilitated by social group characteristics, similar distributions of individual interest or success should be typical of all social groups. This may well be what accounts for the similarity of satisfactions with "yourself" and "friends," but it is difficult to regard medical service, school services, and some job components, other than pay, as not having some differences in quality and access "imposed" by differential membership in some of the social group categories we have been examining. It may be that aspirations or expectations of quality or quantity of service in these areas vary systematically across the social groups in which the quality or quantity of service also varies. If, for instance, low socioeconomic individuals have a distribution of expectations regarding medical service and the quality of education that has a lower "mean" than the distribution of expectations of services in these areas held by high socioeconomic persons, then the distributions of satisfaction with these services, which certainly do vary for socioeconomic levels of the population, might well be similar for various social categories.

Future work on human evaluations will have to cope with the nature and source of reference standards whether they are aspirations, expectations, cultural norms, interests, etc., as well as the degrees of differential satisfaction that result from comparing present conditions with these reference "values."

DISCUSSION

Our data reveal a great range and variety in individuals' evaluations of aspects of their lives. There is even a considerable range and variety in the averages of people's evaluations as they are scanned from topic to topic. Evidence also exists that some of the variability and difference is associated with age, with being an "only" parent with children, with socioeconomic status, and with race. Except for the fact that most divorced, deserted, separated, and widowed parents with children, in our sample, are mothers, we can find no statistically significant differences associated with the sex of the respondent.

Although the pattern of what is satisfying and dissatisfying is different, when separate evaluations are all added together, the poorest quality of life seems to be reported by blacks (not by all of them, of course, just by a larger proportion than whites), by teen-agers, by currently single parents with children, by well-educated people with low incomes, and by people with low education and low incomes (low socioeconomic status). The differences between these groups and other groups that are older, married, richer, etc., are not great, but there are some items on which the differences of conditions and their evaluation are large and clearly significant.

Obviously the combination of low income and limited financial resources is a partially common factor though that is not the only concern that characterizes the quality of life of these various groups. Those respondents that had low income and low education (low socioeconomic status) show a pattern that one might begin to regard as symptomatic of poverty. They tended to be more dissatisfied than others with job pay, family income, financial security, and their standard of living. They felt deprived in meeting their physical needs and they were not as satisfied as others with their health. They had less fun and enjoyment in life and they were discouraged about prospects of achieving more, getting a better job, etc. However, they tended *not* to be more critical than others, on the average, of their neighborhood, their community, or the agencies of government at the local or national level and were even more satisfied than the average with the activities of political leaders and the information they got through the media. Another aspect of this syndrome that seems to go with being poor is a reported less than average satisfaction with their marriages and marital situation where strains seem to cause some stress. These conditions and statements are all relative and poor people still said that they are mostly satisfied with their marriages; it is just that better-off people said they are pleased or delighted, and all groups, except those with broken marriages, put marriage and their families high on their list of gratifications.

Among blacks there is a disproportionate fraction who were poor and thus they tended to show most of this syndrome associated with being poor financially and poor educationally. But they also reported less than average levels of satisfaction with their neighborhoods and neighborhood services and, further distinguishing their pattern from that of the poor, they tended to be less satisfied with the government at local and national levels. Also they reported clearly poorer evaluations than average with how they are treated by others, others' sincerity, the respect they get, and the degree to which they are accepted and included by others.

The picture of poorest quality of life appears among the group that is made up almost entirely of women with children who did not have a marital partner. They were hit by economic dissatisfactions, resentment and unhappiness over their lost marriages and the interpersonal crises that often went with those changes, and very mixed feelings about their neighborhoods. They were unhappy about the pressures they are under and the time they have, their accomplishments and prospects, but they scored higher than average on freedom from bother. In some ways single persons over forty-five years of age without children show some similar conditions, but for those who were once married the marital break or loss is older, their economic situation is more like the average, and they have more than average time to do things but they reported less fun.

Age seems to make some difference in satisfactions but in our data it is a little ambiguous as to what that effect is. An average of domain satisfactions and value–criteria evaluations indicates an uncertain pattern with sampling variations and inconsistencies from study to study. The main result is that feelings about concerns, all taken together, stay about the same over the different age ranges. However, if one looks at individual concerns there are more that seem to increase with the passing years than decrease, but the majority do not change significantly. Older people were not as happy about their health or the chances of getting a different but good job. There also is a slight drop-off, during the passing decades, of the delight people felt about their children. The national average never drops below "pleased," but some of the charm must be lost for some because the mean does drop fairly steadily from the time that the children were very young.

Our middle-aged and older citizens reported that they grow more relaxed, freer from bother and pressure and time restrictions with advancing years. They also became more appreciative of the neighborhood and community and the people they knew. On a number of other topics one begins to wonder whether the satisfactions are growing or whether a cohort of fairly satisfied people is getting older. Older respondents reported greater satisfaction with their religious faith, people's sincerity, and the respect they recieve. They also tended to be more supportive of aspects of government, even including the fact that they felt better about the taxes they pay and even though they were more dissatisfied than satisfied with that demand on their pocketbooks. Only identical data from the past or in the future could answer the question of whether age leads to these improved satisfactions or whether we are witnessing the passing of a cohort whose norm was to feel the way they said they did.

A few topics seem to be uninfluenced by and independent of these social group categories. Being young or old, rich or poor, with children or without, married or unmarried, black or white, seem to have nothing to do with how people felt about their relatives, their friends, and their co-workers. People did not always feel good about them, but however they felt seems to be an individual preference and not a characteristic associated with being in one or another of the social groups we have examined. Similarly, the area of how people felt about themselves, their self-worth, and how they treat other people seems to show variety and diversity but quite independent of group member- ship. How they felt about their jobs also seems to be an evaluation not determined by social group categories, except for job pay which is clearly related. Finally, with respect to local services there was diversity in how people felt about schools and local medical services available to them, whether they are current or recent users of either set of facilities, but the poor or the rich, blacks or whites, young or old, men or women did not seem to have judgments predictable from one or another of those social category identities. This set of conclusions does not say that *combinations* of these group characteristics might not show other relationships. Perhaps poor blacks over fifty, for example, feel somewhat differently or more homogeneously than all blacks or all poor or all people over fifty. Perhaps college-educated married women not working for pay feel differently from all women or all college-educated people, and so forth. The sparse representation in our samples of such complex subgroups has prevented our doing analyses that would permit our drawing any conclusions about them.

However, it is clear that our indicators do reveal a great deal about the conditions and concerns with which certain large aggregates of people live. They do provide some measures against which one might assess a growing feeling by blacks that they are being better accepted into the main mix of society or, perhaps, a growing feeling by the poor that their lot is something to criticize somebody for. Clusters of items hang together. They show some interdepend- ence (as described in chap. 2) and they show similar patterns of relationships across social groups (as discussed here). It is apparent that feelings about different aspects of neighborhood, of economic conditions, of neighborhood and community services, of governmental activity, etc., clump together, that we can measure them, and that we could monitor their change.

The process of asking about a large number of domains and value–criteria also reveals that, in addition to the lower than average evaluations that went with certain constellations of social conditions, there were also some compensa- tory satisfactions that tended to be above average. As people got older and health became something not taken for granted, they had more time to do things, more satisfaction with the neighborhood, and so forth. Even though blacks may seem to have been hit harder than most with dissatisfying condi- tions, they were above average in their feelings about the entertainment they get, their religious faith, and their feelings about themselves. Also, the hard- pressed women who were struggling to get by as the only parent present for their children felt more positive than average about their freedom from bother. It certainly does not all even out for every individual, and despite some meager compensations there were millions of people whose sense of well-being was rather low. Nevertheless, across the varied people who fell within any of the social groups we have examined, the compensations were remarkably prevalent and account for our perhaps surprising finding that these social groups differed only rather modestly in *general* well-being. While people in different groups showed only small differences in their feelings about life-as-a-whole or in their average evaluations across many concerns, underlying this homogeneity is a heterogeneous complex in which members of different groups showed different patterns of positive and negative feelings about specific life concerns.

CHAPTER SUMMARY

Differences in the quality of life perceived by various subgroups in the population is one of the topics that any social indicators program would be interested in detecting and predicting. Our measures do detect significant differences in well-being among certain groups in society and pinpoint the areas in which these differences are felt.

In all, twenty-seven groups were examined and defined on the basis of sex, age, stage in the family life-cycle, socioeconomic status, or race. Contrary to what might be expected by some observers, differences among these groups in *general* well-being were rather modest. With respect to specific concerns, however, groups showed significantly different patterns of positive and negative feelings.

People's feelings about life-as-a-whole were fairly stable across the age groups. Feelings about health and one's children dropped off a little but these were more than counterbalanced by small increases in satisfaction with one's home, neighborhood and community, one's job, government activities and services, one's religious fulfillment, and a number of other domains and values. Some of the differences between age groups may be due to the attitudes of an age cohort but others are clearly an accompaniment of settling-in and maturity.

Stages of the family life-cycle show few differences that could not also be attributed to age except for people who fall off the normative steps of marriage, bearing children, and then experiencing the "empty nest." The worst picture of well-being was reported by those for whom marriage had failed and resulted in economic problems, family disruption, worsened relations in the neighborhood and community, and feelings of not knowing where to turn for a job or help.

As one might expect, socioeconomic status was associated with clear differences in perceived well-being but not in feelings about the neighborhood (except security) or community, not in interpersonal relationships and not in feelings about government activities or services. But economic and familial satisfactions were above average among those with high socioeconomic status, as were feelings about one's success, one's health, and one's job.

Blacks and whites showed some significant differences though there was a large overlap, of course, in individual's reports. Blacks reported lower economic satisfactions and some associated familial discontents (the same was found among poor people). Blacks were considerably lower than whites in how they felt about the treatment they receive from other people; they were unusually critical of their neighborhoods and communities, and of local and federal government agencies.

We found no statistically significant differences in perceived well-being between men and women.

CHAPTER 10

Americans' Well-Being: Life-as-a-Whole

It is uncertain how often people put the parts and pieces of their lives together in clear, all-thing-considered evaluations of their lives-as-a-whole. Most of the time attention is likely to be focused on how do I feel today or how I liked my vacation last month, or directed toward whether I should move, change jobs, go on a diet, buy a new car, or get married. However, big decisions do force some more general evaluations. When one is debating a major move, one has to consider the overall picture and weigh financial benefits, the novelty of new surroundings, weather, leaving friends, uprooting established relations, and so forth. Even in the absence of major events, there is a certain amount of binding of events over time. If one's job is a bore, what helps one through the day is the prospect of going home or having free time to do something exciting. If one's marriage is not very rewarding now, it may yet offer stability, security, and convenience at other times. If one's neighborhood is aggravating for a number of reasons, it may also be the setting for appreciated friendships and enjoyed social occasions. If children are annoying, they may also be the *raison d'être* for one's efforts. In other words, parts and pieces and incidents in one's life do not tend to be evaluated in isolation but rather in a larger context that encompasses a span of life concerns and a span of time.

We felt, therefore, that it was not unreasonable or artifical to ask people for evaluations of their lives-as-a-whole. For some, such evaluations may not represent carefully reasoned, highly organized and developed assessments, but—as noted near the beginning of chapter 3—there are both theoretical considerations and empirical evidence to suggest that most people do perform some sort of global evaluation on their lives. Furthermore, results presented in chapter 6 suggest that evaluations of global well-being can be assessed with roughly the same validities as feelings about more specific life concerns.

The present chapter examines various measures of global well-being to determine how Americans felt about their lives-as-a-whole. The chapter begins with descriptions for the entire adult American population and then turns to data for selected social and demographic groups. The measures examined are those included in one or more of the national-level surveys.[1]

Evaluations of Life-as-a-whole can be made in accord with different perspectives and along different dimensions. In the course of our explorations we have sometimes asked Americans to evaluate their lives from an "absolute" perspective, other times from a "relative" perspective (i.e., how one's own well-being compares with that of other people), and still other times from a "change" perspective (i.e., how one's current well-being compares with what one experienced in the past or expects in the future). We have also experimented with various evaluative dimensions, sometimes asking for assessments on a very general evaluative dimension, other times asking about much more specific dimensions such as Satisfaction, Happiness, Positive affect, Worthwhileness, and the like. Chapter 3 describes a typology for classifying measures of global well-being according to the nature of the evaluation that is being performed, and we will use the same typology in this chapter to group together results from comparable but different measures.

Before turning to the descriptive results, we would note that the present chapter is just one of several that focus on evaluations of Life-as-a-whole. The full set of global measures is detailed in chapter 3, which also described their conceptual and empirical interrelationships and classifies them according to the typology mentioned above. Chapter 5 includes an extended series of analyses that examine the levels and patterns with which many different global measures can be predicted from a standard set of concern-level evaluations. Chapter 6 develops estimates of the reliability and validity with which feelings about Life-as-a-whole were tapped by different measurement methods. Since perceptions of global well-being are centrally important in our investigations, they receive attention—sometimes extended attention—in other chapters as well, but chapters 3, 5, 6, and 10 are the ones that use and compare numerous different global measures.

EVALUATIONS OF LIFE-AS-A-WHOLE BY THE TOTAL POPULATION

General Evaluations of Life-as-a-Whole

Absolute Perspective (Type A and B Measures). How did Americans evaluate their lives when asked to make a very general evaluation from an absolute perspective? The measure we came to call Life 3 is the one that we believe provides the best indications of these evaluations. As described more fully in chapter 3, Life 3 is an index based on two separate interview items, each of which asked respondents how they felt about "your life as a whole."[2] Life 3

---

[1] Appendix N presents additional data from a national survey conducted in October 1974.

[2] In each of the three national surveys that included both of these items, the distribution of answers to the first item was highly similar to the distribution from the second. For the May data, which

EXHIBIT 10.1. Global Well-Being as Assessed by the Life 3 Measure

Scale	Survey		
	May 1972	Nov. 1972	April 1973
7.0 Delighted	7.0%	5.5%	6.8%
6.5	9.2%	7.4%	8.7%
6.0 Pleased	23.5%	23.4%	23.9%
5.5	21.8%	17.8%	19.2%
5.0 Mostly satisfied	23.2%	26.4%	22.4%
4.5	6.8%	8.4%	8.0%
4.0 Mixed	4.7%	6.3%	6.4%
3.5	1.9%	1.7%	1.4%
3.0 Mostly dissatisfied	0.9%	1.1%	1.1%
2.5	0.2%	0.7%	0.6%
2.0 Unhappy	0.2%	0.8%	0.7%
1.5	0.2%	0.3%	0.4%
1.0 Terrible	0.4%	0.2%	0.4%
	100.0%	100.0%	100.0%
Means:	5.5	5.3	5.4

Note: The Life 3 measure used here is described in Exhibit 3.1; see measure G3.

Data sources: 1,297 respondents to May national survey; 1,072 respondents to November Form
2 national survey; and 1,433 respondents to April national survey.

proved to be typical of the group of global measures that involve general evaluations from an absolute perspective (as shown in chap. 3); it proved to be one of the most highly predictable of our global measures (as shown in chap. 5); and its validity seemed to be higher than most other global measures (as shown in chap. 6). Scores on the Life 3 measure could be determined for respondents to three national surveys and are presented in Exhibit 10.1.

Clearly, the distribution of scores on the Life 3 measure was highly stable across the three national surveys. The same hint that we saw in chapter 8 of the November evaluations being slightly lower than either of the spring evaluations appears here also. As noted previously, until we have a longer series of surveys we will not know whether the lower reading in November is part of a recurring cycle or an idiosyncrasy of these particular data. What seems more important, however, is the very substantial similarity of results from the three surveys.

Based on these data we can estimate that close to two-thirds of American adults had feelings about Life-as-a-whole that ranged between Pleased and Mostly satisfied. Another one-sixth or one-seventh felt even more positive about Life-as-a-whole, while the remaining one-quarter to one-fifth of the population felt less well-off than Mostly satisfied. Most of this last group, however, gave answers that suggested they felt Mixed—about equally satisfied

are typical, the means were 5.47 and 5.46, and the standard deviations were 1.03 and 0.99. (Comparable results from the November Form 2 survey are available in Exhibit 6.9.) Chapters 3 and 6 discuss the extent to which respondents gave similar answers to the two questions.

and dissatisfied. Nevertheless, there were *some* people who fell in each possible score category, and the very small proportions of our respondents who answered Terrible still represent roughly a half million Americans.

Life 3 is not the only indication we have of Americans' general evaluations of Life-as-a-whole from an absolute perspective. Three other question formats were used with national samples of respondents to explore this same matter. In each case we tried to detour around the semantic limitation of using words or terms for presenting the answer options. The measures to be presented next, which use the Circles-and-Pie-Slices Scale, the Ladder Scale, and the Thermometer Scale, all depend primarily on graphic relationships rather than verbal meanings.

One device confronted the respondent with nine circles, each divided into eight "pie slices" of equal size and labeled with plus and minus signs. The first circle had eight pie slices, each carrying a plus sign. Each subsequent circle dropped one plus sign and added one minus sign until one reached the limit of a circle with eight pie slices, each one marked with a minus sign (see app. A, April 1973 questionnaire). Respondents were read: "Here are some circles that we can imagine represent the lives of different people. Circle eight has all pluses in it, to represent a person who has all good things in his life. Circle zero has all minuses in it, to represent a person who has all bad things in his life. Other circles are in betweeen." Most respondents grasped the abstraction involved and could make a choice of one of the alternative patterns when they are asked: "Which circle do you think comes closest to matching your life?" This "scale" is not free of semantic meaning since we have used symbolic cues such as "good things," "pluses," "minuses," "zero," etc., but we have provided much less semantic content. Also, this scale has ratios of pluses and minuses, a concept that is not at all apparent in other rating scales.

Results of assessing Life-as-a-whole using the Circles Scale appear in Exhibit 10.2. Before considering those results, however, we turn to the two other question formats that also yield general evaluations from an absolute perspective and that are also included in Exhibit 10.2.

Kilpatrick and Cantril (1960) developed a self-anchoring scale that may not be very different from other scales in a functional sense but that is distinctive in format. Their procedure asks one to picture a ladder (instead of a horizontal linear scale) and then requires the rater to define the end points within his or her own experience and imagination with only some specification of what is being ranked or rated. Sometimes the top and bottom of the ladder are cued to be the best and worst life you can imagine or know of. In our case we asked people to think of the "best life I could expect to have" and the "worst life I could expect to have." We provided nine rungs on our ladder and asked our respondents: "Where was your life most of the time during the past year?" These results also appear in Exhibit 10.2.

The third set of results in Exhibit 10.2 came from the Thermometer Scale. This is a graphic device (printed on a card that was handed to the respondent) that looks like a thermometer and ranges from zero "degrees" to one hundred "degrees." The instructions note that if the respondent doesn't feel "particularly warm or cold" toward what is being rated, then it should be rated at the

EXHIBIT 10.2. Global Well-Being as Assessed by the Circles, Ladder, and Thermometer Measures

Circles: whole life			Ladder: most of the time		Thermometer		
Number of:						Data	
+'s	−'s	April data	Rung number	April data	"Degrees"	Nov-1	Nov-2
8	0	11%	9 (best life)	7%	90–100	17%	19%
7	1	15%	8	11%	80–89	41%	43%
6	2	27%	7	23%	70–79	26%	26%
5	3	20%	6	23%	60–69	8%	7%
4	4	22%	5	23%	50–59	5%	3%
3	5	3%	4	7%	40–49	2%	1%
2	6	1%	3	3%	30–39	<1%	<1%
1	7	0%	2	2%	20–29	<1%	<1%
0	8	1%	1 (worst life)	1%	10–19	<1%	<1%
		100%		100%	0–9	<1%	<1%
						100%	100%
Mean number of +'s:		5.5	Mean rung number:	6.1	Mean "degrees":	78	79

Note: The measures used here are described in Exhibit 3.1; see measures G6, G7, and G8.
Data Sources: 1,118 respondents to November Form 1 national survey; 1,072 respondents to November Form 2 national survey; and 1,433 respondents to April national survey.

middle of the thermometer; if the respondent has a "warm feeling" or feels "favorably" toward it, it should be scored between 50 and 100 degrees, depending on how warm the feeling is; and, conversely, negative feelings are to be indicated by a score between zero and fifty. The scale has been used for measuring reactions to political candidates (e.g., Inter-University Consortium for Political Research, 1975) and seemed potentially useful for ratings of Life-as-a-whole as well.

The results in Exhibit 10.2 are in close accord with those for Life 3 presented in Exhibit 10.1. (This is as it should be, since all these results refer to the same thing, general evaluations of Life-as-a-whole from an absolute perspective.) Most people evaluate Life-as-a-whole in moderately positive terms; a small but significant proportion picked the most positive categories; negative evaluations were rare but did occur. It is clear from the exhibit that respondents were much more willing to place Life-as-a-whole near the extreme top of the Thermometer Scale than at the top of the others.[3] Apparently more people were prepared to say that they felt very "warm" or very favorably toward Life-as-a-whole than were ready to evaluate their lives in the near-perfect terms implied by the eight pluses and zero minuses of the most positive circle, or by the phrase, "the best life I could expect to have," which is associated with the top of the ladder.

In addition to using the ladder format to assess Life-as-a-whole "most of

[3] After comparing the Thermometer Scale with certain others, chapter 6 concludes that this scale has lower construct validity—i.e., is less sensitive to people's true feelings—than the Delighted–Terrible, Circles, or Ladder Scales. The conclusion, of course, is consistent with the present observation of the Thermometer Scale being less discriminating.

the time during the past year," this scale was used to obtain people's feelings about the following:

"Where on the ladder would you say was your best week in the past year—on which rung would you put it?"

"Where on the ladder was your worst week during the past year—on which rung?"

"Where was your life five years ago?"

"Where do you expect your life to be five years from now?"

It is of interest to compare people's ranking of their life "most of the time," with these other references. Exhibit 10.3 presents the figures. Not surprisingly, the average score assigned to the "best week" is somewhat above the typical "most of the time" score, and the "worst week" score is well below this. What is perhaps more surprising is the fact that there was even 1 percent of the population that rated the best week at the level of "the worst life I could expect to have!" One wonders what these individuals were experiencing. There is a similar small but non-zero percentage that placed themselves at the top of the scale even in their worst week. The estimates of global well-being five years ago and five years hence are also interesting. People, in the aggregate, thought their present life was somewhat better than it had been five years ago (but the difference here is rather modest), and people were, on average, remarkably optimistic about the future. In fact, average expectations of well-being five years hence were very similar to what people described as their best week during the past year!

Long-Term Changes in Well-Being (Type E Measures). In contrast to the evaluations of global well-being from an absolute perspective just discussed,

EXHIBIT 10.3. Global Well-Being at Various Time Periods as Assessed by Ladder Measures

	Ladder rung	Time period				
		Most of the time	Best week	Worst week	Five years ago	Five years from now
Best life	9	7%	23%	1%	9%	24%
	8	11%	20%	2%	14%	25%
	7	23%	25%	4%	18%	23%
	6	23%	16%	8%	17%	11%
	5	23%	10%	15%	17%	9%
	4	7%	3%	17%	9%	4%
	3	3%	1%	22%	6%	2%
	2	2%	1%	13%	4%	1%
Worst life	1	1%	1%	18%	6%	1%
		100%	100%	100%	100%	100%
Mean rung number:		6.1	7.1	3.6	5.8	7.1

Note: The measures used here are described in Exhibit 3.1; see measures G6, G17, G23, G64, and G65.
Data Source: 1,433 respondents to April national survey.

we can also examine evaluations of *changes* in global well-being. By how much do people think their lives have improved or deteriorated in the past? What do they expect in the future? By combining respondents' answers to some of the ladder items presented in the previous exhibit, we constructed new measures that let us answer these questions for changes experienced over the past five years, and for changes expected over the coming five years. Exhibit 10.4 shows the results.

In the previous exhibit we saw that the average rating of current global well-being was somewhat higher than what people thought it had been five years previously, and that the average rating for five years in the future was substantially above that for the present. In Exhibit 10.4 we can see some of the conflicting tendencies that lie back of the averages. While people in the aggregate showed some modest sense of progress over the past five years, in the first column of Exhibit 10.4 we can see that approximately one-third of the respondents saw *no* change in their global well-being, and close to another third (30 percent) felt their lives had actually deteriorated. Even among those who saw an advance, most rated their present lives as only slightly better than what they remembered their lives being like five years ago. It would seem that Americans certainly were not perceiving overwhelming improvements in their global well-being over the past five years.

As for the five years in the future, the broad trend was toward optimism, but of a rather muted sort. A third of the population expected no change, and another 40 percent foresaw only slight improvements. On the other hand, the proportion of people who expected more-than-slight declines was very small (about 2 percent), and was more than counterbalanced by the 17 percent who expected more-than-slight gains.

In addition to asking about expected changes in global well-being, we also

EXHIBIT 10.4. Changes in Global Well-Being

Scale	Life now compared to 5 years ago	Life 5 years hence compared to now
Much better	4%	3%
Somewhat better	10%	14%
Slightly better	24%	40%
Same	32%	34%
Slightly worse	21%	7%
Somewhat worse	8%	2%
Much worse	1%	<1%
	100%	100%

Note: The measures used here are described in Exhibit 3.1. See measures G56 and G57; as noted there, these measures were obtained by subtracting answers to one ladder item from answers to another. In the present exhibit the original 17 categories have been collapsed as follows: 8 to 5, 4 to 3, 2 to 1, 0, –1 to –2, –3 to –4, –5 to –8.

Data Source: 1,433 respondents to April national survey.

asked about changes respondents wanted to make in their lives.[4] On an
intuitive basis, one might initially suppose that a consequence of dissatisfaction with life would be at least a wish to change parts or aspects of it, but this
may not be so in terms of the way people think and talk about their lives. One
could reasonably imagine an individual who was dissatisfied with his or her
house but who could not imagine changing it or see any feasible way to change
it without costs or sacrifices that seemed too costly. On the other hand, one
could also imagine people who would express satisfaction and still have a wish
or determination to change parts of their lives to preserve or improve their
situation as they perceive it. However this reasoning might go on the part of
our respondents, we decided to at least ask a question on the topic. We asked:
"Considering the way your life is going, would you like to continue much the
same way, change some parts of it, or change many parts of it?" The distribution of answers appears in Exhibit 10.5.

As noted in chapter 3, answers to this question proved more highly
correlated with people's absolute levels of well-being than with the amount and
direction of expected change in well-being. There was the expected tendency
for people who felt more negative about their well-being to want to make more
changes in their lives ($r = .4$; see Exhibit 3.5). While there was also a tendency
for those who wanted to make more changes to expect more improvement in the
coming five years, this relationship was quite weak in the one set of respondents where it could be examined ($r = .2$ in the July data; see Exhibit 3.7).

**EXHIBIT 10.5. Desires to Change Parts
of Life**

Considering the way your life is going, would you like to:	
Continue the same way	36%
Change some parts	54%
Change many parts	10%
	100%

Note: The measure used here is described in
Exhibit 3.1; see measure G66.
Data source: 1,072 respondents to November Form
2 national survey.

Own Well-Being Relative to That of Others (Type D Measures). Still another
perspective from which well-being can be evaluated is the relative one: where
respondents stand relative to what they think is typical for other Americans.
Using the Circles Scale, described earlier, respondents were asked not only to
rate their own Life-as-a-whole but also to indicate "which circle do you think
would be chosen most often by people in this country?" This latter item
provides information about perceptions of the modal, or most typical, level of

[4]The question on desired changes is classified as a "Supplementary" measure (Type G) rather than
as a measure of long-term change in well-being (Type E); see Exhibit 3.1.

EXHIBIT 10.6. Relative Global Well-Being

Scale	Own well-being compared to that of typical Americans
Much higher	2%
Somewhat higher	17%
Slightly higher	43%
Same	25%
Slightly lower	10%
Somewhat lower	3%
Much lower	<1%
	100%

Note: The measure used here appears in Exhibit 3.1 as G53; as noted there the measure was obtained by subtracting answers from one circles item from answers to another. In the present exhibit the original 17 categories have been collapsed as follows: 8 to 5, 4 to 3, 2 to 1, 0, −1 to −2, −3 to −4, −5 to −8.
Data source: 1,433 respondents to April national survey.

well-being experienced by American adults. The two measures can be compared to determine how respondents perceived their *relative* well-being. These results appear in Exhibit 10.6.

The exhibit shows the interesting but not unexpected result that American adults tended to perceive themselves as being better off than the typical American. Note that 62 percent thought their own well-being was higher than the level Americans would most likely assign to themselves, while about 13 percent scored themselves lower. One cannot "explain away" these findings by appealing to the notion that other people's lives might not suit the preferences of the respondent, because the rating is not with respect to other's lives but with respect to how other people would evaluate their *own* lives. The data indicate a bias in perception.[5] People tended to underestimate the extent to which most people positively evaluate their own lives. Of course, this bias has the self-serving effect of enhancing one's relative position, but one wonders whether there may be certain negative effects—particularly in a democratic society—of the apparently widespread tendency to underestimate the well-being experienced by one's fellow citizens.

Besides noting this bias, however, we would go on to suggest that at least some of the differences between people in their perception of relative well-being undoubtedly reflects reality. Some people *do* feel more positively about their lives than does the typical American, and others feel worse. Not surprisingly, there is a moderate tendency for people who rated their own global well-being unusually high to think that they were more pleased than other people, and for those who rated themselves unusually low to believe that they were less pleased than others ($r = .4$; see Exhibit 3.2).

[5]A portion of chapter 7 compares evaluations of one's own well-being with that of others in greater detail; see the section titled "Exploration 7."

More Specific Evaluations of Life-as-a-Whole (Type C Measures)

In the preceding section we examined assessments of Life-as-a-whole employing a very general evaluative dimension and several different evaluative perspectives. Because of the extreme generality of the assessments, it seems reasonable to think of these measures as indicators of global well-being. We turn now to evaluations of various more specific qualities of Life-as-a-whole. In all, we shall consider eleven qualities: satisfaction, happiness, worries, positive affect, negative affect, affect balance, and the extent to which life is seen as interesting, enjoyable, worthwhile, full, and/or rewarding.

From the results presented in chapter 3 we know that many of these qualities substantially overlap with one another and that most of them bear substantial positive relationships to the more general measures of well-being (as, indeed, they should). Nevertheless, these various measures have some interest in their own right in helping to pin down the sorts and kinds of feelings that characterize the quality of life in America.

All of the qualities we shall discuss in this section have also been examined by previous investigators (chap. 3 details the original sources), and part of the reason for presenting distributions of the answers from our national samples is to facilitate comparisons with previous results and with those that may be obtained in the future. Although our purpose here is not to undertake an analysis of changes in Americans' perceptions of well-being over the years, this clearly is one of the significant potentials of social indicators, and we anticipate that the distributions presented here will contribute to that long-term enterprise.

Satisfaction, Happiness, Worries. Exhibits 10.7, 10.8, and 10.9 present the distributions of reports about satisfaction with Life-as-a-whole, levels of happiness, and the frequency of worrying. The vast majority of Americans claimed to be at least "pretty satisfied" (more than 80 percent) and "pretty happy" (about 90 percent). On the other hand, about 20 percent said they worried "a lot" or

EXHIBIT 10.7. Satisfaction with Life-as-a-Whole

7-point Satisfaction				3-point Satisfaction	
		Nov-1	Nov-2		Nov-2
Completely satisfied	7	13%	14%	Completely satisfying	19%
	6	41%	44%	Pretty satisfying	69%
	5	27%	24%	Not very satisfying	12%
	4	13%	11%		100%
	3	4%	5%		
	2	1%	1%		
Completely dissatisfied	1	1%	1%		
		100%	100%		

Note: The measures used here are described in Exhibit 3.1; see measures G29 and G30.
Data sources: 1,118 respondents to November Form 1 national survey; and 1,072 respondents to November Form 2 national survey.

EXHIBIT 10.8. Happiness

3-point Happiness			Feelings about how happy you are	
	May	Nov.		Nov.
			7. Delighted	13%
Very happy	27%	22%	6. Pleased	40%
Pretty happy	64%	67%	5. Mostly satisfied	33%
Not too happy	9%	11%	4. Mixed	9%
	100%	100%	3. Mostly dissatisfied	3%
			2. Unhappy	1%
			1. Terrible	1%
				100%

Note: The measures used here are described in Exhibit 3.1; see measures G31 and G32.
Data sources: 1,297 respondents to May national survey; and 1,072 respondents to November Form
2 national survey.

EXHIBIT 10.9. Worries

Frequency of worrying	Nov-1	Nov-2
Never	2%	4%
A little	31%	35%
Sometimes	43%	42%
A lot	19%	15%
All the time	5%	4%
	100%	100%

Note: The measure used here is described in Exhibit 3.1;
see measure G33.
Data sources: 1,118 respondents to November Form 1
national survey; and 1,072 respondents to November
Form 2 national survey.

"all the time," 12 percent said their life was "not very satisfying," and 10 percent said they were "not too happy."

Each of the items was included in more than one of our national surveys, and where identical items were asked at identical times, as was the case for both satisfaction and worries, the results were highly similar. For happiness, however, the proportion of respondents claiming to be "very happy" declined from 27 percent in May 1972 to 22 percent in November of that year. One wonders to what extent this represents a continuation of what may have been a trend of declining happiness in the United States[6] and to what extent it may be merely a

---

[6]This same three-point happiness measure has been included in various national surveys over the years. The percentage of people saying they were "very happy" has gradually declined between 1957 and 1972. In 1957 Gurin, Veroff, and Feld (1960) found 35 percent of the American population claiming to be "very happy." In 1963 the figure was 32 percent, in 1965 30 percent (Bradburn, 1969). In 1971 Campbell, Converse, and Rodgers (1976) found it to be 29 percent, and—as noted above—in 1972 we found it to be 27 percent and 22 percent in May and November, respectively. Recent data reported by Davis (1975) based on surveys in 1973, 1974, and 1975, however, show a sharp and unexpected return to the levels of the latter 1950s.

seasonal fluctuation. (Our April data do not include measures of happiness, so we cannot directly answer this question. However, as noted in our discussion of Exhibit 10.1, many other life evaluations showed less positive assessments in November than in either the preceding May or the following April, suggesting that there may indeed have been some seasonal fluctuation.)

Positive Affect, Negative Affect, Affect Balance. As described in chapter 3, our measures of affect were taken directly from earlier work by Bradburn (1969, Bradburn and Caplovitz, 1966). His concept of happiness involved the presence of positive affect and the absence of negative affect and he measured these components independently. To do so, for positive affects, he asked whether one has recently felt:

Particularly excited or interested in something?
Proud because someone complimented you on something you had done?
Pleased about having accomplished something?
On top of the world?
That things were going your way?

For a complementary measure of negative affects, he asked whether one has recently felt:

So restless that you couldn't sit long in a chair?
Very lonely or remote from other people?
Bored?
Depressed or very unhappy?
Upset because someone criticized you?

To get an affect balance measure he (and we also) simply subtracted the number of negative affects that the respondent had experienced from the number of positive ones. We extended Bradburn's approach by also asking about the *frequency* with which the affects were experienced.

Our results on affect appear in Exhibit 10.10. Looking first at the positive affects, one can see that at least half the respondents claimed to have experienced most of them at least "several times" in the past few weeks. (The exception is feelings of being "on top of the world," which were much rarer.) The negative affects, on the other hand, tended to be experienced much less frequently—ranging from feelings of being "restless," which 42 percent experienced at least several times, to being "upset," which was reported with this frequency by only 8 percent. The data for affect balance, also presented in Exhibit 10.10, show that positive affects predominated over negative ones for the substantial majority of Americans (70 percent), but that there was about one-sixth of the population for whom the negative affects predominated.

Selected Other Qualities of Life-as-a-Whole. The May interview included assessments of five other life qualities, selected from a larger list used previously by Campbell, Converse, and Rodgers (1976). These were presented as two polar terms at a time, and respondents were asked to pick some point along the linear scale connecting the two extremes that seemed most descriptive of their lives-as-a-whole.[7] As shown in Exhibit 10.11, the five qualities of life were:

[7]The presentation format is that of the "semantic differential" (Osgood, Suci, Tannenbaum, 1957). As presented to the respondents, some pairs had the undesirable terms first, others the positive terms first; all were later coded from 7 (the "good" end) to 1 (the "undesirable" end).

EXHIBIT 10.10. Positive Affect, Negative Affect, Affect Balance

	Never	Once	Several	A lot	Total
	Frequency of experiencing designated affect in the past few weeks				
Positive affects					
Excited	36%	11%	40%	13%	100%
Proud	30%	16%	47%	7%	100%
Pleased	20%	13%	57%	10%	100%
On top of the world	68%	6%	20%	6%	100%
Things going your way	32%	7%	50%	11%	100%
Negative affects					
Restless	50%	8%	26%	16%	100%
Lonely	76%	7%	12%	5%	100%
Bored	63%	7%	22%	8%	100%
Depressed	69%	8%	18%	5%	100%
Upset	81%	11%	7%	1%	100%

Affect balance

Negative									Positive
−5	−4	−3	−2	−1	0	+1	+2	+3	+4	+5
<1%	1%	2%	5%	8%	13%	17%	17%	16%	14%	6%

Note: The measures used here are described in Exhibit 3.1; see measures G35, G36 and G37.
Data source: 1,072 respondents to November Form 2 national survey.

interesting–boring, enjoyable–miserable, worthwhile–useless, full–empty, and rewarding–disappointing. The distributions of answers to all five items were remarkably similar, with half to two-thirds of the respondents placing their lives at or adjacent to the positive extreme and only 4 percent to 6 percent putting their lives that close to the negative extreme.

EVALUATIONS OF LIFE-AS-A-WHOLE IN POPULATION GROUPS

A comparison of evaluations of Life-as-a-whole by members of different demographic and social groups provides insights into the quality of life experienced by people in different circumstances and casts some light on the nature of

EXHIBIT 10.11. Selected Other Qualities of Life-as-a-Whole

	Positive					Negative		Total	Mean
	7	6	5	4	3	2	1		
Interesting/boring	31%	17%	23%	19%	6%	2%	2%	100%	5.4
Enjoyable/miserable	32%	24%	19%	16%	4%	2%	3%	100%	5.5
Worthwhile/useless	43%	23%	17%	10%	3%	2%	2%	100%	5.8
Full/empty	42%	22%	13%	13%	4%	3%	3%	100%	5.6
Rewarding/disappointing	34%	24%	19%	15%	4%	2%	2%	100%	5.5

Note: The measures used here are described in Exhibit 3.1; see measures G39 through G43.
Data source: 1,297 respondents to May national survey.

our various global measures as well. We turn next to consider the same
divisions of the American population that were examined in chapter 9; i.e., sex,
age, socioeconomic status, family life-cycle, and race. In the exhibits that follow
none of the global measures show large differences between men and women,
but there are some substantial differences when the population is divided
according to other criteria.

As in the first part of the chapter, we shall group the global measures
according to the typology presented in chapter 3, beginning first with the
general evaluations made from various perspectives and concluding with evaluations of several more specific life qualities.

General Evaluations of Life-as-a-Whole

Absolute Perspective (Type A Measures). Exhibit 10.12 shows mean evaluations of global well-being by members of selected groups. The exhibit includes
the results of assessing this by three different measures (Life 3, Circles, Ladder),
all of which are intended to tap the same phenomenon—a very general evaluation from an absolute perspective.

We have already examined the differences on Life 3 for the various groups
in the preceding chapter. The same data are presented here for comparison
purposes. There seem to be no marked differences by age level; evaluations of
life did not get better, and the best conclusion is that they stayed steady or
declined very slightly with advancing age. Life was rated better, however, by
succeeding socioeconomic groups ordered from low to high. Among the status
inconsistent groups, people with high income and low education felt better off
than those with low income and high education. Looking at family life-cycle
stages, there was a clear difference in terms of being married or not. Among the
married respondents, the evaluations were above average and they stayed
relatively steady, as they did with age increases, and perhaps dropped just a
meager decimal point or two. When blacks and whites are compared, the blacks
were always on the slightly lower (less pleased) side. The difference was
statistically significant in one survey, marginally significant in another, and
only one percentage point in the third, but always in the same direction.[8]

When we turn to the circles and slices-of-life measure we replicate the same
picture. Age made no difference. Things improved dramatically with socioeconomic status, principally with income. Being married went with better ratings
than did not being married, and blacks rated themselves as having a poorer
ratio of good to bad parts in their lives than did whites.

The measure using the Ladder Scale showed no differences by age level
except for a hint that the teen-agers in our sample rated their lives higher.

---

[8]Exhibits 4.6 and 4.7 show that six classification variables closely comparable to those used to
define the groups discussed here could, jointly, explain 8 percent to 11 percent of the variance in
Life 3. Thus, while the differences among groups we have just described are of some interest,
membership in the groups accounts for only a small part of the total variation in people's
perceptions of global well-being.

EXHIBIT 10.12. Mean Global Well-Being in Designated Groups as Assessed by the Life 3, Circles, and Ladder Measures

Group		Life 3 May	Life 3 Nov.	Life 3 April	Circles April	Ladder April
Sex:	Men	5.5	5.4	5.4	5.4	5.9
	Women	5.4	5.3	5.4	5.6	6.1
Age:	15–19	5.6	5.4	5.6	5.5	6.4
	20–24	5.5	5.2	5.5	5.4	6.0
	25–29	5.6	5.5	5.4	5.6	6.0
	30–34	5.4	5.4	5.5	5.6	6.1
	35–44	5.5	5.3	5.3	5.5	6.0
	45–54	5.3	5.3	5.4	5.6	6.0
	55–64	5.5	5.4	5.3	5.4	6.1
	65+	5.4	5.3	5.3	5.7	6.2
SES:	(low)1	5.3	5.1	5.0	4.8	5.4
	2	5.4	5.2	5.3	5.1	5.8
	3	5.5	5.4	5.4	5.4	5.9
	4	5.6	5.4	5.5	5.9	6.3
	(high)5	5.7	5.6	5.7	6.2	6.7
	6	5.2	5.1	5.2	5.3	5.7
	7	5.5	5.5	5.4	5.7	6.2
FLC:	1	5.2	5.1	5.2	5.3	5.8
	2	5.7	5.5	5.6	5.8	6.2
	3	5.7	5.4	5.6	5.7	6.0
	4	5.5	5.5	5.6	5.7	6.2
	5	5.5	5.6	5.4	5.7	6.4
	6	5.5	5.5	5.5	5.7	6.4
	7	5.3	5.1	5.0	5.2	5.8
	8	5.1	5.0	4.9	4.6	5.3
Race:	White	5.5	5.4	5.4	5.6	6.1
	Black	5.4	4.8	5.0	4.9	5.4

Note: The measures used here are described in Exhibit 3.1; see measures G3, G6, and G7. Appendix M shows the number of cases in each group. Chapter 9 (section titled "Groups Identified") describes the Socioeconomic Status and Family Life-Cycle Scales.
Data sources: 1,297 respondents to May national survey; 1,072 respondents to November Form 2 national survey; and 1,433 respondents to April national survey.

Again the chosen rung on the ladder was steadily higher for progressive levels of socioeconomic status, and again being married or not married made most of the difference in life-cycle patterns. Blacks, on the average, chose a point a little lower on the ladder than whites did.

In addition to the evaluations of Life-as-a-whole shown in Exhibit 10.12, it is interesting to consider how different groups in the population responded to the item "yourself." Self-evaluation is surely an important component for assessing the totality of one's global well-being, but it can also be regarded as a kind of summative judgment in its own right. For some purposes it might be a better assessment of a person's life feelings than a broader one that encompassed feelings about society, the direction of the economy, and so forth. Although not a "global" measure having to do with Life-as-a-whole, the evaluations we obtained of "yourself" were like the global measures just discussed in employing an absolute perspective and a very general evaluative dimension. (Answers were on the Delighted–Terrible Scale.)

The results from asking, "How do you feel about yourself?" on two surveys were very similar and are shown in Exhibit 10.13. The distributions of means across the groups are very flat. There are small differences but most are not replicated. Perhaps most interesting is the finding that blacks, on the average, rated their feelings about themselves two or three decimal points better than whites did. This difference could be real, in which case it is not very important because it is small, or it could be a chance occurrence that it happened even twice, but it is interesting because it is one of the few comparisons of whites and blacks that goes in the direction of a better evaluation for blacks.

EXHIBIT 10.13. Mean Evaluations of "Yourself" in Designated Groups as Assessed on the Delighted–Terrible Scale

Group		May	April
Sex:	Men	5.3	5.3
	Women	5.1	5.2
Age:	15–19	5.1	5.4
	20–24	5.1	5.3
	25–29	5.3	5.3
	30–34	5.2	5.4
	35–44	5.3	5.2
	45–54	5.1	5.2
	55–64	5.2	5.1
	65+	5.2	5.2
SES:	(low)1	5.3	5.0
	2	5.1	5.3
	3	5.2	5.2
	4	5.2	5.2
	(high)5	5.2	5.3
	6	5.1	5.2
	7	5.1	5.4
FLC:	1	5.1	5.2
	2	5.2	5.2
	3	5.3	5.3
	4	5.3	5.3
	5	4.9	5.2
	6	5.2	5.3
	7	5.2	5.0
	8	5.0	4.9
Race:	White	5.2	5.2
	Black	5.5	5.4

Note: The measure used here is described in Exhibit 2.1; see item 22. Appendix M shows the number of cases in each group. Chapter 9 (section titled "Groups Identified") describes the Socioeconomic Status and Family Life-Cycle Scales.
Data sources: 1,297 respondents to May national survey; and 1,433 respondents to April national survey.

Long-Term Changes in Well-Being (Type E Measures). Exhibit 10.14 brings together two indicators of long-term change in well-being (in columns D and E), the original ladder-based measures from which the change measures were calculated (in columns A–C), and a related item having to do with the number of parts of their lives that respondents *desired* to change (in column F).

By looking at column D one can see that all but one of the age groups perceived improvements in their global well-being over the past five years, the biggest improvements being seen by respondents in their latter twenties and

EXHIBIT 10.14. Mean Global Well-Being in Designated Groups at Various Time Periods, Long-Range Changes in Global Well-Being, and Desires to Change Parts of Life

| Group | | Level of well-being | | | Long-range changes in well-being | | Desire to change parts of life |
| | | Most of the time | Five years ago | Five years from now | Past 5 yrs. | Next 5 yrs. | |
		A	B	C	D	E	F
Sex:	Men	5.9	5.8	7.0	0.1	1.1	1.7
	Women	6.1	5.8	7.2	0.3	1.1	1.7
Age:	15–19	6.4	6.2	7.7	0.2	1.3	2.0
	20–24	6.0	5.8	7.5	0.2	1.5	1.9
	25–29	6.0	5.1	7.7	0.9	1.7	1.9
	30–34	6.1	5.3	7.7	0.8	1.6	1.7
	35–44	6.0	5.6	7.1	0.4	0.9	1.7
	45–54	6.0	5.9	7.0	0.1	1.0	1.6
	55–64	6.1	5.9	6.5	0.2	0.4	1.5
	65+	6.2	6.4	6.3	− 0.2	0.1	1.5
SES:	(low)1	5.4	5.7	6.0	− 0.3	0.6	1.7
	2	5.8	5.6	6.8	0.2	1.0	1.7
	3	5.9	5.5	7.2	0.4	1.3	1.7
	4	6.3	5.7	7.5	0.6	1.2	1.8
	(high)5	6.7	6.3	7.6	0.4	1.1	1.6
	6	5.7	5.6	7.0	0.1	1.3	1.9
	7	6.2	5.8	7.0	0.4	1.8	1.6
FLC:	1	5.8	5.9	7.3	− 0.1	1.5	2.0
	2	6.2	5.4	7.5	0.8	1.3	1.9
	3	6.0	5.4	7.5	0.6	1.5	1.8
	4	6.2	5.7	7.5	0.5	1.3	1.7
	5	6.4	5.6	7.5	0.8	1.1	1.7
	6	6.4	6.2	6.8	0.2	0.4	1.5
	7	5.8	5.9	6.0	− 0.1	0.2	1.6
	8	5.3	4.9	7.2	0.4	1.9	2.1
Race:	White	6.1	5.8	7.1	0.3	1.0	1.7
	Black	5.4	5.2	7.0	0.2	1.6	2.0

Note: Means in the first five columns are based on April data and the Ladder Scale (1 = worst life I could expect to have; 9 = best life); means in the last column come from the November respondents and are based on a 3-point scale (1 = continue life the same way; 3 = change many parts). The measures used here are described in Exhibit 3.1; see G6, G56, G57, G64, G65, and G66. Appendix M shows the number of cases in each group. Chapter 9 (section titled "Groups Identified") describes the Socioeconomic Status and Family Life-Cycle Scales.
Data sources: 1,072 respondents to November Form 2 national survey; and 1,433 respondents to April national survey.

early thirties. After the mid-thirties, the amount of improvement declined with increases in age, and for those sixty-five or more years old there was no sense of improvement at all but a slight decline. By examining columns A and B, the basis for these differences in perceptions can be seen. It is not that people in their twenties and thirties were especially positive about their current well-being and older people more negative; differences in perceptions of current well-being were negligible (column A). Rather, the groups differed in how well-off they thought they had been five years previously. The respondents who put themselves lowest five years prior to the survey were the twenty-five-to twenty-nine-year-olds. (They were then in their early twenties and the year was 1967, notable for urban troubles in America and the Vietnam War abroad.) Each age group progressively older than the twenty-five- to twenty-nine-year-olds rated their level of well-being five years prior to the survey in increasingly rosier terms, resulting in the older age groups seeing progressively less improvement over the past five years.

The estimates of life five years in the future (column C) were all optimistic, all better than now, and (except for people over sixty-four) all better than five years ago. People in their late twenties and early thirties expected the biggest improvement, and were closely followed by people in their teens and early twenties (column E).

Turning next to differences among socioeconomic groups, Exhibit 10.14 shows that all groups except the lowest thought their life had improved over the past five years. People near the top of the SES Scale saw the greatest improvements, and those at the bottom felt things had actually worsened (column D). Interestingly, perceptions of well-being five years ago were virtually the same for most of the different socioeconomic groups (column B), and differences among the groups in their sense of progress arose because they perceived different levels of current well-being (column A).

Expectancies about the future did get higher for progressive steps in the socioeconomic classification so the best-off now and the best-off five years ago (the same group) expected to be the best-off five years from now, too (column C); but the middle groups are the ones who expected the biggest improvements (colume E).

Comparing the family life-cycle groups, the married respondents tended to see more improvement in their well-being over the past five years than unmarried ones, and unmarried people with no children at home (groups 1 and 7) were unusual in seeing slight deterioration in their lives-as-a-whole (column D). Among these people, those who were forty-five years of age or older were also unusual in foreseeing little improvement over the coming five years, though the younger ones were at least as optimistic as those who were married (column E). The group that was most optimistic about the future, however, was the unmarried people with children; their assessments of current well-being were the lowest of any group (column A), and they expected their well-being to rise to about the average level expected by others in the coming five years (column C).

Blacks and whites expected about the same levels of well-being five years from now but they saw different positions in the present and also five years back, so it is clear that expectations were greater among blacks than whites in terms of the expected *rate* or *pace* of improvement.

Also included in Exhibit 10.14 (column F) are results from the question: "Considering how your life is going, would you like to continue much the same way, change some parts of it, or change many parts of it?" The two sexes showed no difference on this measure, but there was a systematic relationship to age, with people in the younger groups wanting to change more parts of their lives than those in older groups. Differences among the socioeconomic status groups were small, and most of the differences among the family life-cycle groups should probably be attributed to age differences rather than family status differences. The exception, however, is for unmarried people with children at home, who were more likely to want to change many parts of their lives than any other group. Comparing the races, blacks tended to want to change more parts of their lives than did whites.

Best Week, Worst Week, Short-Term Changes (Measures of Types B and F). Included among the series of questions using the ladder format were evaluations of Life-as-a-whole during the "best week" and "worst week" in the past year. The results, together with a measure of the range of short-term changes in well-being derived from the difference in the two answers, are presented in Exhibit 10.15.

For the level of well-being during the best week, teen-agers picked the highest position of any age group and people over thirty-five were clearly lower, but when we look at the choice of "worst week," the over-sixty-five-year-olds chose the highest level and the choices got lower and lower for younger age groups. The younger age groups, therefore, were reporting wider swings in their lives than were felt by older people. The differences in group means between "best" and "worst week" went from 4.5 "rungs" (half the scale) for teen-agers to 2.9 "rungs" for the over-sixty-fives by steady steps with no ties or reversals. It is clear that if we asked people to evaluate their lives in terms of how bad a time they had had recently life would appear to be better for successive age groups. If, on the other hand, we asked people to evaluate their lives in terms of the "best week" they had had recently, life evaluations would drop off with advancing age but not nearly as dramatically.

When socioeconomic groups are compared, the findings indicate that low socioeconomic individuals had a somewhat poorer "best week," on the average, and also a poorer "worst week" than people in other categories. High-SES people reported a higher "best week" than the members of any other social group we examined and their "worst week" was also not as bad as anybody else's. The family life-cycle findings are similar to those found on other measures. The worst "worst week" (group average 2.7), not far from the bottom of the ladder, was reported by unmarried respondents with children at home. The difference between "best" and "worst week" was the same for blacks and whites but each average is a shade higher for whites than for blacks.

Own Well-Being Relative to That of Others (Type D Measures). Exhibit 10.16 shows how the groups compared with respect to a measure of relative well-

EXHIBIT 10.15. Mean Global Well-Being in Designated Groups
During Best and Worst Weeks and Short-Range Changes in Well-
Being

Group		Level of well-being		Short-range changes in well-being
		Best week	Worst week	
Sex:	Men	7.1	3.5	3.6
	Women	7.2	3.6	3.6
Age:	15–19	7.5	3.0	4.5
	20–24	7.3	3.0	4.3
	25–29	7.4	3.3	4.1
	30–34	7.3	3.5	3.8
	35–44	7.0	3.5	3.5
	45–54	7.1	3.7	3.4
	55–64	7.0	3.9	3.1
	65+	6.9	4.0	2.9
SES:	(low)1	6.3	3.1	3.2
	2	6.8	3.5	3.3
	3	7.2	3.4	3.9
	4	7.5	3.6	3.9
	(high)5	7.7	4.2	3.5
	6	7.1	2.9	4.2
	7	7.1	3.8	3.3
FLC:	1	7.1	3.1	4.0
	2	7.4	3.5	3.9
	3	7.2	3.3	3.9
	4	7.4	3.6	3.8
	5	7.4	3.7	3.7
	6	7.2	4.1	3.1
	7	6.6	3.6	3.0
	8	6.6	2.7	3.9
Race: White		7.2	3.6	3.6
	Black	6.7	3.1	3.6

Note: Means are based on the Ladder Scale (1 = worst life I could expect to have; 9 = best
life). The measures used here are described in Exhibit 3.1; see G17, G23, and G59.
Appendix M shows the number of cases in each group. Chapter 9 (section titled
"Groups Identified") describes the Socioeconomic Status and Family Life-Cycle Scales.
Data source: 1,433 respondents to April national survey.

being; i.e., how the respondents' rating (on the Circles Scale) of their own lives-
as-a-whole compared with their perceptions of the level of well-being most
likely to be experienced by Americans.

No group, on the average, rated most people as choosing a better picture of
their lives than their own choice (note that there are no negative scores in the
exhibit), and only two groups put their own well-being close to the level they
thought was most common in America. These were the lowest socioeconomic
group and unmarried people with children living at home.

When the population is divided by sex or age, substantial differences in
relative well-being do not appear. Socioeconomic status shows marked but not

EXHIBIT 10.16. Mean Relative Global Well-Being in Designated
Groups

Group		Relative well-being	Index components	
			Own well-being	Typical well-being
Sex:	Men	1.0	5.4	4.4
	Women	1.1	5.6	4.5
Age:	15–19	1.0	5.5	4.5
	20–24	1.1	5.4	4.3
	25–29	1.3	5.6	4.3
	30–34	1.1	5.6	4.5
	35–44	1.1	5.5	4.4
	45–54	1.1	5.6	4.5
	55–64	0.9	5.4	4.5
	65+	1.2	5.7	4.5
SES:	(low)1	0	4.8	4.8
	2	0.7	5.1	4.4
	3	1.0	5.4	4.4
	4	1.5	5.9	4.4
	(high)5	1.7	6.2	4.5
	6	0.7	5.3	4.6
	7	1.5	5.7	4.2
FLC:	1	0.9	5.3	4.4
	2	1.3	5.8	4.5
	3	1.3	5.7	4.4
	4	1.3	5.7	4.4
	5	1.4	5.7	4.3
	6	1.2	5.7	4.5
	7	0.6	5.2	4.6
	8	0.1	4.6	4.5
Race:	White	1.1	5.6	4.5
	Black	0.6	4.9	4.3

Notes: The Relative well-being scores indicate the amount by which the respondents'
own well-being exceeded what they estimated was the most commonly experienced
level of well-being, expressed in terms of the Circles Scale. The measures used here
are described in Exhibit 3.1; see measures G7, G53, and G67. Appendix M shows the
number of cases in each group. Chapter 9 (section titled "Groups Identified")
describes the categories of the Socioeconomic Status and Family Life-Cycle Scales.
Data source: 1,433 respondents to April national survey.

surprising differences: Those at the bottom of the scale saw themselves as least
well-off relative to others, and those at the top as most well-off relative to
others. Dividing the population by stage in the family life-cycle shows all the
married groups as having higher perceived relative well-being than any of the
unmarried groups, and the unmarried people with children at home, as noted
above, were exceptionally low. Between the races, whites saw themselves as
being somewhat further above average levels than did blacks.

The perceptions of relative well-being provide a picture that is much the
same as that which emerged when we considered absolute evaluations of well-
being (Exhibit 10.12), and the "Index components" included in Exhibit 10.16

show why. There was practically no difference among any of the groups examined here in the mean values they assigned for the most typical level of well-being in America. We noted in the first part of this chapter that there seems to have been substantial bias in perceptions of what this typical level of well-being was, and we see here that this bias seems to be remarkably uniform across different social and demographic groups.

More Specific Evaluations of Life-as-a-Whole (Type C Measures)

From among the eleven more specific evaluative dimensions described in the first part of this chapter, we have selected four on which to compare social and demographic groups. These are: satisfaction, happiness, affect balance, and worries. Respondents to the November Form 2 national survey evaluated their lives-as-a-whole with respect to each of these qualities, with the results shown in Exhibit 10.17. In addition, some of these same qualities were assessed by respondents to certain of the other national surveys (satisfaction and worries in the November Form 1 survey, and happiness in the May survey), and although we do not present these other results, the patterns are the same as those that appear in Exhibit 10.17.

Satisfaction. The two different measures of satisfaction with Life-as-a-whole produced identical results, as one can see in Exhibit 10.17. There was hardly any difference between men and women, and no systematic trend with advancing age. As with our more general assessments of well-being, satisfaction increased with higher socioeconomic status; was higher for married people than unmarried ones (and was unusually low for unmarried people with children at home, category 8 of the Family Life-Cycle Scale); and was higher for whites than blacks.

Happiness. Both our measures of happiness show the same general pattern across the different groups as we observed for satisfaction, but with one small yet potentially interesting variation. As with satisfaction, the difference in happiness between men and women was slight, high-SES respondents were happier than low-SES ones, married people were happier than unmarried ones, and whites were happier than blacks. With respect to age, however, both the seven-point and three-point happiness measures showed slight declines in happiness with advancing age. The differences were quite small and within the limits of what might be attributed to sampling error, but a trend is discernible in these data. This is one hint that the happiness and satisfaction measures tapped somewhat different life qualities: While happiness may have declined slightly with advancing age, satisfaction did not seem to.[9]

Positive and Negative Affect. The pattern of results just described for happiness also appeared for positive affect, but with greater clarity. In most respects

[9]In their study of Life quality Campbell, Converse, and Rodgers (1976) report that with increasing age happiness declined and satisfaction *increased.* Our results on happiness are parallel to theirs, but in neither the November Form 2 survey (shown in Exhibit 10.17) nor in the November Form 1 survey did we observe any systematic increase in satisfaction with age, despite our having used the same satisfaction measure as Campbell, Converse, and Rodgers.

EXHIBIT 10.17. Mean Evaluations of Satisfaction, Happiness, Affect, and Worries by Designated Groups

Group		Satisfaction		Happiness		Affect			Frequency of worrying
		7-pt	3-pt	7-pt	3-pt	Pos.	Neg.	Bal.	
Sex:	Men	5.5	3.2	5.5	3.3	3.2	1.5	1.6	2.6
	Women	5.4	3.1	5.4	3.2	3.1	1.7	1.5	2.9
Age:	15–19	5.5	3.3	5.6	3.4	3.5	2.2	1.4	2.7
	20–24	5.2	3.1	5.5	3.1	3.3	2.1	1.2	2.9
	25–29	5.6	3.1	5.5	3.4	3.7	1.8	1.8	2.8
	30–34	5.4	3.1	5.5	3.3	3.3	1.5	1.8	2.8
	35–44	5.3	3.2	5.3	3.2	3.1	1.6	1.5	2.9
	45–54	5.3	3.1	5.5	3.2	3.1	1.6	1.6	2.8
	55–64	5.6	3.3	5.5	3.3	3.0	1.4	1.6	2.8
	65+	5.5	3.1	5.4	3.1	2.8	1.3	1.4	2.6
SES:	(low)1	5.2	2.9	5.3	2.8	2.3	1.8	0.5	2.9
	2	5.4	3.0	5.3	3.1	2.8	1.7	1.1	2.9
	3	5.4	3.1	5.6	3.3	3.2	1.6	1.6	2.8
	4	5.6	3.2	5.5	3.4	3.7	1.5	2.3	2.9
	(high)5	5.7	3.4	5.6	3.6	3.6	1.4	2.2	2.8
	6	5.2	3.0	5.2	3.1	3.2	1.8	1.4	2.6
	7	5.5	3.5	5.7	3.4	3.0	1.7	1.3	2.8
FLC:	1	5.1	3.0	5.2	3.1	3.3	2.3	1.1	2.8
	2	5.5	3.2	5.7	3.4	3.5	1.6	2.0	2.6
	3	5.5	3.2	5.5	3.3	3.5	1.6	1.9	3.0
	4	5.6	3.2	5.5	3.3	3.3	1.4	1.9	2.8
	5	5.6	3.5	5.7	3.4	3.3	1.2	2.1	2.8
	6	5.6	3.3	5.6	3.4	3.0	1.3	1.7	2.7
	7	5.3	3.0	5.2	2.9	2.7	1.6	1.1	2.7
	8	4.9	2.7	5.1	2.8	2.5	2.4	0.1	3.1
Race:	White	5.5	3.2	5.6	3.3	3.3	1.6	1.7	2.8
	Black	4.9	2.6	4.9	2.6	2.2	2.0	0.3	2.8

Notes: The higher the mean in any column, the greater the quality shown at the head of the column. The 7-point scales are coded 7 to 1; the 3-point scales are coded 5, 3, 1; Positive and Negative affect each run from 5 to 0; Affect balance scores run from +5 to −5; the Worries code runs from 5 to 1. All measures used here are described in Exhibit 3.1; see G29–G33 and G35–G37. Appendix M shows the number of cases in each group. Chapter 9 (section titled "Groups identified") describes the categories of the Socioeconomic Status and Family Life-Cycle Scales.

Data source: 1,072 respondents to November Form 2 national survey.

negative affect showed just the opposite pattern, but there was one marked and interesting exception. The exception occurs when the age groups are compared: The experience of positive affects tended to decline with advancing age (paralleling the slight decline in reported happiness), but *so also* did reports of negative affects! Older people experienced fewer "highs," but also experienced fewer "lows." Of course, this result is perfectly consistent with the finding in Exhibit 10.15 that older people had a narrower range of *variation* in their feelings about well-being.

Across the remaining group comparisons, however, the trends for positive affect were mirrored by opposite trends for negative affect. The differences between the sexes were very small, with men reporting just slightly more positive affects, and fewer negative affects, than women. With increases in socioeconomic status, the experience of positive affects showed a marked increase, and negative affects showed a modest decrease. Married people reported more positive affects and fewer negative affects than did nonmarried people of roughly comparable ages. (When comparing the family life-cycle groups with respect to positive and negative affect, one can see the influence of both marital status and age on the means shown in Exhibit 10.17.) Blacks reported substantially fewer positive affects and modestly more negative affects than did whites.

Affect Balance. The pattern of differences between groups with respect to affect balance pretty much repeated that which has been previously described for satisfaction and happiness. As before, the higher scores, which indicate excesses of positive affects over negative affects, appeared for people with higher socioeconomic status, those who were married, and whites. The only variation on the pattern occurred across the age groups. Whereas satisfaction stayed essentially the same as age increased, and happiness showed a faint decrease with advancing age, the predominance of positive affects was most pronounced among those between twenty-five and thirty-four and was slightly less among people who were either younger or older than that. As with happiness, however, the differences were small.

Worries. Exhibit 10.17 also includes data on the reported frequency of worrying. Here the pattern of differences was distinctly different from that observed for any other global measure. There was a modest sex difference, with women reporting that they worried more often than did men, and there were virtually *no* differences associated with socioeconomic status. Although higher status was associated with higher global well-being, both absolutely and relatively, with a sense of having made more progress over the past five years, and with more satisfaction, happiness, and positive affect, higher status apparently did not reduce the frequency of worrying!

Across the various family life-cycle groups the differences in frequency of worrying also showed a pattern distinct from what we have seen before: Although differences were small, it appears that people with children at home worried more frequently than those who did not have children or whose children had grown and left. Clearly, the more "usual" pattern of married people showing more positive scores than unmarried ones did not apply to worrying.

Finally, the split for race also produced a distinctive result. On average, whites and blacks were equal on this indicator of life quality.

COMMENTS ON DEFENSES, ADAPTATIONS, AND COPING MECHANISMS

Evaluating oneself and one's own life situation is not an easy or comfortable process and it is easy to bias the assessment in one's favor. It is undoubtedly quite a strain to come up with a derogatory judgment and our data indicate that only a minority did. We can also get some insight into how people think about this evaluative process and how they cope with it.

It seems clear from our data that evaluation of "yourself" is fairly independent of the economic and social conditions in which one lives. Whether one is young or old, poor or rich, with a family or without, one's evaluation of oneself as an individual seems to be a private judgment not to be predicted from these circumstances. Knowing the social group characteristics of people gives one no toehold at all in predicting how they feel about themselves. Everyone does not feel good about themselves but self-worth is not a diploma or a dollar figure or an age bracket.[10]

It also appears from our data that people tend to see their own lives as better than most other people's lives. This may be partly a matter of ignorance, an attachment to the familiar, or, as attribution theory would suggest, a self-judgment that includes intentions, explanations, etc., while other people are judged on the sparser evidence of observable or intuited conditions. Whatever the process or reasons, "most people" are judged to be near the middle of the scale while the majority of individuals put themselves and their life circumstances above that point. With such a perspective it is certainly reasonable for most people to say that they are "pleased" or "mostly satisfied."

Optimism is another apparent phenomenon that keeps people from assimilating some of the sting of current conditions. Only the elderly seem to be accepting conditions as they are without expectations of future improvement. The pace or gradient of projected improvement does vary considerably from group to group and seems to be tempered by some realistic considerations, but the hope of better things is undoubtedly a help in one's acceptance of present circumstances.

Another factor that seems to account for much of the leveling of life evaluations over the years is a reduction in the range of swings from good to bad times as one gets older. Life's experiences or conditions are not as good nor as bad as they once were when one was younger. If one's life evaluations were a simple averaging this would lead to a moderately steady state, but it undoubtedly also includes some lowering of aspirations, as well as some ability to avoid stressful events or accommodate to them without the extremes of judgment that are felt by younger people.

These ways of coping with life's situations are obviously helpful to the individual and when they break down they are probably indicators of severe circumstances. It is a definition of "threat" to see life as getting worse in the future. To feel that most people's lives are better than one's own is to isolate

[10]It is interesting that, although the *mean* evaluations of "yourself" did not change from social group to social group in any significant way, there were differences in the *shapes of distributions* of self-evaluations that were related to certain group membership. On an index of skewness of a distribution, the closer the measure is to zero, the more symmetrical it is. Positive numbers indicate skewness (tail of curve) toward the low self-evaluation end of our scale; negative numbers indicate the tail of the distribution toward the high or positive end of the scale. The skewness index for evaluations of "yourself" by blacks was +.50, for young people +.10, for low SES +.28, and for high SES −.30. Thus, for instance, low-SES people tended to bunch their self-evaluations toward the "good" end *for that group*, while high-SES people tended to do the opposite, but the two groups ended up with the same average self-evaluation.

oneself somewhat from feelings of shared problems and mutual stresses. To devaluate one's own self because of environmental circumstances is to rob oneself of much that being human is supposed to allow. Obviously, these kinds of considerations must be taken account of in the process of understanding people's judgments about their lives and their experiences.

CHAPTER SUMMARY

The chapter presents data from twenty-four global measures that have been administered to one or more nationally representative samples of American adults. All of the measures involve assessments of Life-as-a-whole, some employing a very general evaluative dimension while other tap specific qualities such as satisfaction, happiness, or worries. Three evaluative perspectives are explored: evaluations of absolute position, of relative position, and of recent or expected changes.

The first part of the chapter focuses on how feelings about life-as-a-whole, evaluated on different dimensions and from different perspectives, were distributed in the American population. In an absolute sense, most people felt quite positive about their lives-as-a-whole. However, there were small proportions (a few percent) who placed themselves at or near the most negative positions of our scales, and only modest proportions (5–20 percent) put themsevles in the topmost categories. Thus, most people saw certain flaws in the quality of their lives, and a few (several hundred thousand out of the 140 million adults our samples represent) felt very negative indeed about the level of their well-being.

With respect to changes in global well-being, Americans on average felt that the present was slightly better than what prevailed five years ago, and that life five years hence would be considerably better than the present. However, not all Americans followed the "typical" pattern. One-third saw no net improvement in their lives in the past five years, and another 30 percent believed their well-being had actually declined. While relatively few expected declines in the coming five years, a substantial minority (34 percent) forsaw no net gains for themselves.

With respect to relative well-being, the "typical" American felt his or her own level of well-being was somewhat above the most commonly experienced level (suggesting an interesting bias in perception), and only a relatively small proportion of Americans (13 percent) thought their own level was even slightly below what was most common.

Distributions are also presented for eleven global measures assessing specific qualities of well-being, and the trends in these measures tend to be consistent with those just described for other assessments of Life-as-a-whole from an absolute perspective.

The second part of the chapter applies most of the global measures to twenty-seven social and demographic subgroups of the American population. These groups are defined on the basis of sex, age, socioeconomic status, stage in the family life-cycle, or race. Men and women showed no major differences on any measure of global well-being, and only with respect to the frequency of worrying was there even a modest difference (women reported worrying more frequently than men).

Comparing across increasing age groups, feelings about the absolute level of well-being remained essentially the same, as did feelings about relative well-being, and satisfaction with life. However, young people believed their well-being had risen more in the past five years and would rise more in the coming five years than did older people, and young people also tended to feel slightly happier. On the other hand, older people desired to make fewer changes in their lives and were less likely to experience big vacillations in feelings about their life situation.

Most of our measures showed substantial associations with socioeconomic status. As SES increased, feelings of general well-being—from both absolute and relative perspectives—increased, as did reports of satisfaction and happiness. High-status people thought they had experienced more progress in the past than low-status people thought they had made, and high-status people were more optimistic about the progress they would make in the future. Nevertheless, high-status people reported worrying just as frequently as did low-status people, and wanted to make just as many changes in their lives.

When the population was divided according to stage in the family life-cycle, two types of "splits" appeared. On most global measures, married people scored higher than unmarried, and unmarried people with children at home scored especially low; this was true for absolute well-being (including feelings of satisfaction and happiness), relative well-being, and people's feelings about improvements in well-being over the past five years. The other split, distinctively different from the first, emerged with respect to the frequency of worrying. Although differences were not large, the presence of children in the home, whatever their ages and whatever the marital status of the respondent, was associated with reports of more frequent worrying.

The final comparison reported in the chapter involves blacks and whites. From an absolute perspective, whites rated their general well-being, and also their satisfaction and happiness, higher than did blacks. Whites also rated their relative well-being higher than did blacks. But the races were about equal in their perceptions of how much net improvement they had experienced in the past five years and in the average frequency with which they reported worrying. As for the future, blacks expected to experience greater improvements in well-being than did whites. They also wanted to change more parts of their lives than did whites.

The chapter concludes with comments about defenses, adaptations, and coping mechanisms: psychological processes that may influence how people evaluate their lives. It is noted that ratings of "yourself" (as distinct from Life-as-a-whole) were quite independent of the economic and social conditions that defined the groups we compared; and it is suggested that being optimistic about the future, positively biased about one's current *relative* position, and able to avoid wide swings in reactions may be some of the ways people manage to justify their present level of well-being to themselves.

PART 3

FUTURE APPLICATIONS

CHAPTER 11

Applications

One of the major goals of our work has been to develop methods for measuring perceived well-being. To this end, preceding chapters have reported an extensive series of investigations designed to provide the fundamental knowledge that, hopefully, will lead the way toward better measurement methods. The quest is for measuring instruments, batteries of questionnaire or interview items, that are broad in their coverage of relevant concerns; that accurately reflect people's true feelings about these concerns; that are statistically efficient (in the sense of avoiding nonproductive redundancies); that are easy and economical to use; and that are sufficiently flexible that they can be tailored to the needs of particular applications and make good use of the resources available.

The uses and applications we foresee are the monitoring of perceived well-being over time, the comparison of findings on perceived well-being in one specific national population with results from other societies and cultures, and the inclusion of well-being measures in studies investigating other variables and interests. We believe that studying the quality of life, and particularly our approach to it via measures of perceived well-being, is feasible and worthwhile in its own right as an assessment of felt evaluations of spheres of living. But the topic and its problems are complex, and further studies that relate evaluations to other variables such as objective conditions, standards, contexts for judgment, and behaviors will further our comprehension.

The purpose of the present chapter is to consider the implications of our results for subsequent measurements of perceived well-being. Drawing upon our results and experiences, the chapter recommends a variety of specific measurement methods, and various batteries of items that would offer effective approaches under specified circumstances. The chapter also offers various suggestions about ways in which the best of the methods we have developed might be improved still further for subsequent applications. The chapter is intended as a guide to those who have responsibilities for designing either large-scale programs for monitoring life quality or one-time measurements, and who would like their designs to be enlightened by what we have learned.

We have argued that perceptions of well-being constitute centrally important components in the quality of the life that a person experiences. It should be noted, however, that we would not propose that perceptions of well-being provide the only useful data about well-being, nor would we propose that well-being is the only topic relevant to life quality. A large-scale program for monitoring life quality will include more than just well-being measures, and even among the well-being measures, we believe, there should be both assessments of people's perceptions and various nonperceptual data.

We suggest that a program designed to assess well-being would be most useful if it included both perceptual and nonperceptual social indicators relevant to the *same* concerns. For example, there might be information about people's affective evaluations of their housing and various "external" or "objective" information about the type, size, condition, and setting of each respondent's dwelling. Similarly, evaluations by the respondents of family income and standard of living would probably be more meaningful if coupled with information about the actual amount of that income, the respondents' current possessions, financial responsibilities, and the like. In short, we would envisage two parallel series of data: one assessing perceptions about well-being with respect to selected life concerns (and at the global levels as well); the other providing various nonperceptual data for the same concerns.

The research results reported in this book speak mainly to the design of instruments for assessing perceived well-being at what we have called the global and concern levels, and it is about these that we shall make specific recommendations. Although we will not consider other matters in detail, the results also have certain further implications for instrument design. If it is granted that the concerns we have identified as important merit inclusion in a social indicators program, then the topical coverage of many of the nonperceptual well-being measures is at least partly determined. In addition, for some of the concerns one might choose to explore people's perceptions regarding particular *components* or subconcerns.

Organization of the Chapter

The chapter consists of two main sections. One is devoted to matters of instrument design, the other to the analysis of the resulting data and its interpretation.

The instrument design section begins with a brief description of some of the parameters that will influence one's choices, and notes how each will affect the configuration of the final battery of items. The section then goes on to consider how such batteries might be assembled by selecting appropriate items at the concern level and at the global level, and by selecting effective response scales. A number of specific batteries of items, ranging from very small to moderately large, are proposed. The section concludes by suggesting how certain exhibits in preceding chapters might be used to develop still other batteries of items.

The second major section of the chapter assumes that the raw data on perceptions of well-being have been collected and considers how summary measures might be derived from them. Once such summary measures are available, the issue becomes one of utilization, and the section makes a number of suggestions regarding possible contexts and comparisons that can be used in interpreting the statistical results.

INSTRUMENT DESIGN

In this section of the chapter we assume that one wishes to assess the well-being perceived by a population, or perhaps well-being with respect to certain specific life aspects perceived by specified segments of a population, and that one is in search of suggestions on how to do it. The collection of data about perceptions usually requires some form of personal survey, usually by interview or questionnaire, and we assume that a survey operation is contemplated. This section suggests various possibilities for effective design of the survey instrument.

Parameters Affecting Instrument Design

The design of a survey instrument for assessing perceptions of well-being will be affected by several factors. These include the breadth of substantive interests of the primary users of the information, the resources that are available for data collection, the degree of precision required of the data, and the approach by which the data will actually be collected.

Substantive Interests. The substantive interests of the information users naturally exert a major impact on the coverage of the instrument. Other things equal, the more broad and heterogeneous those interests, the larger will be the number of items needed in the battery. Our own work has been oriented toward a very broad coverage of well-being, and when we come to propose specific batteries of items later in this chapter, it will be with the expectation that a broad coverage is desired. Nevertheless, some of our results can be usefully applied even when one's interests are more narrowly defined. For example, each of the major "regions" of the perceptual structure mapped in chapter 2—self, family, relations with other people, "economic" matters, the local community, and the larger society—includes within itself a variety of more specific concerns, most of which are tapped by several items. It would be quite possible to construct a battery of items by drawing from just a limited portion of the structure. Furthermore, the measurement methods we identified in chapter 6 as yielding the most sensitive measures of people's true feelings proved to work well for a wide variety of different concerns. We believe one could turn to these methods regardless of the breadth or narrowness of the desired coverage.

Resources. The resources available for data collection is another parameter that exerts a fundamental influence on instrument design. The amount of data to be collected is closely related to the time required to collect it, and time generally costs money. Given that the costs of survey interviewing can be very substantial, even when one depends upon the good will of the respondent and does not pay for the time he or she spends answering questions, it is very important that the data collection procedure be efficient. The procedures we have developed reflect a concern for efficiency. The general format of both questions and answers is standard and easily learned. The questions are short and direct and do not take long to read. The answers are easily arrived at and quickly conveyed.

We have found that with the techniques we have used, the average response time is about twelve to fifteen seconds per item with representative samples of American adults. In other words, the typical respondent can answer four or five of our items each minute. This assumes that the respondent is handed a card showing a modest number of response categories (e.g., the categories of the Delighted–Terrible Scale), and that a significant number of items can all be answered using the same set of categories (hence respondents become "trained" in the use of the answer scale). The figure does not include the approximately one minute required for the interviewer to read instructions at the beginning. These figures are for data collected through personal interviews; however, the experience we have with telephone interviews and group-administered questionnaires suggests that rates are not markedly different for those approaches, perhaps a little slower for the telephone interviews and a little faster for questionnaires.

Using this estimate of four to five items per minute, one can immediately determine the approximate length of the battery of items that could be administered with given resources. It is worth noting that rather substantial numbers of items can be answered in even sharply limited periods of time. Something of potential interest and usefulness can be accomplished in as little as three or four minutes, and by devoting even a modest part (e.g., ten or fifteen minutes) of a general purpose survey to assessment of perceived well-being, substantial information can be obtained.

Precision. Numerous factors affect the accuracy of one's data—the size of the sample, the skill with which the interviewing is done, the efforts at error control in the field and during the data processing stages, the measurement methods used, etc.—but here we wish to focus on the matter of multiple items. Within an item battery of a given length there is a trade-off between breadth of coverage and accuracy. In designing a measuring instrument one faces a range of options running from assessment of many different concerns with just a single item tapping each, to assessment of just a few concerns using many items for each one.

Since many single-item measures, including ours, include a mixture of valid variance and random error variance, and perhaps correlated error variance as well, through appropriate combination of items that tap the same phenomenon one can usually derive a multiple-item measure that includes a higher proportion of valid variance than any of its components. This happens because the common valid variance accumulates when the items are combined, while the random errors partially offset one another. The practical question is how many items should be combined, and results from chapter 6 can be used to provide some rather specific recommendations.

The general pattern is one of rapid gains in validity from combining the first few items, and markedly decreased gains thereafter. For example, given items that yield 65 percent valid variance, 8 percent correlated error variance, and 27 percent random error variance—which, as described in chapter 6, is the estimated composition of single item measures based on the Delighted–Terrible Scale in our July data—the first item yields 65 percent valid variance, a second similar item combined with it would raise the valid variance to 76 percent, a third similar item added to the pair would raise the figure to 79 percent, a fourth item would raise it to 81 percent, and a fifth item would raise it to 83 percent. Even combining an infinite number of similar items, if that were possible, would not raise the valid variance past 89 percent. Although the figures would differ for items having a different variance composition, the basic pattern remains essentially the same.

It follows that using two items to assess feelings about a given concern would be substantially better than just one, three would be somewhat better than two, but that rarely would it be worth using more than four items per concern. Our recommendation then is that when designing an instrument to assess perceptions of well-being, one include at least two and possibly three items per concern. Under austerity conditions one might use just a single item per concern, but even with substantial resources one would rarely need to use as many as four.

Methods of Data Collection. Another parameter that affects instrument design, particularly the length of the instrument, is the method by which the data will be collected. We have collected data on perceived well-being using four different methods: face-to-face interviews, telephone interviews, group-administered questionnaires, and mailed questionnaires. It may be useful to report our experiences with each.

The face-to-face interview is the most widely used method for collecting survey data from nationally representative samples of respondents. This has been the primary approach used by us and also by most others to assess subjective measures of life quality up to now, and probably this approach will continue to be frequently employed. Clearly, batteries of items intended to assess perceived well-being must be usable within this context. Our own work includes four batteries of items administered in face-to-face interviews (those administered to our May, November Form 1, November Form 2, and April respondents). The largest battery contained just over sixty concern-level items answered on the Delighted–Terrible Scale, plus about a dozen other items using other answer scales. Despite some initial hesitancy on the part of the interviewing staff, this relatively large battery went well. Respondents found the material interesting and apparently did not become overly fatigued. We suspect, however, that a battery much longer than this might begin to exceed the patience and attention span of some respondents.

The data from our July respondents were collected using group-administered questionnaires. Our experience with this method was very satisfactory, and we would recommend its use when one wants a large amount of data and it is feasible to bring respondents together. These respondents were given a lengthy questionnaire that consisted of about 640 questions and required about three hours to complete. Within the questionnaire, there was a core battery of somewhat more than a hundred concern-level items, all of which referred to the same D–T response scale. Despite its length, this questionnaire was administered without significant problems, and—as noted in chapter 6—yielded measures with some of the highest estimated validities we have encountered to date. Part of the success of this data collection undoubtedly resulted from the motivation of the respondents—they had been promised a modest payment for their time and had accepted an invitation to participate—and we would urge that this factor be carefully considered by others who may contemplate using a similar approach.

With our sample of several hundred October respondents, we tried a third method of data collection, telephone interviews. While attractive from an economic standpoint, the validity of the information obtained in telephone interviews may be somewhat lower than that collected by face-to-face interviews or group-administered questionnaires. Although the correctness of the validity estimates described in chapter 6 for our telephone interview data depends on more than the usual number of supporting assumptions, most of our estimates suggest that these data were somewhat less valid than the best of the measures generated by other data collection methods.

With respect to the mailed questionnaire method of data collection, we have only limited information. We did obtain a good response rate (over 80 percent), and much usable data from some five hundred people[1] to whom we mailed a questionnaire containing a battery of fourteen items to be answered using the D–T Scale. This suggests that the approach may be feasible. Although the estimated validity of the measures derived from these questionnaires was very low, this is probably because the respondents were not assessing their own well-being, but were giving estimates of how *another* person perceived his or her well-being. We do not have validity estimates for data collected by mailed questionnaires that can be usefully compared with estimates for data collected by other methods.

Specific Proposals on Instrument Design

In assembling a battery of items to assess perceived well-being, three very specific sets of decisions have to be made. One involves the particular concerns to be assessed and the items to use in assessing them; a second involves the global assessments to be made and the items to use for this purpose; the third involves what measurement method—i.e., response scale—to employ. We shall make recommendations about each of these.

Concern-Level Measures. By far the largest part of a battery assessing perceptions of well-being will probably be devoted to concern-level measures.

---

[1]These were the Other raters for our July respondents.

Hence, the number of concerns to be assessed, and the number of items used to assess each, will have major impacts on the total length of the battery.

Effective combinations of concern-level measures can be of almost any size, and this flexibility can be used to tailor the battery to the available resources. At one extreme, one can imagine an extensive collection of questions assessing thirty or forty different concerns and using several items to tap each one. This would provide a rather complete coverage of the total structure of well-being perceptions and would yield measures with close to the maximum achievable validity. At the other extreme, one can imagine a minimal collection using just single items to tap each of perhaps six concerns. Our data suggest that a mere half-dozen items, if properly chosen, could provide moderately valid coverage of the most essential aspects of the perceptual structure. We suspect that in most actual applications the number of concern-level items will fall somewhere between the hundred-odd items required for the "maxi" collection and the half-dozen of the "mini" collection.

Which items should one include? The results reported in chapters 2 and 4 provide a basis for recommending a variety of specific combinations of concern-level items that would yield statistically efficient and reasonably broad assessments of perceived well-being. Before proceeding to make such recommendations, however, we would note that our proposals are intended only as *examples* of reasonably effective instrument designs. The combinations of items we shall propose could be used in precisely the form we suggest, but there are also many possibilities for modification, some of which we shall note as we proceed.

Our general strategy for constructing potentially useful and statistically efficient combinations of concern-level items is to include items that tap a "sample" of concerns chosen to meet the following five criteria: (1) The concerns, taken jointly, should account for a substantial part of the variance in people's feelings about life-as-a-whole; (2) each concern individually should show some real relationship to feelings about life-as-a-whole;[2] (3) the concerns should cover the total structure of perceptions as completely as the available resources permit;[3] (4) the concerns should show minimum redundancy (i.e., covariation) with one another; and (5) the concerns should be of substantial interest from the standpoint of personal and/or societal decision-making.[4]

---

[2] The phrase "real relationship" here is meant to imply an association that is stronger than could be attributed merely to spurious overlaps caused by shared method effects. Chapter 6 includes a detailed discussion of method effects and other forms of correlated errors, and provides quantitative estimates of the magnitudes of them. Given that roughly 10 percent of the variance in measures based on the Delighted–Terrible Scale seems attributable to common method effects, correlations exceeding .10 between such measures probably show some "real relationship."

[3] Our proposals assume that one's basic purpose is to assess the full range of concerns. However, as noted previously in this chapter, if one's interests are more specifically focused, one could pick and choose from among the items relevant to just certain concerns and/or develop new items in the light of what we have found to be effective general formats.

[4] The analyses reported in preceding chapters provide information of direct relevance to the first four of these criteria. The fifth, relevance to personal or societal decision-making, depends on information that is beyond the intended scope of our present research. The accounting analyses presented in Exhibits 4.2 through 4.5 are particularly relevant to the first criterion in showing the extent numerous combinations of concerns jointly predict feelings about life-as-a-whole. The

One of the results of applying our strategy for "sampling" concerns is the combination identified in chapter 4 as the Selected 12 Concerns (see Exhibits 4.2 and 4.4). Included here are assessments of self, family, money, fun, housing, family activities, leisure time, leisure activities, national government, consumer services, health and job. As a set, these concerns meet the criteria we have specified reasonably well: They can jointly explain 50–60 percent[5] of the variance in feelings about life-as-a-whole, which is as much as can be explained by much larger sets of concerns and which is close to 100 percent of the variance potentially explainable with these less than perfectly valid measures; each of the concerns individually shows some relationship to life-as-a-whole beyond what could be attributed to common method effects; the concerns are reasonably well distributed throughout the perceptual structure; and most of these concerns are of substantial interest from a personal and/or social point of view. At a minimum, one would need twelve items to tap these twelve concerns, and the ones we would recommend are the following (item numbers refer to Exhibit 2.1): 21, 4, 83, 28, 87, 6, 38, 30, 106, 101, 7, and 75, respectively. If one wanted to use more items to tap each concern and thereby increase the validity of the assessments, additional items are also available for many of these concerns (as described in chap. 2), or could be easily developed. With twelve concerns being assessed, there would be few occasions when one would need more than a total of thirty-six concern-level items.

The Selected 12 Concerns were chosen at a middle phase of our research and reflect the items that had been developed and the state of our understanding of the perceptual structure at that time. Subsequently, additional items were developed, more data were collected, and further analyses were made. These now permit us to suggest several types of modifications.

One type of modification would be to maintain the present number of concerns but to substitute certain new ones for some of the existing ones. One could argue, for example, that the Selected 12 are somewhat redundant in the family and leisure areas, and a bit sparse with respect to interpersonal relationships and the local area: neighborhood, community, local government, and the like. Affective evaluations of interpersonal relationships and of the local area emerged as major and distinctive "regions" of the perceptual structure in some of our later analyses (see Exhibits 2.2 and 2.3, particularly). Given that the concerns having to do with family activities and leisure activities are not required for maintaining the predictive power of the combination (as shown in Exhibit 4.3), one could delete these from the Selected 12 and substitute the others we have suggested without detracting significantly from the ability of

---

bivariate relationships between individual concerns and feelings about life-as-a-whole, presented in Exhibits 4.1 and 5.1, are relevant to the second criterion. The structural maps of Exhibits 2.2 through 2.8 can be used to estimate the redundancy among concerns and the breadth of coverage provided by any particular combination and hence speak to criteria 3 and 4. These structural maps, particularly Exhibit 2.2, are also useful for identifying multiple items that are located close to one another in the perceptual structure and that might be used to tap the same concern.

[5]The explanatory power is 50 percent in the May national survey, 60 percent in the November national survey.

the combination to meet our first criterion, and these modifications would probably improve the combination with respect to the other criteria. At the single-item level of measurement, these modifications could be achieved by deleting items 6 and 30 from the preceding list and substituting items 90 and 54.

Another type of modification would be to reduce the number of concerns. The data in Exhibit 4.3 show that a mere six concerns—Self, Family, Money, Fun, Housing and National government—have essentially all the explanatory power possessed by the Selected 12. If one were operating with an austerity budget and needed a "mini" set of items, one could use the items 21, 4, 83, 28, 87, and 106 and meet the above criteria reasonably well. Of course, using more than just one item to assess each concern would increase the validity of measurement. This would require using a longer battery of items, but the number of concern-level items probably would not exceed eighteen.

Still a third type of modification would be to expand the number of concerns beyond those covered by the Selected 12, and here the possibilities are very numerous. Although this would not improve the combination with respect to the first criterion, since this criterion is met about as well as it can be even with a very modest number of concerns, it might be desirable for the sake of increasing the coverage of the structure and/or permitting the inclusion of additional concerns for their substantive interest. Exhibit 2.2 portrays thirty-four concerns, and since the boundary of where one concern begins and another ceases is itself somewhat arbitrary, modifying the way the items are clustered could either increase the number of concerns beyond thirty-four or reduce them below that number.

We will not take the space to list the specific items that might be used to assess the thirty-four concerns represented in Exhibit 2.2, as they can be determined from the exhibit itself. There is at least one item for each of the concerns identified there, and multiple items for many. However, if one wished to tap each concern by more than a single item certain new items would have to be developed. Of course, it would be important to demonstrate that any new items tapped the portion of the perceptual structure they were intended to.

As the number of concerns being assessed becomes quite large, they either become redundant or cease to be relevant to general well-being. Our second criterion is designed to ensure that the concerns selected for assessment have some relevance to well-being in general, and we have suggested that if there is no real relationship between a concern and feelings about life-as-a-whole, we believe a rather special reason would have to be present before its presence in a battery should be accepted. Although we believe that thirty-three of the thirty-four concerns shown in Exhibit 2.2 meet this second criterion, we would note that the relevance of one of them, Weather, seems doubtful, and that the relevance of one other, Traditions, seems marginal. (Exhibit 4.1 shows that these two concerns show relationships to life-as-a-whole that are little, if any, above the approximately .10 that one could attribute to common method effects.[6])

[6]Three other concerns from Exhibit 2.2 also show rather low relationships to Exhibit 4.1: Children, Taxes, and Own education. In these cases we suspect the low relationships are idiosyncracies of the July data, for Exhibit 4.1 shows higher relationships for these concerns in one or more national surveys.

Accordingly, we would not recommend that major attention be focused on these two concerns in most future assessments.

Before concluding this discussion on possible combinations of concern-level items, we would briefly consider the distinction between domain-type and criterion-type concerns. Our basic model of the process people use to evaluate their well-being (portrayed graphically in Exhibit 1.1) assumes that feelings about life-as-a-whole can be explained by either domains or criteria. The analyses reported in chapters 4 and 7 support this hypothesis, and it is now time to consider the implications of the finding for potential applications.

It happens that it is domains that fit more neatly with current ideas about what constitutes appropriate topics for assessment by social indicators, and it is domains that are chiefly (but not exclusively) represented in our Selected 12 Concerns and the several modifications we have suggested to that set. Should one consider the alternative possibility of building a battery consisting mainly of items that tap criterion-type concerns?

This is a possibility, but not one that we would recommend for general purposes. It is true that a combination of criterion-type items can be assembled that provides substantial predictions of feelings about life-as-a-whole, one of the elements in our strategy for "sampling" concerns. (Exhibit 4.5 shows numerous possible combinations and the predictive power of each.) It is also true that the criterion-type items with which we have experimented all show, on an individual basis, at least modest relationships to feelings about life-as-a-whole, the second element in our strategy. However, despite our explicit attempts to develop criterion items that would be widely heterogeneous and only modestly redundant, it turns out that these items are substantially more interlinked than are domain-type items (as can be seen by comparing Exhibits 2.7 and 2.8). Furthermore, when domains and criteria are plotted in the same multidimensional space (Exhibit 2.2), the criterion-type items prove to be distributed much less widely. We conclude that criterion-type items, at least those we have developed, cannot, by themselves, provide a statistically efficient coverage of the entire structure of perceptions about well-being. These items are of considerable theoretical interest, and certain of them may have substantial application potential as well, but we would not advocate a general purpose battery based on them alone.

Global Measures. Many investigations of perceived well-being will appropriately include certain assessments of life-as-a-whole. Although this concept is probably too global to contribute directly to many decisions about specific social policies, people's evaluations of their life-as-a-whole are of fundamental interest in their own right and provide a direct summary measure that can be achieved only artificially with nonperceptual indicators.

The presence of summary measures about life-as-a-whole within a data set permits one to assess the perceived "relevance" of whatever concerns have been assessed. If one can demonstrate a substantial relationship between feelings about a particular concern and assessments about life-as-a-whole, the potential importance of that concern is immediately established. On the other hand, if the relationship between a concern and life-as-a-whole turns out to be essentially zero, the usefulness of focusing extended attention on that concern is, at the least, called into question.

Results presented in chapters 3 and 5 lead to a number of recommendations about what global measures to include in a battery assessing perceived well-being. Most useful, we believe, would be the inclusion of at least one Type A measure;[7] i.e., an assessment of the respondent's own life-as-a-whole from an absolute perspective and using the full range of a very general evaluative dimension. These measures seem to come closest to providing a single numerical estimate of the affective and evaluative feelings a person has toward life-as-a-whole. Chapter 5 suggests that it is the phenomenon tapped by the Type A measures that people's affective evaluations of various life concerns "sums" to, and chapter 3 shows that reasonably equivalent Type A measures can be achieved by a variety of measurement methods.

In line with our earlier observation that the validity of measurement is substantially enhanced if two or three items are used to tap each phenomenon of interest, we would here suggest that two or three items be included in the battery as a basis for constructing a Type A global measure. If the D–T Scale were being used as the basic measurement method, one could follow our practice in using Life 1 and Life 2 as the elements from which Life 3 was constructed. (See measures G1, G2, and G3, respectively, in Exhibit 3.1.) We put Life 1 early in our batteries (usually the second item, on the supposition that the first item should be very easy and relatively unimportant), and we put Life 2 near or at the very end of the battery. The intervening items between the two global ones required at least five to ten minutes (more in some batteries), and under these circumstances asking a nearly identical question twice did not seem to bother the respondents.

Although we would give first priority to a Type A global measure, if resources permitted other global assessments, it might prove useful to expand the set somewhat. We would not recommend any of the Type B (part-range) measures, as these seem to involve a difficult and perhaps psychologically artificial judgment for the respondents. However, several of the Type C measures, which tap the extent to which people hold certain specific feelings toward their lives-as-a-whole, have historically and/or conceptually interesting pedigrees. Measures G32, seven-point Happiness, could be easily included within a battery employing the D–T Scale, and it should be no problem to use the same item wording with other response scales. An alternative assessment of happiness is measure G31, three-point Happiness; this has a long history of use with samples of American adults. Bradburn's measures of Positive Affect, Negative Affect, and Affect Balance (measures G35, G36, and G37) are interesting from a conceptual standpoint and were well received by respondents. Generating them, however, requires a special battery of ten items (described in Exhibit 3.1). For other specific feelings about life-as-a-whole, one might consider measures G39 to G48 in Exhibit 3.1. Within this set, measures G39 to G41 and

---

[7]The typology of global measures referenced here and in following paragraphs is fully described in chapter 3.

G43 to G44 were administered by Campbell, Converse, and Rodgers (1976) to their sample of American adults in 1971, and also by us to another nationally representative sample in 1972 (our May respondents), with results described in previous chapters.

Among our Type D global measures—those that tap people's sense of how their well-being compares to that of other people—our Measure G50, Much better, was among those judged most promising in chapter 3. Among the Type D measures included in Exhibit 5.4, this was the one that showed the highest relationships to the concern measures. Hence if one were going to include just a single Type D global measure, our recommendations would be to use Much better (G50). If one wanted a second but slightly different item to tap essentially the same underlying concept, measure G49, Better than everyone, provides an excellent candidate. On the other hand, if one wanted to tap a quite different concept, measure G55, Uniqueness, might be considered. As noted in chapter 3, Uniqueness seemed quite distinct from all of the other Type D measures, and as described in chapter 5, this was the one global measure that gave even a hint of showing a pattern of relationships to the concern measures that was different from the "basic" pattern shown by all other global measures.

The Type E global measures all employ a long-term change perspective and are potentially interesting, at least in part, precisely because they have shown only rather weak associations with assessments of current well-being at either the global or concern levels (as described in chaps. 3 and 5). The Type E measures apparently tap feelings about well-being that are distinctly different from those tapped by the Type A measures. All of the Type E global measures we have used are based on the Ladder Scale, and chapter 6 notes that this measurement method seems to yield somewhat less valid indications of people's feelings than certain others. Hence our recommendation would be to use items with essentially the same wording as measures G64 and G65 (Ladder: five years ago, and Ladder: five years hence, respectively), which together with Measure G6 (Ladder: whole life) were the basis of our long-term change measures; but to move away from the Ladder format and use the D–T, Faces, or Circles Scales instead. (We remind the reader that chapter 3 concludes that one of the Type E measures we constructed—measure G58, Progress past and future—seemed not to represent any psychological reality and should probably be avoided in the future.)

None of the Type F global measures (short-term change) showed much association with other indications of well-being. Arguments for including any of these measures in a battery assessing life quality would have to be made on other grounds. Of the Type F measures, G62, Variation in feelings, seems the most promising.

The Type G global measures are a miscellaneous set, none of which provides a direct assessment of the respondent's current well-being. We have already mentioned G64 and G65, assessments of well-being five years ago and five years hence, in connection with our comments on the long-term change measures. The remaining three measures in this group, two assessments of others' well-being and an indication of the respondent's desire to make changes in his own life, would probably require a rather special justification before they would merit inclusion in a general purpose battery.

Response Scales. Our recommendations regarding response scales have already been made, and we have here only to remind the reader of what is presented in greater detail in chapter 6.

If one were going to use an existing verbal scale, we feel that the Delighted–Terrible Scale would be best. It produces measures that have as high an estimated validity as those from any other scale we have investigated and that are higher than derived from most of the other methods. It employs explicitly labeled categories. It is easy to use. And its distributions, though they tend to show some clustering at the positive end, permit substantial discriminations among respondents.

Chapter 6 also contains some ideas about possible modifications to the existing Delighted–Terrible Scale that might provide still finer discriminations among the group of people who describe themselves as being "Pleased" or "Mostly satisfied," a group that is of substantial size for many concerns.

If one wanted to use a graphic (i.e., nonverbal) scale, our recommendations are the Circles or Faces Scales. Like the D–T Scale, both of these yield measures with relatively high validities and both employ explicitly labeled categories. While these scales are quite usable in their present forms, chapter 6 suggests ways to achieve possible improvements. The Circles Scale might be made easier to use by employing colors or shadings in place of the present plus and minus symbols. The discriminatory power of the Faces Scale at the positive end might be enhanced by substituting three categories for what are now two near the positive end, the present second and third categories.[8]

Whenever one considers modifying a scale that has already been used to generate significant bodies of data, one must consider the benefits possibly gained relative to the added difficulty of comparing the new results with prior ones. When such comparisons are of crucial importance for the analysis and/or interpretation of the data, it may be desirable to forgo an uncertain and at most modest gain for the sake of being able to make a rigorous and true comparison.

When it *does* seem desirable to employ a modified version of a scale, the comparison problem can be at least partially solved by "splicing" the new data to the old. It is often possible to employ both the original and modified versions of a scale to the same respondents, or to equivalent samples of respondents, in order to determine how results from one version of the scale translate into those of the other version. (Chapter 7 provides such translations between the D–T, Circles and Ladder Scales, though it does not include data for any of the proposed modifications to these scales.)

ANALYSIS AND INTERPRETATION

A well-designed instrument for assessing perceptions of well-being, when administered to a set of respondents, generates information—a substantial

[8] If a supplementary category were added near the positive end of the Faces Scale, one also might wish to add a category near the negative end to preserve the symmetry of the scale.

amount of information if the battery of items is lengthy and/or the respondents are numerous. Nearly always the amount of information will be too much to comprehend in its raw state, and some forms of data reduction and analysis will be needed. This section of the chapter suggests analyses that may be appropriate and a few of the ways those analyses may subsequently be interpreted.

Measure Construction and Analysis

Earlier in the chapter we recommend using two or three items to assess feelings about life-as-a-whole, or about any particular concern, in order to increase the validity of measurement. If such multiple assessments are included in the battery, one of the first analysis tasks will be to construct the desired summary measures. Two issues should be addressed: Would it be appropriate to form a single measure by combining the items that were expected to tap the same phenomenon? If so, how should the combination be made?

Answering the first question requires examining the pattern of relationships among the items. If one has the time and resources, perceptual maps, similar to those presented in chapter 2, might be obtained. These would be interesting for a number of reasons. They would show whether items intended to tap the same concern in fact clustered closely together; they would show how any newly developed items fitted in with items that had been used previously; and they would enable one to compare the form and organization of the perceptual structure from the new group of respondents with that from prior groups. Even if a full perceptual mapping were not feasible, however, it would be desirable to check whether the items intended to tap the same concern showed substantial covariation. One would hope to find stronger associations between them than between items intended to tap different concerns, and if this condition were grossly violated it would probably be inappropriate to make the planned item combinations.

Once one has determined that it is appropriate to combine certain items, there arises the practical question of how this is to be done. Our practice, and the one we would recommend, has been to compute a simple mean of the answers given by each respondent to the relevant items. Since we have found that all items pertaining to the same phenomenon (if they use the same response scale) tend to have approximately the same variance, this procedure results in the items making approximately equal contributions to the final measure; i.e., being equally weighted. Use of the mean keeps the new scores on the same scale as the original answers, which makes it possible to tie a given numerical result directly to the meanings of the categories chosen by the respondents. Use of this procedure also facilitates the handling of "missing data" cases: The respondent can be assigned a score on the measure even if some of the data are missing. (Our practice has been to use the mean if at least half the data are present; if less than half are present we would assign the respondent to a missing data category on the new measure.)

Once the items have been combined into various global- and concern-level measures, one would probably want to obtain a variety of descriptive statistics:

means, variances, percentage distributions, etc. These can be computed for one's total set of respondents and perhaps also for various subgroups within it. To examine how the concern measures, both individually and in various combinations, relate to feelings about life-as-a-whole, one may also wish to perform some accounting analyses along the lines of those presented in chapters 4 and 5. If, in addition to the information about perceptions of well-being, one has other data about conditions that characterize the lives of the respondents (as we have suggested might form an optimal design for an investigation of the quality of life), one will probably wish to relate the respondents' affective evaluations of given concerns to life conditions that pertain to those same concerns.

Interpretation Perspectives

The computations one performs, as well as the interpretive efforts one undertakes, of course depend on one's purposes. Information about people's perceptions of well-being is potentially useful for a variety of reasons. It can help in identifying social problems and sensitizing decision-makers and citizens to particular needs; it can help set social goals and priorities; it can contribute evidence relevant for evaluating the effectiveness of particular social programs; it can inform policymakers and "the people" about the nature of their society (or community, organization, region, etc.) and the trends occurring within it; and it may provide some of the raw material from which a better ability to predict future changes can be developed.

Information from the types of measures we have proposed lends itself to a number of interpretive perspectives. Perhaps the simplest of these focuses on the distribution of evaluations about a single life concern. Percentage distributions showing what proportion of the whole population hold given feelings about a particular concern, such as the distributions presented in chapter 8, are of very considerable descriptive interest in their own right. From the basic distribution one can determine the average feeling about a particular life concern, what proportion of the population feels more (or less) positive than some predetermined value, and to what extent people have similar (or different) feelings about that concern. Of course, information about the distribution, central tendency, and dispersion of feelings can be based either on answers to single interview items or, as suggested previously in this chapter, on cluster scores derived by combining answers to several items.

Interpretive possibilities become much broader when one incorporates one or more of the comparisons that seem especially relevant for social indicators. These are comparisons pertaining to (1) different occasions, (2) different population groups, and/or (3) different life concerns. These three bases for comparison, taken one at a time or in various combinations, yield a rich series of interpretive possibilities for social indicator data.

One-time measures gain in value when they are *repeated* so one has knowledge of the direction and magnitude of shift in public response. If one chose, one could compute a derived social indicator from the more basic data

354   FUTURE APPLICATIONS

that would show the mean change in evaluations about a given concern, expressed either as the amount of absolute change on a certain scale, or as the percentage of change from some baseline date when the question was first asked or when particular social conditions existed. Change measures are not limited to changes in the level of satisfaction; one might also be interested in changes in the degree of consensus (i.e., dispersion) in feelings about a particular life concern.

The data in Part 2 of this book showing perceived well-being on a wide range of concerns for representative samples of American adults could contribute to this type of comparison. If a new study were conducted using methods comparable to ours, or using methods that lend themselves to suitable "translation," the new results could be compared with the figures we obtained for the 1972–73 period. Our data are not the only sources of information about perceptions of well-being from representative samples of Americans, but we believe our figures cover a wider range of concerns and are derived by a more sensitive measurement approach than other figures that are currently available.

The *disaggregation* of national data so information is available for one or another social group is a second way to greatly increase interpretive possibilities and potentials for social understanding. The comparison of group means, as in chapters 9 and 10, gives an indication of the differential conditions that are associated with one or another sector of the social structure. Here also, one might be interested in examining dispersions in feelings as well as mean levels of satisfaction, and a comparison of social groups might well focus on differences in dispersion as well as differences in levels.

By combining these first two bases of comparison, differences between occasions and differences between social groups, one generates still richer interpretive possibilities. Changes in the magnitudes of differences among social groups could serve as important indicators of shifting social conditions. (The data presented in Part 2 of this book may prove useful for documenting changes among social groups. Data are presented for groups defined on the basis of sex, age, race, socioeconomic status, and stages in the family life-cycle.[9])

Affective evaluations of life concerns, if made on a standard response scale, can also be interpreted in the light of *differences between concerns*. This is the third base for comparison mentioned previously. For many practical issues having to do with problem identification and setting of social priorities, as well as for more abstract purposes oriented toward the search for greater social understanding, it is important to know the relative positions of different concerns in people's evaluation hierarchies.

This possibility of combining across concerns can be combined with either of the two previous bases of comparison, across occasions or across social

[9]Although we have not published descriptive statistics for other groupings of the American population, numerous other classifications could be made. The basic data are publicly archived in the Social Science Archive, Institute for Social Research, University of Michigan, Box 1248, Ann Arbor, Michigan 48106, USA. Inquiries can be addressed to the archive, which is prepared to either perform desired tabulations and/or distribute raw data and appropriate documentation.

groups. Examining differences between social groups in the relative positions they assign to given concerns would provide much information about both the groups and the concerns. And a consideration of changes over time in the relative positions of particular concerns would tell much about the nature and direction of social change.

Finally, there stands the attractive possibility of utilizing all three bases for comparison simultaneously. At this level of complexity one could address, in a broad, detailed, and sophisticated way, some of the most fundamental issues implicit in the social indicators movement. One might hope to identify certain indicators that "lead" and others that "lag" in the change process. And one might hope for significant increases in understanding about the maintenance, increase, decrease, and redistribution of well-being.

CHAPTER SUMMARY

One of the major goals of our work has been to develop methods for measuring perceived well-being. This chapter considers how our research results can be applied to yield measuring instruments (i.e., batteries of survey items) that are broad in coverage, sensitive to people's true feelings, statistically efficient, easy and economical to use, and with sufficient flexibility that they can be tailored to particular needs and resources. Although our recommendations focus on the design of instruments for assessing perceptions of well-being, a comprehensive quality-of-life instrument might also include a parallel series of nonperceptual measures of well-being and assessments of selected other aspects of life quality as well.

At least four general parameters have an impact on the design of the measuring instrument. One is the substantive interests of the people who will use the data. Although the orientation of our investigations, and the focus of the present recommendations, assume one is interested in well-being in general, much of what we have found can also be applied to the design of instruments assessing just a few specific aspects of well-being.

A second parameter is the amount of interviewing time that can be supported with the available resources. The items and response scales we have developed are designed to make efficient use of whatever time may be available, and experience shows that the typical respondent answers our items at the rate of four or five per minute. Thus, it follows that one can collect evaluations of a substantial number of different aspects of life in rather modest time.

A third parameter affecting instrument design is the precision desired. One way to increase the validity of measurement is to use more than one item to tap the respondents' feelings about a given phenomenon. Given the estimates reported in chapter 6 for the validity and reliability of our measures, substantial gains in precision can be achieved by using two or three items for each phenomenon, but rarely would it be justified to use as many as four.

A fourth parameter is the method of data collection. Using face-to-face interviews, we have administered batteries containing up to sixty concern-level items to nationally representative samples and obtained reasonably high validities with no significant problems. With well-motivated respondents, a battery almost double this length was successfully used in a group-administered questionnaire format. It also yielded measures with relatively high validities. Our experience with telephone interviews, on the other hand, suggests this method may yield measures with somewhat lower validities.

In assembling a battery of items to assess perceived well-being, three specific sets of decisions have to be made. These relate to the particular concerns to be assessed and the items to use in assessing them, the global aspects to be measured and the items to use for this, and what response scale(s) to use. The chapter makes specific recommendations on each of these matters.

Our strategy for selecting the concerns to be assessed includes five elements: The concerns should jointly account for a substantial part of the variation in feelings about life-as-a-whole; each concern should show an individual relationship to life-as-a-whole, the concerns should tap all major portions of the structure of well-being perceptions; the concerns should be minimally redundant; and the concerns should be of substantive interest from a personal and/or societal perspective. Findings presented in chapters 2, 4, and 5 have relevance to the first four of these criteria. One of the results of applying this selection strategy is the Selected 12 Concerns described in chapter 4. The present chapter discusses various possible modifications to the Selected 12—some involving substitutions of new concerns for old, others involving deletion of some concerns, others involving additions—and recommends items that might be used to measure each or notes where relevant items can be found in preceding chapters.

The inclusion of one or more global measures of perceived well-being in a battery generates certain summary information that is of substantial interest in its own right, which is difficult to derive from nonperceptual measures, and which helps one assess the relevance of particular concerns. Chapters 3 and 5 present various results that can be used to help decide which global measures to include in a battery. Our recommendation is to include at least one Type A measure (an assessment of life-as-a-whole made from an absolute perspective and involving the full range of a very general evaluative dimension), and various means of achieving this are suggested. The chapter also identifies the more promising measures of Types C, D, E, and F, and notes that measures of Types B and G could be omitted from most general purpose batteries.

With respect to the selection of response scales, we recommend use of the Delighted–Terrible Scale, if one wants a verbal scale, or either the Circles or Faces Scale, if a graphic scale is desired, for reasons that are detailed in chapter 6. Minor modifications to these scales (also described in chap. 6) might make them still better, but if comparisons to existing data are important the gains from the modifications may not be sufficient to justify the added difficulties when making the comparisons.

Once a battery of items has been administered to a set of respondents, one of the first analytic tasks will usually be to construct the desired measures. If the battery includes several items intended to tap the same phenomenon, one should check to see whether one would be justified in combining them and then, if so, actually make the combination; specific procedures are suggested. With the desired measures in hand, one can proceed to compute various descriptive, accounting, and other analytic statistics.

The statistics one actually computes, of course, depend on one's purposes, which might include the following: identifying social problems, sensitizing decision-makers and citizens to particular needs, helping to set social goals and priorities, contributing evidence relevant for evaluating the effectiveness of social programs, informing policymakers and "the people" about the nature of their society and trends occurring within it, and/or developing the means for predicting future changes. Whatever one's purpose, the interpretation of the data is likely to involve making comparisons between different groups of people, between different life concerns, and/or between different times. For making comparisons between different groups of people and/or different concerns, one can turn to various national baseline data, including some from our own surveys, or generate "internal" comparisons within one's own data. Unfortunately, there is as yet not much information on which to base comparisons between different times, though as this begins to accumulate it promises to contribute to our understanding of various issues having to do with changes in well-being.

APPENDIXES

APPENDIX A

Interview and Questionnaire Schedules

This appendix presents the most relevant portions of the interview and questionnaire schedules from which the data in this book were obtained. The selected portions of the several questionnaires appear in this appendix in the following order:

Interview used with May respondents, pages 362 to 364
Interview used with November Form 1 respondents, pages 365 to 366
Interview used with November Form 2 respondents, pages 367 to 369
Interview used with April respondents, pages 370 to 372
Questionnaire used with July respondents, pages 373 to 387

The complete interview schedules administered to the national samples and/or the complete questionnaire administered to the July respondents can be obtained for a modest processing charge from the Social Science Archive, Institute for Social Research, The University of Michigan, Box 1248, Ann Arbor, Michigan 48106, U.S.A. Each of the national survey interview schedules was about sixty pages in length, and the questionnaire administered to the July respondents was about one hundred pages.

I feel:

[1]	[2]	[3]	[4]	[5]	[6]	[7]
Delighted	Pleased	Mostly Satisfied	Mixed (about equally satisfied and dissatisfied)	Mostly Dissatis- fied	Unhappy	Terrible

[A] Neutral (neither satisfied nor dissatisfied)

[B] I never thought about it

[C] Does not apply to me

I think my life is::

BORING	[1]	[2]	[3]	[4]	[5]	[6]	[7]	INTERESTING
ENJOYABLE	[1]	[2]	[3]	[4]	[5]	[6]	[7]	MISERABLE
USELESS	[1]	[2]	[3]	[4]	[5]	[6]	[7]	WORTHWHILE
FRIENDLY	[1]	[2]	[3]	[4]	[5]	[6]	[7]	LONELY
FULL	[1]	[2]	[3]	[4]	[5]	[6]	[7]	EMPTY
DISCOURAGING	[1]	[2]	[3]	[4]	[5]	[6]	[7]	HOPEFUL
DISAPPOINTING	[1]	[2]	[3]	[4]	[5]	[6]	[7]	REWARDING
BRINGS OUT THE BEST IN ME	[1]	[2]	[3]	[4]	[5]	[6]	[7]	DOESN'T GIVE ME MUCH CHANCE

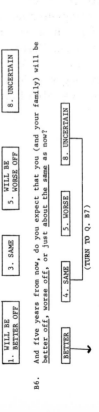

SECTION B: ECONOMIC ATTITUDES

B1. We are interested in how people are getting along financially these days. Would you say that you (and your family) are better off or worse off financially than you were a year ago?

1. BETTER NOW →   3. SAME →   5. WORSE NOW →   8. UNCERTAIN

B2. Why do you say so? _____

B3. Are you (and your family) making as much money now as you were a year ago, or more, or less?

1. MORE NOW   3. ABOUT THE SAME   5. LESS NOW

B4. Now thinking back five years, would you say you (and your family) are better off or worse off financially now than you were five years ago?

BETTER →   4. SAME   5. WORSE   8. UNCERTAIN

B4a. Would you say that you were much better off now or a little better off?

1. MUCH BETTER   2. LITTLE BETTER   3. UNCERTAIN

B5. Now looking ahead - do you think that a year from now you (and your family) will be better off financially, or worse off, or just about the same as now?

1. WILL BE BETTER OFF   3. SAME   5. WILL BE WORSE OFF   8. UNCERTAIN

B6. And five years from now, do you expect that you (and your family) will be better off, worse off, or just about the same as now?

BETTER →   4. SAME   5. WORSE   8. UNCERTAIN

(TURN TO Q. B7)

B6a. Would you say that you expect to be much better off or a little better off?

1. MUCH BETTER   2. LITTLE BETTER   3. UNCERTAIN

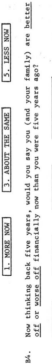
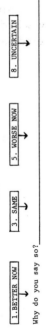

Time now is: _____

In the next section of this interview we want to find out how you feel about parts of your life, and life in this country as you see it. Please tell me the feelings you have now--taking into account what has happened in the last year and what you expect in the near future.

I am going to be asking about a long list of things. (HAND R CARD 4) so just tell me what number on this card gives the best summary of how you feel, "one" for delighted, "two" for pleased, and so forth on to "seven" for you feel terrible about it. If you have no feelings at all on the question, tell me letter "A." If you have never thought about something that I ask you, and this probably will not happen, then tell me letter "B." And I may ask you a question that doesn't apply to you, if so tell me letter "C." Let's try an easy one first. (WRITE NUMBER OR LETTER IN BOX TO LEFT OF EACH QUESTION)

D1. How do you feel about your car? ☐

D2. Now a very general one: How do you feel about your life as a whole? (DO NOT ACCEPT "C" AS AN ANSWER) ☐

D3. How do you feel about your house/apartment? (NO "C") ☐

How do you feel about . . .

D4. The services you get in this neighborhood--like garbage collection, street maintenance, fire and police protection ☐

D5. The outdoor space there is for you to use outside your home (NO "C") ☐

D6. This particular neighborhood as a place to live (NO "C") ☐

D7. This community as a place to live (NO "C") ☐

D8. Outdoor places you can go in your spare time (NO "C") ☐

D9. The weather in this part of the state (NO "C") ☐

D10. How safe you feel in this neighborhood (NO "C") ☐

D11. The way you spend your spare time, your non-working activities (NO "C") ☐

D12. The things you do and the times you have with your friends (NO "C") ☐

D13. Things you do to help people or groups in this community ☐

D14. Your marriage ☐

D15. The things you and your family do together ☐

D16. Your housework--the work you need to do around your home (NO "C") ☐

How do you feel about . . .

D17. Your religious faith ☐

D18. Your job (IF "C," SKIP TO D24) ☐

D19. The people you work with--your co-workers ☐

D20. The work you do on your job--the work itself ☐

D21. The pay and fringe benefits you get, and security of your job ☐

D22. What it is like where you work--the physical surroundings, the hours, and the amount of work you are asked to do ☐

D23. What you have available for doing your job--I mean equipment, information, good supervision, and so on ☐

D24. The people who live in the houses/apartments near yours (NO "C") ☐

D25. People who live in this community (NO "C") ☐

D26. The people you see socially ☐

D27. The organizations you belong to ☐

D28. Your wife/husband ☐

D29. Your children ☐

D30. Close adult relatives--I mean people like parents, in-laws, brothers and sisters ☐

D31. The way young people in this country are thinking and acting (NO "C") ☐

D32. The way people over 40 in this country are thinking and acting (NO "C") ☐

D33. How do you feel about yourself? (NO "C") ☐

D34. Your own health and physical condition (NO "C") ☐

D35. How you get on with other people (NO "C") ☐

D36. The responsibilities you have for members of your family ☐

D37. The way you handle the problems that come up in your life (NO "C") ☐

D38. What you are accomplishing in your life (NO "C") ☐

D39. How much fun you are having (NO "C") ☐

How do you feel about . . .

D40. The amount of time you have for doing the things you want to do (NO "C")

D41. The chance you have to know people with whom you can really feel comfortable (NO "C")

D42. The way other people treat you (NO "C")

D43. The goods and services you can get when you buy in this area-- things like food, appliances, clothes (NO "C")

D44. The services you can get when you have to have someone come in to fix things around your home--like painting, repairs (NO "C")

D45. The doctors, clinics, and hospitals you would use in this area (NO "C")

D46. The way you can get around to work, schools, shopping, etc. (NO "C")

D47. The sports or recreation facilities you yourself use, or would like to use--I mean things like parks, bowling alleys, beaches

D48. The schools in this area (NO "C")

D49. The usefulness, for you personally, of your education (NO "C")

D50. The income you (and your family) have (NO "C")

D51. Your standard of living--the things you have like housing, car, furniture, recreation, and the like (NO "C")

D52. What you have to pay for basic necessities such as food, housing, and clothing (NO "C")

D53. The taxes you pay--I mean the local, state, and national taxes all together (NO "C")

D54. The condition of the natural environment--the air, land, and water in this area (NO "C")

D55. The way the police and courts in this area are operating (NO "C")

D56. The way your local government is operating (NO "C")

D57. The way our national government is operating (NO "C")

D58. What our government is doing about the economy--jobs, prices, profits (NO "C")

D59. Our national military activities (NO "C")

How do you feel about . . .

D60. The way our political leaders think and act (NO "C")

D61. How the United States stands in the eyes of the rest of the world (NO "C")

D62. The information you get from newspapers, magazines, TV, and radio (NO "C")

D63. The entertainment you get from TV, radio, movies, and local events and places (NO "C")

D64. Life in the United States today (NO "C")

D65. And now the last one. How do you feel about your life as a whole? (NO "C")

Here are some words you might use to describe your present life. (HAND R CARD 5) For example, if you think your present life is very "boring," just tell me number "one." If you think it is very "interesting," tell me number "seven." If you think it is somewhere in between, (POINT TO IN BETWEEN NUMBERS) then tell me the number you think is about right. (WRITE NUMBER IN BOX TO LEFT OF EACH QUESTION)

D66. Do you feel your present life is boring, interesting, or some number in between?

D67. Is it enjoyable, miserable, or somewhere in between?

D68. Useless or worthwhile?

D69. Full or empty?

D70. Disappointing or rewarding?

D71. Taking all things together, how would you say things are these days-- would you say you're very happy, pretty happy, or not too happy these days?

| 1. VERY HAPPY | 3. PRETTY HAPPY | 5. NOT TOO HAPPY |

Time now is: _____

CARD K1

"FEELING" THERMOMETER

WARM

100°	Very warm or favorable feeling
85°	Good warm or favorable feeling
70°	Fairly warm or favorable feeling
60°	A bit more warm or favorable than cold feeling
50°	No feeling at all
40°	A bit more cold or unfavorable feeling
30°	Fairly cold or unfavorable feeling
15°	Quite cold or unfavorable feeling
0°	Very cold or unfavorable feeling

COLD

K3. While we have the feeling thermometer in front of us, what about your own life? Where would you put your life as a whole these days on the feeling thermometer?

_____
(RATING)

S: FEELINGS ABOUT LIFE

In the next section of this interview I will be asking how you feel about your life, and life in this country. Please tell me the feelings you have now-- taking into account what has happened in the last year and what you expect in the near future.

(CARD S1, ORANGE) Most of the questions can be answered by telling me what number on this card comes closest to how you feel: "one" for delighted, "two" for pleased, and so forth on to "seven" for terrible. If one of the questions doesn't seem to fit the way you think, you can tell me "A" to indicate that you can't answer that particular question.

I FEEL:

1	2	3	4	5	6	7
DELIGHTED	PLEASED	MOSTLY SATISFIED	MIXED (ABOUT EQUALLY SATISFIED AND DISSATISFIED)	MOSTLY DISSATIS-	UNHAPPY	TERRIBLE

A I CAN'T ANSWER THAT QUESTION

S1. First, a very general question: How do you feel about your
    _____   life as a whole?

S2. Now, try and forget all the things in your life that annoy
    _____   or worry you; how do you feel about the good and pleasant
                 parts of your life? How do these nice aspects, by themselves,
                 make you feel?

S3. Now do the opposite--try and forget all the good and pleasant
    _____   parts of your life; how do you feel about the things that annoy
                 or worry you? How do these poor aspects, by themselves, make
                 you feel?

S5. (CARD S1, ORANGE) Now here are some questions on how you feel about parts of your life. Like before, just tell me the number on the card which gives the best idea of how you feel.

S5a. How do you feel about your house/apartment?

S5b. Thinking only of your own needs, how do you feel about your house/apartment?

S5c. With your values of what is appropriate or fair, how do you feel about your house/apartment?

S5d. Considering what your house/apartment takes in money, time and energy, how do you feel about the house/apartment?

S5e. Thinking of what it would take to move to another dwelling or change this one, how do you feel about your present house/apartment?

S5f. How do you think most people would feel about your house/apartment?

S5g. Thinking of your age and position in life, how do you feel about your house/apartment?

S6. Now let's shift to another part of your life.

S6a. How do you feel about what you are accomplishing in your life?

S6b. Considering just yourself and your own needs, how do you feel about what you are accomplishing in life?

S6c. With your values of what is appropriate or fair, how do you feel about what you are accomplishing in life?

S6d. How do you feel about what you are accomplishing in life considering the resources of money, time and energy you're putting into it?

S6e. Thinking of what it would take to change what you are accomplishing, how do you feel about what you are accomplishing in life?

S6f. How do you think most people would feel about what you are accomplishing in your life?

S6g. Thinking of your age and position in life, how do you feel about what you are accomplishing in life?

7. Here's the last set of these kinds of questions.

S7a. How do you feel about what our national government is doing?

S7b. Thinking only of yourself and your needs, how do you feel about what the national government is doing?

S7c. With your values about what is appropriate and fair, how do you feel about what the national government is doing?

S7d. How do you feel about what our national government is doing considering the resources--money, time and energy--being put into it?

S7e. Considering what it would take to change what the government is doing, how do you feel about what our national government is doing?

S7f. How do you think most people feel about the things that our national government is doing?

S7g. Thinking of your age and position in life, how do you feel about what our national government is doing?

TIME NOW _____

X28. Most people worry more or less about somethings. Would you say you never worry, worry a little, worry sometimes, worry a lot or worry all the time?

| 1. NEVER WORRY | 2. WORRY A LITTLE | 3. WORRY SOMETIMES |

| 4. WORRY A LOT | 5. WORRY ALL THE TIME |

X33. (CARD X2-WHITE) We have talked about various parts of your life; now I want to ask about your life as a whole. How satisfied are you with your life as a whole these days? Which number on this card comes closest to how satisfied or dissatisfied you are with your life as a whole? If you are completely satisfied, you would choose number 1; if you are completely dissatisfied, you would choose number 7. (CHECK NUMBER CHOSEN BY R)

Completely Satisfied   1   2   3   4   5   6   7   Completely Dissatisfied

G11. In general, how satisfying do you find the way you're spending your life these days? Would you call it completely satisfying, pretty satisfying or not very satisfying?

| 1. COMPLETELY | 3. PRETTY | 5. NOT VERY | 8. DK |

CARD K1

"FEELING" THERMOMETER

WARM

100° ——— Very warm or favorable feeling

85° ——— Good warm or favorable feeling

70° ——— Fairly warm or favorable feeling

60° ——— A bit more warm or favorable than cold feeling

50° ——— No feeling at all

40° ——— A bit more cold or unfavorable feeling

30° ——— Fairly cold or unfavorable feeling

15° ——— Quite cold or unfavorable feeling

0° ——— Very cold or unfavorable feeling

COLD

K3. While we have the feeling thermometer in front of us, what about your own life? Where would you put your life as a whole these days on the feeling thermometer?

_____
(RATING)

L1. (ASK L1a THRU L1k BEFORE PROCEEDING TO L2 a-k). Now I have some questions about how you have been feeling recently. You can just answer "yes" or "no." During the past few weeks did you ever feel...

L1a. Particularly excited or interested in something?

| 0. NO | YES |

L1b. Did you ever feel so restless that you couldn't sit long in a chair?

| 0. NO | YES |

L1c. Proud because someone complimented you on something you had done?

| 0. NO | YES |

L1d. Very lonely or remote from other people?

| 0. NO | YES |

L1e. Pleased about having accomplished something?

| 0. NO | YES |

L1f. Bored?

| 0. NO | YES |

L1g. On top of the world?

| 0. NO | YES |

L1h. Depressed or very unhappy?

| 0. NO | YES |

L1j. That things were going your way?

| 0. NO | YES |

L1k. Upset because someone criticized you?

| 0. NO | YES |

(IF ALL "NO," TURN TO P. 37, L3)

L2. (ASK THIS QUESTION FOR EACH ITEM TO WHICH THE RESPONDENT ANSWERED "YES" IN L1.) You mentioned that you had felt _____. How often during the past few weeks did you feel this way? Was it just once, several times, or a lot of times?

L2a. Particularly excited or interested in something...

| 1. ONCE | 2. SEVERAL | 3. A LOT |

L2b. So restless that you couldn't sit long in a chair...

| 1. ONCE | 2. SEVERAL | 3. A LOT |

L2c. Proud because someone complimented you...

| 1. ONCE | 2. SEVERAL | 3. A LOT |

L2d. Very lonely or remote from other people...

| 1. ONCE | 2. SEVERAL | 3. A LOT |

L2e. Pleased about having accomplished something...

| 1. ONCE | 2. SEVERAL | 3. A LOT |

L2f. Bored?

| 1. ONCE | 2. SEVERAL | 3. A LOT |

L2g. On top of the world...

| 1. ONCE | 2. SEVERAL | 3. A LOT |

L2h. Depressed or very unhappy...

| 1. ONCE | 2. SEVERAL | 3. A LOT |

L2j. That things were going your way...

| 1. ONCE | 2. SEVERAL | 3. A LOT |

L2k. Upset because someone criticized you...

| 1. ONCE | 2. SEVERAL | 3. A LOT |

L3. Taking all things together, how would you say things are these days--would you say you're very happy, pretty happy, or not too happy these days?

| 1. VERY HAPPY | 3. PRETTY HAPPY | 5. NOT TOO HAPPY |

In the next section of this interview we want to find out how you feel about parts of your life, and life in this country as you see it. Please tell me the feelings you have now--taking into account what has happened in the last year and what you expect in the near future.

L4. Considering the way your life is going, would you like to continue much the same way, change some parts of it, or change many parts of it?

| 1. CONTINUE SAME WAY | 2. CHANGE SOME PARTS | 3. CHANGE MANY PARTS |

(CARD L1, ORANGE) Now I am going to be asking about a long list of things, so just tell me what number on this card gives the best summary of how you feel, "one" for delighted, "two" for pleased, and so forth on to "seven" for you feel terrible about it. If you have no feelings at all on the question, tell me letter "A." If you have never thought about something that I ask you, and this probably will not happen, then tell me letter "B." And I may ask you a question that doesn't apply to you, if so tell me letter "C." Let's try an easy one first (WRITE NUMBER OR LETTER ON LINE TO LEFT OF EACH QUESTION.)

I FEEL:

| 1 | 2 | 3 | 4 | 5 | 6 | 7 |
| DELIGHTED | PLEASED | MOSTLY SATISFIED | MIXED (ABOUT EQUALLY SATISFIED AND DISSATISFIED) | MOSTLY DISSATIS- FIED | UNHAPPY | TERRIBLE |

A NEUTRAL (NEITHER SATISFIED NOR DISSATISFIED)

B I NEVER THOUGHT ABOUT IT

C DOES NOT APPLY TO ME

L5. How do you feel about your house/apartment? (DO NOT ACCEPT "C" AS AN ANSWER)

L6. And now a very general one: How do you feel about your life as a whole? (NO "C")

How do you feel about . . .

____ L7. This community as a place to live (NO "C")

____ L8. Your housework--the work you need to do around your home (NO "C")

____ L9. The way young people in this country are thinking and acting (NO "C")

____ L10. Your own health and physical condition (NO "C")

____ L11. The things you and your family do together

____ L12. How much you are admired or respected by other people (NO "C")

____ L13. The way you spend your spare time, your non-working activities (NO "C")

____ L14. Your job

____ L15. What our government is doing about the economy--jobs, prices, profits (NO "C")

____ L16. The respect other people have for your rights (NO "C")

____ L17. The reliability of the people you depend on

____ L18. The information and entertainment you get from TV, newspapers, radio, magazines

____ L19. Your friends (NO "C")

____ L20. Your opportunity to change things around you that you don't like (NO "C")

____ L21. Your standard of living--the things you have like housing, car, furniture, recreation, and the like (NO "C")

____ L22. Your sex life

____ L23. How secure you are from people who might steal or destroy your property (NO "C")

____ L24. The privacy you have--being alone when you want to be (NO "C")

____ L25. The goods and services you can get when you buy in this area-- things like food, appliances, clothes (NO "C")

____ L26. Your chance of getting a good job if you went looking for one

____ L27. The sleep you get (NO "C")

____ L28. The standards and values of today's society (NO "C")

How do you feel about . . .

_____ L29. How happy you are   (NO "C")

_____ L30. The amount of time you have for doing the things you want to do (NO "C")

_____ L31. Nearby places you can use for recreation or sports

_____ L32. Yourself--what you are accomplishing and how you handle problems (NO "C")

_____ L33. What you have to pay for basic necessities such as food, housing, and clothing (NO "C")

_____ L34. What our national government is doing (NO "C")

_____ L35. How much fun you are having (NO "C")

_____ L36. How creative you can be (NO "C")

_____ L37. Your chances for relaxation--even for a short time (NO "C")

_____ L38. The income you (and your family) have (NO "C")

_____ L39. How well your family agrees on how family income should be spent

_____ L40. The way our political leaders think and act (NO "C")

_____ L41. Your own family life--your wife/husband, your marriage, your children if any

_____ L42. What your local government is doing (NO "C")

_____ L43. The chance you have to enjoy pleasant or beautiful things (NO "C")

_____ L44. And now the last one of these; How do you feel about your life as a whole? (NO "C")

TIME NOW: _____

Now, a few more general questions.

X28. Most people worry more or less about somethings. Would you say you <u>never</u> worry, <u>worry a little</u>, <u>worry sometimes</u>, <u>worry a lot</u> or <u>worry all the time?</u>

| 1. NEVER WORRY | 2. WORRY A LITTLE | 3. WORRY SOMETIMES |

| 4. WORRY A LOT | 5. WORRY ALL THE TIME |

X33. (CARD X2- WHITE) We have talked about various parts of your life; now I want to ask about your life as a whole. How satisfied are you with your life as a whole these days? Which number on this card comes closest to how satisfied or dissatisfied you are with your life as a whole? If you are completely satisfied, you would choose number 1; if you are completely dissatisfied, you would choose number 7. (CHECK NUMBER CHOSEN BY R)

Completely   Completely
Satisfied   Dissatisfied
_____
 1   2   3   4   5   6   7

SECTION B:

Now we come to some questions on how you feel about your life.

B1. (CARD B1 - ORANGE) Here are some circles that we can imagine represent the lives of different people. Circle eight has all pluses in it, to represent a person who has all good things in his life. Circle zero has all minuses in it, to represent a person who has all bad things in his life. Other circles are in between.

```
    8        7        6        5        4        3        2        1        0
ALL GOOD                                                              ALL BAD
THINGS                                                                 THINGS
```

B1a. Which circle do you think comes closest to matching your life? _____

B1b. Which circle do you think would be chosen most often by people in this country? _____

B2. (CARD B2 - WHITE) Here is a picture of a ladder. At the bottom of the ladder is the worst life you might reasonably expect to have. At the top is the best life you might expect to have. Of course, life from week to week falls somewhere in between.

```
        ┌───┐  9   BEST LIFE I COULD EXPECT TO HAVE
        ├───┤  8
        ├───┤  7
        ├───┤  6
        ├───┤  5
        ├───┤  4
        ├───┤  3
        ├───┤  2
        └───┘  1   WORST LIFE I COULD EXPECT TO HAVE
```

B2a. Where on the ladder would you say was your best week in the past year --on which rung would you put it? _____

B2b. Where on the ladder was your worst week during the past year-- on which rung? _____

B2c. Where was your life most of the time during the past year? _____

B2d. Where was your life five years ago? _____

B2e. Where do you expect your life to be five years from now? _____

(CARD B3 - BLUE) Next I am going to ask a list of things. Just tell me what number on this card best says how you feel about each; "seven" for delighted; "six" for pleased; and so forth on to "one" for terrible. If you have no feelings at all on the question, tell me a letter "A." If you have never thought about something I ask, then tell me letter "B," we just want your first reaction. **Let's start with a very general one....** (WRITE NUMBER OR LETTER ON LINE TO LEFT OF EACH QUESTION)

I FEEL:

7	6	5	4	3	2	1
DELIGHTED	PLEASED	MOSTLY SATISFIED	MIXED (ABOUT EQUALLY SATISFIED AND DISSATISFIED)	MOSTLY DISSATISFIED	UNHAPPY	TERRIBLE

A NO FEELINGS AT ALL

B NEVER THOUGHT ABOUT IT

_____ B3. How do you feel about your life as a whole?

_____ B4. How do you feel about the extent to which your physical needs are met?

How do you feel about . . .

_____ B5. How fairly you get treated

_____ B6. How neat, tidy, and clean things are around you

How do you feel about . . .

_____ B7. Your safety

_____ B8. How interesting your day to day life is

_____ B9. The amount of physical work and exercise in your life

_____ B10. How sincere and honest other people are

I FEEL:

7	6	5	4	3	2	1
DELIGHTED	PLEASED	MOSTLY SATISFIED	MIXED (ABOUT EQUALLY SATISFIED AND DISSATISFIED)	MOSTLY DISSATISFIED	UNHAPPY	TERRIBLE

A NO FEELINGS AT ALL

B NEVER THOUGHT ABOUT IT

How do you feel about . . .

_____ B11. How sincere and honest you are

_____ B12. The extent to which you are developing yourself and broadening your life

_____ B13. How secure you are financially

_____ B14. The amount of pressure you are under

How do you feel about . . .

_____ B15. The amount of respect you get from others

_____ B16. Your independence or freedom--the chance you have to do what you want

_____ B17. The amount of fun and enjoyment you have

How do you feel about . . .

_____ B18. Yourself

_____ B19. The freedom you have from being bothered and annoyed

_____ B20. The religious fulfillment in your life

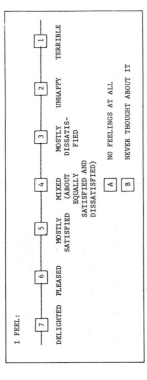

J5. TO BE RATED BY THE INTERVIEWER: CONSIDERING ALL THE THINGS YOU HAVE HEARD FROM THIS RESPONDENT AND THE THINGS THAT YOU HAVE BEEN ABLE TO OBSERVE, WE WOULD LIKE YOU TO RATE HOW YOU THINK THE RESPONDENT REALLY FEELS ABOUT HIS LIFE AS A WHOLE. CHECK ONE.

| 7. DELIGHTED | 6. PLEASED | 5. MOSTLY SATISFIED | 4. MIXED (ABOUT EQUALLY SATISFIED AND DISSATISFIED) |

| 3. MOSTLY DISSATISFIED | 2. UNHAPPY | 1. TERRIBLE |

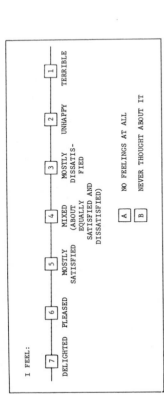

I FEEL:

| 7 | 6 | 5 | 4 | 3 | 2 | 1 |
| DELIGHTED | PLEASED | MOSTLY SATISFIED | MIXED (ABOUT EQUALLY SATISFIED AND DISSATISFIED) | MOSTLY DISSATIS-FIED | UNHAPPY | TERRIBLE |

| A | NO FEELINGS AT ALL |
| B | NEVER THOUGHT ABOUT IT |

How do you feel about . . .

_____ B 21. The amount of beauty and attractiveness in your world

_____ B 22. The extent to which you are achieving success and getting ahead

_____ B23. How much you are accepted and included by others

_____ B 24. The extent to which you can adjust to changes in your life

_____ B 25. How much you are really contributing to other people's lives

_____ B 26. The extent to which you are tough and can take it

_____ B 27. And last, a very general one: How do you feel about your life as a whole

TIME TO NEAREST MINUTE _____

WAS THIS SECTION INTERRUPTED ☐ 1. YES ☐ 2. NO

Survey Research Center
The University of Michigan
Ann Arbor, Michigan

July 1973
#462150

Questionnaire
Number

A Study of Methods of Measuring

THE QUALITY OF PEOPLE'S LIVES

Part 1

People are different. They live in a variety of situations and they don't feel the same way about the events and circumstances that they encounter in day to day life. If people in this country are going to change the quality of their lives, much of it is up to them as individuals, but some improvements can't be made unless more is known about the conditions of people's lives and how they feel about what is happening to them.

This is a questionnaire on how you feel about your life. It is a long questionnaire and it will take a long time to fill it out. When you start, work at your own pace, but as fast as you comfortably can. Most of the questions should be interesting, some may be dull and tiring, many will be easy—it's your life, not some unknown topic—but some questions will be hard. Answer them all as well as you can.

Quite often you may think that you have already covered a topic and we have asked the same kind of question with just a difference in wording. You will be right. We are trying to find the best way to ask questions and we are trying out several different wordings. So keep on going even if some of it looks like a repeat or a return. We aren't trying to trick you. You don't have to be consistent. You don't need to have your answers all agree with each other.

Since we are trying to improve this questionnaire, it would help us if you would indicate in the margins any of the questions which seem particularly hard or unclear by writing "hard," or "unclear" next to those questions.

Your answers to this questionnaire will be confidential.

If you have any problems, please ask a question.

2 Imagine that the lines below represent piles of cards. Each pile has people whose lives are pretty similar. The person in Pile A below has a life like nobody else. People in pile G have lives like quite a lot of other people. In which pile would you put your life? DRAW A CIRCLE AROUND THE LETTER UNDER THE PILE YOU CHOOSE

A	B	C	D	E	F	G

3 If all the adults in the United States were represented by cards—one person per card—and if you were sorting everyone into seven piles ordered from those who had the best kind of life to those who had the worst kind of life, some people would have to fall in the middle pile. We have drawn a line to represent the height of the pile of cards, representing people, in the middle group.

Draw lines up from each of the other six points to show about how many people you think would be in the other piles. Just make your best guess.

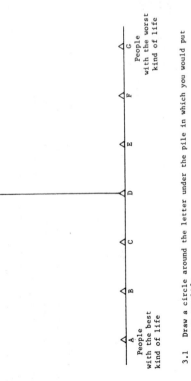

A   B   C   D   E   F   G
People   People
with the best   with the worst
kind of life   kind of life

3.1 Draw a circle around the letter under the pile in which you would put your own life.

7 Here is a circle and we can imagine that it represents your life. The pie slices are parts of your life. There are 8 slices, so let's imagine that you can divide your life up into 8 parts.

Now, put a plus sign (+) in those slices that are good parts of your life.

Put a zero (0) in those slices that are neutral parts of your life—neither good or bad.

And, put a minus sign (-) in those slices that are bad parts of your life.

Put some mark in every slice.

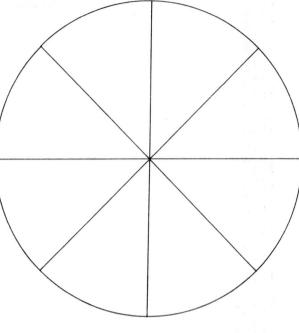

APPENDIX A   375

11 Here is a picture of a ladder. At the bottom of the ladder is the worst life you might reasonably expect to have. At the top is the best life you might expect to have. Of course, life from week to week falls somewhere in between. WRITE A NUMBER ON THE LINE TO THE LEFT OF EACH QUESTION

```
        ___
   9   |___|  Best life I could expect to have
   8   |___|
   7   |___|
   6   |___|
   5   |___|
   4   |___|
   3   |___|
   2   |___|
   1   |___|  Worst life I could expect to have
```

____ 11.1 Where on the ladder was your best week in the past year--on which rung would you put it?

____ 11.2 Where on the ladder was your worst week during the past year-- on which rung?

____ 11.3 Where was your life most of the time during the past year?

____ 11.4 Where was your life five years ago?

____ 11.5 Where do you expect your life to be five years from now?

Here is another picture of a ladder. At the bottom of this ladder is the worst situation you might reasonably expect to have. At the top is the best you might expect to have. The other rungs are in between. WRITE A NUMBER ON THE LINE TO THE LEFT OF EACH QUESTION BELOW

```
        ___
   9   |___|  Best I could expect to have
   8   |___|
   7   |___|
   6   |___|
   5   |___|
   4   |___|
   3   |___|
   2   |___|
   1   |___|  Worst I could expect to have
```

____ 11.6 Where on the ladder is your house or apartment--on which rung would you put it?

____ 11.7 Where on the ladder is the way you spend your spare time, your non-working activities--on which rung?

____ 11.8 Where would you put the way our national government is operating?

____ 11.9 Where would you put your standard of living--the things you have like housing, car, furniture, recreation, and the like?

____ 11.10 Where would you put your independence or freedom--the chance you have to do what you want?

13　Here are some faces expressing various feelings. Below each is a letter.

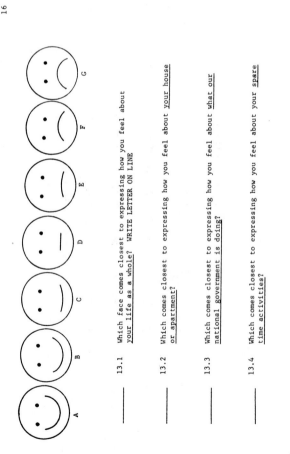

A　B　C　D　E　F　G

13.1　Which face comes closest to expressing how you feel about your life as a whole? WRITE LETTER ON LINE

_____

13.2　Which comes closest to expressing how you feel about your house or apartment?

_____

13.3　Which comes closest to expressing how you feel about what our national government is doing?

_____

13.4　Which comes closest to expressing how you feel about your spare time activities?

_____

13.5　Which comes closest to expressing how you feel about your independence or freedom--the chance you have to do what you want?

_____

13.6　Which comes closest to expressing how you feel about your standard of living--the things you have like housing, car, furniture, recreation, and the like?

_____

14　Taking all things together, how would you say things are these days--would you say you're very happy, pretty happy, or not too happy these days? CHECK ONE BOX

☐ Very happy

☐ Pretty happy

☐ Not too happy

16　Now we would like to go back to some of the things we have asked before and inquire further about how you regard them.

16.1　Check the box next to the words which best describe how you feel about your house or apartment. CHECK ONE BOX

☐ Terrible

☐ Unhappy

☐ Mostly dissatisfied

☐ Mixed--about equally satisfied and dissatisfied

☐ Mostly satisfied

☐ Pleased

☐ Delighted

16.1a　For a place to live at this point in your life, do you think of your house or apartment as:　CHECK ONE BOX

☐ An ideal house or apartment for you

☐ The kind you want most to have

☐ The best house or apartment you are able to get now

☐ A good enough house or apartment for now

☐ A tolerable house or apartment

☐ A very unsatisfactory place for you to live

16.2 Check the box next to the words which best describe how you feel about yourself. CHECK ONE BOX

☐ Terrible
☐ Unhappy
☐ Mostly dissatisfied
☐ Mixed--about equally satisfied and dissatisfied
☐ Mostly satisfied
☐ Pleased
☐ Delighted

16.2a For this point in your life, do you think of your self as: CHECK ONE BOX

☐ An ideal person for you
☐ The kind of person you want most to be
☐ The best kind of person you are able to be now
☐ A good enough person for now
☐ A tolerable and acceptable kind of person
☐ A failure as a person

16.3 Check the box next to the words which best describe how you feel about your work (either for pay or at home). CHECK ONE BOX

☐ Terrible
☐ Unhappy
☐ Mostly dissatisfied
☐ Mixed--about equally satisfied and dissatisfied
☐ Mostly satisfied
☐ Pleased
☐ Delighted

16.3a For this point in your life, do you think of your work as: CHECK ONE BOX

☐ Ideal kind of work for you
☐ What you want most to do
☐ The best kind of work you are able to get now
☐ Good enough work for now
☐ A tolerable way to spend work time
☐ A very unsatisfactory kind of work for you

17   Next we have some questions about your family income--the money that comes
      in for yourself, your spouse (if any), and any children living with you.
      Please answer each of these questions by writing one number of the following
      numbers on the line next to each question.

      1   Less than half of my present family income
      2   Half of my present family income
      3   $1000 per year less than my present family income
      4   My present family income
      5   $1000 per year more than my present family income
      6   My present family income plus half as much again
      7   Double my present family income
      8   More than double my present family income

If it is easier for you to answer the questions, write down somewhere the
dollar amounts which correspond to each of the above answers.

_____   17.1   What amount would correspond to a "dream income" for you?

_____   17.2   What amount would be as much as you think you will ever make?

_____   17.3   What amount would give you almost all you really want?

_____   17.4   What amount would be what you could just get by on?

_____   17.5   What is the smallest amount that would make you feel delighted
                with your income?

_____   17.6   What is the smallest amount that would make you feel pleased
                with your income?

_____   17.7   What is the smallest amount that would make you feel mostly
                satisfied with your income?

_____   17.8   What is the amount that would make you feel about equally
                satisfied and dissatisfied with your income?

_____   17.9   What is the largest amount that would leave you feeling mostly
                dissatisfied about your income?

_____   17.10   What is the largest amount that would leave you feeling unhappy
                about your income?

_____   17.11   What is the largest amount that would leave you feeling terrible
                about your income?

16.4   Check the box next to the words which best describe how you feel
        about your life as a whole.   CHECK ONE BOX

        ☐ Terrible
        ☐ Unhappy
        ☐ Mostly dissatisfied
        ☐ Mixed--about equally satisfied and dissatisfied
        ☐ Mostly satisfied
        ☐ Pleased
        ☐ Delighted

16.4a   For this point in your life, do you think of your life as:
        CHECK ONE BOX

        ☐ An ideal kind of life for you
        ☐ What you want your life most to be
        ☐ The best kind of life you are able to
           have now
        ☐ A good enough life for now
        ☐ A tolerable kind of life
        ☐ A very unsatisfactory life for you

18. Now let's compare your life and some aspects of it with the lives of six people you know well. It does not matter to us who these people are, but for your convenience write down the initials of each person in the boxes provided below. (Think of real people you meet from time to time.)

Under each set of initials put a "B" if you think that on the whole that your life (or in later questions, some aspect of it) is better for you than that person's would be.

Put a "S" if yours seems about the same for you as that person's would be.

Put a "W" if yours seems worse for you than that person's would be.

WRITE ONE LETTER ON EACH OF THE SIX LINES AFTER EACH QUESTION

    B Better than this person's would be

    S About the same as this person's would be

    W Worse than this person's would be

	1st person	2nd person	3rd person	4th person	5th person	6th person
INITIALS →						

18.1 Compared to this person's life as a whole, for me my life is: ____ ____ ____ ____ ____ ____

18.2 Compared to this person's house or apartment, for me my house or apartment is: ____ ____ ____ ____ ____ ____

18.3 Compared to this person's way of spending spare time, for me my way of spending spare time is: ____ ____ ____ ____ ____ ____

18.4 Compared to this person's standard of living, for me my standard of living is: ____ ____ ____ ____ ____ ____

18.5 Compared to this person's independence or freedom, for me my independence or freedom is: ____ ____ ____ ____ ____ ____

Here are some circles that we can imagine represent the lives of different people. Circle 0 has all minuses in it, to represent a person who has all bad things in his or her life. Circle 8 has all plusses in it, to represent a person who has all good things in his or her life. Other circles are in between. WRITE ONE NUMBER ON THE LINE TO THE LEFT OF EACH QUESTION

0
1
2
3
4
5
6
7
8

18.6 ____ Which circle do you think comes closest to matching your life?

18.7 ____ Which circle do you think would be chosen most often by people in this country?

18.8 ____ Which comes closest to matching how you feel about your house or apartment?

18.9 ____ Which comes closest to matching how you feel about your independence or freedom--the chance you have to do what you want?

18.10 ____ Which comes closest to matching how you feel about the way you spend your spare time, your non-working activities?

18.11 ____ Which comes closest to matching how you feel about the way our national government is operating?

18.12 ____ Which comes closest to matching how you feel about your standard of living--the things you have like housing, car, furniture, recreation, and the like?

About my house or apartment I would feel:

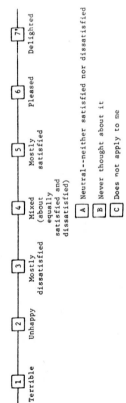

1	2	3	4	5	6	7
Terrible	Unhappy	Mostly dissatisfied	Mixed (about equally satisfied and dissatisfied)	Mostly satisfied	Pleased	Delighted

A Neutral--neither satisfied nor dissatisfied

B Never thought about it

C Does not apply to me

____ 19.2a How would you feel about your house or apartment if you considered only the standard of living it enables you to have?

____ 19.2b How would you feel about your house or apartment if you considered only the fun it enables you to have?

____ 19.2c How would you feel about your house or apartment if you considered only the independence or freedom--the chance you have to do what you want--it enables you to have?

____ 19.2d How would you feel about your house or apartment if you considered only the beauty and attractiveness it enables you to enjoy?

____ 19.2e How would you feel about your house or apartment if you considered only the freedom from bother and annoyance it enables you to have?

____ 19.2f How would you feel about your house or apartment if you considered only the safety it enables you to have?

____ 19.2g How would you feel about your house or apartment if you considered only how it enables you to accomplish what you want?

____ 19.2h How would you feel about your house or apartment if you considered only its effect on your acceptance and inclusion by other people?

19.3 Do you have a job for which you are paid and at which you usually work at least 20 hours per week? CHECK ONE BOX

☐ No →GO TO QUESTION 19.4

☐ Yes →GO TO QUESTION 19.3a

About my job I would feel:

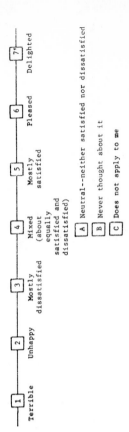

1	2	3	4	5	6	7
Terrible	Unhappy	Mostly dissatisfied	Mixed (about equally satisfied and dissatisfied)	Mostly satisfied	Pleased	Delighted

A Neutral--neither satisfied nor dissatisfied

B Never thought about it

C Does not apply to me

____ 19.3a How would you feel about your job if you considered only the standard of living it enables you to have?

____ 19.3b How would you feel about your job if you considered only the fun you have?

____ 19.3c How would you feel about your job if you considered only its effect on your independence or freedom--the chance you have to do what you want.

____ 19.3d How would you feel about your job if you considered only the beauty and attractiveness you get to enjoy?

____ 19.3e How would you feel about your job if you considered only the freedom from bother and annoyance that you have?

____ 19.3f How would you feel about your job if you considered only your safety?

____ 19.3g How would you feel about your job if you considered only how much it enables you to accomplish things?

____ 19.3h How would you feel about your job if you considered only its effect on your acceptance and inclusion by other people?

19.4 Do you have a husband or a wife or any children?   CHECK ONE BOX

☐ No ——→ GO TO QUESTION 19.5a

☐ Yes ——→ GO TO QUESTION 19.4a

About my family life I would feel:

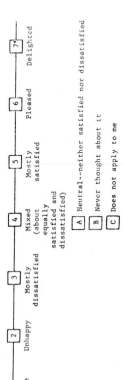

1	2	3	4	5	6	7
Terrible	Unhappy	Mostly dissatisfied	Mixed (about equally satisfied and dissatisfied)	Mostly satisfied	Pleased	Delighted

A Neutral--neither satisfied nor dissatisfied

B Never thought about it

C Does not apply to me

19.4a _____ How would you feel about your own family life--your marriage, husband or wife, and children--if you considered only its effect on your standard of living?

19.4b _____ How would you feel about your own family life if you considered only the fun it enables you to have?

19.4c _____ How would you feel about your own family life if you considered only its effect on your independence or freedom--the chance you have to do what you want?

19.4d _____ How would you feel about your own family life if you considered only the attractiveness and beauty it enables you to enjoy?

19.4e _____ How would you feel about your own family life if you considered only the freedom from bother and annoyance that it enables you to have?

19.4f _____ How would you feel about your own family life if you considered only the safety it enables you to have?

19.4g _____ How would you feel about your own family life if you considered only how it enables you to accomplish what you want?

19.4h _____ How would you feel about your own family life if you considered only its effect on your acceptance and inclusion by other people?

About my neighborhood as a place to live I would feel:

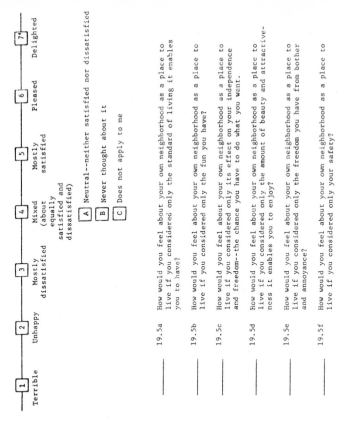

1	2	3	4	5	6	7
Terrible	Unhappy	Mostly dissatisfied	Mixed (about equally satisfied and dissatisfied)	Mostly satisfied	Pleased	Delighted

A Neutral--neither satisfied nor dissatisfied

B Never thought about it

C Does not apply to me

19.5a _____ How would you feel about your own neighborhood as a place to live if you considered only the standard of living it enables you to have?

19.5b _____ How would you feel about your own neighborhood as a place to live if you considered only the fun you have?

19.5c _____ How would you feel about your own neighborhood as a place to live if you considered only its effect on your independence and freedom--the chance you have to do what you want.

19.5d _____ How would you feel about your own neighborhood as a place to live if you considered only the amount of beauty and attractiveness it enables you to enjoy?

19.5e _____ How would you feel about your own neighborhood as a place to live if you considered only the freedom you have from bother and annoyance?

19.5f _____ How would you feel about your own neighborhood as a place to live if you considered only your safety?

19.5g _____ How would you feel about your own neighborhood as a place to live if you considered only how it enables you to accomplish things?

19.5h _____ How would you feel about your own neighborhood as a place to live if you considered only how much you are accepted and included by other people?

About my spare time I would feel:

1	2	3	4	5	6	7
Terrible	Unhappy	Mostly dissatisfied	Mixed (about equally satisfied and dissatisfied)	Mostly satisfied	Pleased	Delighted

A Neutral--neither satisfied nor dissatisfied

B Never thought about it

C Does not apply to me

_____ 19.6a How would you feel about the way you spend your spare time, your non-working activities, if you considered only its effect on your standard of living?

_____ 19.6b How would you feel about the way you spend your spare time, if you considered only how much fun you have?

_____ 19.6c How would you feel about the way you spend your spare time if you considered only your independence or freedom--the chance you have to do what you want?

_____ 19.6d How would you feel about the way you spend your spare time if you considered only the beauty and attractiveness you enjoy?

_____ 19.6e How would you feel about the way you spend your spare time if you considered only the freedom you have from being bothered and annoyed?

_____ 19.6f How would you feel about the way you spend your spare time if you considered only your safety?

_____ 19.6g How would you feel about the way you spend your spare time if you considered only how it enables you to accomplish things?

_____ 19.6h How would you feel about the way you spend your spare time if you considered only how much you are accepted and included by others?

About our national government I would feel:

1	2	3	4	5	6	7
Terrible	Unhappy	Mostly dissatisfied	Mixed (about equally satisfied and dissatisfied)	Mostly satisfied	Pleased	Delighted

A Neutral--neither satisfied nor dissatisfied

B Never thought about it

C Does not apply to me

_____ 19.7a How would you feel about the way our national government is operating if you considered only its effect on your standard of living?

_____ 19.7b How would you feel about the way our national government is operating if you considered only the fun it enables you to have?

_____ 19.7c How would you feel about the way our national government is operating if you considered only the independence or freedom-- the chance you have to do what you want--that it enables you to have?

_____ 19.7d How would you feel about the way our national government is operating if you considered only the beauty and attractiveness it enables you to enjoy?

_____ 19.7e How would you feel about the way our national government is operating if you considered only the freedom from bother and annoyance that you have?

_____ 19.7f How would you feel about the way our national government is operating if you considered only your safety?

_____ 19.7g How would you feel about the way our national government is operating if you considered only how it enables you to accomplish things?

_____ 19.7h How would you feel about the way our national government is operating if you considered only its effect on how much you are accepted and included by other people?

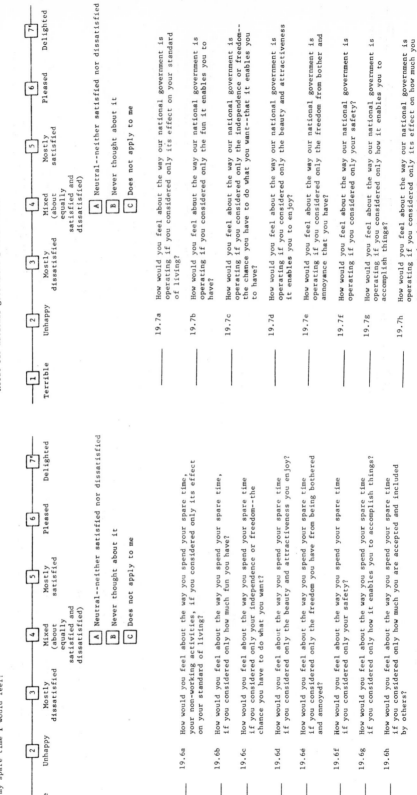

20 Here is a set of things which may--or may not--be important in affecting your overall feelings about the life you are living. For each item, please indicate how important it is to you in influencing your thinking about how well off you are. We do not want to know how you feel about it, but just how important it seems to you.

FOR EACH ITEM PICK THE MOST APPROPRIATE ANSWER FROM THE FOLLOWING LIST OF ANSWERS AND WRITE THE NUMBER ON THE LINE TO THE LEFT OF EACH ITEM

How important in influencing your feelings about your life:

```
1 Not at all important
2 Only slightly important
3 Moderately important
4 Rather important
5 Very important
6 Of utmost importance

0 Doesn't apply to me OR I can't answer OR I
  never thought about it
```

___ 20.1 Your house or apartment

___ 20.2 Your job

___ 20.3 Your own family life--your wife or husband, your marriage, your children (if any)

___ 20.4 Your own neighborhood as a place to live

___ 20.5 The way you spend your spare time, your non-working activities

___ 20.6 The way our national government is operating

___ 20.7 How much fun you are having

___ 20.8 Your standard of living--the things you have like housing, car, furniture, recreation and the like

___ 20.9 Your independence or freedom--the chance you have to do what you want

___ 20.10 The amount of beauty and attractiveness in your day to day life

___ 20.11 The freedom you have from being bothered or annoyed

___ 20.12 Your safety

___ 20.13 What you are accomplishing

___ 20.14 How much you are accepted and included by others

23 Think who is the neighbor who lives nearest to you, who is of the same sex as you, and who is at least 18 years old. (if there are several such neighbors living equally close to your house or apartment, pick the one to the left as you walk into your place.)

The following questions all concern how you think this person feels about aspects of his or her own life. All these questions can be answered by writing one of the following numbers or letters in the space to the left of each item.

I think he or she feels:

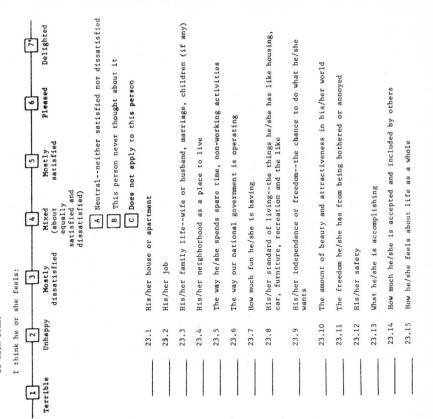

1	2	3	4	5	6	7
Terrible	Unhappy	Mostly dissatisfied	Mixed (about equally satisfied and dissatisfied)	Mostly satisfied	Pleased	Delighted

A Neutral--neither satisfied nor dissatisfied

B This person never thought about it

C Does not apply to this person

___ 23.1 His/her house or apartment

___ 23.2 His/her job

___ 23.3 His/her family life--wife or husband, marriage, children (if any)

___ 23.4 His/her neighborhood as a place to live

___ 23.5 The way he/she spends spare time, non-working activities

___ 23.6 The way our national government is operating

___ 23.7 How much fun he/she is having

___ 23.8 His/her standard of living--the things he/she has like housing, car, furniture, recreation and the like

___ 23.9 His/her independence or freedom--the chance to do what he/she wants

___ 23.10 The amount of beauty and attractiveness in his/her world

___ 23.11 The freedom he/she has from being bothered or annoyed

___ 23.12 His/her safety

___ 23.13 What he/she is accomplishing

___ 23.14 How much he/she is accepted and included by others

___ 23.15 How he/she feels about life as a whole

25 Think back over what your life has been like during the past 10 weeks. It may help to try to remember some of the specific things that happened to you, or which you did during this period.

YOUR ANSWERS SHOULD ADD UP TO 10 WEEKS.

25.1 For what part of that time did you feel delighted about your life as a whole? _____ weeks

25.2 For what part of that time did you feel pleased about your life as a whole? _____ weeks

25.3 For what part of that time did you feel mostly satisfied about your life as a whole? _____ weeks

25.4 For what part of that time did you feel mixed--about equally satisfied and dissatisfied about your life as a whole? _____ weeks

25.5 For what part of that time did you feel mostly dissatisfied about your life as a whole? _____ weeks

25.6 For what part of that time did you feel unhappy about your life as a whole? _____ weeks

25.7 For what part of that time did you feel terrible about your life as a whole? _____ weeks

TOTAL: _____

NOTE: PLEASE CHECK TO MAKE SURE YOUR ANSWERS ADD UP TO 10 WEEKS. IF THEY DON'T, PLEASE GO BACK AND ADJUST YOUR ANSWERS.

26 The next items can all be answered by picking one number from the following to indicate how much you agree with the statement. Write the number in the space provided.

1 Completely false
2 Somewhat false
3 Both true and false
4 Somewhat true
5 Completely true
0 Doesn't apply to me

____ 26.1 Having friends in my house is hard.

____ 26.2 I look for better ways to do my work on the job.

____ 26.3 When I'm not feeling well, my family helps me.

____ 26.4 I have too much spare time.

____ 26.5 I think tax money is wasted.

____ 26.6 I would have trouble borrowing $1000 if I needed it.

____ 26.7 If I wanted to, I could take a vacation starting whenever I wished.

____ 26.8 I enjoy walking around and looking at things, even if I have nowhere in particular to go.

____ 26.9 It would be safe to take an evening stroll in my neighborhood.

____ 26.10 I am not accomplishing what I want.

____ 26.11 I find my house fits my needs.

____ 26.12 I don't see socially the people I work with.

____ 26.13 A lot of people in my neighborhood are strangers to one another.

____ 26.14 I waste most of my spare time.

____ 26.15 I trust the government to find the best solutions to problems.

____ 26.16 I can have a night on the town when I feel like it without worrying about the cost.

____ 26.17 I can't spend my time the way I would like to.

____ 26.18 People are considerate of my feelings.

Scale:

1 Completely false
2 Somewhat false
3 Both true and false
4 Somewhat true
5 Completely true
0 Doesn't apply to me

26.19 If the Fire Department inspected my home, they would find it completely safe.

26.20 I have done things which made a solid contribution in their own way.

26.21 My home is hard to keep up.

26.22 If I had to change jobs, I'd try to get one doing the same kind of work.

26.23 I could count on my neighbors to help out if something were to happen to my family.

26.24 I look foward to weekends.

26.25 My life includes some play.

26.26 I spend all I want and still have money left over at the end of the month.

26.27 I am free to set my own pace in my day-to-day activities.

26.28 I can be alone when I want to.

26.29 When I take my car on a trip, I feel secure.

26.30 People I come in contact with treat me fairly.

26.31 My home is comfortable all year around.

26.32 When I go out for an enjoyable time my family is with me.

26.33 The people in my neighborhood are not very satisfied being there.

26.34 I use my spare time for things I want to do.

26.35 I don't have much fun when I'm alone.

26.36 My home is not very well equipped.

26.37 The things I see on my trips around town are quite pretty.

26.38 There is just too much noise around me.

Scale:

1 Completely false
2 Somewhat false
3 Both true and false
4 Somewhat true
5 Completely true
0 Doesn't apply to me

26.39 I have had medical treatment for an injury in the last five years.

26.40 I get along well with other people.

26.41 My home provides a good place to get away from the cares of the outside world.

26.42 When I need someone to talk to I go to a family member or relative.

26.43 Someone from the neighborhood keeps an eye on our house or apartment, even when no one is there.

26.44 The United States Congress is out of touch with most of the people.

26.45 I look forward to each new day.

26.46 I have all the material things I want.

26.47 I find the people around me attractive.

26.48 Other people annoy me.

26.49 I'm better off than I used to be.

26.50 When I meet someone new at a social gathering, we have trouble talking.

26.51 I look forward to going to work.

26.52 I spend holidays with my relatives.

26.53 Someone keeps an eye on the children in my neighborhood when they play, even if not their parents.

26.54 Decisions at a national level are made for pressure groups, regardless of how the majority of people feel.

26.55 When I want some time for myself I never get it.

26.56 My town is ugly.

26.57 I can finish most things I start without being interrupted.

1 Completely false
2 Somewhat false
3 Both true and false
4 Somewhat true
5 Completely true
0 Doesn't apply to me

26.58   My friends think I'm not doing very well.

26.59   I don't have many friends.

26.60   I take all the sick leave I can.

26.61   When I disagree with a family member, we get into an argument or a fight.

26.62   I have trouble finding the time to run errands and to do the small things that need to be done from day to day.

26.63   I support the President's policies.

26.64   My friends are fun to be with.

26.65   I am tied down by my present situation at home and at work.

26.66   Places I spend most of my time are not very attractive.

26.67   I don't carry much money with me when I go out alone at night.

26.68   I am getting what I want out of life.

26.69   Strangers are nice to me.

26.70   People in my family don't laugh often.

28.54

We would like to contact two or three people who know you pretty well and ask them about a dozen short questions. We would like their guesses as to how you feel about certain things--your house or apartment, your neighborhood, your freedom from annoyance, and the like--the same items we asked you to estimate how your nearest neighbor felt about.

We'll contact these people by mail or phone, and send them a short question-naire, telling us that you gave us their names.

What we need from you are the names of three people who know you pretty well and as good a mailing address for each as you can remember. (This may be any person--including your husband or wife.)

We are not going to tell these people how you answered any questions, nor will we tell you how they answer.

Please print clearly!

People who know you pretty well:

Person #1

Name: _____

Number and street: _____

Town and state: _____

Phone number: _____

Person #2

Name: _____

Number and street: _____

Town and state: _____

Phone number: _____

Person #3

Name: _____

Number and street: _____

Town and state: _____

Phone number: _____

ID number: _____

These questions all concern how you think the person listed at the bottom of the letter feels about aspects of his or her own life. Complete each of the following sentences by writing one of the numbers or letters from the box below on the line to the left of each. Tell how you think the person feels.

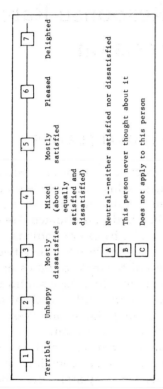

1	2	3	4	5	6	7

Terrible   Unhappy   Mostly   Mixed   Mostly   Pleased   Delighted
                       dissatisfied   (about   satisfied
                                       equally
                                       satisfied and
                                       dissatisfied)

[A] Neutral--neither satisfied nor dissatisfied

[B] This person never thought about it

[C] Does not apply to this person

I think he or she feels . . .

_____ with his/her house or apartment.

_____ with his/her job.

_____ with his/her family life--wife or husband, marriage, children (if any).

_____ with his/her neighborhood as a place to live.

_____ with the way he/she spends spare time, non-working activities.

_____ with the way our national government is operating.

_____ with how much fun he/she is having.

_____ with his/her standard of living--the things he/she has like housing, car, furniture, recreation and the like.

_____ with his/her independence or freedom--the chance to do what he/she wants.

_____ with the amount of beauty and attractiveness in his/her world.

_____ with the freedom he/she has from being bothered or annoyed.

_____ with his/her safety.

_____ with what he/she is accomplishing.

_____ with how much he/she is accepted and included by others.

_____ with how he/she feels about life as a whole.

APPENDIX B

Sampling Designs, Response Rates, Sampling Precision

SAMPLING DESIGNS FOR NATIONAL SURVEYS

The samples for the national surveys were designed to represent people living in households in the coterminus United States exclusive of people on military reservations. The seventy-four sample points, located in thirty-six states and the District of Columbia, included the two Standard Consolidated Areas (New York/Northeastern New Jersey, and Chicago/Northwestern Indiana, the ten largest Standard Metropolitan Statistical Areas (SMSAs), thirty-two other SMSAs and thirty non-SMSAs, which were either single counties or county groups. In the multistage area probability sampling, first stage stratification of SMSAs and counties was carried out independently within each of the four major geographic regions: Northeast, North Central, South, and West, each of which received representation in proportion to its population.

Over all regions, the SMSAs and counties were assigned to relatively homogeneous groups or strata. Twelve of these strata contained only one primary area each; these were the twelve major metropolitan areas that were included with certainty. The remaining sixty-two strata averaged around 2 million population and contained from two to two hundred or more primary areas (SMSAs or county groups). From each stratum one primary area was selected with probability proportionate to population. This sampling process led to approximately equal sample sizes from the sixty-two primary sample areas.

As the multistage area sampling continued within the primary units, the area was divided and subdivided, in two to five stages, into successively smaller sampling units. By definition and procedure, each housing unit belonged uniquely to one sampling unit at each stage. Within the primary areas, cities, towns, and rural areas were the secondary selections. Blocks or clusters of addresses in cities and towns, and chunks of rural areas were the

388

third-stage units. In a fourth stage there was a selection of small segments or clusters of dwellings where interviews were taken for the study. In the last stage of sampling, one eligible person was objectively selected as a respondent from the sample household. Probability selection was enforced at all stages of the sample selection; the interviewers had no choice among households or among household members within a sample household.

Within each household where a responsible person could be contacted, one eligible individual was designated as the respondent. If after repeated calls, no one was at home, or the designated respondent was not at home or refused to be interviewed, no substitution was made.

Although households were sampled at a constant rate, designated respondents had variable selection rates according to the number of eligible persons within the household. Therefore, to be precise, data for each respondent should be weighted by the number of eligible persons in the household. However, because variable weights increase the complexities of data processing and analysis to some degree, both weighted and unweighted estimates were examined for a number of variables. There was a decision to analyze the data unweighted by the number of eligible respondents.

Detailed description of the sampling procedure can be found in Kish and Hess (1965).

RESPONDENT SELECTION IN THE LOCAL (JULY) SURVEY

Nine members of the Survey Research Center's Field Staff who happened to live and work in the Toledo, Ohio, area were each instructed to recruit twenty-five people willing to participate in the study by completing a group-administered questionnaire. The respondents were selected from the Toledo area using an informal quota system based on sex, age, and income. No more than two members from the same family were accepted. (Appendix H compares characteristics of the July respondents with comparable characteristics of a true probability sample of the Toledo area and of American adults in general.)

RESPONDENT ELIGIBILITY AND RESPONSE RATES

May Data. Within each sample household, persons eighteen years of age or older, and married persons under eighteen years of age, were eligible for selection. The overall response rate (i.e., the percentage of the sample with whom interviews were successfully completed) was 76 percent.

November Data. The Form I and Form II data both come from the second wave of a panel survey. Criteria that were used to determine who in a household was eligible as a respondent in the first wave were: (1) the person had to be eighteen years of age or older on or before Election Day, November 7, 1972, and (2) the person had to be a United States citizen. The overall response rate for Wave I was 76 percent, and the reinterview rate for Wave II was 81 percent;

thus, 62 percent of the original sample selections are present as respondents to Wave II. Response rates were virtually identical for the subsamples that received Form I or Form II of the Wave II questionnaire.

April Data. Within each household persons eighteen years of age or older, and married persons under eighteen years of age, were eligible for selection. The overall response rate was 74 percent.

PRECISION OF SAMPLE ESTIMATES OF PERCENTAGES

With a probability design the magnitude of sampling errors, due to taking a sample rather than a census, can be approximated from the sample. The sampling error does not measure the actual error in a sample statistic, but it does allow the construction of a range; i.e., a "confidence interval" that will include the population value with a specified probability.

Exhibit B.1 gives the approximate values of the sampling error associated with percentages according to the magnitude of the percentage and the number of sample individuals on which it is based. An interval that is the width of the indicated sampling error on either side of the sample estimate (plus or minus) has a chance of nineteen in twenty of including the real population value, the value that would have been obtained if a complete census had been taken at the same time and under the same conditions as the sample survey.

As an example, suppose that the sample shows that 50 percent of the approximately fifteen hundred people in our April survey have a high life-satisfaction index; we would like to know what proportion would have been obtained if a census had been taken instead of a sample. By referring to the table and locating the intersection of the row for 50 percent and the column for fifteen hundred interviews, we find the sampling error for that particular combination to be approximately 3.2 percent. Therefore, we can say that there are nineteen chances out of twenty that the proportion of people in the whole population with a high life-satisfaction index is between 46.8 and 53.2 percent (50 Percent ± 3.2 percent).

EXHIBIT B.1. Approximate 95%-Level Sampling Errors for Percentages

Reported percentages	Number of respondents							
	1,500	1,000	750	500	400	300	200	100
50	3.2	3.8	4.4	5.1	5.6	6.4	7.6	10
30 or 70	2.9	3.5	4.0	4.7	5.2	5.9	7.0	9.6
20 or 80	2.6	3.0	3.5	4.1	4.5	5.1	6.1	8.4
10 or 90	1.9	2.3	2.6	3.1	3.4	3.8	4.6	6.3
5 or 95	1.4	1.7	1.9	2.2	2.5	2.8	3.3	4.6

Note: The figures in this table represent two standard errors.

APPENDIX C

Clusters of Concern Items

Included in chapter 2 is a description of how certain concern items were grouped into clusters. For each of these clusters a measure was constructed by combining some or all of the relevant items. This appendix—in Exhibit C.1—indicates the items that were combined to form each measure.

All measures were constructed by a standard procedure. The score on the measure is the *mean* of the scores of the included items that had codes in the 1–7 range of the Delighted–Terrible Scale. If more than half of the included items had scores outside this range (e.g., the respondent said he had never thought about this concern, data missing, etc.), the measure itself was scored as "data missing." Since the variances of the concern items within each cluster were approximately equal, and since the interrelationships within each cluster tended to be approximately equal, this standard procedure for constructing measures resulted in approximately equal weighting of the items in the final cluster score.

EXHIBIT C.1. Measures Constructed from Clusters of Concern Items

Cluster number	Cluster name	Items included
C1	Virtues index	10+48
C2	Self-adjustment index	13+14+16
C3	Efficacy index	14+20+22
C4	Accomplishment index	18+20+33
C5	Self index	22+33
C6	Family index	1+2+3
C7	Marriage index	2+3+4
C8	Family relations index	6+9
C9	Health index	7+29
C10	Acceptance index	55+63+64
C11	Friends index A	59+61
C12	Friends index B	59+60+61
C13	Respect index	52+56+66

EXHIBIT C.1. *(continued)*

Cluster number	Cluster name	Items included
C14	Treatment index	17+54
C15	Independence index	34+44
C16	Central values index	18+23+28+44+64
C17	Respect/Bother-free index	43+53
C18	Leisure index	30+40+41
C19	Money index A	81+83+84
C20	Money index B	83+85
C21	Meet needs index	8+81
C22	Job index A	75+79+80
C23	Job index B	75+76+77+79+80
C24	Neighborhood index	57+58+88+89+90+94
C25	Community index	57+89+90
C26	Safety index	94+95+96
C27	Services index A	91+101
C28	Consumer index	97+99+101
C29	Recreation index A	112+114+115
C30	Recreation index B	112+115
C31	Local government index A	93+104
C32	Local government index B	93+103
C33	National government index A	106+107+109
C34	National government index B	105+107+108+109
C35	Media index A	116+117+118
C36	Media index B	116+117
C37	Cost index	100+102
C38	Religion index	69+70
C39	Beneficience index	71+72
C40	Close people index	1+2+5+57+58+59+60+76
C41	Other people index	47+49+51+52+53+54+55+56+64+65+66
C42	Things index	79+86+87+88+112+113+114+115
C43	Conditions index	7+24+27+40+41+43+44+45+46+62
C44	Activities index	6+26+29+30+42+61+71+74+77+97+116+118
C45	Competence index	11+13+14+16+17+18+19+20+21+33
C46	Services index B	91+92+93+98+99+101+104
C47	Money index C	78+81+83+84+85+100+102
C48	Nature of self index	10+35+36+48+50+68

Item numbers match Exhibit 2.1

Interrelationships Among Concern Items in May and April Surveys, by Population Subgroups

This appendix presents interrelationships among concern items from the May and April national surveys for nine major subgroups of American adults.

To facilitate comparison between results for the subgroup and results for the total population, the arrangement of items in the exhibits of this appendix is based on maps for the *total* population, and relationships for the indicated subgroup have been superimposed. Thus, the items that appeared in the May survey, shown in Exhibits D.1 to D.9, are all plotted as in Exhibit 2.7 (which was itself adapted from Exhibit 2.4). Similarly, the items from the April survey, in Exhibits D.10 to D.18, appear as in Exhibit 2.6 (and 2.8).

Only correlations of at least +.40 are shown (except in Exhibit D.17, where the minimum is +.60). The absence of a line between two items indicates that their relationship was less than this amount. No substantial negative relationships occurred.

EXHIBIT D.1. Interrelationships Among 59 Items of May National Survey, Data from Men (*N* = 547)

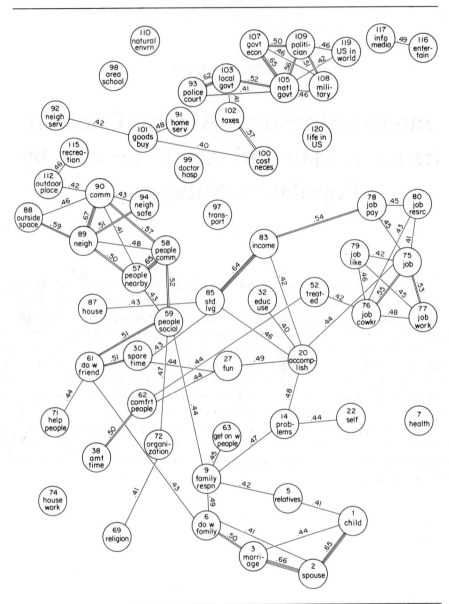

Item numbers match Exhibit 2.1; linkages show *r* ≥ .40.

EXHIBIT D.2. Interrelationships Among 59 Items of May National Survey, Data from Women (*N* = 750)

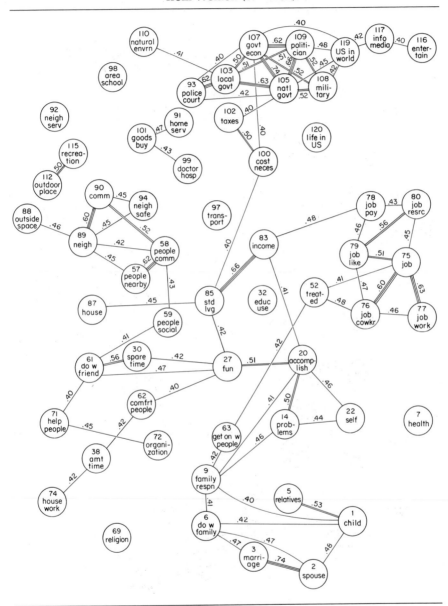

Item numbers match Exhibit 2.1; linkages show *r* ≥ .40.

EXHIBIT D.3. Interrelationships Among 59 Items of May National Survey, Data from People 16–29 Years Old (N = 358)

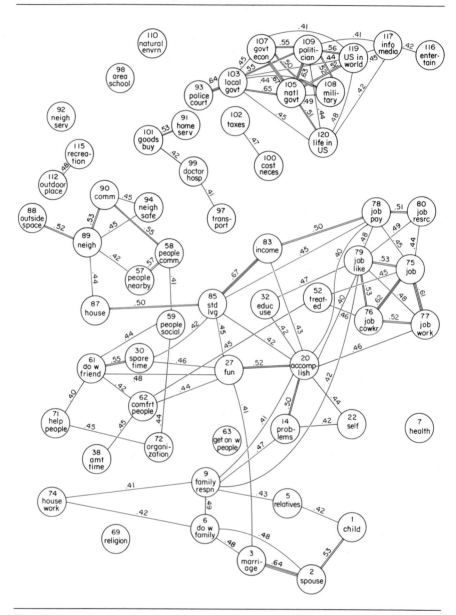

Item numbers match Exhibit 2.1; linkages show r ≥ .40.

EXHIBIT D.4. Interrelationships Among 59 Items of May National Survey, Data from People 30–44 Years Old (*N* = 356)

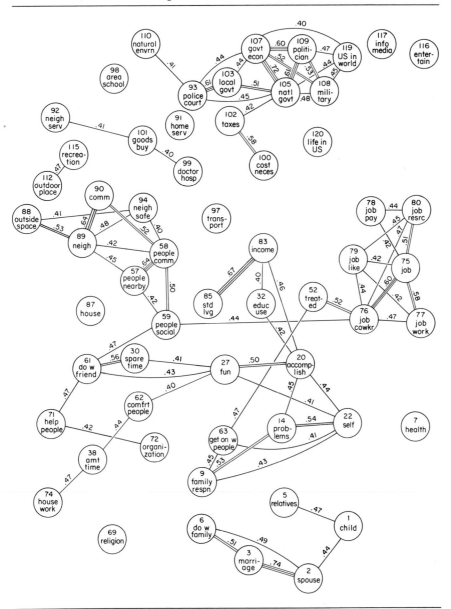

Item numbers match Exhibit 2.1; linkages show *r* ≥ .40.

EXHIBIT D.5. Interrelationships Among 59 Items of May National Survey, Data from People 45–59 Years Old (N = 275)

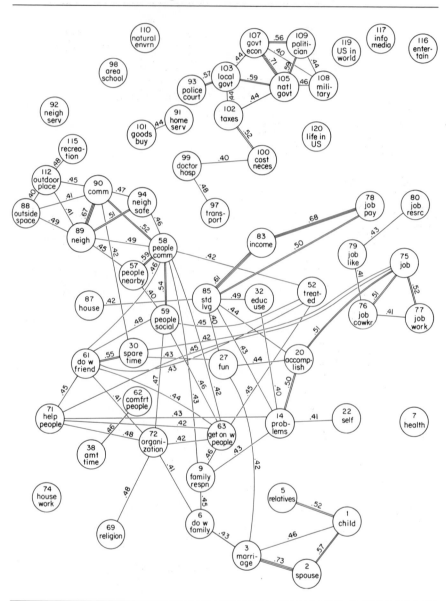

Item numbers match Exhibit 2.1; linkages show $r \geq .40$.

EXHIBIT D.6. Interrelationships Among 59 Items of May National Survey, Data from People 60+ Years Old (N = 305)

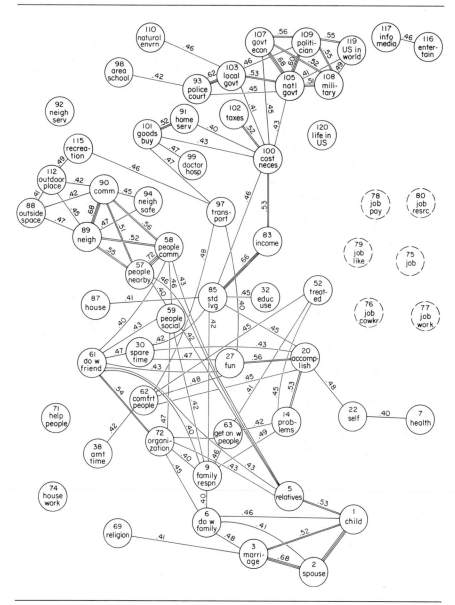

Item numbers match Exhibit 2.1; linkages show $r \geq .40$.

EXHIBIT D.7. Interrelationships Among 59 Items of May National Survey, Data from Blacks (*N* = 115)

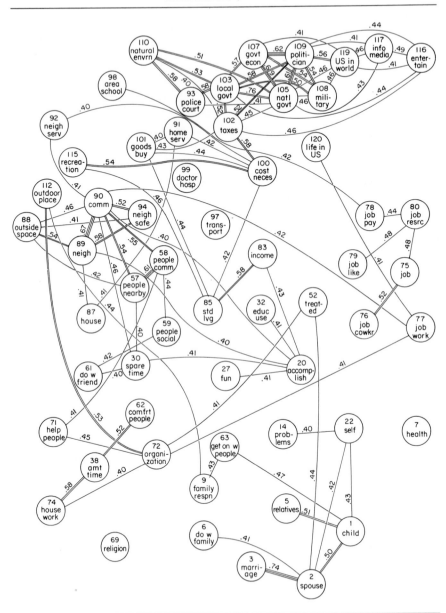

Item numbers match Exhibit 2.1; linkages show *r* ≥ .40.

EXHIBIT D.8. Interrelationships Among 59 Items of May National Survey, Data from People 30+ Years Old and with Low SES (N = 134)

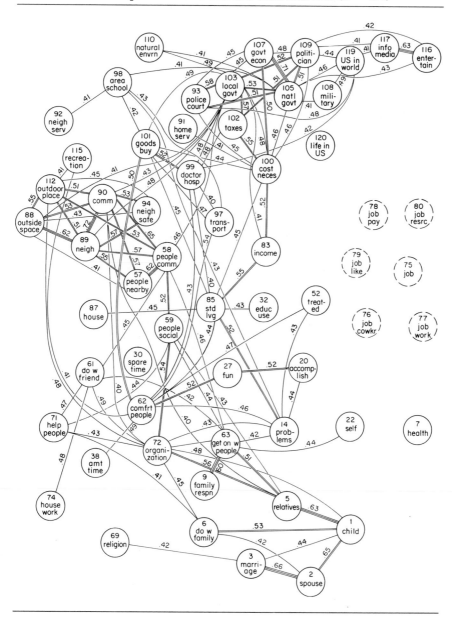

Item numbers match Exhibit 2.1; linkages show $r \geq .40$.

EXHIBIT D.9. Interrelationships Among 59 Items of May National Survey, Data from People 30+ Years Old and with High SES (*N* = 140)

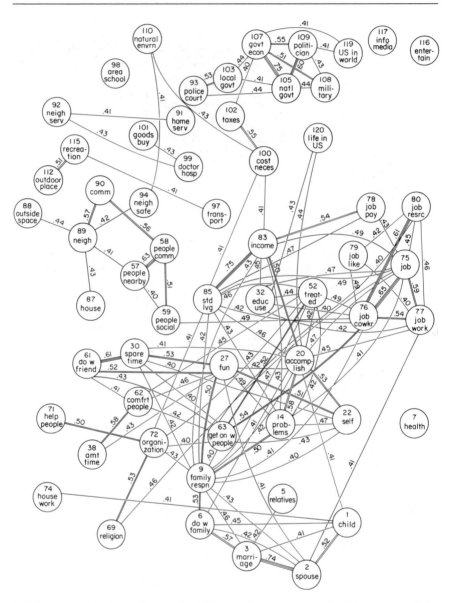

Item numbers match Exhibit 2.1; linkages show *r* ≥ .40.

EXHIBIT D.10. Interrelationships Among 23 Items of April National Survey, Data from Men (*N* = 611)

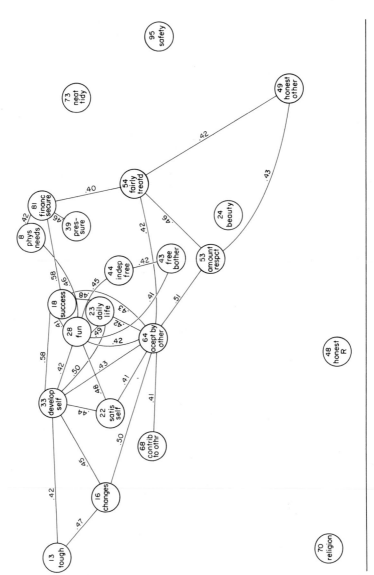

Item numbers match Exhibit 2.1; linkages show *r* ≥ .40.

EXHIBIT D.11. Interrelationships Among 23 Items of April National Survey, Data from Women
(N = 822)

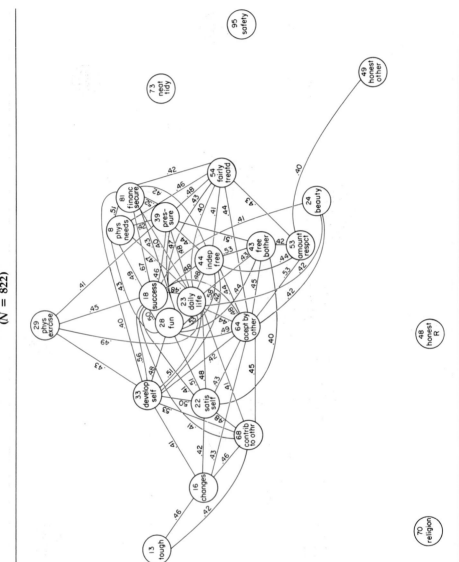

Item numbers match Exhibit 2.1; linkages show $r \geq .40$.

EXHIBIT D.12. Interrelationships Among 23 Items of April National Survey, Data from People 16–29 Years Old (N = 384)

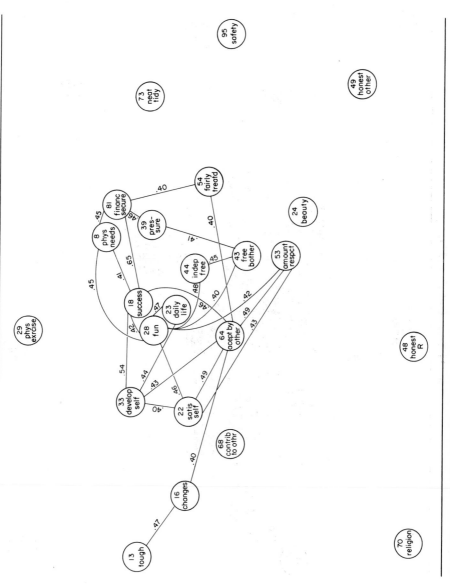

Item numbers match Exhibit 2.1; linkages show $r \geq .40$.

EXHIBIT D.13. Interrelationships Among 23 Items of April National Survey, Data from People 30–44 Years Old (*N* = 393)

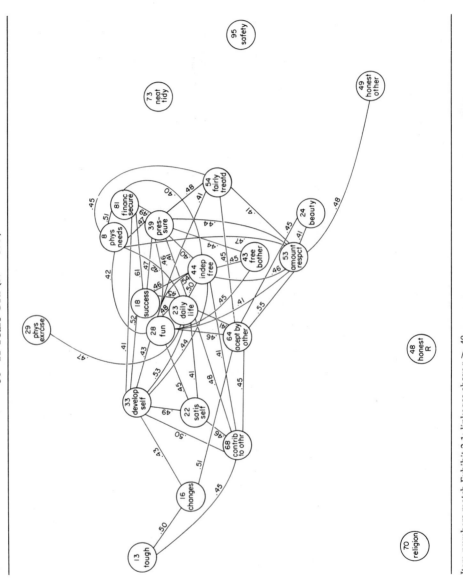

Item numbers match Exhibit 2.1; linkages show *r* ≥ .40.

EXHIBIT D.14. Interrelationships Among 23 Items of April National Survey, Data from People 45–59 Years Old (N = 320)

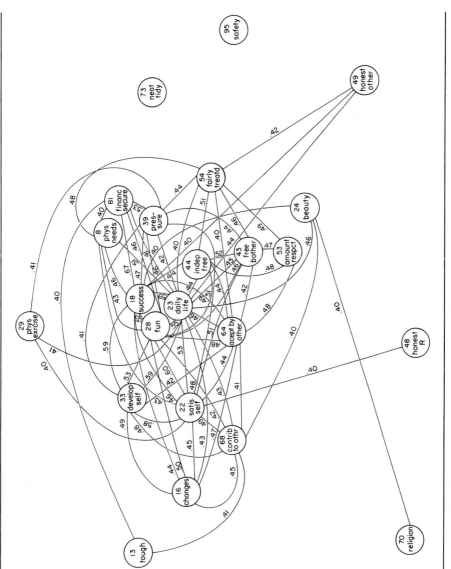

Item numbers match Exhibit 2.1; linkages show r ≥ .40.

EXHIBIT D.15. Interrelationships Among 23 Items of April National Survey, Data from People 60+ Years Old ($N = 334$)

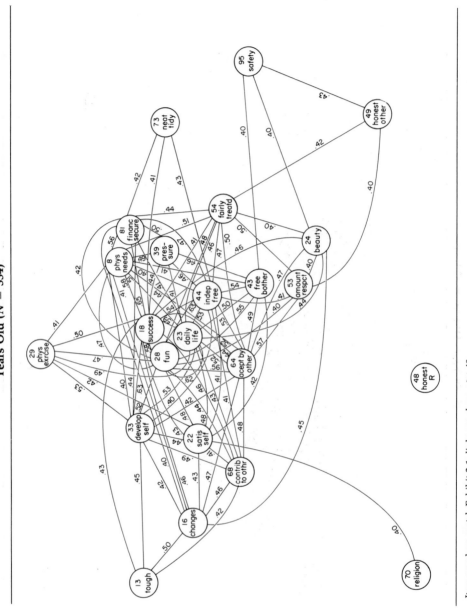

Item numbers match Exhibit 2.1; linkages show $r \geq .40$.

EXHIBIT D.16. Interrelationships Among 23 Items of April National Survey, Data from Blacks (N = 126)

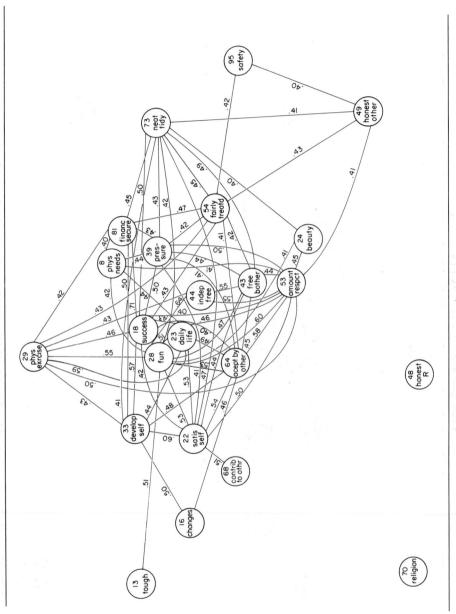

Item numbers match Exhibit 2.1; linkages show $r \geq .40$.

EXHIBIT D.17. Interrelationships Among 23 Items of April National Survey, Data from People 30+ Years Old and with Low SES (N = 172)

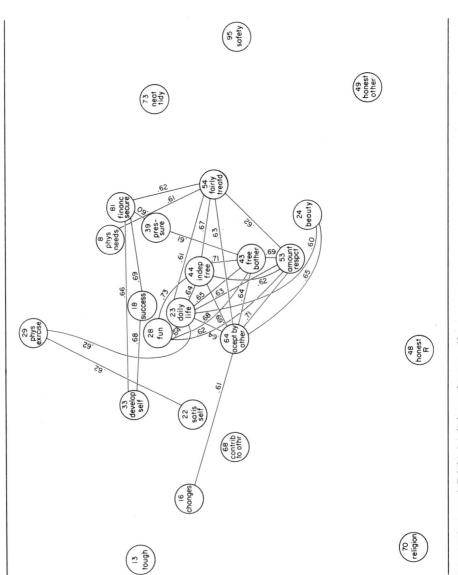

Item numbers match Exhibit 2.1; linkages show r ≥ .60.

EXHIBIT D.18. Interrelationships Among 23 Items of April National Survey, Data from People 30+ Years Old and with High SES (N = 210)

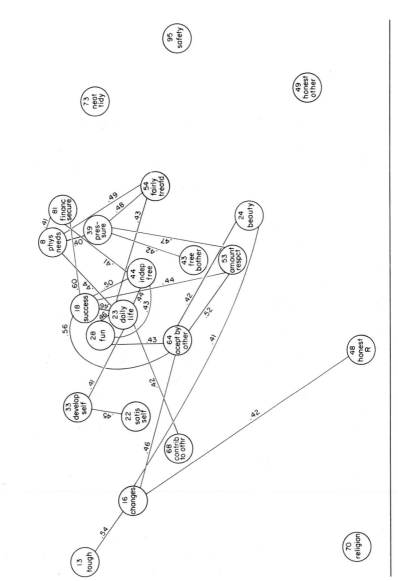

Item numbers match Exhibit 2.1; linkages show $r \geqslant .40$.

APPENDIX E

Factor Analyses of Concern Items from May, November, and April National Surveys

The mapping results presented in Exhibits 2.4 through 2.6 were derived by applying Smallest Space Analysis to the covariations among the concern items included in the May, November, and April national surveys. This appendix describes the results of applying factor analysis to these same data.

Our main purposes in examining the covariation among answers to the concern items were to identify sets of items that represented statistically distinct concerns, to infer how these concerns fit together within an encompassing structure of perceptions, to locate specific concern items according to the portions of this structure that they tapped, and to see whether the internal structure of concerns was stable in different subgroups of the population. While items of one concern were required to be statistically distinct from items of other concerns, this was not taken to imply that items had to be statistically *independent:* It seemed unrealistic to expect that evaluations of one aspect of life would be totally unrelated to evaluations of all other aspects of life.

One approach to achieving these goals through factor analysis would have been to perform an oblique factor analysis on each of our thirty matrices[1] of covariations among concern items and then attempt to match certain of the resulting factors across the subgroups. Given the large number of concern items to be analyzed, the relatively high cost of performing oblique rotations in factor analysis, and the problem of matching factors across analyses, we felt the analysis strategy used in chapter 2 and appendix D was preferable.

Instead, orthogonal factor analyses were performed for the total population (but not the subgroups), using data from each of the three national surveys, to

---

[1] In each of three national surveys, there is one matrix based on data from the total population and nine matrices based on data from major subgroups (listed in chapter 2).

412

check whether this "elegant" and parsimonious approach would yield results significantly different from those described in chapter 2. To the extent that different analysis techniques produced results that were compatible with one another, our confidence in the findings would be increased. The Factor Analysis results proved reasonably consonant with those from Smallest Space Analysis and did not substantially alter our inferences about perceptual structures.

The comparison of the two sets of results was interesting in itself. The underlying structure seemed to be more clearly portrayed in the results from the Smallest Space Analyses than in those from the Factor Analyses. We conclude that if limited resources were to permit application of just one of these techniques when analyzing similar data in the future, some form of nonmetric multidimensional scaling (e.g., Smallest Space Analysis) is likely to be more useful than orthogonal Factor Analysis.

May respondents. For the sixty-three items from the May data, plus three global measures of general well-being, a principal components analysis produced 15 factors with eigenvalues greater than 1.0. These fifteen factors explained 59 percent of the total variance, and 81 percent of the estimated common variance.[2] Prior to rotation, the first factor explained 22 percent of the total variance, and all of the rest were small, most explaining only 2–3 percent of the total variance. After a varimax rotation, the fifteen factors—in nearly all cases—could be closely matched with the concern item clusters that were arrived at using the methods described in chapter 2 and that are shown in Exhibit 2.7. These results appear in Exhibit E.1. Thus, for the May data, the factor analysis provided a rather nice confirmation of the earlier results.

November respondents. A factor analysis was also performed on the thirty-seven items of the November data (plus one global assessment of well-being), with results that were essentially identical to those just described. In these data, nine factors had eigenvalues greater than 1.0 and explained 58 percent of the total variance, with the first factor explaining 28 percent and the others rather small amounts.[3] After a varimax rotation most of these factors could be easily interpreted as representing concerns that had been identified previously in our data. These results appear in Exhibit E.2.

April respondents. A factor analysis was also performed on the twenty-three items of the April data. For these criterion-type concerns, only three factors had eigenvalues greater than 1.0 (jointly, they explained 47 percent of the total variance, 77 percent of the estimated common variance[4]). As in previously described factor analyses, the first factor was by far the most important (36 percent of the total variance), and the other factors relatively inconsequential, from a variance-explained perspective. The varimax rotation criterion did not, in general, locate factors in ways that were conceptually satisfying. The results appear in Exhibit E.3.

---

[2]Communality estimates were entered at 1.0 and iterated downward until stable estimates were obtained.
[3]Communality estimates were entered at 1.0 and not iterated.
[4]Squared multiple correlations were entered as communality estimates and not iterated.

EXHIBIT E.1. Factor Loadings on Items from May Survey
(≥ .40 After Varimax Rotation)

Factors	Item numbers, names and loadings[a]
1. Global satisfaction	G11 Rodgers' X (.77) G3 Life #3 (.74) G32 Happiness (.52) 27 Fun (.50) 20 Accomplishments (.43)
2. Government	105 National govt. (.78) 107 Govt. handles economy (.76) 109 Poli. leaders (.70) 108 Natl. military acts (.64) 104 Local govt. (.55) 119 U.S. in eyes of world (.50); 93 Police and courts (.45)
3. Neighborhood	89 Neighborhood (.77) 90 Community (.67) 88 Space outside home (.57) 58 People in community (.56) 57 People nearby homes (.53)
4. Job	75 Your job (.72) 76 Co-workers (.67) 79 Job: what like there (.64) 77 Work itself (.60) 80 Job: resources (.56)
5. Family	2 Your wife/husband (.79) 3 Marriage (.68) 1 Your children (.68) 6 Things to do w. family (.51) 5 Close adult relatives (.46)
6. Other people	72 Org. belong (.61) 71 Do to help people (.53) 61 Things do w. friends (.48)
7. Services	101 Goods can buy (.61) 91 Services for home (.56) 99 Doctors & hospitals (.48) 97 Get around, transportation (.41)
8. Young and old people	123 Young people think (.68) 122 People over 40 think (.41)
9. Outdoor recreation	112 Outdoor places (.57) 115 Recreation facility (.52)
10. Income	83 Family income (.70) 85 Standard of living (.67)
11. Media	117 Info. media (.65) 116 Entertainment (.54)
12. Time	38 Time to do things (.65)

EXHIBIT E.1. *(continued)*

Factors	Item numbers, names and loadings[a]
13. Self-efficacy	14 Handling problems (.45)
	9 Family responsibility (.43)
	22 Feel about yourself (.42)
	63 Getting on w. people (.42)
14. (not named)	(No items loaded ≥.40)
15. (not named)	(No items loaded ≥.40)

[a] Items included in the analysis but with no loading ≥.40 on any factor were: 7, 30, 32, 52, 62, 69, 74, 86, 87, 92, 98, 100, 102, 110, 111, and 120.

Note: No items loaded ≥ .40 on more than one factor. Item numbers match Exhibits 2.1 or 3.1.

EXHIBIT E.2. Factor Loadings on Items from November Survey (≥.40 After Varimax Rotation)

Items[a]		1 Family, fun	2 House, income	3 Job, etc.	4 Govt.	5 Comm.	6 Relax, time	7 Frnds., others	8 Young people	9 Creat.	h^2
4	Family life	.78									.70
26	Sex life	.77									.62
G32	Happy	.65									.65
6	Things fam. does	.61									.56
27	Fun	.53									.65
87	House		.69								.58
74	Housework		.60								.51
82	Agree on spend.	.45	.55								.58
83	Income		.50	.43							.59
85	Stnd. Lvng.		.50								.61
12	Get good job			.71							.62
57	Job			.57							.54
7	Health			.45							.48
21	Self			.42							.57
106	Natl. govt.				.85						.77

109	Pol. ldrs.	.80					.71
107	Govt. econ.	.78					.68
100	Cost of nec.	.51					.48
90	Community		.66				.62
114	Rec. places		.61				.62
101	Goods & services		.57				.46
104	Local govt.	.48	.52				.53
41	Relax			.73			.68
38	Time do things			.72			.72
42	Sleep			.61			.45
45	Privacy			.50			.56
25	Beaut. thngs.			.44			.58
65	Reliable others				.63		.57
60	Friends				.61		.58
55	Admired by others				.59		.53
56	Respect rights				.47		.55
118	Info. media				.40		.52
123	Young people					.84	.73
96	Secure frm theft					.40	.49
36	Creativity						.62	.54

[a] Item numbers match Exhibits 2.1 or 3.1. Items 11, 30, and 121 (omitted) showed no loadings ≥ .40.

EXHIBIT E.3. Factor Loadings on Concern Items from April Survey (≥ .40 After Varimax Rotation)

Items[a]		Factors			h²
		1	2	3	
53	Respect for respondent	.60			.47
49	Sincerity of others	.58			.36
54	Fairly treated	.53			.44
43	Bother & annoyance	.50			.42
95	Safety	.45			.28
24	Beauty	.45			.33
47	Acceptance by others	.41	.49		.47
16	Adjust to changes		.59		.41
68	Contribute to others		.58		.42
22	Self		.58		.46
33	Self-development		.57	.44	.52
13	Tough		.52		.31
28	Fun		.44	.46	.48
23	Interesting life		.42	.44	.47
81	Financial security			.68	.55
18	Achieve success			.67	.60
8	Meet physical needs			.51	.40
39	Pressure			.46	.40
44	Independence and freedom			.40	.38

[a] Item numbers match Exhibit 2.1. Items 29, 48, 70, and 73 (omitted) showed no loading ≥ .40.

Factor Analysis of Global Measures from the April National Survey

This appendix presents the results of factor analyzing the covariations among the global measures that were assessed by the April respondents. (Two other factor analyses, one of the global measures from the November Form 2 respondents and one of global measures from the July respondents, are presented and/or discussed in chap. 3.)

We felt the factor analysis presented in this appendix was less enlightening than those that are included in chapter 3. However, some readers may be interested in what resulted when commonly used procedures for orthogonal factor analysis were applied to the April data.

For the sixteen global measures, a principal components analysis produced six components with eigenvalues greater than 1.0. These six components explained 88 percent of the total variance, with the first component explaining 34 percent, the second 18 percent, and the remaining four each explaining from 11 percent to 7 percent.

The loadings, both before and after a varimax rotation, appear in Exhibit F.1. Prior to rotation all of the items that assess the respondent's level of current or future well-being loaded on the first factor. The remaining items were distributed among the other factors, heavily influenced by the few high correlations between derived measures and their components. The presence of these purely artifactual correlations strongly influenced the varimax rotation, and four of the six rotated factors reflected little except the mechanics by which the derived measures had been constructed.

EXHIBIT F.1. Factor Analysis of Global Measures from April Survey

Measures		Loading prior to rotation						Loadings after varimax rotation						Variance explained
		1	2	3	4	5	6	1	2	3	4	5	6	
G1	Life 1	.80	.05	-.10	.17	.00	.36	.87	.00	.03	-.06	.04	.23	82%
G2	Life 2	.78	.01	-.12	.21	-.01	.39	.89	-.02	.01	-.02	.06	.19	82%
G3	Life 3	.86	.03	-.11	.21	-.01	.42	.96	-.02	.02	-.04	.05	.21	97%
G6	Ladder: most	.80	.16	.16	-.11	-.28	-.28	.39	-.06	.16	.00	-.17	.81	87%
G7	Circles: whole life	.77	.14	.00	-.15	.07	-.23	.39	.01	.18	-.19	.10	.67	69%
G14	Interviewer rating	.66	.06	.02	.16	.02	.19	.65	-.02	.14	.01	.04	.25	50%
G17	Ladder: best	.72	-.04	-.22	-.20	-.34	-.33	.30	-.15	-.24	.00	.04	.82	83%
G23	Ladder: worst	.53	.38	.61	.18	.25	-.27	.22	-.01	.82	.01	-.06	.41	90%
G53	Circles: R—others	.64	.03	.05	-.64	.32	.00	.27	.02	.11	-.77	.07	.49	92%
G56	Past progress	.34	-.70	.50	-.08	-.33	-.02	.12	-.94	.05	-.02	-.08	.28	98%
G57	Future progress	-.08	-.58	-.49	.25	.58	-.13	-.03	-.09	-.14	-.01	.95	-.23	99%
G58	Progress past & future	.22	-.95	.14	.08	.06	-.06	.09	-.85	-.05	-.03	.49	.06	98%
G59	Ladder: best—worst	.03	-.31	-.75	-.30	-.49	.00	.01	-.03	-.96	.00	.09	.23	99%
G64	Ladder: 5 years ago	.21	.82	-.41	.02	.15	-.19	.14	.92	.05	.04	-.02	.29	96%
G65	Ladder: 5 years hence	.64	-.40	-.31	.16	.31	-.38	.31	-.12	.02	.01	.76	.49	93%
G67	Circles: others	-.01	.11	-.07	.79	-.38	-.31	.06	.07	.07	.93	.03	.10	88%
Factor contributions														
	To total variance	34%	18%	11%	9%	8%	7%	22%	16%	11%	9%	11%	18%	88%
	To explained variance	39%	20%	13%	11%	9%	8%	25%	18%	13%	11%	13%	21%	100%

Notes: Communality estimates were entered at 1.0 and not iterated. Principal components with λ < 1.0 were eliminated. Item numbers match Exhibit 3.1.

Scan for Interactions Involving Concern Measures and Life 3

The purpose of this appendix is to provide an example of the approach used for scanning for first-order interactions and some specific numerical results from one of the scans.

As discussed in chapter 4, one of our general analytic problems was to find an appropriate way to combine feelings about life concerns to arrive at a good prediction of feelings about life-as-a-whole. In statistical terms, this is the problem of finding an appropriate "model." One simple and commonly used model is the additive model, which assumes that the influence of each predictor (upon a dependent variable) "adds on" to the effects of all other predictors; i.e., that the influence of any one predictor is not affected by the *level* of any other predictor(s). If the influence of one predictor is contingent upon the level of one or more other predictors, one has statistical interaction (sometimes called a contingency effect). One of the ways to find out whether an additive model is appropriate for a set of data is to determine whether there are any interactions. The presence of marked interactions usually implies that an additive model is not appropriate.

In this appendix we describe only the means of scanning for *first-order* interactions (i.e., those involving two predictors and one dependent variable), though—as noted in chapter 4—a check was also made for higher-order interactions.

The basic strategy of our procedure follows closely from the above description of "interaction": We look to see whether the level of one predictor affects the strength of relationship between another predictor and the dependent variable. This requires dividing the respondents according to their level on one concern measure (the control measure) and computing the relationship (we used gammas) between another concern measure and Life 3. We did this for many different combinations of predictors. In each case, data were split into approximate thirds (high, medium, low) on the control variable, and—for reasons of economy—relationships between the other predictor and Life 3 were computed for (only) two of the three groups, the top and bottom thirds.

Since it would have been very expensive to check for interaction among all possible pairs of the relevant concern measure (for example, there were 870 such pairs among the thirty predictors from the May data), procedures were devised for selecting the pairs to be checked. In the data from the May respondents, which provide our example here, a preliminary Multiple Classification Analysis identified six concern measures that had the highest betas and another ten with the next highest betas. Among the six predictors with the highest betas, all possible pairs were checked. Among the full set of sixteen, every fifth pair was checked, making the selection in such a way that each predictor was used as a control measure an approximately equal number of times.

Exhibit G.1 shows the seventy-four pairs of concern measures that were selected by one or both of these two procedures and the actual values of the computed relationships. It is clear at a glance that the differences between the gammas, an indication of the magnitude of the interactions, tend to be small (the mean absolute difference is .08). The largest difference is .27 (based on gammas of .46 and .19, and involving the predictors 6 and 30); the next largest is .26 (based on gammas of .65 and .39, predictors C3 and C20). Most of the remaining differences were .10 or less.

Although none of the interactions looked very substantial, we wanted a more precise indication of the magnitude of the interaction effect where our scan had indicated such an effect might exist. Accordingly, we selected the two biggest differences for further investigation. By comparing how well these predictor pairs could predict Life 3 using an additive model with the accuracy of prediction using an approach that was sensitive to both additive and interactive effects, the potency of the interactive effect could be estimated. In neither case did the interaction effect by itself account for as much as 2 percent of the variance of Life 3.[1] Since these were the largest of the interactions, it was clear that there was little to be gained by using the more complicated predictive model that would be required if nonadditive effects were to be included.

---

[1]Operationally, this was achieved by performing two Multiple Classification Analyses for each pair of predictors. The method is fully described in Andrews et $al.$ (1973) and involves comparing an R^2_{adj} from an analysis using the two predictors with an adjusted eta^2 from an analysis using the two predictors combined into a single pattern variable.

EXHIBIT G.1. Scan for First-Order Interactions Involving Selected Pairs of Concern Measures and Life 3

Each cell shows the upper figure over the lower figure (upper / lower).

Measure correlated with Life 3	87	30	6	74	123	7	27	38	C34	C3	C6	C28	C32	C37	C20	C30
87 House/apartment	— / —	— / —	.35 / .29	— / —	.38 / .35	— / —	.33 / .30	— / —	— / —	.32 / .25	.34 / .35	— / —	— / —	— / —	.28 / .20	— / —
30 Spare-time activities	.41 / .37	— / —	— / —	— / —	— / —	.41 / .37	— / —	— / —	— / —	— / —	.43 / .36	— / —	— / —	— / —	— / —	.41 / .36
6 Things do with family	.44 / .30	.46 / .19	— / —	— / —	— / —	— / —	.41 / .21	— / —	— / —	.42 / .31	.38 / .33	.45 / .37	— / —	— / —	.47 / .31	— / —
74 Housework	— / —	— / —	.23 / .12	— / —	— / —	— / —	— / —	.31 / .13	— / —	— / —	— / —	— / —	.32 / .18	— / —	— / —	— / —
123 Young people think	— / —	— / —	— / —	.13 / .13	— / —	— / —	— / —	— / —	.22 / .08	— / —	— / —	— / —	— / —	.17 / .03	— / —	— / —
7 Your health	— / —	— / —	— / —	— / —	.27 / .26	— / —	— / —	— / —	— / —	.19 / .19	— / —	— / —	— / —	— / —	.25 / .28	— / —
27 Amount of fun	.51 / .54	— / —	.49 / .47	— / —	— / —	.54 / .49	— / —	— / —	— / —	.43 / .43	.51 / .49	— / —	— / —	— / —	.49 / .51	.55 / .46
38 Time to do things	— / —	.24 / .02	— / —	— / —	— / —	— / —	.19 / .14	— / —	— / —	— / —	— / —	.27 / .17	— / —	— / —	— / —	— / —
C34 Natl. govt. index	— / —	— / —	.29 / .22	— / —	— / —	— / —	— / —	.20 / .22	— / —	— / —	— / —	— / —	.22 / .14	— / —	— / —	— / —
C3 Efficacy index	.58 / .61	— / —	.49 / .64	.56 / .56	— / —	— / —	.49 / .50	— / —	.41 / .60	— / —	.50 / .57	— / —	— / —	.61 / .56	.39 / .65	— / —
C6 Family index	.50 / .56	— / —	.54 / .51	— / —	.58 / .48	— / —	.50 / .40	— / —	— / —	.46 / .40	— / —	— / —	— / —	— / —	.50 / .48	— / —
C28 Consumer index	.29 / .29	— / —	— / —	.21 / .22	— / —	— / —	.13 / .32	— / —	— / —	— / —	.32 / .26	— / —	— / —	— / —	— / —	.20 / .32
C32 Local govt. index	— / —	.15 / .23	— / —	— / —	— / —	— / —	— / —	— / —	— / —	— / —	— / —	.11 / .18	— / —	— / —	— / —	— / —
C37 Media index	— / —	— / —	.16 / .19	— / —	— / —	— / —	— / —	.11 / .14	— / —	— / —	— / —	— / —	.19 / .09	— / —	— / —	— / —
C20 Money index	.47 / .43	— / —	.51 / .42	.47 / .45	— / —	— / —	.46 / .42	— / —	.49 / .37	.31 / .45	.49 / .45	— / —	— / —	.50 / .44	— / —	— / —
C30 Recreation index	— / —	— / —	— / —	— / —	.29 / .16	— / —	— / —	— / —	— / —	.15 / .20	— / —	— / —	— / —	— / —	.14 / .10	— / —

Data: 1,297 respondents to May national survey. Item numbers match Exhibit 2.1 or C.1.

Upper figure of each pair is the gamma between the indicated measure and Life 3 for the approximately one-third of respondents who gave the least positive evaluations on the indicated control measure; the lower figure is a similar gamma for the one-third who gave the most positive evaluations.

Demographic Characteristics of July Respondents

EXHIBIT H.1. Demographic Characteristics of July Respondents with Comparisons to a Random Sample of Toledo Residents and to American Adults in General

Demographic characteristics	July respondents	Toledo sample[a]	National data[b]
Age			
17–19	6%	3%	6%
20–24	14	12	12
25–34	21	17	19
35–44	18	18	17
45–54	17	18	17
55–64	13	17	14
65+	11	15	15
	100%	100%	100%
Sex			
Male	44%	40%	47%
Female	56	60	53
	100%	100%	100%
Race			
White	87%	87%	89%
Black	13	12	10
Other	0	1	1
	100%	100%	100%
Marital status			
Married	70%	63%	68%
Divorced or separated	6	13	8
Widowed	7	12	11
Never married	17	12	13
	100%	100%	100%

424

EXHIBIT H.1. *(continued)*

Demographic characteristics	July respondents	Toledo sample[a]	National data[b]
Education (highest)			
Grade school	4%	15%	19%
9–11 grades	11	21	16
Completed high school	31	35	34
Some college	26	19	19
Completed college	20	7	9
Advanced degree	8	3	3
	100%	100%	100%
Family income (annual)			
Under $3,000	7%	c	12%
$3,000–4,999	9	—	12
$5,000–7,499	7	—	12
$7,500–9,999	7	—	14
$10,000–12,499	18	—	15
$12,500–14,999	17	—	11
$15,000–19,999	21	—	12
$20,000–24,999	7	—	6
$25,000+	7	—	6
	100%		100%
Working status			
Working	59%	61%	57%
Unemployed, laid off	6	3	6
Retired, disabled	10	11	13
Housewife	19	23	22
Student, not working	6	2	2
	100%	100%	100%

[a] Data in this column are from respondents to a 1973 Survey Research Center study that drew a representative probability sample of Toledo residents.

[b] Data in this column pertaining to age, sex, and race are based on 1970 U.S. Census figures; those pertaining to marital status, education, family income, and working status are from a 1973 survey of adult Americans, our "April respondents."

[c] Figures not tabulated.

Distributions Produced by the Delighted–Terrible, Faces, and Circles Scales on Five Concerns

EXHIBIT I.1. Comparison of Percentage Distributions Produced by the Delighted–Terrible, Faces, and Circles Scales for Feelings About Five Concerns

Life concern and measurement method[a]	Scale categories									
	(negative)			(positive)						
	0	1	2	3	4	5	6	7	8	Total
Independence and freedom										
D–T	[b]	1	4	8	15	36	28	8	[b]	100%
Faces	[b]	2	4	8	9	25	35	17	[b]	100%
Circles	2	2	3	9	12	18	23	22	9	100%
Standard of living										
D–T	[b]	0	0	7	12	39	37	5	[b]	100%
Faces	[b]	1	3	5	9	28	41	13	[b]	100%
Circles	0	0	2	6	16	25	26	18	7	100%
National government										
D–T	[b]	10	23	24	34	7	2	0	[b]	100%
Faces	[b]	28	22	22	16	8	4	0	[b]	100%
Circles	7	14	16	27	24	7	2	2	1	100%
House, apartment										
D–T	[b]	0	1	4	18	31	38	8	[b]	100%
Faces	[b]	1	2	4	13	24	39	16	[b]	100%
Circles	1	0	3	9	18	21	19	22	7	100%
Spare time										
D–T	[b]	1	0	6	15	42	32	4	[b]	100%
Faces	[b]	1	3	5	8	33	35	15	[b]	100%
Circles	0	0	4	8	12	23	26	20	7	100%

Notes: Cases with missing data have been omitted. In no instance did these amount to more than 8 percent of the respondents.
[a] Measurement methods are described in Exhibit 3.1; see measures G1, G5, and G7. The wordings of the concern-level items are shown in Exhibit 2.1; see items 30, 44, 85, 87, and 106.
[b] Nonexistent category for this scale.
Data source: 222 respondents to July survey.

Number of Cases Used in Computing Means Shown in Exhibit 7.1

EXHIBIT J.1. Number of Cases Used in Computing Means Shown in Exhibit 7.1

		Categories of the D–T scale						
Measures[a]		Delighted	Pleased	Mostly sat.	Mixed	Mostly dissat.	Unhappy	Terrible
G1	Life 1	18	86	77	22	6	6	0
G2	Life 2	26	88	74	20	4	2	0
87	House	16	80	64	37	8	2	1
30	Spare time	8	69	89	30	13	1	1
106	Natl. govt.	1	5	14	70	48	45	21
85	Stand. lvg.	11	73	79	24	14	0	0
44	Ind., free.	16	60	76	33	17	8	2

[a] Measure numbers refer to Exhibits 2.1 or 3.1.
Note: These figures show the number of cases used in computing means for the Circles Scale. The cases used for the Faces and Ladder Scales vary slightly due to missing data, but in no instance is the variation more than two cases from the figure shown here.

APPENDIX K

Distributions and Means on Selected Concern Clusters for All May Respondents and for Subgroups

EXHIBIT K.1. Distributions on Concern Clusters

		Delighted–terrible scale category						
Cluster[a]		Delighted	Pleased	Mostly satisfied	Mixed	Mostly dissatisfied	Unhappy	Terrible
C3	Efficacy	3%	31%	47%	16%	2%	1%	<1%
C6	Family	51%	36%	8%	2%	2%	<1%	<1%
C11	Friends	8%	46%	37%	7%	2%	<1%	<1%
C20	Money	3%	26%	40%	19%	8%	3%	1%
C23	Job	10%	40%	37%	10%	2%	<1%	0
C24	Neighborhood	6%	40%	37%	12%	4%	1%	<1%
C28	Consumer	4%	32%	41%	16%	5%	1%	<1%
C30	Recreation	5%	31%	36%	16%	7%	4%	1%
C32	Local government	1%	10%	29%	33%	16%	7%	4%
C34	National government	<1%	3%	15%	41%	25%	11%	4%
C36	Media	1%	10%	31%	34%	18%	5%	1%
C37	Cost	1%	3%	15%	27%	30%	17%	8%

[a] Cluster numbers match Exhibit C.1 in appendix C.
Data source: 1,297 respondents to May national survey.

EXHIBIT K.2. Mean D–T Scale Scores on Concern Clusters for All May Respondents and for Subgroups

Group[b]		C3 Efficacy	C6 Family	C11 Friends	C20 Money	C23 Job	C24 Neighborhood	C28 Consumer	C30 Recreation	C32 Local government	C34 Nat'l. government	C36 Media	C37 Cost
								Concern cluster[a]					
All Rs		5.2	6.3	5.5	4.8	5.4	5.3	5.1	5.1	4.1	3.6	4.2	3.4
Men		5.3	6.4	5.5	4.9	5.4	5.3	5.1	5.1	4.0	3.6	4.2	3.4
Women		5.1	6.3	5.6	4.8	5.5	5.3	5.1	5.1	4.2	3.6	4.2	3.3
Age:	15–19	5.2	6.3	5.6	4.5	5.0	4.7	4.9	4.7	3.8	3.6	4.6	3.3
	20–24	5.0	6.5	5.5	4.7	5.3	5.0	5.0	4.7	3.8	3.5	4.3	3.2
	25–29	5.2	6.4	5.5	4.8	5.4	5.1	5.0	4.9	4.0	3.7	4.4	3.2
	30–34	5.1	6.3	5.5	4.8	5.3	5.1	4.8	4.8	3.9	3.5	4.2	3.3
	35–44	5.2	6.3	5.5	5.0	5.5	5.4	5.1	5.0	4.1	3.5	4.0	3.2
	45–54	5.1	6.2	5.6	4.9	5.5	5.4	5.2	5.2	4.2	3.6	4.0	3.3
	55–64	5.2	6.3	5.6	5.0	5.6	5.5	5.3	5.4	4.4	3.8	4.3	3.7
	65+	5.2	6.2	5.5	4.8	5.5	5.5	5.1	5.4	4.5	3.8	4.2	3.7
Family Life-Cycle:	1	5.0	(N=3)	5.6	4.7	5.3	5.0	4.8	5.0	3.6	3.4	4.2	3.3
	2	5.2	6.4	5.5	4.9	5.2	5.1	5.0	4.7	3.9	3.5	4.2	3.1
	3	5.3	6.6	5.6	4.8	5.5	5.2	5.2	4.8	4.1	3.6	4.3	3.3
	4	5.2	6.4	5.4	4.9	5.5	5.3	5.1	5.0	4.1	3.6	4.1	3.3
	5	5.1	6.4	5.4	5.1	5.6	5.6	5.1	5.0	4.2	3.3	3.9	3.2
	6	5.2	6.3	5.6	5.0	5.5	5.5	5.2	5.4	4.3	3.6	4.0	3.4
	7	5.1	5.2	5.6	4.8	5.5	5.4	5.1	5.4	4.4	3.8	4.4	3.8
	8	5.0	4.3	5.5	4.2	5.5	4.8	4.9	4.8	3.9	3.6	4.6	3.2
Socioeconomic status:	1	5.2	5.9	5.5	4.4	5.5	5.4	4.9	5.2	4.4	3.8	4.6	3.5
	2	5.2	6.2	5.4	4.7	5.4	5.2	5.1	5.2	4.2	3.7	4.4	3.3
	3	5.1	6.4	5.5	4.8	5.4	5.2	5.1	4.9	4.0	3.5	4.2	3.3
	4	5.2	6.5	5.6	5.0	5.5	5.3	5.2	5.2	4.0	3.6	4.1	3.3
	5	5.2	6.5	5.6	5.4	5.2	5.4	5.3	5.1	4.1	3.6	4.0	3.5
	6	5.0	6.1	5.5	4.2	5.2	5.0	4.9	4.8	4.0	3.5	4.1	3.3
	7	5.2	6.2	5.5	5.3	5.4	5.3	5.0	5.0	4.1	3.5	4.3	3.1
Blacks		5.1	6.4	5.5	4.9	5.4	5.3	5.1	5.1	4.2	3.6	4.2	3.4
Whites		5.3	5.8	5.5	4.3	5.5	4.9	4.8	4.6	3.9	3.3	4.5	3.1

[a] Cluster numbers match Exhibit C.1 in appendix C.

[b] Subgroup Ns appear in appendix M; see chapter 9 for description of Family Life-Cycle and Socioeconomic Status Scales.

Data source: 1,297 respondents to May national survey.

Formation of Socioeconomic Status Scale

Respondents were assigned to socioeconomic status categories on the basis of their family income and the educational attainment of the head of their household. A nine by ten matrix was generated using these variables, and respondents were assigned to an SES category according to the scheme shown in Exhibit L.1. Categories numbered 1 through 5 contain respondents whose income levels are roughly commensurate with the education of the head of their household and thus are status consistent; categories 6 and 7 contain respondents whose positions are status inconsistent.

EXHIBIT L.1. Assignment of Socioeconomic Status on the Basis of Household Head's Educational Attainment and Family Income

Head's educational attainment	Annual family unit income									
	Under 3,000	3,000–3,999	4,000–4,999	5,000–5,999	6,000–7,499	7,500–9,999	10,000–12,499	12,500–14,999	15,000–24,999	25,000– or more
5th grade or less	1	1	2	2	2	7	7	7	7	7
6–8th grade	1	1	2	2	2	2	7	7	7	7
9–11th grade	1	1	2	2	2	3	3	3	7	7
9–11th plus noncollege training	1	1	2	2	2	3	3	3	7	7
12th grade	6	6	2	2	3	3	3	4	4	7
12th grade plus noncollege training	6	6	2	2	3	3	3	4	4	7
Some college	6	6	6	6	3	4	4	4	5	5
BA or BS	6	6	6	6	6	4	4	5	5	5
BA plus; higher degree	6	6	6	6	6	6	5	5	5	5

Subgroup *N*s and Percentage Distributions

EXHIBIT M.1. Subgroup *N*s and Percentage Distributions

Group[a]		Number in sample			Distribution		
		May	Nov. F2	April	May	Nov. F2	April
All Rs		1297	1072	1433	100%	100%	100%
Men		547	465	611	42%	43%	43%
Women		750	607	822	58%	57%	57%
Age:	15–19	46	33	43	4%	3%	3%
	20–24	166	123	161	13%	12%	11%
	25–29	146	141	180	11%	13%	13%
	30–34	134	100	139	10%	9%	10%
	35–44	222	182	254	17%	17%	18%
	45–54	191	152	225	15%	14%	16%
	55–64	172	152	202	13%	14%	14%
	65+	217	176	227	17%	17%	16%
Family Life-Cycle:	1	134	122	168	10%	12%	12%
	2	135	66	129	10%	6%	9%
	3	204	188	220	16%	18%	15%
	4	212	195	259	16%	19%	18%
	5	49	38	44	4%	4%	3%
	6	281	215	313	22%	20%	22%
	7	207	164	229	16%	16%	16%
	8	63	55	68	5%	5%	5%
Socioeconomic Status:	1	156	122	172	12%	12%	13%
	2	181	186	189	14%	18%	14%
	3	268	225	280	21%	22%	21%
	4	239	169	280	18%	17%	21%
	5	169	146	210	13%	14%	15%
	6	104	107	128	8%	10%	9%
	7	101	72	102	8%	7%	7%

431

EXHIBIT M.1. *(continued)*

Group[a]	Number in sample			Distribution		
	May	Nov. F2	April	May	Nov. F2	April
Blacks	115	106	126	9%	10%	9%
Whites	1165	950	1248	90%	89%	87%

Note: Subgroup Ns may sum to less than the total number of respondents because some respondents could not be assigned to any of the categories indicated.

[a] See chapter 9 for description of Family Life-Cycle and Socioeconomic Status Scales.

Data sources: 1,297 respondents to May national survey; 1,072 respondents to November Form 2 national survey; and 1,433 respondents to April national survey.

APPENDIX N

Perceived Well-Being in 1974, 1976

Surveys of American adults in October 1974 and April 1976 included well-being measures selected from among those described in this book. Because some readers will be interested in trends across time, it seems important to present these results, even though the results became available only after the text for Part 2 of this book had been completed.

The October 1974 survey was an Omnibus Survey of the Survey Research Center, Institute for Social Research, University of Michigan, highly similar in design to the other national surveys described in Exhibit 1.4 and appendix B. The number of respondents to the October 1974 survey was 1,528. Exhibit N.1 shows the distribution of these respondents on the Life 1 measure of global well-being and on five concern-level measures.

The April 1976 survey was also an Omnibus Survey of the Survey Research Center, basically similar in design to the other national surveys described in Exhibit 1.4 and appendix B. The total sample for this survey was split into

EXHIBIT N.1. Distribution of October 1974 Respondents on Selected Well-Being Measures[a]

Measure[b]		Delig.	Pleas.	Mos. sat.	Mixed	Mos. diss.	Unhap.	Terr.	(Means)
G1	Life-as-a-whole	13%	33%	34%	13%	3%	2%	2%	5.3
18	Extent you are achieving success	6%	25%	31%	18%	9%	7%	4%	4.6
75	Job	13%	39%	28%	12%	4%	3%	1%	5.3
83	Family income	2%	18%	33%	20%	12%	7%	8%	4.2
85	Standard of living	7%	32%	38%	12%	6%	3%	2%	5.1
106	What our national government is doing	1%	3%	9%	34%	23%	18%	12%	3.2

[a] The exhibit shows percentage distributions for respondents who chose one of the categories shown. The percentage of the total respondents who chose some other answer or who were coded missing data varied from 1.3 percent to 10.5 percent with the exception of the job item where it was 38.9 percent.
[b] Measure numbers match Exhibit 2.1 or 3.1.

random halves. In one half, feelings about well-being were assessed using the Delighted–Terrible Scale, in the other half the seven-point Satisfaction scale was used. (These scales are described in chapters 1 and 3 respectively.) The upper portion of Exhibit N.2 shows how 820 respondents who received the Delighted–Terrible Scale were distributed on a measure of global well-being and on four concern-level measures. The lower portion of this exhibit shows similar information for the 728 respondents who answered on the seven-point Satisfaction scale.

EXHIBIT N.2. Distribution of April 1976 Respondents on Selected Well-Being Measures: Delighted–Terrible and Satisfaction Scales[a]

Measure[b]	Delighted–terrible scale							
	Delig.	Pleas.	Mos. sat.	Mixed	Mos. diss.	Unhap.	Terr.	(Means)
G1 Life-as-a-whole (Life 1)	19%	35%	31%	11%	2%	2%	<1%	5.5
3 Marriage	49%	35%	10%	2%	1%	2%	1%	6.2
7 Health	18%	34%	28%	8%	5%	4%	3%	5.3
85 Living standard	14%	38%	29%	11%	5%	2%	1%	5.4
87 House/apartment	19%	34%	29%	10%	4%	2%	2%	5.4

	Seven-point satisfaction scale							
	Compl. Sat. (7)	(6)	(5)	Neutral (4)	(3)	(2)	Compl. Dissat. (1)	
G29 Life-as-a-whole (Sat.)	35%	32%	15%	12%	4%	1%	1%	5.7
3 Marriage	66%	19%	7%	5%	<1%	<1%	3%	6.3
7 Health	35%	22%	13%	14%	7%	3%	6%	5.3
85 Living standard	32%	26%	17%	13%	6%	3%	3%	5.5
87 House/apartment	37%	20%	16%	15%	4%	4%	4%	5.4

[a]The exhibit shows percentage distributions for respondents who chose one of the categories shown. The percentage of total respondents who chose some other answer or who were coded missing data was always under two percent, with the exception of the marriage item where it was 37.6 percent on the Delighted–Terrible Scale and 34.9 percent on the Satisfaction scale.
[b]Measure numbers match Exhibit 2.1 or 3.1.

References

Aberbach, Joel D., and Walker, Jack L. *Race in the City: Political Trust and Public Policy in the New Urban System.* Boston: Little, Brown and Co., 1973.

Abrams, Mark. "This Britain: A Contented Nation?" *New Society* 27:594 (21 February 1974): 439–440.

Adams, J. Stacy. "Toward an Understanding of Inequity." *Journal of Abnormal and Social Psychology* 67:5 (November 1963): 422–436.

Allport, Gordon W., and Vernon, Philip E. *A Study of Values.* Boston: Houghton-Mifflin, 1931.

Althauser, Robert P., and Heberlein, Thomas A. "Validity and the Multitrait-Multimethod Matrix." In *Sociological Methodology 1970,* edited by Edgar F. Borgatta and George W. Bohrnstedt, pp. 151–169. San Francisco: Jossey-Bass, 1970.

Alwin, Duane F. "Approaches to the Interpretation of Relationships in the Multitrait-Multimethod Matrix." In *Sociological Methodology 1973–74,* edited by Herbert L. Costner, pp. 79–105. San Francisco: Jossey-Bass, 1974.

Andrews, Frank M. "Social Indicators and Socioeconomic Development." *The Journal of Developing Areas* 8:1 (October 1973): 3–12.

Andrews, Frank M.; Morgan, James N.; Sonquist, John A.; and Klem, Laura. *Multiple Classification Analysis.* 2d ed. Ann Arbor, Mich: Institute for Social Research, 1973.

Bachman, Jerald G.; Kahn, Robert L.; Mednick, Martha T.; Davidson, Terrence N., and Johnston, Lloyd D. *Youth in Transition,* vol. 1. Ann Arbor, Mich.: Institute for Social Research, 1967.

Bateson, Gregory. *Steps to an Ecology of Mind.* San Francisco: Chandler Publishing Company, 1972.

Bell, Daniel. *The Coming of Post-Industrial Society: A Venture in Social Forecasting.* New York: Basic Books, 1973.

Blalock, H. M., Jr. "Estimating Measurement Error Using Multiple Indicators and Several Points in Time." *American Sociological Review* 35:1 (February 1970): 101–111.

Blalock, Hubert M., Jr. *Causal Inferences in Nonexperimental Research.* Chapel Hill: University of North Carolina Press, 1964.

Blumenthal, Monica D.; Kahn, Robert L.; Andrews, Frank M.; and Head, Kendra B. *Justifying Violence: Attitudes of American Men.* Ann Arbor, Mich.: Institute for Social Research, 1972.

Bohrnstedt, George W. "Observations on the Measurement of Change." In *Sociological Methodology 1969,* edited by Edgar F. Borgatta and George W. Bohrnstedt, pp. 113–133, San Francisco: Jossey-Bass, 1969.

Bohrnstedt, George W., and Carter, T. Michael. "Robustness in Regression Analysis." In *Sociological Methodology 1971,* edited by Herbert L. Costner, pp. 118–146, San Francisco: Jossey-Bass, 1971.

Boruch, Robert F., and Wolins, Leroy. "A Procedure for Estimation of Trait, Method, and Error Variance Attributable to a Measure." *Educational and Psychological Measurement* 30:3 (Autumn 1970): 547–574.

435

Bradburn, Norman M. *The Structure of Psychological Well-Being.* Chicago: Aldine, 1969.

Bradburn, Norman M., and Caplovitz, David. *Reports on Happiness: A Pilot Study of Behavior Related to Mental Health.* Chicago: Aldine, 1965.

Brickman, Philip, and Campbell, Donald T. "Hedonic Relativism and Planning the Good Society." In *Adaptation-Level Theory: A Symposium,* edited by M. H. Appley, pp. 287–302. New York and London: Academic Press, 1971.

Campbell, Angus, and Converse, Philip E., eds. *The Human Meaning of Social Change.* New York: Russell Sage Foundation, 1972.

Campbell, Angus; Converse, Philip E.; and Rodgers, Willard L. *The Quality of American Life: Perceptions, Evaluations, and Satisfactions.* New York: Russell Sage Foundation, 1976.

Campbell, Angus, and Schuman, Howard. "Racial Attitudes in Fifteen American Cities." Ann Arbor, Mich.: Survey Research Center. Also in *Supplemental Studies for the National Advisory Commission on Civil Disorders.* Washington: U.S. Government Printing Office, July 1968, pp. 1–67; and New York, Washington and London: Frederick A. Praeger, Publishers, 1968.

Campbell, Donald T., and Fiske, Donald W. "Convergent and Discriminant Validities by the Multitrait-Multimethod Matrix." *Psychological Bulletin* 56:2 (March 1959): 81–105.

Cantril, Hadley, *The Pattern of Human Concerns.* New Brunswick, N.J.: Rutgers University Press, 1965.

Cantril, Hadley. *The Human Dimension: Experience in Policy Research.* New Brunswick, N.J.: Rutgers University Press, 1967.

Carlisle, Elaine. "The Conceptual Structure of Social Indicators." In *Social Indicators and Social Policy,* edited by Andrew Shonfield and Stella Shaw. London: Heinemann Educational Books, 1972.

Cochran, W. G. "The Effectiveness of Adjustment by Subclassification in Removing Bias in Observational Studies." *Biometrics* 24:2 (June 1968): 295–313.

Cochran, W. G. "Some Effects of Errors of Measurement on Multiple Correlation." *Journal of the American Statistical Association* 65:329 (March 1970): 22–34.

Conger, Anthony J. "Evaluation of Multimethod Factor Analysis." *Psychological Bulletin* 75:6 (June 1971): 416–420.

Conner, Robert J. "Grouping for Testing Trends in Categorial Data." *Journal of the American Statistical Association* 67:339 (September 1972): 601–604.

Costner, Herbert L. "Theory, Deduction, and Rules of Correspondence." *American Journal of Sociology* 75:2 (September 1969): 245–263.

Cronbach, Lee J., and Meehl, Paul E. "Construct Validity in Psychological Tests." *Psychological Bulletin* 52:4 (July 1955): 281–302.

Dalkey, Norman C. *Studies in the Quality of Life: Delphi and Decision-Making.* Lexington, Mass.: Lexington Books, 1972.

David, Henry. "Social Indicators: Reverent and Irreverent Observations." Paper prepared for the NATO Advanced Study Institute on Technology Assessment, Gargnano, Italy, September 18–29, 1972.

Davis, James A. "Does Economic Growth Improve the Human Lot? Yes, Indeed, about .0005 per Year." A paper prepared for the International Conference on Subjective Indicators of Quality of Life, Cambridge, England, September 1975.

Dodd, Stuart C. "On Classifying Human Values: A Step in the Prediction of Human Valuing." *American Sociological Review* 16:5 (October 1951): 645–653.

Duncan, Otis Dudley. "Path Analysis: Sociological Examples." *American Journal of Sociology* 72:1 (July 1966): 1–16.

Executive Office of the President: Office of Management and Budget. *Social Indicators, 1973.* Washington: U.S. Government Printing Office, 1973.

Ezekiel, Mordecai, and Fox, Karl A. *Methods of Correlation and Regression.* 3d ed. New York: Wiley, 1959.

French, John R. P., Jr.; Rodgers, Willard; and Cobb, Sidney. "Adjustment as Person-Environment Fit." In *Coping and Adaptation,* edited by George V. Coelho, David A. Hamburg, and John E. Adams. New York: Basic Books, 1974.

Goldberger, Arthur, and Duncan, Otis Dudley, eds. *Structural Equation Models in the Social Sciences.* New York: Seminar Press, 1974.

Goldberger, Arthur S. "Structural Equation Methods in the Social Sciences." *Econometrica* 40:6 (November 1972): 979–1001.

Guilford, J. P. *Psychometric Methods.* 2d ed. New York: McGraw Hill, 1954.

Gurin, Gerald; Veroff, Joseph; and Feld, Sheila. *Americans View Their Mental Health.* New York: Basic Books, 1960.

Guttman, Louis. "A General Nonmetric Technique for Finding the Smallest Coordinate Space for a Configuration of Points." *Psychometrika* 33:4 (December 1968): 469–506.

Harman, Harry H. *Modern Factor Analysis.* Chicago: University of Chicago Press, 1967.

Hartman, Robert S. "The Science of Value." In *New Knowledge in Human Values,* edited by Abraham H. Maslow. New York: Harper, 1959.

Heise, David R. "Separating Reliability and Stability in Test-Retest Correlation." *American Sociological Review* 34:1 (February 1969): 93–101.

Helson, H. *Adaptation-level Theory: An Experimental and Systematic Approach to Behavior.* New York: Harper and Row, 1964.

Hoffenberg, Marvin. "Comments on 'Measuring Progress Towards Social Goals: Some Possibilities at National and Local Levels.'" *Management Science* 16:12 (August 1970): B779–B783.

Holmes, D. "Conscious Self-Appraisal of Achievement Motivation: The Self-Peer Rank Method Revisited." *Journal of Consulting and Clinical Psychology* 36 (1971): 23–26.

Holmes, D., and Tyler, J. "Direct versus Projective Measurement of Achievement Motivation." *Journal of Consulting and Clinical Psychology* 32 (1968): 712–717.

Hyman, Herbert H., and Singer, Eleanor D., eds. *Readings in Reference Group Theory and Research.* New York: Free Press, 1968.

Inter-University Consortium for Political Research. *The C[enter for] P[olitical] S[tudies'] 1972 American National Election Survey.* Ann Arbor, Mich.: Inter-University Consortium for Political Research, 1975.

Jackson, Douglas N. "Multimethod Factor Analysis in the Evaluation of Convergent and Discriminant Validity." *Psychological Bulletin* 72:1 (July 1969): 30–49.

Jackson, Douglas N. "Comments on [Conger's] 'Evaluation of Multimethod Factor Analysis.'" *Psychological Bulletin* 75:6 (June 1971): 421–423.

Joreskog, K. G. "A General Approach to Confirmatory Maximum Likelihood Factor Analysis." *Psychometrika* 34:2 (June 1969): 183–202.

Joreskog, K. G. "A General Method for Analysis of Covariance Structures." *Biometrika* 57:2 (August 1970): 239–251.

Joreskog, Karl G. "A General Method for Estimating a Linear Structural Equation System." In *Structural Equation Models in the Social Sciences,* edited by Arthur Goldberger and Otis Dudley Duncan, pp. 85–112. New York: Seminar Press, 1973.

Joreskog, Karl G., and van Thillo, Marielle, "LISREL: A General Computer Program for Estimating a Linear Structural Equation System Involving Multiple Indicators of Unmeasured Variables." Unpublished research bulletin RB-72-56. Princeton, N.J.: Educational Testing Service, December 1972.

Kelley, Harold H. "Attribution in Social Interaction." In Edward E. Jones, David E. Kanouse, Harold H. Kelley, Richard E. Nisbet, Stuart Valins, and Bernard Weiner, *Attribution: Perceiving the Causes of Behavior.* Morristown, N.J.: General Learning Press, 1971.

Kilpatrick, F. P., and Cantril, Hadley. "Self-Anchoring Scaling: A Measure of Individuals' Unique Reality Worlds." *Journal of Individual Psychology* 16:2 (November 1960): 158–173.

Kish, Leslie, and Hess, Irene. *The Survey Research Center's National Sample of Dwellings.* Ann Arbor, Mich.: Institute for Social Research, The University of Michigan, 1965.

Kluckhohn, Clyde. "Values and Value-Orientations in the Theory of Action: An Exploration in Definition and Classification." In *Toward a General Theory of Action,* edited by Talcott Parsons and Edward A. Shils, pp. 388–433. Cambridge, Mass.: Harvard University Press, 1951.

Kluckhohn, Florence Rockwood. "Dominant and Variant Value Orientations." In *Personality in Nature, Society and Culture.* 2d ed., revised and enlarged, edited by Clyde Kluckhohn and Henry A. Murray, pp. 342–357. New York: Knopf, 1953.

Kulik, James A.; Revelle, William R.; and Kulik, Chen-Lin. "Scale Construction by Hierarchical Cluster Analysis." Unpublished document. Ann Arbor, Mich.: The University of Michigan Computing Center, 1970.

Labovitz, Sanford. "The Assignment of Numbers to Rank Order Categories." *American Sociological Review* 35:3 (June 1970): 515–524.

Land, Kenneth C. "Principles of Path Analysis." In *Sociological Methodology 1969*, edited by Edgar F. Borgatta and George W. Bohrnstedt, pp. 3–37. San Francisco: Jossey-Bass, 1969.

Land, Kenneth C. "On the Estimation of Path Coefficients for Unmeasured Variables from Correlations among Observed Variables." *Social Forces* 48:4 (June 1970): 506–511.

Land, Kenneth C. "On the Definition of Social Indicators." *American Sociologist* 6 (November 1971), 322–325.

Lansing, John B.; Withey, Stephen B.; and Wolfe, Arthur C. *Working Papers on Survey Research in Poverty Areas.* Ann Arbor, Mich.: The Institute for Social Research, The University of Michigan, 1971.

Lazarsfeld, Paul F. "Notes on the History of Quantification in Sociology—Trends, Sources and Problems." In *Quantification: A History of the Meaning of Measurement in the Natural and Social Sciences*, edited by Harry Woolf. Indianapolis: Bobbs-Merrill, 1961.

Lepley, Ray, ed. *The Language of Value.* New York: Columbia University Press, 1957.

Lewin, Kurt. "Time Perspective and Morale." In *Civilian Morale*, edited by Kurt Lewin. Boston: Houghton-Mifflin, 1942.

Lingoes, James C., and Roskam, Edward E. "A Mathematical and Empirical Analysis of Two Multidimensional Scaling Algorithms." *Psychometrika* 38:4–2 (December 1973): 1–93.

Lord, Frederic M., and Novick, Melvin R. *Statistical Theories of Mental Test Scores.* Reading, Mass.: Addison-Wesley, 1968.

Luce, Gay Gaer. *Biological Rhythms in Psychiatry and Medicine* (Report written for the Program Analysis and Evaluation Branch, Office of Program Planning and Evaluation, National Institute of Mental Health). Washington: U.S. Government Printing Office, 1970.

McNemar, Quinn. *Psychological Statistics* (Fourth Edition). New York: Wiley, 1969.

McRae, Douglas J. "MICKA: A FORTRAN IV Iterative K-Means Cluster Analysis Program." *Behavioral Science,* 16 (1971): 423–424.

Mallman, Carlos A. "On the Satisfaction of Human Aspirations as the Development Objective." Paper prepared for the Symposium on Science, Technology, and Human Values, cosponsored by the American Association for the Advancement of Science and the National Science and Technology Council of Mexico, Mexico City, July 2–3, 1973.

Miller, George A. "The Magical Number Seven, Plus or Minus Two: Some Limits on Our Capacity for Processing Information." *Psychological Review* 63:2 (March 1956): 81–97.

Morris, Charles W. *Paths of Life: A Preface to a World Religion.* New York: Harper, 1942.

Morris, Charles W. *Varieties of Human Value.* Chicago: The University of Chicago Press, 1956.

OECD (Organisation for Economic Co-operation and Development). *Science, Growth and Society— A New Perspective.* Report of the Secretary-General's Ad Hoc Group on New Concepts of Science Policy. Paris: OECD, 1971.

OECD (Organisation for Economic Co-operation and Development). *List of Social Concerns Common to Most OECD Countries.* Paris: OECD, 1973.

Osgood, Charles E.; Suci, George J.; and Tannenbaum, Percy H. *The Measurement of Meaning.* Urbana, Ill.: University of Illinois Press, 1957.

Parducci, Allen. "Category Judgment: A Range-Frequency Model." *Psychological Review* 72:6 (November 1965): 407–418.

Parsons, Talcott, and Shils, Edward, *Toward a General Theory of Action.* Cambridge: Harvard University Press, 1951.

Powers, William T. *Behavior: The Control of Perception.* Chicago: Aldine, 1973.

Quinn, R.; Seashore, S.; Kahn, R.; Mangione, T.; Campbell, D.; Staines, G.; and McCullough, M. *Survey of Working Conditions.* Washington: U.S. Government Printing Office, Document 2916–0001, 1971.

Ramsay, J. O. "The Effect of Number of Categories in Rating Scales on Precision of Estimation of Scale Values." *Psychometrika* 38:4 (December 1973): 513–532.

Rokeach, Milton. *The Nature of Human Values.* New York: The Free Press, 1973.

Rummel, Rudolph J. *Applied Factor Analysis.* Evanston, Ill.: Northwestern University Press, 1971.

Samuelson, Paul A. *Economics.* New York: McGraw Hill, 1955.

Sawhill, Isabel V. "The Role of Social Indicators and Social Reporting in Public Expenditure Decisions." In *The Analysis and Evaluation of Public Expenditures: The PPB System.* A compendium of papers submitted to the Subcommittee on Economy in Government of the Joint Economic Committee, Congress of the United States, Volume I. Washington: U.S. Government Printing Office, 1969.

Schuman, Howard, and Gruenberg, Barry. "Dissatisfaction with City Services: Is Race an Important Factor?" In *People and Politics in Urban Society,* edited by Harlan Hahn, pp. 369–392. Beverly Hills and London: Sage Publications, 1972.

Sheldon, Eleanor Bernert, and Freeman, Howard E. "Notes on Social Indicators: Promises and Potential." *Policy Sciences* 1:1 (Spring 1970): 97–111.

Sonquist, John A.; Baker, Elizabeth Lauh; and Morgan, James N. *Searching for Structure.* Revised edition. Ann Arbor, Mich.: Institute for Social Research, 1973.

Spence, Ian. "A Monte Carlo Evaluation of Three Nonmetric Multidimensional Scaling Algorithms." *Psychometrika* 37:4 (December 1972): 461–486.

Spiegel, John. *Transactions: The Interplay between Individual, Family, and Society.* New York: Science House, 1971.

Survey Research Center, The University of Michigan. *Survey of Working Conditions: Final Report on Univariate and Bivariate Tables.* Washington: U.S. Government Printing Office, 1971.

Thurstone, Louis L. *The Measurement of Value.* Chicago: The University of Chicago Press, 1959.

U. S. Bureau of the Census. "Current Population Reports," Series PC-20, Number 223, October 7. Washington: U.S. Government Printing Office, 1971.

U.S. Bureau of the Census. "Current Population Reports," Series PC-20, Number 239, September. Washington: U.S. Government Printing Office, 1972a.

U.S. Bureau of the Census. *Statistical Abstract of the United States* (93rd Edition). Washington: U.S. Government Printing Office, 1972b.

U.S. Department of Health, Education and Welfare. *Toward a Social Report.* Washington: U.S. Government Printing Office, 1969 (also Ann Arbor, Mich.: Ann Arbor Paperbacks, University of Michigan Press, 1970).

Walster, Elaine; Berscheid, Ellen; and Walster, G. William. "New Directions in Equity Research." *Journal of Personality and Social Psychology* 25:2 (1973): 151–176.

Wessman, A. E., and Ricks, D. F. *Mood and Personality.* New York: Holt Rinehart and Winston, 1966.

White, Ralph K. "Value Analysis: A Quantitative Method for Describing Qualitative Data." *Journal of Social Psychology* 19: Second Half (May 1944): 351–358.

Wiley, David E., and Wiley, James A. "The Estimation of Measurement Error in Panel Data." *American Sociological Review* 35:1 (February 1970): 112–117.

Work in America. Report of a Special Task Force to the Secretary of Health, Education and Welfare. Cambridge, Mass.: MIT Press, 1973.

Index

Aberbach, Joel D., 30n, 435
Aborn, Murray, iv
Abrams, Mark, 20, 435
Acceptance by others, evaluation of
  and global well-being, 112, 135, 156, 159,
    162, 165
  measurement of, 33, 39, 391
  and other concerns, 38-40, 47, 58, 403-
    411, 418
  and perception of neighbor's, 241
  by population groups, 287-307
  and six domains, 237
  by total population, 270-273
Accomplishment, evaluation of own
  and global well-being, 112, 124, 127,
    132, 135, 139, 156, 159, 162, 165,
    169, 423
  measurement of, 32, 39, 55, 391
  and other concerns, 38-40, 44, 47, 58,
    392-411, 414-418
  and perceptions of neighbor's, 241
  by population groups, 287-307, 323-324,
    429
  and six domains, 237
  and six evaluative contexts, 231-233
  by total population, 266-270, 428, 433
Adams, J. Stacy, 16, 435
Affect: positive, negative, balance, total
  comments about, 87, 103-104, 163-164
  distributions on, 321
  evaluation of,
    by population groups, 330-332
    by total population, 320-321
  and indicator battery design, 349
  measurement of, 68, 72-73, 87n
  and other global measures, 84-104

Affect (*cont'd*)
  relationships among, 85, 87, 92-94
  and single concerns, 161-164
Affective evaluations
  as basis for assessing perceptual structure,
    54-55
  as entries in conceptual model, 12-14, 18
  generation of, 15-18, 219-220, 231-233,
    303
  measurement of by Delighted—Terrible
    Scale, 18-20, 223-229
  nature of, 18
  related to perceptions of past and future,
    229-231
Age groups
  concerns and global well-being within,
    146
  evaluations of global well-being by, 322-
    334
  evaluations of life concerns by, 287-290,
    305-306, 429
  and global well-being, 139, 141
  percentages of in various data, 424, 431
  relationships among concerns, 50-51, 396-
    399, 405-408
  relationships among global indicators, 82-
    83
  see also Young people; People over 40
Allport, Gordon W., 31, 435
Althauser, Robert P., 184n, 435
Alwin, Duane F., 184n, 435
Andrews, Frank M., 4, 116n, 123n, 422n
  435,
Apartment, *see* Housing
April 1973 data
  clustering of concern items, 54, 56

441